# STATISTICAL METHODS IN THE BIOLOGICAL AND HEALTH SCIENCES

# STATISTICAL METHODS IN THE BIOLOGICAL AND HEALTH SCIENCES

**J. S. MILTON, Ph.D.**
Professor of Statistics
Radford University

**J. O. TSOKOS, Ph.D.**
Associate Professor of Biochemistry
University of South Florida

INTERNATIONAL STUDENT EDITION

McGRAW-HILL INTERNATIONAL BOOK COMPANY

Auckland Bogotá Guatemala Hamburg Johannesburg Lisbon
London Madrid Mexico New Delhi Panama Paris
San Juan São Paulo Singapore Sydney Tokyo

**JOAN M. SAVAGE**

**STATISTICAL METHODS
IN THE
BIOLOGICAL AND HEALTH SCIENCES**

INTERNATIONAL STUDENT EDITION



1st printing 1983



This book was set in Aster by York Graphic Services, Inc.
The editors were John J. Corrigan and James S. Amar;
the designer was Nicholas Krenitsky;
the production supervisor was Leroy A. Young.
The drawings were done by Danmark & Michaels, Inc.

Library of Congress Cataloging in Publication Data

Milton, J. Susan (Janet Susan)
Statistical methods in the biological and health sciences.

Bibliography: p.
Includes index.
1. Life sciences—Statistical methods. 2. Biometry.
I. Tsokos, Janice O. II. Title. [DNLM: 1. Biometry.
WA 950 M662s]
QH323.5.M54 1983 519.5 82-17310
ISBN 0-07-042359-8

**When ordering this title use ISBN 0-07-066419-6**

KOSAIDO PRINTING CO., LTD. TOKYO, JAPAN

# CONTENTS

# PREFACE

It has become increasingly evident that the interpretation of much of the research in the biological and health sciences depends to a large extent on statistical methods. For this reason, it is essential that students in these fields be exposed to statistical reasoning early in their careers. This text is intended as a *first* course in statistical methods for students in the biological and health sciences. It is hoped that this first course will occur on the undergraduate level. However, this text can be used to advantage by graduate students who have little or no prior experience with statistical methods.

This text is not a statistical cookbook, nor is it a manual for researchers. We attempt to find a middle road—to provide a text that gives the student an understanding of the logic behind statistical techniques as well as practice in using them. Calculus is *not* assumed. The reader with an adequate background in high school algebra should be able to follow the arguments presented.

We chose the examples and exercises specifically for the student of biological and health sciences. They are drawn from genetics, general biology, ecology, and medicine. Except where indicated otherwise, data are simulated. However, the simulation is done with care, so that the results of the analysis are consistent with recently reported research. In this way, the student will gain some insight into the types of problems that interest current workers in the biological sciences. Many exercises are left open-ended, in hopes of stimulating some classroom discussion.

It is assumed that the student has access to some type of electronic calculator. Many such calculators are on the market, and most have some built-in statistical capability. The use of these calculators is encouraged, for it allows the student to concentrate on the interpretation of the analysis rather than the arithmetic computations.

We should point out that most of the data sets presented are rather small, so that the student will not be overwhelmed by the computational aspects of statistical analysis. We do *not* intend to imply that very small samples are acceptable in biological research. In fact, most major research projects involve a tremendous investment in time and money and result in a large body of data. Such data lend themselves to analysis via the electronic computer. For this reason, we include some instruction in the use of computer packages. The package chosen for illustrative purposes is SAS (Statistical Analysis System: SAS Institute, Inc., Raleigh, North Carolina). This was done because of its widespread availability and ease of use. We do not intend to imply that it is superior to other well-known packages such as SPSS (Statistical Package for the Social Sciences, McGraw-Hill), BMD (Biomedical Computer Programs, University of California Press), or MINITAB (Duxbury Press). The computer methods are presented as "computing supplements" at appropriate points in the text. The student with access to the computer is encouraged to give them a try! However, the supplements can be skipped with no loss of continuity.

The appendixes include an introduction to summation notation (Appendix A), and tables of probability distributions (Appendix B). Answers to the odd-numbered exercises also are provided.

A number of different courses can be taught from this book. They can vary in length from one quarter to one year. It is difficult to determine exactly what material can be covered in a given time, since this is a function of class size, academic maturity of the students, and the inclination of the instructor. However, we do offer some guidelines for the use of this text. In particular, the type of course presented can vary from one whose chief aim is to familiarize the student with handling data sets to one of a more theoretical nature. This can be done by means of the starred exercises and sections. Starred problems either are a little more difficult than the routine exercise or are theoretical; starred sections include material that perhaps is a bit out of the mainstream for beginning courses, but which, if used, will enhance the course. Starred exercises and sections can be omitted without loss of continuity.

Chapter 1: This chapter is provided for those who like to begin a course by talking about describing data sets. It can be skipped, for points essential to inference are reiterated as necessary.

Chapters 2 and 3: These chapters provide a background in probability and counting. At least the first two sections of Chapter 2 can be covered as a reading assignment.

Chapter 4: This chapter introduces discrete and continuous random variables, densities, distribution functions, and expectation. It is very important because it provides the theory on which much of the later material depends.

Chapter 5: This chapter discusses the binomial, Poisson, and normal distributions. The material on the Poisson distribution is optional. The other two topics should be covered, for they are used extensively in later chapters.

Chapter 6: This chapter is intended as *only* an introduction to the language underlying inference. It should be covered quickly, perhaps as a reading assignment. The points made in the chapter are reinforced in subsequent discussions.

Chapter 7: The real business of inference is begun here. This chapter should be covered at a slower pace, since the basic notions of inference (estimation, hypothesis testing, $P$ values, confidence intervals) are developed fully for the first time. These ideas are abbreviated in later chapters. This is a crucial chapter for the student.

Chapter 8: This chapter is concerned with inferences on proportions; both one- and two-sample problems are considered.

Chapter 9: The discussion of two-sample problems is concluded by considering inferences on two means and two variances.

Chapter 10: This chapter extends the ideas of Chapter 9 (two-sample problems) to $k$ samples. It introduces experimental design and the language underlying this area of statistics.

Chapter 11: This chapter introduces regression and correlation. In particular, simple linear regression is covered in some detail.

Chapter 12: Categorical data problems are considered here. Problems of goodness of fit as well as tests of association are discussed.

Chapter 13: This chapter presents a collection of distribution-free tests. These tests are chosen to familiarize the student with some of the more commonly encountered distribution-free methods. Also they are selected so that a distribution-free alternative is available for most of the normal theory tests previously presented.

We wish to thank The Chemical Rubber Company, the Macmillan Company, Biometrics, Bell Laboratories, and Biometrika for permission to reprint statistical tables. We also wish to thank the *Chicago Tribune* for use of selected cartoons. A special thanks goes to SAS Institute for permission to use their package for illustrative purposes.

Thanks are also due to Judy Willis and Linda Federspiel for typing the manuscript and to Joan Savage and Charlene Lutes for their help as biological consultants. A very special thanks is offered to the following reviewers for their many helpful suggestions during the preparation of the manuscript: Dr. Jon Cole, St. John's University; Professor Bruce Cowell, University of South Florida; Professor Richard A. Damon, Jr., University of Massachusetts; Dr. Janice Derr, The Pennsylvania State University; Professor Judith K. Dunn, University of Texas, Medical Branch, Galveston; Professor William L. Harkness, The Pennsylvania State University; Dr. Werner G. Hein, The Colorado College; Professor K. Hinkelmann, Virginia Polytechnic Institute and State University; Professor Maita Levine, University of Cincinnati; Professor Charles E. McCulloch, Cornell University; and Professor Norman B. Rushforth, Case Western Reserve University.

**J. S. Milton**
**J. O. Tsokos**

[illegible] estimation, involving [illegible] and [illegible] [illegible] [illegible]. These [illegible] [illegible] [illegible] [illegible] [illegible] for the student.

Chapter 8. This chapter is devoted to inferences on [illegible]; one- and two-sample problems are considered.

Chapter 9. The discussion of two-sample problems is [illegible], giving inferences on two means and two variances.

Chapter 10. This chapter extends the idea of [illegible] to k samples and introduces [illegible] [illegible] underlying the ideas of statistics.

Chapter 11. This chapter introduces regression and correlation [illegible]; simple linear regression is covered in some detail.

Chapter 12. Categorical data problems are considered here. Problems of goodness of fit as well as [illegible] are [illegible].

Chapter 13. This chapter presents a collection of nonparametric tests. These tests are chosen to familiarize the student with some of the more commonly encountered distribution-free [illegible] and to show that a distribution-free alternative is available for most of the [illegible] theory tests previously presented.

We wish to thank The Chemical Rubber Company, the Macmillan Company, [illegible], Bell Laboratories, [illegible] for permission to reprint statistical tables. We also wish to thank [illegible]. A special thanks goes to SAS Institute for permission to use their package for illustrative purposes.

Thanks are also due to Judy [illegible] for typing the manuscript and to Joan Savage and Charlene [illegible] [illegible] consultation. A very special thanks is offered to the following reviewers for their many helpful suggestions during the preparation of the manuscript: [illegible], St. John's University; [illegible], University of South Florida; Professor [illegible], University of Massachusetts; Dr. [illegible], The Pennsylvania State University; Professor Judith [illegible], University of Texas; [illegible]; Professor William L. Harkness, The Pennsylvania State University; Dr. Werner [illegible], The Colorado College; Professor [illegible], Virginia Polytechnic Institute and State University; Professor [illegible], University of Cincinnati; Professor Charles [illegible], [illegible] University; and Professor Norman [illegible], Case Western Reserve University.

[illegible]

[illegible]

"The good Christian should be wary of mathematicians and all those who make a practice of sacrilegious prediction, particularly when they speak the truth. Because the danger exists that these people in league with the devil, may becloud the souls of men and enmesh them in the snares of hell."

(*De genesi ad litteram* 2, XVII, 37)

# 1. DESCRIPTIVE METHODS

This Augustinian admonition expresses (unfortunately) the attitude of many laypeople toward mathematicians and mathematics in general. However, as we endeavor to show in this text, mathematics, in particular that branch of mathematics known as statistics, has become an indispensable tool for most scientists.

Statistics has been defined as the art of decision making in the face of uncertainty. We begin by describing a typical problem that calls for a statistical solution. We use this example to introduce some of the language underlying the field of statistics. The terms are used here on an intuitive level. They are defined in a more technical sense later, as the need arises.

A researcher studying heart disease has identified four factors as being potentially associated with the development of the disease: age, weight, number of cigarettes smoked per day, and family history of heart disease. The researcher wants to gather evidence that either confirms these factors as contributing to the development of the disease or shows them to be unimportant. How should she or he proceed?

This is inherently a statistical problem. What characteristics identify it as such? Simply these:

**1.** Associated with the problem is a large group of objects (in this case, people) about which inferences are to be made. This group of objects is called the *population*.

**2.** Certain characteristics of the members of the population are of particular interest. The value of each of these characteristics may change from object to object within the population. They are called *random variables:*

variables because they change in value; random because their behavior depends on chance and is somewhat unpredictable.

**3.** The population is too large to study in its entirety. So we must make inferences about the population based on what is observed by studying only a portion, or *sample,* of objects from the population.

In the study of factors affecting heart disease, the population is the set of all persons suffering from the disease. The random variables of interest are the patient's age and weight, number of cigarettes smoked per day, and family history. It is impossible to identify and study every person with heart disease. Thus any conclusions that are reached must be based on studying only a portion, or a sample, of these people.

Random variables fall into two broad categories: continuous and discrete. A *continuous random variable* is a variable that can assume any value in some interval or continuous span of real numbers. The variable age in the study of heart disease is continuous, as is the variable weight. A person's age conceivably can lie anywhere between 0 and, say, 110 years, a continuous time span. And that person's weight may lie anywhere from 0 to perhaps 600 pounds! A *discrete random variable* is a variable that assumes its values at isolated points. Thus the set of possible values is either finite or countably infinite. The number of cigarettes smoked per day is discrete. Its set of possible values is $\{0, 1, 2, 3, 4, 5, \ldots\}$, a countably infinite collection. If family history is studied by recording the number of natural parents and grandparents who experienced heart disease, then this variable also is discrete. Its set of possible values is $\{0, 1, 2, 3, 4, 5, 6\}$, a finite collection.

You should realize that there are two types of data sets: those that consist of observations on *every* member of the population and those that consist of observations on only a sample of the population. In the former case, the methods of inferential statistics are *not* needed; population characteristics can be determined by direct observation of the data set. In the latter case, inferential methods are essential. Regardless of the situation, before researchers can draw any conclusions about the population under study from the data collected, they must organize, summarize, and present the data in easily understandable form. The purpose of this chapter is to introduce some commonly encountered methods for doing this. Methods for using this information to make inferences concerning the population as a whole when the data set constitutes only a sample drawn from the population are the topic of much of the rest of the text.

## BAR GRAPHS

**1.1** □ One of the simplest methods for presenting numerical data is a *bar graph.* Bar graphs are just what the name implies, graphs in which the data are presented by means of horizontal or vertical bars. These graphs often allow one to detect visually trends, patterns, or relationships that otherwise might have gone unnoticed. Then these patterns can be investigated more deeply by using analytic statistical techniques. There are various types of bar graphs. Some of the more frequently encountered are illustrated in the following examples.

**EXAMPLE 1.1.1** □ A study of eye injuries incurred during participation in the racket sports of tennis, squash, badminton, and racket ball was conducted in 1978. Table 1.1, concerning the seriousness of these injuries and the age and sex of the patients, reflects a portion of the data collected. A vertical bar graph displaying the distribution of serious eye injuries in males among age groups is constructed by graphing the age categories as reported in Table 1.1 on the horizontal axis and the number of patients in each age category on the vertical axis. The result is shown in Figure 1.1.

**TABLE 1.1** EYE INJURIES

| | Serious Eye Injuries | | Nonserious Eye Injuries | |
|---|---|---|---|---|
| AGE, YR | MALE | FEMALE | MALE | FEMALE |
| <30 | 7 | 1 | 4 | 5 |
| 30–50 | 9 | 10 | 10 | 27 |
| >50 | 4 | 0 | 4 | 1 |
| **Total** | 20 | 11 | 18 | 33 |

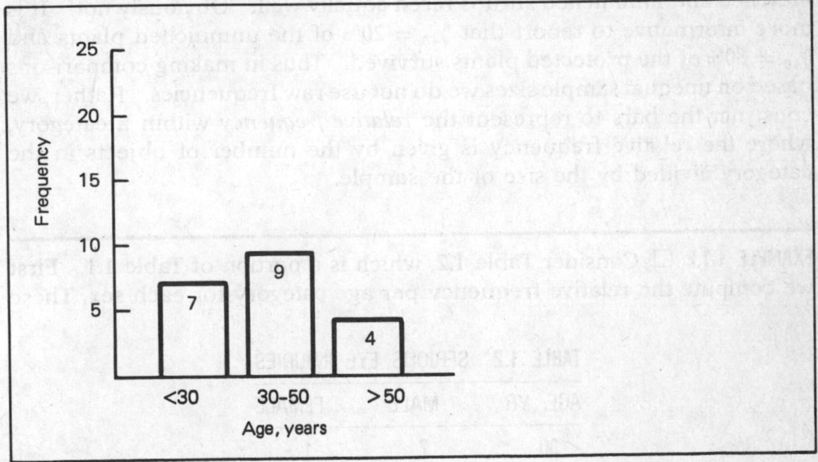


**FIGURE 1.1** Frequency distribution of serious eye injuries among age groups (male). (*JAMA,* 1978, vol. 239, no. 24, pp. 2575–2577, Copyright 1980, American Medical Association. Used with permission.)

Note that the bars are all the *same width.* Since the height of each depends on the number of patients in the respective category, the area of each bar is proportional to the number of patients in the category. That is, the higher the number of patients per category, the larger the area of the bar corresponding to that category. Since differences in area are fairly easy to detect when all the objects are the same general shape, quick visual comparisons among categories are possible. For example, a glance at Figure 1.1 allows one to note that more serious injuries occurred in the 30 to 50 years old age group than in the other two, and that there was a fairly sharp drop in the number of serious injuries after age 50.

---

The bar graph just considered is very simple. However, the technique of graphing categories versus frequency counts has an important practical application, which is discussed in Chapter 12.

One interesting way to use bar graphs is to make comparisons. For example, there is obviously more information in Table 1.1 than has been utilized in Example 1.1.1. In particular, it would be interesting to compare the distribution of serious injuries among age groups in males to that in females. This can be done by constructing bar graphs for each sex on the same axis. However, a word of caution is in order. If the sample sizes are equal, then the comparison can be made by using raw frequencies; if they are not the same, then raw frequencies can be misleading. For example, suppose that, in a study of the effect of wind chill on shrubs, 10 had been mulched and 40 had not. It is reported that eight that had been mulched and eight that had not survived the winter. Is it accurate to conclude that mulched and unmulched shrubs fared equally well? Obviously not! It is more informative to report that $8/40 = 20\%$ of the unmulched plants and $8/10 = 80\%$ of the protected plants survived. Thus in making comparisons based on unequal sample sizes we do not use raw frequencies. Rather, we construct the bars to represent the *relative frequency* within a category, where the relative frequency is given by the number of objects in the category divided by the size of the sample.

---

**EXAMPLE 1.1.2** □ Consider Table 1.2, which is a portion of Table 1.1. First we compute the relative frequency per age category for each sex. These

**TABLE 1.2** SERIOUS EYE INJURIES

| AGE, YR | MALE | FEMALE |
|---|---|---|
| $<30$ | 7 | 1 |
| 30–50 | 9 | 10 |
| $>50$ | 4 | 0 |
| **Total** | 20 | 11 |

**TABLE 1.3** SERIOUS EYE INJURIES

| | Male | | Female | |
|---|---|---|---|---|
| AGE, YR | FREQUENCY | RELATIVE FREQUENCY | FREQUENCY | RELATIVE FREQUENCY |
| <30 | 7 | 7/20 = 35% | 1 | 1/11 = 9% |
| 30-50 | 9 | 9/20 = 45% | 10 | 10/11 = 91% |
| >50 | 4 | 4/20 = 20% | 0 | 0/11 = 0% |
| **Total** | 20 | 20/20 = 100% | 11 | 11/11 = 100% |

are shown in Table 1.3. Graphing the age categories versus the *relative frequency* of serious eye injuries for each sex side by side yields the bar graph of Figure 1.2. To make the categories easier to distinguish, the pairs of bars for each category are separated slightly. Note that the distributions of serious injuries in the two groups are similar in that the highest percentage of injuries occurs in the 30 to 50 years old age group, with a sharp decline after age 50 in both cases. Note also that the distribution for males is more uniform in that the percentages falling into each age category among men (35%, 45%, 20%) do not vary as much as those among women (9%, 91%, 0%). At this point, these statements apply to only the 20 men and 11 women involved in the study. Whether these suggested patterns exist in general cannot be determined from the graph alone. To be able to make statements about serious eye injuries in women and men in general, a detailed statistical analysis of the given data and perhaps even

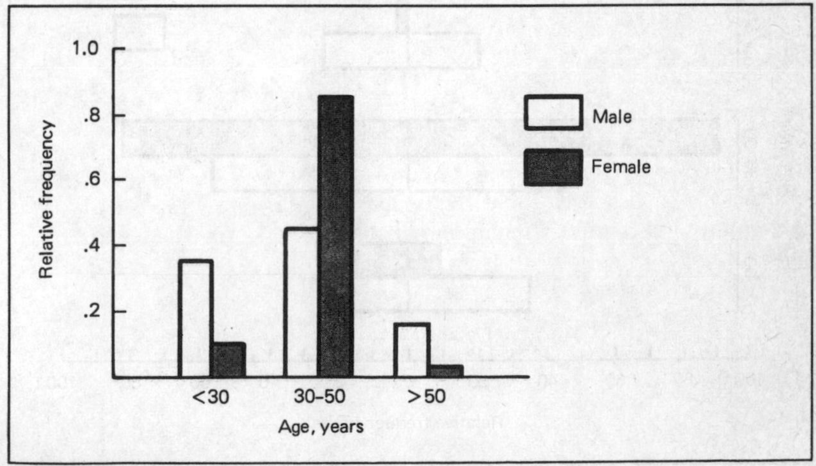


**FIGURE 1.2** Relative frequency distribution of serious eye injuries among age groups (by sex).

more data are needed. Developing the techniques for such an analysis is the task of much of the remainder of this text.

---

To summarize all the data presented in Table 1.1 in one bar graph, a horizontal directional bar graph can be used. This bar graph uses horizontal rather than vertical bars; it is directional in that the left side of the axis is used to graph one data set and the right side is used to graph the other.

---

**EXAMPLE 1.1.3** □ Table 1.1, when modified to include relative frequencies expressed as percentages, yields Table 1.4. A directional horizontal bar

**TABLE 1.4** EYE INJURIES

| | Serious Eye Injuries | | Nonserious Eye Injuries | |
|---|---|---|---|---|
| AGE, YR | MALE | FEMALE | MALE | FEMALE |
| <30 | 7 (35%) | 1 (9%) | 4 (22%) | 5 (15%) |
| 30–50 | 9 (45%) | 10 (91%) | 10 (56%) | 27 (82%) |
| >50 | 4 (20%) | 0 (0%) | 4 (22%) | 1 (3%) |
| **Total** | 20 (100%) | 11 (100%) | 18 (100%) | 33 (100%) |

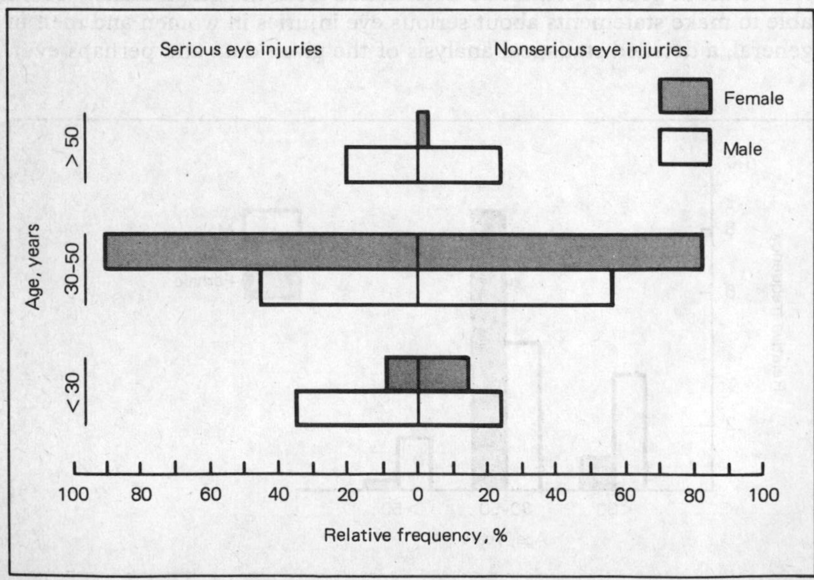


**FIGURE 1.3** Relative frequency distribution of serious and nonserious injuries among age groups (by sex).

graph presenting the data in Table 1.4 is constructed by graphing the data for serious eye injuries on the left of the vertical axis and those for nonserious injuries on the right. The data are still categorized by age, with relative frequency data for the sexes graphed side by side for comparative purposes. Such a graph, shown in Figure 1.3, suggests that the pattern noted in Example 1.1.2 relative to serious eye injuries also holds for nonserious injuries. That is, the distribution for men is more uniform than for women, with the highest percentages for both groups occurring in the 30 to 50 years old age group.

---

Another type of bar graph encountered quite often in scientific literature is the *stratified* bar graph. This type of graph is helpful whenever the objects in each category can be subdivided according to some secondary trait. Consider Example 1.1.4.

---

**EXAMPLE 1.1.4** □ The stratified bar graph shown in Figure 1.4 displays a portion of the data collected in a study of cystic fibrosis. It gives the

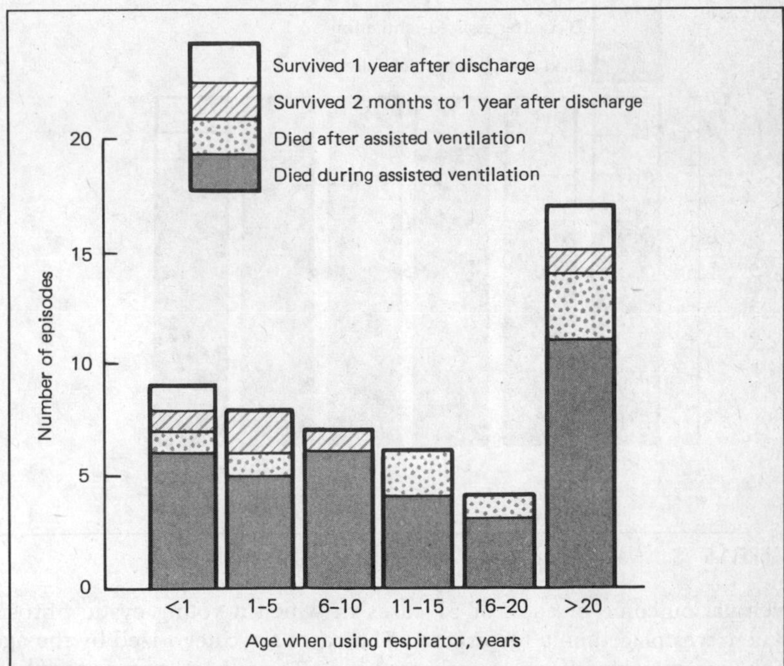


**FIGURE 1.4** Outcome of 51 episodes of assisted ventilation in 46 patients with cystic fibrosis. (*JAMA,* 1978, vol. 239, no. 18, pp. 1851–1854, Copyright 1980, American Medical Association. Used with permission.)

**TABLE 1.5** CYSTIC FIBROSIS PATIENTS PLACED ON RESPIRATORS

| | Age When Using Respirator, yr | | | | | | |
|---|---|---|---|---|---|---|---|
| SURVIVAL STATUS | <1 | 1-5 | 6–10 | 11-15 | 16–20 | >20 | |
| Died during assisted ventilation | 6 (67%) | 5 (62.5%) | 6 (85.7%) | 4 (67%) | 3 (75%) | 11 (64.7%) | |
| Died after assisted ventilation | 1 (11%) | 1 (12.5%) | 0 (0%) | 2 (33%) | 1 (25%) | 3 (17.6%) | |
| Survived 2 months to 1 year after discharge | 1 (11%) | 2 (25%) | 1 (14.3%) | 0 (0%) | 0 (0%) | 1 (5.9%) | |
| Survived 1 year after discharge | 1 (11%) | 0 (0%) | 0 (0%) | 0 (0%) | 0 (0%) | 2 (11.8%) | |
| **Total** | 9 | 8 | 7 | 6 | 4 | 17 | 51 |

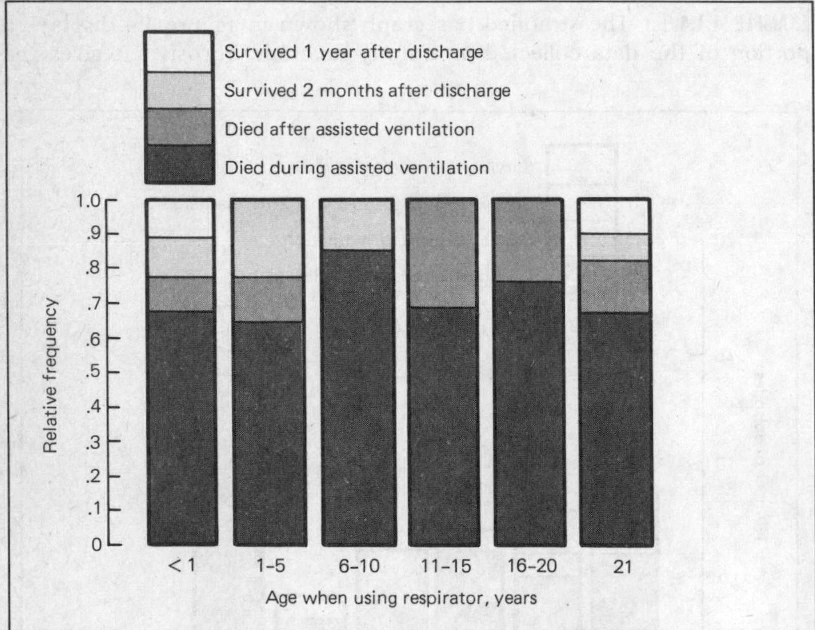


**FIGURE 1.5** Survival status of cystic fibrosis patients by percentage.

eventual outcome of each of 51 cases in which a young cystic fibrosis patient was placed on a respirator. The cases are categorized by the age of the patient when the respirator was used. The age categories are subdivided according to the survival status of the patient.

Several things are immediately noticeable. Probably the most striking observation is that in each age category, over 50% of the cases resulted in death while the patient was on the respirator. This is indicated by the fact that within each bar the solid portion accounts for more than half of the area. Another point of interest is that the only age categories in which a patient survived for a year after discharge were the youngest and the oldest. But again we must be careful! If we want to compare survival patterns across age groups, then we need to convert the frequencies shown in Figure 1.4 to *relative* frequencies, so that comparisons are meaningful. Table 1.5 is extracted from Figure 1.4.

To construct a stratified bar graph from Table 1.5 that can be used for comparative purposes, we graph the age categories along the horizontal axis and subdivide each bar according to the percentage of cases in each survival category. This graph is shown in Figure 1.5. It can be seen from Figure 1.5 that the percentage of patients who died after assisted ventilation in the 11 to 15 years old age group is higher than that in the over 20 years old age group. Note that this relationship is *not* evident from Figure 1.4, which is based on raw frequencies rather than relative frequencies. In fact, Figure 1.4 erroneously gives exactly the opposite impression.

## EXERCISES 1.1

1. Table 1.6 shows a portion of the data gathered in a study of sports injuries in females.
   a. Find the percentage of injuries falling into each category in both parts of the table.
   b. Construct vertical bar graphs summarizing the frequency and relative frequency of injury types. Since only one data set is involved, each graph conveys basically the same information concerning the distribution of injury types. Can you think of a reason why the relative frequency approach might be preferable?

**TABLE 1.6** SPORTS INJURIES IN FEMALES

| Injury Type | NUMBER | PERCENTAGE |
|---|---|---|
| Contusion | 17 | 8.9 |
| Fracture | 8 | |
| Inflammation | 22 | |
| Laceration | 1 | |
| Sprain | 62 | |
| Strain | 59 | |
| Other | 23 | |
| **Total** | 192 | 100 |

**TABLE 1.6** *(Continued)*

| Injury Location | NUMBER | PERCENTAGE |
|---|---|---|
| Head | 7 | 3.6 |
| Spine/trunk | 22 | |
| Upper extremity | | |
| Shoulder | 7 | |
| Wrist/hand | 17 | |
| Other | 13 | |
| Lower extremity | | |
| Thigh | 24 | |
| Knee | 27 | |
| Ankle | 32 | |
| Other | 43 | |
| **Total** | 192 | 100 |

*Source: JAMA,* vol. 239, no. 21, pp. 2245–2248, 1978.

**c.** Construct a horizontal bar graph summarizing distribution of injuries by location.

**2.** Consider Table 1.7 concerning the relationships among player's experience, player's sex, and the seriousness of eye injuries in players of racket sports. Summarize the data shown in the table by a horizontal directional bar graph.

**TABLE 1.7** INJURIES RELATED TO PLAYER EXPERIENCE

| | Serious Injuries | | Nonserious Injuries | |
|---|---|---|---|---|
| EXPERIENCE | MALE | FEMALE | MALE | FEMALE |
| Players | | | | |
| Beginner | 4 | 1 | 0 | 3 |
| Beginner-Intermediate | 3 | 3 | 0 | 3 |
| Intermediate | 7 | 4 | 9 | 15 |
| Intermediate-Superior | 4 | 3 | 2 | 9 |
| Superior | 2 | 0 | 2 | 1 |
| Spectators | 0 | 0 | 3 | 2 |

*Source: JAMA,* vol. 239, no. 24, pp. 2575–2577, 1980.

**3.** The directional bar graph of Figure 1.6 summarizes the results of a study of injury rates in female athletes. Comment on any interesting relationships or patterns suggested by the graph.

**4.** The stratified bar graph of Figure 1.7 concerns the injury rate in female athletes among

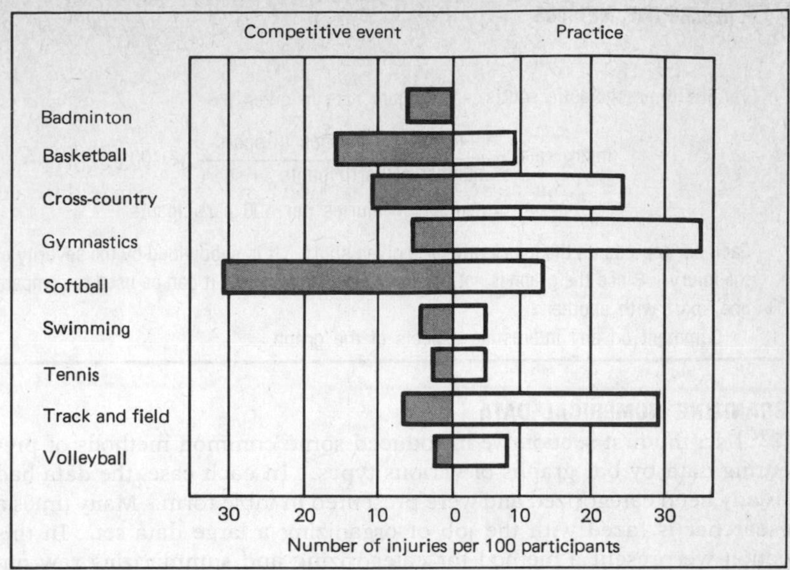


**FIGURE 1.6** Injury rate, injuries per 100 participants. (*JAMA,* 1978, vol. 239, no. 21, pp. 2245–2248, Copyright 1980, American Medical Association. Used with permission.)

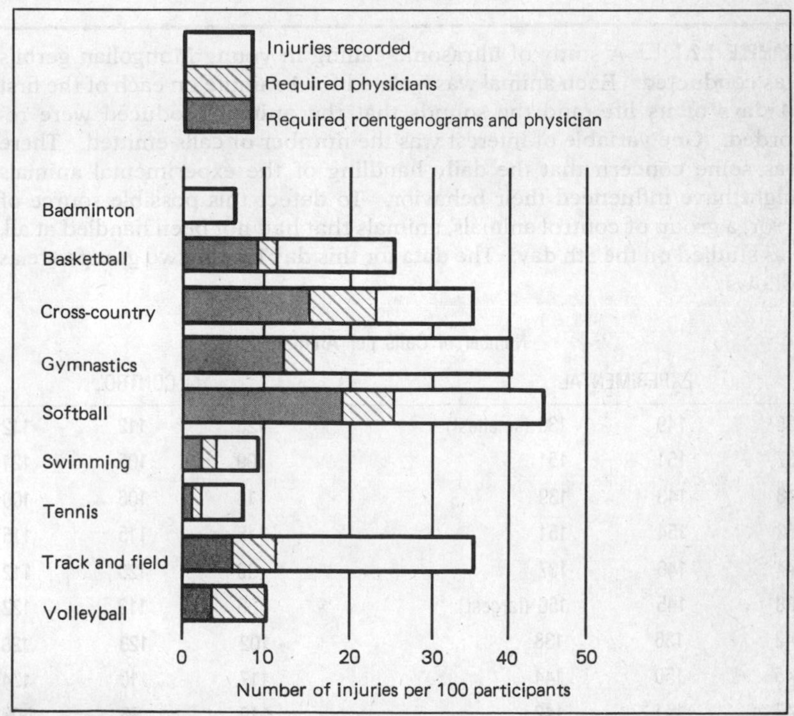


**FIGURE 1.7** Injury rate, injuries per 100 participants. (*JAMA,* 1978, vol. 239, no. 21, pp. 2245–2248, Copyright 1980, American Medical Association. Used with permission.)

various interscholastic sports. The injury rate is given by

$$\text{Injury rate} = \frac{\text{number of injuries in sport}}{\text{number of participants in sport}} \times 100$$
$$= \text{number of injuries per 100 participants}$$

Each bar represents the injury rate for a given sport. It is subdivided by the severity of the injury. Since the graph is not based on raw frequencies, it can be used to compare one sport with another.

Comment on any interesting aspects of the graph.

## ORGANIZING NUMERICAL DATA

**1.2** □ In the first section we introduced some common methods of presenting data by bar graphs of various types. In each case, the data had already been categorized and were presented in table form. Many times a researcher is faced with the job of organizing a large data set. In this section we present a method for categorizing and summarizing raw numerical data. The method is outlined and illustrated step by step in Example 1.2.1.

---

**EXAMPLE 1.2.1** □ A study of ultrasonic calling in young Mongolian gerbils was conducted. Each animal was isolated for 1 minute on each of the first 14 days of its life, and the sounds that the animal produced were recorded. One variable of interest was the number of calls emitted. There was some concern that the daily handling of the experimental animals might have influenced their behavior. To detect this possible source of error, a group of control animals, animals that had not been handled at all, was studied on the 5th day. The data for this day for the two groups are as follows:

Number of Calls per Animal

| EXPERIMENTAL | | | CONTROL | | |
|---|---|---|---|---|---|
| 135 | 149 | 130 (smallest) | 123 | 112 | 112 |
| 137 | 151 | 151 | 109 | 105 | 121 |
| 148 | 143 | 139 | 118 | 106 | 100 |
| 152 | 154 | 151 | 116 | 115 | 115 |
| 144 | 146 | 137 | 96 | 120 | 112 |
| 138 | 145 | 156 (largest) | 88 | 112 | 122 |
| 142 | 136 | 138 | 102 | 123 | 128 |
| 145 | 150 | 144 | 117 | 110 | 124 |
| 147 | 151 | 142 | 119 | 98 | 109 |
| 147 | 138 | 155 | 101 | 111 | 90 |

Consider first the data for the experimental animals. Our task is to separate these data into categories. Generally, 5 to 20 categories of equal length are desirable, with the actual number used being dependent on the number of data points available. Since we have only 30 observations, we use a small number of categories, say five. Now we locate the largest data point (156) and the smallest (130). These are used to find the length of the interval containing all the data points. In this case, the data are covered by an interval of length $156 - 130 = 26$ units. To find the minimum length required for each category, this number is divided by the number of categories desired. Here the minimum category length is $26/5 = 5.2$ units. To find the *actual* category length to be used in splitting the data, we round the minimum length *up* to the same number of decimal places as the data. Here the data are reported in whole numbers. Thus we round the minimum length, 5.2, up to the nearest whole number, 6. The categories actually used will be of length 6. The first category starts $\frac{1}{2}$ unit below the smallest observation. Since the data here are integer-valued, a unit is 1 and we start the first category $\frac{1}{2}$ unit $= \frac{1}{2} \times 1 = .5$ below the smallest observation. That is, the lower boundary for the first category is $130 - .5 = 129.5$. The remaining category boundaries are found by successively adding the actual category length (6) to the preceding boundary length until all data points are covered. In this manner we obtain the following five finite categories for the experimental animals: 129.5 to 135.5, 135.5 to 141.5, 141.5 to 147.5, 147.5 to 153.5, 153.5 to 159.5. Note that since the boundaries have one more decimal place than the data, no data point can fall on a boundary; each data point must fall into one and only one category. Now the data can be summarized in table form by counting the number of observations in each category (see Table 1.8).

The graph of the frequency distribution is shown in Figure 1.8. This graph is now called a frequency *histogram*. The word *histogram* is used to describe any vertical bar graph depicting the distribution of a single variable in which the areas of the rectangles constructed are proportional to the number of objects in the respective categories.

Treating the data for the control animals in the same manner yields Table 1.9 and the histogram shown in Figure 1.9 (smallest observation = 88; largest = 128; data are covered by an interval of length

**TABLE 1.8** EXPERIMENTAL ANIMALS

| CATEGORY | BOUNDARIES | FREQUENCY | RELATIVE FREQUENCY |
|---|---|---|---|
| 1 | 129.5 to 135.5 | 2 | 2/30 = 6.7% |
| 2 | 135.5 to 141.5 | 7 | 7/30 = 23.3% |
| 3 | 141.5 to 147.5 | 10 | 10/30 = 33.3% |
| 4 | 147.5 to 153.5 | 8 | 8/30 = 26.7% |
| 5 | 153.5 to 159.5 | 3 | 3/30 = 10.0% |

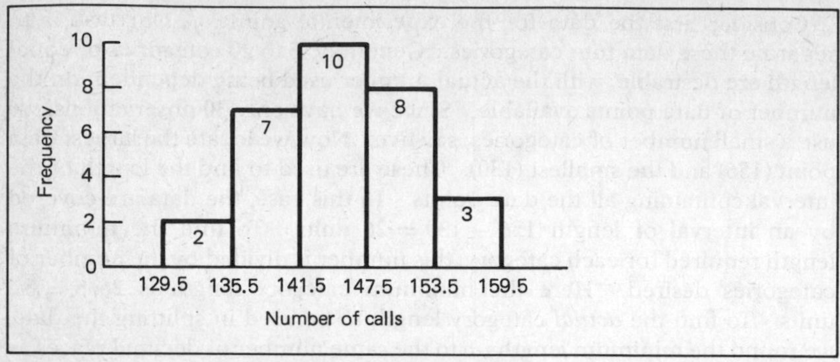


**FIGURE 1.8** Frequency histogram (experimental).

128 − 88 = 40 units; minimum category length = 40/5 = 8; actual category length = 9; lower boundary for the first category is 88 − ½ unit = 88 − ½ × 1 = 87.5).

Both histograms, Figures 1.8 and 1.9, are frequency histograms. If we had graphed categories versus the *relative frequency* per category, the re-

**TABLE 1.9** CONTROL ANIMALS

| CATEGORY | BOUNDARIES | FREQUENCY | RELATIVE FREQUENCY |
|---|---|---|---|
| 1 | 87.5 to 96.5 | 3 | 3/30 = 10.0% |
| 2 | 96.5 to 105.5 | 5 | 5/30 = 16.7% |
| 3 | 105.5 to 114.5 | 9 | 9/30 = 30.0% |
| 4 | 114.5 to 123.5 | 11 | 11/30 = 36.6% |
| 5 | 123.5 to 132.5 | 2 | 2/30 = 6.7% |

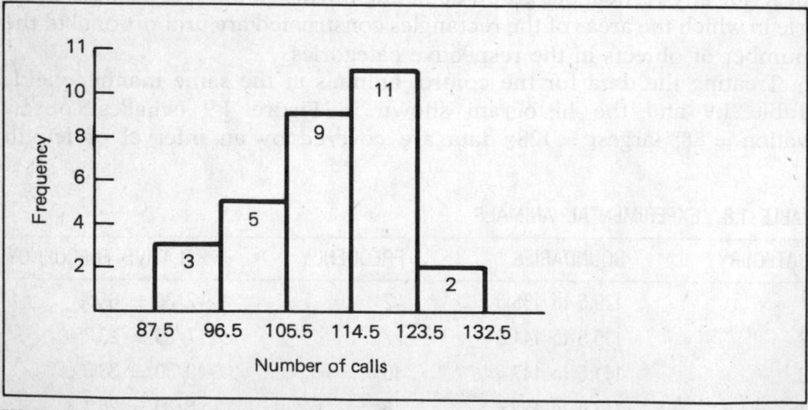


**FIGURE 1.9** Frequency histogram (controls).

sulting graph would have been called a relative frequency histogram. Note that the histograms do have somewhat different shapes and that they are located at different places along the horizontal axis. This implies that there may, in fact, be some basic differences in the behavior of the two groups of animals. These differences can be detected by using the analytic methods introduced in Section 1.3.

---

In addition to the frequency distribution among categories, often it is of interest to consider the *cumulative* frequency distribution of the observations. The cumulative frequency distribution is found by determining for each category the number of observations falling in or below that category. This idea is illustrated in Example 1.2.2.

---

**EXAMPLE 1.2.2** □ Many people experience systemic allergic reactions to insect stings. These reactions differ from patient to patient not only in severity but also in time to onset of the reaction. The following data represent the time to onset of the reaction in 40 patients who experienced a systemic reaction to a bee sting. (Data are in minutes.)

| | | | | | | | |
|---|---|---|---|---|---|---|---|
| 10.5 | 11.2 | 9.9 | 15.0 | 11.4 | 12.7 | <u>16.5</u> | 10.1 |
| 12.7 | 11.4 | 11.6 | 6.2 | 7.9 | 8.3 | 10.9 | 8.1 |
| <u>3.8</u> | 10.5 | 11.7 | 8.4 | 12.5 | 11.2 | 9.1 | 10.4 |
| 9.1 | 13.4 | 12.3 | 5.9 | 11.4 | 8.8 | 7.4 | 8.6 |
| 13.6 | 14.7 | 11.5 | 11.5 | 10.9 | 9.8 | 12.9 | 9.9 |

By using the method of Example 1.2.1 to divide the data into six categories, Table 1.10 is obtained (smallest observation = 3.8; largest = 16.5; data are covered by an interval of length 16.5 − 3.8 = 12.7; minimum category length = 12.7/6 = 2.12; data are reported to the nearest $\frac{1}{10}$, so round the minimum category length *up* to the nearest $\frac{1}{10}$, to get 2.2 for the actual category length; lower boundary for the first category is $\frac{1}{2}$ unit = $\frac{1}{2} \times \frac{1}{10} = \frac{1}{20}$ = .05 below the smallest observation at 3.8 − .05 = 3.75).

**TABLE 1.10** FREQUENCY DISTRIBUTION OF TIME TO ONSET OF REACTION

| CATEGORY | BOUNDARIES | FREQUENCY | RELATIVE FREQUENCY |
|---|---|---|---|
| 1 | 3.75 to 5.95 | 2 | 2/40 = .05 |
| 2 | 5.95 to 8.15 | 4 | 4/40 = .10 |
| 3 | 8.15 to 10.35 | 10 | 10/40 = .25 |
| 4 | 10.35 to 12.55 | 16 | 16/40 = .40 |
| 5 | 12.55 to 14.75 | 6 | 6/40 = .15 |
| 6 | 14.75 to 16.95 | 2 | 2/40 = .05 |

**TABLE 1.11** CUMULATIVE DISTRIBUTION OF TIME TO ONSET OF REACTION

| CATEGORY | BOUNDARIES | CUMULATIVE FREQUENCY | RELATIVE CUMULATIVE FREQUENCY |
|---|---|---|---|
| 1 | 3.75 to 5.95 | 2 | 2/40 = .05 |
| 2 | 5.95 to 8.15 | 6 | 6/40 = .15 |
| 3 | 8.15 to 10.35 | 16 | 16/40 = .40 |
| 4 | 10.35 to 12.55 | 32 | 32/40 = .80 |
| 5 | 12.55 to 14.75 | 38 | 38/40 = .95 |
| 6 | 14.75 to 16.95 | 40 | 40/40 = 1.00 |

To find the cumulative frequency distribution, we sum or accumulate the frequencies and relative frequencies in Table 1.10. (See Table 1.11.) When the data are "continuous" in the sense that the observations conceivably could take on any value in some interval of real numbers, an interesting and useful graph can be constructed from the cumulative table. The graph is a line graph obtained by plotting the upper boundary of each category on the horizontal axis versus the relative cumulative frequency.

The data in this example are continuous since time to onset of the reaction can assume any value between 0 and, say, 2 or 3 hours. The line graph for these data, sometimes called a *relative cumulative frequency ogive,* is shown in Figure 1.10.

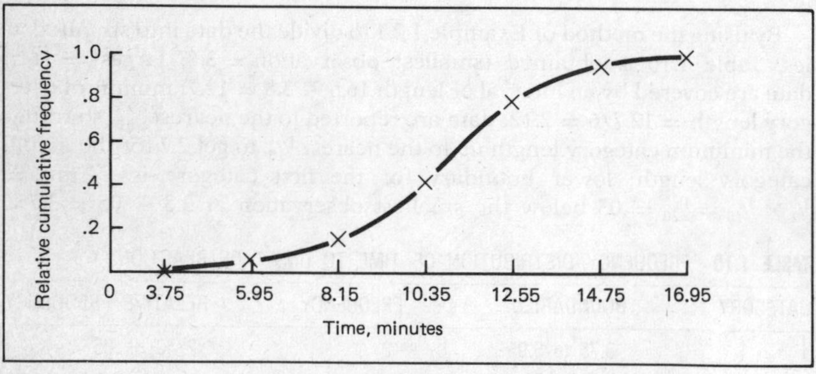


**FIGURE 1.10** Relative cumulative frequency ogive.

We now ask two questions:

Approximately what percentage of patients have experienced a reaction within 10 minutes?

By what time has a reaction occurred in half of the patients?

The first question can be answered graphically by locating 10 on the horizontal axis, projecting a vertical line up to the ogive, and then projecting a horizontal line over to the vertical axis (see Figure 1.11). The desired per-

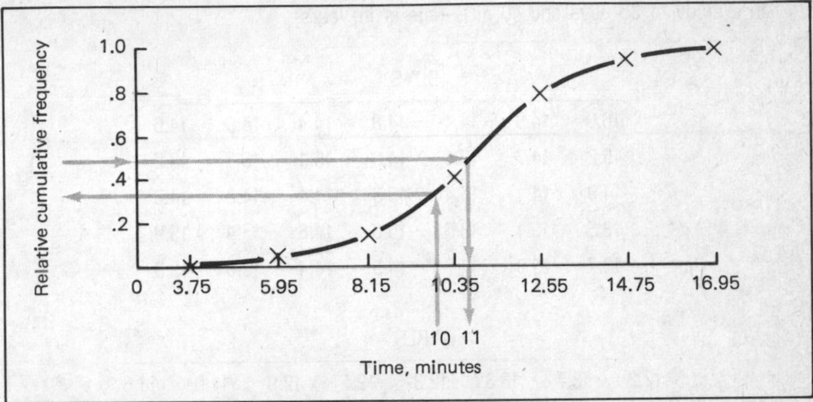


**FIGURE 1.11** Projection method for estimating percentages.

centage is seen to be approximately 37%. The second question is answered by locating .5 on the vertical axis and then reversing the process. The answer is seen to be approximately 11 minutes. (See Figure 1.11.)

---

## EXERCISES 1.2

**1.** One variable of interest in a study of the Xanthid crab, a small crab found near Gloucester Point, Virginia, is the number of eggs spawned per individual. The following observations were obtained for 45 crabs:

| | | | | | | | |
|---|---|---|---|---|---|---|---|
| 1,959 | 4,534 | 7,020 | 6,725 | 6,964 | 7,428 | 9,359 | 9,166 |
| 2,802 | 2,462 | 4,000 | 3,378 | 7,343 | 4,189 | 8,973 | 4,327 |
| 2,412 | 7,624 | 1,548 | 4,801 | 737 | 5,321 | 849 | 5,749 |
| 6,837 | 8,639 | 7,417 | 6,082 | 10,241 | 962 | 3,894 | 1,801 |
| 5,099 | 6,627 | 4,484 | 5,633 | 4,148 | 6,588 | 5,847 | 4,632 |
| 6,472 | 8,372 | 8,225 | 6,142 | 12,130 | | | |

**a.** Find the largest and smallest observations.

**b.** Find the length of the interval that covers the data set.

**c.** What minimum category length is needed to cover the interval of **b** if seven categories are used?

**d.** Find the actual category length to be used in partitioning the data set.
**e.** Find the lower boundary for the first category.
**f.** Determine a frequency table for the data set, and use it to construct a relative frequency histogram.

**2.** In studying growth patterns in children, one important variable is the age of the child when the adolescent growth spurt begins. The following observations were obtained in a study of 35 boys and 40 girls (age is in years):

BOYS

| | | | | | | |
|---|---|---|---|---|---|---|
| 16.0 | 14.9 | 14.1 | 14.8 | 14.4 | 14.0 | 14.6 |
| 15.2 | 14.7 | 13.6 | 14.6 | 16.1 | 13.2 | 13.2 |
| 14.9 | 14.1 | 15.4 | 15.3 | 14.4 | 14.8 | 14.8 |
| 13.5 | 15.1 | 13.5 | 15.0 | 14.6 | 15.4 | 15.9 |
| 13.7 | 15.9 | 14.7 | 14.5 | 14.4 | 13.8 | 15.3 |

GIRLS

| | | | | | | | |
|---|---|---|---|---|---|---|---|
| 12.2 | 13.7 | 13.3 | 12.3 | 12.5 | 12.9 | 11.9 | 11.6 |
| 13.4 | 12.4 | 12.6 | 13.5 | 12.5 | 13.4 | 11.7 | 13.5 |
| 13.7 | 12.1 | 14.1 | 11.8 | 12.8 | 12.9 | 11.6 | 14.3 |
| 13.1 | 13.3 | 13.5 | 14.7 | 12.3 | 11.6 | 13.1 | 12.6 |
| 12.7 | 12.7 | 12.0 | 11.4 | 13.5 | 12.4 | 12.1 | 12.1 |

**a.** Break each data set into six categories, using the method of Example 1.2.1.
**b.** Construct relative frequency histograms for each data set. Comment on any apparent similarities or differences in the histograms.
**c.** For each data set, construct a relative cumulative frequency ogive. Use the ogive to approximate the age by which 50% of the boys have begun the adolescent growth spurt; do the same for the girls. Does there appear to be much difference between the two values?
**d.** By age 12, approximately what percentage of the girls had experienced the beginning of the growth spurt? By age 14, approximately what percentage of the boys had experienced the beginning of the growth spurt?

**3.** In patients with Duchenne muscular dystrophy, serum levels of creatine kinase are dramatically elevated over the normal value of less than 50 units/liter. The following data are serum creatine kinase activities measured in 24 young Duchenne patients (in units per liter):

| | | | | | |
|---|---|---|---|---|---|
| 3720 | 3795 | 3340 | 5600 | 3800 | 3580 |
| 5500 | 2000 | 1570 | 2360 | 1500 | 1840 |
| 3725 | 3790 | 3345 | 3805 | 5595 | 3575 |
| 1995 | 5505 | 2055 | 1575 | 1835 | 1505 |

a. Break the data set into five categories.
b. Find the cumulative frequency distribution of the data set.
c. Plot a relative cumulative frequency ogive for the data set.
d. Based on these data, what percentage of Duchenne patients have serum creatine kinase levels of at least 50 times the normal value?

4. In a study designed to correlate seasonal change in plasma testosterone with the reproductive cycle in lizards, the following data were obtained from a sample of 33 lizards of a particular species captured in the month of August. (Testosterone levels are in nanograms per milliliter.)

| | | | | | | | | | | |
|---|---|---|---|---|---|---|---|---|---|---|
| 7.5 | 7.2 | 3.0 | 12.1 | 15.1 | 12.1 | 11.5 | 11.8 | 7.2 | 13.2 | 13.6 |
| 8.2 | 9.5 | 8.4 | 13.3 | 12.5 | 12.4 | 2.1 | 10.7 | 9.4 | 6.7 | 6.8 |
| 6.1 | 8.3 | 7.9 | 6.0 | 7.6 | 13.2 | 4.5 | 9.3 | 8.1 | 3.5 | 9.0 |

In October a sample of 40 lizards of the same species had the following plasma testosterone levels:

| | | | | | | | |
|---|---|---|---|---|---|---|---|
| 43.7 | 37.2 | 29.0 | 31.6 | 47.5 | 48.3 | 38.3 | 29.7 |
| 32.5 | 45.2 | 36.1 | 30.5 | 37.2 | 50.5 | 36.9 | 44.5 |
| 35.9 | 28.7 | 37.5 | 30.2 | 36.9 | 43.2 | 27.0 | 26.2 |
| 41.8 | 26.4 | 34.3 | 28.6 | 35.9 | 22.0 | 45.4 | 30.3 |
| 29.8 | 46.1 | 42.7 | 31.5 | 37.4 | 25.1 | 27.2 | 45.0 |

a. Find frequency tables for both data sets. (Use six categories in each case.)
b. Construct relative frequency histograms for both data sets.
c. Compare the histograms in light of the additional observation that secondary sex characteristics develop in young lizards in the winter and mating takes place in summer.

---

## DESCRIPTIVE MEASURES

**1.3** □ One way to compare two data sets is by constructing and comparing their histograms, as was done in Section 1.2. This comparison does give some insight into the differences and similarities between the two. However, the method is not very precise. The purpose of this section is to develop some analytic measures that can be used to characterize a data set. In particular, we consider two measures of location or central tendency, the sample mean and the sample median; and three measures of dispersion or variability, the sample variance, sample standard deviation, and sample range. The word *sample* is used to emphasize the fact that the data sets presented are based on experiments involving only a small portion, or "sample," of objects of the type under study. For instance, in the study of the reaction of patients to bee stings in Example 1.2.2, the 40 patients involved do not constitute all persons who are allergic to bees; they represent only a portion, or a "sample," of patients drawn from this larger group.

**EXAMPLE 1.3.1** □ In a study of scholastic sports injuries, 25 school districts within a state were selected and polled. The following data were obtained on the number of serious injuries incurred by male athletes while participating in basketball and football:

| BASKETBALL | | | | | FOOTBALL | | | | |
|---|---|---|---|---|---|---|---|---|---|
| 1 | 2 | 4 | 4 | 7 | 1 | 7 | 7 | 6 | 1 |
| 3 | 3 | 2 | 4 | 5 | 2 | 6 | 1 | 7 | 2 |
| 2 | 4 | 3 | 5 | 3 | 1 | 3 | 2 | 7 | 5 |
| 4 | 4 | 3 | 6 | 5 | 6 | 1 | 7 | 4 | 1 |
| 5 | 6 | 4 | 6 | 5 | 5 | 7 | 6 | 3 | 2 |

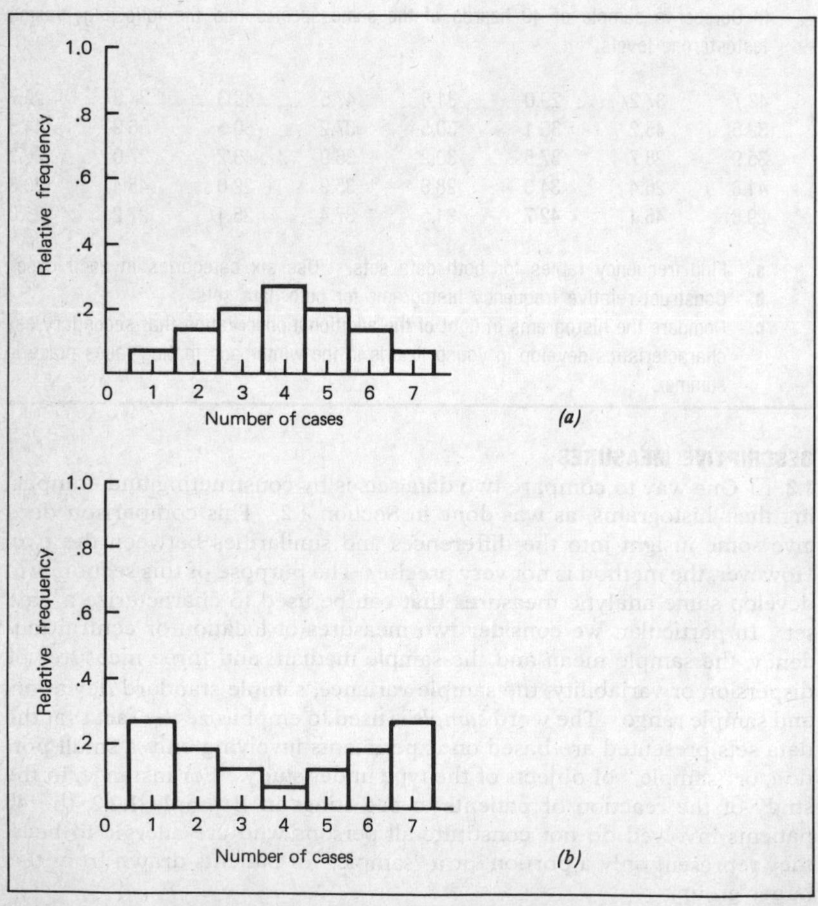


**FIGURE 1.12** Relative frequency histograms: basketball (*a*) and football (*b*).

**TABLE 1.12** FREQUENCY DISTRIBUTIONS OF SCHOLASTIC SPORTS INJURIES

| Basketball Injuries | | | Football Injuries | | |
|---|---|---|---|---|---|
| NUMBER OF CASES | FREQUENCY | RELATIVE FREQUENCY | NUMBER OF CASES | FREQUENCY | RELATIVE FREQUENCY |
| 1 | 1 | .04 | 1 | 6 | .24 |
| 2 | 3 | .12 | 2 | 4 | .16 |
| 3 | 5 | .20 | 3 | 2 | .08 |
| 4 | 7 | .28 | 4 | 1 | .04 |
| 5 | 5 | .20 | 5 | 2 | .08 |
| 6 | 3 | .12 | 6 | 4 | .16 |
| 7 | 1 | .04 | 7 | 6 | .24 |



The frequency table is Table 1.12, and the relative frequency histogram for each data set is shown in Figure 1.12. It is evident that even though both histograms are centered at four, their shapes are quite different. We need to have a method to detect analytically similarities and differences such as these.

---

The most common measure of the center of location of a data set is its mean. The *mean* of a data set is just its arithmetic average. This definition is formalized below. It entails the use of summation notation. The reader who is unfamiliar with this notation is referred to Appendix A.

**Definition 1.3.1** *Sample Mean.* Let $x_1, x_2, \ldots, x_n$ be a set of $n$ observations on a variable $X$. The arithmetic average of these values is called the *sample mean* and is denoted by $\bar{x}$. That is,

$$\text{Sample mean} = \bar{x} = (x_1 + x_2 + \cdots + x_n)/n = (\Sigma x)/n.$$

---

**EXAMPLE 1.3.2** □ Let $X$ denote the number of basketball injuries reported per district and $Y$ the number of football injuries reported per district. Using the data of Example 1.3.1 it can be seen that

$$\bar{x} = (\Sigma x)/25 = (1 + 3 + 2 + 4 + 5 + \cdots + 5)/25 = 4 \text{ cases}$$

and

$$\bar{y} = (\Sigma y)/25 = (1 + 2 + 1 + 6 + 5 + \cdots + 2)/25 = 4 \text{ cases}$$

As expected both data sets have the same sample mean. With respect to this measure of the center of location the data sets are identical. If this were the only measure used to compare the two data sets, we would conclude that there is no difference between them. This is obviously not the case. There is a difference that is not being detected by the mean alone.

The characteristic that is not being detected by the sample mean is *variability*. There is some fluctuation in the observations. They are not all the same. Some lie close to the mean; others do not. We need a measure that detects the extent of this variability. Several have been proposed. Perhaps the most logical way to try to measure variability about the mean is to average the differences between the observations and the mean. A quick example will show that although this proposal is intuitively appealing, it will not work!

---

**EXAMPLE 1.3.3** □ Consider the following set of observations:

$$x_1 = 2 \qquad x_3 = 1 \qquad x_5 = 4$$
$$x_2 = 5 \qquad x_4 = 3$$

The sample mean for this data set is

$$\bar{x} = \frac{\Sigma x}{5} = \frac{2 + 5 + 1 + 3 + 4}{5} = 3$$

The average difference between the observations and the sample mean is

$$\frac{(2 - 3) + (5 - 3) + (1 - 3) + (3 - 3) + (4 - 3)}{5}$$
$$= \frac{(-1) + 2 + (-2) + 0 + 1}{5}$$
$$= 0$$

The proposed method of measuring variability makes it appear that there is no fluctuation in the data. The problem is evident. We are allowing negative differences to cancel positive ones, to give an average difference of zero. This problem must be corrected to obtain a satisfactory measure of variability about the mean.

---

There are several ways to measure variability that avoid the problem of allowing negative differences to cancel positive ones. Two are in common use. Both avoid the problem of negative differences by squaring the differences before averaging them. The most logical measure of variability about the mean is the arithmetic average of these squared differences,

$$\frac{\Sigma(x - \bar{x})^2}{n}$$

This measure is acceptable and is preferred by many. However, the more common measure is obtained by dividing the sum of the squared differences by $n - 1$ instead of $n$. The reason is that the measure obtained, called the *sample variance,* has some mathematical properties that make it especially useful in inferential statistics. These properties are discussed in Chapter 7. The definition is formalized here.

**Definition 1.3.2** *Sample Variance.* Let $x_1, x_2, \ldots, x_n$ be a set of $n$ observations on a variable $X$ with sample mean $\bar{x}$. The *sample variance* is denoted by $s^2$ and is given by

$$s^2 = \frac{\Sigma(x - \bar{x})^2}{n - 1}$$

---

**EXAMPLE 1.3.4** □ The data set

| 2 | 1 | 4 |
|---|---|---|
| 5 | 3 | |

of Example 1.3.3 has a sample mean of 3. Its sample variance is given by

$$\begin{aligned} s^2 &= \frac{\Sigma(x - \bar{x})^2}{(n - 1)} \\ &= \frac{(2-3)^2 + (5-3)^2 + (1-3)^2 + (3-3)^2 + (4-3)^2}{4} \\ &= \frac{(-1)^2 + 2^2 + (-2)^2 + 0^2 + 1^2}{4} \\ &= \frac{1 + 4 + 4 + 0 + 1}{4} = \frac{10}{4} = 2.5 \end{aligned}$$

---

The formula for the sample variance given in Definition 1.3.2 does involve a fair amount of computation, especially if the data set is large. The following formula for $s^2$ is computationally easier than that given in Definition 1.3.2. Its proof is based on the rules for summation which are given in Appendix A.

---

**THEOREM 1.3.1** □ *Computational Formula for* $s^2$. Let $x_1, x_2, \ldots, x_n$ be a set of $n$ observations on a variable $X$ with sample mean $\bar{x}$. The sample variance is given by

$$s^2 = \frac{n\Sigma x^2 - (\Sigma x)^2}{n(n - 1)}$$

The use of this formula is illustrated by recalculating the sample variance for the data of Example 1.3.4.

**EXAMPLE 1.3.5** □ Consider the set of observations

$$\begin{matrix} 2 & 1 & 4 \\ 5 & 3 & \end{matrix}$$

To compute $s^2$ by using the computational formula, two quantities, $\Sigma x$ and $\Sigma x^2$, are required. For these data

$$\Sigma x = 2 + 5 + 1 + 3 + 4 = 15$$

and

$$\Sigma x^2 = 2^2 + 5^2 + 1^2 + 3^2 + 4^2 = 55$$

Thus

$$\begin{aligned} s^2 &= \frac{n\Sigma x^2 - (\Sigma x)^2}{n(n-1)} \\ &= \frac{5(55) - (15^2)}{5(4)} \\ &= \frac{275 - 225}{20} = 2.5 \end{aligned}$$

As expected, this result agrees with that obtained in Example 1.3.4.

Keep in mind the practical interpretation of $s^2$. The measure is defined in such a way that it cannot be negative. Furthermore, if most of the observations lie close to the mean, the variance will be small. However, if the data points exhibit a fair amount of variability in the sense that values quite frequently lie far from the mean, then the variance will be large.

We are now in a position to investigate further the differences that exist between the two data sets of Example 1.3.1.

**EXAMPLE 1.3.6** □ Consider the histograms of Figure 1.12. Most of the observations obtained on basketball injuries lie close to the mean value of 4, as evidenced by the bulge in the center of histogram *a*. However, very few of the observations obtained on football injuries lie near 4. This is apparent from the dip in the center of histogram *b*. Intuitively, then, we would expect the sample variance for the data on basketball injuries to be smaller than that for the data on football injuries. To verify this, let us compute $s^2$ for each data set.

BASKETBALL

$$\Sigma x = 100$$

$$\Sigma x^2 = 452$$

$$s_X^2 = \frac{n\Sigma x^2 - (\Sigma x)^2}{n(n-1)}$$

FOOTBALL

$$\Sigma y = 100$$

$$\Sigma y^2 = 544$$

$$s_Y^2 = \frac{n\Sigma y^2 - (\Sigma y)^2}{n(n-1)}$$

$$= \frac{25(452) - (100^2)}{25(24)} \qquad = \frac{25(544) - (100^2)}{25(24)}$$

$$= 2.17 \qquad = 6$$

As expected, $s_X^2 < s_Y^2$.

---

A second measure of variability is the sample standard deviation. We define this measure now.

**Definition 1.3.3** *Sample Standard Deviation.* Let $x_1, x_2, \ldots, x_n$ be a set of $n$ observations on a variable $X$ with sample variance $s^2$. The *sample standard deviation* is denoted by $s$ and is defined by

$$s = \sqrt{s^2}$$

Note that the sample standard deviation is simply the nonnegative square root of the sample variance. Since these two measures of variability are so closely related, the natural question to ask is, Why bother with both of them? There is one very practical reason for wanting to measure variability by using the standard deviation of the data set. Consider the data on the number of football and basketball injuries reported in 25 school districts. The unit associated with each data point and with each sample mean is an "injury." When the sample variance is calculated, the differences between the observed values and the sample mean are *squared*. The unit associated with the sample variance is therefore a "squared injury"! This does not make any sense. However, since the sample standard deviation is the square root of the sample variance, the unit associated with $s$ is again an "injury." It often happens that the original unit is meaningless when squared. For this reason, generally no unit is attached to a variance. However, the unit associated with a standard deviation will always be the same as that associated with the original data and so will always be physically meaningful.

---

**EXAMPLE 1.3.7** □ The sample variance for the number of basketball-related injuries is 2.17 (see Example 1.3.6). The sample standard deviation is $s = \sqrt{s^2} = \sqrt{2.17} = 1.47$ injuries.

---

The last measure of variability to be considered is the sample range. This measure is the easiest to compute, and we define it here.

**Definition 1.3.4** *Sample Range.* Let $x_1, x_2, \ldots, x_n$ be a set of $n$ observations on a variable $X$. The *sample range* is the difference between the largest and smallest observations with subtraction being in the order of largest minus smallest.

The last measure of central tendency to be considered is the sample median. Roughly speaking, the sample median is the "middle" of the data set.

**Definition 1.3.5** *Sample Median.* Let $x_1, x_2, \ldots, x_n$ be a set of $n$ observations on a variable $X$ arranged in order (smallest to largest). The *sample median* is denoted by $\tilde{x}$ and is given by

$$\tilde{x} = \begin{cases} x_{(n+1)/2} & \text{if } n \text{ is odd} \\ \dfrac{x_{n/2} + x_{n/2+1}}{2} & \text{if } n \text{ is even} \end{cases}$$

This definition appears to be complicated. It is not. It says simply that to find the sample median, first the observations are *ordered* smallest to largest. The sample median is the middle observation if $n$ is odd; it is the arithmetic average of the two middle observations if $n$ is even.

---

**EXAMPLE 1.3.8** □ In a study of water pollution, samples of mussels were taken from two localities in Sweden. The variable of interest is $X$, the lead concentration in the mussel measured in milligrams per gram of dry weight. The data collected are as shown: The data has been ordered from smallest to largest.

| SMYGEHUK (I) | FALSTERBO KANAL (II) |
|---|---|
| 106.3 | 113.0 |
| 209.3 | 140.5 |
| 246.5 | 163.3 |
| 252.3 | 185.7 |
| 294.4 | 202.5 |
| | 207.2 |

The sample range for the data collected at Smygehuk is $294.4 - 106.3 = 188.1$; for the data collected at Falsterbo Kanal, the sample range is $207.2 - 113.0 = 94.2$.

Since there is an odd number of observations in data set I ($n = 5$), the sample median is the middle observation. That is,

$$\tilde{x} = x_{(n+1)/2} = x_{(5+1)/2} = x_3 = 246.5$$

There are an even number of observations in data set II ($n = 6$). Thus the sample median is the average of the two middle observations. That is,

$$\tilde{y} = \frac{y_{n/2} + y_{n/2+1}}{2} = \frac{y_{6/2} + y_{6/2+1}}{2} = \frac{y_3 + y_4}{2}$$

$$= \frac{163.3 + 185.7}{2} = 174.5$$

---

Measures of the central tendency, the variability, and the range provide valuable information about a data set. Often, however, we are concerned with not just a single data set, but the way in which a particular set of measurements behaves as a function of time, or dose of drug, or some other variable. At each time point, drug dose, and so on, a different data set is obtained. This may involve a very large number of data points, so a convenient way of graphing the data that provides maximum information is desirable. One such method is illustrated in Example 1.3.9.

---

**EXAMPLE 1.3.9** □ The concentration of lactate in arterial blood was measured in a sample of six young men before and at several times during controlled exercise and in the recovery period following. The data in Table 1.13 were obtained. The mean and standard deviation for the data

**TABLE 1.13** ARTERIAL CONCENTRATIONS OF LACTATE (MILLIMOLES/LITER)

| | Exercise, minutes | | | | Recovery, minutes | | | |
|---|---|---|---|---|---|---|---|---|
| REST | 5 | 10 | 20 | 30 | 5 | 20 | 35 | 65 |
| 0.93 | 7.60 | 8.25 | 6.70 | 6.49 | 4.35 | 2.05 | 1.35 | 0.85 |
| 0.55 | 3.95 | 4.31 | 8.85 | 4.38 | 6.22 | 2.98 | 2.02 | 0.58 |
| 0.87 | 6.54 | 6.52 | 4.56 | 8.75 | 2.45 | 1.17 | 0.76 | 0.95 |
| 0.62 | 4.27 | 5.15 | 7.29 | 6.72 | 3.57 | 2.71 | 1.21 | 1.10 |
| 0.72 | 5.85 | 7.31 | 5.88 | 4.88 | 3.81 | 1.84 | 1.58 | 0.62 |
| 0.79 | 5.41 | 6.30 | 6.96 | 7.70 | 5.62 | 2.36 | 1.29 | 0.79 |

set at each time point may be computed and are given in Table 1.14. Then a graph can be constructed in which the mean lactate concentration in millimoles per liter is plotted as a function of time. The standard deviation of each time point in the data set is shown as a set of brackets extending above and below the mean value points, as shown in Figure 1.13. Just a glance at this graph gives an idea of the change in blood lactate during

**TABLE 1.14**

| | | Exercise, minutes | | | | Recovery, minutes | | | |
|---|---|---|---|---|---|---|---|---|---|
| | REST | 5 | 10 | 20 | 30 | 5 | 20 | 35 | 65 |
| $\bar{x}$ | 0.75 | 5.60 | 6.31 | 6.71 | 6.49 | 4.34 | 2.19 | 1.37 | 0.82 |
| $s$ | 0.15 | 1.38 | 1.43 | 1.43 | 1.65 | 1.39 | 0.65 | 0.42 | 0.20 |

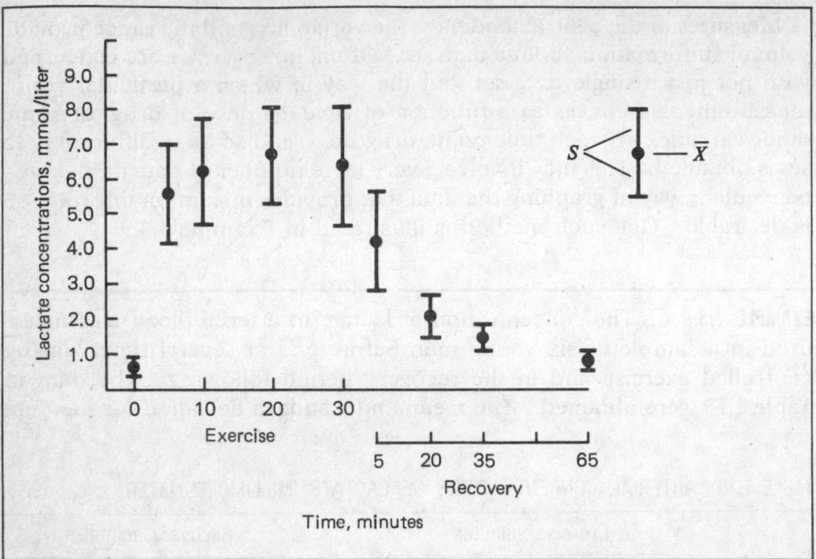


**FIGURE 1.13** Lactate concentration over time.

exercise and recovery and allows a quick assessment of the variability at different time points.

---

You should be warned of one thing. Many graphs of the sort described in Example 1.3.9 appear in the literature. Other graphs of a similar appearance are used also. In these graphs, however, a measure of variability known as the *standard error of the mean* (SE) is used to determine the length of the brackets extending above and below the mean. (See Exercise 1.3.4.) Graphs of either sort should be clearly marked to indicate which measure of variability is being used.

There are other statistical measures to describe data sets. We presented here the most commonly encountered ones. Several others are mentioned in the exercises for reference purposes. The sample mean, variance, and standard deviation are used extensively throughout this text; the sample median plays an important role in our discussion of distribution-free methods in Chapter 13.

---

## EXERCISES 1.3

1. Consider the following data sets:

| DATA SET I | | | DATA SET II | | | |
|---|---|---|---|---|---|---|
| 2 | 4 | 0 | 1 | 1 | 5 | 7 |
| 1 | 4 | 3 | 3 | 4 | 6 | |
| 3 | 1 | 1 | 2 | 1 | 5 | |

For each data set find the sample mean, sample variance, sample standard deviation, sample range, and sample median.

**2.** In a study of parasites, the distribution of the tick *Ixodes trianguliceps* in field mice was considered. The following observations were obtained on the number of ticks found on 44 mice.

| | | | | | | | | |
|---|---|---|---|---|---|---|---|---|
| 0 | 2 | 0 | 0 | 2 | 2 | 0 | 0 | 1 |
| 1 | 3 | 0 | 0 | 1 | 0 | 0 | 1 | 0 |
| 1 | 4 | 0 | 0 | 1 | 4 | 2 | 0 | 0 |
| 1 | 0 | 0 | 2 | 2 | 1 | 1 | 0 | 6 |
| 0 | 5 | 1 | 3 | 0 | 1 | 0 | 1 | |

Find the sample mean, sample variance, sample standard deviation, sample range, and sample median.

***3.** *Outliers.* Often studies of birds are conducted by capturing, banding, and releasing the birds so that their movements can be followed. One variable studied was the flight distance from the point of release of a bird just banded to its first perch. The following data were obtained on two types of birds, the robin and the mourning dove (distance is given in feet):

| ROBIN (I) | | | MOURNING DOVE (II) | | | |
|---|---|---|---|---|---|---|
| 128.8 | 57.2 | 48.2 | 40.0 | 381.7 | 358.9 | 1200.0* |
| 160.0 | 65.2 | 69.2 | 80.0 | 266.8 | 13.9 | |
| 192.1 | 68.9 | 117.3 | 313.9 | 162.7 | 165.5 | |
| 163.4 | 24.7 | 36.5 | 175.7 | 76.0 | 317.2 | |
| 186.4 | 37.4 | 140.8 | 55.5 | 22.1 | 300.6 | |
| 156.2 | 99.7 | 59.3 | 44.7 | 170.0 | 197.7 | |
| 70.0 | 265.0 | 71.3 | 166.7 | 263.7 | 288.1 | |
| 10.0 | 78.7 | 105.3 | 83.4 | 369.7 | 102.0 | |

**a.** Find the sample mean, median, range, variance, and standard deviation for each data set. Do they seem similar with respect to any of these measures?

***b.** Note that the starred observation in the data set for mourning doves is very different from the others. It is called an *outlier.* (An outlier is an observation at either extreme of a sample which is so far removed from the main body of the data that the appropriateness of including it in the sample is questionable.) To see the effect of this outlier, drop it from the data set and calculate the mean, median, range, variance, and standard deviation for the remaining 24 observations. Which measure is least affected by the presence of the outlier? Do you see why it is desirable to report both the mean and the median of a data set? Does there appear to be an outlier in data set I?

*4. *Sample Standard Error.* In the literature, usually researchers report the mean of their sample together with either the sample standard deviation $s$ or a measure called the sample standard error of the mean (SE). These two measures, though related, are not the same. The equations relating the two are

$$\text{SE} = \frac{s}{\sqrt{n}} \qquad \text{or} \qquad (\text{SE})(\sqrt{n}) = s$$

The usefulness of this measure becomes apparent in Chapter 7.

a. One variable of interest in a study of Gambel's sparrow is $X$, the duration of its song in seconds. It is reported that based on a sample of 115 birds, the sample mean is 2.06 seconds with a sample standard deviation of .177 second. What is the value of the standard error of the mean for this sample?

b. In a study of the effects of DDE, one of the principal components of DDT, on the egg shells of great black-backed gulls, one variable of interest is the thickness of the shells in micrometers. Two groups of gulls are studied: those lightly contaminated with the substance and those that have been highly contaminated. The following is reported:

| LIGHTLY CONTAMINATED | HIGHLY CONTAMINATED |
|---|---|
| $n = 8$ | $n = 7$ |
| $\bar{x} = 316$ μm | $\bar{y} = 287$ μm |
| SE = 4 | SE = 9 |

Find the sample standard deviation for each group. Point out the similarities and differences between the two groups.

*5. *Coefficient of Variation.* The coefficient of variation is a measure used to compare the variability in one data set with that in another in situations in which a direct comparison of standard deviations is not convenient or realistic. For example, in a study of milk consumption in the United States, it is reported that the mean number of gallons of milk consumed per family unit per week is 8 with a sample standard deviation of 3 gallons. A similar study in Canada reports the mean consumption to be 12 liters with a sample standard deviation of 4 liters. It makes no sense to compare these standard deviations directly because they are reported in different units. A quick way to compare variability is with the ***coefficient of variation*** (CV), given by

$$\text{CV} = \frac{s}{\bar{x}}(100)$$

a. An experiment is conducted to investigate the effect of a new dog food on weight gain in pups during the first 8 weeks of their lives. It is reported that the mean weight gain in a group of Great Dane pups is 30 pounds with a standard deviation of 10 pounds; the mean weight gain in a group of Chihuahua pups is 3 pounds with a standard deviation of 1.5 pounds. Calculate the coefficient of variation for each group. Which group exhibits the greater variability? Why is a direct comparison of standard deviations misleading here?

**b.** A study of weights of 2-year-old girls in Great Britain yielded a sample mean of 12.74 kilograms with a sample standard deviation of 1.60 kilograms. A similar study in the United States resulted in a sample mean of 29.2 pounds with a sample standard deviation of 2 pounds. Find the coefficient of variation for each group. Which group exhibits greater variability?

---

## HANDLING GROUPED DATA

**1.4** □ In many instances in the literature, data are presented in table or category form. Neither the raw data nor summary measures are given. When this occurs, it is helpful to be able to extract from the table at least a rough approximation of various summary measures for the underlying data set. Methods for doing so are given in the following examples.

---

**EXAMPLE 1.4.1** □ In a study of Down's syndrome, 180 children who were suffering from the disorder were examined. Table 1.15 gives the frequency distribution for the variable $X$, the child's IQ. To use this table to

**TABLE 1.15** FREQUENCY DISTRIBUTION OF IQ

| CLASS | CLASS BOUNDARIES | FREQUENCY |
|---|---|---|
| 1 | 10.5 to 20.5 | 4 |
| 2 | 20.5 to 30.5 | 34 |
| 3 | 30.5 to 40.5 | 0 |
| 4 | 40.5 to 50.5 | 70 |
| 5 | 50.5 to 60.5 | 43 |
| 6 | 60.5 to 70.5 | 19 |
| 7 | 70.5 to 80.5 | 7 |
| 8 | 80.5 to 90.5 | 2 |
| 9 | 90.5 to 100.5 | 1 |

approximate the mean IQ, first we determine the midpoint of each category or class. The *midpoint* is the arithmetic average of the lower and upper class boundaries. Thus the midpoint for the first class, which we denote by $m_1$, is

$$m_1 = \frac{10.5 + 20.5}{2} = 15.5$$

Successive class midpoints $m_2, m_3, \ldots, m_9$ are given in Table 1.16.

**TABLE 1.16** FREQUENCY DISTRIBUTION OF IQ

| CLASS | CLASS BOUNDARIES | CLASS MIDPOINT $m_i$ | FREQUENCY $f_i$ |
|---|---|---|---|
| 1 | 10.5 to 20.5 | 15.5 | 4 |
| 2 | 20.5 to 30.5 | 25.5 | 34 |
| 3 | 30.5 to 40.5 | 35.5 | 0 |
| 4 | 40.5 to 50.5 | 45.5 | 70 |
| 5 | 50.5 to 60.5 | 55.5 | 43 |
| 6 | 60.5 to 70.5 | 65.5 | 19 |
| 7 | 70.5 to 80.5 | 75.5 | 7 |
| 8 | 80.5 to 90.5 | 85.5 | 2 |
| 9 | 90.5 to 100.5 | 95.5 | 1 |

As long as the classes are not excessively wide, the midpoint of each class serves as a good approximation for each of the values in the class. Thus in approximating the sample mean, each of the four observations in class 1, whose actual values are unknown to us, is replaced by the number 15.5; each of the 34 observations in class 2 is replaced by the number 25.5; this procedure is continued for the other classes until finally the one observation in class 9 is replaced by the value 95.5. To approximate $\bar{x}$, we add these values and divide by 180, the total number of children in the study. Thus

$$\bar{x} \doteq \frac{4(15.5) + 34(25.5) + 0(35.5) + \cdots + 2(85.5) + 1(95.5)}{180}$$

$$= 47.4$$

where the symbol $\doteq$ means "approximately equal to." The mean IQ for this group of children is approximately 47.4.

---

A similar procedure can be used to approximate the sample variance for grouped data. Once again, the method is based on the assumption that the class midpoint provides a good approximation for each of the observations in the class. It also utilizes Theorem 1.3.1, the computational formula for $s^2$.

**Definition 1.4.1** *$\bar{x}$ and $s^2$, Grouped Data.* Let $x_1, x_2, x_3, \ldots, x_n$ be a set of $n$ observations on a variable $X$ categorized into $K$ classes. Let $m_i$ and $f_i$ $(i = 1, 2, 3, \ldots, K)$ denote the class midpoint and class frequency, respectively, for each class. Then

$$\bar{x} \doteq \sum_{i=1}^{K} \frac{f_i m_i}{n}$$

and

$$s^2 \doteq \frac{n \sum_{i=1}^{K} f_i m_i^2 - \left(\sum_{i=1}^{K} f_i m_i\right)^2}{n(n-1)}$$

---

**EXAMPLE 1.4.2** □ The approximate value of $s^2$ for the grouped data for Example 1.4.1 is given by

$$s^2 \doteq \frac{n \sum_{i=1}^{K} f_i m_i^2 - \left(\sum_{i=1}^{K} f_i m_i\right)^2}{n(n-1)}$$

$$= \frac{180 \sum_{i=1}^{9} f_i m_i^2 - \left(\sum_{i=1}^{9} f_i m_i\right)^2}{180(179)}$$

For these data

$$\sum_{i=1}^{9} f_i m_i^2 = 4(15.5)^2 + 34(25.5)^2 + \cdots + 2(85.5)^2 + 1(95.5)^2$$
$$= 445{,}595$$

and

$$\sum_{i=1}^{9} f_i m_i = 4(15.5) + 34(25.5) + \cdots + 2(85.5) + 1(95.5)$$
$$= 8540$$

Thus

$$s^2 \doteq \frac{180(445{,}595) - (8540^2)}{180(179)} = 225.8$$

and

$$s \doteq \sqrt{225.8} = 15.03$$

---

We outline here a method that can be used to approximate any specified observation in a data set from grouped data. When the point of interest is the "middle" of the data set, the method can be applied to obtain an approximation for the sample median.

Assume that $x_1, x_2, x_3, \ldots, x_n$ is a linearly ordered set of observations on a variable $X$. Let $x_j$ denote any one of these observations. To approximate $x_j$ from grouped data, the following steps are used:

1. Locate the class in which $x_j$ falls; denote the class frequency for this class by $f$.

2. Find the lower and upper class boundaries for this class; denote them by $l$ and $u$, respectively.

3. Find the difference between $j$ and the cumulative frequency for the class immediately preceding the one in which $x_j$ falls; denote this difference by $d$.

4. The approximate value of $x_j$ is

$$x_j \doteq l + \frac{d}{f}(u - l)$$

This procedure is easier to apply than it is to outline! Consider Example 1.4.3.

**EXAMPLE 1.4.3** □ A study is conducted to assess the effect of alcohol on serum cholesterol levels. One variable of interest is $X$, the amount of alcohol consumed per week per subject. The data for the 923 subjects who participated in the study are given in Table 1.17.

**TABLE 1.17** FREQUENCY DISTRIBUTION OF ALCOHOL CONSUMPTION (IN OUNCES)

| CLASS | CLASS BOUNDARIES | FREQUENCY $f$ | CUMULATIVE FREQUENCY | RELATIVE CUMULATIVE FREQUENCY |
|---|---|---|---|---|
| 1 | 0 to .5 | 201 | 201 | .218 |
| 2 | .5 to 3.5 | 372 | 573* | .621 |
| 3 | 3.5 to 9.5 | 260 | 833 | .903 |
| 4 | 9.5 to 19.5 | 80 | 913 | .989 |
| 5 | $\geq$19.5 | 10 | 923 | 1.000 |

The total number of observations is $n = 923$. Since this number is odd, by Definition 1.3.5 the sample median is $\tilde{x} = x_{(n+1)/2} = x_{462}$. Thus we are trying to approximate $x_j = x_{462}$. From the cumulative frequency distribution it can be seen that the 462d observation lies in the second class (denoted *). The class frequency for this class is $f = 372$. Its lower class boundary is $l = .5$; its upper boundary is $u = 3.5$. The difference between $j$ and the cumulative frequency for class 1 is $d = 462 - 201 = 261$. Thus

$$\begin{aligned}\tilde{x} = x_{462} &\doteq l + \frac{d}{f}(u - l)\\ &= .5 + \frac{261}{372}(3.5 - .5)\\ &= 2.6\end{aligned}$$

The approximate median alcohol consumption is 2.6 ounces per week.

The sample median for data that are continuous also can be approximated graphically. This was done in Section 1.2, although the word *median* was not used then. The method is illustrated in Example 1.4.4.

**EXAMPLE 1.4.4** □ Consider again the data in Table 1.17. Let us construct the relative cumulative frequency ogive for the data by graphing the upper class boundary of each class against its relative cumulative frequency. The graph is shown in Figure 1.14. Since the median is the "middle" of

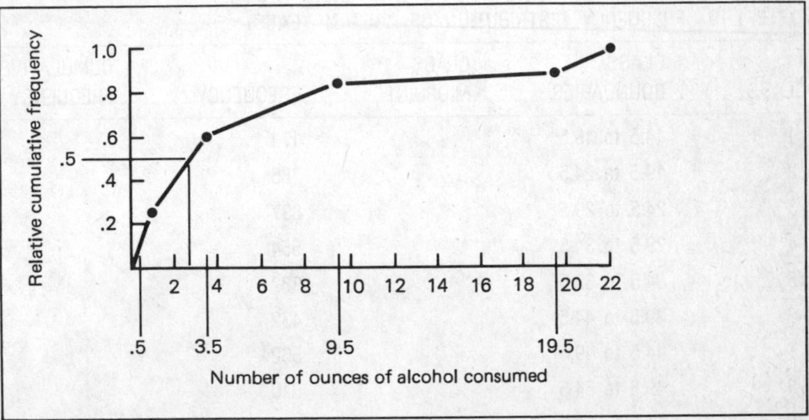


**FIGURE 1.14** Relative cumulative frequency ogive.

the data set, it is the point with the property that half the observations fall on or below it and the rest fall above. To approximate this point graphically, we locate .5 on the vertical axis and use the projection method of Section 1.2 to locate the approximate value of the sample median on the horizontal axis. The value appears to lie near 3, which agrees fairly well with the value obtained previously.

## EXERCISES 1.4

1. Consider Table 1.18.
   a. Complete Table 1.18 by finding the midpoint and cumulative frequency for each class.
   b. Approximate the sample mean, variance, standard deviation, and median.
2. A study is conducted on the age of women using oral contraceptives. The grouped data in Table 1.19 are reported.
   a. Complete Table 1.19 by finding the class midpoint and cumulative frequency for each class.

**TABLE 1.18** FREQUENCY DISTRIBUTION

| CLASS | CLASS BOUNDARIES | CLASS MIDPOINT | FREQUENCY | CUMULATIVE FREQUENCY |
|---|---|---|---|---|
| 1 | 4.5 to 9.5 | | 1 | |
| 2 | 9.5 to 14.5 | | 2 | |
| 3 | 14.5 to 19.5 | | 5 | |
| 4 | 19.5 to 24.5 | | 3 | |

**TABLE 1.19** FREQUENCY DISTRIBUTION OF AGE (IN YEARS)

| CLASS | CLASS BOUNDARIES | CLASS MIDPOINT | FREQUENCY | CUMULATIVE FREQUENCY |
|---|---|---|---|---|
| 1 | 14.5 to 19.5 | | 171 | |
| 2 | 19.5 to 24.5 | | 785 | |
| 3 | 24.5 to 29.5 | | 837 | |
| 4 | 29.5 to 34.5 | | 554 | |
| 5 | 34.5 to 39.5 | | 382 | |
| 6 | 39.5 to 44.5 | | 432 | |
| 7 | 44.5 to 49.5 | | 562 | |
| 8 | 49.5 to 54.5 | | 610 | |
| 9 | 54.5 to 59.5 | | 490 | |
| 10 | 59.5 to 64.5 | | 258 | |
| 11 | 64.5 to 69.5 | | 153 | |
| 12 | 69.5 to 74.5 | | 60 | |

**b.** Approximate the sample mean, variance, standard deviation, and median.

**3.** A study of Hodgkin's disease was conducted. The study was restricted to patients under age 40. One purpose of the study was to compare the distribution of cases by age in men to that in women. The grouped data shown in Table 1.20 were reported.

**a.** Complete Table 1.20 by finding the midpoint and cumulative frequency for each class.

**b.** For each group, approximate the sample mean, variance, standard deviation, and median. Point out the similarities and differences in the two groups.

**TABLE 1.20** DISTRIBUTION OF CASES BY AGE

| CLASS | CLASS BOUNDARIES | CLASS MIDPOINT | FREQUENCY | CUMULATIVE FRQUENCY |
|---|---|---|---|---|
| Men | | | | |
| 1 | 4.5 to 9.5 | | 1 | |
| 2 | 9.5 to 14.5 | | 4 | |
| 3 | 14.5 to 19.5 | | 7 | |
| 4 | 19.5 to 24.5 | | 23 | |
| 5 | 24.5 to 29.5 | | 16 | |
| 6 | 29.5 to 34.5 | | 7 | |
| 7 | 34.5 to 39.5 | | 10 | |
| Women | | | | |
| 1 | 4.5 to 9.5 | | 0 | |
| 2 | 9.5 to 14.5 | | 2 | |
| 3 | 14.5 to 19.5 | | 10 | |
| 4 | 19.5 to 24.5 | | 7 | |
| 5 | 24.5 to 29.5 | | 3 | |
| 6 | 29.5 to 34.5 | | 5 | |
| 7 | 34.5 to 39.5 | | 2 | |

**Computing Supplement**

As can be seen, the calculations necessary to summarize even a relatively small data set can become tedious and time-consuming. To alleviate this problem, several computer systems for data analysis have been developed in recent years. Among the systems currently in widespread use are SPSS (Statistical Package for the Social Sciences, McGraw-Hill), BMD (Biomedical Computer Programs, University of California Press), MINITAB (Pennsylvania State University), and SAS (Statistical Analysis System, SAS Institute Inc.). To use any such system, one needs little background in computer science.

We present here a very brief introduction to SAS programming to give you some experience with computer packages. Once this experience has been gained, it is not difficult to adjust to any of the other packages, for they are similar. We introduce SAS by presenting some sample programs that could be modified to analyze many of the data sets presented in this chapter. Card input is assumed in these programs. You should consult the appropriate expert at your own installation to determine the job cards necessary to access SAS.

**EXAMPLE 1** □ The following observations were obtained on variable $X$, the height, in feet, of a cross-match of yews to be used in hedges.

| | | | | | | | | | |
|---|---|---|---|---|---|---|---|---|---|
| 1.58 | 2.27 | 2.08 | 1.62 | 2.36 | 1.89 | 1.32 | 2.51 | 2.06 | 1.86 |
| 2.09 | 2.00 | 2.37 | 1.39 | 1.91 | 2.00 | 1.87 | 1.75 | 1.95 | 2.31 |

For this data set, find the mean, variance, standard deviation, and range. Also construct a frequency histogram for the data.

The first step in analyzing data via the SAS package is to read the data and get them into an SAS data set. This is done by means of a series of statements which name the data set (the DATA statement), describe the arrangement of the data (the INPUT statement), and signal the beginning of the data lines (the CARDS statement). SAS statements may begin in any column of the card and always end with a semicolon.

The name chosen for the data set should be a one-word name up to eight characters long. The first character must be a letter or an underscore. Later characters can be letters, characters, or underscores. It is usually helpful to choose a name that is in some way related to the data set itself. To name the data set, the SAS key word DATA is used, followed by the name chosen. For instance, in Example 1 we might choose to name the data set ***hedges***. We would inform the computer of this choice by punching the statement.

```
DATA HEDGES;
```

on a single card.

The next statement needed is the INPUT statement. This statement describes the order in which the variables appear on the cards and names the variables. Variable names are chosen at the discretion of the programmer, but they must satisfy the same guidelines as those used in naming the data set. In Example 1, there is only one variable, the height of the plant. The input statement is simple in this case. We need only write

```
INPUT HEIGHT;
```

This tells the computer that each card will contain the value of only one variable, whose name is ***height***.

The INPUT statement is followed by the CARDS statement. The purpose of this statement is to signal SAS that the data cards follow immediately. This statement is written

```
CARDS;
```

The data follow immediately with one observation punched per card. Since SAS recognizes the end of the data cards when it sees a semicolon, make sure that the first card after the data cards contains a semicolon. This can be done by punching a card containing only a semicolon. Thus our program looks like this:

```
DATA HEDGES;      names the data set
INPUT HEIGHT;     names the variable
CARDS;            signals beginning of data lines
  1.58
  2.09
  2.27
   :              data (one observation per card)
  2.31
   ;              signals end of data
```

Now the data are in a SAS data set named ***hedges***. So we must tell the computer what to do with the data, by means of one or more ***procedure*** statements. The procedure statement begins with the SAS key word PROC, followed by the name of the procedure desired. Most of the summary statistics introduced in this chapter can be obtained by using the ***means*** procedure. The key word for this procedure is MEANS, followed by the key words for those summary statistics desired. Some of these key words are as follows:

| | |
|---|---|
| MAXDEC $= n$ | $n$ is an integer from 0 to 8 specifying the number of decimal places that will be used to print the results |
| MEAN | mean |
| STD | standard deviation |
| MIN | smallest value |
| MAX | largest value |
| RANGE | range |
| VAR | variance |
| STDERR | standard error of the mean |
| CV | coefficient of variation |
| N | number of observations |
| SUM | sum of the observations |
| USS | sum of the squares of the observations |

Thus to find the summary statistics called for in Example 1, where the results are reported to two decimal places, we use the command

```
PROC MEANS MAXDEC = 2 MEAN VAR STD RANGE;
```

The frequency histogram requested can be obtained by calling on the ***chart*** procedure. The statements required are

```
PROC CHART;
VBAR HEIGHT;
```

The first statement calls for a chart to be made; the second requests a vertical bar chart or frequency histogram for the variable named ***height***.

One further statement is desirable. This is a ***title*** statement that enables the programmer to print a title at the top of each page of output. The title can contain up to 132 characters. The SAS key word is TITLE[$n$], where $n$ gives the line number at which the title is to be printed. For instance, the statements

```
TITLE1 ANALYSIS;
TITLE2 OF;
TITLE3 YEW DATA;
```

would result in the word ***analysis*** being printed on line 1 of each page of output, the word ***of*** being printed on line 2 of each page, and the words ***yew data*** being printed on line 3.

The entire program is as follows:

```
DATA HEDGES;
INPUT HEIGHT;
CARDS;
1.58
2.09
```

```
2.27
 :
2.31
 ;
TITLE1 ANALYSIS;
TITLE2 OF;
TITLE3 YEW DATA;
PROC MEANS MAXDEC = 2 MEAN VAR STD RANGE;
PROC CHART;
VBAR HEIGHT;
```

To adjust the program to handle another data set, one should change the name of the data set (HEDGES) and the input variable (HEIGHT) to names appropriate to the new data. Also the title should be changed to indicate the data being analyzed. The output of this program is as follows:

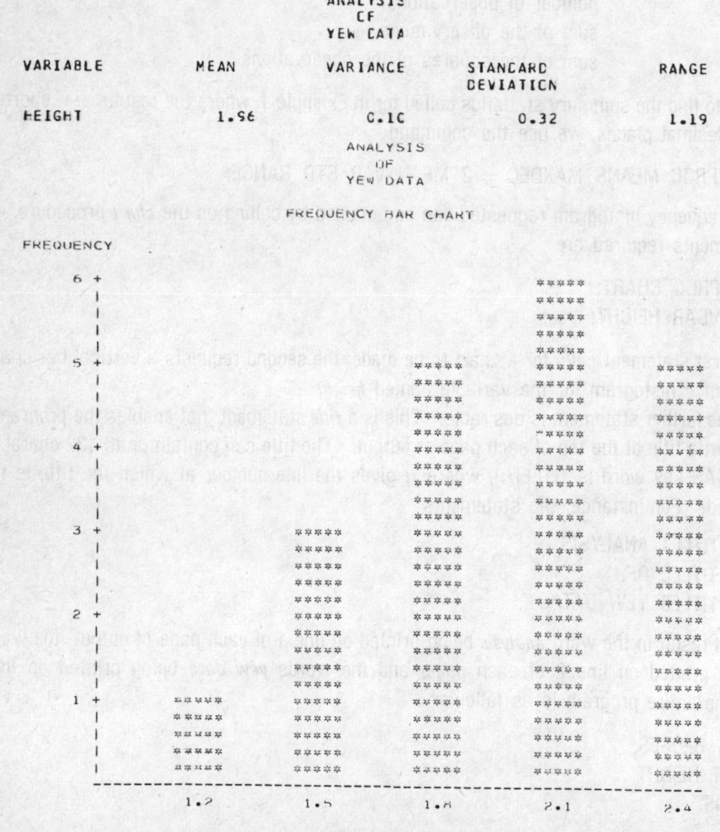

**EXAMPLE 2** □ A researcher has the following data on the sex and systolic blood pressure of 50 randomly selected individuals participating in a physical fitness program:

| | | | | | | | |
|---|---|---|---|---|---|---|---|
| Male | 112 | Male | 130 | Female | 112 | Female | 120 |
| Male | 130 | Male | 120 | Male | 157 | Male | 125 |
| Female | 152 | Female | 130 | Female | 130 | Male | 120 |
| Male | 140 | Male | 110 | Male | 120 | Male | 115 |
| Female | 100 | Female | 120 | Male | 118 | Male | 142 |
| Female | 120 | Female | 120 | Male | 122 | Male | 102 |
| Female | 130 | Male | 110 | Male | 96 | Female | 118 |
| Female | 90 | Male | 120 | Male | 102 | Female | 120 |
| Female | 115 | Male | 126 | Male | 130 | Male | 144 |
| Male | 136 | Female | 140 | Female | 130 | Male | 116 |
| Male | 122 | Male | 108 | Male | 118 | Female | 136 |
| Male | 108 | Male | 135 | Male | 110 | Male | 114 |
| Female | 140 | Female | 150 | | | | |

First let us sort the data set by sex. For each subgroup, let us find the number of observations per group and then determine the mean, variance, and coefficient of variation for each. Then we construct a relative frequency histogram for each subgroup. The program required to do these things is as follows:

| STATEMENT | FUNCTION |
|---|---|
| DATA BPRESS; | names data set |
| INPUT SEX $ PRESSURE; | name variables; $ indicates that variable *sex* is nonnumeric; variables will appear on the cards in the order *sex*, followed by individual's blood pressure |
| CARDS; | signals beginning of data |
| M 112<br>F 112<br>M 130<br>M 157<br>F 152<br>⋮<br>F 150 | data with sex coded by letters M and F |
| ; | signals end of data |
| PROC SORT; BY SEX; | sorts data by sex |
| PROC MEANS MAXDEC = 1 N MEAN VAR CV; BY SEX; | find summary statistics requested for each subgroup and reports these values to 1 decimal place |
| TITLE SUMMARY STATISTICS BY SEX; | titles first page of output |
| PROC CHART; BY SEX; | calls for charts to be made for each subgroup |
| TITLE RELATIVE FREQUENCY | titles remaining pages of output |

| | |
|---|---|
| DISTRIBUTIONS; | |
| VBAR PRESSURE/TYPE = PERCENT; | asks for vertical bar charts for variable *pressure;* the type is to be a percentage or relative frequency histogram |

To adjust this program to analyze another data set, the names of the data set and the input variables should be changed to reflect the new data. If there are no subgroups, then the PROC SORT and BY statements should be deleted.

```
                         SUMMARY STATISTICS BY SEX
                                  SEX=F

VARIABLE               N           MEAN          VARIANCE          C.V.

PRESSURE              19          124.9             239.9          12.4
------------------------------ SEX=M -----------------------------------
PRESSURE              21          121.2             186.4          11.3
```

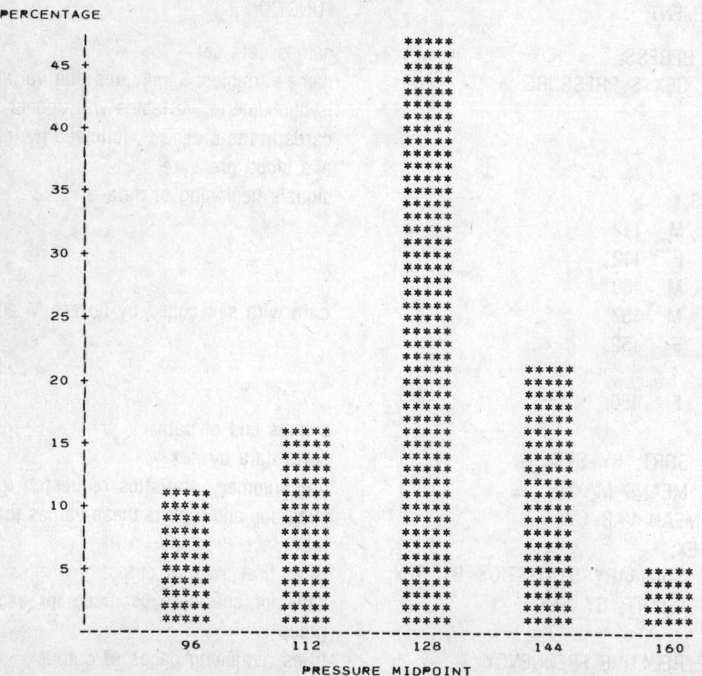

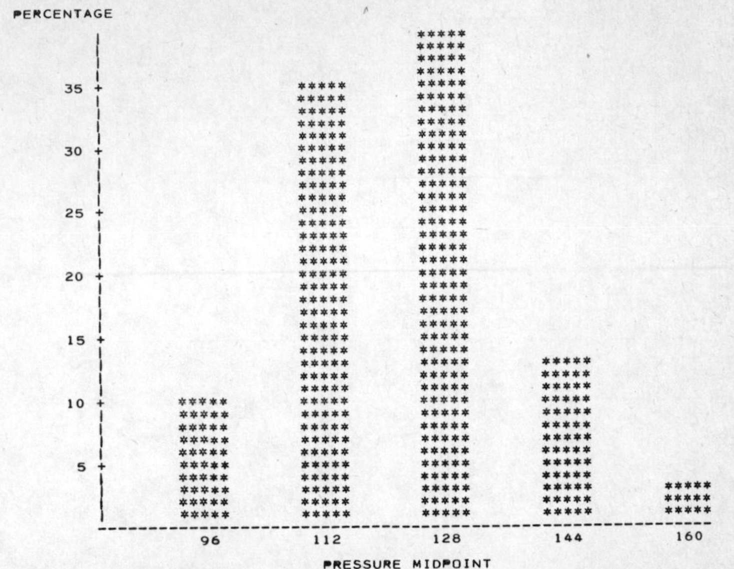
RELATIVE FREQUENCY DISTRIBUTIONS
SEX=M
PERCENTAGE BAR CHART
PERCENTAGE
35
30
25
20
15
10
5
96
112
128
144
160
PRESSURE MIDPOINT

# INTRODUCTION TO PROBABILITY

# 2.

In Chapter 1 we introduced many of the methods used to describe a data set. If the aim of the experimenter is just that, to describe the results of one particular experiment, then the methods of Chapter 1 may be sufficient. However, if the purpose of the experiment is to use the information obtained to draw broad conclusions concerning all objects of the type studied, then the methods of Chapter 1 constitute only the beginning of the analysis. To draw valid conclusions and make accurate predictions concerning a population based on observing only a portion of that population, inferential statistical methods must be employed. These methods entail the intelligent use of probability theory. Therefore we begin by considering the interpretation of probabilities and the special terminology underlying this area of mathematics.

## INTERPRETING PROBABILITIES

**2.1** □ When asked the question "Do you know anything about probability?" most people are quick to answer "no!" But usually that is not the case at all. The ability to correctly interpret probabilities, at least on the intuitive level, is assumed in our culture. One hears the phrases "the probability of rain today is 95%" or "there is a 0% chance of rain today." It is assumed that the general public knows how to properly interpret these values. Briefly, the interpretation of probabilities can be summarized as follows:

**1.** Probabilities are numbers between 0 and 1, inclusive, that reflect the chances of a particular physical event occurring.

**2.** Probabilities near 1 indicate that the event involved is expected to occur. They mean not that the event will occur, only that the event is considered to be a common occurrence.

**3.** Probabilities near 0 indicate that the event is not expected to occur. They mean not that the event will fail to occur, only that the event is considered to be rare.

**4.** Probabilities near $\frac{1}{2}$ indicate that the event is just as likely to occur as not.

The preceding properties are guidelines for interpreting probabilities once these numbers are available, but they do not indicate how to actually go about assigning probabilities to events. Three methods are commonly used: the *personal* approach, the *relative frequency* approach, and the *classical* approach. Each method has its uses, advantages, and disadvantages.

---

**EXAMPLE 2.1.1** □ A patient is suffering from kidney stones, and his condition has not been improved by ordinary means. His physician is contemplating an operation and must answer the question "What is the probability that the operation will be a success?" Many factors come into play, among them the patient's age, general health, and attitude toward the operation. These factors make this patient unique. The physician has not faced this *exact* problem before and will not face it again. It is a "one-shot" situation, and its solution calls for a value judgment to be made. Any probability assigned to the event "the operation is a success" is a *personal opinion.*

---

This example illustrates both the advantages and disadvantages of the personal approach. Its main advantage is that it is always applicable. Anyone can have a personal opinion about anything. Its main disadvantage is obvious: its accuracy depends on the accuracy of the information available and the ability of the scientist to correctly assess that information.

---

**EXAMPLE 2.1.2** □ A researcher is developing a new drug to be used in desensitizing patients to bee stings. Of 200 subjects tested, 180 showed a lessening in the severity of symptoms upon being stung after the treatment was administered. It is natural to assume, then, that the probability of this occurring in another patient receiving treatment is at least *approximately*

$$\frac{180}{200} = .90$$

On the basis of this study, the drug is reported to be 90% effective in lessening the reaction of sensitive patients to stings. This probability is *not* simply a personal opinion. It is a figure based on repeated experimentation and actual observation. It is in fact a *relative frequency.*

---

Example 2.1.2 illustrates the characteristics of the relative frequency approach to probability. It can be used in any situation in which the experiment can be repeated many times and the results observed. Then the approximate probability of the occurrence of event $A$, denoted $P[A]$, is given by

$$P[A] \doteq \frac{f}{n} = \frac{\text{number of times event } A \text{ occurred}}{\text{number of times experiment was run}}$$

The disadvantage in this approach is that the experiment cannot be a one-shot situation; it must be repeatable. The advantage in this approach over the personal approach is that usually it is more accurate, because it is based on actual observation rather than personal opinion. Keep in mind the fact that any probability obtained by using the relative frequency approach is an approximation. It is a value based on $n$ trials. Further testing might result in a different approximate value. However, as the number of trials increases, the changes in the approximate values obtained tend to become slight. Thus for a large number of trials, the approximate probability obtained by using the relative frequency approach is usually quite accurate.

---

**EXAMPLE 2.1.3** □ What is the probability that a child born to a couple, each with genes for both brown and blue eyes, will be brown-eyed? To answer this question, we note that since the child receives one gene from each parent, the possibilities for the child are (brown, blue), (blue, brown), (blue, blue), and (brown, brown), where the first member of each pair represents the gene received from the father. Since each parent is just as likely to contribute a gene for brown eyes as for blue eyes, all four possibilities are equally likely. Since the gene for brown eyes is dominant, three of the four possibilities lead to a brown-eyed child. Hence, the probability that the child is brown-eyed is $3/4 = .75$.

---

The above probability is not a personal opinion, nor is it based on repeated experimentation. In fact, we found this probability by the *classical method*. This method can be used whenever the possible outcomes of the experiment are *equally likely*. In this case, the probability of the occurrence of event $A$ is given by

$$P[A] = \frac{n(A)}{n(S)} = \frac{\text{number of ways } A \text{ can occur}}{\text{number of ways the experiment can proceed}}$$

This method, too, has advantages and disadvantages. Its main drawback is that it is not always applicable; it does require that the possible outcomes be equally likely. Its main advantage is that, when applicable, the probability obtained is exact. Furthermore, it requires neither experimentation nor data gathering and so is easy to use.

All three methods come into play at times and are used frequently in upcoming discussions.

## EXERCISES 2.1

In each of the following exercises, a probability is sought. What method—personal, relative frequency, or classical—do you think is most appropriate in solving the problem? Be ready to defend your choice. Where possible, find the exact or approximate probability called for.

1. A woman contracts German measles while pregnant. What is the probability that her child will be born with a birth defect?
2. A drug is being tested for use in the treatment of poison ivy. Of 190 people tested, 150 gained some relief from the drug. What is the probability that the drug will be effective on the next patient who uses it?
3. A behavioral zoologist studies a large colony of baboons in the wild. She notes that of the 150 animals in the colony, 5 have unusually light-colored fur. What is the probability that the next baboon infant born will be light-colored?
4. A biochemist plans to isolate and purify a newly discovered enzyme from spinach leaves. He consults the literature for guidance in designing a purification procedure, but since this particular enzyme has never been isolated before, no specific guidelines are available. What is the probability that his newly designed purification procedure will be successful?
5. A husband is left-handed, and his wife is right-handed. Two children are born to the couple. Each child is just as likely to be left-handed as right-handed. What is the probability that both children will be left-handed?
6. A laboratory makes an error in cross-matching blood only about once in every 2000 cross-matches. What is the probability that a reported cross-match will be in error?
7. A chemist knows from experience that about 8 out of every 100 samples she receives to test for phosphate have too little phosphate to detect with routine analysis. What is the probability that she will have to use an alternative, more sensitive procedure on the next sample she is asked to assay?
8. An excess number of asbestos bodies were found in 98 of 140 construction workers studied. What is the probability that a randomly selected construction worker will have an undue number of asbestos bodies in the lungs?
9. A blood bank has available five units of blood labeled $A^+$. One unit is mislabeled and is, in fact, type O. A unit is selected at random from the five for use in a transfusion. What is the probability that the mislabled unit will be selected?

## SAMPLE SPACES AND EVENTS

**2.2** □ The problems discussed in Section 2.1 are simple in nature. When experiments become more complex, the mathematics required to analyze them must become more precise. The mathematical basis needed is elementary set theory.

To determine what is "probable," first we must be able to pinpoint what is "possible." That is, the first step in analyzing most probabilistic experiments is to determine a list of possibilities for the experiment. Such a list is called a sample space.

**Definition 2.2.1** *Sample Space and Sample Point.* A *sample space* for an experiment is a set $S$ such that each physical outcome of the experiment corresponds to exactly one element of $S$. An element of $S$ is called a *sample point.*

---

**EXAMPLE 2.2.1** □ A woman is a carrier for classical hemophilia. She gives birth to three sons. What is an appropriate sample space for this experiment?

Since we are primarily concerned with whether each son has the disease, we need generate only a sample space that gives that information. This can be done quickly by means of a simple diagram called a *tree.* A tree may be used conveniently in any experiment that takes place in a small number of distinct stages. In this case, we have three natural stages, one to represent the birth of each son. The first son born either does (yes) or does not (no) have the disease. This is indicated in the tree diagram of Figure 2.1*a,* where yes $= y$ and no $= n$. Likewise, the second son either does or does not have the disease. This fact is shown in Figure 2.1*b.*

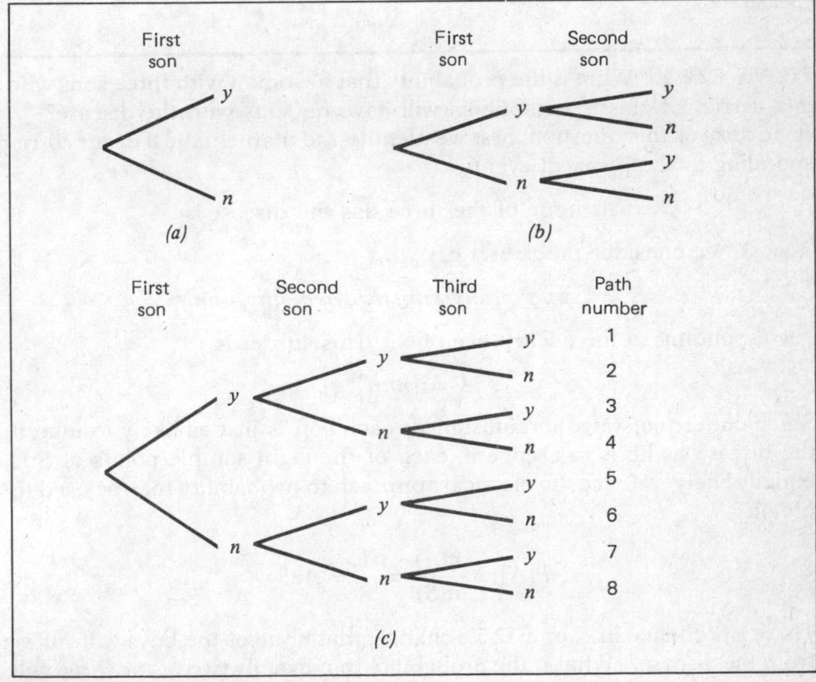


**FIGURE 2.1** Constructing a tree diagram.

Finally, the third son either does or does not have the disease. Therefore the tree is completed as illustrated in Figure 2.1*c*. A sample space $S$ for the experiment can be read from the tree by following each of the eight distinct paths through the tree. Thus

$$S = \{yyy, yyn, yny, ynn, nyy, nyn, nny, nnn\}$$

---

There may be more than one reasonable sample space for an experiment. Generally, the sample space chosen should be detailed enough to allow one to answer whatever questions are of interest. Furthermore, if it is possible to find a sample space in which each sample point occurs with the same probability, then this sample space is usually preferred over any other. Once a suitable sample space has been determined, it can be used to answer probabilistic questions by considering what are called mathematical events.

**Definition 2.2.2** *Event.* Any subset $A$ of a sample space $S$ is called an *event.* We write $A \subseteq S$.

---

**EXAMPLE 2.2.2** □ What is the probability that a woman with three sons who is a carrier of classic hemophilia will have no sons with the disease?

To answer this question, first we identify the mathematical event corresponding to the physical event:

$A$: none of the three has the disease

That is, we consider the subset of

$$S = \{yyy, yyn, yny, ynn, nyy, nyn, nny, nnn\}$$

corresponding to the occurrence of $A$. This subset is

$$A = \{nnn\}$$

Since under the stated circumstances each son is just as likely to inherit the disease as he is to escape it, each of the eight sample points of $S$ is equally likely. Hence the classical approach to probability may be used to obtain

$$P[A] = \frac{n(A)}{n(S)} = \frac{1}{8} = .125$$

There is 1 chance in 8, or a 12.5% chance, that none of the boys will suffer from the disease. What is the probability that exactly two of the three will be afflicted? The mathematical event of interest here is

$$B = \{yny, yyn, nyy\}$$

Hence
$$P[B] = \frac{n(B)}{n(S)} = \frac{3}{8} = .375$$

---

Recall from elementary set theory that any set is a subset of itself. In particular, $S \subseteq S$. That is, the sample space itself is an "event." It corresponds to a physical event that is certain to occur; hence it is called the *sure,* or *certain,* event. It is assigned a probability of 1. Recall also that the empty set, $\varnothing$, is a subset of every set. In particular, $\varnothing \subseteq S$, and hence the empty set is also an event. It corresponds to a physical event that cannot occur and therefore is referred to as the *impossible* event. It is assigned a probability of zero.

Venn diagrams are useful in illustrating problems and in organizing data. Since the sample space $S$ is an ordinary set and an event $A$ is just a subset of $S$, the usual set theory convention can be used to illustrate this relationship diagrammatically, as shown in Figure 2.2. Note that $A'$ repre-

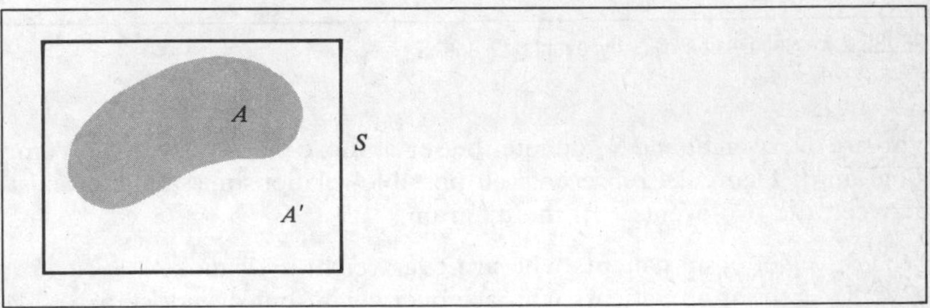


**FIGURE 2.2** $A \subseteq S$ implies that $A$ is an ***event.***

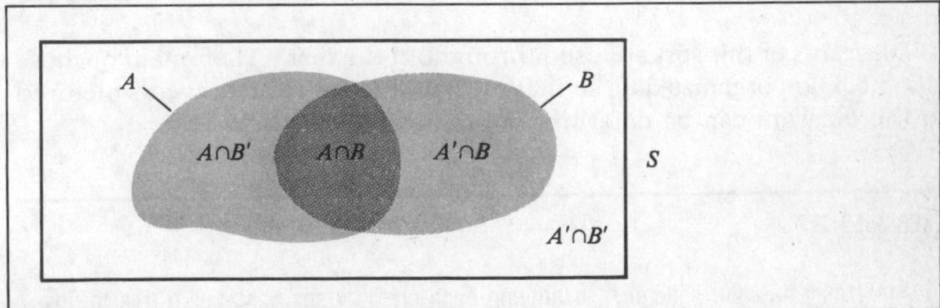


**FIGURE 2.3** Subdivision of $S$ by events $A$ and $B$.

sents all points of $S$ that are not in $A$. Physically it represents the nonoccurrence of event $A$. Note also that $A \cup A' = S$.

Two events, $A$ and $B$, associated with the same sample space also can be represented conveniently, as shown in Figure 2.3. In this way, all relationships that may exist among the events under study can be represented easily. These ideas are illustrated in Example 2.2.3.

**EXAMPLE 2.2.3** □ A study is designed to investigate weight and smoking habits among patients with hypertension. Let $O$ denote the set of patients

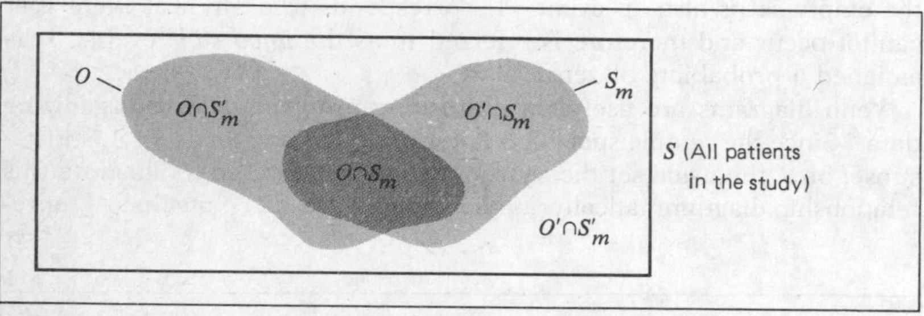


**FIGURE 2.4** Subdivision of $S$ by events $O$ and $S_m$.

who are overweight and $S_m$ denote the set of those that smoke. The Venn diagram of Figure 2.4 represents all possible relationships that can exist between the two events. In the diagram,

$O \cap S_m$ = set of all patients who are overweight *and* smoke
$O \cap S'_m$ = set of all patients who are overweight but do *not* smoke
$O' \cap S_m$ = set of all patients who are *not* overweight but do smoke
$O' \cap S'_m$ = set of all patients who are *not* overweight and do *not* smoke

Diagrams of this sort are used throughout the text. Their main purpose is to help you organize data so that probabilities of various events pictured in the diagram can be determined.

## EXERCISES 2.2

1. A family has four children. Identifying each child by sex only, use a tree to give a sample space for the birth order of the children. List the sample points which constitute the events

$A$: the first child is a boy
$B$: exactly two of the four are boys
$C$: the oldest and youngest are boys
$D$: two are girls and three are boys

What kind of event is $D$?

2. Assume that each child born is just as likely to be a boy as a girl. Find the probability of each event listed in Exercise 2.2.1.
3. A bioactive tetrapeptide (a compound consisting of four amino acids linked into a chain) has the following amino acid composition: alanine (A), glutamic acid (G), lysine (L), and histidine (H).
   a. Using the notation given, draw a tree to represent all possible four amino acid chains made up of these components.
   b. List the elements of the sample space generated by the tree.
   c. List the sample points that constitute the event $A$: glutamic acid is found at one or the other end of the chain.
   d. Assume that each of the 24 sample points of $S$ is equally likely. Find $P[A]$.
   e. List the sample points that constitute the event $B$: lysine is found at the left end of the chain. Find $P[B]$.
4. In a study of immunization in preschool children, interest centers on the mumps and measles vaccines. Let $M$ represent the event that a child has received the mumps vaccine and $M_s$ the event that a child has received the measles vaccine.
   a. Describe the children in $M \cap M_s$ and $M_s' \cap M$.
   b. Describe in set notation the collection of all children who received the measles vaccine but not the mumps vaccine.
   c. Describe in set notation the collection of all children who received neither vaccine.
5. In a study of the effects of sulfur dioxide on trees along major roadways, two events are identified: $L$, the tree has leaf damage; and $S_t$, the tree is stunted.
   a. Describe in set notation the collection of trees that are not stunted.
   b. Describe in set notation the collection of trees that are stunted but show no leaf damage.
   c. Describe in set notation the collection of trees that exhibit neither characteristic.

## PERMUTATIONS AND COMBINATIONS

**2.3** □ As indicated in Section 2.1, there are various ways to determine the probability of a physical event. The classical approach, when applicable, has the advantage of being exact. Recall that to apply the classical method, you must be dealing with an experiment in which the possible physical outcomes are equally likely. In this case, the probability of the occurrence of a specific event $A$ is given by

$$P[A] = \frac{n(A)}{n(S)}$$

Thus to compute a probability by using the classical approach, you must be able to count two things: $n(A)$, the number of ways in which event $A$

can occur, and $n(S)$, the number of ways in which the experiment can proceed. When the experiment involved is rather simple, each can be found by listing or by use of a tree diagram. However, as the experiment becomes more complex, these methods are cumbersome and time-consuming. Alternative methods for counting must be developed. In the remainder of this chapter we introduce briefly counting and classical probability. These methods are applicable to many problems in the biological sciences and underlie much of the elementary theory of genetics.

Two widely encountered types of problems can be solved by using the classical approach, namely, those involving permutations and those involving combinations. Before we consider how to mathematically handle the two, it is necessary to be able to distinguish one from the other.

**Definition 2.3.1** *Permutation.* A *permutation* is an arrangement of objects in a definite order.

**Definition 2.3.2** *Combination.* A *combination* is a selection of objects without regard to order.

It is evident from Definitions 2.3.1 and 2.3.2 that the characteristic that distinguishes a permutation from a combination is *order*. If the order in which some action is taken is important, then the problem is a permutation problem and can be solved by using the multiplication principle discussed in Section 2.4. If order is irrelevant, then it is a "combination" problem and it involves the use of the combination formula developed in Section 2.5.

---

**EXAMPLE 2.3.1**

**a.** Write your social security number. Is this a permutation of numbers or a combination of numbers? It is obviously a permutation. The number 239-62-5558 is *not* the same as the number 329-62-5558. The order in which the digits are written is important.

**b.** Twenty different amino acids are commonly found in peptides and proteins. A pentapeptide consisting of the five amino acids

alanine–valine–glycine–cysteine–tryptophan

has different properties and is, in fact, a different compound from the pentapeptide

alanine–glycine–valine–cysteine–tryptophan

which contains the same amino acids. Are peptides permutations or combinations of amino acid units? They are permutations because the sequence, or order, of the amino acids in the chain is important.

**c.** A biologist has 10 plants with which to experiment. Only eight are needed in the experiment. The eight to be used are selected at random. Does this collection of plants represent a combination or a permutation of plants? It is a combination since interest centers only on which plants are selected and not on the order in which they were chosen.

---

Example 2.3.1 is intended only to convey an intuitive notion of the difference between permutations and combinations. Their significance in the analysis of scientific data is illustrated shortly.

---

## EXERCISES 2.3

In each of the following exercises an experiment is described. For each, state whether a permutation or a combination is involved. Be ready to defend your answer.

1. Write your name.
2. List by sex the birth order of the children in a family with five children.
3. A scientist has six different cages of white rats in the animal room and wants to select three of the six to use in an experiment.
4. Eight patients, each allergic to insect stings, are to be desensitized. Four are to be selected at random and treated with a compound consisting of insect venom. For comparative purposes, the other four are to be treated with a compound made from insect bodies.
5. In running a glucose tolerance test, the blood sugar level of a patient is observed and recorded every half hour for $2\frac{1}{2}$ hours. Each reading is recorded as being either normal ($n$), high ($h$), or low ($l$).
6. A chemist has 10 water samples taken from the wastewater of a paper factory. Three are randomly selected and tested for acidity.



---

## MULTIPLICATION PRINCIPLE

**2.4** □ Once a problem has been identified as being one in which order is important, the next question to be answered is, How many permutations or arrangements of the given objects are possible? This question usually can be answered by means of the *multiplication principle*. This principle is harder to state than it is to use, and most people apply it intuitively even if they have had little formal mathematical training. We illustrate its use in Example 2.4.1.

---

**EXAMPLE 2.4.1** □ Biologists are interested in the order in which the four ribonucleotides adenine (A), uracil (U), guanine (G), and cytosine (C) combine to form small chains. These nucleotides provide the principal subunits of RNA, the intermediate information-carrying molecule involved in

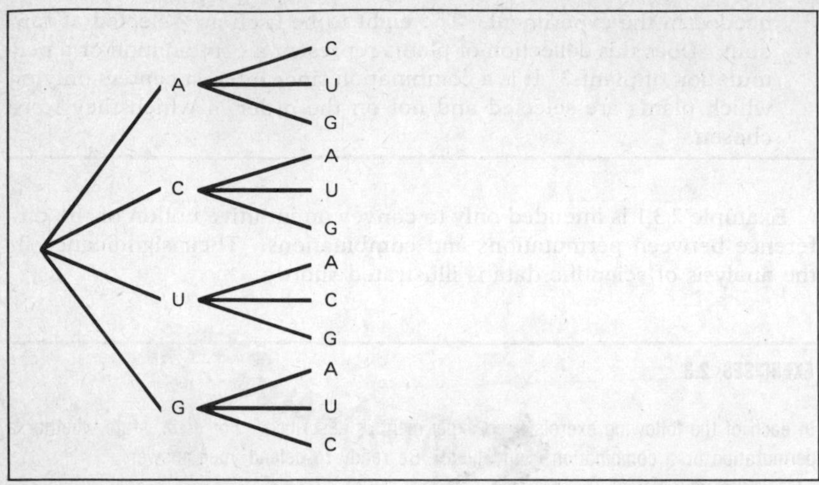


**FIGURE 2.5** Two nucleotide chains.

translating the DNA genetic code. How many chains, each consisting of two *different* nucleotides, can be formed? This question can be answered easily by means of the tree of Figure 2.5.

The answer is evidently 12. Note that we are considering the chain AC to be different from CA. That is, the order in which the nucleotides are arranged is important. Hence we have shown that there are 12 permutations of four distinct objects when used two at a time. This result could have been predicted without recourse to a tree by asking three simple questions.

**1.** How many stages or steps are involved in the experiment as a whole? Answer: two. Stage 1 corresponds to the first nucleotide falling into place; stage 2 corresponds to a second, *different* nucleotide linking with the first. Represent the fact that two stages are involved by drawing two slots.

| ______ | ______ |
|---|---|
| 1st nucleotide | 2d nucleotide |

**2.** In how many ways can the first stage of the experiment be performed? Answer: four. There are four nucleotides available, any one of which could fall into the first position. Indicate this by placing a 4 in the first slot.

| 4 | ______ |
|---|---|
| 1st nucleotide | 2d nucleotide |

**3.** After the first stage is complete, in how many ways can stage 2 be performed? Answer: three. Since each chain is to consist of two *different* nucleotides, repetition is not allowed. The nucleotide appearing first in the chain is no longer in contention. The second member of the chain must be one of the three remaining. Indicate this by placing a 3 in the second slot.

| 4 | 3 |
|---|---|
| 1st nucleotide | 2d nucleotide |

The multiplication principle says that to determine the total number of possible permutations, you need only multiply these two numbers, once again obtaining an answer of 12. Note that the 4 in the first slot corresponds directly to the first-stage branching in the tree diagram and the 3 to the second-stage branching.

---

We now formalize the above discussion by stating the multiplication principle and pointing out some guidelines for its use.

**THEOREM 2.4.1** □ *Multiplication Principle.* Consider an experiment taking place in $k$ stages. Stage 1 can occur in $n_1$ ways. After it has occurred in one of these ways, stage 2 can occur in $n_2$ ways, followed by stages $3, 4, \ldots, k$ which can occur successively in $n_3, n_4, \ldots, n_k$ ways. Altogether the experiment can occur in $n_1 \cdot n_2 \cdot \cdots \cdot n_k$ ways.

There are several guidelines to consider when you apply the multiplication principle:

**1.** Watch out for repetition versus nonrepetition. Sometimes objects can be repeated (such as the digits in a social security number); at other times they cannot (as specified in Example 2.4.1). Generally the physical context of the problem either allows or precludes repetition.

**2.** Watch for subtraction. Consider event $A$. Occasionally it will be difficult, if not impossible, to find $n(A)$ directly. However, $S = A \cup A'$. Since $A$ and $A'$ have no points in common, $n(S) = n(A) + n(A')$. This implies that $n(A) = n(S) - n(A')$.

**3.** If there is a stage in the experiment with a special restriction, then you should worry about the restriction first.

These points are illustrated in Example 2.4.2.

---

**EXAMPLE 2.4.2** □ The DNA-RNA code is a molecular code in which the sequence of molecules provides significant genetic information. Each seg-

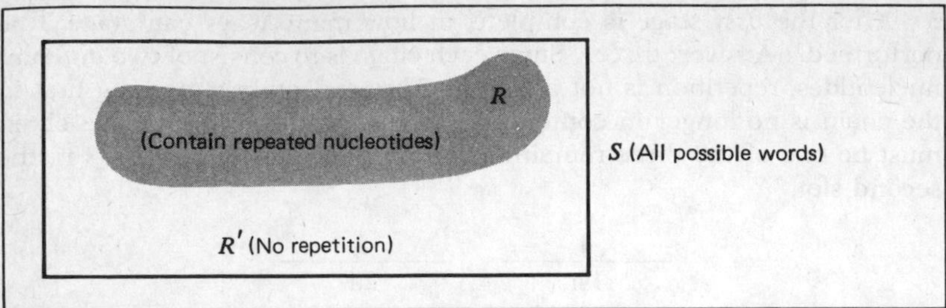


**FIGURE 2.6** Partitioning $S$.

ment of RNA is composed of "words." Each word specifies a particular amino acid and is composed of a chain of three ribonucleotides that are not necessarily all different. For example, the word UUU corresponds to the amino acid phenylalanine, whereas AUG identifies methionine.

**a.** Consider the experiment of forming an RNA word. How many words can be formed? That is, what is $n(S)$? Each of the three ribonucleotides in the chain is one of the four mentioned in Example 2.4.1, namely, adenine (A), uracil (U), guanine (G), and cytosine (C). Thus this is a three-stage experiment with four possibilities at each stage. By the multiplication principle, $n(S) = 4 \cdot 4 \cdot 4 = 64$.

**b.** How many of the words of part **a** have at least two identical nucleotides? This question is easily answered by subtraction. Let $R$ denote the event that the word contains repeated nucleotides. Consider the diagram of Figure 2.6. We already know that $n(S) = 64$. By the multiplication principle, $n(R') = 4 \cdot 3 \cdot 2 = 24$. Hence, by subtraction, the number of words involving some repetition is

$$n(R) = n(S) - n(R') = 64 - 24 = 40$$

**c.** If a word is formed at random, what is the probability that it will contain some repetition of nucleotides? Using classical probability, we have

$$P[R] = \frac{n(R)}{n(S)} = \frac{40}{64} = .625$$

**d.** Consider event $B$ that a randomly formed word ends with U (uracil) and involves no repetition. Find $P[B]$. Since the last position in the word must be filled by uracil, there is only one choice for that position, as indicated:

$$\underline{\qquad} \quad \underline{\qquad} \quad \underline{\quad 1 \quad}$$

Once this restriction has been taken care of, we note that repetition is not allowed. So the first position can be filled with any of the three remaining nucleotides and the second position by either of two.

$$\underline{\quad\quad 3} \quad \underline{\quad\quad 2} \quad \underline{\quad\quad 1}$$

Thus, $n(B) = 6$ and

$$P[B] = \frac{n(B)}{n(S)} = \frac{6}{64}$$

---

Thus far we have been concerned with fairly simple problems that may or may not involve repetition. Now we consider situations in which repetition is inevitable. The question to be answered is, How many distinct arrangements of $n$ objects are possible if some of the objects are identical and therefore cannot be distinguished one from the other? To answer this question, first we must consider a shorthand notation called *factorial notation.* This notation is used extensively throughout the remainder of this text.

**Definition 2.4.1** *n Factorial.* Let $n$ be a positive integer. The product $n(n-1)(n-2)\cdots3\cdot2\cdot1$ is called *n factorial* and is denoted by $n!$.

---

**EXAMPLE 2.4.3**

$$6! = 6\cdot5\cdot4\cdot3\cdot2\cdot1 = 720$$

---

**Definition 2.4.2** *Zero Factorial.*

$$0! = 1$$

Now we return to the problem at hand, that of determining the number of possible permutations when some of the objects being permuted are indistinguishable from others.

---

**EXAMPLE 2.4.4** □ Consider the two nucleotides adenine (A) and uracil (U). How many words—chains of three ribonucleotides not necessarily all different—can be formed by using only these two symbols? Since a word involves three symbols and only two distinct symbols are to be used, repetition is inevitable. By the multiplication principle, there are $2\cdot2\cdot2 = 8$ possible words. This is not new. However, if we now ask, "How many of the eight involve uracil twice and adenine once?" the question is new. We are arranging a total of $n = 3$ objects, but two are identical (namely, two

U's) and therefore are indistinguishable from each other. To answer the question, let us list the possibilities:

AUU UAU UUA

The answer is 3. How could this have been predicted without the use of a list? We note that

$$3 = \frac{3 \cdot 2 \cdot 1}{(2 \cdot 1)(1)} = \frac{3!}{2!1!}$$

The 3 in the numerator represents the fact that a total of three objects are being permuted. There are two numbers in the denominator because there are two types of objects involved, namely, two U's and one A.

---

The above pattern is not coincidental. It can be shown to hold in any situation in which $n$ objects are to be arranged with some objects indistinguishable from others. Theorem 2.4.2 formalizes this idea.

**THEOREM 2.4.2** □ *Permutations of Indistinguishable Objects.* Consider $n$ objects where $n_1$ are of type 1, $n_2$ of type 2, . . . , $n_k$ of type $k$. The number of ways in which the $n$ objects can be arranged is given by

$$\frac{n!}{n_1!n_2!\cdots n_k!} \qquad n_1 + n_2 + \cdots + n_k = n$$

---

**EXAMPLE 2.4.5** □ Fifteen patients are to be used in an experiment to test a standard drug, an experimental drug, and a placebo. Each patient is to be randomly assigned a treatment. In how many different ways can the three treatments be assigned to the 15 patients? What is the probability that a random assignment of treatments would result in 10 patients receiving the placebo, 3 receiving the experimental drug, and 2 receiving the standard?

The first question is not new. There are $3 \cdot 3 \cdot 3 \cdot \cdots \cdot 3 = 3^{15} = 14{,}348{,}907$ ways to assign treatments to patients. The second question is new. To find the desired probability, we must determine how many of the above arrangements involve the placebo 10 times, the experimental drug three times, and the standard drug twice. This is easily found by Theorem 2.4.2 to be

$$\frac{15!}{10!3!2!} = \frac{15 \cdot 14 \cdot 13 \cdot 12 \cdot 11 \cdot \cancel{10!}}{\cancel{10!}(3 \cdot 2 \cdot 1 \cdot 2 \cdot 1)} = 30{,}030$$

The desired probability is therefore

$$\frac{30{,}030}{14{,}348{,}907} \doteq .0021$$

---

## EXERCISES 2.4

1. **a.** How many RNA words can be formed that begin with U (uracil) and end with A (adenine) or G (guanine)? (Remember that four ribonucleotides may be used—A, U, G, and C—and that a word consists of three of these, not necessarily all different.)
   **b.** How many of the words of part **a** have no repetition?
   **c.** What is the probability that a randomly formed word will begin with U, end with A or G, but involve repetition?
   **d.** Check your answers by constructing the tree diagrams corresponding to **a** and **b**.
2. Of the possible 64 RNA words, 61 are known to code for the 20 existing amino acids. The other three code "stops," which cause termination of the peptide. If a word is formed at random, what is the probability that it will code for an amino acid?
3. A word codes for threonine if and only if it begins AC. How many synonyms (words that have identical meanings) are there for threonine?
4. Consider the RNA segment UUUAUUUUA. This segment involves the three nonoverlapping words UUU (phenylalanine), AUU (isoleucine), and UUA (leucine). Note that if a mutation occurs and the string of nucleotides is changed to read UUAAUUUUA, then the segment no longer codes the same sequence of amino acids. There are two synonyms for phenylalanine, three for isoleucine, and six for leucine. In how many different but equivalent ways can the above three-amino-acid sequence be expressed?
5. Consider any segment of three nonoverlapping words. In how many ways could such a segment be expressed? How many of these segments have no repeated words? If a segment is selected at random, what is the probability that it will have some repetition of words? What is the probability that each word will be different and each code an amino acid? (See Exercise 2.4.2.)
6. In treating a patient for high blood pressure, a physician has a choice of five different drugs, two of which are experimental. She can also select any one of four exercise programs, of which two involve indoor activities and the other two outdoor activities. Three choices of diet are available, one of which is completely salt-free.
   **a.** How many treatments consisting of one drug, one exercise program, and one diet are possible?
   **b.** How many of the treatments in **a** involve the use of an experimental drug?
   **c.** All treatments in **a** are assumed to be equally desirable. If a treatment is selected at random, what is the probability that it will involve an experimental drug and an outdoor exercise program?
   **d.** If, in fact, a specific one of the experimental drugs is dangerous when used in conjunction with the salt-free diet, what is the probability that such a treatment will nevertheless be prescribed by chance?
7. Seven drugs are being tested for their effectiveness in controlling acne. A researcher is asked to rank the drugs from 1 to 7, with the most effective drug receiving a rank of 1.
   **a.** In how many ways can the seven ranks be assigned to the seven drugs?
   **b.** Drugs A and B are manufactured by the company running the test, although this is not known by the researcher. If, in fact, the researcher cannot distinguish among

the products and actually randomly assigns ranks, what is the probability that these two drugs will receive the top two ranks?

**c.** If the experiment is run and drugs A and B are ranked in the top two positions, do you feel that the company has evidence that its products are more effective than the competitor's? Explain on the basis of your answer to part **b**.

**8.** A 10-word RNA sequence is to be formed. It involves the word ACU (threonine) three times, GGU (glycine) twice, GAA (glutamic acid) four times, and UAA (stop) once. How many 10-word sequences with this composition are possible? What is the probability that a randomly selected sequence from this group will have the stop somewhere other than at the end of the sequence?

**9.** Fifteen experimental animals are available to use in a study to compare three different diets. Each diet is to be used on five randomly selected animals. In how many ways can the diets be assigned to the experimental subjects?

***10.** Two body colors, gray (*E*) and ebony (*e*), are recognized in fruit flies with gray being dominant. Two wing types are also noted, normal (*V*) and short, or vestigial, (*v*) with normal being dominant. Homozygous flies (*EEVV* and *eevv*) are mated to form double-heterozygous offspring (*EeVv*). These are allowed to mate, and both eggs and sperm contain all possible gamete types (*EV, Ev, eV, ev*) in equal proportions. When an egg is fertilized, the zygote produced will contain four genes—two for body color and two for wing type. For example, if a sperm of the form *EV* fertilizes an egg of the form *ev*, the zygote will be of the form *EeVv* and will produce a gray fly of normal wing span.

**a.** How many different zygotes are possible? Think of the formation of a zygote as a four-stage process as follows:

| ______ | ______ | ______ | ______ |
|---|---|---|---|
| color gene | color gene | wing type | wing type |
| ♂ | ♀ | ♂ | ♀ |

**b.** How many of the above result in a zygote which will produce an ebony fruit fly? A gray fly?

**c.** How many of the zygotes will produce a normal-winged fly?

**d.** If a fly is selected at random from among a large number of flies resulting from the above experiment, what is the probability that it will have normal wings? What is the probability that it will be ebony and have short wings? What is the probability that it will *not* be ebony with short wings?

***11.** Genes determining albinism are denoted *A* and *a*, with *A* dominant and leading to a normal individual with respect to this trait. In order to be an albino, one must receive the recessive gene *a* from each parent. Individuals of the type *Aa*, although normal themselves, can pass on the trait to their offspring and are called ***carriers***.

**a.** A normal couple gives birth to an albino son. What is the gene type of each parent?

**b.** What is the probability that the next child born to the couple also will be an albino? What is the probability that the child will be a carrier of albinism?

**c.** A woman has a normal mother and an albino father. Her maternal grandmother is also albino. What is the probability that the woman is a carrier of albinism?

## COMBINATIONS

**2.5** □ Thus far we have considered counting problems in which order, either natural or imposed, was important. We now turn our attention to situations in which order is irrelevant. That is, we now consider problems involving combinations rather than permutations.

---

**EXAMPLE 2.5.1** □ Five people have volunteered to take part in an experimental program. Only two are needed to complete the study. In how many ways can two people be selected from five?

Order is not important here. Interest centers only on which two are selected, not on the order of selection. Thus we are asking, How many combinations are there of five objects, selected two at a time? The question can be answered by labeling the volunteers *A, B, C, D, E* and then listing all possible subsets of size two as follows:

| | | | |
|---|---|---|---|
| $\{A, B\}$ | $\{A, E\}$ | $\{B, E\}$ | $\{D, E\}$ |
| $\{A, C\}$ | $\{B, C\}$ | $\{C, D\}$ | |
| $\{A, D\}$ | $\{B, D\}$ | $\{C, E\}$ | |

There are obviously 10 combinations. We write ${}_5C_2 = 10$, where the 5 indicates the number of objects available, the 2 shows the number selected, and the $C$ indicates a combination is involved. Alternatively, we may write $\binom{5}{2} = 10$. How could the value 10 have been obtained without the use of the list? We note simply that

$$10 = \frac{5!}{2!3!}$$

The numerator of this expression is 5! because there are five objects from which to choose. There are two numbers in the denominator, 2! and 3!. This is due to the fact that the five objects are split into two groups, namely, those selected for the study (2) and those omitted from the study $(5 - 2 = 3)$.

---

The pattern noted above is not coincidental and is generalized in Theorem 2.5.1.

**THEOREM 2.5.1** □ The number of combinations of $n$ distinct objects, selected $r$ at a time, denoted ${}_nC_r$, or $\binom{n}{r}$, is given by

$${}_nC_r = \binom{n}{r} = \frac{n!}{r!(n-r)!}$$

**EXAMPLE 2.5.2** □ A blood bank has available 10 units of $A^+$ blood. In fact, four are contaminated with serum hepatitis. Three units are randomly selected for use with three patients. What is the probability that all three patients will be exposed to hepatitis from this source? What is the probability that at least two of the three will be so exposed?

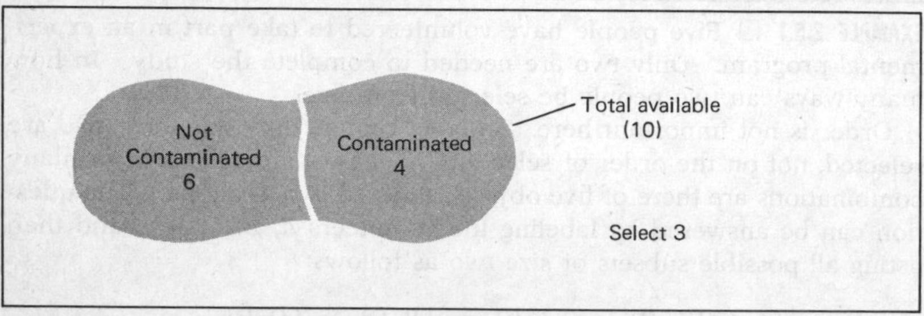


**FIGURE 2.7** Partitioning the set of blood units.

Each of these questions involves combinations, since we are interested in only the final units selected, not the order in which they are selected. Consider the diagram of Figure 2.7. The total number of ways to select three units from the 10 available is

$$_{10}C_3 = \frac{10!}{3!7!} = 120$$

In order for all three patients to be exposed to hepatitis from this source, all three units must be selected from the four contaminated units. The number of ways to make such a selection is

$$_4C_3 = \binom{4}{3} = \frac{4!}{3!1!} = 4$$

Assuming that each of the 120 possible ways to select three units from 10 is just as likely to occur as any other, we may use classical methods to conclude that

$$P[\text{all three exposed to risk}] = \frac{4}{120} = .0333$$

The second question is a bit more complex. In order for exactly two of the three to be exposed to risk from this source, we must select two units from the contaminated group and one from the noncontaminated group. Therefore, there is a two-stage process implied. The first stage, obtaining two contaminated units, can proceed in $_4C_2 = 4!/(2!2!) = 6$ ways; the second stage, obtaining one good unit, can proceed in $_6C_1 = 6!/(1!5!) = 6$ ways. By the multiplication principle, the entire two-stage procedure can proceed in $6 \cdot 6 = 36$ ways. Since "at least two" means two or three, altogether there are $36 + 4 = 40$ ways to expose at least two of the three patients to risk. The probability of this occurring is therefore $^{40}/_{120} = .3333$.

This chapter is intended only as a brief introduction to counting. However, the methods illustrated here should give you sufficient background for reading and understanding the statistical procedures presented later.

## EXERCISES 2.5

1. Evaluate:
   a. ${}_6C_2$
   b. ${}_8C_5$
   c. $\binom{4}{0}$
   d. $\binom{3}{3}$

2. A group of 12 patients is available for use in a study. Five are to be selected to receive an experimental treatment; the other seven are to receive the standard treatment and are to serve as a control. In how many ways can the control group be selected? What is the probability that a specific individual A will be selected into the control group? *Hint:* Think of the group as being split as shown in Figure 2.8.

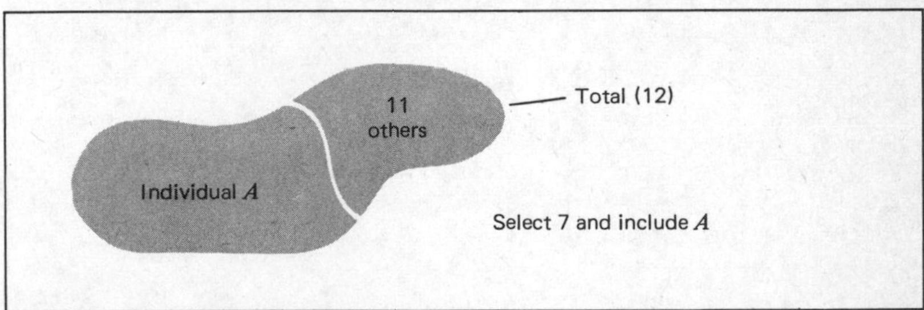


**FIGURE 2.8** Partitioning the set of patients.

3. A new compound has been developed to help reduce skin dryness. Fifteen women, all about the same age with the same skin type, are asked to take part in a test. Seven are randomly selected and asked to use the product on their hands for 2 weeks. The others serve as a control. At the end of the experiment, an impartial judge is asked to select the seven whose hands appear to be in the best condition. If, in fact, the

treatment has had no effect at all, what is the probability that by chance alone the judge will select all seven who used the experimental compound? What is the probability that she will select exactly five of those who used the experimental compound?

4. A scientist has six different cages of white rats in the animal room. Of the six cages, two contain some rats which are diseased. What is the probability in a random selection of three cages that none of the cages containing diseased animals will be selected? What is the probability that exactly one cage with diseased animals will be selected?
5. A chemist has 10 water samples taken from the wastewater of a paper factory. Unknown to the chemist, four samples are excessively acidic. In a random selection of three samples, what is the probability that exactly two will have excess acid?

---

# PROBABILITY AS A MATHEMATICAL SYSTEM

# 3.

In Chapter 2 we considered general properties of probabilities and some elementary methods of determining them. In this chapter we continue our study by discussing how probabilities behave mathematically; that is, we consider probability as an axiomatic system. Although this topic can become quite complex, we do not attempt full coverage here. We present only those axioms, theorems, and definitions that are basic to the understanding of commonly encountered problems.

## AXIOMS OF PROBABILITY

**3.1** □ In developing any axiomatic system, one begins by stating a few basic definitions and axioms that underlie the system. The definitions are the technical terms of the system; axioms are statements that are assumed to be true and therefore require no proof. Generally, one starts with as few axioms as possible and then uses these axioms and the technical definitions to develop whatever theorems follow logically. Luckily, one can develop a useful and powerful system of theorems relative to probability by beginning with only three axioms, each of which is intuitively quite reasonable. The ability to interpret probabilities as in Section 2.1 is a direct consequence of these axioms. Thus, we now justify mathematically the comments made there. Before stating the axioms, we pause to consider one definition.

**Definition 3.1.1** *Mutually Exclusive Events*. Two events $A_1$ and $A_2$ are *mutually exclusive* if and only if $A_1 \cap A_2 = \varnothing$. Events $A_1, A_2, A_3, \ldots$ are mutually exclusive if and only if $A_i \cap A_j = \varnothing$ for every $i \neq j$.

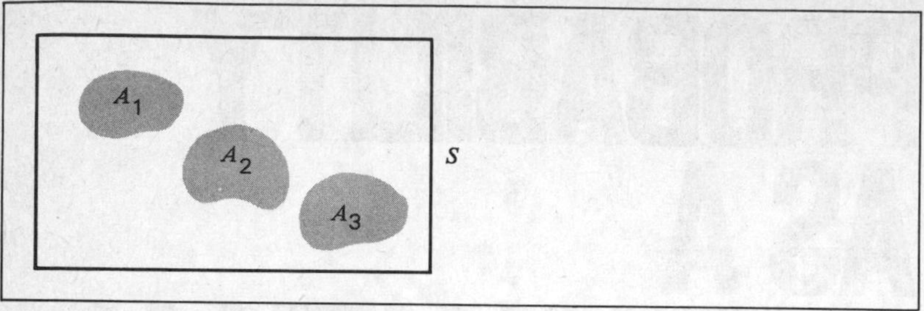


**FIGURE 3.1** Mutually exclusive events.

Note that Definition 3.1.1 is mathematical. In ordinary set theory, the events would be termed *disjoint*. This means that they have no sample points in common (see Figure 3.1). Practically speaking, mutually exclusive events are physical events that cannot occur simultaneously. For example, events $A_1$, the patient recovers from an operation, and $A_2$, the patient dies on the operating table, are mutually exclusive events. It is impossible for both events to occur at the same time; the occurrence of one event precludes the occurrence of the other.

### Axioms of Probability

**1.** Let $S$ denote a sample space for an experiment. Then $P[S] = 1$.

**2.** $P[A] \geq 0$ for every event $A$.

**3.** Let $A_1, A_2, A_3, \ldots$ be a sequence of mutually exclusive events. Then $P[A_1 \cup A_2 \cup A_3 \cup \cdots] = P[A_1] + P[A_2] + P[A_3] + \cdots$

Axiom 1 states a fact that most people would regard as obvious, namely, that the probability assigned to a sure, or certain, event is 1. Axiom 2 ensures that probabilities can never be negative. Axiom 3 is called the *property of countable additivity*. It guarantees that when one deals with mutually exclusive events, the probability of one or the other of the events occurring can be found by adding the individual probabilities. These axioms lead quite easily to Theorems 3.1.1 and 3.1.2.

**THEOREM 3.1.1** □ $P[\varnothing] = 0$. This theorem states that the probability associated with the "impossible" event, $\varnothing$, is 0. Since the impossible event corresponds to a physical event that cannot occur, we would want our axioms to assign a probability of 0 to such an event.

**THEOREM 3.1.2** □ Let $A_1, A_2, \ldots, A_n$ be a finite collection of mutually exclusive events. Then

$$P[A_1 \cup A_2 \cup \cdots \cup A_n] = P[A_1] + P[A_2] + \cdots + P[A_n]$$

Axiom 3 deals with an infinite collection of events. Theorem 3.1.2 guarantees that when one deals with a *finite* collection of mutually exclusive events, the additive property still holds. That is, given a finite collection of mutually exclusive events, the probability of one or the other of the events occurring can be found by adding the individual probabilities. Theorem 3.1.2 is especially important because it gives us the ability to find the probability of an event when the sample points in the sample space for the experiment are not equally likely. To understand this idea, consider Example 3.1.1.

---

**EXAMPLE 3.1.1.** □ The distribution of blood types in the United States is roughly as follows:

| | |
|---|---|
| A: 41% | AB: 4% |
| B: 9% | O: 46% |

An individual is brought into the emergency room after an automobile accident. He is to be blood-typed. What is the probability that he will be of type A, B, or AB?

The sample space for this experiment is

$$S = \{\text{A}, \text{B}, \text{AB}, \text{O}\}$$

The sample points are not equally likely, so the classical approach to probability is not applicable. However, Theorem 3.1.2 can be used to find the desired probability. Let $A_1$, $A_2$, and $A_3$ denote the events that the patient has type A, B, and AB blood, respectively. We are looking for $P[A_1 \cup A_2 \cup A_3]$. Since it is impossible for one individual to have two different blood types, these events are mutually exclusive. By Theorem 3.1.2,

$$\begin{aligned} P[A_1 \cup A_2 \cup A_3] &= P[A_1] + P[A_2] + P[A_3] \\ &= .41 + .09 + .04 \\ &= .54 \end{aligned}$$

There is a 54% chance that the patient will have one of the three blood types mentioned.

---

**THEOREM 3.1.3** □ $P[A'] = 1 - P[A]$.

Theorem 3.1.3 states that the probability that an event will *not* occur is equal to 1 minus the probability that it will occur. For example, based on recently conducted research, it is estimated that the probability of "curing" childhood leukemia is $\frac{1}{3}$. ("Cure" means that the child is free from disease for at least 4 years after treatment ended.) Thus the probability that the disease will not be cured is $1 - \frac{1}{3} = \frac{2}{3}$.

---

## EXERCISES 3.1

1. Which of the following are pairs of mutually exclusive events?
   - **a.** *A:* Jane Doe's son has hemophilia.
     *B:* Jane Doe's daughter is a carrier of hemophilia.
   - **b.** *A:* 65% of pea seeds planted germinate.
     *B:* 50% of pea seeds fail to germinate after planting.
   - **c.** *A:* José is suffering from hypothermia.
     *B:* José's temperature is 102°F.
   - **d.** *A:* The pH of a topsoil sample is equal to 7.0.
     *B:* The sample of topsoil is alkaline.
2. In treating premature babies, the amount of oxygen received can affect vision. Each child treated can be classed as having normal vision, having a mild lesion, having a moderate lesion, having a severe lesion, or being blind. A study shows that the probabilities of each of these events occurring are .80, .10, .06, .02, and .02, respectively.
   - **a.** List the sample points that consitute event $A$, a child is born with a vision defect. Find $P[A]$.
   - **b.** List the sample points that constitute the event $B$, a child is born with a vision defect but is not blind. Find $P[B]$.
3. A particular chemical analysis has a rather limited range. Typically, 15% of the samples are too concentrated to be assayed without dilution, and 20% are contaminated with an interfering material that must be removed before analysis. The rest may

be analyzed without pretreatment. Assume that samples both too concentrated and contaminated never occur. What is the probability that a randomly selected sample can be assayed without pretreatment?

**4.** Diabetes in pregnancy constitutes a major problem in maternal and child welfare. Among pregnant diabetics, toxemia occurs in 25% of the cases, hydramnios in 21% of the cases, and fetal wastage in 15%. Other complications occur in 6% of the cases. Assume that no two of these complications can occur in a single pregnancy. Thus the sample space $S$ for the experiment of observing the pregnancy of a diabetic is

$$S = \{\text{toxemia, hydramnios, fetal wastage, other, normal}\}$$

What is the probability that a randomly selected pregnant diabetic will have a normal pregnancy? What is the probability that a randomly selected pregnant diabetic will have some sort of complication?

**5.** The weather bureau's air pollution index classifies each day as being extremely good, good, fair, poor, or extremely poor. Past experience indicates that 50% of the days are classed as extremely good, 22% as good, 18% as fair, 8% as poor, and 2% as extremely poor. A warning is issued on days that are classed as poor or extremely poor. What is the probability that a warning is issued on a randomly selected day?

**6.** Studies on depression indicate that a particular course of treatment improves the condition of 72% of those on whom it is used, does not affect 10%, and worsens the condition of the rest. A patient suffering from depression is treated by using this method. What is the probability that his condition will worsen? What is the probability that the treatment is not detrimental to his condition?

## GENERAL ADDITION RULE

**3.2** □ In Section 3.1 we saw how to handle questions concerning the probability of one or another event occurring if those events were mutually exclusive. That is, we considered $P[A_1 \cup A_2]$ when events $A_1$ and $A_2$ had no sample points in common. In this section we discuss the general addition rule. Its purpose is to allow us to handle the more general case of finding the probability that at least one of two events will occur when the events themselves are not necessarily mutually exclusive.

We begin by considering the Venn diagram of Figure 3.2. Note that $A_1$

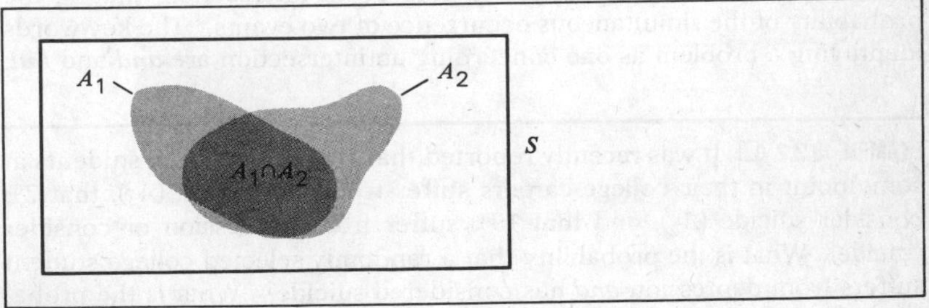


**FIGURE 3.2** $A_1 \cap A_2 \neq \varnothing$.

and $A_2$ are *not* mutually exclusive since $A_1 \cap A_2$, the shaded region shown, is not empty. If we computed $P[A_1 \cup A_2]$ as in Section 3.1, we would conclude that

$$P[A_1 \cup A_2] = P[A_1] + P[A_2]$$

However, since $(A_1 \cap A_2) \subseteq A_1$ and $(A_1 \cap A_2) \subseteq A_2$, obviously we included $P[A_1 \cap A_2]$ twice in the above calculation. In order to correct for this, $P[A_1 \cap A_2]$ must be subtracted from the right-hand side of the equation. The resulting expression is the general addition rule.

**THEOREM 3.2.1** □ *General Addition Rule.* Let $A_1$ and $A_2$ be events. Then

$$P[A_1 \cup A_2] = P[A_1] + P[A_2] - P[A_1 \cap A_2]$$

The key word to watch for in identifying a problem as one in which the general addition rule applies is the word *or.* The use of the rule is illustrated in Example 3.2.1.

---

**EXAMPLE 3.2.1** □ It is thought that 30% of all people in the United States are obese ($A_1$) and that 3% suffer from diabetes ($A_2$). Two percent are obese and suffer from diabetes. What is the probability that a randomly selected person is obese *or* suffers from diabetes?

We have been given $P[A_1] = .3$, $P[A_2] = .03$, and $P[A_1 \cap A_2] = .02$. We are asked to find $P[A_1 \cup A_2]$. Applying the general addition rule, we obtain

$$\begin{aligned} P[A_1 \cup A_2] &= P[A_1] + P[A_2] - P[A_1 \cap A_2] \\ &= .30 + .03 - .02 \\ &= .31 \end{aligned}$$

---

The general addition rule not only is useful in computing the probability of a union but is, in fact, a link between the operations of union and intersection. If we are given the proper information, we can use the general addition rule to find the probability of an intersection, that is, the probability of the simultaneous occurrence of two events. The key words identifying a problem as one concerning an intersection are *and* and *but.*

---

**EXAMPLE 3.2.2** □ It was recently reported that 18% of all college students at some point in their college careers suffer from depression ($A_1$), that 2% consider suicide ($A_2$), and that 19% suffer from depression or consider suicide. What is the probability that a randomly selected college student suffers from depression *and* has considered suicide? What is the probability that a randomly selected student has suffered from depression *but* has not considered suicide?

We know that $P[A_1] = .18$, $P[A_2] = .02$, and $P[A_1 \cup A_2] = .19$. We are asked, first, to find $P[A_1 \cap A_2]$. Applying the general addition rule, we get

$$P[A_1 \cup A_2] = P[A_1] + P[A_2] - P[A_1 \cap A_2]$$

or

$$\begin{aligned} P[A_1 \cap A_2] &= P[A_1] + P[A_2] - P[A_1 \cup A_2] \\ &= .18 + .02 - .19 \\ &= .01 \end{aligned}$$

To answer the second question posed, we display the information given in a Venn diagram. Since $P[A_1 \cap A_2] = .01$, we know that 1% of the total area in the diagram lies in the region representing $A_1 \cap A_2$, as shown in Figure 3.3*a*. Since $P[A_1] = .18$, of the total area, 18% lies in the region labeled $A_1$; since $(A_1 \cap A_2) \subseteq A_1$, 17% of the area lies in the shaded region of Figure 3.3*b*. Similarly, since $P[A_2] = .02$ and $(A_1 \cap A_2) \subseteq A_2$, 1% of the area lies in the shaded region of Figure 3.3*c*. Since $P[S] = 1$ and we have accounted for $17 + 1 + 1 = 19\%$ of the area, the remaining 81% lies in the shaded region of Figure 3.3*d*. Now we can answer the second question by looking for the appropriate region in the Venn diagram, namely, $A_1 \cap A_2'$. It can be seen that the probability associated with this region is .17. Thus, the probability that a randomly selected college student has suffered from depression but has not considered suicide is .17.

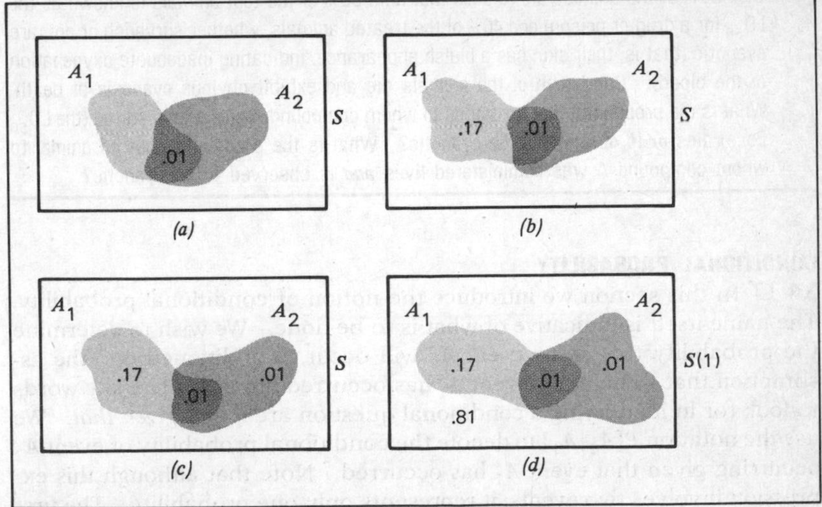


**FIGURE 3.3** Computing probabilities by using Venn diagrams.

## EXERCISES 3.2

1. It has been reported that 62% of all health services are financed through private (nongovernment) funds, that 70% are financed by a combination of employer and employee working together, and that 50% are financed both privately and by the employer and employee. What is the probability that a randomly selected patient will have health services that are funded privately or by the employer and employee? What is the probability that a randomly selected patient will have health services that are funded by the employer and employee but are not funded privately?
2. Studies show that 12% of all persons treated by physicians are admitted to the hospital. Of the persons treated, 1% have an adverse drug reaction of some sort, and 12.4% are admitted to the hospital or have an adverse drug reaction. What is the probability that a randomly selected patient will be admitted to the hospital and have a drug reaction? What is the probability that a randomly selected patient will be admitted to the hospital but have no adverse drug reaction? What is the probability that a randomly selected patient will have an adverse reaction to a drug but will not be admitted to the hospital?
3. A chemist analyzes sea water samples for two heavy metals: lead and mercury. She finds that 38% of the samples taken from near the mouth of a river on which numerous industrial plants are located contain toxic levels of lead or mercury, and 32% contain toxic levels of lead. Of these samples, 10% contain high levels of both metals. What is the probability that a given sample will contain a high level of mercury? What is the probability that a given sample will contain only lead?
4. If Swiss mice are given a dose of 1 mg of compound A per kilogram of body weight, then 50% of the animals die (a dose that kills 50% of the test animals is known as the $LD_{50}$ for a drug or poison) and 40% of the treated animals, whether surviving or not, are cyanotic (that is, their skin has a bluish appearance, indicating inadequate oxygenation of the blood). One-fourth of the animals die and exhibit obvious cyanosis at death. What is the probability that an animal to whom compound A was administered (the $LD_{50}$ dose) dies *or* is observed to be cyanotic? What is the probability that an animal to whom compound A was administered lives *and* is observed to be cyanotic?

## CONDITIONAL PROBABILITY

**3.3** □ In this section we introduce the notion of conditional probability. The name itself is indicative of what is to be done. We wish to determine the probability that some event $A_2$ will occur, "conditioned on" the assumption that some other event $A_1$ has occurred already. The key words to look for in identifying a conditional question are *if* and *given that*. We use the notation $P[A_2|A_1]$ to denote the conditional probability of event $A_2$ occurring given that event $A_1$ has occurred. Note that although this expression involves two events, it represents only one probability. The first event listed is the event whose occurrence is in doubt; the slash is read "given that"; the second event listed is assumed to have occurred already.

**EXAMPLE 3.3.1** □ A woman has three children. What is the probability that the first two are boys ($A_1$)? What is the probability that exactly two of the three are boys ($A_2$)? What is the probability that both conditions are satisfied?

These questions are not conditional and can be easily answered by using a tree diagram (see Figure 3.4). If we assume that each child is just as likely to be a boy as a girl, then the eight sample points represented in the tree are equally likely. Therefore, the classical approach can be used to compute the desired probabilities. In particular,

$$P[A_1] = 2/8$$
$$P[A_2] = 3/8$$
$$P[A_1 \cap A_2] = 1/8$$

Suppose we are told that the first two children are boys. Now, what is the probability that there are exactly two boys in the family? That is, what is $P[A_2|A_1]$? Since we know that the first two children are boys, the sample space for the experiment no longer logically consists of eight points but, in fact, now contains only the two points MMM and MMF. The remaining six points are inconsistent with the known information. The conditional question posed is answered via this new two-point sample space. Since these points are equally likely and only one of them corresponds to having exactly two boys in the family,

$$P[A_2|A_1] = P[\text{exactly two boys}\,|\,\text{first two are boys}] = 1/2$$

In this case note that $1/2 = P[A_2|A_1] \neq P[A_2] = 3/8$. Receipt of the new information did affect the probability assigned to the event that exactly two of the children are boys.

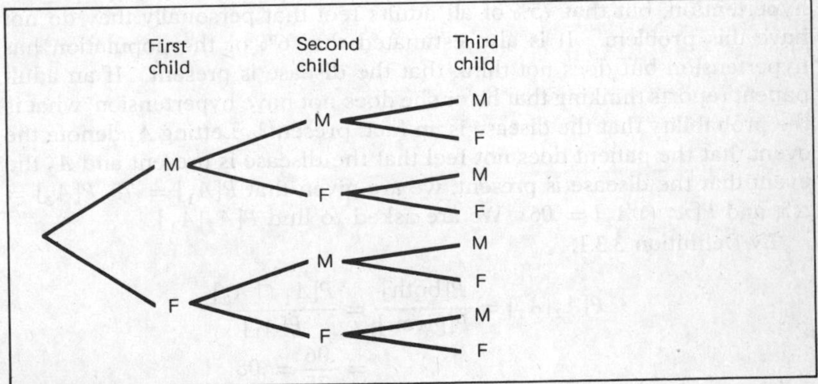


**FIGURE 3.4** Birth orders in a three-child family.

Example 3.3.1 is an oversimplification of the general problem. Most conditional questions are asked relative to situations for which it is not convenient to work directly with an explicitly restricted sample space. Thus, it is necessary to develop a formula for conditional probability that, in essence, automatically reduces the sample space to be consistent with the given information and computes the desired probability relative to this reduced sample space. To discover the formula, we need only look for some pattern in Example 3.3.1. Numerically, the pattern is easy enough to spot. Just note that

$$P[A_2|A_1] = \frac{1}{2} = \frac{1/8}{2/8} = \frac{P[A_1 \cap A_2]}{P[A_1]}$$

This relationship is not unique to this problem. In fact, it is the general definition for the conditional probability of event $A_2$ given $A_1$.

**Definition 3.3.1** *Conditional Probability.* Let $A_1$ and $A_2$ be events such that $P[A_1] \neq 0$. The conditional probability of $A_2$ given $A_1$, denoted $P[A_2|A_1]$, is defined by

$$P[A_2|A_1] = \frac{P[A_1 \cap A_2]}{P[A_1]}$$

Practically speaking, note that the condition that $P[A_1] \neq 0$ is not restrictive. If $A_1$ has occurred, it must have had nonzero probability originally. Definition 3.3.1 is remembered easily as

$$\text{Conditional probability} = \frac{P[\text{both events}]}{P[\text{given event}]}$$

---

**EXAMPLE 3.3.2** □ It is estimated that 15% of the adult population has hypertention, but that 75% of all adults feel that personally they do not have this problem. It is also estimated that 6% of the population has hypertension but does not think that the disease is present. If an adult patient reports thinking that he or she does not have hypertension, what is the probability that the disease is, in fact, present? Letting $A_1$ denote the event that the patient does not feel that the disease is present and $A_2$ the event that the disease is present, we are given that $P[A_1] = .75$, $P[A_2] = .15$, and $P[A_1 \cap A_2] = .06$. We are asked to find $P[A_2|A_1]$.

By Definition 3.3.1,

$$P[A_2|A_1] = \frac{P[\text{both}]}{P[\text{given}]} = \frac{P[A_1 \cap A_2]}{P[A_1]} = \frac{.06}{.75} = .08$$

There is an 8% chance that a patient who expresses the opinion that she or he has no problem with hypertension does, in fact, have the disease.

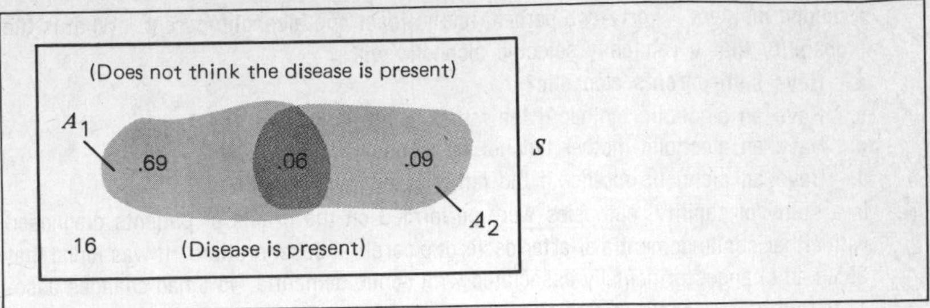


**FIGURE 3.5**

Similarly, we might ask, If the disease is present, what is the probability that the patient will suspect its presence? That is, What is $P[A_1' | A_2]$? Before applying Definition 3.3.1, we organize these data into a Venn diagram, as shown in Figure 3.5. By Definition 3.3.1,

$$P[A_1' | A_2] = \frac{P[\text{both}]}{P[\text{given}]} = \frac{P[A_1' \cap A_2]}{P[A_2]}$$

Reading from the Venn diagram, we have

$$\frac{P[A_1' \cap A_2]}{P[A_2]} = \frac{.09}{.15} = .60$$

That is, if the patient expresses the opinion that he or she has hypertension, there is a 60% chance of the patient being right.

---

## EXERCISES 3.3

1. Suppose a family has four children.
   a. Find the probability that exactly two are male.
   b. What is the probability that exactly two are male if the first child born is male?
   c. Find the probability that the last child born is male.
   d. What is the probability that the last child born is male if the first three are female?
2. A study indicates that 10% of the population in the United States is 65 years old or older and that 1% of the total population is afflicted with mild heart failure. Furthermore, 10.4% of the population is age 65 or older or suffers from mild heart failure. An individual is selected at random.
   a. Find the probability that the individual is 65 or older and suffering from mild heart failure.
   b. Use the answer to part **a** to organize the data into a Venn diagram.
   c. If an individual is 65 or older, what is the probability that the person will suffer mild heart failure?
   d. If an individual is under age 65, what is the probability that he or she will suffer mild heart failure?
3. In a study of alcoholics, it was found that 40% had alcoholic fathers and 6% had

alcoholic mothers. Forty-two percent had at least one alcoholic parent. What is the probability that a randomly selected alcoholic will

**a.** Have both parents alcoholic?
**b.** Have an alcoholic mother if the father is alcoholic?
**c.** Have an alcoholic mother but not an alcoholic father?
**d.** Have an alcoholic mother if the father is not alcoholic?

**4.** In a study of senility, autopsies were performed on the brains of patients diagnosed with either senile dementia or arteriosclerotic cerebral degeneration. It was found that 35% had changes principally associated with senile dementia, 45% had changes associated with arteriosclerotic cerebral degeneration, and 20% showed evidence of both. Based on this information, what is the probability that a patient with brain damage resulting from arteriosclerotic cerebral degeneration also will have brain changes characteristic of senile dementia? What is the probability that a patient who does not have changes owing to senile dementia will have arteriosclerotic cerebral degeneration?

**5.** In a study of waters located near power plants and other industrial plants that release wastewater into the water system, it was found that 5% showed signs of chemical and thermal pollution, 40% showed signs of chemical pollution, and 35% showed evidence of thermal pollution. Assume that the results of the study accurately reflect the general situation. What is the probability that a stream that shows some thermal pollution also will show signs of chemical pollution? What is the probability that a stream showing chemical pollution will not show signs of thermal pollution?

**6.** Studies have shown that snowshoe hares die off periodically, even in the absence of predators and known diseases. Two identifiable causes of death are low blood sugar and convulsions. It is estimated that 7% of the animals dying exhibit both symptoms, 40% have low blood sugar, and 25% suffer from convulsions. What percentage die from causes other than the two mentioned? What is the probability that a randomly selected animal that has low blood sugar also will have suffered from convulsions?

---

## *APPROXIMATING CONDITIONAL PROBABILITIES—SENSITIVITY, SPECIFICITY, AND FALSE-POSITIVE AND FALSE-NEGATIVE RATES

**3.4** □ In most statistical studies, you work with experimental data. Thus probabilities or percentages reported usually are not exact. They are only approximations of the true underlying probabilities, and should be viewed as such.

Many times data are not reported in terms of approximate probabilities as in Section 3.3, but come in the form of a table of raw frequencies. In this case, you are asked to use the raw frequencies to approximate the corresponding true probabilities by using the relative frequency approach discussed in Chapter 2. Consider Example 3.4.1.

---

**EXAMPLE 3.4.1** □ The serum of a pregnant woman may be analyzed by using a procedure known as starch gel electrophoresis. This test may reveal the presence of a protein zone called the *pregnancy zone*. Table 3.1 gives frequency data concerning the sex of the child and the presence or absence of this zone.

**TABLE 3.1**

| | | Pregnancy Zone | | |
|---|---|---|---|---|
| | | PRESENT | ABSENT | |
| Sex | Male | 51 | 96 | 147 |
| | Female | 78 | 75 | 153 |
| | | 129 | 171 | 300 |

Important questions to ask are, If the pregnancy zone is present, what is the probability that the child is male? and If the zone is not present, what is the probability that the child is male? Both are conditional questions, and they can be answered quite easily by using Definition 3.3.1. Let $A_1$ denote the event that the pregnancy zone is present and $A_2$ the event that the child is male. First, we are asked to find $P[A_2|A_1]$. To do so, we must approximate $P[A_1 \cap A_2]$ and $P[A_1]$ from Table 3.1. Using the relative frequency approach to probability gives

$$P[A_1] \doteq \frac{\text{number of times pregnancy zone was present}}{300}$$

$$= \frac{129}{300}$$

and

$$P[A_1 \cap A_2] = \frac{\text{number of times zone was present and child was male}}{300}$$

$$= \frac{51}{300}$$

By Definition 3.3.1,

$$P[A_2|A_1] = \frac{P[A_1 \cap A_2]}{P[A_1]}$$

$$\doteq \frac{51/300}{129/300}$$

$$= \frac{51}{129} = .39$$

Note that this result could have been obtained from Table 3.1 at a glance by realizing that once we know that the pregnancy zone was present, attention is immediately restricted to the 129 cases in column 1. Of these, 51 are male. Hence common sense points to $^{51}/_{129}$ as the conditional probability of the child being male given that the zone is present.

Second, we are asked to find $P[A_2|A_1']$. From Table 3.1

$$P[A_2|A_1'] \doteq {}^{96}/_{171} = .56$$

A word of caution is in order. When you are using a frequency table to approximate a conditional probability, you must be careful. In particular, you must consider whether the marginal totals are free to vary or are fixed by the experimenter. Example 3.4.2 illustrates the reason.

**EXAMPLE 3.4.2** □ A study was run to determine the effect of heavy smoking on vital lung capacity. Five heavy smokers and ten nonsmokers were selected for the study. After moderate exercise, the vital lung capacity of each subject was measured and classified as satisfactory or unsatisfactory. The results are shown in Table 3.2.

**TABLE 3.2** VITAL LUNG CAPACITY

| | SATISFACTORY | UNSATISFACTORY | |
|---|---|---|---|
| **Heavy Smoker** | 1 | 4 | 5 (Fixed by the experimenter) |
| **Nonsmoker** | 5 | 5 | 10 (Fixed by the experimenter) |
| | 6 (Random) | 9 (Random) | 15 |

Some conditional probabilities can be reliably approximated from these data whereas others cannot. For instance,

$$P[\text{heavy smoker} \mid \text{satisfactory lung capacity}]$$

cannot be approximated, but

$$P[\text{satisfactory lung capacity} \mid \text{heavy smoker}]$$

can be. What is the difference between the two? Simply, in finding the former one must approximate from the data the probability of a randomly selected individual having a satisfactory vital lung capacity and being a heavy smoker. Since the experimenter fixed the number of heavy smokers in the experiment at 5, essentially the approximated probability of this event was forced to be at most $5/15$. This is unrealistic, and so the probability that an individual with a satisfactory vital lung capacity is a heavy smoker cannot be approximated from this experiment. However, in finding the latter, the five heavy smokers randomly selected by the experimenter can be viewed as being a random sample from the population of all heavy smokers. Thus we can use the relative frequency approach to approximate the probability that a heavy smoker will have a satisfactory vital lung capacity to be $1/5$. In summary, if all margins are random, then any conditional probability called for can be approximated. If the margins associated with the *given* event are fixed, then conditional probabilities can be found based on the relative frequency approach to probability.

In clinical chemistry, two rates are of particular interest, namely, the false-positive and false-negative rates of the test procedure. These rates are conditional probabilities. They are defined as logic would indicate. The false-positive rate, for instance, is the probability that the test will result in a positive finding when, in fact, the subject does not have the trait to be detected. The false-negative rate is defined analogously. These definitions are formalized here.

**Definition 3.4.1** *False-Positive Rate.* The *false-positive rate* of a test is denoted by $\alpha$ (alpha) and is given by

$$\alpha = P[\text{test results are positive} \mid \text{subject is a true negative}]$$

**Definition 3.4.2** *False-Negative Rate.* The *false-negative rate* of a test is denoted $\beta$ (beta) and is given by

$$\beta = P[\text{test results are negative} \mid \text{subject is a true positive}]$$

Note that each of these probabilities is a probability of error. Hopefully, diagnostic tests used in practice will be such that each is low. Given a frequency table, these rates can be approximated by the techniques of Example 3.4.2.

---

**EXAMPLE 3.4.3** □ In a study of 300 pairs of twins, the twins were questioned as to whether they were identical. Then other factors such as ABO blood group, MN blood type, and Rh blood type were considered. On the basis of these traits, the twins were classified as identical (+) or nonidentical (−). The latter classification procedure is considered to be the true classification. The purpose of the study is to test the ability of twins to self-classify. The results are shown in Table 3.3. All margins are random.

**TABLE 3.3**

| | | Self-Classification | | |
|---|---|---|---|---|
| | | IDENTICAL (+) | NONIDENTICAL (−) | |
| True Classification | (+) | 54 | 4 | 58 |
| | (−) | 12 | 130 | 142 |
| | | 66 | 134 | 200 |

Based on these findings, what are the approximate false-positive and false-negative rates for the self-classification procedure?

Note that $\alpha$ is the probability that a pair of twins will classify themselves as identical when, in fact, they are not. From Table 3.3,

$$\alpha \doteq 12/142 = .08$$

And $\beta$ is the probability that a pair of twins will classify themselves as nonidentical when, in fact, they are identical, so

$$\beta \doteq 4/58 = .07$$

## EXERCISES 3.4

1. Consider Example 3.4.1. Approximate the probability that the child is female if the pregnancy zone is present. Approximate the probability that the pregnancy zone will be present if the child is male.
2. A study is run to investigate the association between flower color and fragrance in wild azaleas found in the Great Smoky Mountains. A 5-acre tract of mountain terrain was selected and found to contain 200 blooming plants. Each was classified both by color and by the presence or absence of fragrance. The results are shown in Table 3.4.

**TABLE 3.4**

| | Flower Color | | |
|---|---|---|---|
| FRAGRANCE | WHITE | PINK | ORANGE |
| **Yes** | 12 | 60 | 58 |
| **No** | 50 | 10 | 10 |

Using these data, approximate, if possible, each of the following probabilities. If it is not possible to approximate a particular probability from the given data, explain why.

**a.** $P$[a randomly selected azalea has a fragrance]
**b.** $P$[a randomly selected azalea is orange]
**c.** $P$[a randomly selected azalea is orange and has a fragrance]
**d.** $P$[a randomly selected azalea is orange given that it has a fragrance]
**e.** $P$[a randomly selected azalea has a fragrance given that it is orange]

3. The results shown in Table 3.5 were obtained in a study designed to test the ability of a surgical pathologist to correctly score surgical biopsy samples as malignant or benign. From the data approximate $\alpha$ and $\beta$.

**TABLE 3.5**

| | Report of Pathologist | | |
|---|---|---|---|
| | POSITIVE (MALIGNANT) | NEGATIVE (BENIGN) | |
| **True Positive** | 79 | 19 | 98 |
| **True Negative** | 7 | 395 | 402 |
| | 86 | 414 | 500 |

4. A study was conducted to investigate a procedure for detecting renal disease in patients with hypertension. Using the new procedure, experimenters screened 137

TABLE 3.6

| | DISEASE PRESENT | DISEASE ABSENT | |
|---|---|---|---|
| **Disease Detected by New Procedure** | 44 | 23 | |
| **Disease Not Detected by New Procedure** | 10 | 60 | |
| | | | 137 |

hypertensive patients. Then the presence or absence of renal disease was determined by another method. The data obtained are shown in Table 3.6. Use the data to approximate the false-positive and false-negative rates for the test.

**5.** *Definition:* The ***specificity*** of a test is the probability that the test results will be negative given that the subject is a true negative. Approximate the specificity of the test of Example 3.4.3. In general, would you want the specificity of a test to be high or low? Explain.

**6.** *Definition:* The ***sensitivity*** of a test is the probability that the test results will be positive given that the subject is a true positive. Approximate the sensitivity of the test of Example 3.4.3. In general, would you want the sensitivity of a test to be high or low? Explain.

**7.** One hundred patients and seventy-five normal subjects were given a diagnostic urine test. Sixty percent were reported positive. There were eight false negatives. What was the approximate false-positive rate?

**8.** Approximate the specificity and sensitivity of the test of Exercise 3.4.1. In general, what is the relationship between the specificity and the false-positive rate? What is the relationship between the sensitivity and the false-negative rate?

## INDEPENDENCE AND THE MULTIPLICATION RULE

**3.5** □ Two important relationships may exist among events. The first, being mutually exclusive, is discussed in Section 3.1; the second, being independent, is described here. The mathematical term has virtually the same meaning as its English counterpart. Webster defines *independent* objects as objects acting "irrespective of each other." Thus two events are independent if one may occur irrespective of the other. That is, the occurrence or nonoccurrence of one has no effect on the occurrence or nonoccurrence of the other. In many cases, we can determine on a purely intuitive basis whether two events are independent. For example, events $A_1$, the patient has tennis elbow, and $A_2$, the patient has appendicitis, are intuitively independent. The fact that the patient has appendicitis should have no bearing on whether she or he has tennis elbow, and vice versa!

In some instances, however, the issue is not clear-cut. Then we need a precise mathematical definition of the term to be able to determine without a doubt whether two events are, in fact, independent. The definition is easy to develop. For example, suppose that, based on the symptoms described, you feel that the probability that the patient has appendicitis is .9 ($A_2$). Now, suppose you are suddenly given the additional information that the patient has tennis elbow ($A_1$). What do you think is the probability of the patient having appendicitis? Obviously, the answer is still .9! Since $A_1$ and $A_2$ are independent, the new information is irrelevant and has no effect at all on the original probability. Thus independence between two events $A_1$ and $A_2$ results in the conditional probability $P[A_2|A_1]$ being equal to the probability originally assigned to event $A_2$. This characterization is taken as the definition of the term *independent events.*

**Definition 3.5.1** *Independent Events.* Let $A_1$ and $A_2$ be events such that $P[A_1] \neq 0$. These events are *independent* if and only if

$$P[A_2|A_1] = P[A_2]$$

---

**EXAMPLE 3.5.1** □ It is estimated that among the U.S. population as a whole, 55% are overweight ($A_1$), 20% have high blood pressure ($A_2$), and 60% are overweight or have high blood pressure. Is the fact that a person is overweight independent of the state of his or her blood pressure? The answer to this question is not obvious. Using the general addition principle yields

$$P[A_1 \cap A_2] = P[A_1] + P[A_2] - P[A_1 \cup A_2]$$

or, in this case,

$$P[A_1 \cap A_2] = .55 + .20 - .60 = .15$$

Thus

$$P[A_2|A_1] = \frac{P[A_1 \cap A_2]}{P[A_1]}$$
$$= \frac{.15}{.55} = \frac{15}{55} = .27$$

Since $P[A_2|A_1] = .27 \neq .20 = P[A_2]$, we may conclude that the events are not independent. Practically speaking, the fact that a person is overweight increases the probability of having high blood pressure.

---

Definition 3.5.1 is logical and easy to understand. However, it is not the definition commonly given for the term *independent events.* The usual definition can be derived by noting the following:

$$P[A_2|A_1] = \frac{P[A_1 \cap A_2]}{P[A_1]} \quad \text{is always true as long as } P[A_1] \neq 0$$

$$P[A_2|A_1] = P[A_2] \quad \text{if } P[A_1] \neq 0 \text{ and the events are independent.}$$

Thus if $A_1$ and $A_2$ are independent, both equations hold simultaneously.

So we have two expressions for $P[A_2|A_1]$, which can be equated to yield

$$\frac{P[A_1 \cap A_2]}{P[A_1]} = P[A_2]$$

Multiplying both sides of this equation by $P[A_1]$, we obtain $P[A_1 \cap A_2] = P[A_1]P[A_2]$, the usual definition of the term *independent events.*

**Definition 3.5.2** *Independent Events.* Let $A_1$ and $A_2$ be events. Then $A_1$ and $A_2$ are *independent* if and only if $P[A_1 \cap A_2] = P[A_1]P[A_2]$.

Definition 3.5.2 can be used as an alternate method for testing for independence. However, it is most useful for determining the probability of the simultaneous occurrence of two events that are physically independent.

---

**EXAMPLE 3.5.2** □ Studies in population genetics indicate that 39% of the available genes for determining the Rh blood factor are negative. Based on this information, what is the probability that a randomly selected individual will have Rh negative blood? Rh negative blood occurs if and only if the individual involved has two negative genes. Since one gene is inherited from each parent, it may be assumed that the gene type of the first gene is independent of that of the second. Hence the probability that an individual has two negative genes is $(.39)(.39) \doteq .15$.

---

Occasionally, we must deal with more than two events. Again, the question arises, When are these events considered independent? Definition 3.5.3 answers this question by extending Definition 3.5.2 to include a finite collection of events.

**Definition 3.5.3** Let $C = \{A_i\colon i = 1, 2, \ldots, n\}$ be a finite collection of events. These events are *independent* if and only if, given any subcollection $A_{(1)}$, $A_{(2)}, \ldots, A_{(m)}$ of elements of $C$,

$$P[A_{(1)} \cap A_{(2)} \cap \cdots \cap A_{(m)}] = P[A_{(1)}]P[A_{(2)}] \cdots P[A_{(m)}]$$

---

**EXAMPLE 3.5.3** □ During the course of a day, a particular diagnostic test is run on three unrelated patients. The test is 90% accurate on both those who do and those who do not have the condition that the test is designed to detect. What is the probability that exactly two of the three test results are in error?

A tree diagram will help answer this question. Within the tree, $C$ represents a correct decision and $E$ an error. Appropriate probabilities are listed in Figure 3.6. Starred paths represent cases of interest. A typical

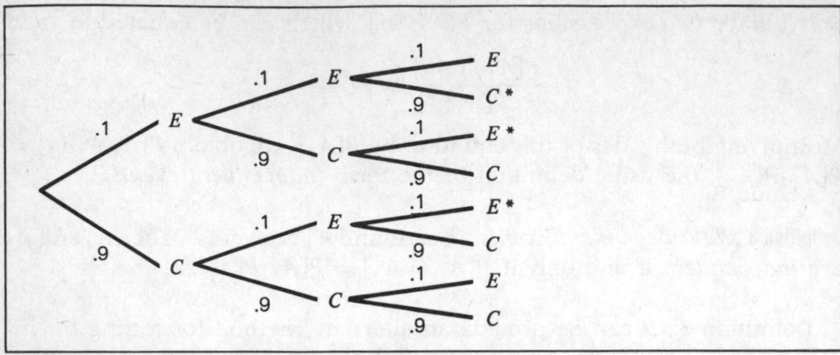


**FIGURE 3.6** Results of a diagnostic test (three patients).

path represents the simultaneous occurrence of three distinct events. For example, the path *EEC* represents the occurrence of an error with the first patient ($E_1$) and an error with the second ($E_2$) and a correct decision with the third ($C_3$). Since the tests are run independently on different patients, we can assume that the results are independent. By Definition 3.5.3, the probability along each path can be found by *multiplying* the probabilities that appear along the path. Thus, for instance, $P[E_1 \cap E_2 \cap C_3] = P[E_1]P[E_2]P[C_3] = (.1)(.1)(.9) = .009$. Since there are three paths which involve exactly two errors, the probability of obtaining exactly two errors in some order is $3(.009) = .027$.

---

There is one further point to be made before we conclude this section. Now we can find $P[A_1 \cap A_2]$ if the events are independent. Furthermore, if the proper information is given, the general addition rule can be used to find this quantity. Is there any other way to find the probability of the simultaneous occurrence of two events if the events are not independent? The answer is yes, and the method used is easy to derive. We know that

$$P[A_2|A_1] = \frac{P[A_1 \cap A_2]}{P[A_1]}$$

regardless of whether the events are independent. Multiplying each side of this equation by $P[A_1]$, we obtain the following formula, called the *multiplication rule*:

$$P[A_1 \cap A_2] = P[A_2|A_1]P[A_1]$$ **Multiplication Rule**

The use of this rule is illustrated in Example 3.5.4.

---

**EXAMPLE 3.5.4** ☐ When a mother is Rh negative and her child is Rh positive, a blood incompatibility exists that may lead to erythroblastosis fetalis, a condition in which the mother forms an antibody against fetal Rh which leads to the destruction of fetal red blood cells. What is the probability that a randomly selected child will be at risk?

Let us use the method of Example 3.5.2 to consider the Rh factor distribution in the general population. If we assume that 39% of the available gene pool is negative and 61% is positive, then independence allows us to conclude that

$$\begin{aligned} P[\text{Rh negative } (--)] &= (.39)(.39) \doteq .15 \\ P[\text{Rh positive homozygous } (++)] &= (.61)(.61) \doteq .37 \\ P[\text{Rh positive heterozygous } (-+) \text{ or } (+-)] &= 2(.39)(.61) \doteq 48 \end{aligned}$$

The incompatibility can arise in two distinct ways:

**1.** The mother is negative ($A_1$), and the father is positive homozygous ($A_2$).

**2.** The mother is negative ($A_1$), the father is positive heterozygous ($A_3$), and the child inherits a positive gene from the father ($A_4$).

Events $A_1$ and $A_2$ may be considered independent. Thus the probability that condition 1 exists is given by

$$\begin{aligned} P[A_1 \cap A_2] = P[A_1]P[A_2] &= (.15)(.37) \\ &= .0555 \end{aligned}$$

Condition 2 is a bit more complex. Note that the mother's gene type has no effect on that of the father or on his ability to convey a positive gene to the child. Thus event $A_1$ is independent of event $A_3 \cap A_4$. This implies that

$$\begin{aligned} P[A_1 \cap (A_4 \cap A_3)] &= P[A_1]P[A_4 \cap A_3] \\ &= (.15)P[A_4 \cap A_3] \end{aligned}$$

However, events $A_3$ and $A_4$ are *not* independent; the fact that the father is positive heterozygous does have a bearing on the child's ability to obtain a positive gene from this source. By the multiplication rule,

$$\begin{aligned} P[A_4 \cap A_3] &= P[A_4 | A_3]P[A_3] \\ &= (.5)(.48) = .24 \end{aligned}$$

Combining these results, we find the probability of a blood incompatibility resulting from condition 2 to be

$$\begin{aligned} P[A_1 \cap (A_4 \cap A_3)] &= P[A_1]P[A_4 | A_3]P[A_3] \\ &= (.15)(.5)(.48) = .0360 \end{aligned}$$

Thus the probability of a blood incompatibility arising from condition 1 or 2 is .0555 + .0360 = .0915.

Independence is an important concept. In the statistical procedures presented in later chapters, often independence is assumed, and the accuracy of the results obtained will depend on the validity of that assumption.

## EXERCISES 3.5

1. Which of the following pairs of events do you think are independent? Which are mutually exclusive?
   $A_1$: A mother has rubella during the first 3 months of pregnancy.
   $B_1$: A mother's child is born dead or deformed.
   $A_2$: A man is sterile.
   $B_2$: A man contracts mumps as an adult.
   $A_3$: A male and female rat are caged together.
   $B_3$: The female rat is sterile.
   $A_4$: A child is nearsighted.
   $B_4$: A child is farsighted.
   $A_5$: An area has been strip-mined.
   $B_5$: The area experiences frequent floods.
   $A_6$: A rabbit is inoculated with polio virus.
   $B_6$: The rabbit's blood contains antibodies to polio.
   $A_7$: A rabbit is inoculated with polio virus.
   $B_7$: The rabbit's blood contains antibodies to measles.
2. Test events $A_1$ and $A_2$ of Example 3.3.2 for independence. Discuss briefly the practical implications of your result.
3. The most common water pollutants are organic. Since most organic materials are broken down by bacteria that require oxygen, an excess of organic matter may result in a depletion of available oxygen. In turn, this can be harmful to other organisms living in the water. The demand for oxygen by the bacteria is called the ***biological oxygen demand*** (BOD). A study of streams located near an industrial complex revealed that 35% have a high BOD, 10% show high acidity, and 4% have both characteristics. Are the events the stream has a high BOD and the stream has high acidity independent? Find the probability that the stream has high acidity given that it has a high BOD.
4. Approximately 50% of the population is male, 68% drinks to some extent, and 38.5% drinks and is male. Given that a randomly selected individual is male, find the probability that he drinks. Is a person's drinking status independent of gender?
5. The probability of contracting serum hepatitis from a unit of blood is .01. A patient receives two units of blood during a hospital stay. What is the probability that he will not contract serum hepatitis from this source?
6. Even though tetanus is rare in the United States, it is fatal 70% of the time. If three persons contract tetanus during one year, what is the probability that at least two of the three will die? (*Hint:* Use a tree.)
7. Studies indicate that 82% of all professional men drink. If they drink, 18% are heavy drinkers. What is the probability that a randomly selected professional man drinks and drinks heavily?
8. Of all cancer patients, 52% are male. Overall 40% of all patients survive for at least 5

years after the original diagnosis. However, for males the 5-year survival rate is only 35%. What is the probability that a randomly selected cancer patient will be male and survive for at least 5 years?

**9.** The probability that a unit of blood was donated by a paid donor is .67. If the donor was paid, the probability of contracting serum hepatitis from the unit is .0144. If the donor was not paid, this probability is .0012. A patient receives a unit of blood. What is the probability of the patient's contracting serum hepatitis from this source?

**10.** An individual's blood group (A, B, AB, O) is independent of the Rh factor classification. Find the probability that a randomly selected individual will have AB negative blood. *Hint:* See Examples 3.5.4 and 3.1.1.

**11.** Two percent of the general population has diabetes. Of these, only half are aware of their condition. If an individual is selected at random, what is the probability that he or she has diabetes but is unaware of the condition?

***12.** It is known that the false-positive rate for a test for a specific disease is 4% and that the false-negative rate is 6%. The test shows 15% of the people to be positive. What is the probability that a randomly selected individual actually has the disease? *Hint:* Let $x = P$[true positive] and $1 - x = P$[true negative]. Note that

$$P[\text{test positive}] = P[\text{test positive and are true positives}] + P[\text{test positive and are true negatives}]$$

***13.** *Hardy-Weinberg Principle.* The Hardy-Weinberg principle from population genetics is named after G. H. Hardy, an English mathematician, and G. Weinberg, a German physician. Basically, the principle states that a population is genetically stable in succeeding generations. The mathematical basis for this principle relies on the notion of independence in two ways: independent mating and independent inheritance of one gene from each parent in offspring. Consider the distribution of a single pair of genes *A* and *a*. Each member of the population will have two of these genes. Thus we have three genotypes: *AA, Aa,* and *aa*. Suppose that these genotypes are present in the population in the ratio $\frac{1}{4}AA$, $\frac{1}{2}Aa$, $\frac{1}{4}aa$. If we assume that members of the population mate

| Mating Type | | | POSSIBLE | PROBABLE | |
|---|---|---|---|---|---|
| MALE | FEMALE | PROBABILITY OF MATCH | OFFSPRING GENOTYPE | OFFSPRING GENOTYPE | PATH PROBABILITY |
| *AA* | *AA* | $\frac{1}{4} \cdot \frac{1}{4}$ | *AA* | 1 | $\frac{1}{16}$ |
| *AA* | *Aa* | $\frac{1}{4} \cdot \frac{1}{2}$ | *AA* | $\frac{1}{2}$ | $\frac{1}{16}$ |
| | | | *Aa* | $\frac{1}{2}$ | $\frac{1}{16}$ |
| *AA* | *aa* | $\frac{1}{4} \cdot \frac{1}{4}$ | *Aa* | 1 | $\frac{1}{16}$ |
| *Aa* | *AA* | | | | |
| *Aa* | *Aa* | | | | |
| *Aa* | *aa* | | | | |
| *aa* | *AA* | | | | |
| *aa* | *Aa* | | | | |
| *aa* | *aa* | | | | |

at random, the nine possible mating types are as listed on page 89. Each mating type leads to one or more possible genotypes among offspring. Given independence, the first few rows are as shown. Complete the table on page 89. Once it is complete, verify that one-fourth of the offspring are of genotype *AA*, half are of *Aa,* and one-fourth are of *aa,* which verifies the Hardy-Weinberg principle.

***14.** Some characteristics in animals are said to be sex-influenced. For example, the production of horns in sheep is governed by a pair of alleles, *H* and *h*. The allele *H* for the production of horns is dominant in males but recessive in females. The allele *h* for hornlessness is dominant in females and recessive in males. Thus, given a heterozygous male (*Hh*) and a heteroxygous female, the male will have horns and the female will be hornless. Assume that two such animals mate.

**a.** Draw a tree to represent the possible genotypes relative to the gene determining horn production.

**b.** Assume that each offspring of this mating is just as likely to be male as female. Find the probability that a given offspring will be male and have horns. Find the probability that a given offspring will be female and have horns.

**c.** Find the probability that a given offspring will have horns. Show that events $A$, the offspring is male, and $B$, the offspring has horns, are not independent.

***15.** In DNA replication, occasionally errors occur that can lead to observable mutations in the organism. Sometimes these errors are chemically induced. Growing bacteria are exposed to a chemical that has a probability of .4 of inducing an error. However, 65% of the errors are "silent" in that they do not lead to an observable mutation. What is the probability of observing a mutated colony? *Hint:* Find *P*[error and observable].

---

## *BAYES' THEOREM

**3.6** □ The topic of this section is the theorem formulated by the Reverend Thomas Bayes (1761). It deals with conditional probability. Bayes' theorem is used to find $P[A \mid B]$ when the available information is not directly compatible with that required in Definition 3.3.1. That is, it is used to find $P[A \mid B]$ when $P[A \cap B]$ and $P[B]$ are not immediately available. Before we state Bayes' theorem, consider Example 3.6.1, which illustrates its usefulness.

---

**EXAMPLE 3.6.1** □ A test has been developed to detect a particular type of arthritis in individuals over 50 years old. From a national survey, it is known that approximately 10% of the individuals in this age group suffer from this form of arthritis. The proposed test was given to individuals with confirmed arthritic disease, and a correct test result was obtained in 85% of the cases. When the test was administered to individuals of the same age group who were known to be free of the disease, a 4% false-positive rate was obtained.

For the test to be useful as a screening test for arthritis, it is necessary that a positive test result be a strong indicator that the disease is present.

Let $D$ denote the event that the disease is present and $T+$ the event that the test result is positive. We want $P[D \mid T+]$ to be high. Since this probability is conditional, the first impulse is to try to use Definition 3.3.1 to find it. However, $P[D \cap T+]$, the probability that the disease is present and the test result is positive, and $P[T+]$, the probability of obtaining a positive result, are not given. Hence Definition 3.3.1 cannot be used directly; another method is needed to compute the desired probability.

To solve the problem, note that these probabilities are given ($T-$ denotes the event that the test result is negative):

$$P[D] = .10 \qquad P[T+ \mid D] = .85 \qquad P[T+ \mid D'] = .04$$
$$P[D'] = .90 \qquad P[T- \mid D] = .15 \qquad P[T- \mid D'] = .96$$

These probabilities are shown in Figure 3.7. Note that the multiplication rule is applied to obtain the path probabilities listed. To find the probability that the disease is present given a positive test result, first we note that

$$P[T+] = .085 + .036 = .121 \qquad \text{(paths 1 and 3, Figure 3.7)}$$
$$P[T-] = .015 + .864 = .879 \qquad \text{(paths 2 and 4, Figure 3.7)}$$

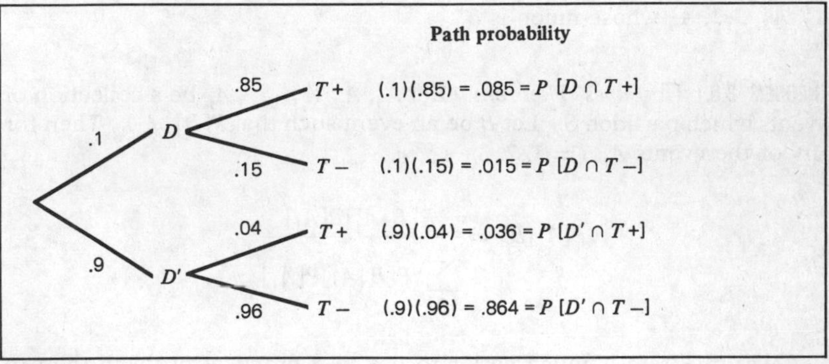


**FIGURE 3.7** Paths and path probabilities.

Next we write the tree in reverse order, keeping the path probabilities the same as shown in Figure 3.8. Let $x = P[D \mid T+]$. From the tree of Figure 3.8 we see that

$$.121x = .085$$

Solving for $x$, we obtain

$$x = P[D \mid T+] = \frac{.085}{.121} \doteq .70$$

That is, if the test result is positive, there is about a 70% chance that the disease is actually present.

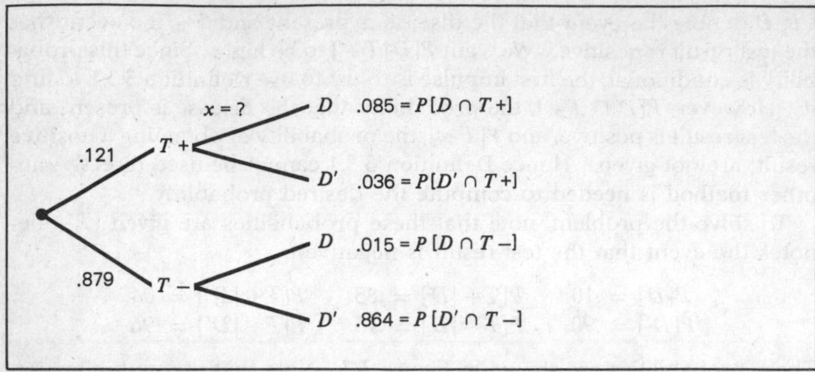


**FIGURE 3.8** Paths and path probabilities in reverse order.

In solving Example 3.6.1 with a tree, we are actually using Bayes' theorem quite naturally. The formal statement of this theorem is given here. By a *partition* of $S$ we mean a collection of mutually exclusive events $A_1$, $A_2$, $A_3$, . . . , $A_n$ whose union is $S$.

**THEOREM 3.6.1** □ *Bayes' Theorem.* Let $A_1, A_2, A_3, \ldots, A_n$ be a collection of events which partition $S$. Let $B$ be an event such that $P[B] \neq 0$. Then for any of the events $A_j$, $j = 1, 2, 3, \ldots, n$,

$$P[A_j \mid B] = \frac{P[B \mid A_j]P[A_j]}{\sum_{i=1}^{n} P[B \mid A_i]P[A_i]}$$

Bayes' theorem is much easier to use in a practical problem than to state formally. To see this, let us reconsider Example 3.6.1 and solve it without use of the tree.

**EXAMPLE 3.6.2** □ In Example 3.6.1, we are asked to find $P[D \mid T+]$, where $D$ is the event that an individual has arthritis and $T+$ is the event that the test result is positive. The two events $D$ and $D'$ partition $S$. (An individual either does or does not have arthritis.) The event $T+$ occurs with nonzero probability. We are given

$$\begin{array}{lll} P[D] = .10 & P[T+ \mid D] = .85 & P[T+ \mid D'] = .04 \\ P[D'] = .90 & P[T- \mid D] = .15 & P[T- \mid D'] = .96 \end{array}$$

Applying Bayes' theorem, we get

$$P[D|T+] = \frac{P[T+|D]P[D]}{P[T+|D]P[D] + P[T+|D']P[D']}$$

$$= \frac{(.85)(.10)}{(.85)(.10) + (.04)(.90)} \doteq .70$$

Note that this is the same result as that obtained by using the tree.

---

Example 3.6.3 illustrates the use of Bayes' theorem when $S$ is partitioned by more than two events.

---

**EXAMPLE 3.6.3** □ The blood type distribution in the United States is type A, 41%; type B, 9%; type AB, 4%; and type O, 46%. It is estimated that during World War II, 4% of inductees with type O blood were typed as having type A; 88% of those with type A blood were correctly typed; 4% with type B blood were typed as A; and 10% with type AB were typed as A. A soldier was wounded and brought to surgery. He was typed as having type A blood. What is the probability that this is his true blood type?

Let

$A_1$: He has type A blood.

$A_2$: He has type B blood.

$A_3$: He has type AB blood.

$A_4$: He has type O blood.

$B$: He is typed as type A.

We want to find $P[A_1|B]$. We are given that

$$\begin{aligned} P[A_1] &= .41 & P[B|A_1] &= .88 \\ P[A_2] &= .09 & P[B|A_2] &= .04 \\ P[A_3] &= .04 & P[B|A_3] &= .10 \\ P[A_4] &= .46 & P[B|A_4] &= .04 \end{aligned}$$

By Bayes' theorem,

$$P[A_1|B] = \frac{P[B|A_1]P[A_1]}{\sum_{i=1}^{4} P[B|A_i]P[A_i]}$$

$$= \frac{(.88)(.41)}{(.88)(.41) + (.04)(.09) + (.10)(.04) + (.04)(.46)}$$

$$\doteq .93$$

Practically speaking, this means that there is a 93% chance that the blood type is A if it has been typed as A. There is a 7% chance that it has been mistyped as A when it is actually some other type.

## EXERCISES 3.6

1. Statistics indicate that the probability that a mother will die during childbirth in the United States is .00022. If the mother is not black, the probability of death is .00017, whereas the figure is .00064 if she is black. Assume that 10% of the births-recorded are to blacks.
   - **a.** Draw a tree indicating these probabilities, and find the path probabilities for each of the four paths. (Let $D$ denote the event that the mother died and $B$ the event that the mother is black.)
   - **b.** Find the tree which reverses the order of the events of part **a.**
   - **c.** Use the tree of part **b** to find the probability that a mother who dies in childbirth is black.
   - **d.** Using Bayes' theorem, find the probability that a mother who dies in childbirth is black, and compare your answer to that obtained in part **c.**
2. Consider Example 3.6.3. If a patient is typed as type A, what is the probability of her actually being type B?

*3. A screening test for cancer of the cervix has a false-negative rate and a false-positive rate, each of .05. Of a certain population of women, 4% have this form of cancer. What is the probability that a randomly selected woman from the population has cancer of the cervix given that she reacts positively to the test?

4. A cancer patient is being treated with a combination of three drugs. It has been observed that when they are used in combination, the probability is $\frac{1}{3}$ that two of the three drugs will be inhibited and that, in fact, only one will be actively fighting the tumor. The effectiveness of each drug alone in producing remission is different. Drug A has been observed to be effective 50% of the time; drug B, 75% of the time; and drug C, 60% of the time. The patient has gone into remission. What is the probability that drug B alone was actually responsible for the remisssion?

*5. The data of Exercise 3.4.4 were collected at a clinic that had an associated renal service. Thus the incidence of renal disease among those screened (39%) is thought to be higher than that in the general population of hypertensive patients. Use the data of Exercise 3.4.4 to estimate the specificity and sensitivity of the test. Use Bayes' theorem to find the probability that a randomly selected patient with hypertension has renal disease given that the test indicates its presence if the rate of renal disease is assumed to be 10% in the general population.

*6. Duchenne muscular dystrophy is a disease of the muscle that affects young boys. The nature of the disorder is such that it prevents transmission by affected males, but it is spread by carrier females who themselves rarely exhibit any symptoms of the disease. Consider a woman who is the daughter of a known carrier of the disease. She has exactly three sons, all normal. Use Bayes' theorem to find the probability that the woman is a carrier. That is, find $P$[carrier | three normal sons].

# RANDOM VARIABLES

# 4.

In Chapter 1, we considered some of the methods currently used to describe data sets. Some of these data sets represented the entire population under study; others represented only a sample drawn from a larger population. In the latter case, we did not attempt to draw more than rough conclusions about the parent population from the sample. In Chapters 2 and 3, we discussed probability theory. We saw how the axioms and theorems of probability can be used to answer many questions of a fairly complex nature. We have not yet considered the implications of probability theory to data analysis. That is, we have not yet begun to show how probability theory can be utilized to draw precise conclusions about a population based on a sample drawn from that population. To do this, first we must turn our attention to a topic that provides the link between probability theory and applied statistics. In particular, we develop the notion of a *random variable*. We show that most statistical studies are, in fact, studies of the properties of one or more random variables. Thus, an understanding of these properties is essential to truly understand the statistical methods presented later in this text.

## DISCRETE AND CONTINUOUS VARIABLES

**4.1** □ The concept of a random variable is not difficult. In fact, many of the problems already presented involve random variables even though the term itself was not used at the time. Intuitively, a random variable is a variable whose actual numerical value is determined by chance. Random variables are denoted by uppercase letters and their observed numerical values by lowercase letters.

---

**EXAMPLE 4.1.1** □ Consider variable $Y$, the number of oil spills per year affecting U.S. coastal waters. This is a random variable. It does not assume exactly the same value every year. It may vary widely from year to year, and the variability is due to chance. If in a particular year there are five spills, we write $y = 5$.

---

**EXAMPLE 4.1.2** □ Let $Z$ denote the number of cc's of a drug that should be prescribed for a patient to control epileptic seizures. This variable changes in value from patient to patient as a result of metabolic and other differences among patients. In fact, its value can change in the same patient from time to time; hence it must be considered a random variable.

---

**EXAMPLE 4.1.3** □ The cephalopods (the "head-foots") are the most highly developed mollusks. One, the octopus, contrary to popular belief, is not large. Variable $D$, the body diameter of an adult octopus, is a random variable. Not all octopuses are the same size. The variability in size is due to both genetic and environmental factors.

---

**EXAMPLE 4.1.4** □ Consider variable $B$, the number of babies born in a given maternity ward before the birth of the first set of Siamese twins. A priori (before the fact), no upper bound can be firmly placed on the set of possible values for $B$. Conceivably, $B$ can assume any of the values $\{0, 1, 2, 3, 4, \ldots\}$. It is a random variable since chance plays a major role in the birth of Siamese twins.

---

There are two easily identifiable types of random variables, discrete and continuous. In the material that follows, you must be able to distinguish the two, for computationally they are handled somewhat differently.

**Definition 4.1.1** A random variable $X$ is *discrete* if it can assume at most a finite or a countably infinite number of possible values.

In Examples 4.1.1 through 4.1.4, $Y$, the number of oil spills per year affecting U.S. coastal waters, and $B$, the number of babies born in a given maternity ward before the birth of the first set of Siamese twins, are both discrete. Variable $Y$ is discrete since the number of possible values for $Y$ is finite. The possible values may reasonably range from 0 to perhaps 50, a finite set of numbers. Variable $B$ is discrete since the set of possible values, $\{0, 1, 2, 3, 4, \ldots\}$, is countably infinite. Usually, discrete variables arise in connection with count data.

**Definition 4.1.2** A random variable $X$ is *continuous* if it can assume any value in some interval (or intervals) of real numbers and the probability that it assumes any specific value is 0.

Variables $Z$, the number of cc's of a drug that should be prescribed for a patient to control seizures, and $D$, the body diameter of an adult octopus, are both continuous. The amount of drug to be prescribed is not restricted to any finite collection of preset possible values. It may lie anywhere between none at all and, say, .3 cc. That is, $Z$ lies in the interval

[0, .3]. Similarly, the body diameter of an adult octopus could lie anywhere within reasonable bounds, say, 10 to 30 centimeters. That is, $D$ lies in the interval [10, 30]. The statement that the probability that a continuous variable assumes any specific value is 0 is *essential* to the definition. Discrete variables have no such restriction. This restriction is intuitively appealing since if we ask *before* the selection is made, What is the probability that a particular octopus will have a body diameter of *exactly* 12.981 321 069 217 031 2 centimeters? the answer is 0. It is virtually impossible to find an octopus with precisely this diameter—not the slightest bit larger or smaller. We discuss this point further from a mathematical standpoint in Section 4.2. Continuous variables generally arise in connection with measurement data.

---

**EXERCISES 4.1**

In each of the following, identify the variable as discrete or continuous.

1. $A$: the number of arms on a chambered nautilis.
2. $V$: the volume of urine output per hour.
3. $B$: the amount of blood lost by a patient during the course of an operation.
4. $H$: the number of hours of light needed per day for a plant to flower.
5. $C$: the number of worker bees in a honeybee society.
6. $R$: the amount of rainfall received per day in a specified region.
7. $S$: the serum bilirubin level in an infant in milligrams per deciliter.
8. $W$: the weight gain of a woman during pregnancy.

---

## DENSITY FUNCTIONS

**4.2** □ When we are dealing with a variable, it is not enough just to admit that the variable is random. We need to be able to predict in some sense the value that the variable will assume at any time. Since the behavior of a random variable is governed by chance, these predictions must be made in the face of a great deal of uncertainty. The best that can be done is to describe the behavior of the variable in terms of probabilities. Two functions are used to accomplish this, the density function and the cumulative distribution function.

**Definition 4.2.1** *Discrete Density.* Let $X$ be *discrete.* The *density* $f$ for $X$ is

$$f(x) = P[X = x]$$

for $x$ real.

There are several things to note concerning the density in the discrete case. First, $f$ is defined on the entire real line, and for any given real number $x$, $f(x)$ is the probability that the random variable $X$ assumes the value $x$. For example, $f(2)$ is the probability that the random variable $X$ assumes the numerical value of 2. Second, since $f(x)$ is a probability, $f(x) \geq 0$ regardless of the value of $x$. That is, $f$ is never negative. Third, if we sum $f$ over all physically possible values of $X$, the sum must be 1. That is,

$$\sum_{\text{all } x} f(x) = 1$$

(See Appendix A for a review of summation notation.) For real values of $x$ that are physically impossible, $f(x) = 0$. Any function that is nonnegative and has the value 1 when summed over its set of possible values can be thought of as being the density for a discrete random variable.

---

**EXAMPLE 4.2.1** □ Batesian mimicry was first described by the British naturalist H. W. Bates in 1862. In Batesian mimicry, an innocuous mimic fools its predator by resembling a stinging or bad-tasting model that the predator has learned to avoid. In an experiment on mimicry, an artificial model is made by dipping mealworms into a solution of quinine to give them a bitter taste. Then they are marked with a green band of cellulose paint, to give them an unusual appearance, and fed to three caged starlings. The starlings learn to associate the special markings with the bitter taste. Next each starling is presented with a mealworm that has not been dipped in

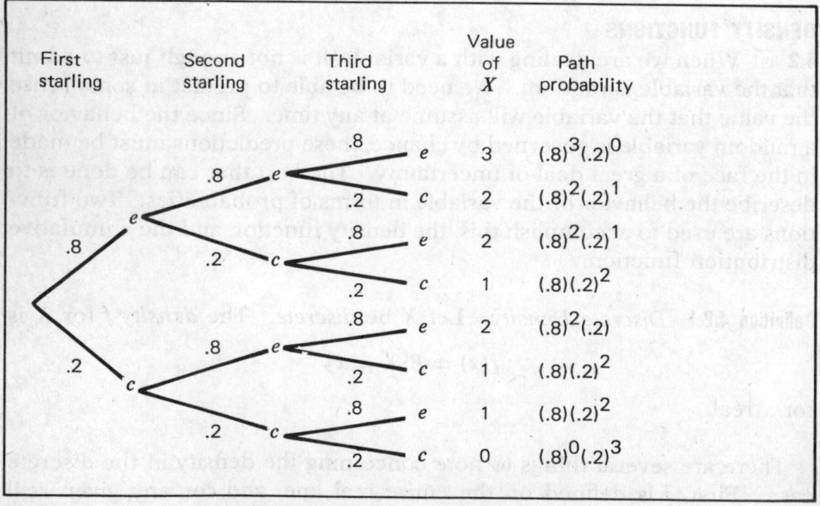


**FIGURE 4.1**

quinine but that has been painted to resemble the model. The probability that the mimic will not be eaten by the starling, which normally eats mealworms voraciously, is .8. Let $X$ denote the number of mimics that escape detection. Since it assumes only the values 0, 1, 2, 3, $X$ is discrete.

To answer probability questions concerning $X$, we must find its density, $f(x)$. This is done by means of the tree diagram of Figure 4.1 ($e$ represents an escape by the mimic; $c$ that the mimic was caught). Since the starlings are reacting independently, the probability of each path is the product of the probabilities found along the path. Thus the density can be read directly from the tree and is summarized as follows:

| $x$ | 0 | 1 | 2 | 3 |
|---|---|---|---|---|
| $f(x) = P[X = x]$ | $(.2)^3$ | $3(.8)(.2)^2$ | $3(.8)^2(.2)$ | $(.8)^3$ |

or

| $x$ | 0 | 1 | 2 | 3 |
|---|---|---|---|---|
| $f(x)$ | $8/1000$ | $96/1000$ | $384/1000$ | $512/1000$ |

Note that, as expected, each entry in row 2 of the table is nonnegative and the entries sum to 1. The table can be used to answer any relevant question posed. For example, the probability that exactly two escape detection is given by $P[X = 2] = f(2) = .384$. The probability that at most two escape is given by

$$\begin{aligned} P[X \leq 2] &= P[X = 0] + P[X = 1] + P[X = 2] \\ &= f(0) + f(1) + f(2) \\ &= .008 + .096 + .384 = .488 \end{aligned}$$

Note also that $P[X < 2] = .104 \neq P[X \leq 2]$. Including or excluding an endpoint in the *discrete* case can affect the numerical value of the answer.

---

Density functions for discrete variables are often given in table form, as in Example 4.2.1. However, in many cases it is more convenient to express the density in functional form. This point is discussed in Chapter 5.

The continuous case is a bit more complex. Since in this case the probability that the variable assumes any specific value is 0, there is no sense in trying to define the density itself as a probability. However, its purpose is the same as in the discrete case, namely, to compute probabilities. But in this case the aim is to compute the probability that the variable will assume some value within a given interval. For example, consider the random variable $T$, the time in hours between the observation of harmonic tremors and the next eruption of the Mount St. Helens volcano. We would like to find the probability that $T$ is less than 24 hours ($P[T < 24]$). Computation of probabilities for the continuous case can be accomplished not arithmetically, but geometrically by the use of density curves as defined here.

**Definition 4.2.2** *Continuous Density.* Let $X$ be a *continuous* random variable. The *density* for $X$ is a function $f$ defined on the entire real line such that

**1.** $f(x) \geq 0$ (nonnegative).

**2.** The area bounded by the graph of $f$ and the $x$ axis is equal to 1.

**3.** For any real numbers $a$ and $b$, $P[a \leq X \leq b]$ is given by the area bounded by the graph of $f$, the lines $x = a$, $x = b$, and the $x$ axis.

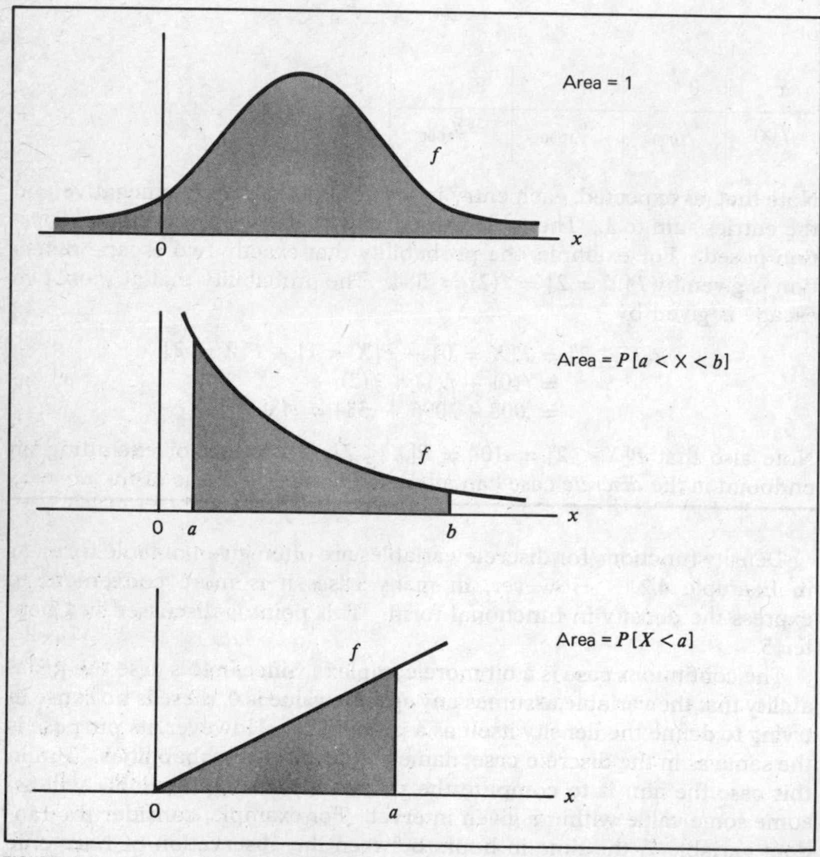


**FIGURE 4.2** Some continuous densities.

This definition looks formidable, but it is not, as we show shortly. Notice that there are similarities between Definitions 4.2.2 and 4.2.1. In both instances, the functions involved are nonnegative, both "sum" to one in some sense, and both are used to calculate probabilities. Graphs of some typical continuous densities are shown in Figure 4.2.

Densities in the continuous case are generally expressed in functional form. We follow the convention of defining $f$ over the range of possible values of variable $X$. It should be understood that $f(x) = 0$ elsewhere.

---

**EXAMPLE 4.2.2** □ The equation for the density for the random variable $Z$, the number of cc's of a drug to be prescribed for control of epileptic seizures, is given by

$$f(z) = \frac{200}{9}z \qquad 0 \leq z \leq .3$$

The graph of this density is shown in Figure 4.3. The fact that this is a density is easily checked. The function is obviously nonnegative. To be a

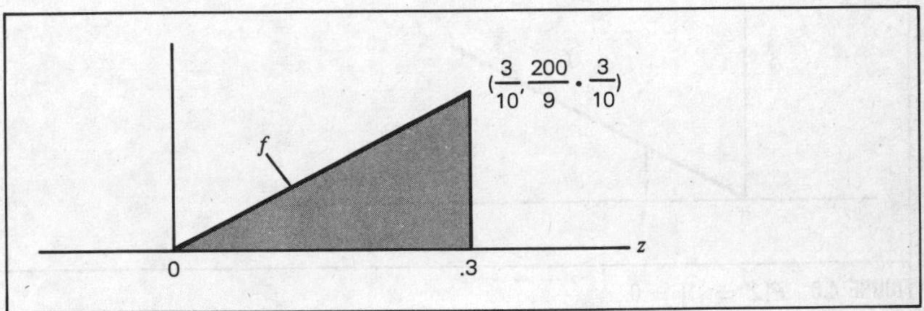


**FIGURE 4.3** Shaded area = 1.

density, the area of the shaded region should be 1. Since the region is triangular, its area can be found by using elementary geometry:

$$\begin{aligned}\text{Area} &= \tfrac{1}{2}(\text{base})(\text{height}) \\ &= \tfrac{1}{2}(\tfrac{3}{10})(\tfrac{3}{10} \times \tfrac{200}{9}) = 1\end{aligned}$$

What is the probability that at most .1 cc should be prescribed? That is, What is $P[Z \leq .1]$? This probability is given by the area of the shaded region in Figure 4.4. Once again, since a triangle is involved, the probability is found to be

$$P[Z \leq .1] = \frac{1}{2}\left(\frac{1}{10}\right)\left(\frac{200}{9} \times \frac{1}{10}\right) = \frac{1}{9}$$

One of every nine patients should receive .1 cc or less. We now ask, What is the probability that a given patient should receive *exactly* .1 cc? Since $Z$

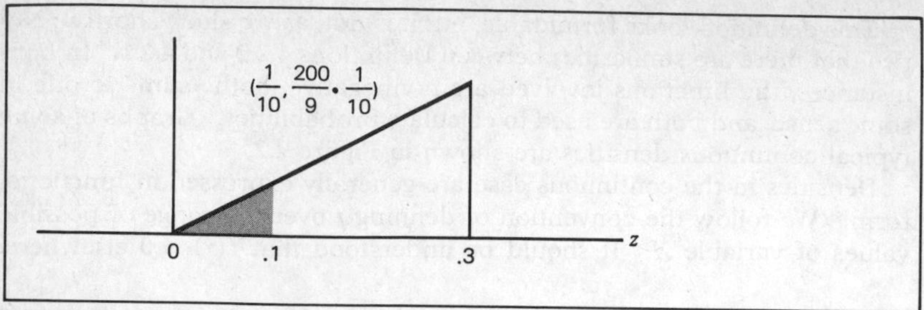


**FIGURE 4.4** Shaded area $= P[Z \leq .1]$.

is continuous, the answer is 0 by definition. This is verified geometrically by realizing that we would be attempting to find the *area* of the dotted line shown in Figure 4.5. Since lines have no width, they have no area. The desired probability is 0.

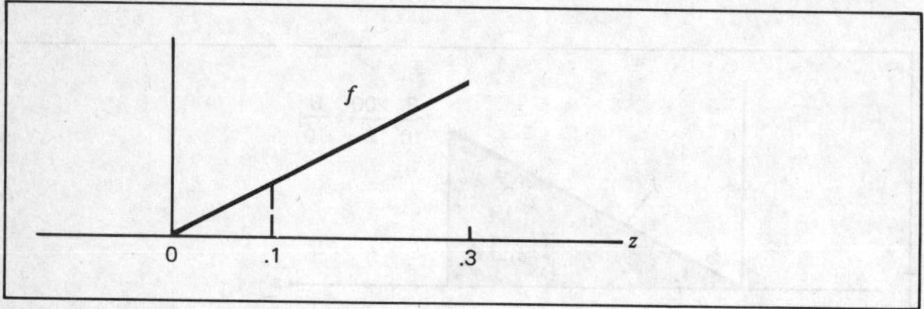


**FIGURE 4.5** $P[Z = .1] = 0$.

This fact points out an important difference between discrete and continuous variables that you must always keep in mind. In the continuous case, adding or deleting an endpoint to an interval makes no difference to the final probability. That is, for example, $P[Z \leq .1] = P[Z < .1]$. In the discrete case, the endpoint may occur with nonzero probability, and hence you cannot simply include or exclude it at will.

---

Part of the art of statistics lies in finding from experimental data and mathematical considerations the proper density for a particular random variable. Over the past years, various densities that seem to come into play in a wide variety of applied fields have been identified and studied in depth. In this text, we make extensive use of these well-known densities, for they provide the foundation for classical methods of applied statistics.

## EXERCISES 4.2

**1.** The following table shows the density for the random variable $X$, the number of persons seeking emergency room treatment unnecessarily per day in a small hospital.

| $x$ | 0 | 1 | 2 | 3 | 4 | 5 |
|---|---|---|---|---|---|---|
| $f(x)$ | .01 | .1 | .3 | .4 | .1 | ? |

**a.** Find $f(5)$.
**b.** Find $P[X \leq 2]$.
**c.** Find $P[X < 2]$.
**d.** Find $P[X > 3]$.

**2.** The following table shows the density for the random variable $X$, the number of wing beats per second of a species of large moth while in flight.

| $x$ | 6 | 7 | 8 | 9 | 10 |
|---|---|---|---|---|---|
| $f(x)$ | .05 | .1 | .6 | .15 | ? |

**a.** Find $f(10)$.
**b.** Find $P[X \leq 8]$.
**c.** Find $P[X < 8]$.
**d.** Find $P[X \geq 7]$.
**e.** Find $P[X > 7]$.

**3.** A compound is developed to give relief from migraine headache. The manufacturer claims that it is 90% effective. It is tried on four patients. Let $X$ denote the number of patients obtaining relief.
**a.** Find the density for $X$, assuming that the claim is correct.
**b.** Find $P[X \leq 1]$.
**c.** If no one receives relief from the compound, do you think that there is reason to suspect the company's claim of a 90% cure rate? Explain on the basis of the probability involved.

**4.** An outbreak of mumps among primary school children is in progress. Ten percent of all primary age children are affected. A pediatrician sees three children of this age during the first hour of her working day. Let $X$ denote the number with mumps. Assume independence and find the density for $X$. Use this to find $P[X = 0]$ and $P[X \leq 1]$.

**5.** Let $X$ denote the percentage of body fluid loss during the first 24 hours by a person suffering from a severe burn. Assume that $X$ has the density shown in Figure 4.6.
**a.** What probability is represented by the shaded area in Figure 4.6?
**b.** What is the probability that $X = 15\%$?
**c.** Shade the area corresponding to $P[X \geq 20\%]$.

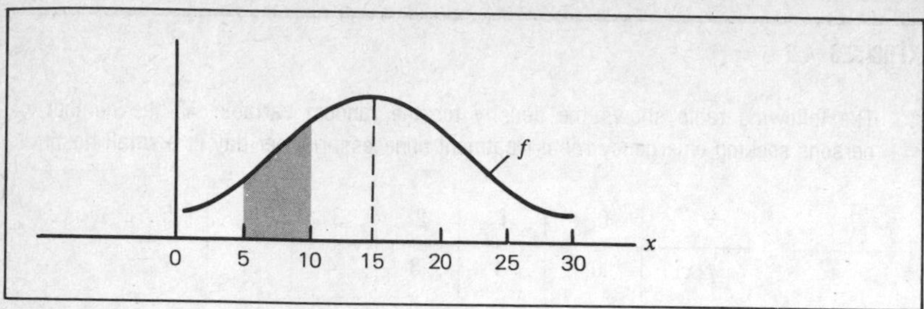


FIGURE 4.6

6. Let $X$ denote the survival time in years after the diagnosis of acute leukemia. The density for $X$ is given by $f(x) = -\frac{1}{2}x + 1, 0 \leq x \leq 2$, and is shown in Figure 4.7.

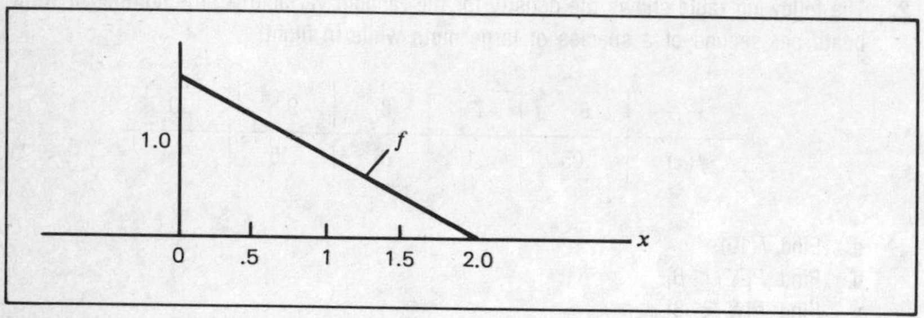


FIGURE 4.7 $f(x) = -\frac{1}{2}x + 1, 0 \leq x \leq 2.$

a. Verify that $f$ is a density.
b. Find $P[X \geq 1]$.
c. Find $P[X > 1]$.
d. Find $P[X = 1]$.
e. Find the probability that a patient will survive less than 6 months.
f. Find the probability that a patient will survive between 6 months and 1 year.

7. Chemical communication among animals is widespread. The major chemical communication in insects is by means of externally released hormones called pheromones. Such a hormone is used as a trail marker by ants. As an ant goes from the nest to a source of food and back, it leaves a chemical trail by touching its abdomen to the ground. Once no more food is available, the ants using the trail secrete no more markers and the trail dissipates. Assume that the density for $X$, the time in minutes that a pheromone trail persists after the last secretion of hormone, is as shown in Figure 4.8.

a. What value of $h$ makes this a density?
b. Find $P[X \leq 1]$.
c. Find $P[X < 1]$.
d. Find $P[X > 3]$.
e. Find $P[X \leq 3]$.

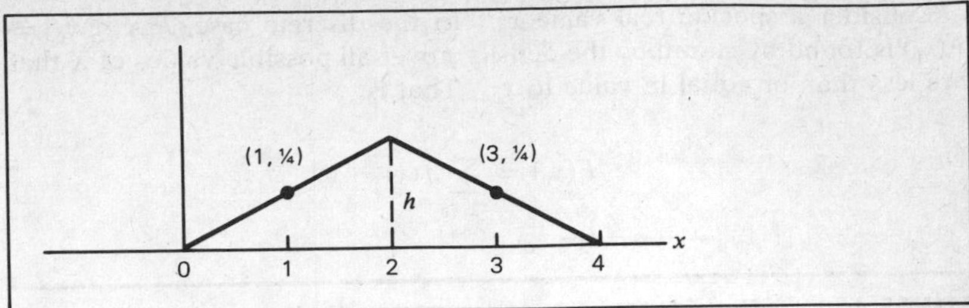


**FIGURE 4.8**

f. Find $P[1 \leq X \leq 3]$.
g. Find $P[X = 2]$.

8. The density for $X$, the time in minutes that it takes a nurse to respond to a patient's call, is given by $f(x) = c$, $0 \leq x \leq 5$, where $c$ is a constant. (Any variable whose density is constant over its set of possible values is said to be uniformly distributed.) Its graph is shown in Figure 4.9.

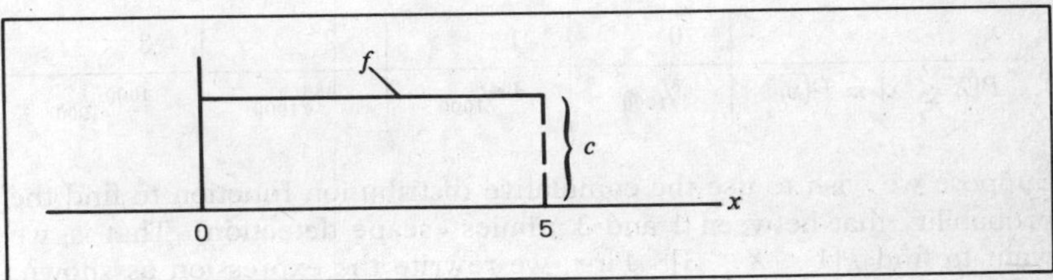


**FIGURE 4.9** $f(x) = c$, $0 \leq x \leq 5$.

a. Find the value of $c$ that makes this a density.
b. Find $P[X \leq 1]$.
c. Find the probability that it takes between 1 and 3 minutes for the nurse to respond.

## CUMULATIVE DISTRIBUTION FUNCTION

**4.3** □ Unlike the density, the cumulative distribution function can be defined for both discrete and continuous variables simultaneously. Its purpose is also to compute probabilities. In fact, as we shall see, most of the statistical tables used extensively in the material that follows are tables of the cumulative distribution function for some pertinent random variable.

**Definition 4.3.1** *Cumulative Distribution Function.* Let $X$ be a random variable with density $f$. The *cumulative distribution function* for $X$, denoted $F$, is defined by

$$F(x) = P[X \leq x] \qquad \text{for } x \text{ real}$$

Consider a specific real value $x_0$. In the discrete case, $P[X \leq x_0] = F(x_0)$ is found by summing the density $f$ over all possible values of $X$ that are less than or equal in value to $x_0$. That is,

$$F(x_0) = \sum_{x \leq x_0} f(x)$$

---

**EXAMPLE 4.3.1** □ Consider the random variable $X$, the number of mimics escaping detection, of Example 4.2.1. The density $f$ for $X$ is given by

| $x$ | 0 | 1 | 2 | 3 |
|---|---|---|---|---|
| $P[X = x] = f(x)$ | $8/1000$ | $96/1000$ | $384/1000$ | $512/1000$ |

The cumulative distribution function (or just the distribution function) for $X$ is given by

| $x$ | 0 | 1 | 2 | 3 |
|---|---|---|---|---|
| $P[X \leq x] = F(x)$ | $8/1000$ | $104/1000$ | $488/1000$ | $1000/1000$ |

Suppose we wish to use the cumulative distribution function to find the probability that between 1 and 3 mimics escape detection. That is, we want to find $P[1 \leq X \leq 3]$. First, we rewrite the expression as shown:

$$P[1 \leq X \leq 3] = P[X \leq 3] - P[X \leq 0]$$

In this form, it is evident that

$$\begin{aligned} P[1 \leq X \leq 3] &= F(3) - F(0) \\ &= 1000/1000 - 8/1000 = 992/1000 = .992 \end{aligned}$$

To find $P[X \geq 2]$, next we rewrite the expression as

$$\begin{aligned} P[X \geq 2] &= 1 - P[X \leq 1] \\ &= 1 - F(1) \\ &= 1 - 104/1000 = 896/1000 \end{aligned}$$

Note that $F$ does what its name, cumulative distribution function, implies. It sums or accumulates probabilities up to and including the point of interest.

---

Again, the continuous case is a bit more complex and is handled graphically.

**EXAMPLE 4.3.2** □ Consider the random variable $Z$, the number of cc's of a drug to be prescribed to control epileptic seizures. Its density from Example 4.2.2 is

$$f(z) = \frac{200}{9}z \qquad 0 \leq z \leq .3$$

and is shown in Figure 4.10. Consider a specific point $z_0$. By definition, $F(z_0) = P[Z \leq z_0]$. Graphically, this probability is given by the area of the shaded region of Figure 4.10.

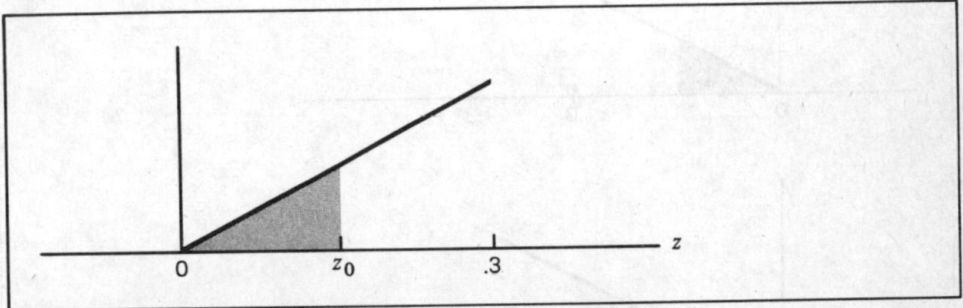


**FIGURE 4.10** $F(z_0) = P[Z \leq z_0]$ = shaded area.

More complex questions also can be expressed in terms of $F$ and corresponding areas under the graph of the density. For example, to find the probability that between .1 and .2 cc inclusive should be prescribed, we must find $P[.1 \leq Z \leq .2]$. Rewriting this expression in terms of $F$, we obtain

$$\begin{aligned} P[.1 \leq Z \leq .2] &= P[Z \leq .2] - P[Z < .1] \\ &= P[Z \leq .2] - P[Z \leq .1] \qquad (Z \text{ is continuous}) \\ &= F(.2) - F(.1) \end{aligned}$$

Graphically, we are finding the area of the shaded region in Figure 4.11*a*, finding the area of the shaded region in Figure 4.11*b*, and subtracting the two to obtain the area of the shaded region in Figure 4.11*c*. The area of this shaded region is equal to the desired probability.

In summary, the cumulative distribution function for a random variable, whether it be discrete or continuous, gives the probability that the variable will assume a value which is *less than or equal to* that specified.

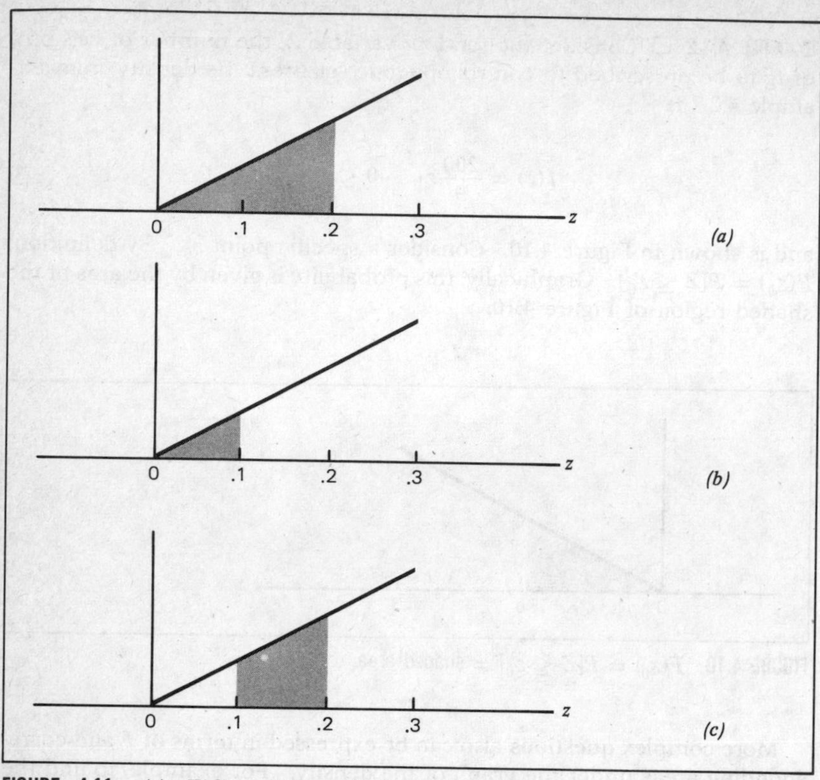


**FIGURE 4.11** (*a*) $F(.2) = P[Z \leq .2]$; (*b*) $F(.1) = P[Z \leq .1]$; (*c*) $F(.2) - F(.1) = P[.1 \leq Z \leq .2]$.

## EXERCISES 4.3

1. The following table shows the density for the random variable $X$, the number of wing beats per second of a species of large moth while in flight:

| $x$ | 6 | 7 | 8 | 9 | 10 |
|---|---|---|---|---|---|
| $f(x)$ | .05 | .1 | .6 | .15 | .1 |

**a.** Find the table for the cumulative distribution function $F$.
**b.** Use $F$ to find $P[X \leq 8]$.
**c.** Use $F$ to find $P[X > 7]$.
**d.** Use $F$ to find $P[7 \leq X \leq 9]$.

2. The density for the random variable $X$, the number of persons seeking emergency room treatment unnecessarily, per day in a small hospital is given by

| $x$ | 0 | 1 | 2 | 3 | 4 | 5 |
|---|---|---|---|---|---|---|
| $f(x)$ | .01 | .1 | .3 | .4 | .1 | .09 |

a. Find the table for the cumulative distribution function.
b. Find $P[X \leq -2]$.
c. Using $F$, find $P[2 \leq X \leq 4]$.
d. Find $P[X \leq 6]$.
e. Find $P[X = 3]$.
f. Using $F$, find the probability that more than two will seek emergency room help unnecessarily.

3. Cells in sections of damaged tissue being examined under the microscope are graded for extent of damage by the following scale: 0, undamaged; 1, slightly damaged; 2, moderately damaged; 3, extensively damaged. Cells of tissue exposed to 20 minutes of anoxia, an abnormally low oxygen supply, before preparation for microscopic study exhibit the following density, where $x$ is the classification value for damage:

| $x$ | 0 | 1 | 2 | 3 |
|---|---|---|---|---|
| $f(x)$ | 0.15 | 0.25 | 0.50 | 0.10 |

a. Find the table for the cumulative distribution function $F$.
b. Use $F$ to find the probability that a randomly selected cell will be only slightly damaged or undamaged.
c. Use $F$ to obtain the probability that at least moderate damage is observed in a randomly selected cell.

4. Grafting, the uniting of the stem of one plant with the stem or root of another, is widely used commercially to grow the stem of one variety that produces fine fruit on the root system of another variety with a hardy root system. Most Florida sweet oranges grow on trees grafted to the root of a sour orange variety. An experiment is done with five grafts of this type. The density for $X$, the number of grafts that fail, is given by

| $x$ | 0 | 1 | 2 | 3 | 4 | 5 |
|---|---|---|---|---|---|---|
| $f(x)$ | .7 | .2 | .05 | .03 | .01 | .01 |

a. Find the table for $F$.
b. Use $F$ to find the probability that at most three grafts fail.
c. Use $F$ to find the probability that at least two grafts fail.
d. Use $F$ to verify that the probability of three failures is .03.

5. Figure 4.12 shows the density for random variable $X$, the time in years to failure of an artificial pacemaker.

a. Which region(s) represents $F(4)$?

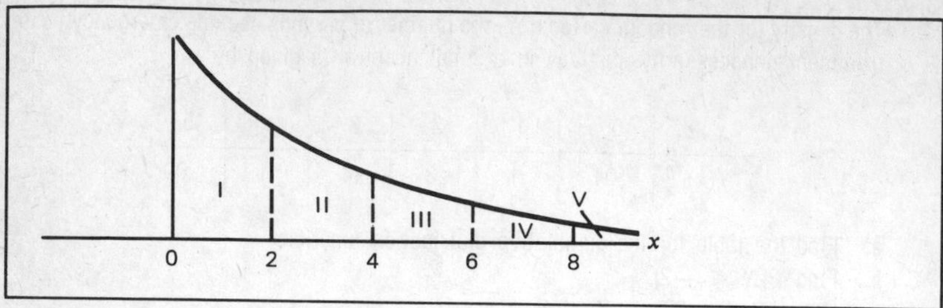


FIGURE 4.12

b. What probability is represented by regions II and III together? Express this probability in terms of $F$.
c. What probability is represented by region V? Express this probability in terms of $F$.
d. Express $P[X \leq 4]$ and $P[X < 4]$, each in terms of $F$.

6. Figure 4.13 shows the graph of the density for random variable $X$, the time in minutes required for a sedative to take effect.

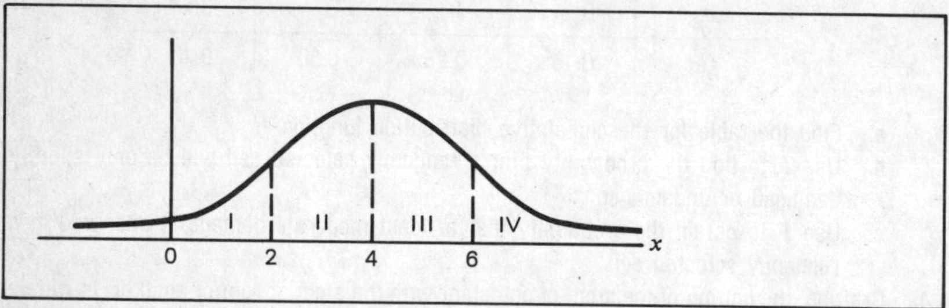


FIGURE 4.13

a. Which region(s) in the diagram corresponds to $F(2)$?
b. Which region(s) in the diagram corresponds to $F(6)$?
c. Express region III in terms of $F$.
d. Express region IV in terms of $F$.

7. Consider random variable $X$, the effective lifetime in months of a pH electrode. Its density is pictured in Figure 4.14.
a. Which regions in the graph correspond to $F(27)$?
b. Express, in terms of $F$, the probability that a randomly selected pH electrode will work effectively for at least 18 months. What regions correspond to this probability?
c. Express, in terms of $F$, the probability that a randomly selected pH electrode will have an effective lifetime of 27 to 36 months. What regions correspond to this probability?

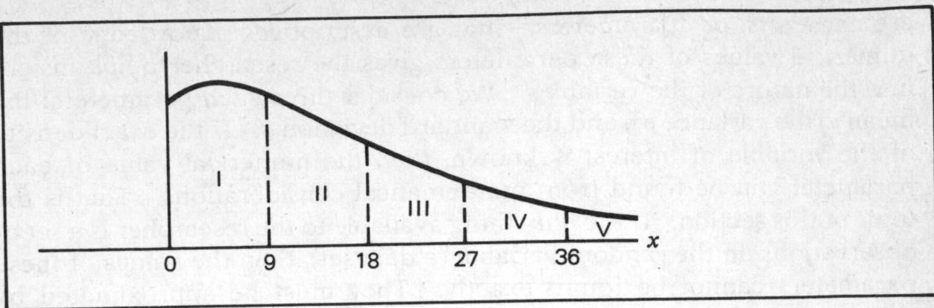


**FIGURE 4.14**

8. When heated coolant from a power plant is released suddenly into a stream, thermal shock, a sudden shift in stream temperature, can occur. Often this results in the death of organisms living in the stream. Let $X$ denote the river temperature in degrees Celsius at a point $\frac{1}{4}$ mile downstream from a power plant just before coolant is released into the stream. Let $Y$ denote the river temperature at the same point 5 minutes after the coolant is released. Let $D = Y - X$, the change in river temperature. Figure 4.15 gives the graph of the density $f$ for $D$.

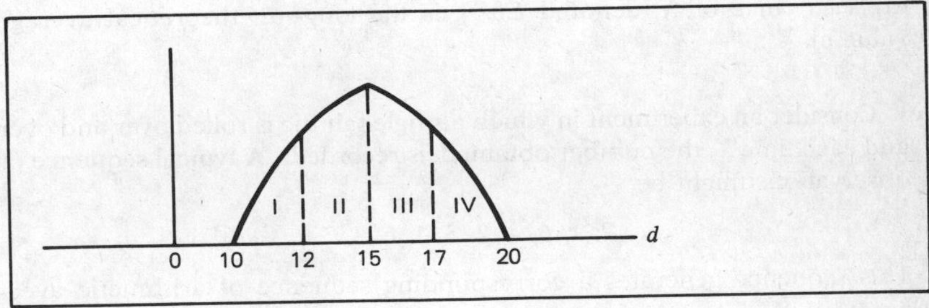


**FIGURE 4.15**

a. Which region(s) represents $F(12)$?
b. What probability is represented by the combined area of regions I and II? Assuming that $f$ is symmetric about 15, what is the numerical value of the probability represented by the area of regions I and II?
c. What probability is represented by region III?
d. What regions represent $F(17) - F(12)$? What probability corresponds to $F(17) - F(12)$?
e. What is $F(5)$?
f. What is the probability that the temperature change will be at most 25°C?

## EXPECTATION AND DISTRIBUTION PARAMETERS

**4.4** □ The density function of a random variable completely describes the behavior of the variable. However, associated with any random variable are constants, or "parameters," that are descriptive. Knowledge of the numerical values of these parameters gives the researcher quick insight into the nature of the variables. We consider three such parameters: the mean $\mu$, the variance $\sigma^2$, and the standard deviation $\sigma$. If the exact density of the variable of interest is known, then the numerical value of each parameter can be found from mathematical considerations. That is the topic of this section. If the only thing available to the researcher is a set of observations on the random variable (a data set), then the values of these parameters cannot be found exactly. They must be approximated by using statistical techniques. That is the topic of much of the remainder of this text.

To understand the reasoning behind most statistical methods, it is necessary to become familiar with one general concept, namely, the idea of mathematical expectation or expected value. This concept is used in defining most statistical parameters and provides the logical basis for most of the methods of statistical inference presented later in this text. We begin with an intuitive definition of the term.

**Definition 4.4.1** *Expected Value, Intuitive.* Let $X$ be a random variable. The *expected value* of $X$, denoted $E[X]$, is the long-run theoretical average value of $X$.

Consider an experiment in which a single fair die is rolled over and over and each time $X$, the number obtained, is recorded. A typical sequence of observations might be

$$2, 1, 6, 4, 2, 5, 1, 6, 3, \ldots$$

This sequence generates a corresponding sequence of arithmetic averages:

$$2, \frac{2+1}{2}, \frac{2+1+6}{3}, \frac{2+1+6+4}{4}, \frac{2+1+6+4+2}{5},$$
$$\frac{2+1+6+4+2+5}{6}, \ldots$$

or $\quad 2, 1.5, 3, 3.25, 3, 3.33, \ldots$

These averages are obviously not constant. They vary as the experiment proceeds, but generally the magnitude of the changes decreases as more and more observations are made. That is, as the number of rolls of the die becomes very large, the sequence of averages tends to settle down around some numerical value. This value is the expected value, or the "long-run theoretical average value," for $X$. Note that if $X$ is a random variable, then $X^2$, $X - 1$, $\sqrt{X}$, and any other variable that can be expressed in terms of $X$ also are random variables. Each will have an expected, or long-run theoretical average, value that we denote by $E[X^2]$, $E[X - 1]$, and $E[\sqrt{X}]$, respectively. Our job is to find a way to determine these expectations from knowledge of the density for $X$ without having to resort to experimentation. This is done by means of Definition 4.4.2.

**Definition 4.4.2** *Expected Value, Discrete.* Let $X$ be a *discrete* random variable with density $f(x)$. Let $H(X)$ be a random variable. The *expected value* of $H(X)$ is given by

$$E[H(X)] = \sum_{\text{all } x} H(x)f(x)$$

Here $H(X)$ represents any function of $X$. When, in particular, $H(X) = X$, the above equation defines the expected value of $X$, $E[X]$. Other functions of primary interest to statisticians are $H(X) = X^2$ and $H(X) = (X - c)^2$ for $c$ a constant, because these functions come into play later in defining the variance for $X$.

---

**EXAMPLE 4.4.1** □ Consider the experiment of rolling a fair die with the variable $X$ being the number obtained per roll. Variable $X$ is uniformly distributed with density as given:

| $x$ | 1 | 2 | 3 | 4 | 5 | 6 |
|---|---|---|---|---|---|---|
| $f(x)$ | $1/6$ | $1/6$ | $1/6$ | $1/6$ | $1/6$ | $1/6$ |

Using Definition 4.4.2, we have

$$\begin{aligned} E[X] &= \sum_{\text{all } x} xf(x) \\ &= 1 \cdot 1/6 + 2 \cdot 1/6 + 3 \cdot 1/6 + 4 \cdot 1/6 + 5 \cdot 1/6 + 6 \cdot 1/6 \\ &= 3.5 \end{aligned}$$

Intuitively, we should have expected this. Notice the symmetry of the density. In the long run, we would expect to roll as many 6s as 1s, as many 2s as 5s, and as many 3s as 4s. Each of these pairs averages to 3.5. Then common sense points to 3.5 as the expected value of $X$. Note also that 3.5 is not a possible value for $X$. The expected value of a random variable need not be among the physically feasible values of $X$. Now consider $H(X) = X^2$, a function of $X$ used extensively in the material that follows:

$$\begin{aligned} E[X^2] &= \sum_{\text{all } x} x^2 f(x) \\ &= 1^2 \cdot 1/6 + 2^2 \cdot 1/6 + 3^2 \cdot 1/6 + 4^2 \cdot 1/6 + 5^2 \cdot 1/6 + 6^2 \cdot 1/6 \\ &= 91/6 \end{aligned}$$

**EXAMPLE 4.4.2** □ Consider the random variable $X$, the number of mimics escaping detection in the Batesian mimicry experiment of Example 4.2.1. The density for $X$ is given by

| $x$ | 0 | 1 | 2 | 3 |
|---|---|---|---|---|
| $f(x)$ | $8/1000$ | $96/1000$ | $384/1000$ | $512/1000$ |

This density is not symmetric, so it is impossible to predict $E[X]$ by inspection. Using Definition 4.4.2, we have

$$E[X] = 0 \cdot 8/1000 + 1 \cdot 96/1000 + 2 \cdot 384/1000 + 3 \cdot 512/1000$$
$$= \frac{2400}{1000} = \frac{12}{5} = 2.4$$

That is, in repeated trials of the same experiment, we would expect the average number of mimics escaping detection to be 2.4. Note that

$$E\left[\left(X - \frac{12}{5}\right)^2\right] = \sum_{\text{all } x}\left(x - \frac{12}{5}\right)^2 f(x)$$
$$= \left(0 - \frac{12}{5}\right)^2 \frac{8}{1000} + \left(1 - \frac{12}{5}\right)^2 \frac{96}{1000}$$
$$+ \left(2 - \frac{12}{5}\right)^2 \frac{384}{1000} + \left(3 - \frac{12}{5}\right)^2 \frac{512}{1000}$$
$$= \frac{144}{25}\frac{8}{1000} + \frac{49}{25}\frac{96}{1000} + \frac{4}{25}\frac{384}{1000} + \frac{9}{25}\frac{512}{1000}$$
$$= \frac{12{,}000}{25(1000)} = \frac{12}{25}$$

Without calculus we cannot compute the expected value of a continuous random variable in any but the simplest cases. However, it is possible to view $E[X]$ geometrically. Consider the graph of the density $f$ for $X$. Imagine cutting the region bounded by the graph of $f$ and the $x$ axis out of a piece of thin, rigid metal and attempting to balance this region on a knife edge held parallel to the vertical axis of the graph. The point at which the region would balance is $E[X]$. Typical densities are shown in Figure 4.16.

When used in a statistical context, the expected value of $X$ is referred to as being the *mean* of $X$ and is denoted $\mu$. That is, the terms *expected value* and *mean* are interchangeable, as are the symbols $E[X]$ and $\mu$. As can be seen from the preceding discussion, the mean of $X$ can be thought of as a measure of the "center of location," in the sense that it indicates where the "center" of the density of $X$ is located along the horizontal axis. For this reason, the mean is often referred to as being a "location" parameter.

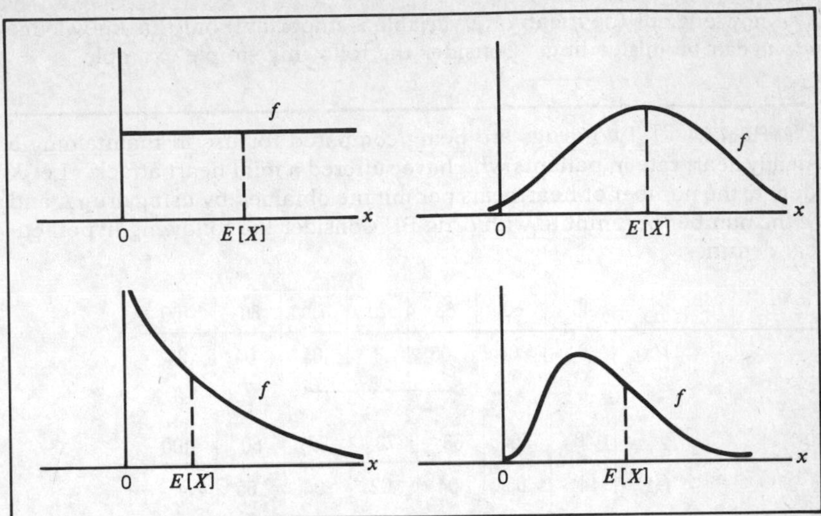


**FIGURE 4.16** $\mu = E[X] =$ balance point.

There are three rules for handling expected values that are useful in justifying statistical procedures in later chapters. These rules are stated and illustrated here.

**THEOREM 4.4.1** □ *Rules for Expectation.* Let $X$ and $Y$ be random variables, and let $c$ be any real number.

1. $E[c] = c$ (The expected value of any constant is that constant.)
2. $E[cX] = cE[X]$ (Constants can be factored from expectations.)
3. $E[X + Y] = E[X] + E[Y]$. (The expected value of a sum is equal to the sum of the expected values.)

---

**EXAMPLE 4.4.3** □ Let $X$ and $Y$ be random variables such that $E[X] = 3$ and $E[Y] = -2$. Then

$$\begin{aligned} E[X + Y] &= E[X] + E[Y] = 3 + (-2) = 1 \\ E[2X + Y] &= E[2X] + E[Y] \\ &= 2E[X] + E[Y] \\ &= 2(3) + (-2) = 4 \\ E[X - 3Y + 1] &= E[X] + E[-3Y] + E[1] \\ &= E[X] + (-3)E[Y] + E[1] \\ &= 3 + (-3)(-2) + 1 \\ &= 10 \end{aligned}$$

---

Knowledge of the mean of a variable is important, but this knowledge *alone* can be misleading. Consider the following simple example.

---

**EXAMPLE 4.4.4** □ Two drugs are being compared for use in maintaining a steady heart rate in patients who have suffered a mild heart attack. Let $X$ denote the number of heartbeats per minute obtained by using drug A and $Y$ the number per minute with drug B. Consider the following hypothetical densities:

| $x$ | 40 | 60 | 68 | 70 | 72 | 80 | 100 |
|---|---|---|---|---|---|---|---|
| $f(x)$ | .01 | .04 | .05 | .8 | .05 | .04 | .01 |

| $y$ | 40 | 60 | 68 | 70 | 72 | 80 | 100 |
|---|---|---|---|---|---|---|---|
| $f(y)$ | .4 | .05 | .04 | .02 | .04 | .05 | .4 |

Since each of the densities is symmetric, inspection shows that $\mu_X = \mu_Y = 70$. Each drug produces *on the average* the same number of heartbeats per minute. However, there is obviously a drastic difference between the two drugs that is not being detected by the mean. On one hand, drug A produces fairly consistent reactions in patients, with 90% differing from the mean by at most 2; very few (2%) have an extreme reaction to the drug. On the other hand, drug B produces highly diverse responses. Only 10% of the patients have heart rates within 2 units of the mean, whereas 80% show an extreme reaction. If we examined only the mean, we would conclude that the two drugs had identical effects—but nothing could be farther from the truth!

---

It is obvious from Example 4.4.4 that something is not being measured by the mean. That something is *variability*. We must develop a parameter that reflects consistency or the lack of it. We want the measure to assume a large positive value if variable $X$ fluctuates to the extent that it often assumes values far from its mean; the measure should assume a small positive value if the values of $X$ tend to cluster closely about the mean. There are several ways to try to develop such a measure.

The most widely used measure is $E[(X - \mu)^2]$. This measure is called the *variance* of $X$.

**Definition 4.4.3** *Variance.* Let $X$ be a random variable with mean $\mu$. The *variance* of $X$, denoted Var $X$, or $\sigma^2$, is given by

$$\text{Var } X = \sigma^2 = E[(X - \mu)^2]$$

Note that the variance essentially measures variability by considering $X - \mu$, the difference between the variable and its mean. The difference is squared so that negative values will not cancel positive ones in the process of finding the expected value.

---

**EXAMPLE 4.4.5** □ Consider random variables $X$ and $Y$ of Example 4.4.4.

$$\begin{aligned}\text{Var } X &= \sum_{\text{all } x} (x - 70)^2 f(x) \\ &= (-30^2)(.01) + (-10)^2(.04) + (-2)^2(.05) + 0^2(.8) + (2^2)(.05) \\ &\quad + (10^2)(.04) + (30^2)(.01) \\ &= 26.4\end{aligned}$$

$$\begin{aligned}\text{Var } Y &= \sum_{\text{all } y} (y - 70)^2 f(y) \\ &= 730.32\end{aligned}$$

As expected, $\text{Var } Y > \text{Var } X$. Even though the two drugs produce the same mean number of heartbeats per minute, they do not behave in the same way. Drug B induces greater variability than drug A. It is not as consistent in its effect as drug A.

---

Note that the variance of a random variable reported alone is not very informative. Is a variance of 26.4 large or small? Only when this value is compared with the variance of a similar variable does it take on meaning. Hence variances are often used for comparative purposes to choose between two variables which otherwise appear to be identical. Also note that the variance of a random variable is essentially a pure number whose associated units often are physically meaningless. For example, if any unit were attached to the variances of Example 4.4.5, it would have to be a "squared heartbeat." This is obviously absurd, and so usually variance is reported with no unit attached. To overcome this problem, a second measure of variability is employed. This measure is the nonnegative square root of the variance, and it is called the *standard deviation*. It has the advantage of having associated with it the same unit as the original data.

**Definition 4.4.4.** *Standard Deviation.* Let $X$ be a random variable with variance $\sigma^2$. The *standard deviation* of $X$, denoted $\sigma$, is given by

$$\sigma = \sqrt{\text{Var } X} = \sqrt{\sigma^2}$$

---

**EXAMPLE 4.4.6** □ The standard deviations of variables $X$ and $Y$ of Example 4.4.5 are, respectively,

$$\sigma_X = \sqrt{\text{Var } X} = \sqrt{26.4} = 5.14 \text{ heartbeats per minute}$$
$$\sigma_Y = \sqrt{\text{Var } Y} = \sqrt{730.32} = 27.02 \text{ heartbeats per minute}$$

---

Examples 4.4.1 through 4.4.6 have all been discrete. Definition 4.4.3 holds for continuous as well as discrete variables. However, calculus is needed to determine the numerical value of $\sigma^2$ in the continuous case. Nevertheless, a useful geometric interpretation is possible in that a variable with a large variance will tend to have a density that is rather flat, whereas one with a small variance will have a peaked density, as illustrated in Figure 4.17. For this reason $\sigma^2$ is referred to as a "shape" parameter.

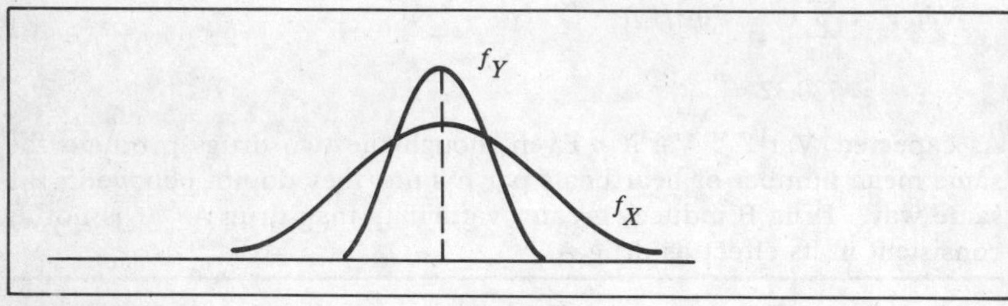


**FIGURE 4.17** $\mu_X = \mu_Y$ and Var $X >$ Var $Y$.

Although Definition 4.4.3 defines $\sigma^2$ in a manner that makes it easy to see what variance is measuring, it does not provide the easiest method for computing $\sigma^2$ and is seldom used for that purpose. The rules for expectation can be applied to develop a simpler computational formula for variance.

**THEOREM 4.4.2** □ *Computational Formula for* $\sigma^2$.

$$\text{Var } X = E[X^2] - (E[X])^2$$

---

**EXAMPLE 4.4.7** □ Consider the random variable $X$, the number of mimics escaping detection in the Batesian mimicry experiment of Example 4.2.1. The density for $X$ is given by

| $x$ | 0 | 1 | 2 | 3 |
|---|---|---|---|---|
| $f(x)$ | $^{8}/_{1000}$ | $^{96}/_{1000}$ | $^{384}/_{1000}$ | $^{512}/_{1000}$ |

From Example 4.4.2 we know that $E[X] = {}^{12}\!/_5$. Thus

$$\begin{aligned} E[X^2] &= \sum_{\text{all } x} x^2 f(x) \\ &= 0^2 \cdot \frac{8}{1000} + 1^2 \cdot \frac{96}{1000} + 2^2 \cdot \frac{384}{1000} + 3^2 \cdot \frac{512}{1000} \\ &= \frac{6240}{1000} = \frac{624}{100} \end{aligned}$$

and

$$\begin{aligned} \operatorname{Var} X &= E[X^2] - (E[X])^2 \\ &= \frac{624}{100} - \left(\frac{12}{5}\right)^2 \\ &= \frac{624}{100} - \frac{576}{100} = \frac{12}{25} \end{aligned}$$

Note that this is the same result as was obtained in Example 4.4.2 by using Definition 4.4.3 to compute $\sigma^2$.

---

Just as there are three rules for expectation that help in simplifying complex expressions, there are three rules for variance. These rules parallel those for expectation and, for the most part, are direct consequences of those rules.

**THEOREM 4.4.3** □ *Rules for Variance.* Let $X$ and $Y$ be random variables and $c$ any real number. Then

1. $\operatorname{Var} c = 0$.
2. $\operatorname{Var} cX = c^2 \operatorname{Var} X$.
3. If $X$ and $Y$ are independent, then $\operatorname{Var}(X + Y) = \operatorname{Var} X + \operatorname{Var} Y$. (Two variables are independent if the value assumed by one has no influence on the value assumed by the other.)

---

**EXAMPLE 4.4.8** □ Let $X$ and $Y$ be independent with $\mu_X = 2$, $\mu_Y = 6$, $\sigma_X{}^2 = 9$, and $\sigma_Y{}^2 = 3$. Then

$$\begin{aligned} E[2X - 3Y - 6] &= 2E[X] - 3E[Y] - 6 \\ &= 2(2) - 3(6) - 6 \\ &= -20 \end{aligned}$$

$$\begin{aligned} \operatorname{Var}[2X - 3Y - 6] &= \operatorname{Var} 2X + \operatorname{Var}(-3Y) + \operatorname{Var}(-6) \\ &= 4 \operatorname{Var} X + 9 \operatorname{Var} Y + 0 \\ &= 4(9) + 9(3) \\ &= 63 \end{aligned}$$

---

In this section we discussed three *theoretical* parameters associated with a random variable $X$. We showed not only how to determine their numerical values from knowledge of the density, but also how to interpret them physically. Keep these things in mind, for much of the remaining material in the text centers on these three parameters. They play a major role in the study of statistical methods and applications to experimental data.

## EXERCISES 4.4

1. Consider the following density:

| $x$ | $-2$ | $-1$ | 0 | 1 | 2 |
|---|---|---|---|---|---|
| $f(x)$ | .1 | .2 | .3 | .2 | .2 |

Find $E[X]$, $\mu_X$, $E[X^2]$, Var $X$, $\sigma_X{}^2$, and $\sigma_X$.

2. The following table shows the density for random variable $X$, the number of adult females in a band of howler monkeys:

| $x$ | 1 | 2 | 3 | 4 | 5 |
|---|---|---|---|---|---|
| $f(x)$ | .1 | .15 | .5 | .15 | .1 |

Find $E[X]$, $\mu$, $E[X^2]$, Var $X$, $\sigma^2$, and $\sigma$.

3. Three patients receive injections to desensitize them to insect stings. The serum used is said to be 90% effective. Let $X$ denote the number of patients who actually become desensitized.
   **a.** Use a tree to derive the table for $f(x)$.
   **b.** Find and interpret $E[X]$.
   **c.** Find $\mu_X$.
   **d.** Find $E[X^2]$.
   **e.** Find Var $X$ and $\sigma_X$.

*4. Certain genes produce such a tremendous deviation from normal that the organism is unable to survive. Such genes are called lethal genes. An example is the gene that produces a yellow coat in mice, $Y$. This gene is dominant over that for gray, $y$. Normal genetic theory predicts that when two yellow mice that are heterozygous for this trait ($Yy$) mate, $\frac{1}{4}$ of the offspring will be gray and $\frac{3}{4}$ will be yellow. Biologists have observed that these predicted proportions do not, in fact, occur, but that the actual percentages produced are $\frac{1}{3}$ gray and $\frac{2}{3}$ yellow. It has been established that this shift is caused by the fact that $\frac{1}{4}$ of the embryos, those homozygous for yellow ($YY$), do not develop. This leaves only two genotypes, $Yy$ and $yy$, occurring in a ratio of 2 to 1, with the former producing a mouse with a yellow coat. For this reason, the gene $Y$ is said to be lethal.

a. Use a tree diagram to verify that normal genetic theory predicts a 3 to 1 ratio of yellow mice to gray when two heterozygous yellow mice mate.

b. A mating experiment is conducted in which a pair of heterozygous yellow mice are to be mated. Consider three offspring of this mating. Let $X$ denote the number of yellow mice among the offspring. The density for $X$ is

| $x$ | 0 | 1 | 2 | 3 |
|---|---|---|---|---|
| $f(x)$ | $1/27$ | $6/27$ | $12/27$ | $8/27$ |

Verify the values in this table.

c. Find the expected number of yellow mice in a litter of size 3. Find the variance and standard deviation for $X$.

**5.** Let $X$ and $Y$ be independent such that $\mu_X = 2$, $\mu_Y = 6$, $\sigma_X{}^2 = 9$, and $\sigma_Y{}^2 = 16$. Find the numerical values of **a** through **f**.

a. $\sigma_X$, $\sigma_Y$

b. $E[X^2]$, $E[Y^2]$

c. $E[X + 2Y]$, Var$[X + 2Y]$

d. $E[3X - 2Y - 2]$, Var$[3X - 2Y - 2]$

e. $E[(X - 2)/3]$; Var$[(X - 2)/3]$

f. $E[(Y - 6)/4]$, Var$[(Y - 6)/4]$

g. The results of parts **e** and **f** are not coincidental. Try to generalize the pattern observed there.

***6.** ***Chebyshev's Inequality.*** This inequality points out another useful property of the standard deviation. In particular, it states that "The probability that any random variable $X$ falls within $k$ standard deviations of its mean is at least $1 - 1/k^2$." For example, if we know that $X$ has mean 3 and standard deviation 1, then we can conclude that the probability that $X$ lies between 2 and 5 ($k = 2$ standard deviations from the mean) is at least $1 - 1/2^2 = .75$.

a. Let $X$ denote the amount of rainfall received per week in a region. Assume that $\mu_X = 1.00$ inch and $\sigma_X = .25$ inch. Would it be unusual for this region to receive more than 2 inches of rain in a given week? Explain on the basis of Chebyshev's inequality.

b. Let $X$ denote the number of cases of rabies reported in a given state per week. Assume that $\mu_X = 1/2$ and $\sigma_X{}^2 = 1/25$. Would it be unusual to observe two cases in a given week? Explain on the basis of Chebyshev's inequality.

# BINOMIAL, POISSON, AND NORMAL DISTRIBUTIONS

# 5.

We consider here three groups, or "families," of random variables: the binomial, the Poisson, and the normal. Each of these families has been found useful in describing physical phenomena in almost every area of scientific and social research. The first two are families of discrete random variables, whereas the third involves variables of the continuous type. The variables within each group form a family in the sense that each is characterized by a density of the same mathematical form, differing only with respect to the numerical value of some pertinent parameter(s).

## BINOMIAL DISTRIBUTION

**5.1** □ We considered the general properties of discrete random variables in some detail in Chapter 4. Here we discuss a specific type of discrete variable, the binomial random variable. Binomial variables arise in connection with experiments that may, on the surface, appear to be quite different in nature. However, upon careful examination, certain common underlying traits become evident. Consider the following experiments.

---

**EXAMPLE 5.1.1** □ **a.** A man and woman, each with one recessive (blue) and one dominant (brown) gene for eye color, parent three children. What is the probability distribution for the number of blue-eyed children?
**b.** A carrier of tuberculosis has a 10% chance of passing the disease on to anyone with whom he comes into close contact who has had no prior exposure. During the course of a day, a carrier comes into contact with 10 such individuals. How many would you expect to contract the disease from this source?

**c.** A new variety of corn is being developed at an agricultural experimental station. It is hoped that it has a 90% germination rate. To verify this figure, 20 seeds are planted in soil of identical composition and given the same care. If the 90% figure is correct, how many seeds are expected to germinate? If 15 or fewer seeds do germinate, is there reason to suspect the 90% figure?
**d.** A survey is being conducted to determine public opinion concerning the construction of a dam to control flooding in the New River Valley. Fifteen residents of the area are to be randomly selected and surveyed. If, in fact, 80% of the people living in the area oppose the dam, what is the probability that a majority of those surveyed will be in opposition? What is the probability that between 10 and 14, inclusive, will oppose the construction?

---

What do these seemingly unrelated experiments have in common? There are essentially four points to be noted:

**1.** *Each can be viewed as consisting of a fixed number of identical trials n.* In Example 5.1.1*a*, a trial consists of the birth of a child; $n = 3$. In Example 5.1.1*b*, a trial is observing an individual who has come into contact with a carrier of tuberculosis to see whether the individual contracts the disease; $n = 10$. A trial in Example 5.1.1*c* consists of observing a corn seed to see whether it will germinate; $n = 20$. In Example 5.1.1*d*, a trial consists of determining a resident's opinion concerning the construction of the dam; $n = 15$.

**2.** *The outcome of each trial can be classified as a "success" or a "failure."* Generally, *success* is defined as observing that characteristic which is being counted. Thus in Example 5.1.1, success consists of obtaining a blue-eyed child, observing an individual who does contract tuberculosis, observing a corn seed that does germinate, and finding a resident of the New River Valley who opposes construction of the dam.

**3.** *The trials are independent in the sense that the outcome of one trial has no effect on the outcome of any other trial and the probability of success p remains the same from trial to trial.* In Example 5.1.1*a*, these conditions are obviously satisfied with $p = \frac{1}{4}$. Since the fact that one person is susceptible to tuberculosis should have no influence on another's susceptibility, independence may be assumed in Example 5.1.1*b* with $p = .1$. If we assume that the seeds in Example 5.1.1*c* are planted so that the growth of one does not impede the growth of any other, then the trials are independent, with $p = .9$. There is some room for debate in Example 5.1.1*d*. Opinion polling generally involves sampling without replacement. Once an individual has been polled, he or she is removed from the population. Thus the composition of the population changes, and the probability of success changes slightly from trial to trial. However, if the group being sampled is large, as is usually the case, then the change is so slight as to be negligible. We conclude that for all practical purposes, we have independence with $p = .8$.

4. *The variable of interest is the number of successes in n trials.*

The four traits listed are the general assumptions underlying the *binomial model.* Any random variable $X$ that represents the number of successes in $n$ independent, identical trials, with probability of success $p$ remaining constant from trial to trial, is called a *binomial random variable* with parameters $n$ and $p$.

To answer the questions posed in Example 5.1.1 or any other probabilistic questions concerning these variables, we must have available the appropriate densities. To see what these densities are, we consider in detail Example 5.1.1*a* in which the number of trials is small. If a pattern can be found, then this pattern can be generalized to obtain the densities for the variables of the remaining experiments.

---

**EXAMPLE 5.1.2** □ A man and woman, each with one recessive and one dominant gene for eye color, parent three children. What is the probability distribution for $X$, the number of blue-eyed children?

This can be viewed as a three-stage process. The sample space and the density for $X$ can be found by considering the tree of Figure 5.1. In the tree, $b$ denotes the birth of a blue-eyed child; $B$, the birth of a brown-eyed child. Since the eye color of one child has no effect on the eye color of

| First child | Second child | Third child | Sample point | Value of $X$ | Path probability |
|---|---|---|---|---|---|
| 1/4 $b$ | 1/4 $b$ | 1/4 $b$ | $b\,b\,b$ | 3 | $(1/4)^3(3/4)^0$ |
| | | 3/4 $B$ | $b\,b\,B$ | 2 | $(1/4)^2(3/4)^1$ |
| | 3/4 $B$ | 1/4 $b$ | $b\,B\,b$ | 2 | $(1/4)^2(3/4)^1$ |
| | | 3/4 $B$ | $b\,B\,B$ | 1 | $(1/4)^1(3/4)^2$ |
| 3/4 $B$ | 1/4 $b$ | 1/4 $b$ | $B\,b\,b$ | 2 | $(1/4)^2(3/4)^1$ |
| | | 3/4 $B$ | $B\,b\,B$ | 1 | $(1/4)^1(3/4)^2$ |
| | 3/4 $B$ | 1/4 $b$ | $B\,B\,b$ | 1 | $(1/4)^1(3/4)^2$ |
| | | 3/4 $B$ | $B\,B\,B$ | 0 | $(1/4)^0(3/4)^3$ |

**FIGURE 5.1** Eye color in a three-child family.

any other, the trials are independent and the path probability can be found by multiplying the probabilities that appear along the path. So the density for $X$ is given by

| $x$ | 0 | 1 | 2 | 3 |
|---|---|---|---|---|
| $f(x)$ | $1(\frac{1}{4})^0(\frac{3}{4})^3$ | $3(\frac{1}{4})^1(\frac{3}{4})^2$ | $3(\frac{1}{4})^2(\frac{3}{4})^1$ | $1(\frac{1}{4})^3(\frac{3}{4})^0$ |

To express this density as an equation, we need only look for patterns. It is evident that the success rate of $\frac{1}{4}$ and the failure rate of $\frac{3}{4}$ appear in each probability listed, with the exponent of the success rate being $x$. Also the sum of the two exponents in each case is 3, the number of trials. Thus, in general, the exponent associated with the failure rate is $3 - x$. The general form of the density is therefore

$$f(x) = K(\tfrac{1}{4})^x(\tfrac{3}{4})^{3-x} \qquad x = 0, 1, 2, 3$$

The only question to be answered is, What is $K$? This coefficient counts the number of paths through the tree that involve a specified value of $X$. A path is just a permutation of three letters, $x$ of them being $b$'s and $3 - x$ being $B$'s. By using the formula for finding the number of permutations of indistinguishable objects (Theorem 2.4.2), it is easy to see that

$$K = \frac{3!}{x!(3-x)!} = \binom{3}{x}$$

Thus the expression for the density for $X$ is

$$f(x) = \binom{3}{x}\left(\frac{1}{4}\right)^x\left(\frac{3}{4}\right)^{3-x} \qquad x = 0, 1, 2, 3$$

---

The method used to derive the density for $X$ in Example 5.1.2 is independent of both the number of trials involved and the actual numerical value of the success rate. Given any number of trials $n$ and any success rate $p$, similar reasoning can be employed to find the density. The density found will have the same general form as that of Example 5.1.2, with the number of trials, 3, being replaced by $n$ and the success rate of $\frac{1}{4}$ being replaced by $p$. This fact is summarized in Theorem 5.1.1.

**THEOREM 5.1.1** □ Let $X$ be a binomial random variable with parameters $n$ and $p$. The density for $X$ is given by

$$f(x) = \binom{n}{x}p^x(1-p)^{n-x} \qquad x = 0, 1, 2, 3, \ldots, n$$

Consider the second type of question posed in Example 5.1.1. Namely, given a binomial random variable $X$ with parameters $n$ and $p$, what is the expected value of $X$? Once again, we turn to a numerical example to guide our thinking.

---

**EXAMPLE 5.1.3** □ Ten individuals, each susceptible to tuberculosis, come into contact with a carrier of the disease. The probability that the disease will be passed from the carrier to any given subject is .10. How many are expected to contract the disease?

Since each individual has a 10% chance of contracting the disease, common sense leads us to expect that 10% of those so exposed will become infected. That is, common sense points to $10(.1) = 1$ for the expected number contracting tuberculosis. Note that this value is obtained by multiplying the number of trials, 10, by the success rate, .1.

---

Once again, the reasoning used to answer the question is independent of the actual number of trials involved or of the numerical value of the success rate. This suggests at least a portion of Theorem 5.1.2. The fact that the variance is as stated cannot be seen from an intuitive argument. It must be derived mathematically.

**THEOREM 5.1.2** □ Let $X$ be binomial with parameters $n$ and $p$. Then $E[X] = np$ and $\text{Var } X = np(1 - p)$.

Recall that the purpose of any density is to help answer probabilistic questions concerning the variable of interest. Recall also that the cumulative distribution function for the variable can be used for the same purpose. The binomial variable has such universal appeal that extensive tables have been developed for both the density and cumulative distribution functions for selected values of $n$ and $p$. Thus the primary task of researchers is to recognize the fact that they are dealing with a binomial variable, to frame their questions in terms of appropriate probabilities, and then to correctly use available tables to answer those questions. Table I of Appendix B is an abbreviated binomial table. It shows values of the cumulative distribution function for binomial variables with $n = 5$, 10, 15, 20 and $p = .1, .2, .25, .3, .4, .5, .6, .7, .8, .9$. Other more extensive tables are available. They are all similar to the one presented, and mastery of the use of Table I in Appendix B should enable you to adjust to the use of more complete tables with little difficulty. We illustrate the use of Table I in Example 5.1.4.

---

**EXAMPLE 5.1.4** □ A new variety of corn is being developed at an agricultural experimental station. It is hoped that 90% of all seed from this corn will germinate. To verify this figure, 20 seeds are planted in soil of identical composition and given the same care. If the 90% figure is correct, how many seeds are expected to germinate?

This question is not new. We are being asked to find $E[X]$, where $X$ is the number of seeds that germinate. From Theorem 5.1.2, $E[X] = np = 20(.9) = 18$. If the 90% figure is correct, we would expect to see about 18 seeds germinate. If at most 15 seeds germinate, is there reason to suspect the 90% figure? On the surface, there appears to be some reason for doubt, because 15 is somewhat below the expected figure of 18. The question is, If the 90% success rate is correct, what is the probability of seeing 15 or fewer seeds germinate? If this probability is fairly large, then there is no reason to suspect the 90% figure. However, if this probability is small, there are two possible explanations. Either a rare event has occurred, or the actual rate of germination is smaller than the rate claimed. Thus our decision is clearly based on determining and interpreting $P[X \leq 15]$. Using the methods of Chapter 4 concerning the cumulative distribution function, we have

$$P[X \leq 15] = F(15) = \sum_{x=0}^{15} f(x) = \sum_{x=0}^{15} \binom{20}{x} (.9)^x (.1)^{20-x}$$

Evaluating this probability directly entails a prohibitive amount of arithmetic. So we turn to Table I in Appendix B. Since Table I lists directly the cumulative distribution function, we can find the answer to our question by looking at the group of values labeled $n = 20$. The desired probability of .0432 is found in the column labeled .9 and the row labeled 15. That is,

$$P[X \leq 15] = F(15) = .0432$$

Is this value large or small? The answer is not clear-cut. Most researchers would tend to consider this small and would conclude that the stated germination rate of .9 was too high.

---

Questions not of the form $P[X \leq x]$ cannot be answered directly from Table I. They must be first rewritten in terms of the cumulative distribution function and then answered by means of the table. This point is illustrated in Example 5.1.5.

---

**EXAMPLE 5.1.5** □ A survey is being conducted to determine public opinion concerning the construction of a dam to control flooding in the New River Valley. Fifteen residents of the area are to be randomly selected and surveyed. If, in fact, 80% of the people living in the area oppose the dam, what is the probability that a majority of those surveyed will be in opposition? Since a majority consists of eight or more individuals, we are being asked to find $P[X \geq 8]$. In terms of the cumulative distribution function,

$$P[X \geq 8] = 1 - P[X \leq 7] = 1 - F(7)$$

From Table I with $n = 15$ and $p = .8$, it can be seen that $F(7) = .0042$. Thus the probability that a majority of those sampled will be in opposition to the dam is $1 - .0042 = .9958$. What is the probability that between 10 and 14, inclusive, will oppose the construction? Expressing this question in terms of the cumulative distribution function, we see that

$$\begin{aligned} P[10 \leq X \leq 14] &= P[X \leq 14] - P[X \leq 9] \\ &= F(14) - F(9) \\ &= .9648 - .0611 \\ &= .9037 \end{aligned}$$

---

## EXERCISES 5.1

1. In each of the following, a random variable is described. For each decide whether the variable is binomial, approximately binomial, or not binomial. If the variable is binomial or approximately so, determine the numerical values of $n$ and $p$. If the variable is not binomial, what binomial assumption is violated? (By ***approximately binomial*** we mean that even though $p$ may vary slightly from trial to trial, the change is so small as to be negligible. Thus probabilities computed by using the binomial density, though not exact, are good approximations to the actual probabilities involved.)

   **a.** An accident has occurred, and six units of AB negative blood are needed. There is none in the laboratory. Five unrelated employees are contacted as possible donors, and their blood types are determined. The number of employees with AB negative blood is $X$. (See Exercise 3.5.10.)

   **b.** In the RNA code, UGG codes tryptophan and UGA codes a stop. In a particular segment, the word UGA appears 5 times. Assume that nucleotides U and G will not mutate but that nucleotide A (adenine) will mutate to G (guanine) .1% of the time. The number of mutations in the sequence in which the word ***stop*** (UGA) is mutated to tryptophan (UGG) is $X$.

   **c.** A chemical reaction is run in which the usual yield is 70%. A new process has been devised that should improve the yield. Proponents of the new process claim that it produces better yields than the old process 90% of the time. The new process is tried 10 times, and the yields are recorded. Variable $X$ is the number of times that the yield has improved over the 70% figure.

   **d.** A biologist has eight plants available for experimentation. The experiment calls for the use of only four plants. Unknown to the biologist, three of the plants are diseased. She randomly selects four plants to use in the experiment. Variable $X$ is the number of diseased plants selected.

   **e** In studying the migratory habits of Canadian geese, approximately 5% of the entire population has been tagged. During a given day eight geese are captured. The number that are tagged is $X$.

f. A couple is determined to have a daughter. They decide to continue having children until a daughter is born, at which time they will produce no more children. The number of children born before the birth of the first daughter is $X$.

2. An oil company has 10 offshore rigs scattered throughout a wide area in the Gulf of Mexico. Officials feel that under normal operating conditions, each rig has only a 1% chance of having an oil spill during the year. Let $X$ denote the number of rigs experiencing a spill during the year.
   a. Argue that $X$ is binomial.
   b. Find the expression for the density.
   c. Find $E[X]$, Var $X$, and $\sigma_X$.
   d. If the rigs were located close together and some unusual situation occurred (such as a hurricane or an earthquake), is it safe to assume that $X$ was binomial? Explain.
3. For each of the binomial or approximate binomial variables $X$ of Exercise 5.1.1, find
   a. The expression for the density
   b. The mean of $X$
   c. The variance of $X$
   d. The standard deviation of $X$
4. A forester is interested in the spread of pine blight in the Great Smoky Mountains. After surveying five key areas, the forester records 0 if no blight is found in the area and 1 if the disease is present. These data are fed into a computer that has probability .001 of reversing a digit upon transmission (reading a 0 as a 1, or vice versa). The number of transmission errors is $X$.
   a. Find the expression for the density for $X$.
   b. Find $E[X]$, $\sigma_X^2$, and $\sigma_X$.
   c. Use the density for $X$ to find the probability that no transmission errors were made.
   d. Use the density for $X$ to find $P[X \leq 1]$.
5. In humans, geneticists have identified two sex chromosomes, *R* and *Y*. Every individual has an *R* chromosome, and the presence of a *Y* chromosome distinguishes the individual as male. Thus the two sexes are characterized as *RR* (female) and *RY* (male). Color blindness is caused by a recessive allele on the *R* chromosome, which we denote by *r*. The *Y* chromosome has no bearing on color blindness. Thus relative to color blindness, there are three genotypes for females and two for males:

| FEMALE | MALE |
|---|---|
| *RR* (normal) | *RY* (normal) |
| *Rr* (carrier) | *rY* (color-blind) |
| *rr* (color-blind) | |

A child inherits one sex chromosome randomly from each parent.
   a. A carrier of color blindness parents a child with a normal male. Construct a tree to represent the possible genotypes for the child.

**b.** What is the probability that a given child born to this couple will be a color-blind male?

**c.** If the couple has three children, what is the probability that exactly two are color-blind males?

**d.** If the couple has five children, what is the expected number of color-blind males? What is the probability that at most two will be color-blind males? What is the probability that three or more will be color-blind males?

**6.** A nuclear power plant is to be built. Local public opinion is sought. A random sample of 20 individuals is selected and polled. It is thought that 60% of the local inhabitants favor the project. If this is true, how many would you expect to express a favorable opinion? If nine or fewer express such an opinion, do you think that there is strong reason to suspect the 60% figure? Explain on the basis of the probability involved.

**7.** Albino rats used to study the hormonal regulation of a metabolic pathway are injected with a drug that inhibits body synthesis of protein. Generally, 4 out of 20 rats die from the drug before the experiment is over. If 10 animals are treated with the drug, what is the probability that at least 8 will be alive at the end of the experiment?

---

## *POISSON DISTRIBUTION

**5.2** □ The second discrete family considered is the Poisson family, named for the French mathematician Siméon Denis Poisson (1781–1840). Poisson random variables arise in connection with what are termed *Poisson processes*. Poisson processes involve observing discrete events in a continuous "interval" of time, length, or space. We use the word *interval* in describing the general Poisson process with the understanding that we may not be dealing with an interval in the usual mathematical sense. For example, we might observe the number of white blood cells in a drop of blood. The discrete event of interest is the observation of a white cell, whereas the continuous "interval" involved is a drop of blood. We might observe the number of times radioactive gases are emitted from a nuclear power plant during a 3-month period. The discrete event of concern is the emission of radioactive gases. The continuous interval consists of a period of 3 months. With this in mind, we describe the general characteristics of a Poisson process.

**Definition 5.2.1** *Poisson Process.* A *Poisson process* with parameter $\lambda > 0$ is an experiment in which discrete events are observed in a continuous interval of time, length, area, or space in such a way that the following conditions are satisfied:

1. There exists an interval of size $h$ sufficiently small that the probability of exactly one occurrence of the event in any interval of size $h$ is $\lambda h$. That is, the probability of exactly one occurrence in an interval of size $h$ is proportional to the size of the interval.

2. The probability of two or more occurrences of the event in any interval of length $h$ is, for all practical purposes, 0.

3. The occurrence of the event in one interval of length $h$ has no effect on the occurrence of the same event in any other nonoverlapping interval of length $h$.

The variable of interest in a Poisson process is $X$, the number of occurrences of the event in an interval of length $s$ units. Variable $X$ is said to be a Poisson random variable with parameter $\lambda s$, where $\lambda$ is the parameter that characterizes the underlying Poisson process. The derivation of the general form for the Poisson density requires some knowledge of calculus. Hence Theorem 5.2.1 is offered without proof.

**THEOREM 5.2.1** □ Let $X$ be a Poisson random variable with parameter $\lambda s$. The density $f$ for $X$ is given by

$$f(x) = \frac{e^{-\lambda s}(\lambda s)^x}{x!} \qquad x = 0, 1, 2, 3, \ldots$$

$$e \doteq 2.7183$$

The expected value of any Poisson random variable also can be derived using calculus. This expectation is of special interest, for it will clearly demonstrate the physical meaning of the parameter $\lambda$ associated with the underlying Poisson process.

**THEOREM 5.2.2** □ Let $X$ be a Poisson random variable with parameter $\lambda s$. Then $E[X] = \lambda s$.

From the above result, we see that the average number of occurrences of the event of interest in an interval of $s$ units is $\lambda s$. Thus the average number of occurrences of the event in 1 unit of time, length, area, or space is $\lambda s/s = \lambda$. That is, physically, *the parameter $\lambda$ of a Poisson process represents the average number of occurrences of the event in question per measurement unit.*

These concepts are illustrated in Example 5.2.1.

---

**EXAMPLE 5.2.1** □ The white blood cell count of a healthy individual can average as low as 6000 per cubic millimeter of blood. To detect a white cell deficiency, a .001 cubic millimeter drop of blood is taken and the number of white cells $X$ is found. How many white cells are expected in a healthy individual? If at most two are found, is there evidence of a white cell deficiency?

This experiment can be viewed as a Poisson process. The discrete event of interest is the occurrence of a white cell; the continuous interval is a drop of blood. It is reasonable to assume that the probability of seeing a white cell in a small drop of blood is proportional to the size of the drop and that, for a sufficiently small drop, the probability of seeing two or more such cells is 0. Since cells move independently, the presence of a white cell in one small drop of blood does not appreciably affect the presence or absence of such a cell in any other drop of the same size. Thus conditions 1, 2, and 3 of Definition 5.2.1 are met. Let the measurement unit be a cubic millimeter; then $s = .001$ and $\lambda$, the average number of occurrences of the event per unit, is 6000. Thus $X$ is a Poisson random variable with parameter $\lambda s = 6000(.001) = 6$. By Theorem 5.2.2, $E[X] = \lambda s = 6$. In a healthy individual, we would expect, on the average, to see six white cells. How rare is it to see at most two? That is, what is $P[X \leq 2]$? From Theorem 5.2.1,

$$P[X \leq 2] = \sum_{x=0}^{2} f(x) = \sum_{x=0}^{2} \frac{e^{-6}6^x}{x!}$$

$$= \frac{e^{-6}6^0}{0!} + \frac{e^{-6}6^1}{1!} + \frac{e^{-6}6^2}{2!}$$

Evaluating this type of expression directly does entail some arithmetic.

Once again, because of the wide appeal of the Poisson model, the values of the cumulative distribution function for selected values of the parameter $\lambda s$ have been tabled. Table II in Appendix B is one such table. The desired probability of .062 is found by looking under the column labeled $\lambda s = 6$ in the row labeled 2. Is there evidence of a white cell deficiency? Since .062 seems moderate in size, there appears to be no clear-cut answer to this question.

---

One other important application of the Poisson density should be mentioned. Consider a binomial variable with large $n$ and small $p$. In this case, it can be shown that the Poisson density with parameter $\lambda s = np$ gives a good approximation to the desired binomial density. A rule of thumb is that the Poisson approximation is good if $n \geq 20$ and $p \leq .05$ and very good if $n \geq 100$ and $np \leq 10$. Since the approximation is used whenever the probability of success $p$ is small, often the Poisson density is referred to as the distribution of "rare" events.

---

**EXAMPLE 5.2.2** □ In *Escherichia coli,* a bacterium often found in the human digestive tract, 1 cell in every $10^9$ will mutate from streptomycin sensitivity to streptomycin resistence. This mutation can cause the individual involved to become resistant to the antibiotic streptomycin. In observing 2 billion ($2 \times 10^9$) such cells, what is the probability that none will mutate? What is the probability that at least one will mutate?

This problem is actually binomial, with $n = 2 \times 10^9$ and $p = 1/10^9$. Since $1/10^9$ is extremely small, the mutation of a cell is a very rare event. Thus $X$, the number of cells mutating, can be thought of as being approximately Poisson with $\lambda s = np = (2 \times 10^9)(1/10^9) = 2$. From Table II in Appendix B, $P[X = 0] = .135$. The probability of at least one mutation is $P[X \geq 1]$. This probability is found by subtraction. That is, $P[X \leq 1] = 1 - P[X = 0] = 1 - .135 = .865$.

## EXERCISES 5.2

1. A Poisson random variable $X$ has parameter $\lambda s = 10$.
   a. Find $E[X]$.
   b. Find the expression for the density for $X$.
   c. Find $P[X \leq 4]$.
   d. Find $P[X \geq 6]$.
   e. Find $P[4 \leq X \leq 12]$.
   f. Find $P[X = 9]$.
2. In studying sleep patterns in humans, five stages of sleep (drowsiness, light, intermediate, deep, REM) are recognized by using the electroencephalogram. Intermediate sleep is characterized by the presence of high-amplitude waves averaging about 2 waves per second. What is the probability that during intermediate sleep none of these waves will occur during a 5-second period? What is the probability that at most 15 such waves will appear in a 5-second period? If 20 or more such waves appeared during a 5-second period, would you suspect that the subject was not in the intermediate sleep stage? Explain on the basis of the probability involved.
3. A particular nuclear plant releases a detectable amount of radioactive gases twice a month on the average. Find the probability that there will be no such emissions during a 3-month period. Find the probability that there will be at most four such emissions during the period. What is the expected number of emissions during a 3-month period? If, in fact, 12 or more emissions are detected, do you feel that there is reason to suspect the reported average figure of twice a month? Explain on the basis of the probability involved.
4. The average number of deaths from lung cancer in a certain population per year has been observed to be 12. If the number of deaths from the disease follows the Poisson distribution, what is the probability that during the current year
   a. There will be exactly 10 deaths from lung cancer?
   b. Fifteen or more people will die from the disease?
   c. Ten or fewer people will die from the disease?
5. In a certain culture, the average number of ***Rickettsia typhi*** cells (cells which cause typhus) is 5 per 20 square micrometers (1/10,000 of a centimeter). How many such cells would you expect to find in a culture of size 16 square micrometers? What is the probability that none will be found in a 16 square micrometer culture? What is the probability that at least nine such cells will be found in a culture of this size?
6. Many samples of water, all the same size and taken from the Hillbank River, were

suspected of having been polluted by irresponsible operators at a sewage treatment plant. The number of coliform organisms in each sample was counted. The average number of organisms per sample was 15. Assuming the number of organisms to be Poisson-distributed, find the probability that

a. The next sample will contain at least 17 organisms.

b. The next sample will contain 18 or fewer organisms.

c. The next sample will contain exactly two organisms.

7. Some strains of paramecia produce and secrete "killer" particles that will cause the death of a sensitive individual if contact is made. All paramecia unable to produce killer particles are sensitive. The mean number of killer particles emitted by a killer paramecium is 1 every 5 hours. What is the probability that a killer paramecium would emit no such particles in a $2\frac{1}{2}$-hour period? What is the probability that it would emit at least one killer particle?

8. In fruit flies, 4 sperm cells in every $10^5$ carry a mutation for red eye to white eye, or vice versa. How many mutations would you expect to occur in 200,000 sperm cells? What is the probability that at most 10 would occur? What is the probability that between 6 and 10, inclusive, would occur?

9. In human beings, mutations for Huntington's disease occur in about 5 of every $10^6$ gametes. What is the probability that in 2 million gametes there will be at least one mutation?

10. It is estimated that only 1 in every 50 parrots captured in the Amazon Basin for use as household pets will survive the transition. During the course of a day, 700 birds are captured. What is the expected number of survivors? What is the probability that at most 10 birds will survive? During a given 3-day period, 700 birds are captured each day. What is the probability that on each of the 3 days at most 10 birds will survive?

11. By damaging the chromosomes in the egg or sperm, mutations can be caused which lead to abortions, birth defects, or other genetic defects. The probability that such a mutation is produced by radiation is .10. Of the next 150 mutations caused by damage to the chromosomes, how many would you expect to have been produced by radiation? What is the probability that exactly 10 were produced by radiation?

12. The probability that a randomly selected baby will be albino is 1/20,000. Of the next 40,000 babies born, what is the probability that none will be albino? What is the probability that at least one will be albino?

## NORMAL DISTRIBUTION

**5.3** □ The normal family is a family of continuous random variables. The normal distribution was first described in 1733 by De Moivre as being the limiting form of the binomial density as the number of trials becomes infinite. This discovery did not get much attention, and the distribution was "discovered" again by both Laplace and Gauss a half-century later. Both men dealt with problems of astronomy, and each derived the normal distribution as a distribution that seemingly described the behavior of errors in astronomical measurements.

The normal distribution is of tremendous importance in the analysis and evaluation of every aspect of experimental data in science and medicine. In fact, the majority of the basic statistical methods that we study in the next chapters is based on the normal distribution. Thus, you should make every effort to master completely its basic structure and usage. We begin with its definition.

**Definition 5.3.1** *Normal Random Variable.* Let $X$ be a random variable with mean $\mu$ and variance $\sigma^2$. Variable $X$ is said to be a *normally distributed random variable* with parameters $\mu$ and $\sigma^2$ if and only if its density is given by

$$f(x) = \frac{1}{\sqrt{2\pi}\sigma} \cdot e^{-\frac{1}{2}[(x-\mu)/\sigma]^2}$$

where $-\infty < x < \infty$
$-\infty < \mu < \infty$
$\sigma > 0$
$e \doteq 2.7183$
$\pi \doteq 3.1416$

Techniques of elementary calculus can be used to verify the following properties.

**1.** The graph of the density of any normal random variable is a symmetric, bell-shaped curve centered at its mean, $\mu$. See Figure 5.2. Note that, as mentioned in Chapter 4, $\mu$ is a location parameter in the sense that it indicates where the curve is centered or located along the horizontal axis.

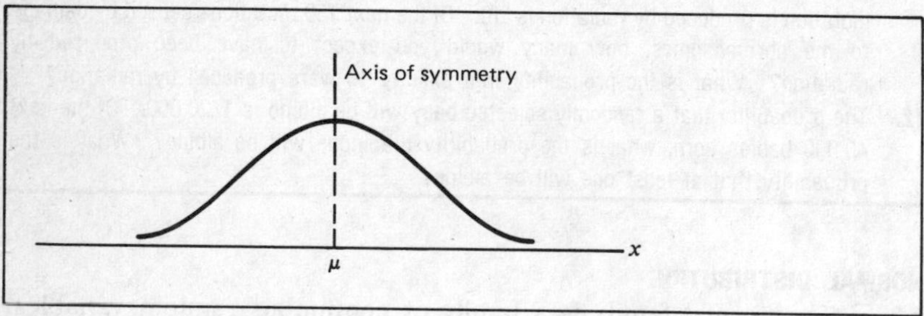


**FIGURE 5.2** $\mu$ is a location parameter.

**2.** The points of inflection, or "dips" in the curve, occur for values of $X$ one standard deviation to either side of the mean ($x = \mu \pm \sigma$). The location of these points determines the shape of the curve. The larger the value of $\sigma$, the farther the inflection points will lie from the mean and thus the flatter the curve will be. Hence, as indicated earlier, $\sigma$ is a shape parameter. See Figure 5.3.

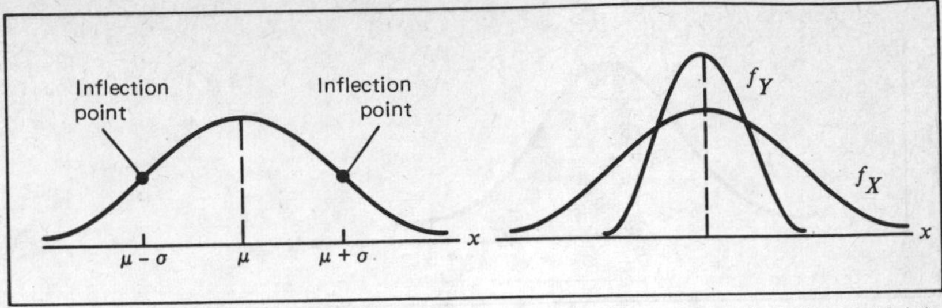


**FIGURE 5.3** $\sigma$ determines the points of inflection (left); $\mu_X = \mu_Y$ and $\sigma_X > \sigma_Y$ (right).

**3.** Every normal random variable is continuous. All the general properties of continuous variables discussed in Chapter 4 apply here. In particular, for any normal density $f$, $f(x) \geq 0$ and the area bounded by the graph of $f$ and the horizontal axis is 1. Probabilities can be found by finding appropriate areas.

---

**EXAMPLE 5.3.1** □ One of the major contributors to air pollution is hydrocarbons emitted from the exhaust systems of automobiles. Let $X$ denote the number of grams of hydrocarbons emitted by an automobile per mile. Assume that $X$ is normally distributed with a mean of 1 gram and a standard deviation of .25 gram. The density for $X$ is given by

$$f(x) = \frac{1}{\sqrt{2\pi}(.25)} \cdot e^{-\frac{1}{2}[(x-1)/.25]^2}$$

The graph of this density is a symmetric, bell-shaped curve centered at $\mu = 1$ with inflection points at $\mu \pm \sigma$, or $1 \pm .25$. A rough sketch of the density is given in Figure 5.4.

One point must be made. Theoretically speaking, a normal random variable must be able to assume any value whatsoever. This is clearly unrealistic here. It is impossible for an automobile to emit a negative amount of hydrocarbons. When we say that $X$ is normally distributed, we

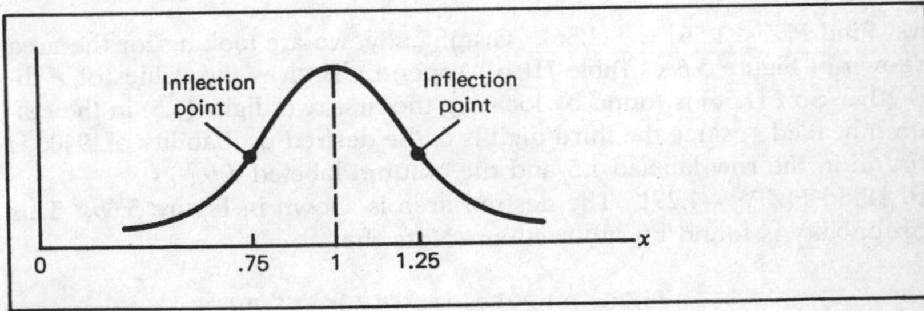


**FIGURE 5.4**

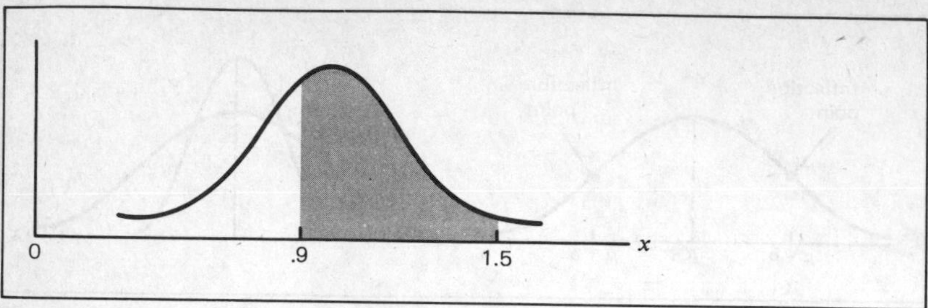


**FIGURE 5.5** Shaded area $= P[.9 \leq X \leq 1.5]$.

mean that over the range of physically reasonable values of $X$, the given normal curve yields acceptable probabilities. With this understanding we can at least approximate the probability that a randomly selected automobile will emit between .9 and 1.5 grams of hydrocarbons by finding the area under the graph of $f$ bounded by the horizontal axis and the lines $x = .9$ and $x = 1.5$, as shown in Figure 5.5.

---

There are infinitely many normal random variables, each uniquely characterized by the two parameters $\mu$ and $\sigma^2$. To calculate probabilities associated with a specific normal curve directly requires the use of calculus. A simple algebraic transformation is employed to overcome this problem. By means of this transformation, called the *standardization procedure,* any question about any normal random variable can be transformed to an equivalent question concerning a normal random variable with mean 0 and variance 1. This particular normal variable is denoted by $Z$ and is called the *standard normal* random variable. The cumulative distribution function for $Z$ is given in Table III of Appendix B. That is, Table III gives $P[Z \leq z]$ for selected values of $z$. The use of Table III is illustrated in Example 5.3.2.

---

**EXAMPLE 5.3.2**

**a.** Find $P[Z \leq 1.56] = F(1.56)$. Graphically, we are looking for the area shown in Figure 5.6*a*. Table III of Appendix B gives the values of $F$ directly. So $F(1.56)$ is found by locating the first two digits (1.5) in the column headed $z$; since the third digit is 6, the desired probability of .9406 is found in the row labeled 1.5 and the column labeled .06.

**b.** Find $P[Z \geq -1.29]$. The desired area is shown in Figure 5.6*b*. This probability is found by subtraction. Note that

$$\begin{aligned} P[Z \geq -1.29] &= 1 - P[Z < -1.29] \\ &= 1 - P[Z \leq -1.29] \qquad (Z \text{ is continuous}) \\ &= 1 - F(-1.29) \end{aligned}$$

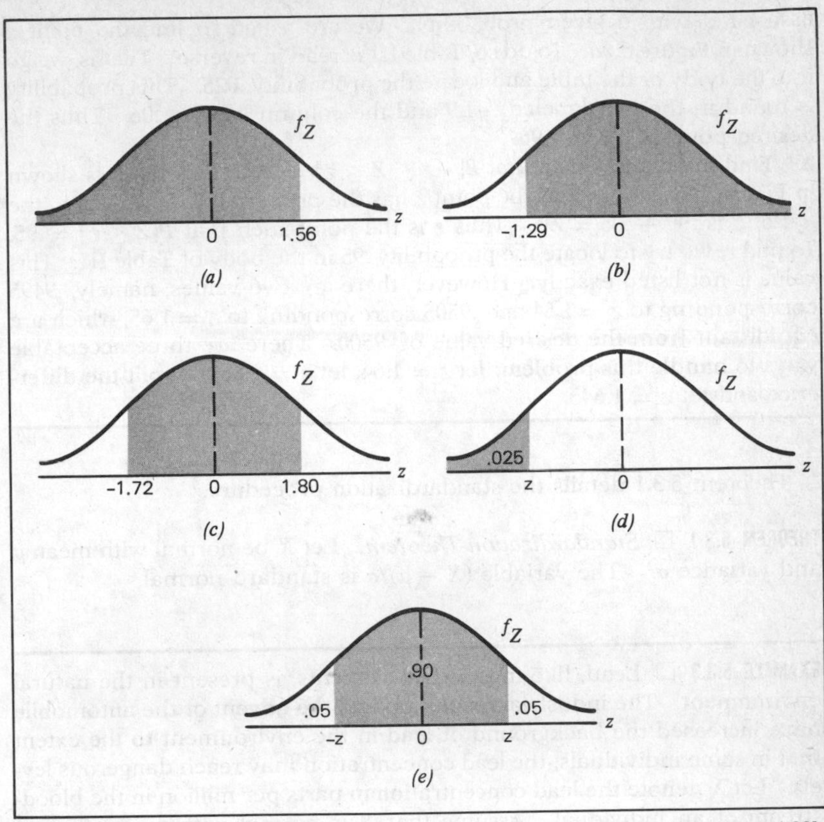


**FIGURE 5.6** (*a*) $P[Z \leq 1.56]$; (*b*) $P[Z \geq -1.29]$; (*c*) $P[-1.72 \leq Z \leq 1.80]$; (*d*) $P[Z \leq z] = .025$; (*e*) $P[-z \leq Z \leq z] = .90$.

From Table III, $F(-1.29) = .0985$ is found in the row labeled $-1.2$ and the column labeled .09. The desired probability is therefore $1 - .0985 = .9015$.

**c.** Find $P[-1.72 \leq Z \leq 1.80]$. This probability is shown in Figure 5.6*c*. In terms of the cumulative distribution function,

$$\begin{aligned} P[-1.72 \leq Z \leq 1.80] &= P[Z \leq 1.80] - P[Z < -1.72] \\ &= P[Z \leq 1.80] - P[Z \leq -1.72] \quad \text{(Z is continuous)} \\ &= F(1.80) - F(-1.72) \\ &= .9641 - .0427 = .9214 \end{aligned}$$

**d.** Find the point $z$ such that $P[Z \leq z] = .025$. This question is of a different type from those asked previously. The former involved finding the probability associated with a given point; the latter involves finding a point associated with a given probability. We are asked to find the point $z$ shown in Figure 5.6*d*. To do so, Table III is read in reverse. That is, we go into the body of the table and locate the probability .025. This probability is found in the row labeled $-1.9$ and the column labeled .06. Thus the desired point is $z = -1.96$.

**e.** Find the point $z$ such that $P[-z \leq Z \leq z] = .90$. This point is shown in Figure 5.6*e*. Note that the point $z$ has the property that the area to the *left* of $z$ is $.90 + .05 = .95$. Thus $z$ is the point such that $P[Z \leq z] = .95$. To find $z$, we try to locate the probability .95 in the body of Table III. This value is not listed exactly. However, there are two values, namely, .9495 corresponding to $z = 1.64$ and .9505 corresponding to $z = 1.65$, which are equidistant from the desired value of .9500. There are three acceptable ways to handle this problem: let $z = 1.64$, let $z = 1.65$, or split the difference and let $z = 1.645$.

---

Theorem 5.3.1 details the standardization procedure.

**THEOREM 5.3.1** □ *Standardization Theorem.* Let $X$ be normal with mean $\mu$ and variance $\sigma^2$. The variable $(X - \mu)/\sigma$ is standard normal.

---

**EXAMPLE 5.3.3** □ Lead, like most other elements, is present in the natural environment. The industrial revolution and the advent of the automobile have increased the background of lead in the environment to the extent that in some individuals, the lead concentration may reach dangerous levels. Let $X$ denote the lead concentration in parts per million in the bloodstream of an individual. Assume that $X$ is normal with mean .25 and standard deviation .11. A concentration of .6 or more is considered to be extremely high. What is the probability that a randomly selected individual will fall in the extremely high range?

To answer this question, we must find $P[X \geq .6]$. This can be done by standardizing $X$, that is, by subtracting the mean of .25 and dividing by the standard deviation of .11 on both sides of the inequality. Thus,

$$\begin{aligned} P[X \geq .6] &= P\left[\frac{X - .25}{.11} \geq \frac{.6 - .25}{.11}\right] \\ &= P[Z \geq 3.18] \\ &= 1 - P[Z \leq 3.18] \\ &= 1 - .9993 = .0007 \end{aligned}$$

Concentrations between .4 and .6 represent occupational exposure to lead. The probability that a randomly selected individual will fall into this range is

$$P[.4 \le X \le .6] = P\left[\frac{.4 - .25}{.11} \le Z \le \frac{.6 - .25}{.11}\right]$$
$$= P[1.36 \le Z \le 3.18]$$
$$= .9993 - .9131 = .0862$$

---

**EXAMPLE 5.3.4** □ Let $X$ denote the amount of radiation that can be absorbed by an individual before death ensues. Assume that $X$ is normal with a mean of 500 roentgens and a standard deviation of 150 roentgens. Above what dosage level will only 5% of those exposed survive?

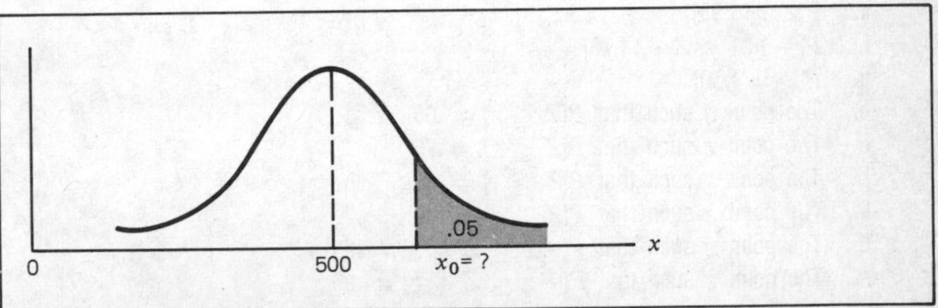


**FIGURE 5.7** $P[X \ge x_0] = .05.$

Here we are asked to find the point $x_0$ shown in Figure 5.7. In terms of probabilities, we want to find the point $x_0$ such that

$$P[X \ge x_0] = .05$$

Standardizing gives

$$P[X \ge x_0] = P\left[\frac{X - 500}{150} \ge \frac{x_0 - 500}{150}\right]$$
$$= P\left[Z \ge \frac{x_0 - 500}{150}\right] = .05$$

Thus $(x_0 - 500)/150$ is the point on the standard normal curve with 5% of the area under the curve to the right and 95% to the left. From Table III in Appendix B, the numerical value of this point is 1.645. Equating these, we get

$$\frac{x_0 - 500}{150} = 1.645$$

Solving this equation for $x_0$ gives the desired dosage level:

$$x_0 = 150(1.645) + 500 = 746.75 \text{ roentgens}$$

---

## EXERCISES 5.3

1. A random variable $X$ is normal with mean 5 and variance 4.
   a. Find the equation for the density $f$ for $X$.
   b. At what values of $X$ are the inflection points of the graph of $f$ located?
   c. Give a rough sketch of the graph of $f$.
   d. Shade in the region in the sketch corresponding to $P[3 \leq X \leq 7]$.
2. Use Table III of Appendix B to find each of the following:
   a. $P[Z \leq -1.52]$
   b. $P[Z \leq 1.37]$
   c. $F(1.37)$
   d. $P[Z \geq -1.42]$
   e. $P[Z \geq 1.98]$
   f. $P[-1.21 \leq Z \leq 1.73]$
   g. $P[Z = 1.50]$
   h. The point $z$ such that $P[Z \leq z] \doteq .05$
   i. The point $z$ such that $P[Z \leq z] \doteq .75$
   j. The point $z$ such that $P[Z \geq z] \doteq .10$
   k. The point $z$ such that $P[Z \geq z] \doteq .80$
   l. The point $z$ such that $P[-z \leq Z \leq z] \doteq .95$
   m. The point $z$ such that $P[-z \leq Z \leq z] \doteq .99$
3. Let $X$ be normal with mean 4 and variance 9. What is the distribution of the variable $(X - 4)/3$?

*4. The following three results, known as the ***empirical rule,*** have applications in sampling theory. Basically, they state that regardless of the normal variable involved, approximately 68% of the values will lie within 1 standard deviation of $\mu$, approximately 95% will lie within 2 standard deviations of $\mu$, and approximately 99% will lie within 3 standard deviations of $\mu$. Let $X$ be normal with mean $\mu$ and variance $\sigma^2$.
   a. Find $P[\mu - \sigma \leq X \leq \mu + \sigma]$.
   b. Find $P[\mu - 2\sigma \leq X \leq \mu + 2\sigma]$.
   c. Find $P[\mu - 3\sigma \leq X \leq \mu + 3\sigma]$.

*5. Consider the random variable $X$ of Example 5.3.4. Use the empirical rule to find $P[350 \leq X \leq 650]$.

*6. Consider the random variable $X$ of Example 5.3.3. Without doing any calculations, what is the approximate probability that the lead concentration in a randomly selected individual will lie between .03 and .47?

7. The number of Btu's of petroleum and petroleum products used per person in the United States in 1975, $X$, was normally distributed with mean 153 million Btu and standard deviation 25 million, Btu.
   a. Find $P[X \leq 100 \text{ million}]$.
   b. Find $P[X \geq 180 \text{ million}]$.
   c. Find $P[100 \text{ million} \leq X \leq 175 \text{ million}]$.
   d. Find $P[128 \text{ million} \leq X \leq 178 \text{ million}]$.
   e. Find the point $x_0$ such that $P[X \leq x_0] \doteq .10$.
   f. Find the point $x_0$ such that $P[X \geq x_0] \doteq .06$.

**8.** In 1969, pheasants in Montana were found to have an appreciable mercury contamination that was thought to have been caused by their eating seed from plants grown from seed treated with methyl mercury. Let $X$ denote the mercury level of a bird in parts per million. Assume that $X$ is normally distributed with mean .25 and standard deviation .08. A pheasant is killed, and the mercury level is determined. Find $P[X \leq .3]$, $P[X \geq .17]$, $P[.2 \leq X \leq .4]$, and $P[.01 \leq X \leq .49]$.

**9.** Among diabetics, the fasting blood glucose level $X$ may be assumed to be approximately normally distributed with mean 106 mg/100 ml and standard deviation 8 mg/100 ml.

- **a.** Find $P[X \leq 120$ mg/100 ml$]$.
- **b.** What percentage of diabetics have levels between 90 and 120 mg/100 ml?
- **c.** Find $P[106 \leq X \leq 110]$.
- **d.** Find $P[X \geq 121$ mg/100 ml$]$.
- **e.** Find the point $x_0$ that has the property that 25% of all diabetics have a fasting glucose level $X$ lower than $x_0$.

**10.** Among a certain population of primates, the volume of the cranial cavity $X$ is approximately normally distributed with mean 1200 cc and standard deviation 140 cc.

- **a.** Find the probability that a randomly chosen member of the population will have a cranial cavity larger than 1400 cc.
- **b.** Find $P[1000 \leq X \leq 1050]$.
- **c.** Find $P[X \leq 1060]$.
- **d.** Find $P[X \leq 920]$.
- **e.** Find the point $x_0$ such that 20% of these primates have a cranial cavity smaller than $x_0$.
- **f.** Find the point $x_0$ such that 10% of these primates have a cranial cavity larger than $x_0$.

---

## NORMAL APPROXIMATIONS

**5.4** □ We saw in Section 5.2 that for large values of $n$, the Poisson density can be used to approximate the binomial. Also the normal curve can be utilized to approximate probabilities associated with either variable. The theoretical justification for either approximation procedure is based on the Central Limit Theorem, which is presented in Chapter 7. The argument given here is based strictly on intuition and empirical evidence.

To see how binomial probabilities can be reasonably approximated, we consider a series of binomial variables. In particular, consider four binomial variables, each with probability of success .4 and with values of $n$ of 5, 10, 15, and 20. The densities for these variables, obtained from Table I of Appendix B, together with a rough sketch for each, are given in Figure 5.8*a* to *d*.

The point to note from these diagrams is made in Figure 5.8*d*. Namely, it is not hard to imagine a smooth bell curve that closely fits the block diagram shown. This suggests that binomial probabilities represented by one or more blocks in the diagram can be approximated reasonably well by a carefully selected area under an appropriately chosen normal curve.

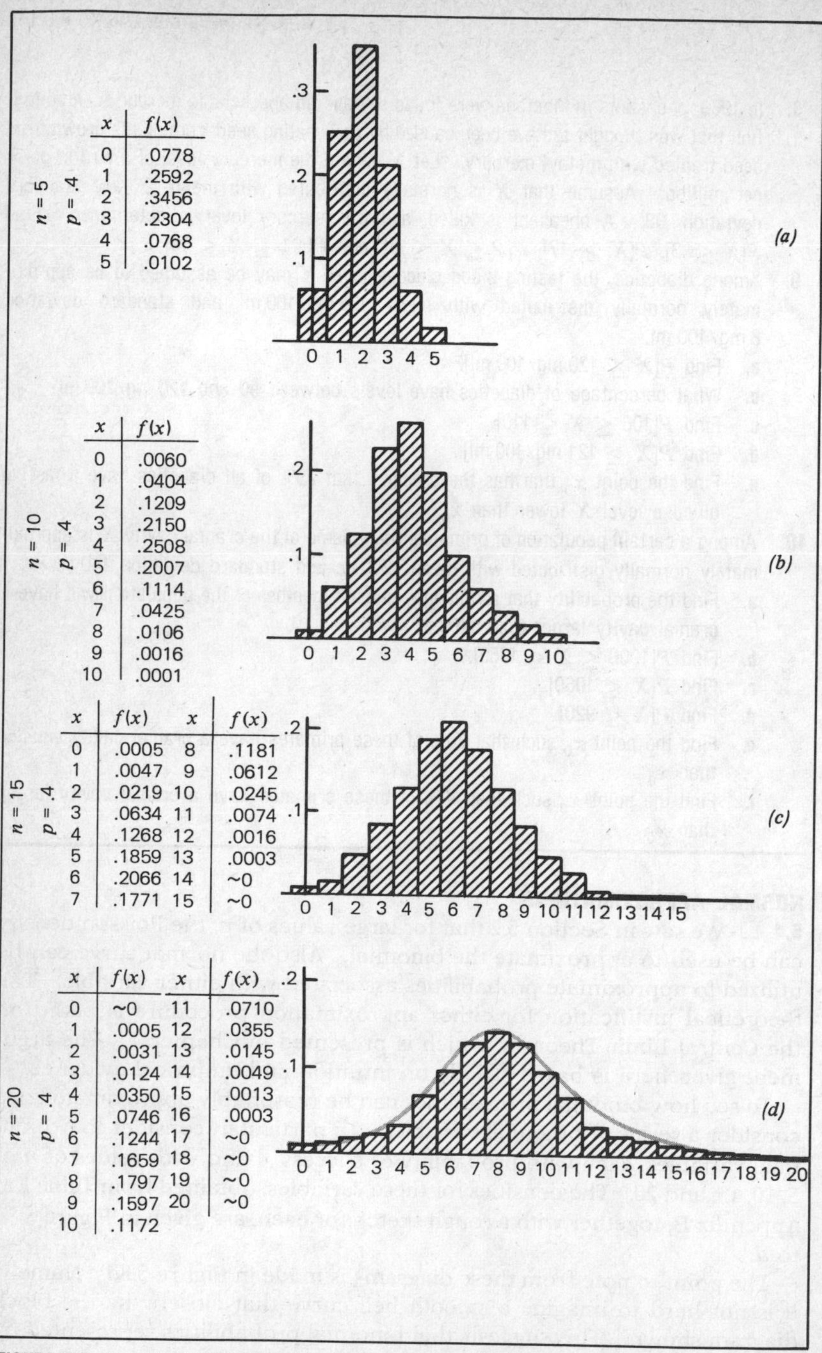


$n = 5$, $p = .4$

| $x$ | $f(x)$ |
|---|---|
| 0 | .0778 |
| 1 | .2592 |
| 2 | .3456 |
| 3 | .2304 |
| 4 | .0768 |
| 5 | .0102 |

$n = 10$, $p = .4$

| $x$ | $f(x)$ |
|---|---|
| 0 | .0060 |
| 1 | .0404 |
| 2 | .1209 |
| 3 | .2150 |
| 4 | .2508 |
| 5 | .2007 |
| 6 | .1114 |
| 7 | .0425 |
| 8 | .0106 |
| 9 | .0016 |
| 10 | .0001 |

$n = 15$, $p = .4$

| $x$ | $f(x)$ | $x$ | $f(x)$ |
|---|---|---|---|
| 0 | .0005 | 8 | .1181 |
| 1 | .0047 | 9 | .0612 |
| 2 | .0219 | 10 | .0245 |
| 3 | .0634 | 11 | .0074 |
| 4 | .1268 | 12 | .0016 |
| 5 | .1859 | 13 | .0003 |
| 6 | .2066 | 14 | ~0 |
| 7 | .1771 | 15 | ~0 |

$n = 20$, $p = .4$

| $x$ | $f(x)$ | $x$ | $f(x)$ |
|---|---|---|---|
| 0 | ~0 | 11 | .0710 |
| 1 | .0005 | 12 | .0355 |
| 2 | .0031 | 13 | .0145 |
| 3 | .0124 | 14 | .0049 |
| 4 | .0350 | 15 | .0013 |
| 5 | .0746 | 16 | .0003 |
| 6 | .1244 | 17 | ~0 |
| 7 | .1659 | 18 | ~0 |
| 8 | .1797 | 19 | ~0 |
| 9 | .1597 | 20 | ~0 |
| 10 | .1172 | | |

**FIGURE 5.8** Density for $X$ binomial: (*a*) $n = 5$, $p = .4$; (*b*) $n = 10$, $p = .4$; (*c*) $n = 15$, $p = .4$; (*d*) $n = 20$, $p = .4$.

Which of the infinitely many normal curves is appropriate? Common sense indicates that the normal variable selected should have the same mean and variance as the binomial variable that it approximates. Theorem 5.4.1, offered without formal proof, summarizes these ideas.

**THEOREM 5.4.1** □ *Normal Approximation to the Binomial Distribution.* Let $X$ be binomial with parameters $n$ and $p$. For large $n$, $X$ is approximately normal with mean $np$ and variance $np(1-p)$.

Admittedly, Theorem 5.4.1 is a bit vague in the sense that the word *large* is not well defined. In the strictest mathematical sense, *large* means as $n$ approaches infinity. For all practical purposes, the approximation is acceptable for values of $n$ and $p$ such that either $p \leq .5$ and $np > 5$ or $p > .5$ and $n(1-p) > 5$.

---

**EXAMPLE 5.4.1** □ A study is performed to investigate the connection between maternal smoking during pregnancy and birth defects in children. Of the mothers studied, 40% smoke and 60% do not. When the babies were born, 20 were found to have some sort of birth defect. Let $X$ denote the number of children whose mother smoked while pregnant. If there is no relationship between maternal smoking and birth defects, then $X$ is binomial with $n = 20$ and $p = .4$. What is the probability that 12 or more of the affected children had mothers who smoked?

To answer this question, we need to find $P[X \geq 12]$ under the assumption that $X$ is binomial with $n = 20$ and $p = .4$. This probability can be read from Table I of Appendix B.

$$\begin{aligned} P[X \geq 12] &= 1 - P[X \leq 11] \\ &= 1 - .9435 \\ &= .0565 \end{aligned}$$

Note that since $p = .4 \leq .5$ and $np = (20)(.4) = 8 > 5$, the normal approximation should give a result quite close to .0565. Graphically, we are dealing with a normal random variable $Y$ with mean $np = 20(.4) = 8$ and variance $np(1-p) = 20(.4)(.6) = 4.8$. The exact probability of .0565 is given by the sum of the areas of the blocks centered at 12, 13, 14, 15, 16, 17, 18, 19, and 20, as shown in Figure 5.9. The approximate probability is given by the area under the normal curve above 11.5. That is,

$$P[X \geq 12] \doteq P[Y \geq 11.5]$$

The number .5 is called the *half-unit correction* for continuity. It was subtracted from 12 in the approximation because otherwise half of the area of the block centered at 12 would have been inadvertently ignored, leading to an unnecessary error in the calculation. From this point on, the calculation is routine.

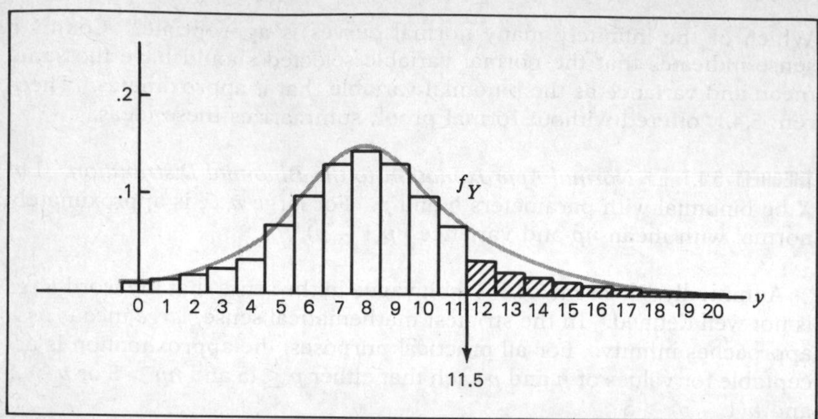


**FIGURE 5.9** $P[X \geq 12]$ = area of shaded blocks $\doteq$ area under curve beyond 11.5.

$$\begin{aligned} P[X \geq 12] &\doteq P[Y \geq 11.5] \\ &= P\left[\frac{Y - 8}{\sqrt{4.8}} \geq \frac{11.5 - 8}{\sqrt{4.8}}\right] \\ &= P[Z \geq 1.59] \\ &= 1 - P[Z \leq 1.59] \\ &= 1 - .9441 = .0559 \end{aligned}$$

Note that even with $n$ as small as 20, the approximated value of .0559 compares quite favorably with the exact value of .0565. In practice, of course, one would not approximate a probability that could be found directly from a binomial table. This was done here only for comparative purposes.

---

The normal approximation to the Poisson distribution is handled similarly to the binomial. Its theoretical basis is also the Central Limit Theorem. It is reasonably accurate for large values of the Poisson parameter $\lambda s$, and it employs the half-unit correction factor to adjust for the fact that a discrete distribution is being approximated by a continuous curve. The procedure is based on Theorem 5.4.2.

***THEOREM 5.4.2** □ *Normal Approximation to the Poisson Distribution.* Let $X$ be Poisson with parameter $\lambda s$. Then for large values of $\lambda s$, $X$ is approximately normal with mean $\lambda s$ and variance $\lambda s$.

---

***EXAMPLE 5.4.2** □ A healthy adult male has on the average 5,400,000 red cells per cubic millimeter of blood. A drop of size 1/10,000 cubic millimeter is examined. What is the probability that the number of red cells $X$ will lie between 500 and 580?

Variable $X$ is Poisson with parameter

$$\lambda s = 5{,}400{,}000 \frac{1}{10{,}000} = 540$$

By Theorem 5.4.2, $X$ is approximately normal with mean and variance each equal to 540. Thus, using the half-unit correction factor, we get

$$\begin{aligned} P[500 \le X \le 580] &\doteq P[499.5 \le Y \le 580.5] \\ &= P\left[\frac{499.5 - 540}{\sqrt{540}} \le Z \le \frac{580.5 - 540}{\sqrt{540}}\right] \\ &= P[-1.74 \le Z \le 1.74] \\ &= .9591 - .0409 = .9182 \end{aligned}$$

---

## EXERCISES 5.4

1. Let $X$ be binomial with $n = 20$ and $p = .3$. Use the normal approximation to the binomial to approximate each of the following. Then compare your results with the values obtained from Table I of Appendix B.
   a. $P[X \le 3]$
   b. $P[3 \le X \le 6]$
   c. $P[X \ge 4]$
   d. $P[X = 4]$
2. It is reported that 10% of all human beings have some sort of allergy. One hundred individuals are randomly selected and interviewed. Find the probability that at least 12 will have some sort of allergy. Find the probability that at most eight will have an allergy.
3. The probability of death resulting from the use of contraceptive pills is 3/100,000. Of 1,000,000 women using this form of birth control, how many deaths are expected to be attributable to this use? What is the probability that there will be at most 25 such deaths? What is the probability that the number of deaths owing to this cause is between 25 and 35, inclusive?
4. A laboratory test for heroin in blood samples has a record of 92% accuracy. If 72 samples are analyzed in a month, what is the probability that
   a. 60 or fewer are accurately evaluated
   b. Fewer than 60 are accurately evaluated
   c. Exactly 60 are accurately evaluated
5. One out of every 400 babies born in a large metropolitan hospital is afflicted with the genetic disease phenylketonuria (PKU). Of the next 2000 babies born in this hospital, what is the probability that at least one will have PKU?

6. Assume that male and female rat pups are equally likely to be born to breeding females in the laboratories of a large laboratory animal supply company. What is the probability that of 1000 animals born, 445 or more will be female?

*7. Let $X$ be Poisson with parameter $\lambda s = 100$. Use the normal approximation to find the following:
   a. $P[X \geq 95]$
   b. $P[X \leq 80]$
   c. $P[90 \leq X \leq 110]$
   d. $P[X = 99]$

*8. The average number of jets either arriving at or departing from O'Hare airport is one every 40 seconds. What is the probability that at least 75 such flights will occur during a randomly selected hour? What is the probability that fewer than 100 such flights will take place in an hour?

*9. A medium contains 20 killer paramecia (see Exercise 5.2.7). What is the probability that in a $2\frac{1}{2}$-hour period none of these will emit a killer particle? What is the probability that between 5 and 10, inclusive, of these will each emit at least one killer particle?

# INTRODUCTION TO INFERENCE

# 6.

Thus far the emphasis in this text has been on probability theory. However, a few judgmental questions have been asked to indicate how practical decisions can be made based on probability. The reason is that the study of statistics is the study of decision making in the presence of uncertainty. The decisions made are almost always based on probability. Thus a solid grounding in the basics of probability is essential to understanding the statistical procedures presented later.

In this chapter we are concerned with the language of statistical inference. We consider when a statistical approach to a practical problem is the reasonable approach to take. We also distinguish between the two broad categories of statistical inference, namely, estimation and hypothesis testing. In the remainder of the text, we apply these general concepts to specific problems arising in the biological and health sciences.

## GENERAL STATISTICAL PROBLEM

**6.1** □ Consider the following examples. Each calls for a statistical solution to the question posed.

---

**EXAMPLE 6.1.1** □ A researcher is interested in studying the diastolic blood pressure while under stress of males between the ages of 20 and 30. He wants to answer the question, What is the mean diastolic pressure under stress for this group?

---

---

**EXAMPLE 6.1.2** □ A researcher from the President's advisory board on energy wants to answer the question, What proportion of U.S. homeowners have stopped heating with oil during the last year? She wants to be able to report on the accuracy of her figure.

---

---

**EXAMPLE 6.1.3** □ In the United States in 1976, the mean number of children born to white married women in the 18 through 24 years old age group was

.8. An environmentalist feels that this figure has been reduced. Does experimental evidence tend to support or refute this contention?

---

**EXAMPLE 6.1.4** □ There has been some concern recently that doctors are ordering an excessive number of laboratory tests for their hospitalized patients. A hospital administrator is interested in studying the situation at her institution. One question to be answered is, What was the mean number of tests ordered per patient visit in this hospital last year?

---

**EXAMPLE 6.1.5** □ A study is run to compare the rate of hypertension among black males in the 25 to 34 years old age group to the rate among white males in the same age category in the United States. It is felt that the rate for blacks is the higher. Is this contention supported by experimental evidence?

---

These examples have one important characteristic in common: they each involve a study of a potentially large group of objects. The group of objects under study in a statistical problem is called the *population*. The populations in Examples 6.1.1 through 6.1.4, respectively, consist of all males between the ages of 20 and 30, the set of all U.S. homeowners, all white married women in the United States in the 18 to 24 years old age group, and the set of all records of patient visits at a particular hospital last year. Two populations are studied in Example 6.1.5: the set of all white males in the United States in the 25 to 34 years old age group and the set of all black males in the United States of this age. Note that the word *population* is used regardless of the type of object under study. The objects in a population can be people, animals, trees, records, bacteria, blood cells, plants, or any other object of interest. Furthermore, the population of concern may be either real or hypothetical. The populations in the given examples are all real in the sense that the groups described, though large, do exist. However, the population of Example 6.1.1 is at least potentially hypothetical. Here interest centers not just on the present group of males 20 to 30 years old, a real collection of young men, but also on future groups of males in this age group, a hypothetical collection.

The purpose of a statistical study is to draw some conclusions about the nature of the population. This population is large—so large that it cannot be studied in its entirety. Hence the conclusions reached must be based on the examination of only a portion of the population. That is, some sampling must be done. Although there are a number of different schemes for obtaining a scientific sample from a population, the most commonly encountered is called a *simple random sample*. This type of sampling is intuitively appealing and is what generally comes to mind when a layperson hears the term "random sample." The term is defined thus:

**Definition 6.1.1** *Simple Random Sample.* A *simple random sample* of size *n* is a collection of *n* objects drawn from the population in such a way that every subset of size *n* has an equal chance of being selected.

One of the easiest ways to select a simple random sample from a finite population is by means of a table of random digits. This table is generated in such a way that each of the digits 0 to 9 has the same probability of appearing in a given position in the table as every other digit. One such table is Table IV of Appendix B. Its use is illustrated in Example 6.1.6.

---

**EXAMPLE 6.1.6** □ Consider Example 6.1.4. The number of patient visits at the hospital during the past year was 8000. Since this population is large, we draw a simple random sample of size 5 from the population, and based on the sample, we approximate the mean number of laboratory tests ordered per patient visit for the entire population. To do so, first note that the records of patient visits are listed in the files and can be numbered from 1 to 8000. We use Table IV to obtain five random four-digit numbers (0001 to 8000). Patient records corresponding to the numbers selected are chosen for study and therefore constitute our simple random sample of size 5. In this way, control of the visits sampled has been taken out of our hands, and there can be no charge that we manipulated the results of the study in any way. A portion of Table IV is shown in Table 6.1.

To begin, a random starting point is selected. This is done by closing your eyes and touching the table with a pencil. Suppose the pencil point lands on the digit 5 circled in Table 6.1. We begin reading the table at that

**TABLE 6.1**

| | | |
|---|---|---|
| 77921 | 06907 | 11008 |
| 99562 | 72905 | (5)6420 |
| 96301 | 91977 | 05463 |
| 89579 | 14342 | 63661 |
| 85475 | 36857 | 43342 |
| 28918 | 69578 | 88231 |
| 63553 | 40961 | 48235 |
| 09429 | 93969 | 52636 |
| 10365 | 61129 | 87529 |
| 07119 | 97336 | 71048 |

point. The table may be read in a variety of ways: across the row, down the column, every other digit down the column, or by any other arbitrary scheme desired. The easiest way is to read the first four digits across the row to obtain the random number 5642. Thus patient visit 5642 has been selected as the first member of our simple random sample. Reading down the column, we find the next random four-digit number is 0546, corresponding to visit number 546. The third and fourth visits selected are numbers 6366 and 4334, respectively. As we continue down the column, the next random number is 8823. Since we have only 8000 patient visits, this number is too large and is discarded. Thus the final member of the random sample corresponds to the next number in the table, 4823. If the same random number had been obtained more than once, it would have been discarded after the first selection. At this point we have a simple random sample that consists of the *files on five patient visits*. Note that we have taken a very small sample for illustrative purposes only. We do *not* mean to imply that samples this small are sufficient for making inferences about large populations.

---

Consider a statistical study in which interest centers on one population trait. This is essentially a study in which interest centers on one random variable $X$. Many questions can be asked concerning $X$. In particular, we might ask, Is $X$ normal? What is $\mu_X$? Is the variance of $X$ larger than 10? We hope to use information obtained from a random sample to help answer these and other questions of a similar nature. In this sense, then, a statistical study is a study of the behavior of one or more random variables. To think of a statistical study in this light requires that the term *random sample* be phrased in terms of random variables. This results in what will be called the "mathematical" definition of the term. It is not equivalent to Definition 6.1.1, although the two do go hand in hand.

**Definition 6.1.2** *Mathematical Random Sample.* A *random sample* of size $n$ from the distribution of $X$ is a collection of $n$ independent random variables $X_1, X_2, X_3, \ldots, X_n$, each with the same distribution as $X$.

---

**EXAMPLE 6.1.7** □ Consider again the population of all patient visits at the given hospital over the past year. The particular variable of interest is $X$, the number of laboratory tests ordered per patient visit. Variable $X$ has a probability distribution, a mean $\mu_X$, and a variance $\sigma_X{}^2$. Neither the exact distribution of $X$ nor the actual numerical value of $\mu_X$ or of $\sigma_X{}^2$ is known. They are *population* characteristics that can be precisely determined only by reviewing each of the 8000 patient records for the past year. To get an idea of the value of $\mu_X$, we draw a simple random sample of size 5 from the population. Let

$X_1$ = number of laboratory tests ordered on first patient visit selected into sample
$X_2$ = number of laboratory tests ordered on second patient visit selected into sample
⋮
$X_5$ = number of laboratory tests ordered on fifth patient visit selected into sample

Since the visits selected into the sample are determined by *chance* via the random digit table, $X_1$, $X_2$, $X_3$, $X_4$, and $X_5$ are *random variables.* They are assumed to be independent, each with the same distribution as $X$. In a mathematical sense, the term *random sample* refers not to the five files selected for study, but to the *five random variables* $X_1, X_2, X_3, X_4, X_5$ associated with the files.

---

The mathematical definition of the term *random sample* is theoretical. In order to draw practical conclusions about the population based on such a sample, the numerical values of variables $X_1, X_2, X_3, \ldots, X_n$ must be determined. At this point, we are dealing not with a collection of randomly selected objects, nor with a group of theoretical variables, but rather with *n numbers* $x_1, x_2, x_3, \ldots, x_n$. These numbers are the observed values of the variables $X_1, X_2, \ldots, X_n$ for a specific simple random sample of objects drawn from the population. This idea leads to the following "applied statistics" definition of the term *random sample.*

**Definition 6.1.3** *Applied Random Sample.* A *random sample* of size $n$ is a collection of $n$ observations $x_1, x_2, x_3, \ldots, x_n$ on the independent and identically distributed random variables $X_1, X_2, X_3, \ldots, X_n$.

---

**EXAMPLE 6.1.8** □ Consider again the problem of approximating the mean number of laboratory tests ordered per patient visit in a particular hospital last year. Once the five files to be sampled have been identified, we can determine the numerical values of the five random variables $X_1, X_2, X_3, X_4, X_5$. Assume that for the first file selected, number 5642, the physician had ordered six laboratory tests. In this case, the random variable $X_1$ has assumed the value $x_1 = 6$. If the second file selected, number 546, reveals that eight tests had been ordered, then the random variable $X_2$ assumes the value $x_2 = 8$. Similarly, the random variables $X_3$, $X_4$, and $X_5$ assume numerical values depending on the number of tests ordered for patient visits 6366, 4334, and 4823, respectively. At this point, when we use the term *random sample,* we refer not to the files themselves or to the random variables associated with the files, but to the five numerical values $x_1, x_2, x_3, x_4, x_5$ assumed by those variables.

---

There are, then, three ways of looking at the term *random sample*. The first deals with the actual objects under study, the second with theoretical random variables associated with those objects, and the third with the numerical values assumed by the variables. The definitions are not equivalent, but they are closely related. Usually it is obvious from the context of the problem which is intended.

---

## EXERCISES 6.1

In Exercises 6.1.1 through 6.1.6, a problem is described. In each case, decide whether a statistical study is called for. If so, identify the population under study and determine whether it is real and/or potentially hypothetical.

1. In studying population growth, city officials want to compare the number of live births at the city's hospitals in 1980 to the number this year.
2. The Council on Alcohol and Drug Abuse wants to determine the percentage of young people in the United States in the 14 to 18 years old age group who have a serious problem with alcohol.
3. A botanist feels that indoleacetic acid is effective in stimulating the formation of roots in cuttings from lemon trees. In an experiment to verify this contention, two groups of cuttings are to be used. One group is to be treated with a dilute solution of indoleacetic acid; the other is given only water. Later a comparison of the root systems of the two will be made.
4. A park official wants to study trail usage on the Appalachian Trail. She is interested in the percentage of hikers going into the wilderness areas of the trail.
5. A biologist is interested in studying the effects of infrared light on petunia plants. The parameters of interest are mean plant height and mean number of flowers per plant.
6. A public health nurse is interested in the percentage of children in the school he serves who have been immunized to mumps either naturally or by means of the mumps vaccine.

---

## ESTIMATION

**6.2** □ There are two broad categories of problems in statistical inference: estimation and hypothesis testing. These areas are closely related, and statistics developed to handle problems in one area often find application in the other.

In either category, there is a population trait of interest and usually at least one population parameter, $\theta$, under study. The parameter may be a mean, a variance, a proportion, a total, or any other population characteristic. To distinguish the two areas, we need only look at the type of question being asked. In an estimation problem, the experimenters usually will have no *preconceived* notion as to the value of $\theta$. They will be going into the experiment with the intent of answering the question, What is the numerical value of $\theta$? Examples 6.1.1, 6.1.2, and 6.1.4 are all estimation problems. In Example 6.1.1, the parameter of interest $\theta$ is the mean diastolic blood pressure of a group of young men; in Example 6.1.2, $\theta$ is the proportion of U.S. homeowners who stopped heating with oil during the last year; in Example 6.1.4, $\theta$ is the mean number of laboratory tests ordered per patient visit in a particular hospital during the year. In none of these problems was there any indication that the experimenters had some prior notion as to the value of these parameters.

In a hypothesis testing problem, the experimenters usually do have a prior notion as to the value of $\theta$ or the structure of the population. The purpose of the study is to gather evidence that either affirms or refutes the hypothesized theory. Examples 6.1.3 and 6.1.5 are of this type. In Example 6.1.3, it is hypothesized that the mean number of births $\theta$ for a certain group of women has fallen below .8; in Example 6.1.5, it is hypothesized that the hypertension rate among a group of blacks $\theta_1$ is greater than the rate $\theta_2$ among a similar group of whites.

Thus to decide whether to approach a problem as an estimation problem or as a test of hypothesis, we need only ask, What is the purpose of the experiment? If it is purely investigative, then an estimation approach is reasonable; if it is to gain support for or refute a previously stated theory, then a hypothesis test is called for.

In this section we consider the language underlying estimation. The first term that must be defined is *statistic.* The concept is not new. It is simply a matter of giving a particular name to a certain class of random variables.

**Definition 6.2.1** *Statistic.* A *statistic* is a random variable whose value can be determined from the observations in a random sample.

---

**EXAMPLE 6.2.1** □ Let $X_1, X_2, X_3, X_4$ represent the diastolic blood pressure of a sample of four randomly selected males. Here $X_1$, $X_1^2$, $X_1 + X_2 + X_3 + X_4$, and $X_1^2 + X_2^2 + X_3^2 + X_4^2$ are all statistics. Given a particular set of observations on these variables, the numerical value of each of these statistics could be found. For example, if $x_1 = 80$, $x_2 = 72$, $x_3 = 70$, and $x_4 = 82$, then the statistics assume the values 80, 6400, 304, and 23,208, respectively. An expression such as $X_1 + X_2 - \mu$ in which $\mu$ is unknown is not a statistic. When the observed values of $X_1$ and $X_2$ are substituted into this expression we get $80 + 72 + \mu$. We still do not know the value of this random variable.

---

The most important feature to notice about Definition 6.2.1 is that *every statistic is a random variable.* Thus everything that has been said concerning the behavior of random variables applies to the behavior of statistics.

It makes sense to classify statistics as discrete or continuous. It makes sense to talk about the distribution of a statistic, its mean, its variance, and the probability that it will assume specific values. In this sense, the study of statistics began in Chapter 4.

Recall that in an estimation problem usually there is at least one parameter $\theta$ whose value is to be approximated on the basis of a sample. The approximation is done by using appropriate statistics. A statistic utilized to approximate or estimate a population parameter $\theta$ is called a *point estimator* for $\theta$ and is denoted by $\widehat{\theta}$. Thus, for example, an estimator for a mean $\mu$ would be denoted $\widehat{\mu}$; an estimator for $\sigma$ would be denoted $\widehat{\sigma}$. Once the sample has been taken and some observations have been made, the numerical value of the statistic $\widehat{\theta}$ can be obtained. Such a number is called a *point estimate* for $\theta$. Note that there is a difference in the terms *estimator* and *estimate*. The estimator is the statistic used to generate the estimate. An estimator is a random variable; an estimate is a number.

---

**EXAMPLE 6.2.2** □ A study is run to estimate the proportion $p$ of U.S. homeowners who stopped heating with oil during the past year. A sample of size $n$ is to be selected at random. The proportion of homeowners in the sample who have turned from oil to another heat source is to be found. This proportion is given by $X/n$, where $X$ is the number in the sample who have switched from oil to another heat source and $n$ is the sample size. So $X/n$ is a statistic. It is intuitively reasonable to use $X/n$, the sample proportion, as an *estimator* for $p$, the population proportion. That is,

$$\widehat{p} = \frac{X}{n}$$

When the experiment was run, 500 of 6000 homeowners interviewed had switched from oil. For this sample, $x = 500$ and thus the point *estimate* for $p$ is

$$\frac{x}{n} = \frac{500}{6000} = .08$$

---

There is one drawback to point estimation. It yields a single value for $\theta$. How good is the figure generated? Is there any assurance that it is even close to the actual value of the parameter being estimated? The best answer is that in most cases, the point estimators derived are at least intuitively logical and in some sense mathematically desirable.

To get an idea of not only the value of the parameter $\theta$ being estimated, but also the accuracy of the estimate, researchers turn to the method of *interval estimation*, or *confidence intervals*. An interval estimator is what the name implies. It is a random interval, an interval whose endpoints $L_1$

and $L_2$ are each statistics. It is used to determine a numerical interval based on a sample. It is hoped that the numerical interval obtained will contain the population parameter being estimated. By expanding from a point to an interval, we create a little room for error and in so doing gain the ability, based on probability theory, to report the confidence that we have in the estimator.

---

**EXAMPLE 6.2.3** □ In Example 6.2.2 a point estimate of $\hat{p} = .08$ was found for the proportion of U.S. homeowners changing from oil heat to another energy source. An interval estimator $(L_1, L_2)$ will expand $\hat{p}$ to an interval

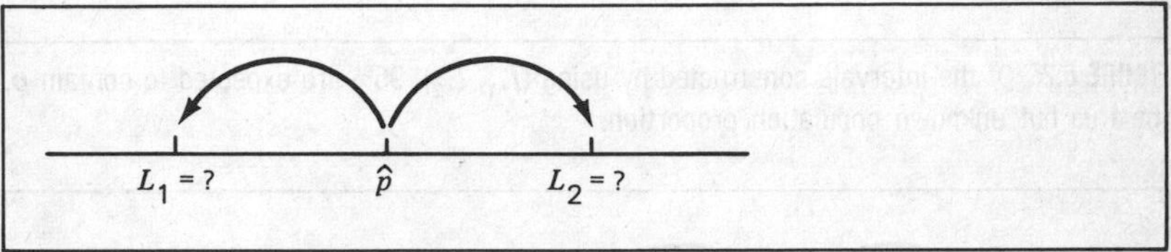


**FIGURE 6.1** Expanding $\hat{p}$ to an interval of values.

of real numbers that will contain the true population proportion $p$ with some degree of certainty. See Figure 6.1. One such estimator, whose derivation is given in Chapter 8, is

$$(L_1, L_2) = \left(\hat{p} - 1.96\sqrt{\frac{1}{4n}}, \hat{p} + 1.96\sqrt{\frac{1}{4n}}\right)$$

where $\hat{p}$ is the sample proportion and $n$ is the sample size. The degree of certainty associated with this estimator is 95%. That is, the estimator is such that in repeated random sampling from the population, 95% of the numerical intervals generated are expected to contain $p$; by chance, 5% will not. See Figure 6.2.

For the data of Example 6.2.2, the observed value of $L_1$ is

$$\hat{p} - 1.96\sqrt{\frac{1}{4n}} = .08 - 1.96\sqrt{\frac{1}{4(6000)}} = .067$$

and the observed value of $L_2$ is

$$\hat{p} + 1.96\sqrt{\frac{1}{4n}} = .08 + 1.96\sqrt{\frac{1}{4(6000)}} = .093$$

See Figure 6.3. For this sample the interval estimate for $p$ is (.067, .093). Does the true proportion $p$ of homeowners changing over from oil really lie between .067 and .093? Unfortunately, there is no way of knowing. The interval (.067, .093) is a 95% confidence interval. All this means is that

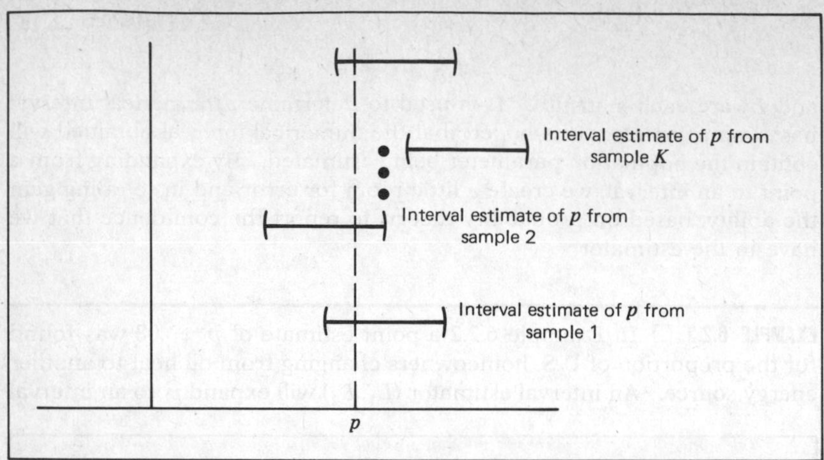


**FIGURE 6.2** Of the intervals constructed by using $(L_1, L_2)$, 95% are expected to contain $p$, the true but unknown population proportion.

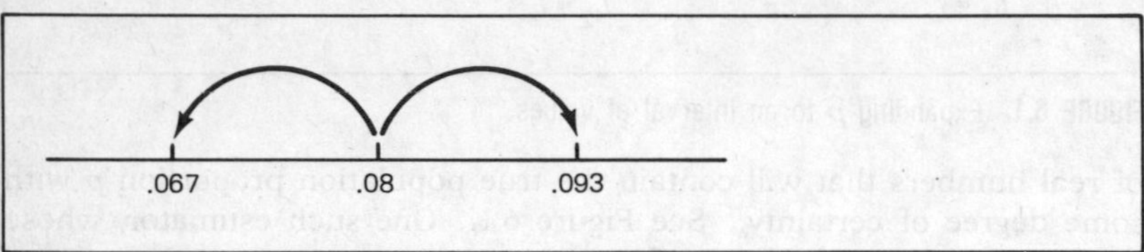


**FIGURE 6.3** A numerical 95% confidence interval on $p$.

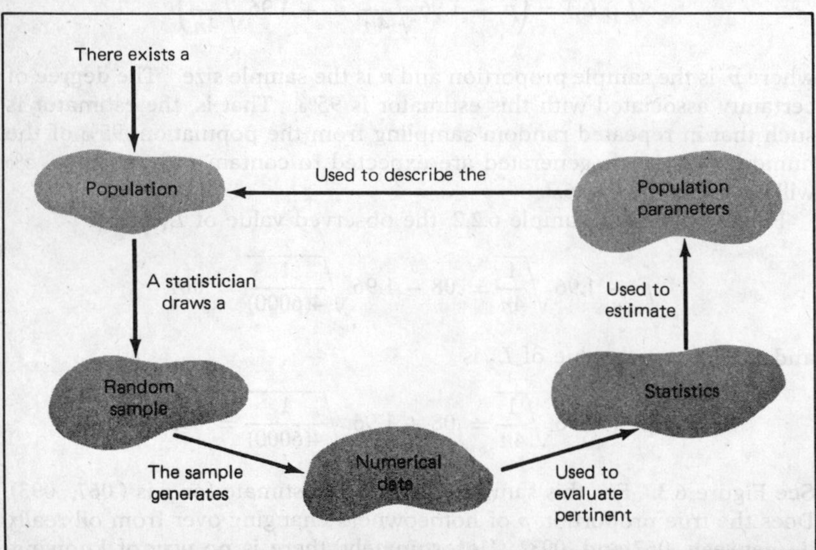


**FIGURE 6.4** A summary of the manner in which a statistical study is conducted.

the procedure used is expected to trap $p$ 95% of the time. We hope that the interval obtained from our particular sample does so.

---

The points made in this section are summarized in Figure 6.4.

---

**EXERCISES 6.2**

In Exercises 6.2.1 to 6.2.5, a problem is described. Would you approach it as an estimation problem or a hypothesis-testing problem? Be ready to support your answer.

1. In order to determine how large a landfill is needed for a town, officials need to ascertain roughly the average number of pounds of garbage produced per household unit per month.
2. The statutory standard for automobile emissions is 3.4 grams of carbon monoxide per mile. General Motors wants to make sure that the average emission for its new model will fall below this standard.
3. Public health officials feel that the smoking rate among males in the 17 to 24 years old age group has increased over the 1974 figure of 36%. They want to verify their contention.
4. Conservationists want to get a rough idea of the number of polar bears living free in Alaska.
5. There is some concern that as combustion products pour more and more carbon dioxide into the atmosphere, it will accumulate faster than it can be absorbed by the sea. This could result in a rise in the earth's mean temperature. In 1971 the mean carbon dioxide concentration in the northern hemisphere was 330 ppm. Now ecologists feel that this figure is too low and want to verify their contention.
6. Foresters want to estimate the proportion $p$ of maples along the main motor roads in the Great Smoky Mountains that have been damaged by sulfur emissions from motor vehicles. A sample of 1000 maples yielded 250 showing signs of some damage.
   **a.** Find a point estimate for $p$.
   **b.** Find a 95% confidence interval for $p$.
7. Emergency room officials want to estimate the proportion of cases handled that are true emergencies. Of 500 cases handled during a 2-month period, 100 were actual emergencies.
   **a.** Find a point estimate for the proportion $p$ of true emergencies.
   **b.** Find a 95% confidence interval for $p$.
8. Measurements of the lung capacity of a sample of 10 coal miners gave the following values in liters:

$$x_1 = 2.75 \quad x_4 = 2.98 \quad x_7 = 3.14 \quad x_{10} = 3.20$$
$$x_2 = 3.50 \quad x_5 = 3.30 \quad x_8 = 2.90$$
$$x_3 = 3.02 \quad x_6 = 3.60 \quad x_9 = 3.20$$

Find the value of $X_3$, $\Sigma_{i=1}^{10}(X_i - 1)$, and $\Sigma_{i=1}^{10} X_i^2$.

9. In monitoring the progress of a flu epidemic, health officials are interested in $X$, the number of new cases reported each day. A random sample of size 8 yielded the following observations for a given day:

$$x_1 = 8 \quad x_3 = 20 \quad x_5 = 22 \quad x_7 = 10$$
$$x_2 = 10 \quad x_4 = 15 \quad x_6 = 9 \quad x_8 = 12$$

Find the values of the following statistics for that day: $X_6$, $\Sigma_{i=1}^{4} X_i$, $\Sigma_{i=1}^{8} X_i^2$, and $\Sigma_{i=1}^{8}(X_i - 1)$. Is $\Sigma_{i=1}^{8}(X_i - \mu)$ a statistic? Explain.

---

## HYPOTHESIS TESTING

**6.3** □ Recall that in a hypothesis testing problem, there is a preconceived theory concerning the population characteristic under study. This implies that there are, in fact, two theories, or hypotheses, involved in any statistical study: the hypothesis being proposed by the experimenter and the negation of this hypothesis. The former, denoted $H_1$, is called the *alternative,* or *research, hypothesis,* whereas the latter is denoted by $H_0$ and is called the *null hypothesis*. The purpose of the experiment is to decide whether the evidence tends to support or refute the null hypothesis. You should keep in mind three general statements when framing $H_0$ and $H_1$:

1. The null hypothesis is the hypothesis of "no difference." Practically speaking, this will result in the statement of equality being a part of $H_0$.

2. Make whatever is to be detected or supported the alternative hypothesis.

3. Statistical hypotheses are always framed in hopes of being able to reject $H_0$ and thereby accept $H_1$.

---

**EXAMPLE 6.3.1** □ A new drug is being developed for use in the treatment of skin cancer. It is hoped that it will be effective on a majority of those patients on whom it is used. The company developing the drug wants to get statistical evidence to support such a claim. Let $p$ denote the proportion of patients for whom the drug will be effective. Since we make whatever is to be supported or detected the alternative hypothesis, the alternative here is that $p > .5$. This automatically implies that the null hypothesis is the negation of $H_1$, namely, that $p \leq .5$. Thus the two hypotheses involved are

$$H_0: p \leq .5$$
$$H_1: p > .5$$

Note that the statement of equality appears as part of the null hypothesis. Note also that from the manufacturer's point of view, it is hoped that $H_0$ will be rejected, thus allowing the acceptance of $H_1$, the manufacturer's claim.

---

Once a sample has been selected and the data have been collected, a decision must be made. The decision will be either to reject $H_0$ or to fail to do so. The decision is made by observing the value of some statistic whose probability distribution is known under the assumption that $H_0$ is true. Such a statistic is called a *test statistic*. If the observed value of the test statistic is unusual when $H_0$ is true, we reject the null hypothesis in favor of the alternative; if the value observed is a commonly occurring one under the assumption that $H_0$ is true, then we do not reject the null hypothesis. This means that at the end of any hypothesis testing study, we will be forced into exactly one of the following situations:

**1.** We will have rejected $H_0$ when it was true; therefore we will have committed what is known as a *Type I error*.

**2.** We will have made the correct decision of rejecting $H_0$ when the alternative $H_1$ was true.

**3.** We will have failed to reject $H_0$ when the alternative $H_1$ was true; therefore we will have committed what is known as a *Type II error*.

**4.** We will have made the correct decision of failing to reject $H_0$ when $H_0$ was true.

---

**EXAMPLE 6.3.2** □ Consider the drug testing problem of Example 6.3.1. The hypothesis being tested is

$$H_0: p \leq .5$$

$$H_1: p > .5 \quad \text{(Drug is effective for majority of patients)}$$

If a Type I error is made, we will have rejected $H_0$ when $H_0$ is true. Practically speaking, we will have concluded that the drug is effective for a majority of users when it is not. This error c[illegible]d lead to the marketing of a drug which is worthless for most patients. A Type II error occurs if we fail to reject $H_0$ when $H_1$ is true. Here this amounts to concluding that the effectiveness rate of the drug is 50% or less when, in fact, it would be useful for a majority of the patients on whom it is tried. This error could lead to failure to market a useful drug. Both errors are serious. The Type I error generally would be considered more serious, since it could result in a delay in the proper treatment of the disease.

---

Note that regardless of what is done, an error is possible. Anytime $H_0$ is rejected, a Type I error might occur; anytime $H_0$ is not rejected, a Type II error might occur. There is no way to avoid this dilemma. The job of the statistician is to design methods for testing hypotheses that will keep the probabilities of making either error reasonably small. Philosophically, there are two ways to distinguish between $H_0$ and $H_1$. The first, used extensively in the past, involves a procedure in which the values of the test statistic that lead to rejection of the null hypothesis are set before the experiment is conducted. These values constitute what is called the *critical, or rejection, region* for the test. The probability of committing a Type I error is the probability that the test statistic will fall into the rejection region by chance, even though the null hypothesis is true. This probability is referred to as *alpha* ($\alpha$), *the size of the test or the level of significance of the test.* This idea is illustrated in Example 6.3.3.

---

**EXAMPLE 6.3.3** □ To test the hypotheses of Example 6.3.1 that

$$H_0\colon p \leq .5$$
$$H_1\colon p > .5$$

a random sample of 20 patients is selected and the drug is used on each. Let us design a test so that $\alpha$, the probability of rejecting $H_0$ when $H_0$ is true, will be about 5%. The test statistic that we shall use is $X$, the number of patients for whom the drug is effective. If the null hypothesis is true, then X is binomial with $n = 20, p = .5$, and $E[X] = np = 10$. Thus if $H_0$ is true, we would expect the drug to be effective on about 10 patients; if $H_1$ is true and the effectiveness rate is actually higher than .5, then we would expect to see more than 10 persons helped by the drug. Note from Table I of Appendix B that

$$\begin{aligned} P[X \geq 14 \mid p = .5] &= 1 - P[X \leq 13 \mid p = .5] \\ &= 1 - .9423 \\ &= .0577 \end{aligned}$$

Let us agree to reject $H_0$ in favor of $H_1$ if the observed value of the test statistic, $X$, is 14 or greater. Thus we have split the possible values of $X$ into two sets: $C = \{14, 15, 16, 17, 18, 19, 20\}$ and $C' = \{0, 1, 2, \ldots, 13\}$. If the observed value of $X$ lies in $C$, we reject $H_0$ and conclude that the drug is effective on a majority of patients on whom it is used. The set of values of the test statistic that leads to rejection of the null hypothesis, $C$, is the *critical, or rejection, region* for the test. We chose $C$ so that the probability that the test statistic will fall into $C$ by chance, even though $H_0$ is true, is .0577. That is, we designed the test so that the probability of committing a Type I error ($\alpha$) is approximately 5%, as desired.

---

Note that the set of possible values of the test statistic has been divided into two sets—those that lead to the rejection of $H_0$ (the rejection region) and those that do not. It is possible that the observed value of the test statistic does not fall into the rejection region even though $H_0$ is not true and should be rejected. If this occurs, a Type II error will be committed. The probability of this occurring is called *beta* ($\beta$). Beta is a little harder to handle than alpha, which can be determined by the experimenter. For a particular test, $\beta$ depends on the alternative. That is, $\beta$ can be found only if a particular value of the alternative is specified. To illustrate, let us find $\beta$ for the test designed in Example 6.3.3.

---

**EXAMPLE 6.3.4** □ The critical region for the test of Example 6.3.3 is $C = \{14, 15, 16, 17, 18, 19, 20\}$. Let us find $\beta$ for the test if the actual effectiveness rate is .7. By definition,

$$\begin{aligned}\beta &= P[\text{Type II error}]\\ &= P[\text{fail to reject } H_0 \mid H_1 \text{ is true}]\\ &= P[X \text{ is not in the critical region} \mid H_1 \text{ is true}]\\ &= P[X \le 13 \mid p = .7] = .3920 \qquad \text{(Table I)}\end{aligned}$$

That is, for the test as designed, there is a 39.2% chance that an effectiveness rate of .7 will not be detected. Beta is a function of the alternative in that if $p$ is changed from .7 to .8, then $\beta$ will change also. In this case,

$$\beta = P[X \le 13 \mid p = .8] = .0867$$

Note that as the difference between the null value of .5 and the alternative value of $p$ increases, $\beta$ decreases.

---

The method illustrated for distinguishing between $H_0$ and $H_1$ entails deciding on the level of significance ($\alpha$) before the data are gathered. That is, it involves presetting $\alpha$. There are several reasons for wanting to do this. It gives a clear-cut way of making a decision. Once $\alpha$ is set, the critical region for the test is fixed also. If the observed value of the test statistic falls in this region, we reject $H_0$; otherwise, we do not. There is no room for debate after the data are gathered. Hence there can be no charge that the statisticians are manipulating the results to suit themselves. In addition, if the consequences of making a Type I error are very serious, then by presetting $\alpha$ we are able to specify before the fact exactly how large a risk we are willing to tolerate.

The terminology introduced thus far is summarized in Figure 6.5.

The second method of choosing between the null hypothesis ($H_0$) and the research ($H_1$) hypothesis is to evaluate the test statistic and then determine the probability of observing a value of the test statistic at least as extreme as the value noted under the assumption that the null hypothesis is true. This probability is referred to by a variety of names, including the *critical level,* the *descriptive level of significance,* and the *probability, or P, value* of the test. We use the term *P value* in this text. Most writers of

| | $H_0$ True | $H_1$ True |
|---|---|---|
| Reject $H_0$ | Type I error (Probability $\alpha$) | Correct decision |
| Fail to reject $H_0$ | Correct decision | Type II error (Probability $\beta$) |

**FIGURE 6.5**

scientific literature have begun to report $P$ values as a routine part of their research results. This idea is illustrated in Example 6.3.5.

---

**EXAMPLE 6.3.5** □ It is felt that the proportion $p$ of females who have begun the adolescent growth spurt by age 11 is over 80%. To gather evidence to verify this claim, the growth of 100 girls is monitored. Based on the data gathered, we want to choose between the research hypothesis $H_1$: $p > .80$ and the null hypothesis $H_0$: $p \leq .80$. The test statistic that we use is $X$, the number of girls in the sample who have begun the growth spurt by their 11th birthday. If $H_0$ is true, then $X$ is binomial with $n = 100$, $p = .8$, $E[X] = np = 80$, and $\text{Var } X = np(1 - p) = 16$. Thus an observed value of the test statistic near or smaller than 80 tends to support $H_0$; an observed value somewhat larger than 80 lends support to the research hypothesis.

When the experiment was completed, 85 of the girls in the sample had begun the growth spurt by their 11th birthday. Is this value enough larger than 80 to cause us to reject $H_0$ in favor of $H_1$? To answer this question, we compute the probability of obtaining a value this large or larger if, in fact, $H_0$ is true. That is, we compute the $P$ value for the test. For this test,

$$P = P[X \geq 85 \mid p = .80]$$

Since $n$ is large, this binomial probability must be approximated by using the procedure of Chapter 5. That is, we approximate the binomial variable $X$ with mean 80 and variance 16, using a normal variable $Y$ with mean 80 and variance 16. Thus

$$\begin{aligned} P &= P[X \geq 85 \mid p = .80] \\ &\doteq P[Y \geq 84.5] \\ &= P\left[Z \geq \frac{84.5 - 80}{4}\right] \\ &= P[Z \geq 1.125] \\ &= 1 - P[Z \leq 1.125] = 1 - .8708 = .1292 \end{aligned}$$

This means that a value as extreme as that observed occurs about 12.92% of the time by chance, even though $H_0$ is true. Since this value is moderately large, we did not observe a result that is particularly unusual. Hence we would not reject $H_0$ based on the data obtained in this experiment.

---

**EXERCISES 6.3**

**1.** In 1969 in the United States on the average 8% of household waste was metal. Because of the increase in recycling efforts, it is hoped that this figure has been reduced. An experiment is run to verify this contention.
   **a.** Set up the appropriate null and alternative hypotheses for the experiment.
   **b.** Explain in a practical sense what has occurred if a Type I error has been committed.
   **c.** Explain in a practical sense what has occurred if a Type II error has been committed.
   **d.** Explain in a practical sense what it means to say that the test is of size .05.

**2.** The probability of making the correct decision of rejecting $H_0$ when $H_1$ is true is called the *power* of the test. Thus power $= 1 - \beta$. Where does power fit into the chart of Figure 6.5? What is the power for the test of Example 6.3.4 when $p = .7$? When $p = .8$? When $p = .9$?

**3.** In 1974, 38% of the females in the United States in the 17 to 24 years old age group, had smoked or were smokers at the time. It is feared that this figure has increased. An experiment is conducted to gain evidence to support this contention.
   **a.** Set up the appropriate null and alternative hypotheses for the experiment.
   **b.** Explain in a practical sense what has occurred if a Type I error has been committed.
   **c.** Explain in a practical sense what has occurred if a Type II error has been committed.
   **d.** The test is to be run in such a way that $\alpha = .1$. Explain in a practical sense exactly what this means.

**4.** Past studies show that the biocide DDT can accumulate in the body. In 1965 the mean concentration of DDT in the body fat of individuals in the United States was 9 ppm. It is hoped that as a result of stricter controls, this concentration has decreased.
   **a.** Set up the appropriate null and alternative hypotheses for documenting this claim.
   **b.** Explain in a practical sense the consequences of making a Type I error and a Type II error.
   **c.** The test is run so that the power for detecting a mean concentration of 6 ppm is .8. Explain in a practical sense what this means.

**5.** The mean level of background radiation in the United States is .3 rem per year. It is feared that as a result of the increased use of radioactive materials, this figure has increased.
   **a.** Set up the appropriate null and alternative hypotheses to document this claim.
   **b.** Explain in a practical sense the consequences of making a Type I error and a Type II error.

c. When the test is conducted, the $P$ value obtained is .01. Explain exactly what this means.

d. With a $P$ value of .01, would you be willing to reject $H_0$ in favor of $H_1$? Explain.

**6.** Set up the null and alternative hypotheses for the experiments of Examples 6.1.3 and 6.1.5.

**7.** A public health official feels that more than 70% of the children under age 3 who are treated at a certain clinic get less than the recommended daily allowance of vitamin A. To substantiate this claim, he will take a random sample of 15 children and determine the average vitamin A dosage for each. The test statistic is $X$, the number receiving less than the recommended daily average of .6 mg. The hypothesis being tested is

$$H_0: p \leq .7$$
$$H_1: p > .7$$

where $p$ is the proportion receiving less than the recommended daily average.

**a.** If $H_0$ is true, how many children would be expected to have a vitamin A deficiency?

**b.** The critical region chosen for the test is $\{13, 14, 15\}$. Find $\alpha$.

**c.** Find $\beta$ if, in fact, $p = .8$.

**d.** Find the power of the test for $p = .8$.

**e.** If when the test is run 12 children appear to be receiving less than the daily minimum, will $H_0$ be rejected? What type of error might be committed?

**8.** A new method for grafting oranges has been devised. It is felt that the proportion of grafts that fail to take, $p$, will be reduced from the current rate of .2. To verify this claim, the new method is used on 20 randomly selected trees, and the number of grafts which fail to take, $X$, is the test statistic.

**a.** Set up the appropriate null and alternative hypotheses for running the test.

**b.** If $H_0$ is true, how many failures would you expect to see?

**c.** The critical region selected for the test is $\{0, 1\}$. What is the value of $\alpha$ for this test?

**d.** What is the value of $\beta$ if, in fact, $p = .1$? What is the power for $p = .1$?

**e.** When the test was run, there were no failures. What practical conclusion should be drawn? What type of error might be made?

**9.** A chemical spill occurred in the Xavier River, and wildlife biologists are concerned about toxic accumulation of the chemical in tissues of fish downstream. Previous measurements have shown that only 15% of the fish contain more than 1.5 mg of the chemical per kilogram of body weight. A sample of 100 fish is to be collected following the spill. The statistic to be used to detect the effects of the spill is $X$, the number of fish that exceed the 1.5-mg limit.

**a.** Set up the appropriate null and alternative hypotheses for detecting a situation in which the proportion $p$ of fish that exceeds the accepted limit of 1.5 mg per kilogram of body weight has become larger than 15%.

**b.** If $H_0$ is true, how many of the 100 fish sampled would you expect to exceed the limit?

**c.** If the observed value of $X$ is too large to have occurred by chance, $H_0$ should be rejected. Suppose that of 100 fish examined, 20 are found to exceed the 1.5-mg level. Should $H_0$ be rejected? Explain by computing the $P$ value of the test.

**10.** A new surgical procedure is to be tested. The current procedure is effective with 50% of the patients on whom it is tried. If the new procedure can be shown to be 60% effective, then it will be put into widespread use. Thus we want to test

$$\text{H}_0\text{: } p = .5$$
$$\text{H}_1\text{: } p = .6$$

The test statistic is $X$, the number of patients for whom the new procedure is effective. Thus if $\text{H}_0$ is true, $X$ is binomial with parameters $n$ and $p = .5$, $E[X] = n(.5)$, and Var $X = n(.5)(.5)$; if $\text{H}_1$ is true, $X$ is binomial with parameters $n$ and $p = .6$, $E[X] = n(.6)$, and Var $X = n(.6)(.4)$.

**a.** For a sample of size 10, we reject $\text{H}_0$ if and only if $X$ is in the set $\{8, 9, 10\}$. That is, the critical region is $\{8, 9, 10\}$. Find $\alpha$ for this test. Find the power of the test. That is, find the probability that $X = 8$, $X = 9$, or $X = 10$ if $p = .6$. With a sample this small, is there a good chance of being able to detect an effectiveness rate of .6 while maintaining an $\alpha$ level of approximately .05?

**b.** For a sample of size 15, we use a critical region of $\{11, 12, 13, 14, 15\}$. What is the value of $\alpha$ for this test? What is the power if $p = .6$? Is this sample large enough to expect to detect a $p$ of .6 while maintaining an $\alpha$ level of approximately .05?

**c.** If $n$ is increased to 20, what critical region should be chosen to obtain an $\alpha$ level of approximately .05? What is the power for this test if $p = .6$?

**d.** It should be clear that to distinguish between $p = .5$ and $p = .6$ with $\alpha \doteq .05$, we must use a sample larger than 20. Use the normal approximation to the binomial distribution to show that for a sample of size 100, $P[X \geq 59] \doteq .05$. Show that when $p = .6$, the power for this test is over .50. That is, find $P[X \geq 59]$ if $X$ is binomial with $n = 100$ and $p = .6$.

# INFERENCES ON A SINGLE PARAMETER

# 7.

Chapter 6 was intended as only an introduction to the basic ideas and terminology underlying the two major areas of statistical inference, estimation and hypothesis testing. In this chapter we consider specific methods used to make inferences about a single population based on a random sample drawn from that population. In particular, we discuss inferences concerning $\mu$, $\sigma^2$, and $\sigma$.

## INFERENCES ON $\mu$ WHEN $\sigma^2$ IS KNOWN

**7.1** □ We consider first the problem of point estimation of the mean of a population. Example 7.1.1 indicates a logical method for solving this problem.

---

**EXAMPLE 7.1.1** □ Researchers at the Environmental Protection Agency (EPA) are interested in air quality. One indicator of air quality is the mean number of micrograms of particulates per cubic meter of air. That is, interest centers on $\mu_X$, where $X$ is the number of micrograms of particulates per cubic meter of air. To monitor the situation, a reading is taken every 6 days by drawing a cubic meter of air through a filter and determining the number of micrograms of particulates trapped. Over a 30-day period, a random sample $X_1, X_2, X_3, X_4, X_5$ of size 5 is generated. Assume that the observed values of these variables for a given 30-day period are

$$x_1 = 58 \quad x_3 = 57 \quad x_5 = 59$$
$$x_2 = 70 \quad x_4 = 61$$

How can these observations be used to estimate $\mu_X$? Recall that $\mu_X = E[X]$ is the long-run theoretical *average* value of $X$. Common sense points to the sample average as a logical estimate for this theoretical population average. That is, intuitively, we would use the arithmetic average of the sample values to approximate $\mu_X$. In this case,

$$\widehat{\mu}_X = \frac{x_1 + x_2 + x_3 + x_4 + x_5}{5} = 61$$

---

Example 7.1.1 suggests the following statistic as a logical estimator for the mean of any population.

**Definition 7.1.1** *Sample Mean.* Let $X_1, X_2, X_3, \ldots, X_n$ be a random sample of size $n$ from a distribution with mean $\mu$. The statistic

$$\bar{X} = \frac{\sum_{i=1}^{n} X_i}{n}$$

is called the *sample mean.*

Note that $\mu_X$ and $\bar{X}$ are *not* the same: the parameter $\mu_X$ is the theoretical mean of the population, and the statistic $\bar{X}$ is the mean of a sample drawn from that population. In other words, $\bar{X}$ is an *estimator* for $\mu_X$. How good an estimator is it? Before this question can be answered, we must decide what properties are desirable in a point estimator. Obviously, we want the estimator to generate estimates that can be expected to be close in value to the parameter $\theta$ being estimated. This can be expected to occur if the estimator $\widehat{\theta}$ possesses two properties. In particular, we would like

1. $\widehat{\theta}$ to be *unbiased* for $\theta$
2. $\widehat{\theta}$ to have small variance for large sample sizes

The word *unbiased* is a technical term whose definition is given here.

**Definition 7.1.2** *Unbiased.* An estimator $\widehat{\theta}$ is an *unbiased* estimator for a parameter $\theta$ if and only if $E[\widehat{\theta}] = \theta$.

Recall that $\widehat{\theta}$ is a statistic; therefore, it is also a random variable and, as such, has a mean, or an expected, value. To say that $\widehat{\theta}$ is unbiased for $\theta$ implies that the mean of the estimator $\widehat{\theta}$ is equal to the parameter $\theta$ that $\widehat{\theta}$ is estimating. Thus an estimator $\widehat{\mu}$ is an unbiased estimator for $\mu$ if and only if $E[\widehat{\mu}] = \mu$; an estimator $\widehat{\sigma}^2$ is unbiased for $\sigma^2$ if and only if $E[\widehat{\sigma}^2] = \sigma^2$; an estimator $\widehat{\sigma}$ for a standard deviation is unbiased for $\sigma$ if and only if $E[\widehat{\sigma}] = \sigma$.

Theorem 7.1.1 shows that not only is the sample mean $\bar{X}$ a logical estimator for the population mean $\mu$, but also it is unbiased for $\mu$.

**THEOREM 7.1.1.** □ Let $\bar{X}$ be the sample mean based on a random sample of size $n$ from a distribution with mean $\mu$. Then $E[\bar{X}] = \mu$.

It is important to realize that since $\hat{\theta}$ is a statistic, in repeated sampling the estimates generated will vary from sample to sample. To say that $\hat{\theta}$ is unbiased for $\theta$ implies that these estimates vary about $\theta$; it also implies that the *average* value of these estimates can be expected to lie reasonably close to $\theta$. For example, since $\bar{X}$ is unbiased for $\mu$, for $k$ repetitions of an experiment the observed sample means $\bar{x}_1, \bar{x}_2, \ldots, \bar{x}_k$ will vary about $\mu$ and the *average* value of these $k$ estimates should lie reasonably close to $\mu$. (See Figure 7.1.)

It is equally important to understand what the term *unbiased* does *not* imply. It does not imply that any *one* estimate will be close in value to the parameter being estimated. In reference to Example 7.1.1, the estimated mean particulate reading was $\hat{\mu} = \bar{x} = 61$ micrograms per cubic meter of air. This estimate is unbiased in the sense that it was generated by means of the unbiased estimator $\bar{X}$. This alone does not guarantee that the actual mean particulate level is anywhere close to 61 micrograms per cubic meter of air. This is unfortunate. Usually, statistical studies are not repeated over and over, so that estimates obtained can be averaged. Usually only one sample is drawn; one estimate is obtained. To have some assurance that this estimate is close in value to $\theta$, the parameter being estimated, ideally the estimator used not only should be unbiased, but also should have small variance for large sample sizes. In this way, even though the estimator fluctuates about $\theta$, the variability is small. Each estimate produced can be expected to be fairly close in value to $\theta$.

Note that the properties of being unbiased with small variance are desirable, but not essential. Later we see examples of acceptable estimators for which one or both properties fail.

Theorem 7.1.2 shows that the sample mean $\bar{X}$ has small variance for large sample sizes. Thus, it is not only logical but also mathematically desirable as an estimator for $\mu$.

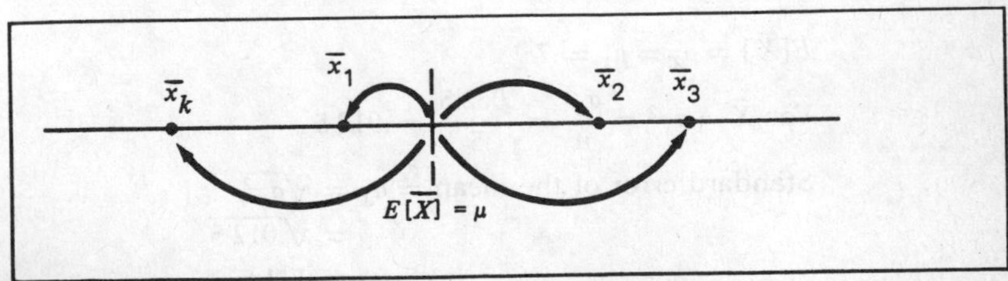


**FIGURE 7.1** $\bar{X}$ varies about $\mu$.

**THEOREM 7.1.2** □ Let $\bar{X}$ be the sample mean based on a random sample of size $n$ from a distribution with mean $\mu$ and variance $\sigma^2$. Then

$$\operatorname{Var} \bar{X} = \sigma_{\bar{X}}^2 = \frac{\sigma^2}{n}$$

Note that since $\sigma^2$ is constant, as the sample size $n$ increases the variance of $\bar{X}$, $\sigma^2/n$, decreases and can be made as small as we wish by choosing *n sufficiently large*. This implies that a sample mean based on a large sample can be expected to lie reasonably close to $\mu$; one based on a small sample may vary widely from the actual population mean. This points out again the advantages of working with a large sample and the danger of placing too much emphasis on conclusions drawn from small samples. Keep in mind that many of the examples and exercises presented in this text are based on small samples. This is done for illustrative purposes only. It is *not* meant to imply that samples this small are acceptable in research.

Note also that since the standard deviation of any random variable is defined to be the nonnegative square root of the variance, the standard deviation of $\bar{X}$ is given by

$$\begin{aligned} \sigma_{\bar{X}} = \sqrt{\sigma_{\bar{X}}^2} &= \sqrt{\operatorname{Var} \bar{X}} \\ &= \sqrt{\frac{\sigma^2}{n}} \\ &= \frac{\sigma}{\sqrt{n}} \end{aligned}$$

The standard deviation of $\bar{X}$ is sometimes referred to as the *standard error* of the mean.

---

**EXAMPLE 7.1.2** □ One of the variables considered in blood tests is $X$, the number of milligrams of billirubin per deciliter of blood. Empirical studies have shown that in a healthy adult $X$ is normally distributed with mean .7 and variance .062 5. During a 2-day period, five blood samples are to be analyzed for a given patient, thus giving rise to a random sample $X_1$, $X_2$, $X_3$, $X_4$, $X_5$ of size 5 from the distribution of $X$. Based on a sample of this size,

$$E[\bar{X}] = \mu_{\bar{X}} = \mu_X = .7$$

$$\operatorname{Var} \bar{X} = \sigma_{\bar{X}}^2 = \frac{\sigma_X^2}{n} = \frac{.062\,5}{5} = .012\,5$$

$$\begin{aligned} \text{Standard error of the mean} = \sigma_{\bar{X}} = \sqrt{\sigma_{\bar{X}}^2} &\\ = \sqrt{.012\,5} &\\ = .111\,8 & \end{aligned}$$

---

Now we are able to find a point estimate for the mean of any population. The problem is that the estimate obtained cannot be expected to be absolutely accurate. To get an idea of not only the numerical value of $\mu$ but also the accuracy of the estimate, we turn to the method of confidence interval estimation. This topic is introduced in Section 6.2. Recall that a confidence interval is a random interval, an interval of the form $(L_1, L_2)$ in which $L_1$ and $L_2$ are each statistics. It is hoped that when these statistics are evaluated for a particular sample, the numerical interval obtained will contain the population parameter of interest. To determine the form of the statistics $L_1$ and $L_2$ for estimating $\mu$, the definition of the term *confidence interval* must be formalized.

**Definition 7.1.3** *Confidence Interval.* A $100(1 - \alpha)\%$ confidence interval on a parameter $\theta$ is a random interval $(L_1, L_2)$ such that

$$P[L_1 \le \theta \le L_2] \doteq 1 - \alpha$$

regardless of the value of $\theta$.

The following general statement will guide in the construction of the confidence intervals presented in this text:

> To construct a $100(1 - \alpha)\%$ confidence interval on a parameter $\theta$, we shall find a random variable whose expression involves $\theta$ and whose probability distribution is known at least approximately.

Relative to the problem at hand, this means that a random variable should be found whose expression involves $\mu$ and whose distribution is known. The desired variable can be found by first considering the distribution of the sample mean. Theorem 7.1.3, offered without proof, shows that if the variable $X$ under study is itself normally distributed, then the sample mean $\bar{X}$ based on a random sample of size $n$ from the distribution of $X$ is normally distributed also.

**THEOREM 7.1.3** □ Let $X_1, X_2, \ldots, X_n$ be a random sample of size $n$ from a distribution that is normal with mean $\mu$ and variance $\sigma^2$. Then $\bar{X}$ is normal with mean $\mu$ and variance $\sigma^2/n$. Furthermore, the random variable

$$\frac{\bar{X} - \mu}{\sigma/\sqrt{n}}$$

is *standard normal.*

Note that the random variable $(\bar{X} - \mu)/(\sigma/\sqrt{n})$ involves the parameter $\mu$, and its distribution is known to be standard normal. This variable can be used to determine the general formula for a $100(1 - \alpha)\%$ confidence interval on $\mu$. We illustrate the method by considering first the construction of a 95% confidence interval. The technique used can be generalized easily to obtain any desired degree of confidence.

---

**EXAMPLE 7.1.3** □ Let us find a 95% confidence interval on $\mu$, the mean number of micrograms of particulate per cubic meter of air, based on the random sample of size 5 given in Example 7.1.1. From Example 7.1.1 it is known that an unbiased point estimate for $\mu$ is $\bar{x} = 61$. Assume that from past experience $X$, the number of micrograms of particulate per cubic meter of air, is known to be normally distributed with variance $\sigma^2 = 9$. We want to extend the point estimate to an interval of real numbers in such a way that we can be 95% confident that the interval obtained contains the true value of $\mu$. That is, we want to determine $L_1$ and $L_2$ so that $P[L_1 \leq \mu \leq L_2] = .95$. (See Figure 7.2.)

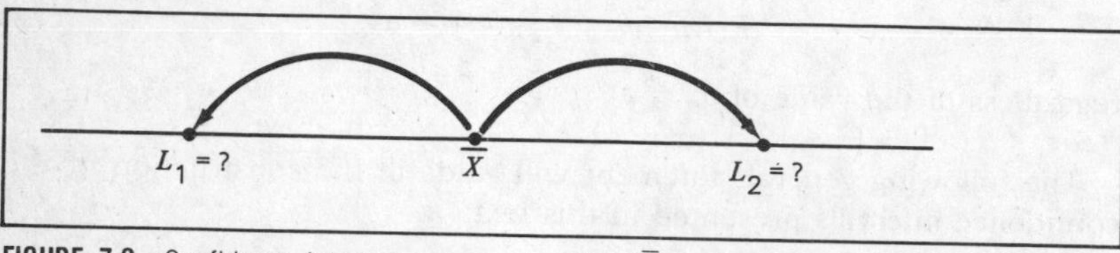


FIGURE 7.2 Confidence interval on $\mu$ centered at $\bar{X}$.

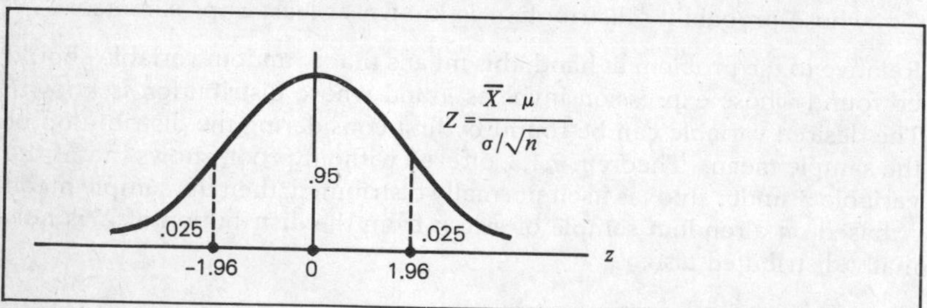


FIGURE 7.3 Partition of $Z$ to obtain a 95% confidence interval on $\mu$.

To do so, consider the partition of the standard normal curve shown in Figure 7.3. It can be seen that

$$P[-1.96 \leq Z \leq 1.96] = .95$$

In this case, $Z = (\bar{X} - \mu)/(\sigma/\sqrt{n})$, and hence we may conclude that

$$P\left[-1.96 \leq \frac{\bar{X} - \mu}{\sigma/\sqrt{n}} \leq 1.96\right] = .95$$

To find the endpoints for a 95% confidence interval on $\mu$, we algebraically isolate $\mu$ in the center of the preceding inequality:

$$P\left[-1.96 \le \frac{\bar{X} - \mu}{\sigma/\sqrt{n}} \le 1.96\right] = .95$$

$$P\left[\frac{-1.96\sigma}{\sqrt{n}} \le \bar{X} - \mu \le \frac{1.96\sigma}{\sqrt{n}}\right] = .95$$

$$P\left[-\bar{X} - \frac{1.96\sigma}{\sqrt{n}} \le -\mu \le -\bar{X} + \frac{1.96\sigma}{\sqrt{n}}\right] = .95$$

$$P\left[\bar{X} + \frac{1.96\sigma}{\sqrt{n}} \ge \mu \ge \bar{X} - \frac{1.96\sigma}{\sqrt{n}}\right] = .95$$

$$P\left[\bar{X} - \frac{1.96\sigma}{\sqrt{n}} \le \mu \le \bar{X} + \frac{1.96\sigma}{\sqrt{n}}\right] = .95$$

From this we see that the lower and upper bounds for the 95% confidence interval are

$$L_1 = \bar{X} - \frac{1.96\sigma}{\sqrt{n}} \qquad L_2 = \bar{X} + \frac{1.96\sigma}{\sqrt{n}}$$

Since it is assumed that $\sigma^2$ is known to be 9, $L_1$ and $L_2$ are statistics. Their observed values for the sample at hand are

$$\bar{x} - 1.96\frac{3}{\sqrt{5}} = 61 - 2.63 = 58.37$$

$$\bar{x} + 1.96\frac{3}{\sqrt{5}} = 61 + 2.63 = 63.63$$

(See Figure 7.4.) Since this interval was generated by using a procedure that, in repeated sampling, will trap the mean 95% of the time, we can be 95% confident that $\mu$ actually lies between 58.37 and 63.63.

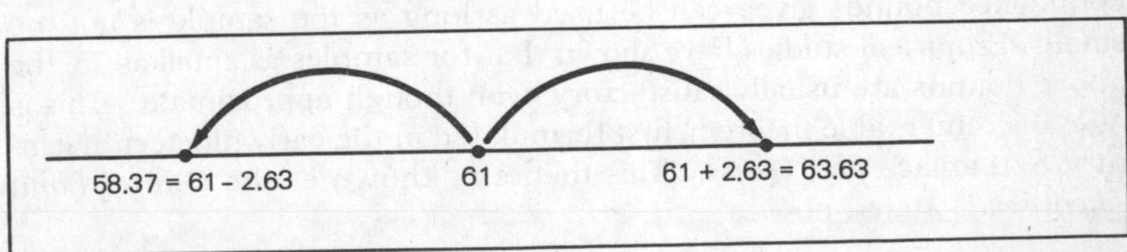


**FIGURE 7.4** The 95% confidence interval on $\mu$.

To generalize this procedure to obtain any desired degree of confidence, one notational convention must be made. We let $z_r$ denote the point such that the area to the *right* of $z_r$ is $r$. For instance, in Example 7.1.3 the number 1.96 has 2.5% of the area under the normal curve lying to its right. Hence we denote 1.96 by $z_{.025}$. The point $-1.96$ can be denoted by $z_{.975}$, or, because of the symmetry of the normal curve, by $-z_{.025}$.

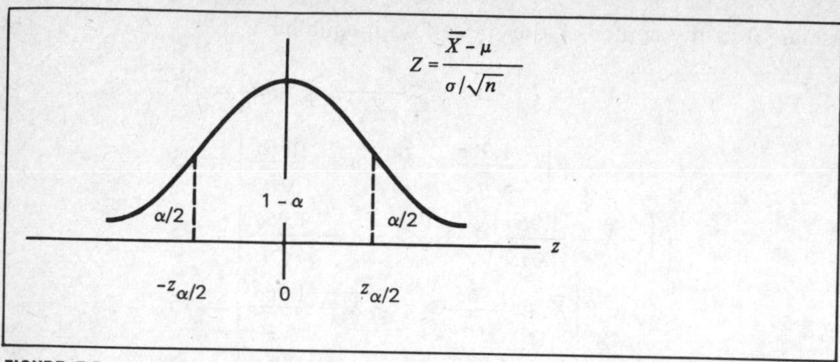


**FIGURE 7.5** Partition of $Z$ to obtain a $100(1 - \alpha)\%$ confidence interval on $\mu$.

To obtain the general formula for a $100(1 - \alpha)\%$ confidence interval on the mean of a normal population whose variance is known, we need only partition the standard normal curve as shown in Figure 7.5. The algebraic argument of Example 7.1.3 goes through exactly as outlined with $z_{.025} = 1.96$ being replaced by $z_{\alpha/2}$, the value 3 being replaced by $\sigma$, and 5 being replaced by $n$. These changes result in Theorem 7.1.4.

**THEOREM 7.1.4** □ $100(1 - \alpha)\%$ *Confidence Interval on $\mu$ When $\sigma^2$ Is Known.* Let $X_1, X_2, \ldots, X_n$ be a random sample of size $n$ from a normal distribution with mean $\mu$ and variance $\sigma^2$. Then a $100(1 - \alpha)\%$ confidence interval on $\mu$ is given by

$$\bar{X} \pm z_{\alpha/2} \frac{\sigma}{\sqrt{n}}$$

There is one further point to be made. Theorem 7.1.4 does require that the base variable $X$ be normal. If this condition is not satisfied, then the confidence bounds given can be used as long as the sample is not too small. Empirical studies have shown that for samples as small as 25, the above bounds are usually satisfactory even though approximate. This is due to a remarkable theorem, first formulated in the early nineteenth century by Laplace and Gauss. This theorem, known as the *Central Limit Theorem,* is stated now.

**THEOREM 7.1.5** □ *Central Limit Theorem.* Let $X_1, X_2, \ldots, X_n$ be a random sample of size $n$ from a distribution with mean $\mu$ and variance $\sigma^2$. Then for large $n$, $\bar{X}$ is approximately normal with mean $\mu$ and variance $\sigma^2/n$. Furthermore, for large $n$, the random variable $(\bar{X} - \mu)/(\sigma/\sqrt{n})$ is approximately standard normal.

Thus, even if $X$ is not normally distributed, we can apply the Central Limit Theorem to justify the use of Theorem 7.1.4.

**EXAMPLE 7.1.4** □ Certain mineral elements required by plants are classed as macronutrients. Macronutrients are measured in terms of their percentage of the dry weight of the plant. Proportions of each element vary in different species and in the same species grown under various conditions. One macronutrient is sulfur. Assume that it is known from past experience that $X$, the percentage of sulfur per plant by dry weight in the mustard family, is normally distributed with standard deviation .25. A study of winter cress, a member of the mustard family, revealed the following observations on $X$ based on a random sample of size 9:

$$
\begin{array}{lll}
x_1 = .7 & x_4 = .65 & x_7 = .9 \\
x_2 = .8 & x_5 = .95 & x_8 = .2 \\
x_3 = .6 & x_6 = 1.0 & x_9 = .55
\end{array}
$$

Based on this information, an unbiased estimate for $\mu$, the mean percentage of sulfur by dry weight in winter cress, is

$$\hat{\mu} = \bar{x} = \sum_{i=1}^{9} \frac{x_i}{9} = \frac{6.35}{9} = .706$$

To extend this point estimate to a 90% confidence interval on $\mu$, consider the partition of the standard normal curve of Figure 7.6. By Theorem 7.1.4, the bounds for a 90% confidence interval on $\mu$ are

$$\bar{X} \pm \frac{z_{.05}\sigma}{\sqrt{n}}$$

In this case, the numerical bounds are

$$.706 \pm 1.645 \frac{.25}{\sqrt{9}}$$

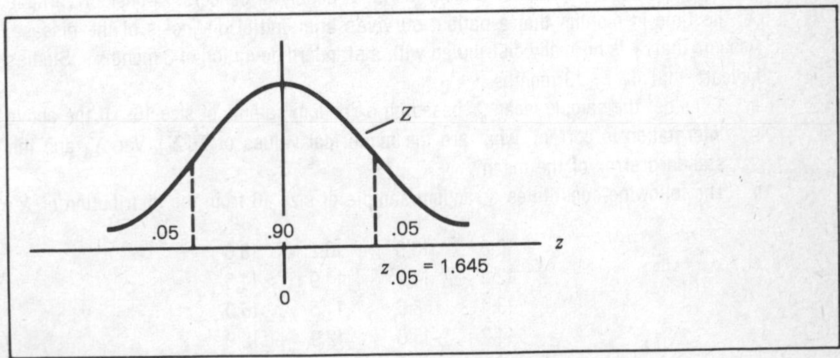


**FIGURE 7.6** Partition of $Z$ to obtain a 90% confidence interval on $\mu$.

or .706 ± .137. Thus we can report that we are 90% confident that the mean percentage of sulfur by dry weight in winter cress lies between .569 and .843.

---

## EXERCISES 7.1

1. A random sample of size 9 yielded the following observations on random variable $X$, the coal consumption in millions of tons by electric utilities:

| | | | | |
|---|---|---|---|---|
| 406 | 395 | 400 | 450 | 390 |
| 410 | 415 | 401 | 408 | |

Find a point estimate for $\mu_X$, the mean coal consumption of electric utilities.

2. Most species of conifers have both pollen cones and seed cones. Pollen released by the male cone is carried by the wind to the female cone where the eggs are fertilized. Consider variable $X$, the elapsed time between pollination and fertilization. Assume that for pines $X$ is normally distributed with a mean of 6 months and a standard deviation of 2 months.
   **a.** Consider the statistic $\bar{X}$ based on a random sample of 25 female cones. What is $E[\bar{X}]$? Var $\bar{X}$? $\sigma_{\bar{X}}$? What type of variable is $\bar{X}$?
   **b.** The following represents a random sample of size 25 from the distribution of $X$:

| | | | | |
|---|---|---|---|---|
| 7.2 | 5.9 | 8.7 | 5.8 | 5.5 |
| 6.3 | 6.5 | 3.4 | 6.9 | 8.2 |
| 7.5 | 10.3 | 3.5 | 7.1 | 8.7 |
| 4.2 | 7.5 | 7.8 | 6.3 | 6.3 |
| 4.7 | 9.0 | 5.5 | 6.7 | 5.7 |

   Use these values to estimate $\mu_X$. Find a 90% confidence interval on $\mu_X$. Does the confidence interval tend to refute the assumed mean of 6 months? Explain.

3. Acute myeloblastic leukemia is among the most deadly of cancers. Consider variable $X$, the time in months that a patient survives after initial diagnosis of the disease. Assume that $X$ is normally distributed with a standard deviation of 3 months. Studies indicate that $\mu_X = 13$ months.
   **a.** Consider the sample mean $\bar{X}$ based on a random sample of size 16. If the above information is correct, what are the numerical values of $E[\bar{X}]$, Var $\bar{X}$, and the standard error of the mean?
   **b.** The following constitutes a random sample of size 16 from the distribution of $X$:

| | | | |
|---|---|---|---|
| 10.8 | 13.6 | 13.2 | 13.6 |
| 12.5 | 14.2 | 14.9 | 14.5 |
| 13.4 | 8.6 | 11.5 | 16.0 |
| 14.2 | 15.0 | 12.9 | 12.9 |

   Use this information to find a point estimate for $\mu_X$. Find a 99% confidence interval on $\mu_X$. Does this confidence interval tend to support or refute the quoted mean survival time of 13 months? Explain.

4. Consider the data of Example 7.1.4. Use these data to find a 95% confidence interval on $\mu$ and a 99% confidence interval on $\mu$. Compare the three intervals that are now available. Can you suggest a general relationship between the length of a confidence interval and the confidence that can be placed in the interval?
5. An important population in the ocean is the zooplankton. This consists of all animals carried passively in moving water. A sample haul near the Isle of Man yielded the following observations on variable $X$, the number of zooplankton per cubic meter of water:

| | | | |
|---|---|---|---|
| 5000 | 5700 | 4450 | 4250 |
| 4500 | 4825 | 4025 | |
| 3700 | 4900 | 3750 | |

Assuming that $X$ is normally distributed with a variance of 90,000, find a 96% confidence interval on $\mu_X$, the mean number of zooplankton per cubic meter of water. Prior to the experiment, a researcher had posed 4200 as the value of the parameter $\mu_X$. Does the confidence interval tend to refute this value? Explain.

## *T* DISTRIBUTION

**7.2** □ Note that to obtain a point estimate for a population mean $\mu$, it is not necessary to know the population variance; the sample mean $\bar{X}$ provides an unbiased estimate for $\mu$ regardless of the value of $\sigma^2$. However, the bounds for a $100(1 - \alpha)\%$ confidence interval on $\mu$ given in Section 7.1 are $\bar{X} \pm z_{\alpha/2}\sigma/\sqrt{n}$. It is assumed that, even though the population mean is unknown, the population variance is known. Practically speaking, this assumption is unrealistic. In most instances, when a statistical study is being conducted, it is being done for the first time; there is no way to know prior to the study either the mean or the variance of the population of interest. We consider in this section the more realistic problem of making inferences on a population mean when the population variance is assumed to be *unknown.*

To derive a general formula for a $100(1 - \alpha)\%$ confidence interval on $\mu$ under these circumstances, it is natural to begin by considering the random variable used earlier, namely,

$$\frac{\bar{X} - \mu}{\sigma/\sqrt{n}}$$

Now there are two problems to overcome:

1. The value of $\sigma$ is not known and must be estimated.
2. The distribution of the variable obtained by replacing $\sigma$ by an estimator is not known.

The first problem is easy to overcome. Recall that the population variance is given by

$$\sigma^2 = E[(X - \mu)^2]$$

We want to estimate this theoretical *average* value based on a random sample $X_1, X_2, X_3, \ldots, X_n$ of size $n$. We do not know the value of $\mu$, but we do have available an unbiased estimator for $\mu$, namely $\bar{X}$. We cannot observe the difference $(X - \mu)^2$ for all $X$, but we can observe the difference $(X_i - \bar{X})^2$ for each element $X_i$ of the random sample. Since $\sigma^2$ is a theoretical average value, it is natural to approximate this parameter by an arithmetic average of sample values. Thus the natural estimator for $\sigma^2$ is

$$\widehat{\sigma}^2 = \sum_{i=1}^{n} \frac{(\bar{X}_i - \bar{X})^2}{n}$$

This estimator is acceptable and is often used to estimate $\sigma^2$. In fact, many electronic calculators with built-in statistical capability utilize this formula to compute the variance of a sample. However, it is not an unbiased estimator for $\sigma^2$. To obtain this property, we divide not by $n$, but by $n - 1$. The resulting estimator is called the sample variance and is defined formally now. Except where specifically indicated otherwise, we estimate $\sigma^2$ by means of this unbiased estimator.

**Definition 7.2.1** *Sample Variance and Sample Standard Deviation.* Let $X_1, X_2, X_3, \ldots, X_n$ be a random sample of size $n$ from a distribution with variance $\sigma^2$. Then the statistic

$$S^2 = \sum_{i=1}^{n} \frac{(X_i - \bar{X})^2}{n - 1}$$

is called the *sample variance.* Furthermore, the statistic $S = \sqrt{S^2}$ is called the *sample standard deviation.*

It should be pointed out that even though $S^2$ is an unbiased estimator for $\sigma^2$, $S$ is not unbiased for $\sigma$. A proof of this is outlined in Exercise 7.2.9.

Recall that when we computed the value of $\sigma^2$ in Chapter 4, the actual definition of the term *variance* was seldom used; a computational formula was developed that was arithmetically easier to handle than the definition. The same is true here. When $S^2$ is computed from a sample, Definition 7.2.1 is not used. Rather, we use the computational formula of Theorem 7.2.1.

**THEOREM 7.2.1** □ *Computational Formula for $S^2$.* Let $X_1, X_2, X_3, \ldots, X_n$ be a random sample of size $n$. The sample variance is given by

$$S^2 = \frac{n \sum_{i=1}^{n} X_i^2 - \left(\sum_{i=1}^{n} X_i\right)^2}{n(n - 1)}$$

---

**EXAMPLE 7.2.1** □ In studying blood coagulation, variable $X$, the partial thromboplastin time in seconds, is used. The following values represent a random sample of 10 observations on $X$ for a given patient:

| | | | | |
|---|---|---|---|---|
| 45 | 40 | 47 | 46 | 42 |
| 50 | 47 | 48 | 49 | 49 |

For these data, an unbiased estimate for the mean partial thromboplastin time is $\hat{\mu} = \bar{x} = 46.3$ seconds. To estimate $\sigma^2$, two quantities, $\Sigma x$ and $\Sigma x^2$, must be found. For these data,

$$\Sigma x = 45 + 50 + 40 + \cdots + 49 = 463$$
$$\Sigma x^2 = 45^2 + 50^2 + 40^2 + \cdots + 49^2 = 21{,}529$$

An unbiased estimate for $\sigma^2$ is given by

$$\widehat{\sigma^2} = s^2 = \frac{n\Sigma x^2 - (\Sigma x)^2}{n(n-1)}$$
$$= \frac{10(21{,}529) - 463^2}{10(9)}$$
$$= 10.23$$

An estimate for $\sigma$ is given by

$$\hat{\sigma} = s = \sqrt{s^2} = \sqrt{10.23} = 3.19 \text{ seconds}$$

---

Consider again the random variable $(\bar{X} - \mu)/(\sigma/\sqrt{n})$, which is at least approximately standard normal. Replace the population standard deviation $\sigma$, now assumed to be unknown, by its estimator $S$ to obtain the random variable $(\bar{X} - \mu)/(S/\sqrt{n})$. To use this random variable to derive a general formula for a $100(1 - \alpha)\%$ confidence interval on $\mu$ when $\sigma^2$ is unknown, one question must be answered: What is the distribution of this variable? It can be shown that the distribution is no longer standard normal. In fact, if the base variable $X$ is normal, then the random variable $(\bar{X} - \mu)/(S/\sqrt{n})$ follows what is called a *student's T,* or simply a *T, distribution* with $n - 1$ degrees of freedom. We pause briefly to consider the general characteristics of a $T$ random variable:

**1.** There are infinitely many $T$ random variables, each identified by one parameter $\gamma$, called *degrees of freedom.* Parameter $\gamma$ is always a positive integer. The notation $T_\gamma$ denotes a $T$ random variable with $\gamma$ degrees of freedom.

**2.** Each $T$ random variable is continuous.

**3.** The graph of the density of each $T$ random variable is a symmetric bell-shaped curve centered at zero.

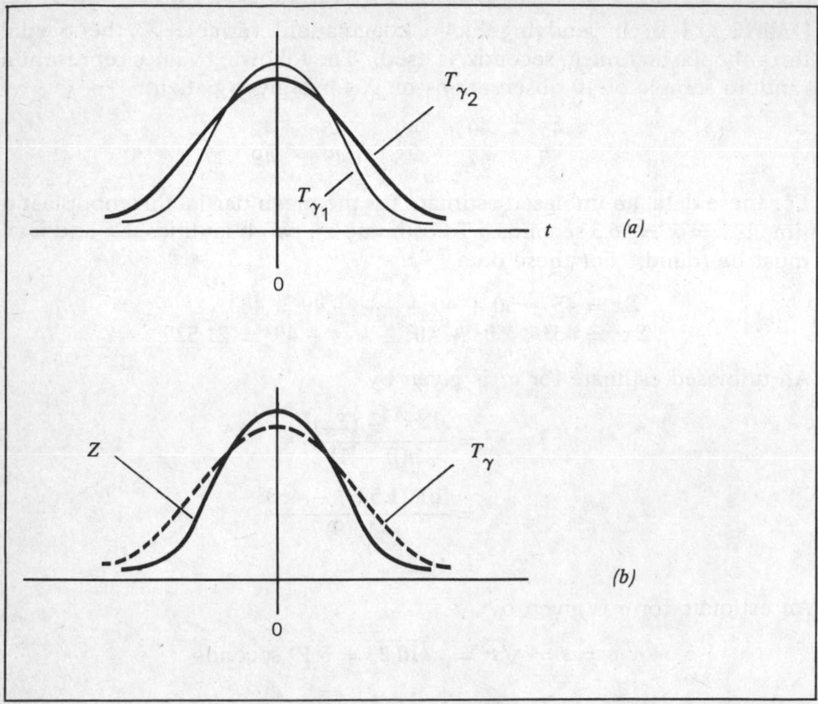


**FIGURE 7.7** (*a*) Typical relationship between two $T$ curves with $\gamma_1 > \gamma_2$, (*b*) typical relationship between a $T$ curve and the standard normal curve.

**4.** Gamma is a shape parameter in the sense that as $\gamma$ increases, the variance of the $T_\gamma$ random variable decreases. Thus, the larger the number of degrees of freedom, the more compact the bell curve associated with the variable becomes.

**5.** As the number of degrees of freedom increases, the $T$ curve approaches the standard normal curve. (See Figure 7.7.)

A partial summary of the cumulative distribution function $F$ for selected $T$ variables is given in Table V of Appendix B. Table V is constructed so that the degrees of freedom are listed as row headings, pertinent probabilities are listed as column headings, and the points associated with those probabilities are listed in the body of the table. We use our previous convention of denoting by $t_r$ the point on the $T_\gamma$ curve such that the area to the right of the point is $r$. Note that technically speaking we should perhaps write $t_{r,\gamma}$ to indicate both the area to the right of the point and the number of degrees of freedom. However, in applications the number of degrees of freedom will be clear from the context of the problem. Thus the double subscript is unnecessary.

---

**EXAMPLE 7.2.2** □ Consider the random variable $T_{10}$.

**a.** From Table V of Appendix B, $P[T_{10} \leq 1.372] = F(1.372) = .90$. (See Figure 7.8.)

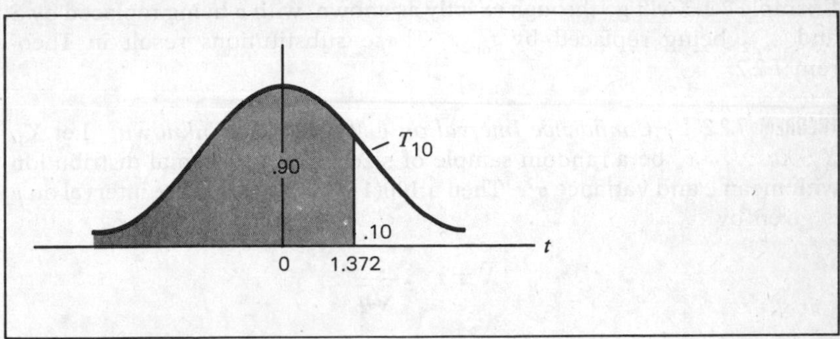


**FIGURE 7.8** $P[T_{10} \leq 1.372] = .90$.

**b.** By using the standard notational convention, $t_{.10} = 1.372$.

**c.** Because of the symmetry of the $T$ distribution, $t_{.90} = -t_{.10} = -1.372$.

**d.** The point $t$ such that $P[-t \leq T_{10} \leq t] = .95$ is $t_{.025} = 2.228$. (See Figure 7.9.)

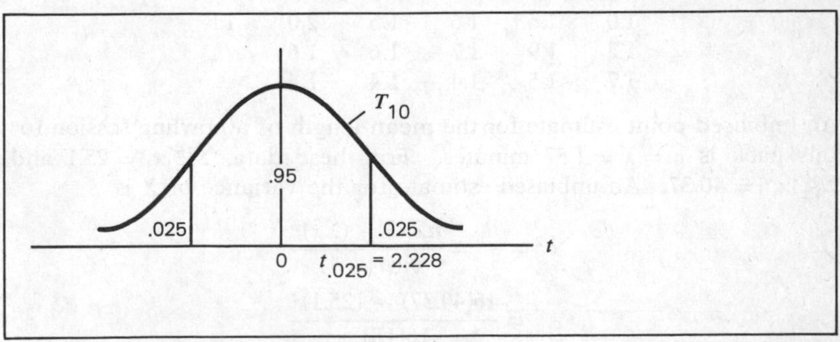


**FIGURE 7.9** $P[-2.228 \leq T_{10} \leq 2.228] = .95$.

---

The last row in Table V of Appendix B is labeled ∞. The points listed in that row are actually points associated with the standard normal curve. Note that as $\gamma$ increases, the values in each column of Table V approach the value listed in the last row.

It is now easy to determine the general form for a $100(1-\alpha)\%$ confidence interval on $\mu$ when $\sigma^2$ is unknown. We need only note that the two random variables

$$Z = \frac{\bar{X} - \mu}{\sigma / \sqrt{n}} \quad \text{and} \quad T_\gamma = \frac{\bar{X} - \mu}{S / \sqrt{n}}$$

have the same algebraic structure. Thus the algebraic argument given in Example 7.1.3 will go through exactly as shown, with $\sigma$ being replaced by $S$ and $z_{\alpha/2}$ being replaced by $t_{\alpha/2}$. These substitutions result in Theorem 7.2.2.

**THEOREM 7.2.2** □ *Confidence Interval on $\mu$ When $\sigma^2$ Is Unknown.* Let $X_1$, $X_2, X_3, \ldots, X_n$ be a random sample of size $n$ from a normal distribution with mean $\mu$ and variance $\sigma^2$. Then a $100(1-\alpha)\%$ confidence interval on $\mu$ is given by

$$\bar{X} \pm t_{\alpha/2} \frac{S}{\sqrt{n}}$$

---

**EXAMPLE 7.2.3** □ Wolf packs are territorial with territories of 130 square kilometers or more. Howling in wolves, which communicates information about both the location and the composition of the pack, is thought to be related to territoriality. The following observations were obtained on $X$, the length in minutes of a howling session of a particular pack under study. Assume that $X$ is normally distributed.

| | | | | | |
|---|---|---|---|---|---|
| 1.0 | 1.8 | 1.6 | 1.5 | 2.0 | 1.8 |
| 1.2 | 1.9 | 1.7 | 1.6 | 1.6 | |
| 1.7 | 1.5 | 1.4 | 1.4 | 1.4 | |

An unbiased point estimate for the mean length of a howling session for this pack is $\hat{\mu} = \bar{x} = 1.57$ minutes. For these data, $\Sigma_{i=1}^{16} x_i = 25.1$ and $\Sigma_{i=1}^{16} x_i^2 = 40.37$. An unbiased estimate for the variance of $X$ is

$$\begin{aligned} \widehat{\sigma^2} = s^2 &= \frac{n\Sigma x^2 - (\Sigma x)^2}{n(n-1)} \\ &= \frac{16(40.37) - (25.1)^2}{16(15)} \\ &= .07 \end{aligned}$$

An estimate for $\sigma$ is

$$\hat{\sigma} = s = \sqrt{.07} = .26 \text{ minute}$$

A 95% confidence interval on $\mu$ is found by considering the partition shown in Figure 7.10 of the $T_{15}$ curve obtained from Table V of Appendix B. The

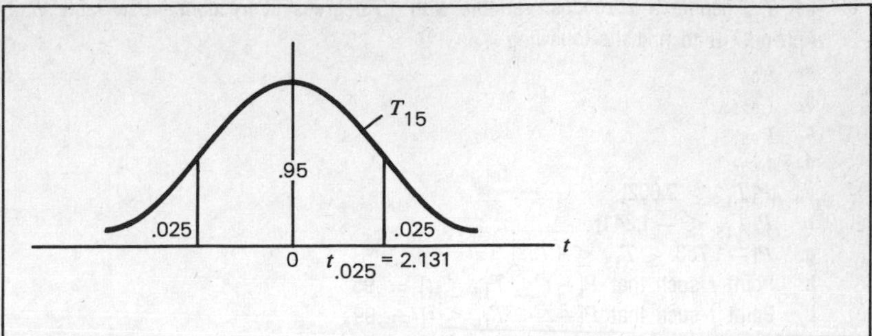


**FIGURE 7.10** Partition of $T_{15}$ to obtain a 95% confidence interval on $\mu$.

bounds for a 95% confidence interval on $\mu$ are

$$\bar{x} \pm t_{.025}\frac{s}{\sqrt{n}} = 1.57 \pm 2.131\frac{.26}{\sqrt{16}}$$

$$= 1.57 \pm .14$$

We can be 95% confident that the mean length of a howling session for this particular pack lies between 1.43 and 1.71 minutes.

---

Several things should be pointed out. First, the number of degrees of freedom involved in finding a confidence interval on $\mu$ when $\sigma^2$ is unknown is $n - 1$, the sample size minus 1. For large samples, this value may not be listed in Table V of Appendix B. In this case, the last line in the table ($\infty$) is used to find points of interest. Second, once again a normality assumption has been made. The validity of this assumption can be checked by using the methods of Chapter 12. If there is reason to suspect that the variable under study has a distribution that is far from normal, then statistical procedures based on the $T$ distribution should not be used. Rather, some distribution-free technique should be employed. Such techniques are discussed in Chapter 13.

---

## EXERCISES 7.2

1. Find $\Sigma x$, $\Sigma x^2$, $\bar{x}$, $s^2$, and $s$ for these data: 2, 3, 1, 4, 2, 0.
2. The following is a random sample of 16 observations on random variable $X$, the number of pounds of beef consumed last year per person in the United States:

| | | | | | |
|---|---|---|---|---|---|
| 118 | 110 | 117 | 120 | 119 | 126 |
| 115 | 112 | 112 | 113 | 122 | |
| 125 | 130 | 115 | 118 | 123 | |

Use these data to find unbiased estimates for $\mu$ and $\sigma^2$. Estimate $\sigma$.

3. Let $T_{15}$ denote a $T$ random variable with 15 degrees of freedom. Use Table V of Appendix B to find the following:
   a. $t_{.05}$
   b. $t_{.025}$
   c. $t_{.95}$
   d. $t_{.975}$
   e. $P[T_{15} \geq 2.602]$
   f. $P[T_{15} \leq -1.341]$
   g. $P[-1.753 \leq T_{15} \leq 1.753]$
   h. Point $t$ such that $P[-t \leq T_{15} \leq t] = .95$
   i. Point $t$ such that $P[-t \leq T_{15} \leq t] = .99$
4. Researchers studying photoperiodism used the cocklebur as an experimental plant. The variable observed was $X$, the number of hours of uninterrupted darkness per day required to produce flowering. The following data were obtained:

| | | | | |
|---|---|---|---|---|
| 15.0 | 13.0 | 15.1 | 16.0 | 13.5 |
| 15.5 | 13.2 | 14.9 | 14.7 | |

   Find unbiased estimates for $\mu$ and $\sigma^2$. Estimate $\sigma$.
5. In a study of water usage in a small town, a random sample of 25 homes is obtained. The variable of interest is $X$, the number of gallons of water utilized per day. The following observations are obtained on a randomly selected weekday. Assume $X$ is normal.

| | | | | |
|---|---|---|---|---|
| 175 | 185 | 186 | 118 | 158 |
| 150 | 190 | 178 | 137 | 175 |
| 180 | 200 | 189 | 200 | 180 |
| 172 | 145 | 192 | 191 | 181 |
| 183 | 169 | 172 | 178 | 210 |

   For these data, $\Sigma x = 4394$ and $\Sigma x^2 = 782{,}666$. Verify these figures. Use the information to estimate $\mu$, $\sigma^2$, and $\sigma$. Find a 90% confidence interval on $\mu$. The town reservoir is large enough to handle an average usage of 160 gallons per day. Does there appear to be a water shortage problem in the town? Explain your answer on the basis of the confidence interval obtained.
6. Duck farms lining the shores of Great South Bay have seriously polluted the water. One pollutant is nitrogen in the form of uric acid. The following is a random sample of nine observations on $X$, the number of pounds of nitrogen produced per farm per day:

| | | | | |
|---|---|---|---|---|
| 4.9 | 5.8 | 5.9 | 6.5 | 5.5 |
| 5.0 | 5.6 | 6.0 | 5.7 | |

   Assume $X$ is normal, and construct a 99% confidence interval on $\mu_X$.
7. To set a standard for what is to be considered a "normal" calcium reading, a random sample of 1000 apparently healthy adults is obtained. A blood sample is draw from each adult. The variable studied is $X$, the number of milligrams of calcium per deciliter of blood. A sample mean of 9.5 and a sample standard deviation of .5 are

found. Assume that $X$ is approximately normally distributed. Find a 95% confidence interval on $\mu$.

**8.** A process called abscission in photobiology is being tested in hopes of increasing the fruit set (the percentage of fruit held on the trees) in orange trees in Florida. The process involves exposing the trees to colored light for 15 minutes each night. The fruit set for 10 experimental trees was obtained first under normal conditions and then after the new treatment. The following observations were obtained on $X$, the percentage increase in the fruit set from one year to the next:

| | | | | |
|---|---|---|---|---|
| 29 | 37 | 32 | 34 | 39 |
| 30 | 36 | 35 | 27 | 40 |

Assume that $X$ is normal, and construct a 95% confidence interval on the mean percentage increase in the fruit set. The developer of the new process claims that it will increase the fruit set by an average of 40%. Do you believe this statement? Explain your answer on the basis of the confidence interval found.

***9.** *$S$ is* not ***an unbiased estimator for $\sigma^2$.*** Here we use proof by contradiction. That is, we show that assuming that $S$ is unbiased for $\sigma$ leads to a contradiction of a known fact. This implies that $S$ cannot be unbiased for $\sigma$. Note that since $S$ is a statistic, it will vary from sample to sample and Var $S > 0$. Assume that $S$ is unbiased for $\sigma$. That is, assume that $E[S] = \sigma$. Use the fact that

$$\text{Var } S = E[S^2] - (E[S])^2$$

to obtain a contradiction.

---

**Computing Supplement**

If you have not read the computing supplement at the end of Chapter 1, do so now. We present here an SAS program to construct a 95% confidence interval on $\mu$ when $\sigma^2$ is assumed to be unknown. The program is written to analyze the data of Example 7.2.3.

| **Statement** | **Function** |
|---|---|
| DATA WOLF; | names data set |
| INPUT TIME @@; | indicates there is only one variable in data set, TIME; @@ indicates that more than one data point will appear per card |
| CARDS; | signals beginning of data |
| 1.0 1.8 1.6 1.5<br>1.2 1.9 1.7 1.6<br>1.7 1.5 1.4 1.4<br>2.0 1.6 1.4 1.8 | data; more than one observation is punched per card; each data point is separated by at least one blank |
| ; | signals end of data |
| PROC MEANS MAXDEC=<br>2 MEAN STDERR VAR; | calls for mean, standard error of mean ($s/\sqrt{n}$), and variance to be computed and reported to two decimal places |
| TITLE SUMMARY STATISTICS; | titles first page of output |

| | |
|---|---|
| OUTPUT OUT=STAT MEAN= XBAR STDERR=XSTDERR; | creates new data set, STAT, whose only members are XBAR and XSTDERR; these variables have as values the values of mean and standard error of mean, respectively, of original data; purpose of this step is to get these values into a data set so they may be used in later computations |
| DATA CI;SET STAT; | places variables XBAR and XSTDERR from data set STAT into new data set, CI |
| T=2.131; | adds variable $T$ to CI; its value is the value of point $t_{.025}$ needed to create a 95% confidence interval on $\mu$; it is found by reading Table V of Appendix B with 15 degrees of freedom |
| LB=XBAR−(T*XSTDERR); | finds lower bound for 95% confidence interval on $\mu$ |
| UB=XBAR+(T*XSTDERR); | finds upper bound for 95% confidence interval on $\mu$ |
| PROC PRINT; VAR LB UB; | asks lower and upper 95% confidence bounds to be printed |
| TITLE1 95% CONFIDENCE INTERVAL; TITLE2 ON THE MEAN; TITLE3 VARIANCE UNKNOWN; | titles second page of output |

The output of this program, looks like this:

```
                    SUMMARY STATISTICS
VARIABLE         MEAN        STD ERROR         VARIANCE
                              OF MEAN
TIME             1.57          0.06              0.07


                  95% CONFIDENCE INTERVAL
                       ON THE MEAN
                    VARIANCE UNKNOWN
               OBS      LB          UB
                1     1.43158     1.70592
```

To adjust this program to analyze another data set, we need only change the name of the original data set and the input variable to fit the new situation. Any confidence level desired can be obtained by adjusting the value of variable $T$. The confidence level indicated in the title also should be adjusted.

## HYPOTHESIS TESTING ON $\mu$

**7.3** □ We consider now the problem of testing a hypothesis concerning the mean of a population. Recall from Chapter 6 that this implies that prior to running the experiment, one has in mind a value for $\mu$. The purpose of the experiment is to gain evidence that tends to support or refute the hypothesized value.

---

**EXAMPLE 7.3.1** □ The U.S. Department of Health has set an average bacteria count of 70 bacteria per cubic centimeter of water as its maximum acceptable level for clam digging waters. An average value larger than 70 is felt to be dangerous, for eating clams taken from such waters may cause hepatitis. In monitoring the waters for the government, one would be interested in testing

$$H_0: \mu \leq 70$$
$$H_1: \mu > 70$$

---

**EXAMPLE 7.3.2** □ A recent study of the ecosystem in a deciduous forest indicated that in the natural forest, the average net change in nitrate nitrogen is an increase of 2 kilograms per hectare per year. Foresters feel that defoliation of forest undergrowth would lead to a decrease in this value. The hypothesis of interest is

$$H_0: \mu \geq 2$$
$$H_1: \mu < 2$$

---

**EXAMPLE 7.3.3** □ The average total blood protein in a healthy adult is 7.25 grams per deciliter. In running a blood test, the technician is testing

$$H_0: \mu = 7.25$$
$$H_1: \mu \neq 7.25$$

---

There is one general statement to keep in mind when you test a hypothesis on any parameter:

> In order to test a hypothesis concerning a parameter $\theta$, you must find a statistic whose probability distribution is known at least approximately under the assumption that the hypothesized value of the parameter is correct.

Such a statistic will serve as the *test statistic*. In the case at hand, we must find a statistic whose distribution is known under the assumption that the hypothesized value of the mean $\mu_0$ is correct. This is not difficult. From the discussion of Section 7.2, we know that the statistic $(\bar{X} - \mu_0)/(\sigma/\sqrt{n})$ is at least approximately standard normal if $\sigma$ is known. The statistic

$(\bar{X} - \mu_0)/(S/\sqrt{n})$ is, for samples drawn from normal or near normal distributions, at least approximately $T$ with $n - 1$ degrees of freedom if $\sigma$ is unknown. Depending on the situation relative to $\sigma$, one or the other of these statistics will be used as the test statistic for testing a hypothesis on a population mean. We concentrate on the latter, because it arises more often in practice.

As can be seen from Examples 7.3.1 through 7.3.3, a hypothesis on $\mu$ may take three general forms. These are given, with $\mu_0$ representing the hypothesized value of the population mean:

| I | II | III |
|---|---|---|
| $H_0: \mu \leq \mu_0$ | $H_0: \mu \geq \mu_0$ | $H_0: \mu = \mu_0$ |
| $H_1: \mu > \mu_0$ | $H_1: \mu < \mu_0$ | $H_1: \mu \neq \mu_0$ |
| Right-tailed test | Left-tailed test | Two-tailed test |

Form I is called a right-tailed test because when a hypothesis of this form is tested, the natural critical region will consist of the upper, or right-tail, region of the $Z$ or $T$ distribution, as the case may be. This point is explained in Example 7.3.4. Similarly, form II is a left-tailed test because the critical region is the lower, or left-tail, region of the appropriate distribution. In a two-tailed test, the critical region consists of both the lower and upper tail regions of the distribution of the test statistic. This is easy to remember because in a one-sided test, the inequality in the *alternative* hypothesis points toward the critical region. (See Figure 7.11.)

---

**EXAMPLE 7.3.4** □ Consider Example 7.3.1. The statistician for the U.S. Department of Health is to monitor the fishing waters. The job is to detect a situation in which the mean bacteria count has risen above the maximum safe level of 70. Since what is to be detected is taken as the alternative hypothesis, we are testing

$$H_0: \mu \leq 70 \qquad \text{(waters are safe)}$$
$$H_1: \mu > 70 \qquad \text{(waters are unsafe)}$$

A random sample of size 9 is drawn, and the bacteria count $X$ for each case is determined. Since $\sigma$ is not known, the test statistic is

$$T_{n-1} = \frac{\bar{X} - \mu_0}{S/\sqrt{n}}$$

or

$$T_8 = \frac{\bar{X} - 70}{S/3}$$

Since $\bar{X}$ is an unbiased estimator for the mean, we expect the observed value of $\bar{X}$ to be close to 70 if $H_0$ is true. This forces the numerator of the test statistic, $\bar{X} - 70$, to be small, causing the observed value of the test statistic to be small. However, if $H_1$ is true, we expect $\bar{X}$ to be larger than 70, forcing $\bar{X} - 70$ to be large and *positive*. This, in turn, results in a large

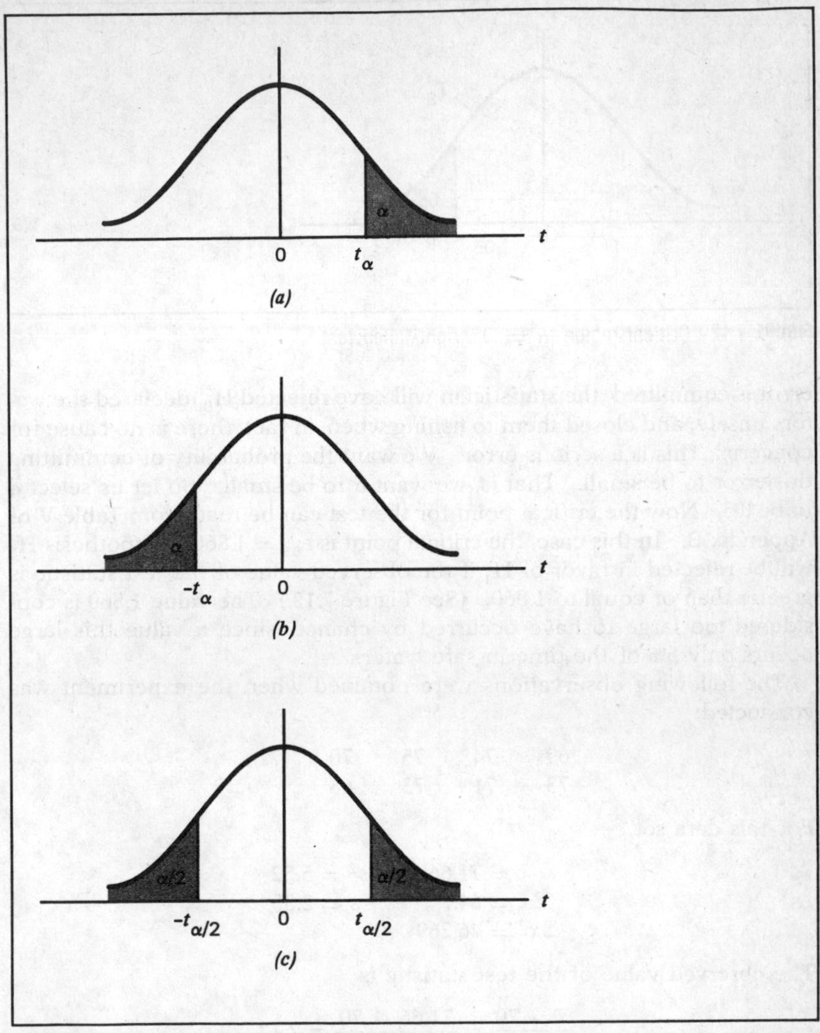


**FIGURE 7.11** (*a*) Critical region: right-tailed test ($H_1$: $\mu > \mu_0$); (*b*) critical region: left-tailed test ($H_1$: $\mu < \mu_0$); (*c*) critical region: two-tailed test ($H_1$: $\mu \neq \mu_0$).

positive value for the test statistic. Hence logically we should reject $H_0$ in favor of $H_1$ whenever the observed value of the test statistic is positive and too large to have reasonably occurred by chance. Thus the natural critical region for the test is the right-tail, or upper, region of the $T_8$ distribution. How large is "too large to have reasonably occurred by chance"?

To answer this question, consider the Type I error. Here, if a Type I

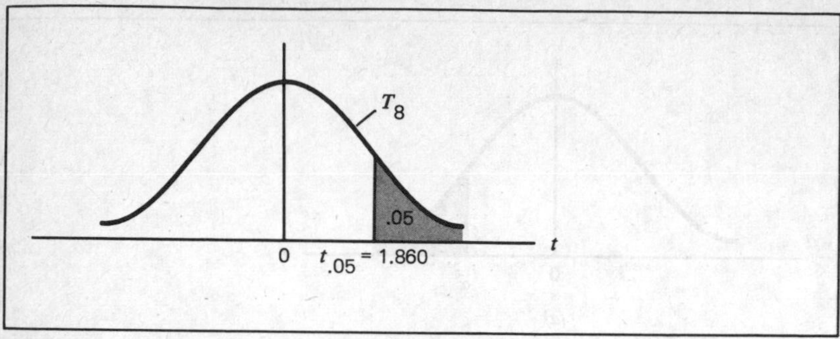


**FIGURE 7.12** Critical region: $\alpha = .05$, right-tailed test.

error is committed, the statistician will have rejected $H_0$, declared the waters unsafe, and closed them to fishing when, in fact, there is no cause for concern. This is a serious error. We want the probability of committing this error to be small. That is, we want $\alpha$ to be small. So let us select $\alpha$ to be .05. Now the critical point for the test can be read from Table V of Appendix B. In this case, the critical point is $t_{.05} = 1.860$. Hypothesis $H_0$ will be rejected in favor of $H_1$ if the observed value of the test statistic is greater than or equal to 1.860. (See Figure 7.12.) The value 1.860 is considered too large to have occurred by chance, since a value this large occurs only 5% of the time in safe waters.

The following observations were obtained when the experiment was conducted:

| | | | | |
|---|---|---|---|---|
| 69 | 74 | 75 | 70 | 72 |
| 73 | 71 | 73 | 68 | |

For this data set,

$$\bar{x} = 71.66 \qquad s^2 = 5.52$$
$$\Sigma x = 645 \qquad s = 2.35$$
$$\Sigma x^2 = 46{,}269$$

The observed value of the test statistic is

$$\frac{\bar{x} - 70}{s/3} = \frac{71.66 - 70}{2.35/3} = 2.12$$

Since $2.12 > 1.86$, we reject $H_0$ and declare the waters unsafe for fishing. There is only a 5% chance that we are doing so unnecessarily.

---

Recall from Chapter 6 that two errors are associated with any test of hypothesis. Interest centers mainly on the Type I error, which occurs with probability $\alpha$. The reason is that $\alpha$ can be controlled by the experimenter. Its value always will be known at least approximately. The same is not true for $\beta$, the probability of committing a Type II error. This value rarely can be determined by elementary methods. However, $\alpha$ and $\beta$ are related in the sense that for a fixed sample size, an increase in $\alpha$ results in a decrease in $\beta$, and vice versa. In setting $\alpha$, you should give some thought to the seriousness of the Type II error. If the consequences of making a Type II error are grave, then $\alpha$ should be chosen to be moderate in size, thus forcing $\beta$ to be relatively small.

---

**EXAMPLE 7.3.5** □ The hypothesis

$$H_0: \mu \geq 2 \qquad H_1: \mu < 2$$

of Example 7.3.2 was tested by removing the undergrowth in a 15-hectare area of an experimental forest. The area was sprayed to prevent regrowth. At the end of a year, the change in nitrate nitrogen per hectare was determined by analyzing runoff water at 15 locations within the forest. The following data resulted:

$$\bar{x} = -3 \qquad \text{(average } \textit{loss} \text{ of 3 kilograms per hectare)}$$
$$s = 7.5 \text{ kilograms per hectare}$$

Is this evidence at the $\alpha = .01$ level that removal of forest undergrowth results in a decrease in the mean net change in nitrate nitrogen per hectare per year?

The critical region for the test based on a sample of size 15 is shown in Figure 7.13. The value of the test statistic based on these data is

$$\frac{\bar{x} - \mu_0}{s/\sqrt{n}} = \frac{-3 - 2}{7.5/\sqrt{15}} = -2.58$$

Since $-2.58 \not< -2.624$, we are unable to reject $H_0$ at the $\alpha = .01$ level. Note, however, that the critical point for an $\alpha = .025$ test of this hypothesis is $-2.145$. At that level, $H_0$ could be rejected. Many statisticians prefer to

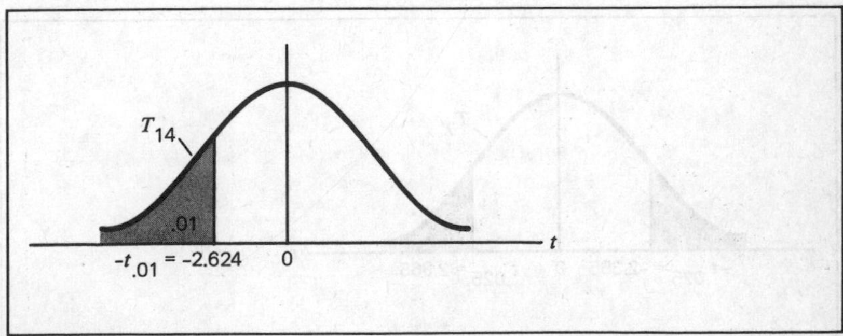


**FIGURE 7.13** Critical region: $\alpha = .01$, left-tailed test.

report both these facts rather than simply state that $H_0$ could not be rejected at the .01 level of significance. Then it is the responsibility of the subject matter expert to make some practical decisions based on these facts.

---

**EXAMPLE 7.3.6** □ A series of eight blood tests were run on a particular patient over several days. The variable monitored is the total protein level. Since the blood protein level should be neither too large nor too small, it is desirable to detect either situation. Thus we are testing

$$H_0: \mu = 7.25 \qquad \text{(normal for healthy adult)}$$
$$H_1: \mu \neq 7.25$$

based on a sample of size 8. The test is two-tailed. To run the test at an $\alpha = .05$ level, the critical region is split into two parts, each with an associated probability of .025. The critical points for such a test are shown in Figure 7.14. We reject $H_0$ if the observed value of the test statistic lies on or above 2.365 or if it lies on or below $-2.365$.

Based on the following observations, what conclusion can be drawn?

| | | | |
|---|---|---|---|
| 7.23 | 7.25 | 7.28 | 7.29 |
| 7.32 | 7.26 | 7.27 | 7.24 |

For these data,

$$\bar{x} = 7.267 \qquad s^2 = .000\,8$$
$$\Sigma x = 58.14 \qquad s = .029\,2$$
$$\Sigma x^2 = 422.538$$

The observed value of the test statistic is

$$\frac{\bar{x} - 7.25}{s/\sqrt{n}} = \frac{7.267 - 7.25}{.029\,2/\sqrt{8}} = 1.647$$

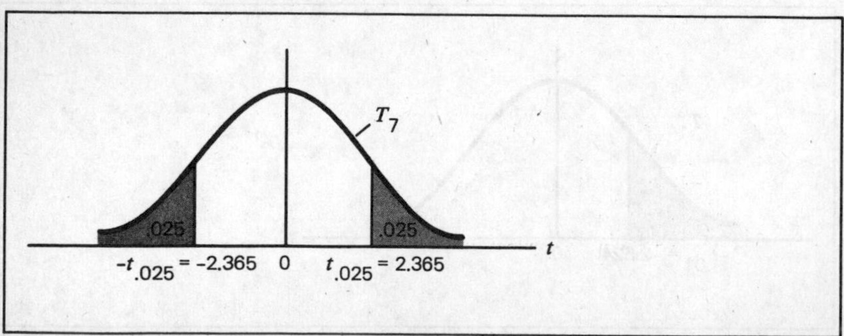


**FIGURE 7.14** Critical region: $\alpha = .05$, two-tailed test.

Since $1.647 \nless -2.365$ and $1.647 \ngtr 2.365$, we are unable to reject $H_0$. At this point, we do not have sufficient statistical evidence that a problem exists.

---

Recall that there are several points of view concerning statistical hypothesis testing. Some researchers prefer to set an $\alpha$ level based on consideration of the seriousness of the Type I and Type II errors before the experiment is run, as in Example 7.3.4. Then no deviation from that level is allowed. Others like to report both the level at which $H_0$ can be rejected and the level at which it cannot be rejected, as in Example 7.3.5. Still others prefer to report the "$P$ value" of the test. Recall that the $P$ value for a test is the probability of observing a value of the test statistic as extreme as that observed under the assumption that the null hypothesis is true. All three methods are acceptable, and you are free to choose the most appealing one. The latter method is illustrated here.

---

**EXAMPLE 7.3.7** □ Each species of firefly has a unique flashing pattern. One species has a pattern that consists of one short pulse of light followed by a resting period thought to have an average length of less than 4 seconds. The following data were obtained on the resting time between flashes of a sample of 16 fireflies of this species:

| | | | | | |
|---|---|---|---|---|---|
| 3.9 | 4.1 | 3.6 | 3.7 | 4.0 | 4.3 |
| 3.8 | 3.2 | 3.7 | 4.2 | 4.0 | |
| 3.5 | 3.5 | 3.8 | 3.4 | 3.6 | |

Does the evidence support the proposed mean resting time of less than 4 seconds?

For this data set,

$$\bar{x} = 3.77 \qquad \text{and} \qquad \frac{\bar{x} - 4}{s/\sqrt{n}} = \frac{3.77 - 4}{.30/4} = -3.06$$

$$s = .30$$

From Table V of Appendix B, the $P$ value for the test, $P[T_{15} \leq -3.06]$, is less than .005. Since the probability is very small, we conclude that there is sufficient evidence to claim that the mean resting time is less than 4 seconds.

---

## EXERCISES 7.3

1. The maximum acceptable level for exposure to microwave radiation in the United States is an average of 10 microwatts per square centimeter. It is feared that a large

television transmitter may be polluting the air nearby by pushing the level of microwave radiation above the safe limit.

**a.** Set up the null and alternative hypotheses needed to gain evidence to support this contention.

**b.** The following is a random sample of nine observations on $X$, the number of microwatts per square centimeter, taken at locations near the transmitter:

| | | | | |
|---|---|---|---|---|
| 9 | 11 | 14 | 10 | 10 |
| 12 | 13 | 8 | 12 | |

Can $H_0$ be rejected at the $\alpha = .1$ level? What practical conclusion can be drawn? What type of error might be committed?

**2.** Normally the leaves of the ***Mimosa pudica*** are horizontal. However, if one of them is touched lightly, the leaflets will fold. It is reported that the mean time from touch to complete closure is 2.5 seconds. An experiment is run to test this value.

**a.** Set up the appropriate two-tailed hypothesis.

**b.** Determine the critical points for an $\alpha = .1$ level test of the hypothesis of Part **a** based on a sample of size 10.

**c.** The following observations were obtained on variable $X$, the elapsed time between touch and closure:

| | | | | |
|---|---|---|---|---|
| 3.0 | 2.9 | 2.8 | 2.7 | 2.6 |
| 2.4 | 2.5 | 2.4 | 2.6 | 2.7 |

Can $H_0$ be rejected? To what type of error are you now subject?

**3.** Bats in flight locate a solid object by emitting shrill squeaks and listening for the echo. It is thought that the mean maximum effective range for this echolocation system is more than 6 meters. To support this hypothesis, a random sample of 16 bats was selected. Each bat was released in a large, enclosed area that contained only one obstruction. The distance from the object at which the bat was observed to veer away from the obstruction was noted. The experiment was repeated several times for each bat, and the mean veer distance for each was determined. The following observations were obtained:

| | | | | | | | |
|---|---|---|---|---|---|---|---|
| 6.2 | 6.8 | 6.1 | 5.7 | 6.1 | 6.3 | 5.8 | 6.3 |
| 5.9 | 6.3 | 6.4 | 6.0 | 6.3 | 6.2 | 5.9 | 6.1 |

Find the $P$ value for this data set. What practical conclusion can you draw from these data? What type of error might you be committing?

**4.** One of the effects of DDT on birds is to inhibit the production of the enzyme carbonic anhydrase. This enzyme controls calcium metabolism. The end result is thought to be the formation of egg shells that are much thinner and weaker than normal. To test this theory, a study was run in which sparrow hawks were fed a mixture of 3 parts per million (ppm) dieldrin and 15 ppm DDT. The thickness of the shells of these birds was compared to the known mean thickness for birds not affected by DDT. The percentage decrease in shell thickness was noted. A random sample of size 16 yielded a sample mean percentage decrease of 8% with a sample standard deviation of 5%. Use this information to test

$$H_0: \mu \leq 0$$
$$H_1: \mu > 0 \qquad \text{(shell thickness decreases)}$$

What is the approximate $P$ value for the test? Do you feel that the theory has been supported statistically? Explain your answer on the basis of the $P$ value.

**5.** The mean carbon dioxide concentration in the air is .035%. It is thought that the concentration immediately above the soil surface is higher than this.

**a.** Set up the null and alternative hypotheses required to gain statistical support for this contention.

**b.** One hundred and forty-four randomly selected air samples taken from within 1 foot of the soil were analyzed. A sample mean of .09% and sample standard deviation .25% resulted. What is the $P$ value for this test? Do you feel that the stated contention has been supported statistically?

---

**Computing Supplement**

The following SAS program is used to test a hypothesis on the value of $\mu$ when $\sigma^2$ is assumed to be unknown. It utilizes the data of Example 7.3.7.

| **Statement** | **Function** |
|---|---|
| DATA FIREFLY; | names data set |
| INPUT TIME @@; | indicates there is only one variable, TIME, in data set; @@ indicates that more than one data point will appear per card |
| HOMEAN = 4; | indicates the hypothesized value of mean is 4 |
| STIME = TIME − HOMEAN; | creates new variable, STIME, by subtracting hypothesized value of mean from each value of TIME; $E$[STIME] = 0 and Var[STIME] = Var[TIME]; so testing $E$[TIME] = 4 is equivalent to testing $E$[STIME] = 0 |
| CARDS; | signals that data follow |
| 3.9 3.8 3.5 ... 4.3 | data all on one card with blank between each data point |
| ; | signals end of data |
| PROC MEANS T PRT; VAR STIME; | asks for observed value of test statistic and $P$ value for two-tailed test of $H_0$: $E$[STIME] = 0 to be printed |
| TITLE TESTING H0: MEAN TIME = 4; | titles output |

The output of this program is as follows:

```
            TESTING HO:MEAN TIME=4

VARIABLE             T        PR>|T|

STIME              -3.06      0.0080
```

So −3.06 is the observed value of the test statistic, and .008 0 is the $P$ value for a two-tailed test. The $P$ value for the left-tailed test

$$H_0: \mu \geq 4 \qquad H_1: \mu < 4$$

is half this value, or .004.

To adjust this program to other problems, the names of the data set, the input variable, and the variable STIME must be changed to be in accord with the new data. Also the value of the variable HOMEAN must be changed to that of the new hypothesized value of the mean. The title statement should be adjusted accordingly.

## INFERENCES ON $\sigma^2$

**7.4** □ Point estimation of $\sigma^2$ is discussed in Section 7.2 in connection with the problem of making inferences on a population mean when the population variance is unknown. On some occasions interest centers not on the mean, but on the variance itself. Thus it is necessary to be able not only to find a point estimate for $\sigma^2$, but also to construct a confidence interval on or test a hypothesis concerning this parameter.

---

**EXAMPLE 7.4.1** □ Copper, a mineral required to some degree by most plants, is classed as a micronutrient. Its concentration in a plant is measured in parts per million and is determined by burning the plant completely and analyzing the ash. The copper concentration varies from species to species. An experiment is run to estimate this variability.

---

**EXAMPLE 7.4.2** □ The Lhasa Apso is a dog of Tibetan ancestry. The breed was introduced in England in 1921 and was first bred for show in 1933. The desired shoulder height in males is 10.5 inches. However, there is a fair amount of natural variability in height. A breeder is attempting to reduce this variability in the animals by selective breeding.

---

**EXAMPLE 7.4.3** □ In manufacturing a drug, its potency varies from time to time. This variability must not be allowed to become too large. A large variance could result in some batches of the drug being too weak to be effective while others are too strong and potentially dangerous. Periodically tests are run to monitor the variance of the drug being produced.

---

Each of these three examples calls for an inference to be made concerning a population variance. To construct a confidence interval on $\sigma^2$ or to test a hypothesis concerning its value, it is necessary to introduce another

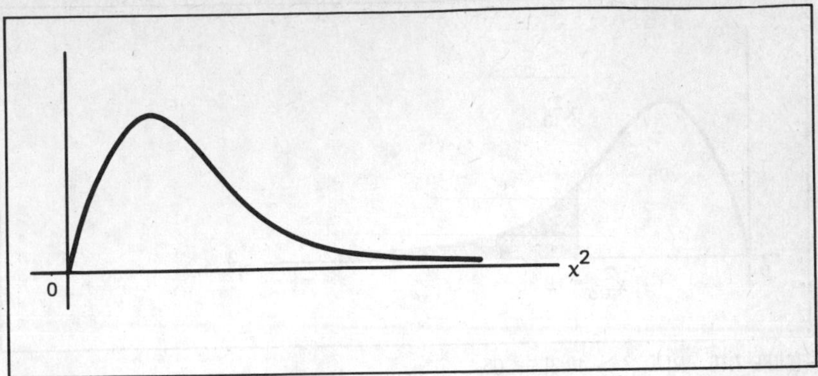


**FIGURE 7.15** Typical chi-square curve.

family of continuous random variables. The general characteristics of members of this family, called *chi-square variables* ($X^2$), are as follows:

**1.** There are infinitely many chi-square random variables, each identified by one parameter $\gamma$, called *degrees of freedom*. Parameter $\gamma$ is always a positive integer. The notation $X_\gamma{}^2$ denotes a chi-square variable with $\gamma$ degrees of freedom.

**2.** Each chi-square variable is continuous.

**3.** The graph of the density of each chi-square variable is an asymmetric curve of the general shape shown in Figure 7.15.

**4.** Chi-square variables cannot assume negative values.

**5.** Parameter $\gamma$ is both a shape and a location parameter in that

$$E[X_\gamma{}^2] = \gamma \qquad \text{and} \qquad \text{Var } X_\gamma{}^2 = 2\gamma.$$

A partial summary of the cumulative distribution function for chi-square variables with various degrees of freedom is given in Table VI of Appendix B. In that table, degrees of freedom appear as row headings, probabilities appear as column headings, and points associated with those probabilities are listed in the body of the table. Once again, we denote by $\chi_r{}^2$ that point on the $X_\gamma{}^2$ curve such that the area to the right of the point is $r$.

---

**EXAMPLE 7.4.4** □ Consider a $X^2$ random variable with 10 degrees of freedom. (Also see Figures 7.16 and 7.17.)

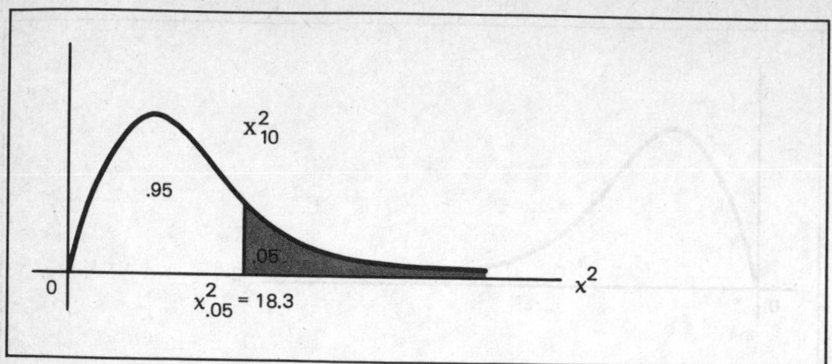


**FIGURE 7.16** $P[X_{10}{}^2 \geq 18.3] = .05$.

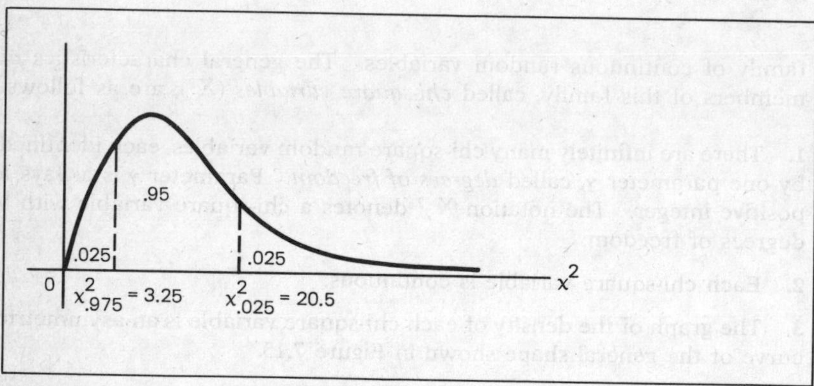


**FIGURE 7.17** $P[3.25 \leq X_{10}{}^2 \leq 20.5] = .95$.

**a.** $P[X_{10}{}^2 \leq 2.56] = F(2.56) = .01$

**b.** $P[X_{10}{}^2 \geq 16] = 1 - F(16) = 1 - .90 = .1$

**c.** $\chi_{.05}{}^2 = 18.3$

**d.** $\chi_{.95}{}^2 = 3.94$

**e.** $P[3.25 \leq X_{10}{}^2 \leq 20.5] = .95$

---

Theorem 7.4.1, offered without proof, provides a random variable that can be used to construct a confidence interval on $\sigma^2$ or to test a hypothesis about its value.

**THEOREM 7.4.1** □ Let $X_1, X_2, X_3, \ldots, X_n$ be a random sample of size $n$ from a distribution that is normal with mean $\mu$ and variance $\sigma^2$. The random

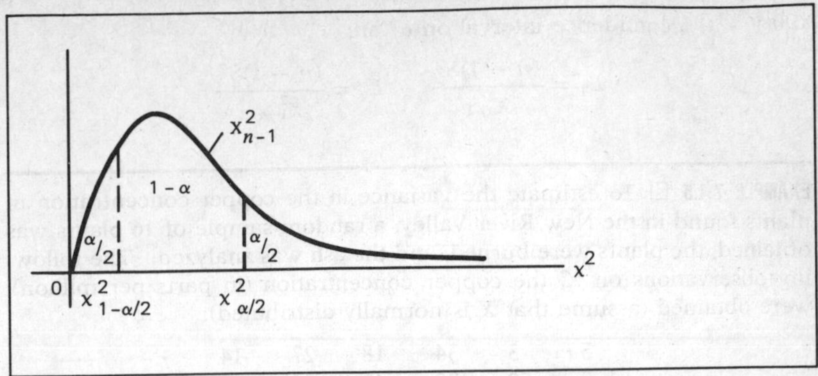


**FIGURE 7.18** Partition of $X^2_{n-1}$ to obtain a $100(1-\alpha)\%$ confidence interval on $\sigma^2$.

variable $(n-1)S^2/\sigma^2$ is distributed as a chi-square random variable with $n-1$ degrees of freedom.

To use Theorem 7.4.1 to construct a confidence interval on $\sigma^2$, note that the variable $(n-1)S^2/\sigma^2$ satisfies the general condition stated earlier. It involves the parameter $\sigma^2$ to be estimated, and its distribution is known to be chi-square with $n-1$ degrees of freedom. The bounds for a $100(1-\alpha)\%$ confidence interval on $\sigma^2$ can be found by considering the partition of the $X^2_{n-1}$ curve shown in Figure 7.18. From this diagram we can see that

$$P[\chi^2_{1-\alpha/2} \le X^2_{n-1} \le \chi^2_{\alpha/2}] = 1-\alpha$$

In this particular application,

$$X^2_{n-1} = \frac{(n-1)S^2}{\sigma^2}$$

Thus

$$P\left[\chi^2_{1-\alpha/2} \le \frac{(n-1)S^2}{\sigma^2} \le \chi^2_{\alpha/2}\right] = 1-\alpha$$

Isolating $\sigma^2$ in the middle of this inequality, we obtain

$$P\left[\frac{(n-1)S^2}{\chi^2_{\alpha/2}} \le \sigma^2 \le \frac{(n-1)S^2}{\chi^2_{1-\alpha/2}}\right] = 1-\alpha$$

From this inequality the desired lower and upper confidence bounds can be read. The result is summarized in Theorem 7.4.2.

**THEOREM 7.4.2** □ *Confidence Interval on $\sigma^2$.* Let $X_1, X_2, X_3, \ldots, X_n$ be a random sample of size $n$ from a distribution that is normal with mean $\mu$ and variance $\sigma^2$. The lower and upper bounds, respectively, for a

$100(1-\alpha)\%$ confidence interval on $\sigma^2$ are

$$L_1 = \frac{(n-1)S^2}{\chi^2_{\alpha/2}} \qquad L_2 = \frac{(n-1)S^2}{\chi^2_{1-\alpha/2}}$$

---

**EXAMPLE 7.4.5** □ To estimate the variance in the copper concentration in plants found in the New River Valley, a random sample of 16 plants was obtained, the plants were burned, and the ash was analyzed. The following observations on $X$, the copper concentration (in parts per million), were obtained (assume that $X$ is normally distributed):

| | | | | | |
|---|---|---|---|---|---|
| 5 | 3 | 34 | 18 | 27 | 14 |
| 8 | 50 | 38 | 43 | 35 | |
| 20 | 70 | 25 | 60 | 19 | |

For these data $\Sigma x = 469$, $\Sigma x^2 = 19{,}407$, and $s^2 = 377.30$. The partition of the $\chi_{15}{}^2$ curve needed to construct a 90% confidence interval on $\sigma^2$ is shown in Figure 7.19.

The bounds for the 90% confidence interval based on this information are

$$L_1 = \frac{(n-1)s^2}{\chi_{.05}{}^2} = \frac{15(377.30)}{25.0} = 226.38$$

and

$$L_2 = \frac{(n-1)s^2}{\chi_{.95}{}^2} = \frac{15(377.30)}{7.26} = 779.54$$

We are 90% sure that the true variance in the copper concentration of plants in the New River Valley lies between 226.38 and 779.54. To find a 90% confidence interval on the population standard deviation $\sigma$, we need only take the square root of these numerical bounds. Thus we can report

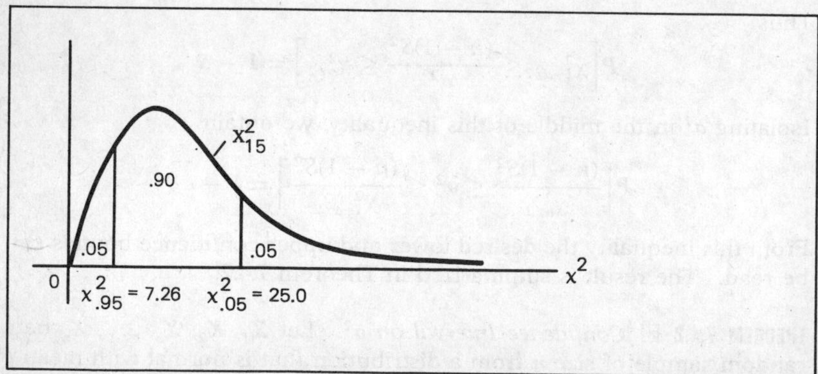


**FIGURE 7.19** Partition of $\chi_{15}{}^2$ to obtain a 90% confidence interval on $\sigma^2$.

that we are 90% confident that the true population standard deviation lies between $\sqrt{226.38} = 15.05$ and $\sqrt{779.54} = 27.92$ parts per million.

---

Hypothesis tests on $\sigma^2$ take the same three general forms as those on the mean. These are summarized below, with $\sigma_0^2$ representing the hypothesized value of the population variance.

| I $H_0: \sigma^2 \leq \sigma_0^2$ | II $H_0: \sigma^2 \geq \sigma_0^2$ | III $H_0: \sigma^2 = \sigma_0^2$ |
|---|---|---|
| $H_1: \sigma^2 > \sigma_0^2$ | $H_1: \sigma^2 < \sigma_0^2$ | $H_1: \sigma^2 \neq \sigma_0^2$ |
| Right-tailed test | Left-tailed test | Two-tailed test |

The test statistic for testing each of these is $(n - 1)S^2/\sigma_0^2$, which, under the assumption that the hypothesized value of $\sigma^2$ is correct, follows a chi-square distribution with $n - 1$ degrees of freedom. The critical region for each test is shown in Figure 7.20. Again, these critical regions can easily be justified intuitively, as is shown in Example 7.4.6.

---

**EXAMPLE 7.4.6** □ The current variance in the height of male Lhasa Apsos is .25. A breeder is attempting to reduce this figure. After a period of selective breeding, a random sample of 15 males is to be chosen from among the animals and measured. Since the researcher's contention is taken as the alternative hypothesis, the purpose of the experiment is to test

$$H_0: \sigma^2 \geq .25 \qquad H_1: \sigma^2 < .25$$

The test statistic to be used is

$$\frac{(n-1)S^2}{\sigma_0^2} = \frac{14S^2}{.25}$$

which, if $H_0$ is true, has a chi-square distribution with $n - 1 = 14$ degrees of freedom. Since $S^2$ is an unbiased estimator for $\sigma^2$, if $H_0$ is true, we expect the numerical value of $S^2$ to lie close to .25, the hypothesized value of $\sigma^2$. This forces the ratio $S^2/.25$ to lie close to 1 and the value of the test statistic to be close to 14, its expected value. If, however, the alternative is true and the population variance is actually smaller than the hypothesized value of .25, we expect $S^2$ to have a value smaller than .25. This, in turn, must force the ratio $S^2/.25$ to be smaller than 1, resulting in a value smaller than 14 for the test statistic. Thus it is logical to reject $H_0$ in favor of $H_1$ if the observed value of the test statistic is too small to have occurred by chance. That is, a left-tailed critical region is the natural choice for this test. The critical region for an $\alpha = .05$ level test is shown in Figure 7.21. Hypothesis $H_0$ will be rejected in favor of $H_1$ if the observed value of the test statistic lies on or below the point 6.57. When the experiment was run, a sample variance of .21 was obtained. The value of the test statistic

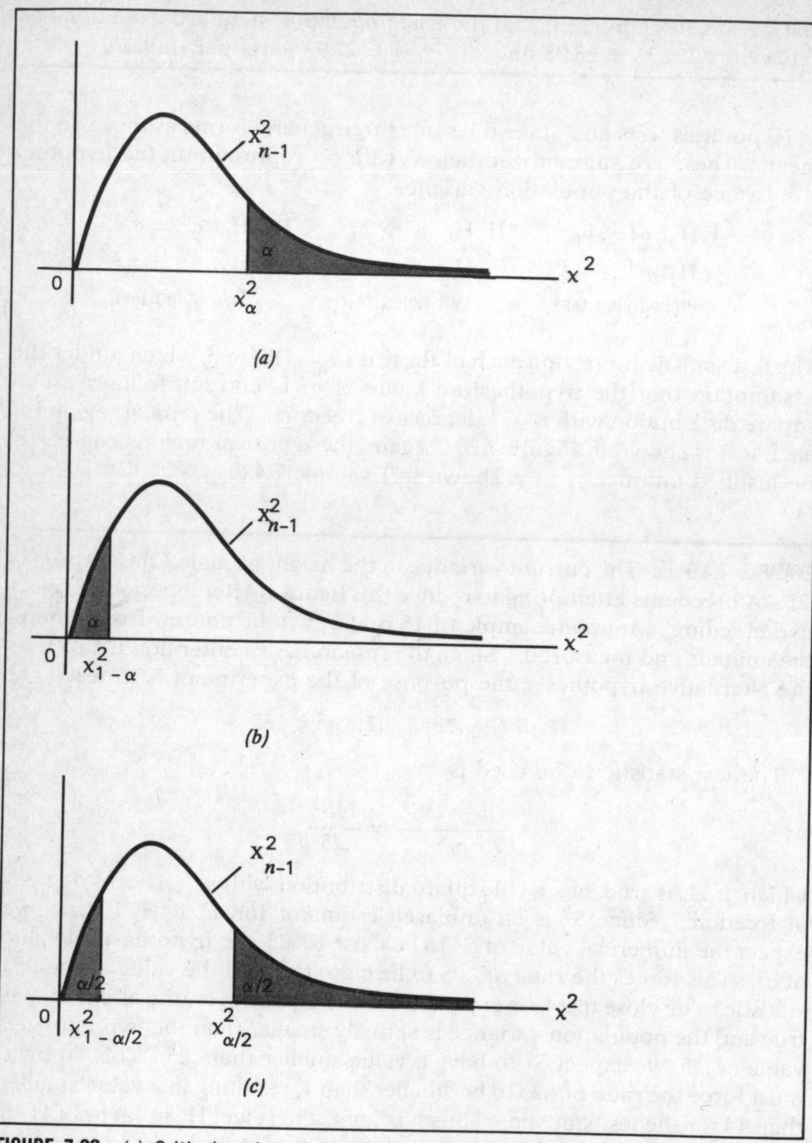


**FIGURE 7.20** (*a*) Critical region: right-tailed test ($H_1$: $\sigma^2 > \sigma_0{}^2$); (*b*) critical region: left-tailed test ($H_1$: $\sigma^2 < \sigma_0{}^2$); (*c*) critical region: two-tailed test ($H_1$: $\sigma^2 \neq \sigma_0{}^2$).

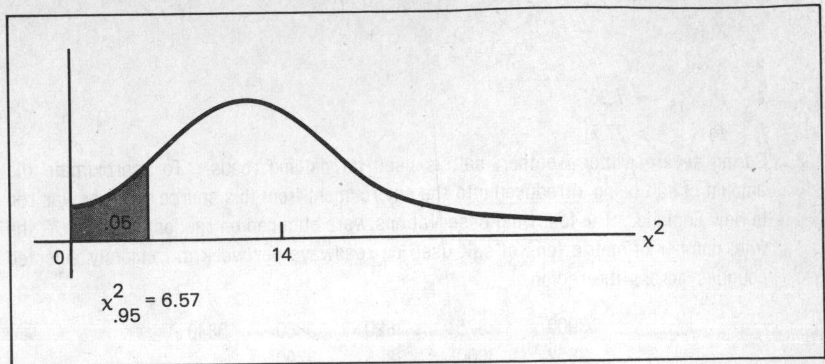


**FIGURE 7.21** Critical region: $\alpha = .05$, left-tailed test.

is $14(.21)/.25 = 11.76$. This value is not sufficiently small to be able to claim that the variability in height has been reduced. On the basis of the available data, we are unable to reject $H_0$.

---

There are two further points to be made. Table VI of Appendix B lists degrees of freedom from 1 to 30. What do you do if the sample size is such that the desired number of degrees of freedom is larger than 30? A procedure for handling this case is given in end-of-book reference [10]. Note also that once again an assumption of normality has been made. In the case of the chi-square statistic violating this assumption can lead to serious errors. If the population from which the sampling is done appears not to be normal, then another method must be used to test hypotheses on $\sigma^2$. One such method is given in [8].

---

## EXERCISES 7.4

1. Consider the random variable $X_9{}^2$.
   a. Find $P[X_9{}^2 \leq 2.09]$.
   b. Find $P[X_9{}^2 \geq 11.4]$.
   c. Find $P[14.7 \leq X_9{}^2 \leq 16.9]$.
   d. Find $\chi^2_{.025}$.
   e. Find $\chi_{.99}{}^2$.
   f. Find $P[\chi_{.95}{}^2 \leq X_9{}^2 \leq \chi_{.05}{}^2]$.
2. Consider the random variable $X_{15}{}^2$. Find:
   a. $E[X_{15}{}^2]$
   b. Var $X_{15}{}^2$

c. $\chi_{.05}^2$
d. $\chi_{.90}^2$
e. $P[X_{15}^2 \leq 7.26]$
f. $P[X_{15}^2 \geq 27.5]$

3. During severe winter weather, salt is used for deicing roads. To approximate the amount of salt being introduced into the environment from this source, a study was run in New England. The following observations were obtained on random variable $X$, the total number of metric tons of salt used on roadways per week in randomly selected counties across the region:

| | | | | |
|---|---|---|---|---|
| 3900 | 3875 | 3820 | 3860 | 3840 |
| 3852 | 3800 | 3825 | 3790 | |

a. Find a point estimate for $\mu_X$.
b. Find a point estimate for $\sigma_X^2$.
c. Assume that $X$ is normally distributed. Find a 90% confidence interval on $\mu_X$.
d. Find 90% confidence intervals on $\sigma_X^2$ and $\sigma_X$.

4. The typical plant cell has a large amount of cytoplasm bounded by a cell membrane called the plasma membrane. The mean thickness of this membrane varies from species to species. A random sample of 20 species yielded the following observations on $X$, the mean thickness of the cell membrane, in angstroms:

| | | | | | | |
|---|---|---|---|---|---|---|
| 80 | 90 | 85 | 82 | 75 | 58 | 70 |
| 84 | 87 | 81 | 87 | 61 | 73 | 84 |
| 85 | 70 | 78 | 95 | 77 | 52 | |

a. Find a point estimate for $\sigma_X^2$.
b. Assume that $X$ is normally distributed. Find 95% confidence intervals on $\mu_X$, $\sigma_X^2$, and $\sigma_X$.

5. One variable studied by biologists is the internal body temperature of poikilothermic animals (animals whose body temperature fluctuates with the surroundings). The lethal dose ($LD_{50}$) for desert lizards is 45°C. It has been observed that most of these animals hide during the heat of a summer day to avoid approaching this lethal dose. An experiment was conducted to study $X$, the time (in minutes) required for the body temperature of a desert lizard to reach 45°C, starting from its normal body temperature while in the shade. The following observations were obtained:

| | | | | | |
|---|---|---|---|---|---|
| 10.1 | 12.5 | 12.2 | 10.2 | 12.8 | 12.1 |
| 11.2 | 11.4 | 10.7 | 14.9 | 13.9 | 13.3 |

a. Find point estimates for $\mu_X$, $\sigma_X^2$, and $\sigma_X$.
b. Assume $X$ is normal. On the basis of these data, can it be concluded that the mean time required to reach the lethal dose is less than 13 minutes? Explain your answer on the basis of the $P$ value.
c. On the basis of these data, can it be concluded that the standard deviation of $X$ is less than 1.5 minutes? Explain your answer on the basis of the $P$ value. ***Hint:***

Testing

$$H_0: \sigma \geq 1.5 \qquad H_1: \sigma < 1.5$$

is equivalent to testing

$$H_0: \sigma^2 \geq (1.5)^2 \qquad H_1: \sigma^2 < (1.5)^2$$

6. Calcium is normally present in mammalian blood in concentrations of about 6 milligrams per 100 milliliters of whole blood. The normal standard deviation of this variable is 1 milligram of calcium per 100 milliliters of whole blood. Variability larger than this can lead to severe disturbances in blood coagulation. A series of nine tests on a patient revealed a sample mean of 6.2 milligrams of calcium per 100 milliliters of whole blood and a sample standard deviation of 2 milligrams of calcium per 100 milliliters of blood. Is there evidence at the $\alpha = .05$ level that the mean calcium level for this patient is higher than normal? Is there evidence at the $\alpha = .05$ level that the standard deviation of the calcium level is higher than normal?
7. To meet the respiratory needs of warm-water fish, the dissolved oxygen content should average 6.5 parts per million with a standard deviation of no more than 1.2 parts per million. As the water temperature increases, the dissolved oxygen decreases. This can cause fish to suffocate. A study is run on the effects of hot summer weather on a large lake. After a particularly hot period, water samples are taken from 25 randomly selected locations in the lake, and the dissolved oxygen content is determined. A sample mean of 6.3 parts per million and a sample standard deviation of 1.7 resulted.
   a. Is this evidence at the $\alpha = .05$ level that the mean oxygen content in the lake has decreased from the acceptable level of 6.5 parts per million?
   b. Find the critical point for an $\alpha = .05$ test of the hypothesis

$$H_0: \sigma \leq 1.2$$
$$H_1: \sigma > 1.2$$

   On the basis of the given data, can $H_0$ be rejected at the $\alpha = .05$ level?

---

**Computing Supplement**

The following SAS program illustrates its use in finding a 90% confidence interval on both the variance and the standard deviation of a variable. The data used are those of Example 7.4.5.

| **Statement** | **Function** |
|---|---|
| DATA COPPER; | names data set |
| INPUT CONC @@; | indicates there is only one variable, CONC, in data set; more than one data point will appear per card |
| CARDS; | indicates that data follow |
| 5 3 34 18<br>8 50 38 43<br>20 70 25 60<br>27 35 19 14 | data; more than one data point per card; at least one blank between each data point |

| | |
|---|---|
| ; | signals end of data |
| PROC MEANS MAXDEC=2 VAR N; | asks for variance and number of observations to be found and reported to two decimal places |
| TITLE SUMMARY STATISTICS; | titles first page of output |
| OUTPUT OUT=STAT VAR=XVAR N=NO; | creates new data set, STAT, whose only members are XVAR and NO; these variables have as values the values of variance and number of observations, respectively, of original data set; these values can now be used in future computations |
| DATA CI; SET STAT; | places variables XVAR and NO from STAT into new data set, CI |
| CHISQRL = 7.26; CHISQRU = 25; | adds variables CHISQRL and CHISQRU to CI; their values are chi-square values from Table VI of Appendix B needed for 90% confidence interval |
| LB = (NO-1)*XVAR/CHISQRU; | computes lower bound for confidence interval on $\sigma^2$ |
| UB = (NO-1)*XVAR/CHISQRL; | computes upper bound for confidence interval on $\sigma^2$ |
| LBS = SQRT (LB); | computes lower bound for confidence interval on $\sigma$ |
| UBS = SQRT (UB); | computes upper bound for confidence interval on $\sigma$ |
| PROC PRINT; VAR LB UB LBS UBS; | asks for confidence bounds to be printed |
| TITLE1 90% CONFIDENCE INTERVAL; | titles output |
| TITLE2 ON THE VARIANCE; | |
| TITLE3 AND THE STANDARD DEVIATION; | |

The output of this program looks thus:

```
                    SUMMARY STATISTICS

          VARIABLE         VARIANCE            N

          CONC              377.30            16


                  90% CONFIDENCE INTERVAL
                      ON THE VARIANCE
                AND THE STANDARD DEVIATION

       OBS       LB         UB          LBS         UBS

        1     226.377    779.537     15.0458     27.9202
```

To adjust this program to other data, the names of the original data set and the input variable should be changed to reflect the new data. Also the values of CHISQRL and

CHISQRU should be altered to the appropriate values depending on the degree of confidence desired and the number of degrees of freedom involved.

**Computing Supplement**
The following illustrates how SAS can be used to test a null hypothesis on $\sigma^2$. The data used are found in Exercise 7.4.5.

| **Statement** | **Function** |
|---|---|
| DATA TEMP; | names data set |
| INPUT TIME @@; | indicates there is only one variable, TIME, in data set; more than one observation will appear per card |
| CARDS; | indicates the data follow |
| 10.1 11.2 12.8<br>12.5 11.4 13.9<br>12.2 10.7 12.1<br>10.2 14.9 13.3 | data; more than one observation per card; at least one blank between data points |
| ; | signals end of data |
| PROC MEANS MEAN VAR STD MAXDEC=2 N; | asks for summary statistics |
| TITLE SUMMARY STATISTICS; | titles first page of output |
| OUTPUT OUT=STAT VAR=XVAR N=XN; | creates new data set called STAT whose only members are XVAR and XN, variance and sample size, respectively, of original data set |
| DATA TEST; SET STAT; | places XVAR and XN in new data set, TEST |
| HOVAR=2.25; | adds variable HOVAR, whose value is the null-hypothesis variance, to TEST |
| CHISQR = (XN−1)*XVAR/HOVAR; | computes value of chi-square test statistic needed to test $H_0$ and adds this value to TEST |
| PROC PRINT; VAR CHISQR; | asks for observed value of test statistic to be printed |
| TITLE1 TESTING HO:VAR=2.25; | titles last page of output |

The output of this program is as follows:

```
                              SUMMARY STATISTICS

VARIABLE            MEAN            VARIANCE          STANDARD            N
                                                      DEVIATION

TIME                12.11           2.19              1.48               12


                              TESTING HO:VAR=2.25

                              OBS      CHISQR

                               1       10.6685
```

Now the observed value of the test statistic, 10.688 5, should be located in Table VI of Appendix B to determine the $P$ value for the test.

To adjust this program to another data set, the names of the data set, input variable, and title should be changed to reflect the new data. Also HOVAR should be set equal to the new null-hypothesis variance.

# INFERENCES ON PROPORTIONS

# 8.

In this chapter we discuss inferences on one proportion and the comparison of two proportions. The study of proportions actually began in Chapter 5 with the discussion of the binomial distribution since, as we show, the binomial model provides the theory on which inferences on proportions are based. We treat the usual problems of statistical inference, namely, point estimation, interval estimation, and hypothesis testing.

## ESTIMATING PROPORTIONS

**8.1** □ The general situation being considered is thus: There is a population of interest, a particular trait is being studied, and each member of the population can be classed as either having or failing to have the trait. Inferences are to be made on parameter $p$, the proportion of the population with the trait. (See Figure 8.1.)

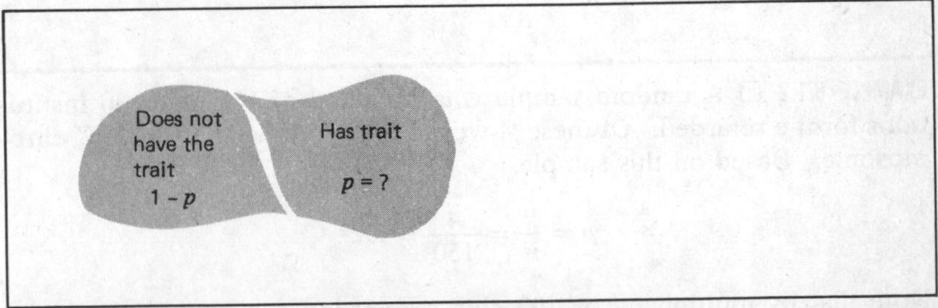


**FIGURE 8.1** Population partitioned by the presence of the trait.

**EXAMPLE 8.1.1** □ More males than females suffer from some form of mental retardation. One possible explanation for this phenomenon, the fragile $X$ syndrome, has been proposed recently. This inherited defect usually is

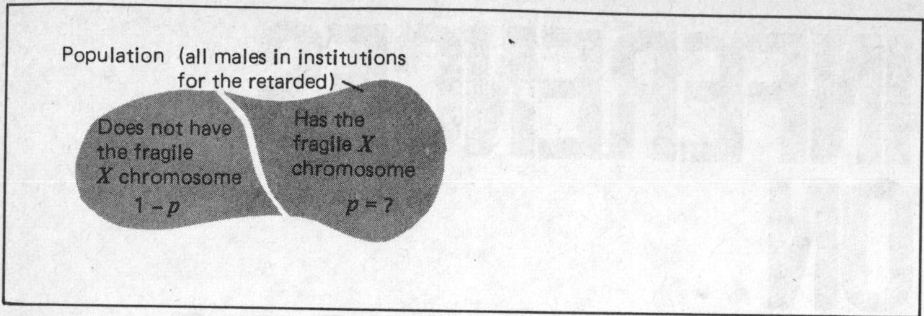


**FIGURE 8.2** Population partitioned by the presence of the fragile $X$ chromosome.

passed on from mother to son, and it appears as a defect on the $X$, or female, chromosome. A study is run to estimate the proportion of males in institutions for the retarded who have this defect. In this case, the population of interest is males in institutions for the retarded; the trait under study is having the fragile $X$ chromosome. We wish to obtain a point estimate for the proportion $p$ of males in these institutions who have this particular defect. Schematically, this is shown in Figure 8.2.

---

What is a logical point estimator for $p$? Common sense indicates that we should draw a random sample from the population of interest, determine the proportion of objects in the sample with the trait, and use this "sample proportion" as an estimate of the population proportion $p$. That is, common sense points to

$$\frac{X}{n} = \frac{\text{number of objects in sample with trait}}{\text{sample size}} = \hat{p} = \text{sample proportion}$$

as a logical estimator for $p$.

---

**EXAMPLE 8.1.2** □ A random sample was obtained of 150 males in institutions for the retarded. Of these, 4 were found to have the fragile $X$ chromosome. Based on this sample,

$$\hat{p} = \frac{x}{n} = \frac{4}{150} = .027$$

Note that by multiplying by 100, this proportion can be converted to a percentage (2.7%). If, in fact, this estimate accurately reflects the true percentage of male retardates with this defect, this could mean that the disorder is the second greatest known cause of mental retardation after Down's syndrome (mongolism).

---

How good is the sample proportion $\hat{p}$ as an estimator for the population proportion $p$? Using the criteria introduced in Chapter 7, we are asking two questions: Is $\hat{p}$ unbiased as an estimator for $p$? That is, is $E[\hat{p}] = p$? And, does $\hat{p}$ have small variance for large sample sizes? To answer either question, we must take a closer look at the situation. Consider a random sample of $n$ objects drawn from the population. Since the population from which the sample is drawn is considered to be large, the number of objects in the sample with the trait of interest is at least approximately binomial with parameters $n$ and $p$. Thus the expected number in the sample with the trait, $E[X]$, is given by $E[X] = np$, and the variance in the number having that trait is given by $\text{Var } X = np(1 - p)$. These points can be understood best by considering their implications to Example 8.1.2.

---

**EXAMPLE 8.1.3** □ The sample of 150 patients from institutions for the retarded can be viewed as constituting a series of 150 identical trials. Each trial results in either a success, observation of a male with the fragile $X$ chromosome, or a failure, observation of a male with a normal $X$ chromosome. Since the population is large, obtaining an individual with a fragile $X$ chromosome on any given trial has no appreciable effect on the result of any other trial; that is, the trials are essentially independent. Furthermore, since the removal of several individuals from a large population has no significant effect on the composition of the group, we may assume that the probability of success $p$, for all practical purposes, remains the same from trial to trial. Thus $X$, the number of individuals with the fragile $X$ chromosome, satisfies at least approximately the underlying assumptions of the binomial model.

---

The preceding discussion allows us to answer easily the two questions posed earlier. In particular, now it is easy to show that the sample proportion is an unbiased estimator for the population proportion and that it has small variance for large sample sizes. Thus we can use the sample proportion as a point estimator for $p$ with some assurance that usually the estimates generated will, in fact, be close in value to $p$.

**THEOREM 8.1.1** □ The sample proportion

$$\hat{p} = \frac{X}{n} = \frac{\text{number of objects in sample with trait}}{\text{sample size}}$$

is unbiased for $p$. Furthermore,

$$\text{Var } \hat{p} = \frac{p(1 - p)}{n}$$

"OH, OH, I JUST DISCOVERED 79% OF MY RATS HAVE CANCER ... AND I DIDN'T INJECT THEM WITH ANYTHING YET!"



Now we turn to the problem of confidence interval estimation of $p$. That is, we would like to extend our point estimate of $p$ to an interval of values so that a confidence level can be reported. To do so, we must find a random variable whose expression involves $p$ and whose probability distribution is known at least approximately. This is easily done. Theorem 5.4.1, which provides the basis for the normal approximation to the binomial distribution, states that for large sample sizes, a binomial variable $X$ with parameters $n$ and $p$ is approximately normal with mean $np$ and variance $np(1 - p)$. By standardizing $X$, it is found that $(X - np)/\sqrt{np(1 - p)}$ is approximately standard normal. Dividing both the numerator and denominator of this expression by $n$, we see that the variable

$$\frac{X/n - p}{\sqrt{p(1 - p)/n}}$$

is also approximately standard normal. This variable does involve $p$, and its probability distribution is known at least approximately. So it can be used to construct the formula for a $100(1 - \alpha)\%$ confidence interval on $p$. That is, it can be utilized to find *statistics* $L_1$ and $L_2$ such that $P[L_1 \le p \le L_2] \doteq 1 - \alpha$.

To do so, consider the partition of the standard normal curve shown in Figure 8.3. From the diagram we can see that

$$P\left[-z_{\alpha/2} \le \frac{X/n - p}{\sqrt{p(1 - p)/n}} \le z_{\alpha/2}\right] \doteq 1 - \alpha$$

We algebraically isolate $p$ in the middle of this inequality to obtain the expressions for the lower and upper confidence bounds on $p$:

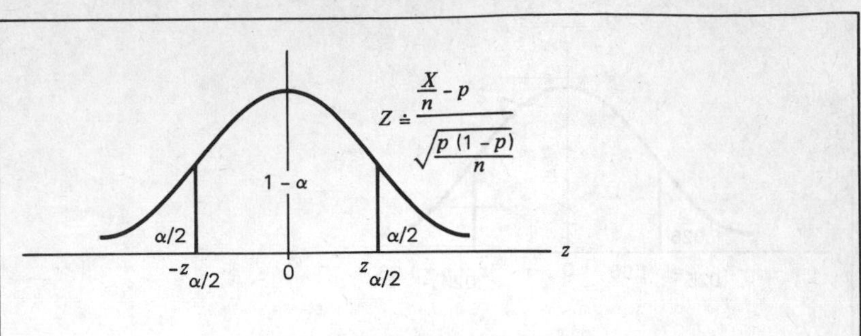


**FIGURE 8.3** Partition of $Z$ to obtain a $100(1-\alpha)\%$ confidence interval on $p$.

$$P\left[-z_{\alpha/2}\sqrt{\frac{p(1-p)}{n}} \le \frac{X}{n} - p \le z_{\alpha/2}\sqrt{\frac{p(1-p)}{n}}\right] \doteq 1-\alpha$$

$$P\left[\frac{X}{n} + z_{\alpha/2}\sqrt{\frac{p(1-p)}{n}} \ge p \ge \frac{X}{n} - z_{\alpha/2}\sqrt{\frac{p(1-p)}{n}}\right] \doteq 1-\alpha$$

$$P\left[\frac{X}{n} - z_{\alpha/2}\sqrt{\frac{p(1-p)}{n}} \le p \le \frac{X}{n} + z_{\alpha/2}\sqrt{\frac{p(1-p)}{n}}\right] \doteq 1-\alpha$$

It appears that the confidence bounds $L_1$ and $L_2$ are given by

$$L_1 = \frac{X}{n} - z_{\alpha/2}\sqrt{\frac{p(1-p)}{n}} = \hat{p} - z_{\alpha/2}\sqrt{\frac{p(1-p)}{n}}$$

$$L_2 = \frac{X}{n} + z_{\alpha/2}\sqrt{\frac{p(1-p)}{n}} = \hat{p} + z_{\alpha/2}\sqrt{\frac{p(1-p)}{n}}$$

However, there is a problem here that has not been encountered before. The bounds $L_1$ and $L_2$ must be *statistics*. Unfortunately, this is not the case. As written, $L_1$ and $L_2$ both involve the unknown parameter $p$. This means that we are attempting to use $p$ to estimate $p$–a seemingly impossible situation! This problem can be overcome in two ways. The obvious method is to replace $p$ by its unbiased point estimator $\hat{p}$, to yield bounds

$$L_1 = \hat{p} - z_{\alpha/2}\sqrt{\frac{\hat{p}(1-\hat{p})}{n}}$$

$$L_2 = \hat{p} + z_{\alpha/2}\sqrt{\frac{\hat{p}(1-\hat{p})}{n}}$$

method I

This method is illustrated in Example 8.1.4.

---

**EXAMPLE 8.1.4** □ The adult screwworm fly is metallic blue and triple the size of a housefly. The screwworm lays eggs in wounds of warm-blooded

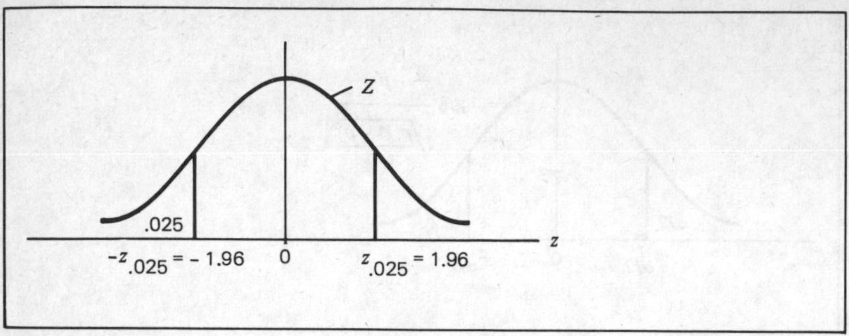


**FIGURE 8.4** Partition of $Z$ to obtain a 95% confidence interval on $p$.

animals and causes severe infection. An experiment was conducted to learn how to control this population. Screwworm pupae were exposed to a radiation dose of 2500 rad in hopes of sterilizing most males. Since the females mate but once, mating with a sterilized male results in sterile eggs. It was found that after radiation, 415 of the 500 matings observed resulted in sterile eggs. The point estimate for the proportion of sterile matings produced by this dosage level is $\hat{p} = 415/500 = .83$. To construct a 95% confidence interval on $p$, consider the partition of the standard normal curve in Figure 8.4.

By using method I, a 95% confidence interval on $p$ is given by

$$\hat{p} \pm z_{\alpha/2}\sqrt{\frac{\hat{p}(1-\hat{p})}{n}} = .83 \pm 1.96\sqrt{\frac{.83(.17)}{500}}$$
$$= .83 \pm .03$$

Converting to percentages, we can be approximately 95% confident that the true percentage of sterile matings resulting from this level of radiation is between 80% and 86%. Note that the word *approximately* is employed since we are approximating a binomial distribution with a normal curve and also are estimating $p$ by $\hat{p}$ to obtain the confidence bounds.

---

Recall that the troublesome term in the proposed expressions for $L_1$ and $L_2$ is $p(1-p)$, for it involves the unknown parameter $p$. The second method for constructing confidence intervals on $p$ is based on a result from elementary calculus. This result states that regardless of the value of $p$, the term $p(1-p)$ will never exceed $1/4$. Therefore, we may replace the troublesome term by its *largest* possible value, $1/4$, to obtain bounds

$$L_1 = \hat{p} - z_{\alpha/2}\sqrt{\frac{1}{4n}}$$
$$L_2 = \hat{p} + z_{\alpha/2}\sqrt{\frac{1}{4n}}$$

method II

Method II is more conservative than method I in that it yields intervals that are, in fact, a bit *longer* than they need be. Confidence intervals obtained by using method II will be longer than those obtained from method I. Since $p(1-p) = \frac{1}{4}$ if and only if $p = \frac{1}{2}$, the closer $\hat{p}$ lies to $\frac{1}{2}$, the more close the agreement between the two will be. Either method can be used in practice at the discretion of the experimenter.

---

**EXAMPLE 8.1.5** □ For comparative purposes, let us construct a 95% confidence interval on the proportion of sterile matings in screwworm flies based on the data of Example 8.1.4. By using method II, this interval is

$$\hat{p} \pm z_{\alpha/2}\sqrt{\frac{1}{4n}} = .83 \pm 1.96\sqrt{\frac{1}{4(500)}}$$
$$= .83 \pm .04$$

That is, we are approximately 95% confident that the true percentage of sterile matings resulting from a radiation dose of 2500 rad is between 79% and 87%. Note that this interval is, as expected, a bit longer than the previous one (80 to 86%). This interval is conservative in the sense that it is the maximum necessary length. Hence, the actual confidence that can be placed in this interval is somewhat higher than the apparent level of 95%.

---

**EXAMPLE 8.1.6** □ The newest development in the treatment of acne is a drug called *cis*-13-retinoic acid. A recent study tested this drug on 14 patients suffering from severe acne. Of the 14 patients tested, 13 showed dramatic clearing of their active lesions. To construct a 99% confidence interval on $p$, the proportion of patients on whom the drug will be effective, the partition of the standard normal curve shown in Figure 8.5 is needed. By using method II, a 99% confidence interval on $p$ is found to be

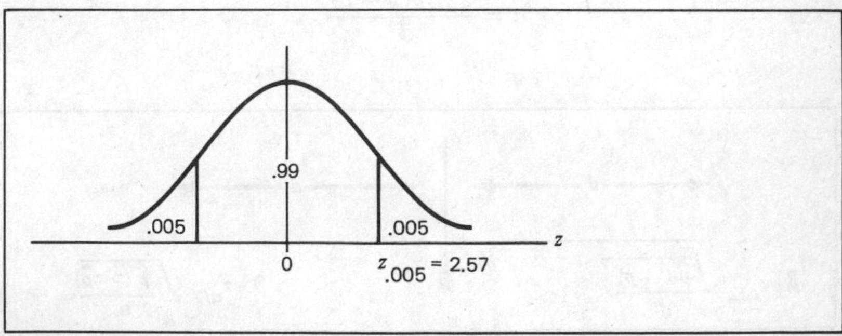


**FIGURE 8.5** Partition of $Z$ to obtain a 99% confidence interval on $p$.

$$\hat{p} \pm z_{\alpha/2}\sqrt{\frac{1}{4n}} = \frac{13}{14} \pm 2.57\sqrt{\frac{1}{4(14)}}$$
$$= .93 \pm .34$$

We can be 99% confident that the drug will be effective on 59% to 100% of those patients on whom it is used.

---

There is a point to be made from Example 8.1.6. It is obvious that the interval obtained is not very informative. It is much too long to give the experimenter any clear indication of the actual value of $p$. The problem is caused by two factors: the degree of confidence required is very high (99%), and the sample size is too small. Thus we can correct the problem by reducing the level of confidence or increasing the sample size or doing both.

This brings up one other important question. How large a sample should be selected so that $\hat{p}$ lies within a specified distance $d$ of $p$ with a stated degree of confidence? There are two ways to answer this question. The first, based on method I for constructing a confidence interval, is applicable when an estimate of $p$ based on some prior experiment is available. This method is illustrated schematically in Figure 8.6.

Since we are $100(1-\alpha)\%$ sure that $p$ lies in the above interval, we are also $100(1-\alpha)\%$ sure that $\hat{p}$ and $p$ differ by at most $d$, where $d$ is given by

$$d = z_{\alpha/2}\sqrt{\frac{\hat{p}(1-\hat{p})}{n}}$$

This equation is solved for $n$ as follows:

$$d = z_{\alpha/2}\sqrt{\frac{\hat{p}(1-\hat{p})}{n}}$$
$$d^2 = z^2_{\alpha/2}\frac{\hat{p}(1-\hat{p})}{n}$$
$$n = \frac{z^2_{\alpha/2}\hat{p}(1-\hat{p})}{d^2}$$

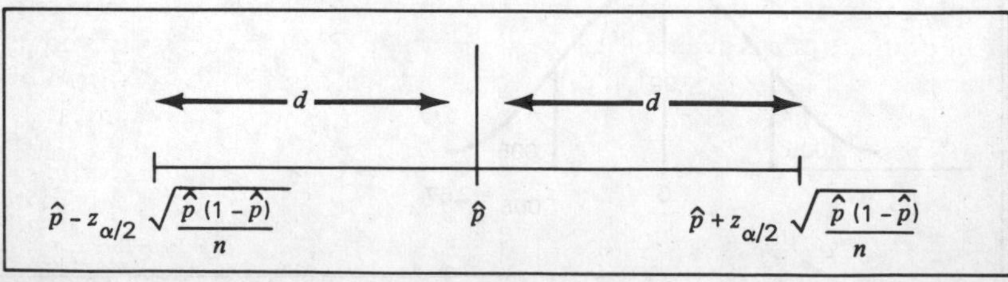


**FIGURE 8.6** Confidence interval on $p$: method I.

Thus we obtain the following formula for finding the sample size needed to estimate $p$ with a stated degree of accuracy and confidence when a prior estimate of $p$ is available:

$$n \doteq \frac{z^2_{\alpha/2}\widehat{p}(1-\widehat{p})}{d^2} \qquad \text{(prior estimate available)}$$

The use of this formula is illustrated in Example 8.1.7.

**EXAMPLE 8.1.7** □ If we wish to further test the acne-combating drug of Example 8.1.6, how large a sample should we use to estimate $p$ to within $d = .02$ with 90% confidence? Since a prior estimate $\widehat{p} = .93$ is available, the above formula is applicable. The point $z_{\alpha/2}$ called for in the formula is the same point required to construct a 90% confidence interval on $p$. This point is shown in Figure 8.7. Thus the sample size required is

$$n = \frac{z^2_{\alpha/2}\widehat{p}(1-\widehat{p})}{d^2} = \frac{(1.65)^2(.93)(.07)}{(.02)^2}$$
$$\doteq 444$$

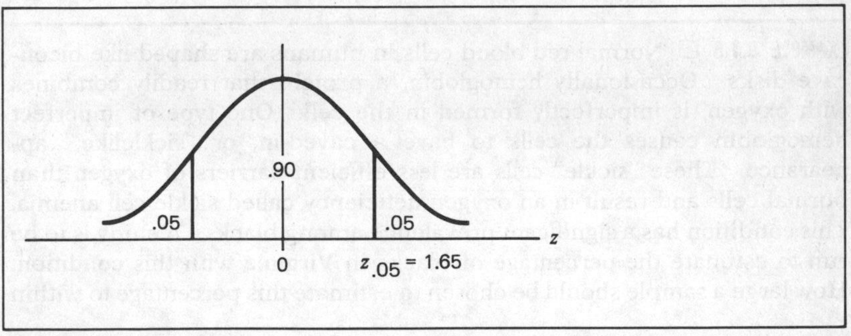


**FIGURE 8.7** Point required to obtain a 90% confidence interval on $p$.

The second method for determining sample size for estimating proportions is based on method II for constructing a confidence interval on $p$. It is applicable when the study is being run for the first time, and hence no prior estimate of $p$ is available to the researcher. The formula is derived in a manner similar to that used previously. We begin with the diagram of Figure 8.8. In this case, $d = z_{\alpha/2}\sqrt{1/(4n)}$. Solving this equation for $n$, we obtain

$$d^2 = z^2_{\alpha/2}\frac{1}{4n}$$

or

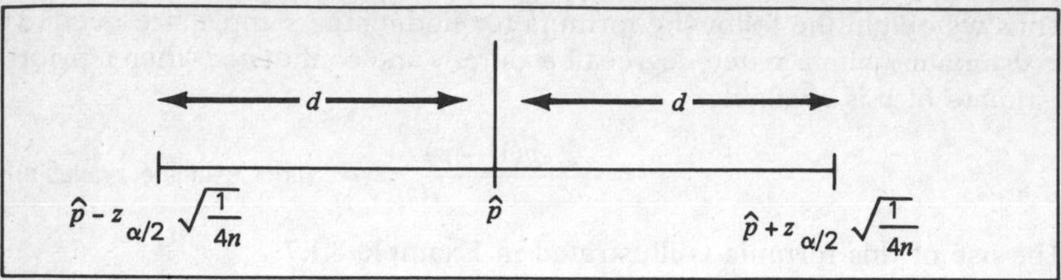


**FIGURE 8.8** Confidence interval on $p$: method II.

$$n \doteq \frac{z^2_{\alpha/2}}{4d^2}$$

Thus the formula for finding the sample size required to estimate $p$ with a stated degree of accuracy and confidence when *no* prior estimate of $p$ is available is

$$n \doteq \frac{z^2_{\alpha/2}}{4d^2} \qquad \text{(no prior estimate available)}$$

The use of this formula is illustrated in Example 8.1.8.

---

**EXAMPLE 8.1.8** □ Normal red blood cells in humans are shaped like biconcave disks. Occasionally hemoglobin, a protein that readily combines with oxygen, is imperfectly formed in the cell. One type of imperfect hemoglobin causes the cells to have a caved-in, or "sicklelike," appearance. These "sickle" cells are less efficient carriers of oxygen than normal cells and result in an oxygen deficiency called sickle cell anemia. This condition has a significant prevalence among blacks. A study is to be run to estimate the percentage of blacks in Virginia with this condition. How large a sample should be chosen to estimate this percentage to within

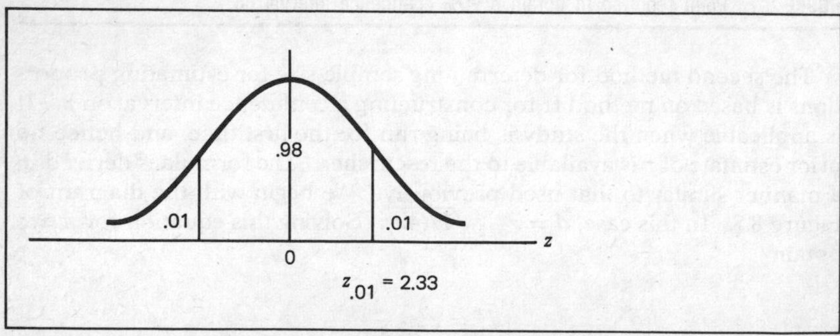


**FIGURE 8.9** Point required to obtain a 98% confidence interval on $p$.

1 percentage point with 98% confidence? No prior estimate of $p$ is assumed available. The $z$ point required is shown in Figure 8.9. Since 1 percentage point is .01, the desired sample size is

$$n \doteq \frac{z_{\alpha/2}^2}{4d^2} = \frac{(2.33)^2}{4(.01)^2} = 13{,}573$$

## EXERCISES 8.1

1. One of the most troublesome forms of venereal disease is caused by the common herpes simplex virus. A recent study tested an ointment containing the sugar 2-deoxy-D-glucose on 36 women with genital herpes infections. Within 4 days, the symptoms were cleared up in 32 of the 36 cases. Find a point estimate for $p$, the proportion of women for whom this treatment will be effective.
2. A national survey was run to estimate the proportion $p$ of individuals 16 years old and under who smoke regularly. Of 1000 individuals interviewed, 200 smoked regularly. Find a point estimate for $p$.
3. A recent study indicates that acute stress can induce changes in the heart that may lead to death. Evidence was obtained by examining 15 cases in which people died after a physical assault even though the injuries alone were not severe enough to cause death. Of the cases, 11 showed a type of heart-cell death called myofibrillar degeneration.
   **a.** Find a point estimate of $p$, the proportion of deaths due to myofibrillar degeneration in assault cases.
   **b.** Find a 90% confidence interval on $p$ by using method I. Is $n$ large enough to get a good idea of the value of $p$ based on this interval?
4. Using the data of Exercise 8.1.1 and method I, find a 95% confidence interval on $p$.
5. Find a 96% confidence interval on $p$ by using the data of Exercise 8.1.2 and method II.
6. In running a white cell count, a drop of blood is smeared thinly and evenly on a glass slide, stained with Wright's stain, and examined under a microscope. Of 200 white cells counted, 125 were neutrophils, a white cell produced in the bone marrow whose function, in part, is to take up infective agents in the blood.
   **a.** Find a point estimate for $p$, the proportion of neutrophils found among the white cells of this individual.
   **b.** Find a 90% confidence interval on $p$ by using method I.
   **c.** In a normally healthy individual, the percentage of neutrophils among the white cells is 60% to 70%. Based on the interval obtained in part **b**, is there clear evidence of a neutrophil imbalance in this individual? Explain.
7. One defense that organisms have against predators is that of being obnoxious, that is, having a disagreeable taste, odor, or spray. One such insect is the walkingstick. Of 50 bluejays that had been sprayed by a walkingstick, 42 remained aloof from the insect for at least 2 weeks. Use this information to find a 94% confidence interval on $p$, the proportion of bluejays that will avoid further contact with the walkingstick for as long as 2 weeks.

**8.** When the study of Example 8.1.8 was conducted, of the 13,573 blacks sampled, 1085 were found to have sickle cell anemia. Use this information to find a 98% confidence interval on the percentage of blacks in the state who have the disease.

**9.** How large a sample would be required to estimate the proportion of deaths due to myofibrillar degeneration in assault cases to within .02 with 95% confidence? (Use the data of Exercise 8.1.3.)

**10.** One problem associated with the use of the supersonic transport (SST) is the sonic boom. In the late 1960s and early 1970s, preliminary tests were run over Oklahoma City, St. Louis, and other areas. After the tests were run, a survey was to be conducted to estimate the percentage of people who felt that they could not live with the sonic booms. How large a sample should have been chosen to estimate the percentage to within 3 percentage points with 94% confidence?

**11.** The Environmental Protection Agency recently identified 30,000 waste dumping sites in the United States that were considered to be at least potentially dangerous. How large a sample is needed to estimate the percentage of these sites that do pose a serious threat to health to within 2 percentage points with 90% confidence?

***12.** *Capture-Recapture Method for Sampling Wildlife Populations.* One parameter of interest to foresters is $N$, the population size of certain species of wild animals. For example, it is important to know the number of bears in the wild in the Great Smoky Mountains so that this population can be protected or controlled. Unfortunately, it is impossible to take a census of this population because of its mobility and the large geographical area involved. Hence $N$ must be approximated statistically. In the capture-recapture method, a number of animals are caught, tagged, and released. They are allowed to disperse. Several days or weeks later, a second sample of animals is obtained. The proportion of tagged animals in this sample is determined. This sample proportion is used as an estimate for the proportion of tagged animals in the population. Let

$T$ = number of animals captured and tagged originally

$p$ = proportion of tagged animals in population $= \dfrac{T}{N}$

$C$ = number of animals caught in second sample

$R$ = number of animals recaptured
= number of tagged animals in second sample

$\hat{p}$ = proportion of tagged animals in second sample $= \dfrac{R}{C}$

Since $\hat{p}$ estimates $p$, $\hat{p} \doteq p$. Substituting, we may conclude that

$$\frac{R}{C} \doteq \frac{T}{N}$$

Solving this equation for $N$, we see that

$$N \doteq \frac{CT}{R}$$

For example, if originally $T = 20$ bears were tagged, $C = 15$ were caught in the second sample, and of these $R = 3$ were tagged, then the estimated number of bears living in the wild is

$$\widehat{N} = \frac{CT}{R} = \frac{15(20)}{3} = 100$$

a. A study is conducted of falcons in northwest Canada. Thirty falcons were tagged, twenty falcons were caught in the second sample, and of these two were tagged. Use this information to estimate $N$, the number of falcons living free in the area.

b. In the mid 1930s, the trumpeter swan of North America was in danger of extinction. At this time, Yellowstone Park and an adjacent hot springs area at Red Rock Lakes, Montana, were designated as a refuge. In the late 1960s, a study was conducted of the swans in this area. Fifty swans were captured and tagged. A second sample of 30 swans contained 5 that were tagged. Use this information to estimate the total swan population in this region at this time.

c. The capture-recapture method is to be used to roughly estimate the number of drug addicts in New York City. For 6 months note is made of the drug addicts arrested for the first time for minor offenses. Then they are released. In this way, 500 addicts are "tagged." During the next year 1800 addicts were arrested for various offenses, and 20 were from the tagged group. Based on this information, estimate the total number of drug addicts in New York City.

---

## HYPOTHESIS TESTING ON $p$

**8.2** □ We consider now the problem of testing a hypothesis on a proportion $p$. This implies that a value for $p$ has been proposed prior to conducting the study. The purpose of the experiment is to gather statistical evidence that either supports or refutes this value. The hypotheses tested can assume any one of the usual three forms, depending on the purpose of the study. Let $p_0$ denote the hypothesized value of $p$. Then these forms are as follows:

| I | II | III |
|---|---|---|
| $H_0: p \leq p_0$ | $H_0: p \geq p_0$ | $H_0: p = p_0$ |
| $H_1: p > p_0$ | $H_1: p < p_0$ | $H_1: p \neq p_0$ |
| Right-tailed test | Left-tailed test | Two-tailed test |

---

**EXAMPLE 8.2.1** □ One theory of learning that has caused a great deal of controversy is that of "transfer of training by cannibalism." In one study to gain statistical support for this theory, a group of planarians was trained to avoid electric shock. Then they were ground up and fed to a group of 100 untrained planarians. If no training is transferred to the untrained planarians by this cannibalism, then the probability that an untrained planarian can avoid the shock is assumed to be $1/2$; otherwise, this probability is greater than $1/2$. Since the purpose of the study is to gain support for the

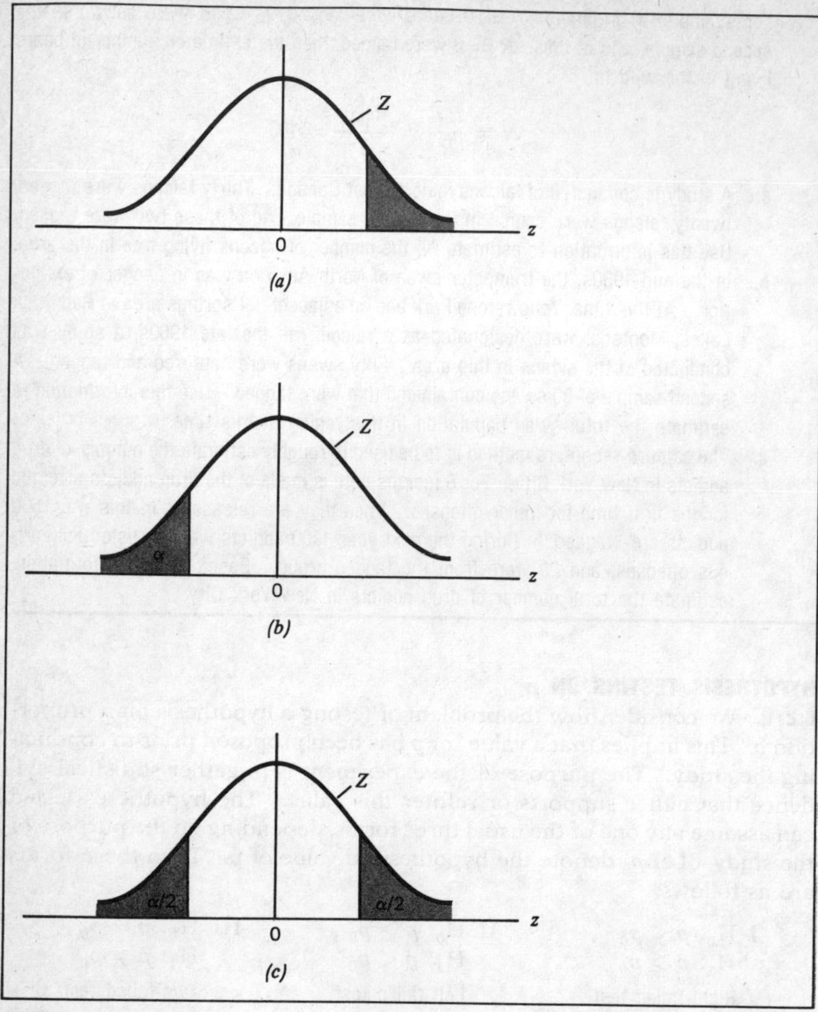


**FIGURE 8.10** (*a*) Critical region: right-tailed test (H$_1$: $p > p_0$); (*b*) critical region: left-tailed test (H$_1$: $p < p_0$); (*c*) critical region: two-tailed test (H$_1$: $p \neq p_0$).

theory, the statement that $p > 1/2$ becomes the alternative hypothesis. So we are testing

$$H_0: p \leq \frac{1}{2}$$

$$H_1: p > \frac{1}{2}$$

**EXAMPLE 8.2.2** □ Until recently, $p$, the death rate from a highly fatal viral infection of the brain, herpes simplex virus encephalitis, has been 70%. A study is run to test the new drug vidarabine for use in treating this disease. Since it is hoped that vidarabine will reduce the death rate, this statement becomes the alternative hypothesis. That is, we are testing

$$H_0: p \geq .70$$
$$H_1: p < .70$$

To test a hypothesis on $p$, a test statistic must be developed. The statistic should be logical. Furthermore, to find the level of significance of the test, its probability distribution must be known at least approximately under the assumption that the null hypothesis is true. Again, the test statistic chosen is the same as the random variable used to generate the confidence bounds for $p$. In particular,

$$\frac{X/n - p_0}{\sqrt{p_0(1 - p_0)/n}}$$

will serve as the test statistic. This statistic is logical in that basically it compares the unbiased estimate for $p$, namely $\hat{p} = X/n$, with the hypothesized value of $p$, namely $p_0$. If these are close in value, indicating that $H_0$ is true, then the observed value of the statistic will be close to zero. If $p$ and $p_0$ differ greatly, indicating that $H_0$ is false, then the observed value of the test statistic will be either a very large positive value or a very large negative value. For large sample sizes, the test statistic is approximately standard normal. The critical region and critical point(s) for each of the three test types are shown in Figure 8.10.

**EXAMPLE 8.2.3** □ The theory of learning by cannibalism is to be confirmed by testing

$$H_0: p \leq .5$$
$$H_1: p > .5$$

(cannibalism increases the probability of avoiding shock)

at the $\alpha = .1$ level. Since the inequality in the alternative points to the right, a right-tailed test is run. The critical point and critical region for the test are shown in Figure 8.11.

We reject $H_0$ in favor of $H_1$ and conclude that cannibalism does increase the probability of avoiding shock if and only if the observed value of the test statistic is greater than or equal to 1.28. When the experiment was conducted, 57 of the 100 planarians tested did avoid the shock. The observed value of the test statistic is

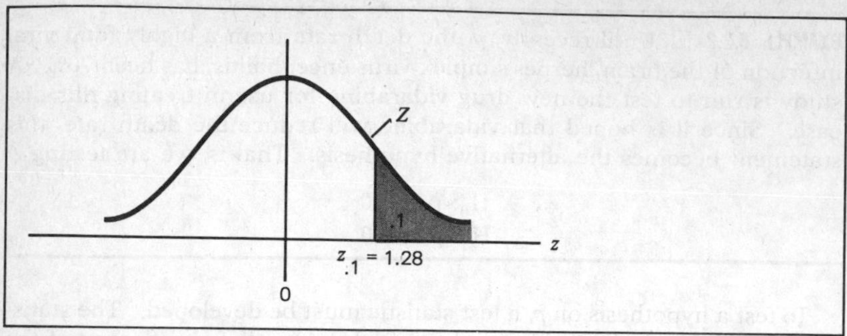


**FIGURE 8.11** Critical region: $\alpha = .1$, right-tailed test.

$$\frac{x/n - p_0}{\sqrt{p_0(1 - p_0)/n}} = \frac{{}^{57}\!/_{100} - .5}{\sqrt{.5(.5)/100}} = 1.4$$

Since 1.4 exceeds the critical point of 1.28, we reject $H_0$. Keep in mind that we are now subject to making a Type I error, but the probability that we have done so is only 10%. That is, there is a 10% chance that we erroneously concluded that cannibalism increases the probability of avoiding shock.

---

Note that the method for testing hypotheses on $p$ illustrated in Example 8.2.3 does assume that the sample size is "large." Following the guidelines of Chapter 5, the word *large* is interpreted to mean that $n$ and $p_0$ are such that $p_0 \leq .5$ and $np_0 > 5$ or $p_0 > .5$ and $n(1 - p_0) > 5$. These criteria are met in Example 8.2.3.

## EXERCISES 8.2

1. Opponents of the construction of a dam on the New River claim that a majority of residents living along the river also are opposed to its construction. A survey is conducted to gain support for this point of view.
   a. Set up the appropriate null and alternative hypotheses.
   b. Find the critical point for an $\alpha = .05$ test of this hypothesis.
   c. Of 500 people surveyed, 270 opposed the construction. Is this sufficient evidence at the $\alpha = .05$ level to claim that a majority of residents are opposed? Explain your answer based on the observed value of the test statistic.
   d. To what type of error are you subject now? Discuss the practical consequences of making such an error.
2. A new type of Japanese beetle trap is being tested. The manufacturer claims that the trap attracts and kills more than 90% of the beetles that come within 30 feet of the trap. An experiment is conducted to gain evidence to support this claim.
   a. Set up the appropriate null and alternative hypotheses.

b. Find the critical point for an $\alpha = .1$ test of this hypothesis.
c. The experiment is conducted by releasing 900 beetles near the trap. If $H_0$ is true, what is the maximum number that you would expect to see attracted to the trap? Of the 900, in fact, 825 were attracted to the trap and killed. Is this sufficient evidence at the $\alpha = .1$ level to support the claim?
d. To what type of error are you now subject? Discuss the practical consequences of making such an error.

3. Consider Example 8.2.2. Of 50 subjects on which vidarabine was tested, 14 died. Find the $P$ value for this test.
4. Among patients with lung cancer, generally 90% or more die within 3 years. As a result of new forms of treatment, it is felt that this rate has been reduced.
   a. Set up the null and alternative hypotheses needed to support this contention.
   b. In a recent study of 150 patients diagnosed with lung cancer, 128 died within 3 years. Can $H_0$ be rejected at the $\alpha = .1$ level? At the $\alpha = .05$ level? Do you think that there is sufficient evidence to claim that the new methods of treatment are more effective than the old? Explain.
5. The current method for treating acute myeloblastic leukemia is to give the patient intensive chemotherapy at the time of diagnosis. Historically this has resulted in a 70% remission rate. In studying a new method of treatment, 50 volunteers are used. How many of the patients would have to go into remission for researchers to claim at the $\alpha = .025$ level that the new method produced a higher remission rate than the old?

---

## COMPARING TWO PROPORTIONS: ESTIMATION

**8.3** □ The problem of comparing two proportions arises frequently in biological and medical studies. The general situation can be described as follows: There are two populations of interest, the same trait is studied in each population, each member of each population can be classed as either having the trait or failing to have it, and in each population the proportion having the trait is unknown. Inferences are to be made on $p_1$, $p_2$, and $p_1 - p_2$, where $p_1$ and $p_2$ are the proportions in the first and second populations with the trait, respectively. (See Figure 8.12.)

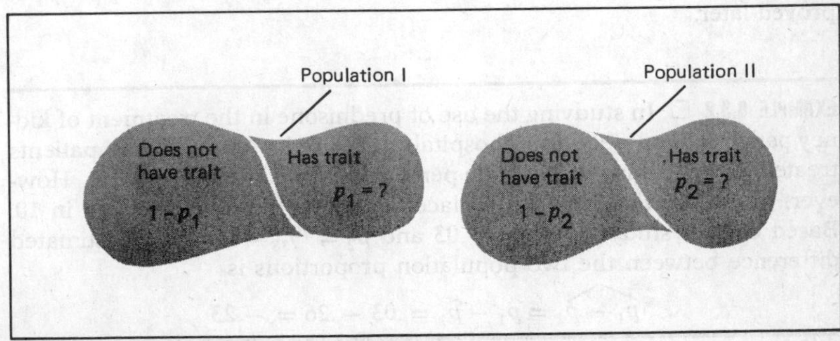


**FIGURE 8.12** $p_1 - p_2 = ?$

**EXAMPLE 8.3.1** ☐ Annually kidney failure claims the lives of many people. A study is conducted among kidney patients to compare the rate of kidney failure among those treated with the steroid drug prednisone to those who received a placebo. Here the two populations of interest are kidney patients treated with the drug and those not receiving it. The trait under study in each case is that of suffering kidney failure. (See Figure 8.13.)

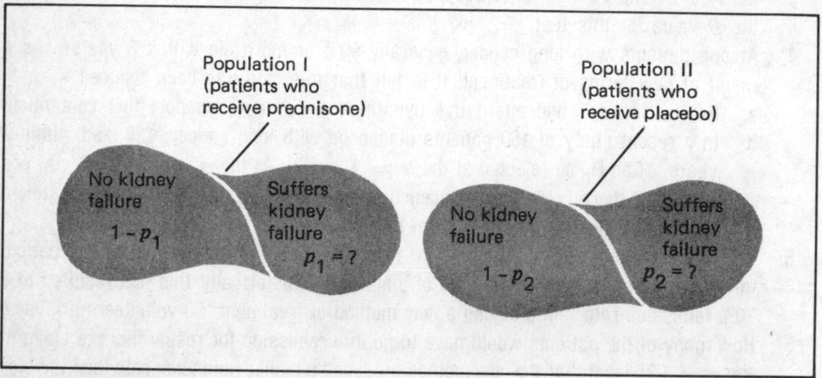


**FIGURE 8.13** $p_1 - p_2 = ?$

The problem of point estimation of the difference between two proportions is solved in the obvious way. We simply estimate $p_1$ and $p_2$ individually and then take as our estimate for $p_1 - p_2$ the difference between the two. That is,

$$\widehat{p_1 - p_2} = \hat{p}_1 - \hat{p}_2 = \frac{X_1}{n_1} - \frac{X_2}{n_2}$$

where $n_1$ and $n_2$ are the sizes of the samples drawn from the two populations and $X_1$ and $X_2$ are the number of objects, respectively, in the samples with the trait. The fact that this estimator is unbiased for $p_1 - p_2$ is proved later.

**EXAMPLE 8.3.2** ☐ In studying the use of prednisone in the treatment of kidney patients, 72 subjects at 19 hospitals were used. Among the 34 patients treated with prednisone, only one person developed kidney failure. However, of the 38 who received a placebo, kidney failure developed in 10. Based on this study, $\hat{p}_1 = 1/34 \doteq .03$ and $\hat{p}_2 = 10/38 \doteq .26$. The estimated difference between the two population proportions is

$$\widehat{p_1 - p_2} = \hat{p}_1 - \hat{p}_2 = .03 - .26 = -.23$$

To extend the point estimator $\hat{p}_1 - \hat{p}_2$ to an interval estimator, we must pause to consider the probability distribution of this variable. Its approximate distribution is given in Theorem 8.3.1.

**THEOREM 8.3.1** □ For large sample sizes, the estimator $\hat{p}_1 - \hat{p}_2$ is approximately normal with mean $p_1 - p_2$ and variance

$$\frac{p_1(1-p_1)}{n_1} + \frac{p_2(1-p_2)}{n_2}$$

To construct a $100(1-\alpha)\%$ confidence interval on $p_1 - p_2$, we must find a random variable whose expression involves this parameter and whose probability distribution is known at least approximately. This is done easily now. We simply standardize the variable $\hat{p}_1 - \hat{p}_2$ to conclude that the variable

$$\frac{\hat{p}_1 - \hat{p}_2 - (p_1 - p_2)}{\sqrt{p_1(1-p_1)/n_1 + p_2(1-p_2)/n_2}}$$

is approximately *standard* normal. Rather than repeat an algebraic argument given previously, let us consider three intervals that have been derived already and note their similarities:

| PARAMETER BEING ESTIMATED | BEGAN DERIVATION WITH | DISTRIBUTION | BOUNDS |
|---|---|---|---|
| $\mu$ ($\sigma^2$ known) | $\dfrac{\bar{X}-\mu}{\sigma/\sqrt{n}}$ | $Z$ | $\bar{X} \pm z_{\alpha/2}\dfrac{\sigma}{\sqrt{n}}$ |
| $\mu$ ($\sigma^2$ unknown) | $\dfrac{\bar{X}-\mu}{S/\sqrt{n}}$ | $T$ | $\bar{X} \pm t_{\alpha/2}\dfrac{S}{\sqrt{n}}$ |
| $p$ | $\dfrac{\hat{p}-p}{\sqrt{p(1-p)/n}}$ | $\sim Z$ | $\hat{p} \pm z_{\alpha/2}\sqrt{\dfrac{p(1-p)}{n}}$ |

The algebraic structure of each of the beginning variables is the same and is of the form

$$\frac{\text{Estimator} - \text{parameter}}{D}$$

where $D$ is related to the standard deviation of the estimator. This is also the algebraic form assumed by the variable

$$\frac{\hat{p}_1 - \hat{p}_2 - (p_1 - p_2)}{\sqrt{p_1(1-p_1)/n_1 + p_2(1-p_2)/n_2}} \sim Z$$

The confidence bounds in the previous cases took the form

$$\text{Estimator} \pm \text{probability point} \times D$$

Applying this notion to the above random variable, we find the proposed confidence bounds for a confidence interval on $p_1 - p_2$ to be

$$\hat{p}_1 - \hat{p}_2 \pm z_{\alpha/2}\sqrt{\frac{p_1(1-p_1)}{n_1} + \frac{p_2(1-p_2)}{n_2}}$$

Once again, there is a slight problem. The proposed bounds are not *statistics*. They include the unknown population proportions $p_1$ and $p_2$. As in the one-sample case, this problem can be overcome either by replacing the population proportions with their estimators $\hat{p}_1$ and $\hat{p}_2$ or by replacing the terms $p_1(1-p_1)$ and $p_2(1-p_2)$ with their maximum possible value of $\frac{1}{4}$. Then the following formulas are obtained for finding confidence intervals on the difference between two population proportions:

$$\hat{p}_1 - \hat{p}_2 \pm z_{\alpha/2}\sqrt{\frac{\hat{p}_1(1-\hat{p}_1)}{n_1} + \frac{\hat{p}_2(1-\hat{p}_2)}{n_2}} \qquad \text{(method I)}$$

$$\hat{p}_1 - \hat{p}_2 \pm z_{\alpha/2}\sqrt{\frac{1}{4n_1} + \frac{1}{4n_2}} \qquad \text{(method II, conservative)}$$

These methods are illustrated in Examples 8.3.3 and 8.3.4.

---

**EXAMPLE 8.3.3** □ To use method I to construct a 95% confidence interval on the difference in the rate of kidney failure between those receiving prednisone and those not receiving the drug, the partition of the standard normal curve shown in Figure 8.4 is needed. From Example 8.3.2, $n_1 = 34$, $n_2 = 38$, $\hat{p}_1 = .03$, $\hat{p}_2 = .26$, and $\hat{p}_1 - \hat{p}_2 = -.23$. The desired confidence bounds are

$$\hat{p}_1 - \hat{p}_2 \pm z_{\alpha/2}\sqrt{\frac{\hat{p}_1(1-\hat{p}_1)}{n_1} + \frac{\hat{p}_2(1-\hat{p}_2)}{n_2}} = -.23 \pm 1.96\sqrt{\frac{.03(.97)}{34} + \frac{.26(.74)}{38}}$$
$$= -.23 \pm .15$$

We can be 95% confident that the difference in failure rates is between −38% and −8%. Note that zero is not in this interval. This is important since we can interpret this to mean that we are 95% confident that the two rates are, in fact, different. Since both bounds are negative, we can further infer that the failure rate for those on the drug is smaller than that for those not on the drug by at least 8%.

---

**EXAMPLE 8.3.4** □ A study is conducted of survival rates of adult birds in the tropics and in the temperature zone. Initially 500 adult birds were tagged with leg bands and released in Panama, a tropical region. A year later, 445 were recaptured. If we assume that those not recovered had fallen victim to a predator, the estimated 1-year survival rate for adult birds in the region is $\widehat{p}_1 = {}^{445}\!/\!_{500} = .89$. A similar experiment in Illinois, in the temperate zone, resulted in recovery of 252 of the 500 birds for an estimated survival rate of approximately .50. A 90% confidence interval on the difference in survival rates depends on the partition of the standard normal curve shown in Figure 8.7.

By using method II, the desired confidence interval is

$$\widehat{p}_1 - \widehat{p}_2 \pm z_{\alpha/2}\sqrt{\frac{1}{4n_1} + \frac{1}{4n_2}} = .89 - .50 \pm 1.65\sqrt{\frac{1}{4(500)} + \frac{1}{4(500)}}$$

$$= .39 \pm .05$$

Note that since zero is not contained in this interval, we can be 90% confident that there is, in fact, a difference in these survival rates. Since both bounds are positive, we can claim that the survival rate in Panama is higher than that in Illinois. This does lend some support to the theory that the survival rate of adult birds in the tropics is generally higher than that in the temperate zone.

---

## EXERCISES 8.3

1. The drug Anturane, marketed since 1959 for the treatment of gout, is being studied for use in preventing sudden deaths from a second heart attack among patients who have already suffered a first attack. In the study, 733 patients received Anturane and 742 were given a placebo. After 8 months it was found that of 42 deaths from a second heart attack, 29 had occurred in the placebo group and 13 in the Anturane group. Use these data to estimate the difference in the percentage of sudden deaths among Anturane users and among patients not receiving the drug.
2. An antibiotic called doxycycline is being tested for use in preventing "traveler's diarrhea." The drug was tested on 38 Peace Corps volunteers who were going to Kenya. Half were given doxycycline, and half were given a dummy dose. Of those on doxycycline, 17 were protected from the disorder while only 11 from the other group were protected. Find a point estimate on the difference in the protection rates among those using doxycycline and those not using it.
3. One of the best studied examples of natural selection is that of the peppered moth. Until 1845 all reported species had been light in color, but in that year a black moth was captured at Manchester. Because of industrialization in the area, the trunks of trees, rocks, and even the ground in the region had become blackened by soot. This mutant black form quickly spread. H. B. D. Kettlewell felt that the spread was due in part to the fact that the black color protected the moth from natural predators, in particular birds. Entomologists at the time claimed that they had never seen a bird eat a peppered moth of any color and discounted his idea. In an experiment to study the theory, Kettlewell marked a sample of 100 moths of each color and then released

them. He returned at night with light traps and recovered 40% of the black moths but only 19% of the light-colored ones. Assume that the moths not recovered had fallen prey to a predator. Find a point estimate for the difference in the survivàl rates.

4. Use method I to construct a 95% confidence interval on the difference in the percentage of sudden deaths among Anturane users and among patients not on the drug, based on the data of Exercise 8.3.1. If a 90% confidence interval were constructed based on the same data, which interval would be longer? Why? Verify your answer. Have you gained evidence to support the statement that the death rate from second attacks is lower among patients on the drug than among patients not on the drug? Explain.
5. Using method I and the data of Exercise 8.3.2, construct a 90% confidence interval on the difference in protection rates among those using doxycycline and those not on the drug. If method II were used to construct an interval of the same confidence level, which would be longer? Why? Verify your answer. Have you gained evidence to support the theory that doxycycline tends to give protection against "traveler's diarrhea"? Explain.
6. Use the data of Exercise 8.3.3 and method II to construct a 98% confidence interval on the difference in survival rates among black moths and light-colored moths in the Manchester region. Does the interval lend support to the statement that the black color tends to protect these moths from predators? Explain.

---

## COMPARING TWO PROPORTIONS: HYPOTHESIS TESTING

**8.4** □ Frequently problems arise in which it is theorized prior to the experiment that one proportion or percentage differs from another by a specified amount. The purpose of the experiment is to gain statistical support for the contention. These hypotheses take any one of the following three forms, where $(p_1 - p_2)_0$ represents the hypothesized value of the difference in proportions:

I $H_0\colon p_1 - p_2 \le (p_1 - p_2)_0$
$H_1\colon p_1 - p_2 > (p_1 - p_2)_0$
Right-tailed test

II $H_0\colon p_1 - p_2 \ge (p_1 - p_2)_0$
$H_1\colon p_1 - p_2 < (p_1 - p_2)_0$
Left-tailed test

III $H_0\colon p_1 - p_2 = (p_1 - p_2)_0$
$H_1\colon p_1 - p_2 \ne (p_1 - p_2)_0$
Two-tailed test

For instance, consider Example 8.4.1.

---

**EXAMPLE 8.4.1** □ Proponents of vitamin C claim that it will improve the chances of survival in cancer patients. Further, it is felt that the percentage of patients showing improvement among those who take a vitamin C supplement exceeds that of those who do not take a supplement by more than 4 percentage points. The situation is pictured in Figure 8.14. From the point of view of the proponents of vitamin C, we are testing

$$H_0\colon p_1 - p_2 \le .04 \qquad H_1\colon p_1 - p_2 > .04$$

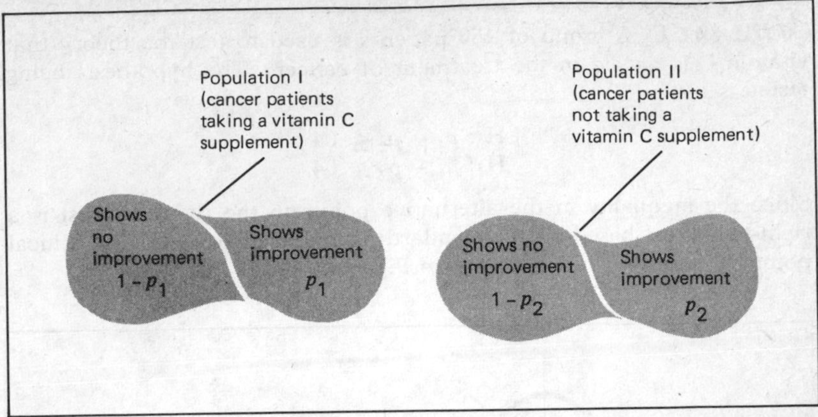


**FIGURE 8.14** Is $p_1 - p_2 > .04$?

To test such hypotheses, a test statistic must be found that is logical and whose probability distribution is known at least approximately under the assumption that the null hypothesis is true. To derive such a statistic, consider the random variable

$$\frac{\hat{p}_1 - \hat{p}_2 - (p_1 - p_2)_0}{\sqrt{p_1(1 - p_1)/n_1 + p_2(1 - p_2)/n_2}}$$

This is the same random variable as that used in Section 8.3 to construct confidence intervals on $p_1 - p_2$. If the null hypothesis is true, then this random variable is approximately standard normal. However, there is one problem. A test statistic must be a statistic! The random variable above is *not* a statistic, for it contains the unknown population proportions $p_1$ and $p_2$. The logical way to overcome this problem is to replace $p_1$ and $p_2$ with their unbiased estimators $\hat{p}_1$ and $\hat{p}_2$, to obtain the approximately standard normal *statistic:*

$$\frac{\hat{p}_1 - \hat{p}_2 - (p_1 - p_2)_0}{\sqrt{\hat{p}_1(1 - \hat{p}_1)/n_1 + \hat{p}_2(1 - \hat{p}_2)/n_2}}$$

This is a logical choice for a test statistic since it compares the estimated difference in proportions $\hat{p}_1 - \hat{p}_2$ with the hypothesized difference $(p_1 - p_2)_0$. If the hypothesized value is correct, then the estimated difference and the hypothesized difference should be close in value. This forces the numerator above to be close to zero and thus yields a small value for the test statistic. Large positive or large negative values of the test statistic indicate that the null hypothesis is not true and should be rejected in favor of an appropriate alternative.

The use of this statistic is illustrated in Example 8.4.2.

**EXAMPLE 8.4.2** □ A group of 150 patients is used to test the theory that vitamin C is an aid in the treatment of cancer. The hypothesis being tested is

$$\begin{aligned} H_0&: p_1 - p_2 \le .04 \\ H_1&: p_1 - p_2 > .04 \end{aligned}$$

Since the inequality in the alternative points to the right, the test is a right-tailed test based on the standard normal distribution. The critical point for an $\alpha = .1$ test is shown in Figure 8.15.

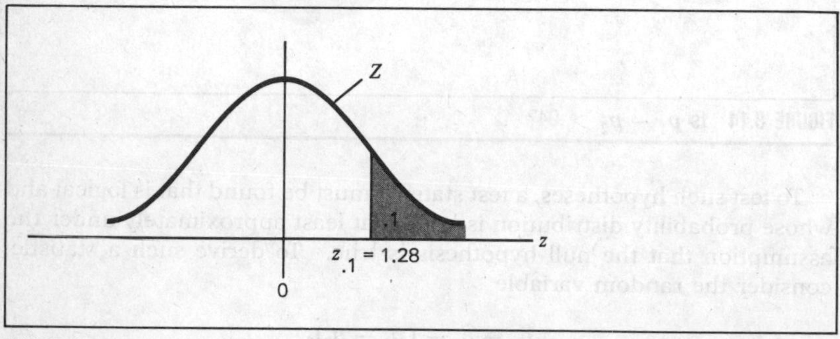


**FIGURE 8.15** Critical point for an $\alpha = .1$, right-tailed test.

The 150 patients were divided into two groups of 75. One group received 10 grams of vitamin C per day; the other received a placebo every day. Of those receiving vitamin C, 47 showed some improvement within 4 weeks; of those on the placebo, only 43 showed any improvement. Based on these data, $\hat{p}_1 = 47/75 \doteq .63$ and $\hat{p}_2 = 43/75 \doteq .57$. The observed value of the test statistic is

$$\frac{\hat{p}_1 - \hat{p}_2 - (p_1 - p_2)_0}{\sqrt{\hat{p}_1(1-\hat{p}_1)/n_1 + \hat{p}_2(1-\hat{p}_2)/n_2}} = \frac{.63 - .57 - .04}{\sqrt{(.63)(.37)/75 + (.57)(.43)/75}} = .25$$

Since .25 is not larger than the critical point of 1.28, we are unable to reject $H_0$ at the $\alpha = .1$ level. Practically speaking, this means that there is not sufficient evidence in this study to support the contention that vitamin C helps in treating cancer to the extent claimed.

Although the hypothesized difference $(p_1 - p_2)_0$ can be any value at all, the most commonly encountered proposed value is zero. In this case, in effect, the hypotheses considered previously compare $p_1$ with $p_2$ and take the following form:

| I $H_0: p_1 \leq p_2$<br>$H_1: p_1 > p_2$ | II $H_0: p_1 \geq p_2$<br>$H_1: p_1 < p_2$ | III $H_0: p_1 = p_2$<br>$H_1: p_1 \neq p_2$ |
|---|---|---|
| Right-tailed test | Left-tailed test | Two-tailed test |

**EXAMPLE 8.4.3** □ An important enemy of the snail (*Cepaea nemoralis*) is the song thrush. These birds select snails from snail colonies and take them to nearby rocks. There the birds break open the snails, eat the soft parts, and leave the shells. In a study of natural selection, the proportion of unbanded shells in the rocks was compared to the proportion of unbanded snails in the nearby colony, a bog near Oxford, England. The background in the bog was fairly uniform. It was felt that, because of their ability to blend into the background, the unbanded snails would be better protected from predators than the banded members of the colony. This would result in the proportion of unbanded shells in the rocks being smaller than that of unbanded snails in the colony. The situation is pictured in Figure 8.16.

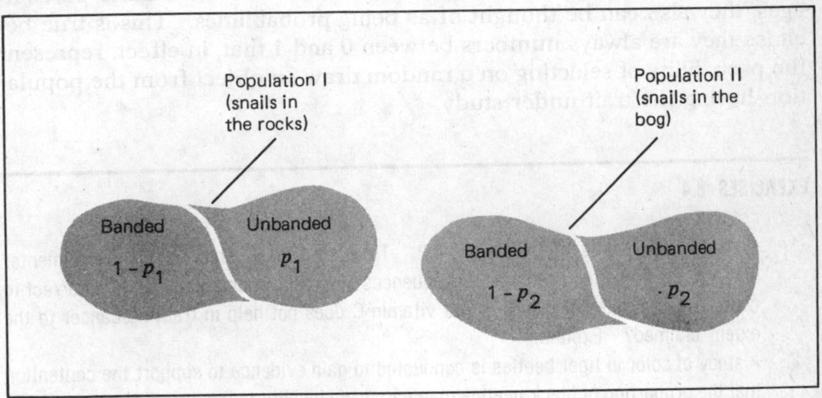


**FIGURE 8.16** Is $p_1 < p_2$?

By taking the theory to be supported as the alternative hypothesis, the purpose of the study is to test

$$H_0: p_1 \geq p_2$$
$$H_1: p_1 < p_2 \quad \text{(unbanded snails are protected in bog)}$$

Of 863 broken shells around the rocks, 377 were unbanded. This yields a point estimate for $p_1$ of $\hat{p}_1 \doteq 377/863 = .44$. Of 560 individuals collected in the bog, 296 were unbanded, which gives a point estimate for $p_2$ of $\hat{p}_2 = 296/560 \doteq .53$. Thus the observed value of the test statistic is

$$\frac{\hat{p}_1 - \hat{p}_2 - (p_1 - p_2)_0}{\sqrt{\hat{p}_1(1-\hat{p}_1)/n_1 + \hat{p}_2(1-\hat{p}_2)/n_2}} = \frac{.44 - .53 - 0}{\sqrt{.44(.56)/863 + .53(.47)/560}} = -3.33$$

The fact that this value is negative is not surprising. The test is a left-tailed test that calls for the rejection of $H_0$ for large negative values of the test statistic. Is $-3.33$ "large"? To answer this question, note from Table III in Appendix B that $P[Z \leq -3.33] = .000\,4$. Thus the $P$ value for the test is .000 4. There are two possible explanations for this small $P$ value:

**1.** The unbanded snails are not really protected by their coloration. We simply *by chance* observed an event that occurs only about 4 times in every 10,000 trials.

**2.** The unbanded snails are protected in the bog by their ability to blend into the uniform background.

We prefer the latter explanation!

---

There is one further point to make: While $p_1$ and $p_2$ have been referred to as proportions, and on occasion they have been converted to percentages, they also can be thought of as being probabilities. This is true because they are always numbers between 0 and 1 that, in effect, represent the probability of selecting on a random draw an object from the population having the trait under study.

---

## EXERCISES 8.4

1. Consider the results of Example 8.4.2. To what type of error is the experimenter subject? Discuss the practical consequences of making such an error. Is it correct to contend that it has been shown that vitamin C does not help in treating cancer to the extent claimed? Explain.
2. A study of color in tiger beetles is conducted to gain evidence to support the contention that the proportion of black beetles may vary from locality to locality. A sample of 500 beetles caught in one season near Providence, Rhode Island, yielded 95 black ones. A catch of 112 beetles from Aqueduct, New York, contained 17 black individuals.
   - **a.** Set up the appropriate two-tailed hypothesis.
   - **b.** Find the critical points for an $\alpha = .05$ test.
   - **c.** Find a point estimate for the difference between the proportions of black beetles in the two regions. Do you think, based on this estimate, that there is a difference in the two proportions?
   - **d.** Test the hypothesis of part **a** at the $\alpha = .05$ level. Do you get the evidence desired in the study? To what type of error are you subject now? Discuss the practical consequences of making such an error.
3. A study is conducted to detect the effectiveness of mammographies. From 31 cases of breast cancer detected in women in the 40 to 49 years old age group, 6 were found by the use of mammography alone. In older women, 38 of 101 cancers detected were found by mammography alone. Is this evidence at the $\alpha = .05$ level that the probabil-

ity of detecting cancer by mammography alone is higher with older women than with younger? Explain your answer by setting up and testing the appropriate statistical hypothesis.

**4.** In a 1970 study, blood tests were run on 759 patients suffering from various infections of the bloodstream. In 46 of these cases, at least two different organisms were isolated from the same blood sample. A similar study of 838 patients conducted in 1975 yielded 109 with two or more organisms present. Based on these samples, can you safely claim that the proportion of such cases has increased by more than 6 percentage points during the 5-year period? Explain your answer by setting up the appropriate hypothesis and finding its $P$ value.

**5.** In a recent study of knee injuries among football players playing on natural grass, two types of shoes were compared. In 266 players wearing multicleated soccer shoes, 14 knee injuries were incurred. Of 2055 players wearing conventional seven-post football shoes, 162 such injuries were reported. Is this evidence at the $\alpha = .1$ level that the probability of sustaining a knee injury while wearing the football shoe is higher than that of doing so while wearing the soccer shoe? Could the same statement be made at the $\alpha = .05$ level? At the $\alpha = .01$ level?

# COMPARING TWO MEANS

# 9.

In this chapter we continue the study of two sample problems by considering methods for comparing the means of two populations. This problem is considered under two different experimental conditions, namely, when the samples drawn are independent and when the data are paired. These terms are explained in depth in the following sections.

## POINT ESTIMATION: INDEPENDENT SAMPLES

**9.1** □ The general situation can be described as follows: There are two populations of interest, each with unknown mean; one random sample is drawn from the first population and one from the second in such a way that objects selected from population I have no bearing on the objects selected from population II (such samples are said to be independent); the population means are to be compared by using point estimation. (See Figure 9.1.)

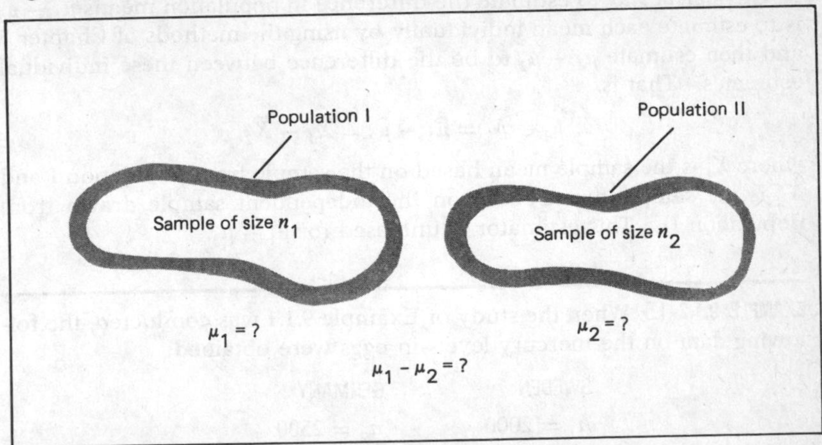


**FIGURE 9.1** Independent random samples drawn from two populations.

---

**EXAMPLE 9.1.1** □ Until recently, Swedish farmers dusted up to 80% of all grains sown with a fungicide containing methyl mercury. A study is run to compare the mean mercury level in eggs produced in Sweden with that of eggs produced in Germany, where methyl mercury is not used. A random sample of eggs produced in Sweden is selected; a random sample of eggs produced in Germany is chosen. These samples are independent in the sense that the eggs selected in one country in no way affect those selected in the other. The study can be visualized as shown in Figure 9.2.

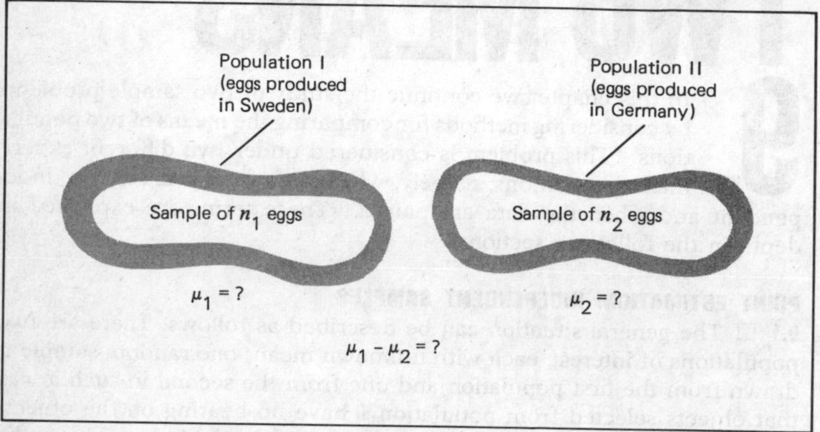


**FIGURE 9.2** Two independent random samples of eggs from Germany and Sweden.

The logical way to estimate the difference in population means $\mu_1 - \mu_2$ is to estimate each mean individually by using the methods of Chapter 7 and then estimate $\mu_1 - \mu_2$ to be the difference between these individual estimates. That is,

$$\widehat{\mu_1 - \mu_2} = \hat{\mu}_1 - \hat{\mu}_2 = \bar{X}_1 - \bar{X}_2$$

where $\bar{X}_1$ is the sample mean based on the sample from population I and $\bar{X}_2$ is the sample mean based on the independent sample drawn from population II. This estimator is unbiased for $\mu_1 - \mu_2$.

**EXAMPLE 9.1.2** □ When the study of Example 9.1.1 was conducted, the following data on the mercury levels in eggs were obtained:

| SWEDEN | GERMANY |
|---|---|
| $n_1 = 2000$ | $n_2 = 2500$ |
| $\bar{x}_1 = .026$ ppm | $\bar{x}_2 = .007$ ppm |
| $s_1 = .01$ | $s_2 = .004$ |

Based on this information, an unbiased estimate for the difference in mean mercury levels in eggs from the two countries is

$$\widehat{\mu_1 - \mu_2} = \hat{\mu}_1 - \hat{\mu}_2 = \bar{x}_1 - \bar{x}_2$$
$$= .026 - .007$$
$$= .019 \text{ ppm}$$

---

Theorem 9.1.1, which concerns the distribution of the estimator $\bar{X}_1 - \bar{X}_2$, provides the theoretical basis for confidence interval estimation and hypothesis testing on $\mu_1 - \mu_2$.

**THEOREM 9.1.1** □ *Distribution of* $\bar{X}_1 - \bar{X}_2$. Let $\bar{X}_1$ and $\bar{X}_2$ be the sample means based on independent samples of sizes $n_1$ and $n_2$, drawn from normal distributions with means $\mu_1$ and $\mu_2$ and variances $\sigma_1{}^2$ and $\sigma_2{}^2$, respectively. Then the random variable $\bar{X}_1 - \bar{X}_2$ is normal with mean $\mu_1 - \mu_2$ and variance $\sigma_1{}^2/n_1 + \sigma_2{}^2/n_2$.

As in the one-sample case, because of the Central Limit Theorem it is safe to assume that for large sample sizes, $\bar{X}_1 - \bar{X}_2$ is at least approximately normal even if the samples are drawn from populations that are not themselves normal.

---

## EXERCISES 9.1

1. It is generally accepted that sex differences in response to heat stress do exist. A group of 10 men and 8 women were put through a vigorous exercise program that involved the use of the treadmill. The environment was hot, and a minimal amount of water was available to the subjects. The variable of interest is the percentage of body weight lost. These data resulted:

| MEN | | WOMEN | |
|---|---|---|---|
| 2.9 | 3.7 | 3.0 | 3.8 |
| 3.5 | 3.8 | 2.5 | 4.1 |
| 3.9 | 4.0 | 3.7 | 3.6 |
| 3.8 | 3.6 | 3.3 | 4.0 |
| 3.6 | 3.7 | | |

   Find a point estimate for the difference in percentage of body weight lost between men and women exercising under these conditions.

2. A study is run to compare some of the physical attributes of female Olympic swimmers with those of female Olympic runners. One variable of interest is the total body fat in kilograms. Samples of 12 runners and 10 swimmers were obtained. These data resulted:

| RUNNERS | | SWIMMERS | |
|---|---|---|---|
| 11.2 | 7.6 | 14.1 | 12.7 |
| 10.1 | 7.3 | 15.1 | 13.7 |
| 9.4 | 6.9 | 11.4 | 11.9 |
| 9.2 | 5.5 | 14.3 | 10.7 |
| 8.3 | 5.0 | 9.2 | 8.7 |
| 8.2 | 3.7 | | |

Find a point estimate for the difference in mean total body fat between female Olympic runners and swimmers.

3. A sample of size 20 is to be chosen from a normal distribution with mean 15 and variance 16. An independent sample of size 25 is selected from a normal distribution with mean 10 and variance 18. What is the mean of the random variable $\bar{X}_1 - \bar{X}_2$? What is its variance? What is its standard deviation? What type of variable $(Z, T, X^2, \ldots)$ is this variable?

$$\frac{\bar{X}_1 - \bar{X}_2 - 5}{\sqrt{16/20 + 18/25}}$$

## COMPARING VARIANCES

**9.2** □ To use confidence intervals or hypothesis tests to compare means based on independent samples, we consider two distinct experimental situations:

1. $\sigma_1{}^2$ and $\sigma_2{}^2$ are unknown but assumed to be equal.
2. $\sigma_1{}^2$ and $\sigma_2{}^2$ are unknown and not assumed to be equal.

In both situations it is assumed that the populations from which the sampling is done are normal. The procedures used in the two cases are not the same. The former is handled by what is called a pooled, independent or uncorrelated $T$ procedure; the latter, by the Smith-Satterthwaite procedure. To determine which method to employ to compare means, obviously it is necessary to be able to decide statistically whether $\sigma_1{}^2$ and $\sigma_2{}^2$ are equal. Thus, we begin by considering a method for comparing the variances of two normal populations. We restrict this discussion to hypothesis testing since we usually want to answer the question, Is $\sigma_1{}^2 = \sigma_2{}^2$?

**EXAMPLE 9.2.1** □ A study of prescribing practices is conducted. The purpose is to analyze the prescribing of digoxin, an important and commonly used drug that is potentially toxic. It is known that generally the dosage level for those over age 64 should be lower than that for younger persons. To run the study, independent samples are drawn from each group. The digoxin dosage level is obtained for each patient selected.

Two questions are posed. Each is to be answered statistically, based on information obtained from the samples. The primary question is this: Is $\mu_1 < \mu_2$? However, before this question can be answered, we must consider the question, Is $\sigma_1^2 = \sigma_2^2$? If the answer to the latter appears to be yes, then a pooled $T$ procedure can be used to compare means; otherwise, the Smith-Satterthwaite procedure should be employed.

---

Hypothesis tests on the relationship between two variances can take any one of the usual three forms, depending on the purpose of the study. These forms are

| I | II | III |
|---|---|---|
| $H_0: \sigma_1^2 \leq \sigma_2^2$ | $H_0: \sigma_1^2 \geq \sigma_2^2$ | $H_0: \sigma_1^2 = \sigma_2^2$ |
| $H_1: \sigma_1^2 > \sigma_2^2$ | $H_1: \sigma_1^2 < \sigma_2^2$ | $H_1: \sigma_1^2 \neq \sigma_2^2$ |
| Right-tailed test | Left-tailed test | Two-tailed test |

To test any one of these hypotheses, a test statistic must be developed. It should be logical, but more importantly, it must be such that its probability distribution can be found or approximated under the assumption that the null hypothesis is true. That is, its distribution must be known if it is to be assumed that the population variances are equal.

It is easy to find a logical statistic for comparing variances. Recall that the sample variances $S_1^2$ and $S_2^2$ are unbiased estimators for the population variances $\sigma_1^2$ and $\sigma_2^2$, respectively. Thus to compare $\sigma_1^2$ with $\sigma_2^2$, we simply compare $S_1^2$ with $S_2^2$. This is done not by looking at the difference between the two, but by looking at $S_1^2/S_2^2$, the ratio of the two. If the null hypothesis is true and the population variances are really equal, then we would expect $S_1^2$ and $S_2^2$ to be close in value, forcing $S_1^2/S_2^2$ to be close to 1. If the ratio is close to zero, then we naturally conclude that the population variances are not equal and that, in fact, $\sigma_1^2 < \sigma_2^2$. Conversely, if $S_1^2/S_2^2$ is much larger than 1, we also conclude that the population variances are different and, in this instance, that $\sigma_1^2 > \sigma_2^2$.

When we use the phrases *close to zero* and *much larger than one,* we are speaking in terms of probabilities. That is, an observed value of the statistic is "close to zero" when it is too *small* to have reasonably occurred by chance if, in fact, the population variances are equal. Similarly, an observed value is "much larger than one" if it is too *large* to have reasonably occurred by chance. To determine the probability of observing various values of the statistic $S_1^2/S_2^2$, we must know its probability distribution. We show that this statistic follows a distribution previously unencountered. In particular, if the population variances are equal, it follows what is called an $F$ distribution. This distribution is defined in terms of a distribution previously studied, namely, the chi-square distribution. In particular, an $F$ random variable can be written as the ratio of two independent chi-square random variables, each divided by their respective degrees of freedom.

**Definition 9.2.1** *F Distribution.* Let $X_{\gamma_1}{}^2$ and $X_{\gamma_2}{}^2$ be independent chi-square random variables with $\gamma_1$ and $\gamma_2$ degrees of freedom, respectively. Then the random variable

$$\frac{X_{\gamma_1}{}^2/\gamma_1}{X_{\gamma_2}{}^2/\gamma_2}$$

follows what is called an *F distribution* with $\gamma_1$ and $\gamma_2$ degrees of freedom.

The important properties of the family of $F$ random variables are summarized:

1. There are infinitely many $F$ random variables, each identified by two parameters $\gamma_1$ and $\gamma_2$, called *degrees of freedom.* These parameters are always positive integers; $\gamma_1$ is associated with the chi-square random variable of the numerator of the $F$ variable, and $\gamma_2$ is associated with the chi-square variable of the denominator. The notation $F_{\gamma_1, \gamma_2}$ denotes an $F$ random variable with $\gamma_1$ and $\gamma_2$ degrees of freedom.
2. Each $F$ random variable is continuous.
3. The graph of the density of each $F$ variable is an asymmetric curve of the general shape shown in Figure 9.3.
4. The $F$ variables cannot assume negative values.

A partial summary of the cumulative distribution function for $F$ variables with various degrees of freedom is given in Table VII of Appendix B.

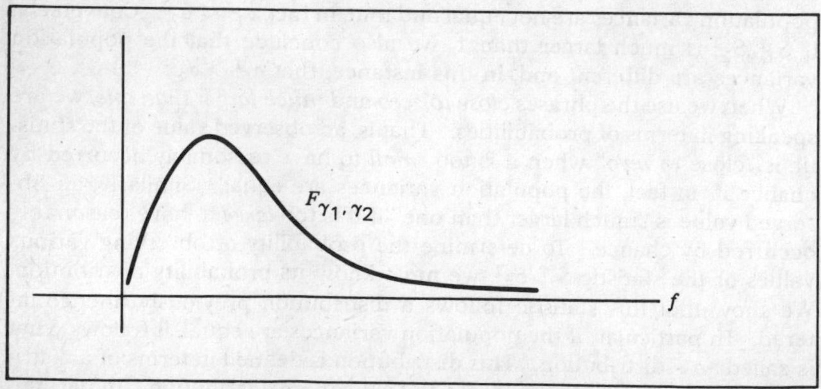


**FIGURE 9.3** A typical $F$ density.

There $\gamma_1$, the degrees of freedom for the numerator, appears as column headings; $\gamma_2$, the degrees of freedom for the denominator, appears as row headings. Once again, we denote by $f_r$ the point of the $F_{\gamma_1,\gamma_2}$ curve such that the area under the curve to the right of the point is $r$. Table VII allows us to read the right-tail points $f_{.01}$, $f_{.025}$, $f_{.05}$, and $f_{.1}$ directly for various degrees of freedom. The left-tail points $f_{.99}$, $f_{.975}$, $f_{.95}$, and $f_{.90}$ must be calculated. This is done by using the fact that a left-tail point for an $F$ variable with $\gamma_1$ and $\gamma_2$ degrees of freedom is the reciprocal of the corresponding right-tail point with the degrees of freedom reversed. This sounds harder than it is! Example 9.2.2 illustrates the use of Table VII in Appendix B.

---

**EXAMPLE 9.2.2** □ Consider $F_{10,15}$, the $F$ random variable with 10 and 15 degrees of freedom.

**a.** $P[F_{10,15} \leq 2.54] = .95$
**b.** $P[F_{10,15} \geq 3.06] = .025$
**c.** $f_{.025} = 3.06$
**d.** $f_{.05} = 2.54$
**e.** $f_{.01} = 3.80$
**f.** $f_{.975} = ?$ To find this point, note that it has an area .975 to its right. It is the left-tail point shown in Figure 9.4. The point cannot be read directly from Table VII. It is calculated by taking the reciprocal of the corresponding right-tail point for an $F$ random variable with the degrees of freedom (DF) reversed. That is,

$$f_{.975}(10, 15\text{ DF}) = \frac{1}{f_{.025}(15, 10\text{ DF})} = \frac{1}{3.52} \doteq .28$$

**g.** $f_{.95}(10, 15\text{ DF}) = \dfrac{1}{f_{.05}(15, 10\text{ DF})} = \dfrac{1}{2.85} \doteq .35$

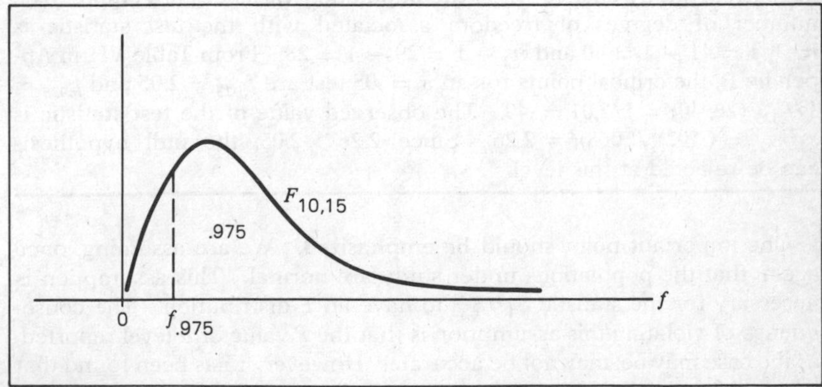


FIGURE 9.4

---

We are now in a position to state Theorem 9.2.1, which will provide a test statistic for comparing two population variances.

**THEOREM 9.2.1** □ Let $S_1{}^2$ and $S_2{}^2$ be sample variances based on independent random samples of sizes $n_1$ and $n_2$ drawn from normal populations with means $\mu_1$ and $\mu_2$ and variances $\sigma_1{}^2$ and $\sigma_2{}^2$, respectively. If $\sigma_1{}^2 = \sigma_2{}^2$, then the statistic $S_1{}^2/S_2{}^2$ follows an $F$ distribution with $n_1 - 1$ and $n_2 - 1$ degrees of freedom, respectively.

Note that the degrees of freedom associated with the statistic $S_1{}^2/S_2{}^2$ are $n_1 - 1$ and $n_2 - 1$. That is, the number of degrees of freedom for the numerator is 1 less than the size of the sample drawn from population I; that of the denominator is 1 less than the size of the sample drawn from population II. We illustrate the use of the statistic $S_1{}^2/S_2{}^2$ as a test statistic in Example 9.2.3.

---

**EXAMPLE 9.2.3** □ In the digoxin study of Example 9.2.1, we wish to test

$$\text{H}_0\text{: } \sigma_1{}^2 = \sigma_2{}^2$$
$$\text{H}_1\text{: } \sigma_1{}^2 \neq \sigma_2{}^2$$

at the $\alpha = .05$ level. These data were obtained:

| PATIENTS OVER AGE 64 | PATIENTS AGED 64 AND UNDER |
|---|---|
| $n_1 = 41$ | $n_2 = 29$ |
| $\bar{x}_1 = .265$ mg/day | $\bar{x}_2 = .268$ mg/day |
| $s_1 = .102$ mg/day | $s_2 = .068$ mg/day |

The test is a two-tailed test. Hypothesis $\text{H}_0$ should be rejected in favor of $\text{H}_1$ if the observed value of the test statistic is too large or too small to have occurred by chance when the population variances are equal. The number of degrees of freedom associated with the test statistic is $n_1 - 1 = 41 - 1 = 40$ and $n_2 - 1 = 29 - 1 = 28$. From Table VII in Appendix B, the critical points for an $\alpha = .05$ test are $f_{.025} = 2.05$ and $f_{.975} = 1/f_{.025}\,(28, 40) \doteq 1/2.01 = .49$. The observed value of the test statistic is $s_1{}^2/s_2{}^2 = (.102)^2/(.068)^2 \doteq 2.26$. Since $2.26 > 2.05$, the null hypothesis can be rejected at this level.

---

One important point should be emphasized. We are assuming, once again, that the populations under study are normal. This assumption is necessary for the statistic $S_1{}^2/S_2{}^2$ to have an $F$ distribution. The consequence of violating this assumption is that the $P$ value or $\alpha$ level reported, as the case may be, may not be accurate. However, it has been found that this problem is minimized if the samples are of *equal size*. It is advisable to verify the normality assumption by using the methods of Chapter 12 before testing for equality of variance by using an $F$ statistic.

---

## EXERCISES 9.2

1. Use Table VII in Appendix B to find each of the following:
   **a.** $P[F_{24,15} \leq 2.29]$
   **b.** $P[F_{20,3} \leq 14.17]$
   **c.** $P[F_{\infty,29} \leq 2.03]$
   **d.** $f_{.05}(15, 12 \text{ DF})$
   **e.** $f_{.01}(30, 5 \text{ DF})$
   **f.** $f_{.1}(40, 9 \text{ DF})$
   **g.** $f_{.1}(50, 9 \text{ DF})$
   **h.** $f_{.9}(24, 15 \text{ DF})$
   **i.** $f_{.95}(40, 30 \text{ DF})$
   **j.** $f_{.975}(20, 20 \text{ DF})$
   **k.** $f_{.99}(20, 35 \text{ DF})$
2. In each part of Figure 9.5, find the points $a$ and $b$ indicated.
3. A study is conducted of airspeed in various bird species. The brown pelican is to be compared to the American oystercatcher. The birds are clocked flying cross-wind with a wind speed of 5 to 8 mph. The following information is obtained (assume normality):

| BROWN PELICAN | OYSTERCATCHER |
|---|---|
| $n_1 = 9$ | $n_2 = 12$ |
| $\bar{x}_1 = 26.05$ mph | $\bar{x}_2 = 30.19$ mph |
| $s_1 = 6.34$ mph | $s_2 = 3.20$ mph |

   Can it be concluded at the $\alpha = .05$ level that $\sigma_1^2 \neq \sigma_2^2$?
4. In a study of carbohydrate metabolism, the root growth in peas grown in water at 6°C is to be compared with the growth of plants grown in a fructose solution at the same temperature. It is thought that the variance will be larger among plants grown in water. The following information is available (assume normality):

| GROWN IN WATER | GROWN IN FRUCTOSE |
|---|---|
| $n_1 = 16$ | $n_2 = 25$ |
| $\bar{x}_1 = 9.48$ mm/120 h | $\bar{x}_2 = 9.46$ mm/120 h |
| $s_1 = .53$ | $s_2 = .25$ |

   Can it be concluded that $\sigma_1^2 > \sigma_2^2$? What is the approximate $P$ value for the test?
5. Consider the study described in Exercise 9.1.1. It is thought that the variance for men is less than that for women. Find $s_M^2$ and $s_W^2$, the sample variances for the percentage of body weight lost by the men and the women, respectively. Find $s_M^2/s_W^2$. Can it be concluded at the $\alpha = .05$ level that $\sigma_M^2 < \sigma_W^2$? (Assume normality.)
6. Consider the study described in Exercise 9.1.2. It is thought that the variance for runners is smaller than that for swimmers. Find $s_R^2$ and $s_S^2$, the sample variances for the total body fat for female Olympic runners and swimmers, respectively. Find $s_R^2/s_S^2$. Can it be concluded at the $\alpha = .05$ level that $\sigma_R^2 < \sigma_S^2$? (Assume normality.)

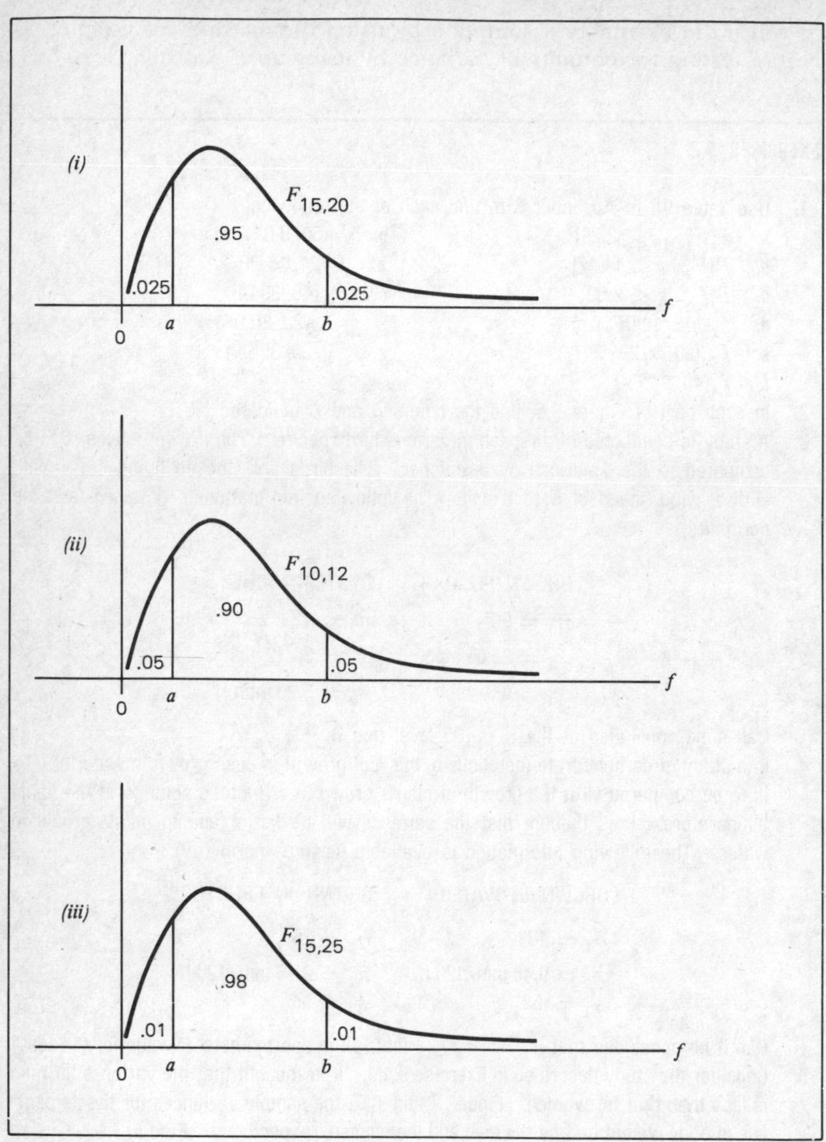


**FIGURE 9.5**

7. A study is run to consider the effect of maternal smoking on unborn babies. The study involves a random sample of 3461 nonsmokers and 2238 smokers. All subjects in the study are white women. The variable of interest is the baby's birth weight in

grams. Assume that this variable is normally distributed. The following information is available:

| NONSMOKERS | SMOKERS |
|---|---|
| $n_1 = 3461$ | $n_2 = 2238$ |
| $\bar{x}_1 = 3480.1$ g | $\bar{x}_2 = 3256.5$ g |
| $s_1 = 8.68$ g | $s_2 = 11.02$ g |

Is there sufficient evidence to claim that $\sigma_2^2 \neq \sigma_1^2$? Explain your answer. (For samples this large, use the row and column labeled $\infty$ in Table VII in Appendix B.)

## INFERENCES ON $\mu_1 - \mu_2$: POOLED $T$

**9.3** □ Recall that in many studies the primary objective is to compare population means. In this section we discuss methods for doing so when no difference has been detected in population variances. Again, normality is assumed throughout.

**EXAMPLE 9.3.1** □ In a study of angina in rats, 18 animals with a history of angina were randomly split into two groups of 9 each. One group was given a placebo and the other an experimental drug FL113. After controlled exercise on a treadmill, the recovery time of each rat was determined. It is thought that FL113 will reduce the average recovery time. The following information is available:

| PLACEBO | FL113 |
|---|---|
| $n_1 = 9$ | $n_2 = 9$ |
| $\bar{x}_1 = 329$ seconds | $\bar{x}_2 = 283$ seconds |
| $s_1 = 45$ seconds | $s_2 = 43$ seconds |

The ratio $s_1^2/s_2^2 = 45^2/43^2 = 1.09$ is used to compare variances. Based on the $F_{8,8}$ distribution, we cannot reject $H_0: \sigma_1^2 = \sigma_2^2$ even at the $\alpha = .2$ level since the right critical point is $f_{.1} = 2.59$. We do not have sufficient evidence to claim that $\sigma_1^2 \neq \sigma_2^2$. Therefore, in comparing means, we assume that the population variances, although unknown, are equal. A point estimate for the difference in mean recovery time is $\bar{x}_1 - \bar{x}_2 = 329 - 283 = 46$ seconds.

It has been stated that $\bar{X}_1 - \bar{X}_2$, the point estimator for the difference in population means, is unbiased for $\mu_1 - \mu_2$. To extend this point estimator to a confidence interval, once again we must find a random variable whose expression involves the parameter of interest, in this case $\mu_1 - \mu_2$, whose distribution is known. Such a random variable is provided by Theorem 9.1.1. This theorem states that when normal populations are sampled, the random variable $\bar{X}_1 - \bar{X}_2$ is normal with mean $\mu_1 - \mu_2$ and variance $\sigma_1^2/n_1 + \sigma_2^2/n_2$. By standardizing this variable it can be concluded that the random variable

$$\frac{\bar{X}_1 - \bar{X}_2 - (\mu_1 - \mu_2)}{\sqrt{\sigma_1^2/n_1 + \sigma_2^2/n_2}}$$

is standard normal. If the population variances have been compared and no difference has been detected, then there is no alternative but to assume that they are equal. Let $\sigma^2$ denote this common population variance. That is, let $\sigma_1^2 = \sigma_2^2 = \sigma^2$. Substituting into the above expression, we conclude that

$$\frac{\bar{X}_1 - \bar{X}_2 - (\mu_1 - \mu_2)}{\sqrt{\sigma^2(1/n_1 + 1/n_2)}}$$

is standard normal. Since $\sigma^2$ is unknown, it must be estimated from the data. This is done by a *pooled* sample variance. Note that we already have two unbiased estimators for $\sigma^2$, namely, $S_1^2$ and $S_2^2$. The idea is to pool, or combine, these estimators to form a single unbiased estimator for $\sigma^2$ in such a way that sample sizes are taken into account. It is natural to want to attach greater importance, or "weight," to the sample variance associated with the larger sample. The pooled variance does exactly this. We define it thus:

**Definition 9.3.1** *Pooled Variance.* Let $S_1^2$ and $S_2^2$ be sample variances based on independent samples of sizes $n_1$ and $n_2$, respectively. The *pooled variance,* denoted $S_p^2$, is given by

$$S_p^2 = \frac{(n_1 - 1)S_1^2 + (n_2 - 1)S_2^2}{n_1 + n_2 - 2}$$

Note that we weight $S_1^2$ and $S_2^2$ by multiplying by $n_1 - 1$ and $n_2 - 1$, respectively. The more natural way to weight is to multiply by the corresponding sample sizes, $n_1$ and $n_2$, respectively. We choose to weight in this somewhat odd way so that the random variable $(n_1 + n_2 - 2)S_p^2/\sigma^2$ will follow a chi-square distribution. This is necessary so that the test statistic that we use to test for equality of means will follow a $T$ distribution.

---

**EXAMPLE 9.3.2** □ Consider a sample variance $s_1^2 = 24$ based on a sample size 16 and a second sample variance $s_2^2 = 20$ based on a sample size 121. The value of the ratio $s_1^2/s_2^2$ is $24/20 = 1.20$. Based on these sample variances, the population variances $\sigma_1^2$ and $\sigma_2^2$ cannot be declared to be different ($f_{.1} = 1.55$). Thus the pooled estimate for the common population variance is

$$s_p^2 = \frac{(n_1 - 1)s_1^2 + (n_2 - 1)s_2^2}{n_1 + n_2 - 2}$$

$$= \frac{15(24) + 120(20)}{16 + 121 - 2}$$

$$= \frac{2760}{135} = 20.44$$

Note that this estimate is quite different from 22, the value that would be obtained by ignoring sample sizes and arithmetically averaging $s_1^2$ and $s_2^2$.

---

To obtain a random variable that can be used to construct a $100(1 - \alpha)\%$ confidence interval on $\mu_1 - \mu_2$, we replace the unknown population variance $\sigma^2$ in the $Z$ random variable

$$\frac{\bar{X}_1 - \bar{X}_2 - (\mu_1 - \mu_2)}{\sqrt{\sigma^2(1/n_1 + 1/n_2)}}$$

by the pooled estimator $S_p^2$, to obtain the random variable

$$\frac{\bar{X}_1 - \bar{X}_2 - (\mu_1 - \mu_2)}{\sqrt{S_p^2(1/n_1 + 1/n_2)}}$$

As in the one-sample case, replacing the population variance by its estimator does affect the distribution. The former random variable is a $Z$ variable; the latter has a $T$ distribution with $n_1 + n_2 - 2$ degrees of freedom. The algebraic structure of this variable is the same as that encountered previously, namely,

$$\frac{\text{Estimator} - \text{parameter}}{D}$$

where $D$ is related to the standard deviation of the estimator. Therefore, the confidence interval on $\mu_1 - \mu_2$ takes the same general form as most of the intervals encountered previously.

**THEOREM 9.3.1** □ *Confidence Interval on $\mu_1 - \mu_2$: Pooled Variance.* Let $\bar{X}_1$ and $\bar{X}_2$ be sample means based on independent random samples drawn from normal distributions with means $\mu_1$ and $\mu_2$, respectively, and common variance $\sigma^2$. Let $S_p^2$ denote the pooled sample variance. The bounds for a $100(1 - \alpha)\%$ confidence interval on $\mu_1 - \mu_2$ are

$$\bar{X}_1 - \bar{X}_2 \pm t_{\alpha/2}\sqrt{S_p^2(1/n_1 + 1/n_2)}$$

where the point $t_{\alpha/2}$ is found relative to the $T_{n_1+n_2-2}$ distribution.

**EXAMPLE 9.3.3** □ In a study of the feeding habits of bats, 25 females and 11 males are tagged and tracked by radio. One variable of interest is $X$, the distance flown per feeding pass. The experiment yielded the following information (assume normality):

| FEMALES | MALES |
|---|---|
| $n_1 = 25$ | $n_2 = 11$ |
| $\bar{x}_1 = 205$ meters | $\bar{x}_2 = 135$ meters |
| $s_1 = 100$ meters | $s_2 = 90$ meters |

Note that $s_1^2/s_2^2 = 100^2/90^2 = 1.23$. Based on the $F_{24,10}$ distribution we cannot reject $H_0: \sigma_1^2 = \sigma_2^2$. ($f_{.1} = 2.18$.) Since no differences can be detected in population variances, we pool $s_1^2$ and $s_2^2$ to obtain

$$s_p^2 = \frac{(n_1 - 1)s_1^2 + (n_2 - 1)s_2^2}{n_1 + n_2 - 2}$$
$$= \frac{24(100^2) + 10(90^2)}{25 + 11 - 2} = 9441.18$$

To compare means, let us find a 90% confidence interval on $\mu_1 - \mu_2$. The partition of the $T_{34}$ curve needed is shown in Figure 9.6. The bounds for the confidence interval are

$$\bar{x}_1 - \bar{x}_2 \pm t_{\alpha/2}\sqrt{s_p^2\left(\frac{1}{n_1} + \frac{1}{n_2}\right)} = 205 - 135 \pm 1.697\sqrt{9441.18(1/25 + 1/11)}$$
$$= 70 \pm 59.66$$

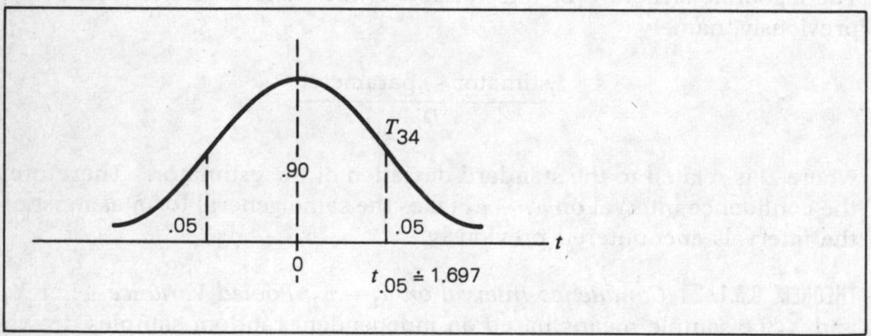


**FIGURE 9.6** Partition of the $T_{34}$ curve needed to obtain a 90% confidence interval on $\mu_1 - \mu_2$.

We can be 90% confident that the difference in mean feeding pass distances between female and male bats is between 10.34 and 129.66 meters. This interval does not contain the number 0 and is positive-valued throughout, an indication that the mean distance for females is higher than that for males. Some biologists have interpreted this to mean that the females are being driven from the closer feeding grounds by the more aggressive males. This theory, however, has not been confirmed.

---

As in previous instances, the random variable used to derive confidence bounds for a parameter also serves as a test statistic for testing various hypotheses concerning the parameter. In this case, the random variable

$$\frac{\bar{X}_1 - \bar{X}_2 - (\mu_1 - \mu_2)_0}{\sqrt{S_p{}^2(1/n_1 + 1/n_2)}} = T_{n_1+n_2-2}$$

serves as a test statistic for testing any of the usual hypotheses, where $(\mu_1 - \mu_2)_0$ denotes the hypothesized difference in population means. The hypothesized difference can be any value whatever. However, the most commonly encountered hypothesized value is zero. In this case, the purpose is to determine whether the population means differ and, if so, which is the larger. That is, the hypotheses take this form:

| I | II | III |
|---|---|---|
| $H_0$: $\mu_1 \leq \mu_2$ | $H_0$: $\mu_1 \geq \mu_2$ | $H_0$: $\mu_1 = \mu_2$ |
| $H_1$: $\mu_1 > \mu_2$ | $H_1$: $\mu_1 < \mu_2$ | $H_1$: $\mu_1 \neq \mu_2$ |
| Right-tailed test | Left-tailed test | Two-tailed test |

The results of the tests can be reported in any of the three ways mentioned previously: by reporting a single $\alpha$ level, by reporting the levels at which $H_0$ can and cannot be rejected, or by reporting the $P$ value of the test. The last method is becoming more common in biological and medical literature. Hence we emphasize this procedure in the remainder of this chapter.

---

**EXAMPLE 9.3.4** □ The summary data for the study of angina in rats of Example 9.3.1 are as follows:

| PLACEBO | FL113 |
|---|---|
| $n_1 = 9$ | $n_2 = 9$ |
| $\bar{x}_1 = 329$ seconds | $\bar{x}_2 = 283$ seconds |
| $s_1 = 45$ seconds | $s_2 = 43$ seconds |

The point estimate for the difference in mean recovery time between those on a placebo and those receiving the experimental drug is $\bar{x}_1 - \bar{x}_2 = 46$ seconds. Is this difference great enough for us to conclude that the experimental drug tends to reduce recovery time? To answer this question, we must find the pooled estimate for the common population variance. This estimate is

$$s_p^2 = \frac{(n_1 - 1)s_1^2 + (n_2 - 1)s_2^2}{n_1 + n_2 - 2}$$

$$= \frac{8(45) + 8(43)}{9 + 9 - 2}$$

$$= \frac{45 + 43}{2} = 44$$

Note that since the sample sizes are the *same,* in this case the pooled estimate is the arithmetic average of the individual estimates $s_1^2$ and $s_2^2$. Now we evaluate the test statistic:

$$\frac{\bar{x}_1 - \bar{x}_2 - (\mu_1 - \mu_2)_0}{\sqrt{s_p^2(1/n_1 + 1/n_2)}} = \frac{46 - 0}{\sqrt{44(1/9 + 1/9)}}$$

$$= 14.71$$

Based on the $T_{16}$ distribution, the $P$ value, the probability of observing a value of 14.71 or larger, is less than .000 5 ($t_{.000\,5} = 4.015$). We do have evidence to support the contention that the experimental drug is effective in reducing the recovery time in rats with angina.

---

## EXERCISES 9.3

1. **a.** Let $s_1^2 = 42$, $s_2^2 = 37$, $n_1 = 10$, $n_2 = 14$. Find $s_p^2$.
   **b.** Let $s_1^2 = 28$, $s_2^2 = 30$, $n_1 = 20$, $n_2 = 20$. Find $s_p^2$. (Do not use your calculator!)
   **c.** Let $s_1^2 = 20$, $s_2^2 = 40$, $n_1 = 10$, $n_2 = 50$. Find $s_p^2$. Why is $s_p^2$ closer in value to $s_2^2$ than to $s_1^2$?
2. The feeding habits of two species of net-casting spiders are studied. These species, the ***Dinopis*** and ***Menneus,*** coexist in eastern Australia. One variable of interest is the size of the prey of each species. The adult ***Menneus*** is about the same size as the juvenile ***Dinopis.*** It is known that there exists a difference in prey size between the adult and juvenile ***Dinopis*** because of their size difference. Is there a difference in mean prey size between adult ***Dinopis*** and adult ***Menneus?*** If so, what is the cause? To answer these questions, the following observations were obtained on the size, in millimeters, of the prey of the two species:

| ADULT *DINOPIS* | | ADULT *MENNEUS* | |
|---|---|---|---|
| 12.9 | 11.9 | 10.2 | 5.3 |
| 10.2 | 7.1 | 6.9 | 7.5 |
| 7.4 | 9.9 | 10.9 | 10.3 |
| 7.0 | 14.4 | 11.0 | 9.2 |
| 10.5 | 11.3 | 10.1 | 8.8 |

a. Use the data to compare population variances.
b. If no differences are detected in population variances, find a 90% confidence interval on $\mu_1 - \mu_2$.
c. On the basis of the interval of part **b**, is there evidence of a difference in mean prey size between the two species? Explain. (Biologists think that any difference detected may be explained by differences in placement and size of the webs built by the two.)

**3.** Consider the data of Exercise 9.1.1. Assuming normality and equal variances, find a 95% confidence interval on the difference in population means. Based on this interval, do you think that a difference exists between men and women in the mean response to heat stress in the two environments described? Explain.

**4.** Consider the data of Exercise 9.1.2. Assuming normality, and equal variances, find a 98% confidence interval on the difference in population means. Based on this interval, do you think that a difference exists between the mean total body fat of female Olympic runners and swimmers? Explain.

**5.** A study is conducted of two drug treatments for potential use in heart transplants. The purpose of the drugs is to act as an immunosuppressant—to repress the body's natural tendency to reject the transplant. Male ACI rats serve as donors; male Lewis-Brown Norway rats, as recipients. These rats are known to be poor matches. The variable of interest is $X$, the survival time in days. The following summary statistics are obtained:

| SODIUM SALICYLATE ALONE | SODIUM SALICYLATE AND AZATHIOPRINE |
|---|---|
| $n_1 = 9$ | $n_2 = 9$ |
| $\bar{x}_1 = 16$ days | $\bar{x}_2 = 15$ days |
| $s_1 = 10.1$ days | $s_2 = 10$ days |

Use this information to compare population variances. Find a 90% confidence interval on the difference in mean survival times between the two treatments. Interpret this interval in terms of its practical implications.

**6.** In a study of diverticular disease and diet, 23 vegetarians were used. One variable of interest was total dietary fiber. The following information was obtained for two groups, those without the disease and those with it (assume normality):

| WITHOUT | WITH |
|---|---|
| $n_1 = 18$ | $n_2 = 5$ |
| $\bar{x}_1 = 42.7$ g | $\bar{x}_2 = 27.7$ g |
| $s_1 = 9.9$ g | $s_2 = 9.5$ g |

Test for equality of population variances. Is there sufficient evidence to claim that the mean total dietary fiber content in the diets of those without the disease is higher than that of those with it? Explain your answer on the basis of the $P$ value of the test.

**7.** Another variable of interest in the study of angina in rats (see Example 9.3.1) is the oxygen intake, measured in milliliters per minute. The experiment provided the following information:

| PLACEBO | FL113 |
|---|---|
| $n_1 = 9$ | $n_2 = 9$ |
| $\bar{x}_1 = 1509$ ml/min | $\bar{x}_2 = 1702$ ml/min |
| $s_1 = 169$ | $s_2 = 181$ |

Use this information to compare population variances. Based on this experiment, is there sufficient evidence to claim that the mean oxygen intake of rats on FL113 is higher than that of those taking the placebo? Explain your answer based on the $P$ value of the test.

**8.** In a study of body characteristics of the ring-billed gull, the variable considered is the bill length. The following data are available:

| FEMALE | MALE |
|---|---|
| $n_1 = 51$ | $n_2 = 41$ |
| $\bar{x}_1 = 59.1$ mm | $\bar{x}_2 = 65.2$ mm |
| $s_1 = 1.9$ mm | $s_2 = 2.0$ mm |

No difference has been detected in population variances. Is there evidence to support the contention that the mean bill length in males is longer than in females? Explain your answer on the basis of the $P$ value of the test.

**9.** One variable used to compare the physical attributes of female Olympic swimmers with runners is the circumference of the upper arm, in centimeters, while relaxed. The following data are available:

| SWIMMERS | RUNNERS |
|---|---|
| $n_1 = 10$ | $n_2 = 12$ |
| $\bar{x}_1 = 27.3$ cm | $\bar{x}_2 = 23.5$ cm |
| $s_1 = 1.9$ cm | $s_2 = 1.7$ cm |

Assuming normality, test for equality of variances. Is there sufficient evidence to claim that the mean circumference of the upper arm is larger in swimmers than in runners? Explain your answer on the basis of the $P$ value of the test.

## INFERENCES ON $\mu_1 - \mu_2$: UNEQUAL VARIANCES

**9.4** □ If a difference is detected when the population variances are compared, then pooling is inappropriate. It is still possible to compare means by using an approximate $T$ statistic. Again, the desired statistic is found by modifying the $Z$ variable

$$\frac{\bar{X}_1 - \bar{X}_2 - (\mu_1 - \mu_2)}{\sqrt{\sigma_1^2/n_1 + \sigma_2^2/n_2}}$$

in a logical way. Since now there is evidence that $\sigma_1^2 \neq \sigma_2^2$, each population variance is estimated separately; these estimates are *not* combined. Instead, the population variances in the $Z$ random variable above are replaced by their respective estimators, $S_1^2$ and $S_2^2$, to obtain the random variable

$$\frac{\bar{X}_1 - \bar{X}_2 - (\mu_1 - \mu_2)}{\sqrt{S_1^2/n_1 + S_2^2/n_2}}$$

As in the past, making this change results in a change in distribution from $Z$ to an approximate $T$. The number of degrees must be estimated from the data. Several methods have been suggested for doing this. Here we demonstrate the Smith-Satterthwaite procedure. According to this procedure, $\gamma$, the number of degrees of freedom, is given by

$$\gamma \doteq \frac{[S_1^2/n_1 + S_2^2/n_2]^2}{\dfrac{[S_1^2/n_1]^2}{n_1 - 1} + \dfrac{[S_2^2/n_2]^2}{n_2 - 1}}$$

The value for $\gamma$ will not necessarily be an integer. If it is not, we round it *down* to the nearest integer. We round down rather than up in order to take a conservative approach. Recall that as the number of degrees of freedom associated with $T$ random variables increases, the corresponding bell-shaped curves become more compact. Practically speaking, this means that, for example, the point $t_{.05}$ associated with the $T_{10}$ curve (1.812) is a little larger than the point $t_{.05}$ associated with the $T_{11}$ curve (1.796). If we can reject a null hypothesis based on the $T_{10}$ distribution, it will also be rejected based on the $T_{11}$ distribution. The converse does not necessarily hold.

This procedure is illustrated in Example 9.4.1.

---

**EXAMPLE 9.4.1** □ A study of energy requirements for growth and maintenance of nestling house martins was conducted in Perthshire, Scotland. The following summary statistics were obtained on the normal variable $X$, the number of kilocalories per gram per hour required per bird:

| INCUBATING ADULTS | PREBREEDING ADULTS |
|---|---|
| $n_1 = 57$ | $n_2 = 12$ |
| $\bar{x}_1 = .016\,7$ kcal/(g)(hr) | $\bar{x}_2 = .014\,4$ kcal/(g)(hr) |
| $s_1 = .004\,2$ | $s_2 = .002\,4$ |

The observed value of the statistic $S_1^2/S_2^2$ is $(.004\,2)^2/(.002\,4)^2 = 3.06$. Based on the $F_{56,11}$ distribution, we can reject $H_0$: $\sigma_1^2 = \sigma_2^2$ at $\alpha \doteq .05$ [$f_{.025}(40, 11 \text{ DF}) = 3.06$]. Since this value is small, we conclude that $\sigma_1^2 \neq \sigma_2^2$ and do not pool the variance. The value of the $T_\gamma$ statistic is

$$\frac{\bar{x}_1 - \bar{x}_2 - (\mu_1 - \mu_2)_0}{\sqrt{s_1^2/n_1 + s_2^2/n_2}} = \frac{.016\,7 - .014\,4}{\sqrt{(.004\,2)^2/57 + (.002\,4)^2/12}} = 2.59$$

The number of degrees of freedom associated with this statistic is

$$\gamma \doteq \frac{[s_1^2/n_1 + s_2^2/n_2]^2}{\dfrac{[s_1^2/n_1]^2}{n_1 - 1} + \dfrac{[s_2^2/n_2]^2}{n_2 - 1}}$$

$$= \frac{[(.004\,2)^2/57 + (.002\,4)^2/12]^2}{[(.004\,2)^2/57]^2/56 + [(.002\,4)^2/12]^2/11} = 27.5$$

Since degrees of freedom must be a positive integer, we round this down to 27. Based on the $T_{27}$ distribution, the probability of obtaining a value of 2.59 or larger is between .01 and .005. That is, the $P$ value for the test of $H_0$: $\mu_1 \leq \mu_2$ is between .01 and .005. Since this value is very small, we conclude that the mean energy requirement for incubating birds is higher than for prebreeding ones.

---

The procedure for finding a confidence interval on $\mu_1 - \mu_2$ when the population variances are unequal is outlined in Exercise 9.4.7.

---

## EXERCISES 9.4

**1.** Consider Example 9.4.1. If one failed to test for equality of variances and mistakenly pooled variances, what would be the observed value of the test statistic? How many degrees of freedom would be used? Would the $P$ value be affected?

**2.** Strontium 90, a radioactive element produced by nuclear testing, is closely related to calcium. In dairy lands, strontium 90 can make its way into milk via the grasses eaten by dairy cows. Then it becomes concentrated in the bones of those who drink the milk. In 1959 a study was conducted to compare the mean concentration of strontium 90 in the bones of children to that of adults. It was thought that the level in children was higher because the substance was present during their formative years. Is this contention supported by the following data? Explain (assume normality).

| CHILDREN | ADULTS |
|---|---|
| $n_1 = 121$ | $n_2 = 61$ |
| $\bar{x}_1 = 2.6$ picocuries per gram | $\bar{x}_2 = .4$ picocurie per gram |
| $s_1 = 1.2$ | $s_2 = .11$ |

**3.** A study is conducted to compare tortoises found on Malabar to those found on Grande-Terre, islands in the Aldabra atoll in the Indian Ocean. One variable of interest is $X$, the weight of an egg at the time of lay. Randomly selected samples from the two islands yield the following summary data (assume normality):

| GRANDE-TERRE | MALABAR |
|---|---|
| $n_1 = 31$ | $n_2 = 148$ |
| $\bar{x}_1 = 64.0$ grams | $\bar{x}_2 = 82.7$ grams |
| $s_1 = 6.5$ grams | $s_2 = 3.6$ grams |

Is there evidence that the mean weight of an egg at the time of lay on Malabar is higher than that on Grande-Terre? Explain.

**4.** A study of red-billed gueleas is conducted. The purpose is to compare a colony located near Lake Chad to one located in Botswana. The Lake Chad colony failed because the adults abandoned the nests; the Botswana colony survived. One variable thought to influence the ability of a female to maintain the nest is $X$, her muscle protein level. One aim of the study is to compare the muscle protein levels of females in the two colonies.

**a.** At the beginning of the laying cycle, the following data were collected:

| LAKE CHAD | BOTSWANA |
|---|---|
| $n_1 = 100$ | $n_2 = 100$ |
| $\bar{x}_1 = .99$ gram | $\bar{x}_2 = 1.00$ gram |
| $s_1 = .01$ gram | $s_2 = .01$ gram |

Compare population variances and test for equality of means, using the appropriate $T$ statistic. Relative to this variable, do the populations seem to be identical at the beginning of the laying cycle?

**b.** At the end of the laying cycle, the following data were obtained:

| LAKE CHAD | BOTSWANA |
|---|---|
| $n_1 = 100$ | $n_2 = 100$ |
| $\bar{x}_1 = .87$ gram | $\bar{x}_2 = .90$ gram |
| $s_1 = .02$ gram | $s_2 = .01$ gram |

Compare population variances and test for equality of means, using the appropriate $T$ statistic. Relative to this variable, do the populations now seem to be identical?

**5.** Consider the data of Exercise 9.2.7. The purpose of the study is to gain evidence to support the contention that the mean weight of newborns is lower among mothers who are smokers than among nonsmokers. Do the data support this contention? Be ready to defend your choice of a test statistic.

**6.** A study is conducted to investigate the ability of monocytes to kill certain yeast cells found in patients with cirrhosis of the liver. These cells are harmful in that they leave the patient open to recurrent infections of various sorts. Blood samples are taken from 16 cirrhosis patients and 9 healthy controls. The following data are obtained on the percentage of yeast cells killed by monocytes in the culture (assume normality):

| CONTROLS | PATIENTS |
|---|---|
| $n_1 = 9$ | $n_2 = 16$ |
| $\bar{x}_1 = 44.22\%$ | $\bar{x}_2 = 28.22\%$ |
| $s_1 = 6.17$ | $s_2 = 4.11$ |

Compare population variances. Based on the results of this test, compare population means, using the appropriate $T$ statistic. Is there sufficient evidence to claim that the mean percentage of yeast cells killed by monocytes among controls is higher than among patients? Explain.

***7.** *Confidence Interval on $\mu_1 - \mu_2$: Unequal Variances.* Confidence bounds for $100(1-\alpha)\%$ confidence intervals on $\mu_1 - \mu_2$ when the population variances are unequal are based on the random variable

$$T_\gamma = \frac{\bar{X}_1 - \bar{X}_2 - (\mu_1 - \mu_2)}{\sqrt{S_1^2/n_1 + S_2^2/n_2}} = \frac{\text{estimator} - \text{parameter}}{D}$$

where $\gamma$ is given by the Smith-Satterthwaite approximation. Again, as a result of the algebraic structure of this variable, the confidence bounds can be determined by inspection:

$$\bar{X}_1 - \bar{X}_2 \pm t_{\alpha/2}\sqrt{\frac{S_1^2}{n_1} + \frac{S_2^2}{n_2}}$$

**a.** A study is conducted of preoperative cross-matching in elective surgery. The operation studied is elective abdominal hysterectomy. The variable of interest is $X$, the number of cross-matched units of blood immediately available. The purpose is to compare the mean number of units available in 1974 to that in 1976. The following summary data are available:

| 1974 | 1976 |
|---|---|
| $n_1 = 25$ | $n_2 = 25$ |
| $\bar{x}_1 = 2.73$ | $\bar{x}_2 = 1.27$ |
| $s_1 = .65$ | $s_2 = 1.0$ |

After comparing population variances, find a 95% confidence interval on $\mu_1 - \mu_2$. Is there evidence of a decrease in the mean number of units available from 1974 to 1976? Explain.

**b.** Consider the data of Exercise 9.2.3. Find a 90% confidence interval on the difference in the mean airspeed of brown pelicans and oystercatchers when flyng cross-wind. Based on this interval, is there evidence that a difference in population means exists? Explain.

**c.** Consider the data of Exercise 9.2.4. Find a 95% confidence interval on the difference in the mean growth of peas grown in water and those grown in the fructose solution. Based on this interval, is there evidence of any difference in growth rates? Explain.

---

**Computing Supplement**

The procedure PROC TTEST can be used to test for equality of both variances and means by utilizing either the pooled $T$ test or the Smith-Satterthwaite procedure. This procedure is illustrated by using the data of Exercise 9.3.2 to test $H_0$: $\mu_1 = \mu_2$.

| **Statement** | **Function** |
|---|---|
| DATA SPIDER; | names data set |
| INPUT GROUP SIZE @@; | indicates two variables named GROUP and SIZE to be entered; GROUP identifies population from which observation is drawn; @@ indicates there will be more than one observation per card |
| CARDS; | indicates that data follow |
| 1 12.9 1 11.9<br>1 10.2 1 7.1<br>1 7.4 1 9.9<br>1 7.0 1 14.4<br>1 10.5 1 11.3<br>2 10.2 2 5.3<br>2 6.9 2 7.5<br>2 10.9 2 10.3<br>2 11.0 2 9.2<br>2 10.1 2 8.8 | data values |
| ; | signals end of data |
| PROC TTEST; | calls for $T$ test to be run |
| CLASS GROUP; | names variable that identifies two groups (populations) being compared |
| TITLE1 TESTING FOR EQUALITY;<br>TITLE2 OF;<br>TITLE3 MEANS AND VARIANCES; | titles output |

The output of this program is as follows:

```
                         TESTING FOR EQUALITY
                                  OF
                          MEANS AND VARIANCES

                            TTEST PROCEDURE

VARIABLE: SIZE

GROUP      N          MEAN        STD DEV      STD ERROR       MINIMUM        MAXIMUM

  1       10   10.26000000     2.51360741     0.79487246    7.00000000    14.40000000
  2       10    9.02000000     1.89666374     0.59977774    5.30000000    11.00000000

VARIANCES          T          DF    PROB > |T|
                 (6)      (5)              (7)
UNEQUAL      1.2453       16.7      0.2303
EQUAL        1.2453       18.0      0.2290
                 (3)                       (4)

FOR HO: VARIANCES ARE EQUAL, F'=      1.76 WITH 9 AND 9 DF        PROB > F'= 0.4142
                                       (1)                                   (2)
```

Note that (1) gives the observed value of the test statistic for testing $H_0$: $\sigma_1{}^2 = \sigma_2{}^2$ and (2) gives the $P$ value for this test. The observed value of the test statistic for testing

$H_0$: $\mu_1 = \mu_2$ by using the *pooled* $T$ test is given by (3), with the $P$ value for the two-tailed alternative shown in (4). The approximate number of degrees of freedom for the Smith-Satterthwaite procedure is shown in (5). The observed value of the test statistic and the $P$ value for the two-sided alternative, using the Smith-Satterthwaite procedure, are shown in (6) and (7), respectively. One should first consider the results of the $F$ test for equality of variances and then use whichever $T$ test is appropriate for testing for equality of means.

This program can be adjusted by making appropriate changes in the names of the data set and the input variables. Also the output of the program can be used to compute confidence intervals on $\mu_1 - \mu_2$, since all the required summary statistics are given on the printout.

## INFERENCES ON $\mu_1 - \mu_2$: PAIRED $T$

**9.5** □ In many instances problems arise in which two random samples are available but they are *not* independent; rather, each observation in one sample is naturally or by design paired with an observation in the other. Consider Example 9.5.1.

---

**EXAMPLE 9.5.1** □ A study was conducted to investigate the effect of physical training on the serum cholesterol level. Eleven subjects participated in the study. Prior to training, blood samples were taken to determine the cholesterol level of each subject. Then the subjects were put through a training program that centered on daily running and jogging. At the end of the training period, blood samples were taken again and a second reading on the serum cholesterol level was obtained. Thus, two sets of observations on the serum cholesterol level of the subjects are available. The data sets are not independent; they are based on the same subjects taken at different times and so are naturally paired by subject. These data were collected:

| SUBJECT | PRETRAINING LEVEL $x$, MG/DL | POSTTRAINING LEVEL $y$, MG/DL |
|---|---|---|
| 1 | 182 | 198 |
| 2 | 232 | 210 |
| 3 | 191 | 194 |
| 4 | 200 | 220 |
| 5 | 148 | 138 |
| 6 | 249 | 220 |
| 7 | 276 | 219 |
| 8 | 213 | 161 |
| 9 | 241 | 210 |
| 10 | 480 | 313 |
| 11 | 262 | 226 |

The purpose is to estimate the difference between the mean cholesterol level before and after training.

---

When pairing such as just illustrated occurs, the methods of Sections 9.3 and 9.4 are no longer applicable. Rather, a procedure for comparing means must take into account the fact that the observations are paired. This is easily done. Consider the generalization of the problem shown in Figure 9.7. Note that associated with this situation is a population of differences $D = X - Y$ and a random sample of differences selected from that population, $D_i = X_i - Y_i$, $i = 1, 2, 3, \ldots, n$. (See Figure 9.8.) Since, by the rules for expectation,

$$\mu_X - \mu_Y = E[X] - E[Y] = E[X - Y] = E[D] = \mu_D$$

the original question, What is $\mu_X - \mu_Y$? is equivalent to, What is $\mu_D$? We are reduced from the original two-sample problem to the *one*-sample problem of making an inference on the mean of the population of differences. This problem is not new, and it can be handled by using the methods of Chapter 7. In particular, the formula for the $100(1 - \alpha)\%$ confidence bounds on $\mu_X - \mu_Y = \mu_D$ is

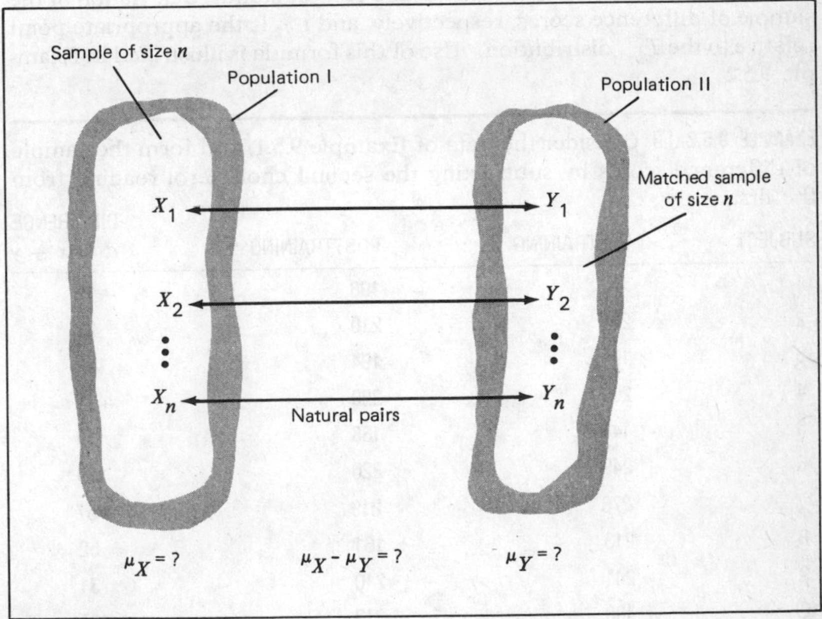


**FIGURE 9.7** Paired data.

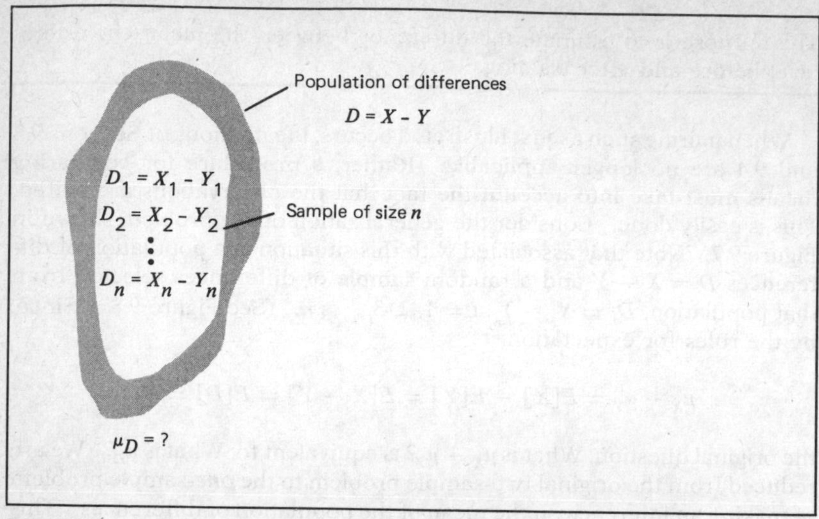


**FIGURE 9.8** Paired data generate a population of differences.

$$\bar{D} \pm \frac{t_{\alpha/2} S_d}{\sqrt{n}}$$

where $\bar{D}$ and $S_d$ are the sample mean and sample standard deviation of the sample of difference scores, respectively, and $t_{\alpha/2}$ is the appropriate point relative to the $T_{n-1}$ distribution. Use of this formula is illustrated in Example 9.5.2

**EXAMPLE 9.5.2** □ Consider the data of Example 9.5.1, and form the sample of difference scores by subtracting the second cholesterol reading from the first.

| SUBJECT | PRETRAINING $x$ | POSTTRAINING $y$ | DIFFERENCE $d = x - y$ |
|---|---|---|---|
| 1 | 182 | 198 | −16 |
| 2 | 232 | 210 | 22 |
| 3 | 191 | 194 | −3 |
| 4 | 200 | 220 | −20 |
| 5 | 148 | 138 | 10 |
| 6 | 249 | 220 | 29 |
| 7 | 276 | 219 | 57 |
| 8 | 213 | 161 | 52 |
| 9 | 241 | 210 | 31 |
| 10 | 480 | 313 | 167 |
| 11 | 262 | 226 | 36 |

To construct a 90% confidence on $\mu_D$, we need to compute the sample mean and the sample standard deviation for the set of difference scores:

$$\bar{d} = \sum_{i=1}^{11} \frac{d_i}{11} = \frac{-16 + 22 + (-3) + \cdots + 36}{11}$$

$$= 33.18$$

$$s_d^{\,2} = \frac{11 \sum_{i=1}^{11} d_i^{\,2} - \left[\sum_{i=1}^{11} d_i\right]^2}{11(10)} = \frac{11(38{,}189) - (365^2)}{11(10)} = 2607.76$$

$$s_d = \sqrt{s_d^{\,2}} = \sqrt{2607.76} = 51.07$$

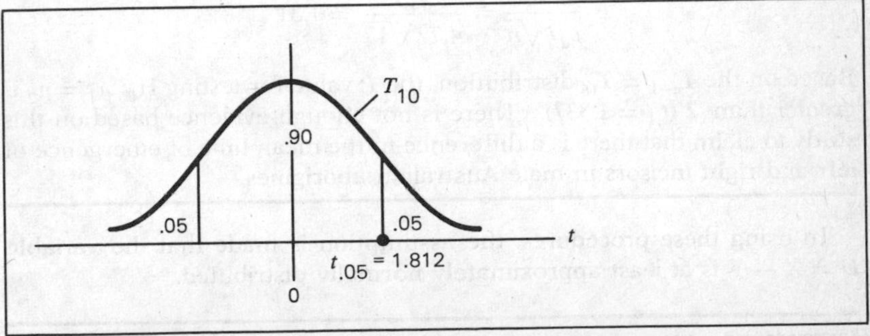


**FIGURE 9.9** Partition of the $T_{10}$ curve needed to obtain a 90% confidence interval on $\mu_D$.

The partition of the $T_{n-1} = T_{10}$ curve needed is shown in Figure 9.9. The desired confidence bounds are

$$\bar{d} \pm t_{\alpha/2} \frac{s_d}{\sqrt{n}} = 33.18 \pm 1.812 \frac{51.07}{\sqrt{11}}$$

$$= 33.18 \pm 27.90$$

We can be 90% confident that the mean difference in serum cholesterol levels is between 5.28 and 61.08 mg/dl. That is, we can be 90% confident that the mean cholesterol level will be reduced by at least 5.28 mg/dl.

Means can be compared by using the hypothesis testing approach also. The null hypothesis $\mu_X = \mu_Y$ is equivalent to the hypothesis $\mu_D = 0$. The test statistic for testing this hypothesis based on the sample of difference scores is

$$\frac{\bar{D} - 0}{S_d / \sqrt{n}}$$

which follows a $T$ distribution with $n - 1$ degrees of freedom if $H_0$ is true. The use of this statistic is illustrated in the following example.

**EXAMPLE 9.5.3** □ A study is conducted of tooth emergence in Australian aborigines. The purpose is to detect differences, if they exist, in the time of emergency of left- and right-side permanent teeth. One tooth studied is the incisor. All subjects are male. The age of the subject at the time of emergence of the left incisor and his age at the time of emergence of the right incisor are determined. Thus each subject produces a pair of observations. Summary statistics for the study are as shown, where the order of subtraction is left-side age minus right-side age:

$$n = 17 \qquad \bar{d} = 1.5 \text{ yr} \qquad s_d = 4.7$$

The observed value of the test statistic is

$$\frac{\bar{d} - 0}{s_d / \sqrt{n}} = \frac{1.5}{4.7 / \sqrt{17}} = 1.31$$

Based on the $T_{n-1} = T_{16}$ distribution, the $P$ value for testing $H_0$: $\mu_1 = \mu_2$ is greater than .2 ($t_{.1} = 1.337$). There is not enough evidence based on this study to claim that there is a difference in the mean time of emergence of left and right incisors in male Australian aborigines.

In using these procedures, the assumption is made that the variable $D = X - Y$ is at least approximately normally distributed.

## EXERCISES 9.5

1. The effect of physical training on the triglyceride level was also studied by using the 11 subjects of Example 9.5.1. The following pretraining and posttraining readings (in milligrams of triglyceride per 100 milliliters of blood) were obtained:

| SUBJECT | PRETRAINING | POSTTRAINING |
|---|---|---|
| 1 | 68 | 95 |
| 2 | 77 | 90 |
| 3 | 94 | 86 |
| 4 | 73 | 58 |
| 5 | 37 | 47 |
| 6 | 131 | 121 |
| 7 | 77 | 136 |
| 8 | 24 | 65 |
| 9 | 99 | 131 |
| 10 | 629 | 630 |
| 11 | 116 | 104 |

Find a 90% confidence interval on the mean change in triglyceride level. Is there evidence that a difference exists? If so, what is the direction of the change?

**2.** A study was conducted to compare the sodium content in the plasma of young southern fur seals with the level in the milk of these seals. The following observations on the sodium content [in millimoles per liter of milk (or plasma)] were obtained in 10 randomly selected seals:

| SUBJECT | MILK | PLASMA |
|---|---|---|
| 1 | 93 | 147 |
| 2 | 104 | 157 |
| 3 | 95 | 142 |
| 4 | 81.5 | 141 |
| 5 | 95 | 142 |
| 6 | 95 | 147 |
| 7 | 76.5 | 148 |
| 8 | 80.5 | 144 |
| 9 | 79.5 | 144 |
| 10 | 87.0 | 146 |

Find a 95% confidence interval on the mean difference in sodium levels in the two body fluids. Is there evidence that a difference exists? If so, what is the direction of the difference?

**3.** A study is conducted to determine the effect of a home meter for helping diabetics control their blood glucose levels. A random sample of 36 diabetics participate in the study. Blood glucose levels were obtained for each patient before they were taught to use the meter and again after they had utilized the meter for several weeks. A mean sample difference of 2.78 mmol/liter with a sample standard deviation of 6.05 mmol/liter was recorded (subtraction done in the order of "before" minus "after"). Is there sufficient evidence to claim that the monitor is effective in helping patients to reduce their blood glucose levels? Support your answer based on the $P$ value of the test.

**4.** It was thought that a program of regular, moderately strenuous exercise could benefit patients who had suffered a previous myocardial infarction. Eleven subjects participated in a study to test this contention. Before the program was begun, the working capacity of each person was determined by measuring the time it took to reach a heart rate of 160 beats per minute while walking on a treadmill. After 25 weeks of controlled exercise, the treadmill measurements were repeated and the difference in times for each subject recorded. The following data resulted:

| SUBJECT | PRETEST | POSTTEST |
|---|---|---|
| 1 | 7.6 | 14.7 |
| 2 | 9.9 | 14.1 |
| 3 | 8.6 | 11.8 |
| 4 | 9.5 | 16.1 |
| 5 | 8.4 | 14.7 |
| 6 | 9.2 | 14.1 |
| 7 | 6.4 | 13.2 |
| 8 | 9.9 | 14.9 |
| 9 | 8.7 | 12.2 |
| 10 | 10.3 | 13.4 |
| 11 | 8.3 | 14.0 |

Do these data support the contention of the investigators? Support your answer based on the $P$ value of the test.

---

**Computing Supplement**

The SAS procedure PROC MEANS can be used to run a paired $T$ test. The method is illustrated by using the data of Exercise 9.5.4.

| Statement | Function |
|---|---|
| DATA EXERCISE; | names data set |
| INPUT X Y; | indicates two variables, $X$ and $Y$, will be used; each card will contain $X$ value, followed by $Y$ value, with at least one blank between |
| DIFF=X−Y; | forms new variable named DIFF that is difference between $X$ value and corresponding $Y$ value |
| CARDS; | indicates that data follow |
| 7.6 14.7<br>9.9 14.1<br>8.6 11.8<br>...........<br>8.3 14.0 | data |
| ; | signals end of data |

| | |
|---|---|
| PROC MEANS MEAN STD STDERR T PRT; VAR DIFF; | asks for mean, standard deviation, and standard error to be printed for variable DIFF; asks for test of $H_0$: $\mu_{\mathbf{DIFF}} = 0$ and $P$ value to be reported |
| TITLE PAIRED T TEST; | titles output |

The output of this program is as follows:

PAIRED T TEST

| VARIABLE | MEAN | STANDARD DEVIATION | STD ERROR OF MEAN | T | PR>\|T\| |
|---|---|---|---|---|---|
| DIFF | -5.12727273 | 1.48195203 | 0.44682535 | -11.47 | 0.0001 |

Note that since $d$ and the standard error $s_d/\sqrt{n}$ are part of this output, a $100(1-\alpha)\%$ confidence interval on the mean difference can be computed quickly by using the information from this program.

# *k*-SAMPLE PROCEDURES: INTRODUCTION TO DESIGN

# 10.

In Chapter 7 we discuss methods for making inferences on the mean and variance of a single population. Chapter 9 is concerned with methods for comparing the means and variances of two populations. Now we extend the methods of Chapter 9 to include more than two populations. We also introduce some of the elementary aspects of experimental design and *an*alysis *o*f *va*riance (ANOVA). The term *experimental design* refers to a broad area of applied statistics that concerns itself with methods for collecting and analyzing data which attempt to maximize the amount and improve the accuracy of the information from a given experiment. The term *analysis of variance* refers to an analytic procedure whereby the total variation in some measured response is subdivided into components that can be attributed to some recognizable source and used to test various hypotheses of interest.

## ONE-WAY CLASSIFICATION, COMPLETELY RANDOM DESIGN WITH FIXED EFFECTS

**10.1** □ The first design that we present is the *one-way classification, completely random design with fixed effects.* While describing this design, we introduce some of the general concepts and terminology underlying the areas of experimental design and analysis of variance. We begin by considering Examples 10.1.1 and 10.1.2.

---

**EXAMPLE 10.1.1** □ A study is run to compare the effectiveness of three comprehensive therapeutic programs for the treatment of mild to moderate acne. Three methods are employed:

**I.** This older method entails twice-daily washing with a polyethylene scrub and an abrasive soap together with the use of 250 mg of tetracycline daily.

**II.** This method, currently in use, entails the use of tretinoin cream, avoidance of the sun, twice-daily washing with an emollient soap and water, and utilization of 250 mg of tetracycline twice daily.

**III.** This new method entails water avoidance, twice-daily washing with a lipid-free cleanser, and use of tretinoin cream and benzoyl peroxide.

These three treatments are to be compared for effectiveness in reducing the number of acne lesions in patients. Thirty-five patients participate in the study. These patients are randomly split into three subgroups of size 10, 12, and 13. One group is assigned treatment I; another treatment, II; and the third, treatment III. At the end of 16 weeks, the percentage improvement in the number of lesions is noted for each patient.

---

**EXAMPLE 10.1.2** □ One source of water pollution is industrial and agricultural runoff that is rich in phosphorus. Too much phosphorus can cause a population explosion of plants and microorganisms referred to as a *bloom*. In a given region, the phosphorus level in four major lakes is to be determined by drawing and analyzing water samples from each lake. It is thought that one of the lakes is being unduly polluted by the runoff from a nearby industrial plant. It is hoped that by comparing the phosphorus level of this lake with that of others in the area this fact will become evident.

---

Examples 10.1.1 and 10.1.2 illustrate two commonly encountered experimental situations in which the *one-way classification, completely random design with fixed effects,* comes into play. They are described in general as follows:

**1.** We have a collection of $N$ experimental units and wish to study the effects of $k$ different treatments. These units are randomly divided into $k$ groups of size $n_1, n_2, \ldots, n_k$, and each subgroup receives a different treatment. A response is noted. The $k$ subgroups are viewed as constituting independent random samples of size $n_1, n_2, \ldots, n_k$ drawn from populations with mean responses $\mu_1, \mu_2, \ldots, \mu_k$, respectively. We want to test the null hypothesis that the treatments have the same mean effect:

$$H_0: \mu_1 = \mu_2 = \cdots = \mu_k$$ (no difference in mean treatment effects)

$$H_1: \mu_i \neq \mu_j \text{ for some } i \text{ and } j$$ (at least one mean differs from others)

2. We have $k$ populations, each identified by some common characteristic to be studied in the experiment. Independent random samples of sizes $n_1, n_2, \ldots, n_k$ are selected from each of the $k$ populations, respectively. Each sample receives the same treatment, and any differences observed in the measured responses are attributed to basic differences among the $k$ populations. The hypothesis is

$$H_0: \mu_1 = \mu_2 = \cdots = \mu_k$$ (no difference in population means)

$$H_1: \mu_i \neq \mu_j \text{ for some } i \text{ and } j$$ (at least one mean differs from others)

where $\mu_i$ denotes the mean response for the $i$th population.

Although these situations are experimentally somewhat different, they are similar in that each results in $k$ independent random samples drawn from $k$ populations with means $\mu_1, \mu_2, \ldots, \mu_k$, respectively. The purpose of the experiment in each case is to compare population means. This design represents the natural extension of the two-sample unpaired problem of Chapter 9 to more than two samples. The situation can be visualized as shown in Figure 10.1.

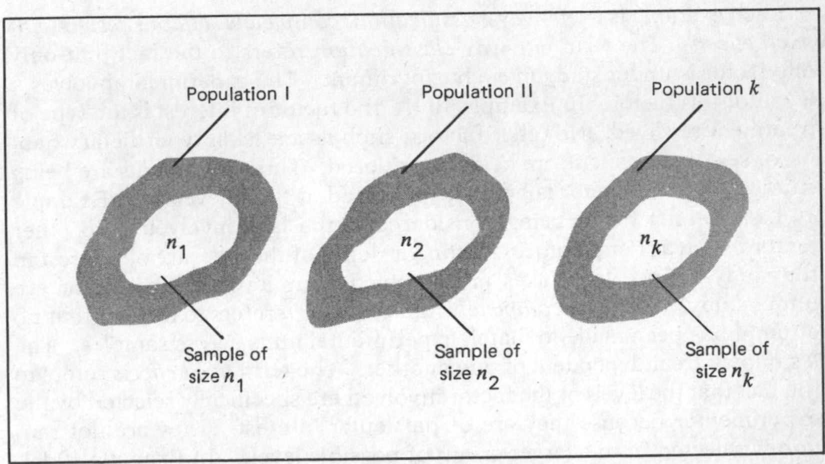


**FIGURE 10.1** $H_0: \mu_1 = \mu_2 = \cdots = \mu_k$. (Are the population means equal?)

---

**EXAMPLE 10.1.3** □ Example 10.1.1 satisfies the first general description. A collection of $N = 35$ patients, each suffering from mild to moderate acne, is available for experimentation. There are $k = 3$ treatments to be compared. The patients are randomly divided into three subgroups of sizes $n_1 = 10$, $n_2 = 12$, and $n_3 = 13$. Each subgroup receives a different treatment, and the response noted is the percentage improvement in the number of lesions observed at the end of 16 weeks of treatment. The three subgroups are viewed as constituting independent random samples drawn from the populations of all patients receiving treatments I, II, and III, respectively. Based on the data obtained, we wish to test

$H_0$: $\mu_1 = \mu_2 = \mu_3$ (no difference in mean response among three treatments)

$H_1$: $\mu_i \neq \mu_j$ for some $i$ and $j$ (at least one treatment differs from others)

---

**EXAMPLE 10.1.4** □ Example 10.1.2 satisfies the second general description. We are studying $k = 4$ lakes. Each lake constitutes a population. Independent samples are selected from each lake. Each sample receives the same treatment in that each is analyzed for phosphorus by the same method. Any differences in mean phosphorus levels that appear are attributed to the fact that the samples were drawn from different lakes with various water compositions.

---

Each example is a *one-way classification, completely random design with fixed effects*. The term *one-way classification* refers to the fact that only one factor is under study in each experiment. The experiment involves $k$ levels of this factor. In Example 10.1.1, the factor of interest is the type of treatment received. No other factors, such as age, skin type, dietary habits, or sex of the patient, are being considered. Three treatments are being studied; thus the factor is being investigated at three levels. In Example 10.1.2, the only factor being considered is the lake involved. No other factors, such as temperature, season, or depth of the lake, are of interest in the study. Since four lakes are involved, four levels of the factor are under study. The term *completely random design* refers to the fact that no attempt has been made to match experimental units across samples. The $k$ samples are independent of one another. The term *fixed effects* refers to the fact that the levels of the factor involved are specifically selected by the experimenter because they are of particular interest. They are not randomly selected from a larger group of possible levels. In Example 10.1.1, the purpose of the experiment is to compare the three specific treatments. The treatments are not randomly selected from a large group of acne treatments available. In Example 10.1.2, the four lakes selected for the study are chosen specifically because they are the major lakes in the region. They are not randomly selected from all the lakes in the region.

The data collected in a single-factor experiment are conveniently recorded in the following format:

DATA LAYOUT FOR ONE-WAY CLASSIFICATION

| Factor Level | | | | |
|---|---|---|---|---|
| 1 | 2 | 3 | ... | $k$ |
| $X_{11}$ | $X_{21}$ | $X_{31}$ | ... | $X_{k1}$ |
| $X_{12}$ | $X_{22}$ | $X_{32}$ | ... | $X_{k2}$ |
| $X_{13}$ | $X_{23}$ | $X_{33}$ | ... | $X_{k3}$ |
| ⋮ | ⋮ | ⋮ | | ⋮ |
| $X_{1n_1}$ | $X_{2n_2}$ | $X_{3n_3}$ | ... | $X_{kn_k}$ |

Note that $n_i$ is the size of the sample drawn from the $i$th population and that $N = \Sigma_{i=1}^{k} n_i$ denotes the total number of responses. Furthermore, $X_{ij}$, $i = 1, 2, \ldots, k$, $j = 1, 2, \ldots, n_i$, is a random variable denoting the response of the $j$th experimental unit to the $i$th level of the factor. In using sample data to compare population means, certain statistics are required:

$$T_{i\cdot} = \sum_{j=1}^{n_i} X_{ij} = \text{total of all responses in } i\text{th level, } i = 1, 2, \ldots, k$$

$$\bar{X}_{i\cdot} = \frac{T_{i\cdot}}{n_i} = \text{sample mean for } i\text{th level, } i = 1, 2, \ldots, k$$

$$T_{\cdot\cdot} = \sum_{i=1}^{k} \sum_{j=1}^{n_i} X_{ij} = \sum_{i=1}^{k} T_{i\cdot} = \text{total of all responses}$$

$$\bar{X}_{\cdot\cdot} = \frac{T_{\cdot\cdot}}{N} = \text{sample mean of all responses}$$

$$\sum_{i=1}^{k} \sum_{j=1}^{n_i} X_{ij}^2 = \text{sum of square of each response}$$

In this notation note that the dot indicates the subscript over which summation is being conducted.

The evaluation of these statistics is illustrated in Example 10.1.5.

---

**EXAMPLE 10.1.5** □ When the experiment of Example 10.1.1 was conducted, the following data resulted. Recall that the observed response is the percentage improvement in the number of acne lesions noted per patient at the end of 16 weeks of treatment.

Factor (Treatment Received) Level

| I | | II | | III | |
|---|---|---|---|---|---|
| 48.6 | 50.8 | 68.0 | 71.9 | 67.5 | 61.4 |
| 49.4 | 47.1 | 67.0 | 71.5 | 62.5 | 67.4 |
| 50.1 | 52.5 | 70.1 | 69.9 | 64.2 | 65.4 |
| 49.8 | 49.0 | 64.5 | 68.9 | 62.5 | 63.2 |
| 50.6 | 46.7 | 68.0 | 67.8 | 63.9 | 61.2 |
| | | 68.3 | 68.9 | 64.8 | 60.5 |
| | | | | 62.3 | |

Note that $n_1 = 10$, $n_2 = 12$, $n_3 = 13$, and $N = \Sigma_{i=1}^{3} n_i = 10 + 12 + 13 = 35$. The observation 70.1 corresponds to the response of the 3d experimental unit to the 2d factor level and thus is the observed value of the random variable $X_{23}$. The observed values of the other pertinent statistics are

$$T_{1\cdot} = \sum_{j=1}^{10} X_{1j} = \text{sum of responses to treatment I}$$

$$= 48.6 + 49.4 + 50.1 + \cdots + 46.7 = 494.6$$

$$T_{2\cdot} = \sum_{j=1}^{12} X_{2j} = \text{sum of responses to treatment II}$$

$$= 68.0 + 67.0 + 70.1 + \cdots + 68.9 = 824.8$$

$$T_{3\cdot} = \sum_{j=1}^{13} X_{3j} = \text{sum of responses to treatment III}$$

$$= 67.5 + 62.5 + 64.2 + \cdots + 60.5 = 826.8$$

$$\bar{X}_{1\cdot} = \frac{T_{1\cdot}}{n_1} = \text{sample mean of responses to treatment I}$$

$$= \frac{494.6}{10} = 49.46$$

$$\bar{X}_{2\cdot} = \frac{T_{2\cdot}}{n_2} = \text{sample mean of responses to treatment II}$$

$$= \frac{824.8}{12} = 68.73$$

$$\bar{X}_{3\cdot} = \frac{T_{3\cdot}}{n_3} = \text{sample mean of responses to treatment III}$$

$$= \frac{826.8}{13} = 63.60$$

$$T.. = \sum_{i=1}^{3} T_i. = T_1. + T_2. + T_3. = \text{grand total of all responses}$$
$$= 494.6 + 824.8 + 826.8 = 2146.2$$
$$\bar{X}.. = \frac{T..}{N} = \text{sample mean of all responses}$$
$$= \frac{2146.2}{35} = 61.32$$
$$\sum_{i=1}^{3} \sum_{j=1}^{n_i} X_{ij}^2 = (48.6)^2 + (49.4)^2 + (50.1)^2 + \cdots + (60.5)^2$$
$$= 133{,}868.94$$

---

To see how these statistics can be used to test the hypothesis that the population means are equal, we must introduce a model for the *one-way classification, completely random design with fixed effects.* A model is a mathematical representation of a typical response that breaks the response into components attributable to various identifiable sources. The following notation is used in writing the model:

$\mu_i$ = theoretical average or expected response at $i$th level, $i = 1, 2, \ldots, k$
= mean of $i$th population (unknown constant)

$\mu$ = theoretical average or expected response, ignoring factor levels (unknown constant)
= mean of population that results by combining $k$ populations into one

Note that if the levels of the factor have no effect on the response, then the means $\mu_1, \mu_2, \ldots, \mu_k$ will all be the same and will equal the grand mean $\mu$; if the factor levels do affect the response, then this will not be the case. Thus the difference between the mean of the $i$th level and the grand mean $\mu_i - \mu$ indicates the effect, if any, of the $i$th level of the factor. Furthermore, note that even though each member of the $i$th population receives the same treatment, the responses obtained will still vary somewhat because of random influences. That is, within each population there is some natural variability about the population mean. For a particular response $X_{ij}$, this variability is given by the difference $X_{ij} - \mu_i$. This difference is referred to as the *random error.* With these comments in mind, the model for the *one-way classification, completely random design with fixed effects,* can be expressed as follows:

**Model** $$X_{ij} \equiv \mu + (\mu_i - \mu) + (X_{ij} - \mu_i) \qquad i = 1, 2, \ldots, k \quad j = 1, 2, \ldots, n_i$$

This model expresses mathematically the idea that each response can be partitioned into three recognizable components as follows:

| Response of $j$th experimental unit to $i$th treatment ($X_{ij}$) | $\equiv$ overall mean response ($\mu$) | + deviation from overall mean due to fact that unit received $i$th treatment ($\mu_i - \mu$) | + random deviation from $i$th population mean due to random influences ($X_{ij} - \mu_i$) |
|---|---|---|---|

As in the past, to test the null hypothesis, a test statistic must be derived. The statistic should be logical, but more importantly, its probability distribution must be known under the assumption that the null hypothesis is true and the $k$ population means are equal. For this to occur, certain assumptions must be made about the populations from which the samples are drawn. In particular, we assume the following:

**Model Assumptions**

1. The $k$ samples represent independent random samples drawn from $k$ specific populations with means $\mu_1, \mu_2, \ldots, \mu_k$, where $\mu_1, \mu_2, \ldots, \mu_k$ are unknown constants.
2. Each of the $k$ populations is *normal.*
3. Each of the $k$ populations has the *same* variance, $\sigma^2$.

Note that these assumptions parallel those made in Chapter 9 relative to the pooled $T$ procedure for comparing two means.

Analysis of variance has been defined as a procedure whereby the total variation in some measured response is subdivided into components that can be attributed to recognizable sources. Since $\mu, \mu_1, \mu_2, \ldots, \mu_k$ are theoretical population means, the model does this in only the theoretical sense. To partition an observation in a practical way, these theoretical means must be replaced by their unbiased estimators $\bar{X}_{\cdot\cdot}, \bar{X}_{1\cdot}, \bar{X}_{2\cdot}, \ldots, \bar{X}_{k\cdot}$, respectively. By replacing the theoretical means by their estimators in the model, the following identity is obtained:

$$X_{ij} \equiv \bar{X}_{\cdot\cdot} + (\bar{X}_{i\cdot} - \bar{X}_{\cdot\cdot}) + (X_{ij} - \bar{X}_{i\cdot})$$

Note that $\bar{X}_{\cdot\cdot}$ is an estimator for $\mu$, the overall mean of the combined population; $\bar{X}_{i\cdot} - \bar{X}_{\cdot\cdot}$ is an estimator for $\mu_i - \mu$, the effect of the $i$th treatment; and $X_{ij} - \bar{X}_{i\cdot}$ is an estimator for $X_{ij} - \mu_i$, the random error. The term $X_{ij} - \bar{X}_{i\cdot}$ is usually called a *residual.* This identity is equivalent to

$$X_{ij} - \bar{X}_{\cdot\cdot} \equiv (\bar{X}_{i\cdot} - \bar{X}_{\cdot\cdot}) + (X_{ij} - \bar{X}_{i\cdot})$$

If each side of the above identity is squared and then summed over all possible values of $i$ and $j$, the following identity, called the *sum-of-squares identity for the one-way classification design,* results.

**Sum-of-Squares Identity**

$$\sum_{i=1}^{k}\sum_{j=1}^{n_i}(X_{ij} - \bar{X}_{..})^2 \equiv \sum_{i=1}^{k} n_i(\bar{X}_{i.} - \bar{X}_{..})^2 + \sum_{i=1}^{k}\sum_{j=1}^{n_i}(X_{ij} - \bar{X}_{i.})^2$$

The derivation of this identity is a straightforward application of the rules of summation. Note that there are three components in this identity. Each has a practical interpretation that should not be overlooked. In particular,

$\sum_{i=1}^{k}\sum_{j=1}^{n_i}(X_{ij} - \bar{X}_{..})^2$ = sum of squares of deviations of observations from grand mean
= measure of total variability in data
= total sum of squares = $SS_{\text{Total}}$

$\sum_{i=1}^{k} n_i(\bar{X}_{i.} - \bar{X}_{..})^2$ = weighted sum of squares of deviations of level or treatment means from grand mean
= measure of variability in data attributed to fact that different levels or treatments are used
= treatment sum of squares = $SS_{\text{Tr}}$

$\sum_{i=1}^{k}\sum_{j=1}^{n_i}(X_{ij} - \bar{X}_{i.})^2$ = sum of squares of deviations of observations from treatment mean associated with observation
= measure of variability in data attributed to random fluctuation among subjects within same factor level
= residual, or error, sum of squares = $SS_E$

By using this shorthand notation, the sum-of-squares identity can be written

$$SS_{\text{Total}} = SS_{\text{Tr}} + SS_E$$

To test

$$H_0\colon \mu_1 = \mu_2 = \cdots = \mu_k$$

we need to define two statistics that are functions of $SS_{\text{Tr}}$ and $SS_E$. The first, called the *treatment mean square* $MS_{\text{Tr}}$, is found by dividing $SS_{\text{Tr}}$ by $k - 1$; the second, called the *error mean square* $MS_E$, is found by dividing $SS_E$ by $N - k$. That is, we define

$$MS_{\text{Tr}} = \frac{SS_{\text{Tr}}}{k - 1} = \text{treatment mean square}$$

$$MS_E = \frac{SS_E}{N - k} = \text{residual mean square}$$

Since each of these mean squares is a statistic, it is also a random variable. As such, it has a probability distribution and a mean, or an expected, value. These expected values are particularly important, for they provide the logical basis for testing for equality of means by the ANOVA procedure. Although the proofs are beyond the scope of this text, it can be shown that

$$E[MS_{\text{Tr}}] = \sigma^2 + \sum_{i=1}^{k} \frac{n_i(\mu_i - \mu)^2}{k - 1}$$

and

$$E[MS_E] = \sigma^2$$

How can $MS_{\text{Tr}}$ and $MS_E$ be used to test $H_0$? To answer this question, we need only note that if $H_0$ is true, then $\mu_1 = \mu_2 = \cdots = \mu_k = \mu$ and hence

$$\sum_{i=1}^{k} \frac{n_i(\mu_i - \mu)^2}{k - 1} = 0$$

If $H_0$ is not true, this term will be positive. Thus if $H_0$ is true, we would expect $MS_{\text{Tr}}$ and $MS_E$ to be close in value, since both estimate the same parameter, namely $\sigma^2$; if $H_0$ is not true, we would expect $MS_{\text{Tr}}$ to be somewhat larger than $MS_E$. This suggests the ratio

$$\frac{MS_{\text{Tr}}}{MS_E}$$

as a logical test statistic. If $H_0$ is true, its value should lie close to 1; otherwise, it should have a value larger than 1. The ratio can be used as a test statistic since if $H_0$ is true, it is known to have an $F$ distribution with $k - 1$ and $N - k$ degrees of freedom. The test is always a right-tailed test with rejection of $H_0$ occurring for values of the statistic

$$F_{k-1,\,N-k} = \frac{MS_{\text{Tr}}}{MS_E}$$

that appear to be *too large* to have occurred by chance.

Computing $SS_{\text{Total}}$, $SS_{\text{Tr}}$, and $SS_E$ directly from the definitions given is awkward. For this reason computational formulas have been developed that are easier to handle and especially convenient for use with electronic calculators. These formulas are a direct consequence of the rules of summation.

**Computational Formulas**

$$SS_{\text{Total}} = \sum_{i=1}^{k} \sum_{j=1}^{n_i} X_{ij}^2 - \frac{T_{..}^2}{N}$$

$$SS_{\text{Tr}} = \sum_{i=1}^{k} \frac{T_{i\cdot}^2}{n_i} - \frac{T_{..}^2}{N}$$

$$SS_E = SS_{\text{Total}} - SS_{\text{Tr}}$$

**TABLE 10.1** ANALYSIS OF VARIANCE: ONE-WAY CLASSIFICATION, COMPLETELY RANDOM DESIGN WITH FIXED EFFECTS

| SOURCE OF VARIATION | DEGREES OF FREEDOM $DF$ | SUM OF SQUARES $SS$ | MEAN SQUARE $MS$ | EXPECTED MEAN SQUARE | $F$ RATIO |
|---|---|---|---|---|---|
| Treatment, or level | $k - 1$ | $\sum_{i=1}^{k} \frac{T_{i\cdot}^2}{n_i} - \frac{T_{\cdot\cdot}^2}{N}$ $(SS_{\text{Tr}})$ | $\frac{SS_{\text{Tr}}}{k-1}$ | $\sigma^2 + \sum_{i=1}^{k} \frac{n_i(\mu_i - \mu)^2}{k-1}$ | $F_{k-1,N-k} = \frac{MS_{\text{Tr}}}{MS_E}$ |
| Residual, or error | $N - k$ | $SS_{\text{Total}} - SS_{\text{Tr}}$ $(SS_E)$ | $\frac{SS_E}{N-k}$ | $\sigma^2$ | |
| **Total** | $N - 1$ | $\sum_{i=1}^{k}\sum_{j=1}^{n_i} X_{ij}^2 - \frac{T_{\cdot\cdot}^2}{N}$ $(SS_{\text{Total}})$ | | | |

Everything that has been said here can be summarized conveniently in tabular form. Keep in mind that $k$ denotes the number of treatments or levels of the factor being investigated; $n_i$, the number of observations selected from the $i$th population; $T_{i\cdot}$, the sum of the observations for the $i$th level; $N$, the total number of observations; and $T_{\cdot\cdot}$, the sum of all observations. See Table 10.1. Note that the columns labeled "degrees of freedom" and "sum of squares" are additive. That is, the degrees of freedom for treatments and for error add to $N - 1$, the total number of degrees of freedom. Furthermore, $SS_{\text{Tr}} + SS_E = SS_{\text{Total}}$.

The ANOVA procedure is illustrated in Example 10.1.6.

---

**EXAMPLE 10.1.6** □ In Example 10.1.5, we began the calculations necessary to test the null hypothesis that the three acne treatments have the same mean effect. In particular, the following values were obtained:

$$T_{1\cdot} = 494.6 \qquad \sum_{i=1}^{3}\sum_{j=1}^{n_i} X_{ij}^2 = 133{,}868.94 \qquad n_1 = 10$$
$$T_{2\cdot} = 824.8 \qquad n_2 = 12$$
$$T_{3\cdot} = 826.8 \qquad n_3 = 13$$
$$T_{\cdot\cdot} = 2146.2 \qquad N = 35$$

From these basic statistics we can evaluate $SS_{\text{Total}}$, $SS_{\text{Tr}}$, and $SS_E$:

$$SS_{\text{Total}} = \sum_{i=1}^{3}\sum_{j=1}^{n_i} X_{ij}^2 - \frac{T_{\cdot\cdot}^2}{N}$$
$$= 133{,}868.94 - \frac{(2146.2)^2}{35} = 2263.96$$

$$SS_{\text{Tr}} = \sum_{i=1}^{3} \frac{T_{i\cdot}^2}{n_i} - \frac{T_{\cdot\cdot}^2}{N}$$
$$= \frac{(494.6)^2}{10} + \frac{(824.8)^2}{12} + \frac{(826.8)^2}{13} - \frac{(2146.2)^2}{35} = 2133.66$$

$$SS_E = SS_{\text{Total}} - SS_{\text{Tr}}$$
$$= 2263.96 - 2133.66 = 130.30$$

The corresponding mean squares are given by

$$MS_{\text{Tr}} = \frac{SS_{\text{Tr}}}{k-1} = \frac{SS_{\text{Tr}}}{2} = \frac{2133.66}{2} = 1066.83$$

$$MS_E = \frac{SS_E}{N-k} = \frac{SS_E}{32} = \frac{130.30}{32} = 4.07$$

The observed value of the test statistic is

$$F_{k-1,\,N-k} = F_{2,\,32} = \frac{MS_{\text{Tr}}}{MS_E}$$
$$= \frac{1066.83}{4.07} = 262.12$$

Remember that $H_0$ is to be rejected if this value is significantly larger than 1. This certainly appears to be the case! To be sure, we check the $F$ tables. The critical point for an $\alpha = .01$ test is approximately 5.39. Since the observed value of 262.12 is much larger than this, the $P$ value for the test is less than .01. We do have statistical evidence that the three treatments differ in mean effect. It is customary to summarize the results in an ANOVA table such as this:

ANOVA

| SOURCE | *DF* | *SS* | *MS* | *F* |
|---|---|---|---|---|
| Treatment | 2 | 2133.66 | 1066.83 | 262.12 |
| Error | 32 | 130.30 | 4.07 | |
| **Total** | 34 | 2263.96 | | |

A few comments of a practical nature should be made. In particular, it is assumed that the $k$ populations under study are normal. This assumption can and should be checked before an analysis of variance is performed to compare population means. There are several methods for doing so. One such method, the chi-square goodness of fit test is presented in Chapter 12. It is also assumed that the $k$ populations have equal variances. To check this assumption, Bartlett's test, Cochran's test, and the maximum $F$ ratio test are commonly used. Although we do not discuss these tests here, we do mention them for reference purposes. It should also be noted that in the one-way classification model, sample sizes can be unequal. However, there are some distinct advantages to having equal sample sizes. First, the consequences of violating the assumption of equal variances are not serious if the samples are the same size. Thus, in this case, running Bartlett's test or some other test for equal variances, though desirable, is not essential. Second, if $H_0$ is rejected and the population means are declared unequal, usually some further tests are desirable. Many of these tests are designed with equal sample sizes in mind.

## EXERCISES 10.1

1. Carbon dioxide is known to have a critical effect on microbiological growth. Small amounts of $CO_2$ stimulate the growth of many organisms while high concentrations

inhibit the growth of most. The latter effect is used commercially when perishable food products are stored. A study is conducted to investigate the effect of $CO_2$ on the growth rate of ***Pseudomonas fragi,*** a food spoiler. Carbon dioxide is administered at five different atmospheric pressures. The response noted is the percentage change in cell mass after a 1-hour growing time. Ten cultures are used at each level. The following data are found:

| Factor ($CO_2$ Pressure in Atmospheres) Level | | | | |
|---|---|---|---|---|
| 0.0 | .083 | .29 | .50 | .86 |
| 62.6 | 50.9 | 45.5 | 29.5 | 24.9 |
| 59.6 | 44.3 | 41.1 | 22.8 | 17.2 |
| 64.5 | 47.5 | 29.8 | 19.2 | 7.8 |
| 59.3 | 49.5 | 38.3 | 20.6 | 10.5 |
| 58.6 | 48.5 | 40.2 | 29.2 | 17.8 |
| 64.6 | 50.4 | 38.5 | 24.1 | 22.1 |
| 50.9 | 35.2 | 30.2 | 22.6 | 22.6 |
| 56.2 | 49.9 | 27.0 | 32.7 | 16.8 |
| 52.3 | 42.6 | 40.0 | 24.4 | 15.9 |
| 62.8 | 41.6 | 33.9 | 29.6 | 8.8 |

**a.** We assume fixed effects. What does this imply concerning the atmospheric levels chosen?
**b.** State the null hypothesis to be tested.
**c.** Find the values of $T_{i\cdot}$, $\bar{X}_{i\cdot}$, $T_{\cdot\cdot}$, $\bar{X}_{\cdot\cdot}$, and $\Sigma_{i=1}^{5}\Sigma_{j=1}^{10}X_{ij}^{2}$.
**d.** Find $SS_{\text{Total}}$, $SS_{\text{Tr}}$, and $SS_E$.
**e.** Find $MS_{\text{Tr}}$ and $MS_E$.
**f.** Evaluate the $F$ statistic used to test $H_0$.
**g.** Can $H_0$ be rejected at the $\alpha = .01$ level? Explain. What assumptions are you making concerning the five populations?

**2.** Chlorpropamide/alcohol flushing (CPAF) is a facial flushing experienced by diabetic patients on chlorpropamide after consumption of alcohol. An experiment is run to study the ability of indomethacin to block this reaction. Three groups of diabetics participated in the study: I, diabetics with no complications; II, diabetics with severe retinopathy; and III, diabetics with large-vessel disease. Each patient's facial temperature is taken at the beginning of the experiment, and then 250 mg of chlorpropamide is given. After 12 hr, the patient is given 40 ml of sherry and the facial temperature is noted. The experiment is repeated, with each patient receiving 100 mg of indomethacin 75 min before receiving the sherry. Again the change in facial temperature is noted. The following observations are obtained on $X$, the difference in temperature (temperature after indomethacin is used minus temperature before indomethacin is taken):

Factor (Type of Diabetic) Level

| I | II | III |
|---|---|---|
| −.23 | .32 | −.35 |
| −.76 | .25 | −.13 |
| −.15 | .29 | .16 |
| −.34 | .07 | .12 |
| −.54 | .10 | −.43 |
| −1.90 | .18 | .49 |
| −2.07 | .16 | −.30 |
| −1.21 | .23 | .44 |

**a.** State the null hypothesis to be tested.

**b.** Test the null hypothesis by completing the ANOVA table. Assume normality.

**c.** Practically speaking, what is the significance of the negative signs associated with some of the observations?

**3.** A study is run of the sulfur content of five major coal seams in Texas. Core samples are taken at random from each of the seams and analyzed. The following data of the percentage of sulfur per plug are found:

Factor (Coal Seam) Level

| 1 | 2 | 3 | 4 | 5 |
|---|---|---|---|---|
| 1.51 | 1.69 | 1.56 | 1.30 | .73 |
| 1.92 | .64 | 1.22 | .75 | .80 |
| 1.08 | .90 | 1.32 | 1.26 | .90 |
| 2.04 | 1.41 | 1.39 | .69 | 1.24 |
| 2.14 | 1.01 | 1.33 | .62 | .82 |
| 1.76 | .84 | 1.54 | .90 | .72 |
| 1.17 | 1.28 | 1.04 | 1.20 | .57 |
| | 1.59 | 2.25 | .32 | 1.18 |
| | | 1.49 | | .54 |
| | | | | 1.30 |

Assuming normality and equal variances, test for equality of means. What conclusions can be drawn from these data?

**4.** A study is run to determine the effects of a chloralkali plant on fish living in the river that flows past the plant. The variable of interest is the total mercury level in micrograms per gram of body weight per fish in the area. Fish samples are taken from four sites along the river:

**I.** 5.5 km above the plant
**II.** 3.7 km below the plant
**III.** 21 km below the plant
**IV.** 133 km below the plant

The following data are found:

| Factor (Location along River) Level | | | |
|---|---|---|---|
| I | I | III | IV |
| .45 | 1.64 | 1.56 | .65 |
| .35 | 1.67 | 1.55 | .59 |
| .32 | 1.85 | 1.69 | .69 |
| .68 | 1.57 | 1.67 | .62 |
| .53 | 1.59 | 1.60 | .70 |
| .34 | 1.61 | 1.68 | .64 |
| .61 | 1.53 | 1.65 | .81 |
| .41 | 1.40 | 1.59 | .58 |
| .51 | 1.70 | 1.75 | .53 |
| .71 | 1.48 | 1.49 | .75 |

Assuming normality, test for equality of means.

**5.** A study is conducted of several species of birds that are similar in nature and share a common environment. The song of each species has a distinctive set of features that permits recognition. One characteristic under investigation is the length of the song in seconds. Three species are studied: the towhee, the common yellowthroat, and the brown thrasher. The following data are obtained:

| Factor (Species) Level | | |
|---|---|---|
| TOWHEE | COMMON YELLOWTHROAT | BROWN THRASHER |
| 1.11 | 2.17 | .42 |
| 1.23 | 1.85 | .93 |
| .91 | 1.99 | .77 |
| .95 | 1.74 | .37 |
| .99 | 1.54 | .50 |
| 1.08 | 1.86 | .48 |
| 1.18 | 1.87 | .68 |
| 1.29 | 2.04 | .62 |
| 1.12 | 1.69 | .39 |
| .88 | | .67 |
| 1.34 | | 1.03 |
| | | .79 |

Assuming normality and equal variances, test the null hypothesis that the mean song lengths are the same for all three species.

---

## MULTIPLE COMPARISONS

**10.2** □ Once a one-way classification analysis of variance has been run to compare $k$ population means, we shall be in exactly one of two possible situations:

1. We have been unable to reject $H_0$. Based on the available data, we have been unable to detect any differences among the $k$ population means. In this case, the analysis of the data is complete.

2. We have been able to reject $H_0$ and therefore conclude that there are some differences among the $k$ population means. In this case, the analysis of the data has just begun, since it is natural to continue the investigation to try to pinpoint where the differences lie.

There are several methods for detecting differences among population means once the hypothesis of equality has been rejected. We present here a method that has found wide acceptance. It is due to D. B. Duncan and is called *Duncan's multiple range test.* The test was originally designed for use with samples of equal size. However, the test has been extended by C. Y. Kramer to include samples of unequal size. We illustrate first the procedure for *equal* sample sizes.

---

**EXAMPLE 10.2.1** □ Water samples from each of four lakes are analyzed for phosphorus. The phosphorus level is given in parts per million (ppm). The following summary statistics, based on 20 randomly selected samples from each lake, are obtained:

$$T_{1\cdot} = .40 \qquad T_{4\cdot} = 1.00$$

$$T_{2\cdot} = .20 \qquad T_{\cdot\cdot} = 1.62$$

$$T_{3\cdot} = .20 \qquad \sum\sum X_{ij}^2 = .288\,0$$

The ANOVA for the experiment is as follows:

ANOVA

| SOURCE | $DF$ | $SS$ | $MS$ | $F$ |
|---|---|---|---|---|
| Treatment | 3 | .027 2 | .009 1 | 3.033 3 |
| Error | 76 | .228 0 | .003 0 | |
| **Total** | 79 | .255 2 | | |

The critical points for $\alpha = .05$ and $\alpha = .025$ tests of

$$H_0: \mu_1 = \mu_2 = \mu_3 = \mu_4$$

based on the $F_{3, 76}$ distribution are approximately 2.76 and 3.34, respectively. Thus the $P$ value for the test is small, lying somewhere between .025 and .05. So we reject $H_0$ and conclude that there are differences in the mean phosphorus levels in the four lakes. Just what these differences are remains to be seen.

---

Duncan's multiple range test is designed to detect differences in population means by comparing sample means. This is done by dividing the $k$ sample means, and therefore the $k$ population means, into subgroups so that means within subgroups are not considered to be significantly different. The test is performed as follows:

**1.** Linearly order the $k$ sample means.

**2.** Consider any subset of $p$ sample means $2 \leq p \leq k$. For the means of any of the corresponding populations to be considered different, the range of the means in the subgroup (largest to smallest) must exceed a specific value, called the *shortest significant range* $SSR_p$.

**3.** The shortest significant range is calculated by means of Table VIII in Appendix B and the following formula:

$$SSR_p = r_p\sqrt{\frac{MS_E}{n}}$$

where $r_p$ = least significant studentized range obtained from Table VIII

$MS_E$ = error mean square from ANOVA

$n$ = common sample size

$\gamma$ = degrees of freedom for $MS_E$

**4.** Results are summarized by underlining any subset of adjacent means that are not considered to be significantly different at the $\alpha$ level selected.

The procedure is illustrated by continuing the analysis of the data of Example 10.2.1.

**EXAMPLE 10.2.2** □ The estimated mean phosphorus levels for the four lakes are

$$\bar{x}_{1\cdot} = \frac{T_{1\cdot}}{20} = \frac{.40}{20} = .02 \text{ ppm}$$

$$\bar{x}_{2\cdot} = \frac{T_{2\cdot}}{20} = \frac{.20}{20} = .01 \text{ ppm}$$

$$\bar{x}_{3\cdot} = \frac{T_{3\cdot}}{20} = \frac{.02}{20} = .001 \text{ ppm}$$

$$\bar{x}_{4\cdot} = \frac{T_{4\cdot}}{20} = \frac{1.00}{20} = .05 \text{ ppm}$$

In linear order, these are

| $\bar{x}_{3\cdot}$ | $\bar{x}_{2\cdot}$ | $\bar{x}_{1\cdot}$ | $\bar{x}_{4\cdot}$ |
|---|---|---|---|
| .001 | .01 | .02 | .05 |

Next we construct a chart giving the values of $SSR_p$ for $\alpha = .05$. The chart is based on $\gamma = 60$ degrees of freedom, since this value is closest to the 76 value required for the Duncan test. Note that $MS_E = .003\,0$ is obtained from the ANOVA of Example 10.2.1, the value of $r_p$ reported is given in Table VIII of Appendix B, and $SSR_p = r_p\sqrt{MS_E/20}$.

| $p$ | 2 | 3 | 4 |
|---|---|---|---|
| $r_p$ | 2.829 | 2.976 | 3.073 |
| $SSR_p$ | .034 6 | .036 4 | .037 6 |

The differences in population means are detected by comparing the largest sample mean with the smallest, the largest with the next smallest, and so forth. Thus potentially we need to consider pairs of sample means in the order

**1.** $\bar{x}_{4\cdot} - \bar{x}_{3\cdot}$
**2.** $\bar{x}_{4\cdot} - \bar{x}_{2\cdot}$
**3.** $\bar{x}_{4\cdot} - \bar{x}_{1\cdot}$
**4.** $\bar{x}_{1\cdot} - \bar{x}_{3\cdot}$
**5.** $\bar{x}_{1\cdot} - \bar{x}_{2\cdot}$
**6.** $\bar{x}_{2\cdot} - \bar{x}_{3\cdot}$

However, once a group of means has been found to be not significantly different, no further test will declare them to differ. Thus, in practice, it may not be necessary to perform all the comparisons indicated. The needed comparisons are shown in Table 10.2.

No further comparisons need be made at this point since no differences have been detected among the mean phosphorus levels of lakes 1, 2, and 3. In summary, we may conclude that $\mu_4 \neq \mu_3$ and $\mu_4 \neq \mu_2$. No other

**TABLE 10.2**

| DIFFERENCE $d$ | NUMBER IN SUBGROUP $p$ | $SSR_p$ (FROM CHART) | IS $d > SSR_p$? | GROUPINGS |
|---|---|---|---|---|
| $\bar{x}_{4\cdot} - \bar{x}_{3\cdot} = .049\,0$ | 4 | .037 6 | yes | $\bar{x}_{3\cdot}\ \bar{x}_{2\cdot}\ \bar{x}_{1\cdot}\ \bar{x}_{4\cdot}$ |
| $\bar{x}_{4\cdot} - \bar{x}_{2\cdot} = .04$ | 3 | .036 4 | yes | $\bar{x}_{3\cdot}\ \bar{x}_{2\cdot}\ \bar{x}_{1\cdot}\ \bar{x}_{4\cdot}$ |
| $\bar{x}_{4\cdot} - \bar{x}_{1\cdot} = .03$ | 2 | .034 6 | no | $\bar{x}_{3\cdot}\ \bar{x}_{2\cdot}\ \underline{\bar{x}_{1\cdot}\ \bar{x}_{4\cdot}}$ |
| $\bar{x}_{1\cdot} - \bar{x}_{3\cdot} = .019$ | 3 | .036 4 | no | $\underline{\bar{x}_{3\cdot}\ \bar{x}_{2\cdot}\ \underline{\bar{x}_{1\cdot}\ \bar{x}_{4\cdot}}}$ |

differences have been detected. The value $\alpha = .05$ is the probability that at least one of these conclusions is incorrect.

---

C. Y. Kramer in 1956 extended Duncan's multiple range test to include unequal sample sizes. The test is performed in a manner similar to Duncan's original procedure with two variations. In particular, the shortest significant range for the adjusted test, denoted $SSR'_p$, is given by

$$SSR'_p = \sqrt{MS_E}\, r_p$$

where $r_p$ = least significant studentized range obtained from Table VIII

$MS_E$ = error mean square from ANOVA

In addition, the test statistic for comparing two population means $\mu_i$ and $\mu_j$ is

$$(\bar{x}_{i\cdot} - \bar{x}_{j\cdot})\sqrt{\frac{2n_i n_j}{n_i + n_j}}$$

This test statistic reflects the sample sizes, and the means $\mu_i$ and $\mu_j$ are considered different if and only if the observed value of the statistic exceeds $SSR'_p$. The procedure is illustrated in Example 10.2.3.

---

**EXAMPLE 10.2.3** □ In Example 10.1.6, it was concluded that the three acne treatments under study did differ in mean effect. To pinpoint the differences, we use Duncan's multiple range test. Since the sample sizes are not equal, Kramer's adjustment is appropriate. From previous results it is known that

$$n_1 = 10 \quad \bar{x}_{1\cdot} = 49.46 \quad MS_E = 4.07$$
$$n_2 = 12 \quad \bar{x}_{2\cdot} = 68.73 \quad \sqrt{MS_E} \doteq 2.02$$
$$n_3 = 13 \quad \bar{x}_{3\cdot} = 63.60$$

In linear order, the sample means are

| $\bar{x}_{1\cdot}$ | $\bar{x}_{3\cdot}$ | $\bar{x}_{2\cdot}$ |
|---|---|---|
| 49.46 | 63.60 | 68.73 |

Using Table VIII of Appendix B with $\alpha = .01$ and $\gamma = 30$ degrees of freedom (as an approximation to $\gamma = 32$ degrees of freedom) and the formula $SSR'_p = \sqrt{MS_E}\, r_p$, we obtain the following adjusted values for the shortest significant range:

| $p$ | 2 | 3 |
|---|---|---|
| $r_p$ | 3.889 | 4.506 |
| $SSR'_p$ | 7.85 | 9.10 |

To compare $\mu_2$ to $\mu_1$, we evaluate the test statistic thusly:

$$(\bar{x}_{2\cdot} - \bar{x}_{1\cdot})\sqrt{\frac{2n_1n_2}{n_1 + n_2}} = (68.73 - 49.46)\sqrt{\frac{2 \cdot 10 \cdot 12}{10 + 12}}$$
$$= 63.65$$

Since this value exceeds $SSR'_3 = 9.10$, we can conclude that $\mu_1 \neq \mu_2$. The statistic

$$(\bar{x}_{2\cdot} - \bar{x}_{3\cdot})\sqrt{\frac{2n_2n_3}{n_2 + n_3}} = (68.73 - 63.60)\sqrt{\frac{2 \cdot 12 \cdot 13}{12 + 13}}$$
$$= 18.12$$

is used to compare $\mu_2$ with $\mu_3$. Since this value exceeds $SSR'_2 = 7.85$, we can conclude that $\mu_2 \neq \mu_3$. The last comparison is $\mu_3$ with $\mu_1$. The necessary statistic is

$$(\bar{x}_{3\cdot} - \bar{x}_{1\cdot})\sqrt{\frac{2n_3n_1}{n_3 + n_1}} = (63.60 - 49.46)\sqrt{\frac{2 \cdot 13 \cdot 10}{13 + 10}}$$
$$= 47.54$$

Since this value also exceeds $SSR'_2$, we conclude that $\mu_1 \neq \mu_3$. Summarizing these results, we have

| Old | new | current |
|---|---|---|
| $\underline{\bar{x}_{1\cdot}}$ | $\underline{\bar{x}_{3\cdot}}$ | $\underline{\bar{x}_{2\cdot}}$ |

That is, at the $\alpha = .01$ level we may conclude that each of the means is significantly different from each of the others.

## EXERCISES 10.2

1. Continue the analysis of the data of Exercise 10.1.1 by applying Duncan's multiple range test.
2. Continue the analysis of the data of Exercise 10.1.2 by applying Duncan's multiple range test.
3. Continue the analysis of the data of Exercise 10.1.3 by applying Duncan's multiple range test with Kramer's adjustment.
4. Continue the analysis of the data of Exercise 10.1.4 by applying Duncan's multiple range test.
5. Continue the analysis of the data of Exercise 10.1.5 by applying Duncan's multiple range test with Kramer's adjustment.

**Computing Supplement**

Two SAS programs are available for running analysis-of-variance tests: PROC ANOVA and PROC GLM. The former is used only if sample sizes are equal; the latter is applicable regardless of the sample sizes. We illustrate PROC GLM by analyzing the data of Examples 10.1.6 and 10.2.3 via SAS. Note that there will be some discrepancies in the values reported because SAS retains more decimal places in its calculations than is generally done with a handheld calculator.

| **Statement** | **Function** |
|---|---|
| DATA ACNE; | names data set |
| INPUT TRTMENT IMPROVE @@; | two variables, TRTMENT and IMPROVE, are involved; TRTMENT assumes values 1, 2, 3 to identify treatment group from which observation comes |
| CARDS; | data follow |
| 1 48.6 1 49.4 1 50.1<br>1 49.8 1 50.6 1 50.8<br>1 47.1 1 52.5 1 49.0<br>1 46.7 2 68.0 2 67.0<br>. . . . . . . . . . .<br>3 63.2 3 61.2 3 60.5 | data |
| ; | signals end of data |
| PROC GLM; | calls on procedure for analysis of variance |
| CLASSES TRTMENT; | signals data are to be grouped according to value of TRTMENT |
| MODEL IMPROVE=TRTMENT; | identifies variable on left, IMPROVE, as dependent, or response, variable |
| MEANS TRTMENT/DUNCAN; | asks for appropriate Duncan's multiple range test |
| TITLE ONE WAY CLASSIFICATION; | titles output |

The output of this program is shown on page 294. Note that the source which we labeled "treatments" is called MODEL by SAS. The $F$ value for testing $H_0$: $\mu_1 = \mu_2 = \mu_3$, 262.02, is given by (1). The $P$ value for the test, .000 1, is given by (2). Since this value is small, we reject $H_0$ and conclude that the treatments differ in mean effect. The results of Duncan's multiple range test with the Kramer adjustment for unequal sized samples are given. Note that the results agree with those of Example 10.2.3.

```
                         ONE WAY CLASSIFICATION

                    GENERAL LINEAR MODELS PROCEDURE

                       CLASS LEVEL INFORMATION

                       CLASS        LEVELS      VALUES

                       TRTMENT        3         1 2 3

               NUMBER OF OBSERVATIONS IN DATA SET = 35



                         ONE WAY CLASSIFICATION

                    GENERAL LINEAR MODELS PROCEDURE

DEPENDENT VARIABLE: IMPROVE

SOURCE                 DF     SUM OF SQUARES        MEAN SQUARE         F VALUE

MODEL                   2     2133.66533333      1066.83266667     (1)  262.02

ERROR                  32      130.29066667         4.07158333          PR > F

CORRECTED TOTAL        34     2263.95600000                        (2)  0.0001

R-SQUARE             C.V.           STD DEV          IMPROVE MEAN

0.942450           3.2906        2.01781648           61.32000000

SOURCE                 DF        TYPE I SS    F VALUE     PR > F

TRTMENT                 2    2133.66533333     262.02     0.0001

SOURCE                 DF       TYPE IV SS    F VALUE     PR > F

TRTMENT                 2    2133.66533333     262.02     0.0001



                         ONE WAY CLASSIFICATION

                    GENERAL LINEAR MODELS PROCEDURE

              DUNCAN'S MULTIPLE RANGE TEST FOR VARIABLE IMPROVE

           MEANS WITH THE SAME LETTER ARE NOT SIGNIFICANTLY DIFFERENT.

                ALPHA LEVEL=.05        DF=32         MS=4.07158

                GROUPING              MEAN         N     TRTMENT

                       A         68.733333        12     2

                       B         63.600000        13     3

                       C         49.460000        10     1
```

## RANDOM EFFECTS

**10.3** □ The model presented in Section 10.1 is called the *fixed-effects model.* Recall that this implies that the factor levels, or "treatments," are selected specifically by the experimenter because they are of particular interest. The purpose of the experiment is to make inferences about the means of the particular populations from which the samples are drawn. No other populations are of interest. If, however, we want to make a broad generalization concerning a larger set of populations, and not just the $k$ populations from which we sample, then the model is called a *random-effects model.* In this case, the $k$ sampled populations are considered to be a random sample of populations drawn from the larger set. The hypothesis of interest is not that $\mu_1 = \mu_2 = \cdots = \mu_k$. Rather, we want to determine whether some variability exists among the population means of the larger set. Consider Example 10.3.1.

---

**EXAMPLE 10.3.1** □ Bacteriological media in use in hospital laboratories are obtained from different manufacturers. It is suspected that the quality of the media varies from manufacturer to manufacturer. To test this theory, a list of manufacturers of a particular medium is compiled, the names of three are randomly selected from the list, and samples of the media from these three sources are tested. The tests are conducted by placing 2 drops of a measured suspension of a standard organism, *Escherichia coli,* on the plate, allowing the culture to grow for 24 hours, and then determining the number of colonies (in thousands) of the organism present at the end of this period. The purpose is not to compare these particular three manufacturers—they were chosen at random and constitute only a sample of all manufacturers of the media. Rather, we wish statistical support for the general statement that the quality of the media differs among manufacturers.

---

Mathematically, the random-effects model can be written as follows:

**Model**

$$X_{ij} \equiv \mu + T_i + E_{ij} \qquad \begin{array}{l} i = 1, 2, \ldots, k \\ j = 1, 2, \ldots, n_i \end{array}$$

where $\mu =$ overall mean effect

$T_i = \mu_i - \mu$ ($\mu_i$ is mean of $i$th population selected for study)

$E_{ij} = X_{ij} - \mu_i$ residual, or random, error

We assume the following:

**Model Assumptions** 1. The $k$ samples represent independent random samples drawn from $k$ populations randomly selected from a larger set of populations.

2. Each of the populations in the larger set is normal, and thus each of the $k$ sampled populations is also normal.

3. Each of the populations in the larger set has the same variance, $\sigma^2$, and thus each of the $k$ sampled populations also has variance $\sigma^2$.

4. Variables $T_1, T_2, \ldots, T_k$ are independent normal random variables, each with mean 0 and common variance $\sigma_{\text{Tr}}^2$.

The model itself and the first three model assumptions are similar to those of the fixed-effects model. However, one important difference between the two is expressed mathematically as model assumption 4. In the fixed-effects, model, the treatments, or levels, used in the experiment are purposely chosen by the experimenter because they are of particular interest. If the experiment were replicated (repeated), the same treatments would be used. That is, the same populations would be sampled each time, and the $k$ treatment effects $\mu_i - \mu$ would not vary. This implies that in the fixed-effects model, the $k$ terms $\mu_i - \mu$ are considered *unknown constants*. In the random-effects model, this is not the case. Since the first step in a random-effects experiment is to randomly select $k$ populations for study, those actually chosen will vary from replication to replication. Thus in the random-effects model, the $k$ terms $T_i = \mu_i - \mu$ are not constants, but are, in fact, *random variables* whose values for a given replication depend on the choice of the $k$ populations to be studied. These variables are assumed to be independent normal random variables with mean 0 and common variance $\sigma_{\text{Tr}}^2$.

If the population means in the larger set are equal, then the treatment effects $T_i = \mu_i - \mu$ will not vary. That is, $\sigma_{\text{Tr}}^2$ will be zero. Thus in the random-effects model, the hypothesis of equal means is tested by considering

$$H_0: \sigma_{\text{Tr}}^2 = 0 \qquad \text{(no variability in treatment effects)}$$
$$H_1: \sigma_{\text{Tr}}^2 \neq 0$$

Even though theoretically the random-effects model differs from the fixed-effects one, the data are handled in exactly the same way. The only change necessary in the analysis-of-variance table occurs in the column of the expected mean square. For this model $E[MS_{\text{Tr}}]$ is changed to read

$$E[MS_{\text{Tr}}] = \sigma^2 + n_0\sigma_{\text{Tr}}^2$$

where

$$n_0 = \frac{N - \sum_{i=1}^{k} n_i^2/N}{k - 1}$$

**TABLE 10.3** ANALYSIS OF VARIANCE: ONE-WAY CLASSIFICATION, COMPLETELY RANDOM DESIGN WITH RANDOM EFFECTS

| SOURCE OF VARIATION | DEGREES OF FREEDOM $DF$ | SUM OF SQUARES $SS$ | MEAN SQUARE $MS$ | EXPECTED MEAN SQUARE | $F$ RATIO |
|---|---|---|---|---|---|
| Treatment, or level | $k - 1$ | $\sum_{i=1}^{k} \frac{T_{i.}^2}{n_i} - \frac{T_{..}^2}{N}$ | $\frac{SS_{Tr}}{k-1}$ | $\sigma^2 + n_0 \sigma_{Tr}^2$ | $\frac{MS_{Tr}}{MS_E}$ |
| Residual, or error | $N - k$ | $SS_{Total} - SS_{Tr}$ | $\frac{SS_E}{N-k}$ | $\sigma^2$ | |
| **Total** | $N - 1$ | $\sum_{i=1}^{k} \sum_{j=1}^{n_i} X_{ij}^2 - \frac{T_{..}^2}{N}$ | | | |

The analysis of variance is summarized in Table 10.3. Again note that if $H_0$ is true ($\sigma_{Tr}^2 = 0$), we would expect $MS_{Tr}$ and $MS_E$ to be close in value, since both estimate the same parameter, $\sigma^2$. If $H_0$ is not true, we would expect $MS_{Tr}$ to be larger than $MS_E$, thus forcing the $F$ ratio to larger than 1. Thus the test is to reject $H_0$ for observed values of the $F_{k-1, N-k}$ statistic that are too large to have occurred by chance.

**EXAMPLE 10.3.2** □ In the experiment of Example 10.3.1, three manufacturers of bacteriological media are randomly chosen. Samples of size 10 are drawn from the stock of each and tested. The following summary data result:

$$T_{1\cdot} = 527 \qquad T_{3\cdot} = 480$$
$$T_{2\cdot} = 502 \qquad T_{\cdot\cdot} = 1509$$

$$\sum_{i=1}^{3} \sum_{j=1}^{10} X_{ij}^2 = 76{,}511$$

The ANOVA for these data is as follows:

ANOVA

| SOURCE | *DF* | *SS* | *MS* | *F* |
|---|---|---|---|---|
| Treatment | 2 | 110.6 | 55.3 | 3 |
| Error | 27 | 497.7 | 18.43 | |
| **Total** | 29 | 608.3 | | |

The critical point for an $\alpha = .1$ test of $H_0$: $\sigma_{Tr}^2 = 0$ based on the $F_{2, 27}$ distribution is 2.51. Since $3 > 2.51$, $H_0$ can be rejected at this level. The $P$ value of the test lies between .1 and .05 (critical value, 3.35). We do have evidence of some variability in quality among manufacturers.

In the random-effects model, no further tests are necessary even if $H_0$ is rejected. The purpose of the experiment is to make a general statement concerning the populations from which the $k$ sampled populations are drawn. This has been done.

## EXERCISES 10.3

1. A study is run of the behavior of the male great titmouse. The purpose is to determine whether there is a difference in the mean height (in meters) at which the bird performs various activities. A list of 10 of the most important activities is compiled. Four—singing, feeding, preening, and resting—are randomly chosen for monitoring. These data, based on 20 observations each, result:

| SINGING | FEEDING | PREENING | RESTING |
|---|---|---|---|
| $T_{1\cdot} = 186$ | $T_{2\cdot} = 44$ | $T_{3\cdot} = 120$ | $T_{4\cdot} = 70$ |

$$\sum_{i=1}^{4} \sum_{j=1}^{20} X_{ij}^2 = 7915.8$$

On the basis of these data, can it be concluded that activities are performed at different heights? Explain your answer on the basis of the ANOVA and the $P$ value involved.

2. Which model, fixed effects or random effects, is more likely to be encountered in practice? Explain your reasoning.

## RANDOMIZED COMPLETE BLOCKS

**10.4** □ The procedure presented in this section is an extension of the paired $T$ procedure for comparing the means of two normal populations (see Chapter 9). Recall that the purpose of pairing is to minimize the effect of some extraneous variable (a variable not under study in the experiment) by pairing experimental units that are similar with respect to this variable. Each member of the pair receives a different treatment, and any differences in response are attributed to treatment effects since the effect of the extraneous variable has been neutralized by pairing. This pairing is illustrated in Figure 10.2.

When we want to compare the means of $k$ populations in the presence of an extraneous variable, a procedure known as *blocking* is used. A *block* is a collection of $k$ (rather than two) experimental units that are as nearly alike as possible relative to the extraneous variable. Each treatment is randomly assigned to one unit within each block. Since once again the

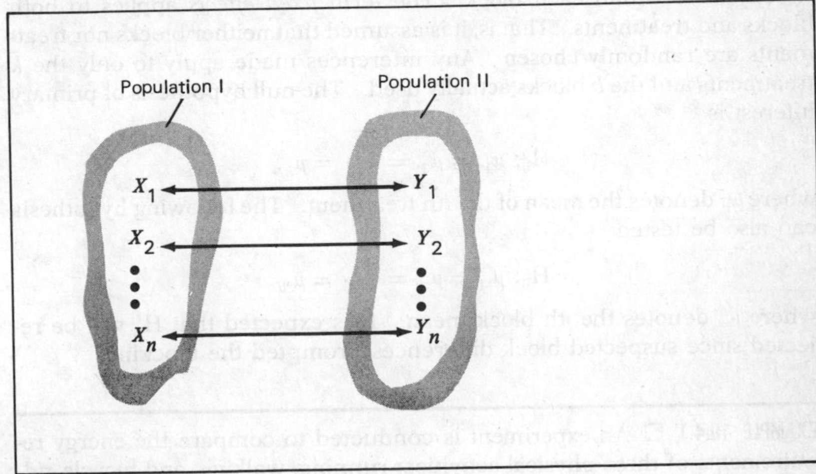


**FIGURE 10.2** Paired data. Is $\mu_1 = \mu_2$?

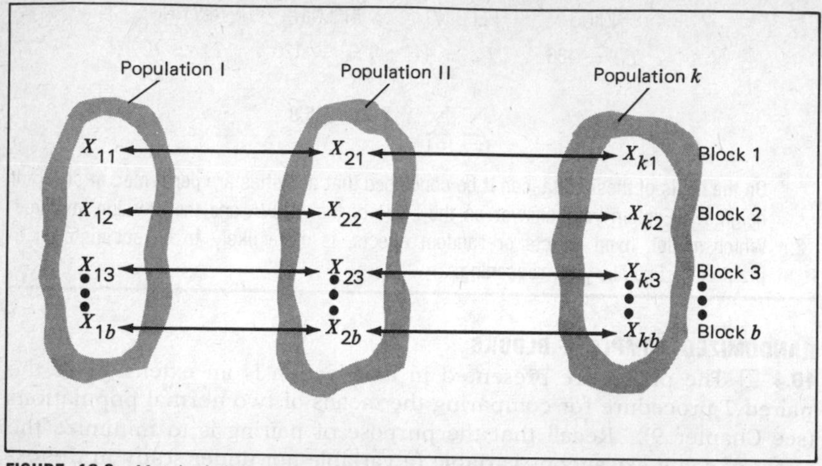


**FIGURE 10.3** Matched data. Is $\mu_{1\cdot} = \mu_{2\cdot} = \cdots = \mu_{k\cdot}$?

effect of the extraneous variable has been neutralized among treatments by matching like experimental units, any differences in response are attributed to treatment effects. The blocking procedure is illustrated in Figure 10.3.

The design presented here is called the *randomized complete block* design with fixed effects. The word *blocks* refers to the fact that experimental units have been matched relative to some extraneous variable; *randomized* refers to the fact that treatments are randomly assigned within blocks; and to say that the design is *complete* implies that each treatment is used exactly once within each block. The term *fixed effects* applies to both blocks and treatments. That is, it is assumed that neither blocks nor treatments are randomly chosen. Any inferences made apply to only the $k$ treatments and the $b$ blocks actually used. The null hypothesis of primary interest is

$$H_0: \mu_{1\cdot} = \mu_{2\cdot} = \cdots = \mu_{k\cdot}$$

where $\mu_{i\cdot}$ denotes the mean of the $i$th treatment. The following hypothesis can also be tested:

$$H_0': \mu_{\cdot 1} = \mu_{\cdot 2} = \cdots = \mu_{\cdot b}$$

where $\mu_{\cdot j}$ denotes the $j$th block mean. It is expected that $H_0'$ will be rejected since suspected block differences prompted the blocking.

---

**EXAMPLE 10.4.1** □ An experiment is conducted to compare the energy requirements of three physical activities: running, walking, and bicycle riding. The variable of interest is $X$, the number of kilocalories expended per kilometer traveled. Since it is thought that metabolic differences among individuals may affect the number of kilocalories required for a given activity, we want to control this extraneous variable. To do so, eight subjects are selected. Each is asked to run, walk, and bicycle a measured distance, and the number of kilocalories expended per kilometer is determined for each subject during each activity. The activities are run in random order with time for recovery between activities. Each individual serves as a block. Each activity is monitored exactly once for each individual, and thus the design is complete. Any differences in the mean number of kilocalories expended will be attributed to differences among the activities themselves, since the effect of individual differences among subjects has been neutralized by blocking. The null hypothesis of particular interest is

$$H_0: \mu_{1\cdot} = \mu_{2\cdot} = \mu_{3\cdot}$$

where $\mu_{1\cdot}$, $\mu_{2\cdot}$, $\mu_{3\cdot}$ denote the mean number of kilocalories expended per kilometer while running, walking, and bicycle riding, respectively. The secondary hypothesis is

$$H_0': \mu_{\cdot 1} = \mu_{\cdot 2} = \cdots \mu_{\cdot 8}$$

where $\mu_{\cdot j}$ denotes the mean energy expended by the $j$th subject. It is suspected that these means differ because of metabolic differences among subjects. This is what prompted us to block.

---

The data collected in a randomized complete block design are conveniently recorded in the following format:

DATA LAYOUT OF RANDOMIZED COMPLETE BLOCK DESIGN

| | | Treatment | | | | |
|---|---|---|---|---|---|---|
| | | 1 | 2 | 3 | ... | $k$ |
| B | 1 | $X_{11}$ | $X_{21}$ | $X_{31}$ | ... | $X_{k1}$ |
| l | 2 | $X_{12}$ | $X_{22}$ | $X_{32}$ | ... | $X_{k2}$ |
| o | 3 | $X_{13}$ | $X_{23}$ | $X_{33}$ | ... | $X_{k3}$ |
| c | ⋮ | ... | ... | ... | ... | ... |
| k | $b$ | $X_{1b}$ | $X_{2b}$ | $X_{3b}$ | ... | $X_{kb}$ |

Note that $b$ denotes the number of blocks used in the experiment and the number of observations per treatment; $k$ denotes the number of treatments being investigated and the number of observations per block; $N = kb$ denotes the total number of responses. Variable $X_{ij}$, $i = 1, 2, \ldots, k$ and $j = 1, 2, \ldots, b$, is a random variable denoting the response to the $i$th treatment in the $j$th block. In using sample data to compare population means, these sample statistics are required:

$$T_{i\cdot} = \sum_{j=1}^{b} X_{ij} = \text{total of all responses to } i\text{th treatment, } i = 1, 2, \ldots, k$$

$$\bar{X}_{i\cdot} = \frac{T_{i\cdot}}{b} = \text{sample mean for } i\text{th treatment, } i = 1, 2, \ldots, k$$

$$T_{\cdot j} = \sum_{i=1}^{k} X_{ij} = \text{total of all responses in } j\text{th block, } j = 1, 2, \ldots, b$$

$$\bar{X}_{\cdot j} = \frac{T_{\cdot j}}{k} = \text{sample mean for } j\text{th block, } j = 1, 2, \ldots, b$$

$$T_{\cdot\cdot} = \sum_{i=1}^{k}\sum_{j=1}^{b} X_{ij} = \sum_{i=1}^{k} T_{i\cdot} = \sum_{j=1}^{b} T_{\cdot j} = \text{total of all responses}$$

$$\bar{X}_{\cdot\cdot} = \frac{T_{\cdot\cdot}}{N} = \text{sample mean for all responses}$$

$$\sum_{i=1}^{k}\sum_{j=1}^{b} X_{ij}^{2} = \text{sum of square of each response}$$

The evaluation of these statistics is illustrated in Example 10.4.2.

---

**EXAMPLE 10.4.2** □ When the experiment of Example 10.4.1 was conducted, the data shown in Table 10.4 on the number of kilocalories expended per kilometer by each subject in each of the three activities resulted. Sample treatment totals and means, block totals and means, and the grand total and mean are given in the margins of the table.

---

To write the model for the randomized complete block design with fixed effects, the following notation is needed:

$\mu$ = overall mean effect

$\mu_{i\cdot}$ = mean of $i$th treatment, $i = 1, 2, \ldots, k$

$\mu_{\cdot j}$ = $j$th block mean, $j = 1, 2, \ldots, b$

$\mu_{ij}$ = mean for $i$th treatment and $j$th block

$\tau_i = \mu_{i\cdot} - \mu$ = effect due to fact that experimental unit received $i$th treatment

$\beta_j = \mu_{\cdot j} - \mu$ = effect due to fact that experimental unit is in $j$th block

$E_{ij} = X_{ij} - \mu_{ij}$ = residual, or random, error

**TABLE 10.4**

| | | Treatment | | | | |
|---|---|---|---|---|---|---|
| | | 1 (RUNNING) | 2 (WALKING) | 3 (BICYCLING) | BLOCK TOTAL | BLOCK MEAN |
| Block | 1 | 1.4 | 1.1 | .7 | 3.2 ($T_{\cdot 1}$) | 1.07 ($\bar{X}_{\cdot 1}$) |
| | 2 | 1.5 | 1.2 | .8 | 3.5 ($T_{\cdot 2}$) | 1.17 ($\bar{X}_{\cdot 2}$) |
| | 3 | 1.8 | 1.3 | .7 | 3.8 ($T_{\cdot 3}$) | 1.27 ($\bar{X}_{\cdot 3}$) |
| | 4 | 1.7 | 1.3 | .8 | 3.8 ($T_{\cdot 4}$) | 1.27 ($\bar{X}_{\cdot 4}$) |
| | 5 | 1.6 | .7 | .1 | 2.4 ($T_{\cdot 5}$) | .8 ($\bar{X}_{\cdot 5}$) |
| | 6 | 1.5 | 1.2 | .7 | 3.4 ($T_{\cdot 6}$) | 1.13 ($\bar{X}_{\cdot 6}$) |
| | 7 | 1.7 | 1.1 | .4 | 3.2 ($T_{\cdot 7}$) | 1.07 ($\bar{X}_{\cdot 7}$) |
| | 8 | 2.0 | 1.3 | .6 | 3.9 ($T_{\cdot 8}$) | 1.30 ($\bar{X}_{\cdot 8}$) |
| | **Treatment Total** | 13.2 ($T_{1\cdot}$) | 9.2 ($T_{2\cdot}$) | 4.8 ($T_{3\cdot}$) | 27.2 ($T_{\cdot\cdot}$) | |
| | **Treatment Mean** | 1.65 ($\bar{X}_{1\cdot}$) | 1.15 ($\bar{X}_{2\cdot}$) | .6 ($\bar{X}_{3\cdot}$) | 1.13 ($\bar{X}_{\cdot\cdot}$) | |

For these data, $\sum_{i=1}^{3} \sum_{j=1}^{8} X_{ij}^2 = 36.18$.

Using this notation, we can express the model thus:

**Model**

$$X_{ij} = \mu + \tau_i + \beta_j + E_{ij} \qquad \begin{array}{l} i = 1, 2, \ldots, k \\ j = 1, 2, \ldots, b \end{array}$$

This model expresses symbolically the notion that each observation can be partitioned into four recognizable components: an overall mean effect $\mu$, a treatment effect $\tau_i$, a block effect $\beta_j$, and a random deviation attributed to unexplained sources $E_{ij}$. We make the following assumptions:

**Model Assumptions**

1. The $k \cdot b$ observations constitute independent random samples, each of size 1, from $k \cdot b$ populations with means $\mu_{ij}$, $i = 1, 2, \ldots, k$ and $j = 1, 2, \ldots, b$.

2. Each of the $k \cdot b$ populations is normal.

3. Each of the $k \cdot b$ populations has the same variance, $\sigma^2$.

4. Block and treatment effects are additive; that is, there is no interaction between blocks and treatments.

Assumptions 1 through 3 are identical to those made in the one-way classification model except that $k \cdot b$, rather than $k$, populations are under consideration. The fourth assumption is new and needs to be examined more closely. Briefly, to say that block and treatment effects are additive means that the treatments behave consistently across blocks and that the blocks behave consistently across treatments. Mathematically, this means that the difference in the mean values for any two treatments is the same in every block, and the difference in the means for any two blocks is the same for each treatment. If this is not the case, then we say that there is interaction between blocks and treatments. Some numerical examples will help clarify this concept.

---

**EXAMPLE 10.4.3** □ Three programs have been developed to help patients who have suffered their first heart attacks to adjust physically and psychologically to their condition. The variable of interest is the time in months needed for the patient to return to an active life. Since it is thought that men and women may react differently to illness, this variable is controlled by blocking. Thus we are dealing with $k \cdot b = 3 \cdot 2 = 6$ normal populations, each assumed to have the same variance. Assume that the means for these six populations are thus:

| | | Treatment | | |
|---|---|---|---|---|
| | | *A* | *B* | *C* |
| Block | Men | $\mu_{11} = 4$ | $\mu_{21} = 5$ | $\mu_{31} = 7$ |
| | Women | $\mu_{12} = 3$ | $\mu_{22} = 4$ | $\mu_{32} = 6$ |

Note that the mean for treatment *A* is 1 less than that for *B* and 3 less than that for *C* in each block; the mean for treatment *B* is 2 less than that for *C* in each block. That is, the treatments behave consistently across blocks. Similarly, the mean for block 1 (men) always exceeds the mean for block 2 (women) by 1, regardless of the treatment involved. That is, the blocks behave consistently across treatments. When this occurs, we say that block and treatment effects are additive, or that there is *no* interaction between treatments and blocks. This idea is illustrated graphically in Figure 10.4.

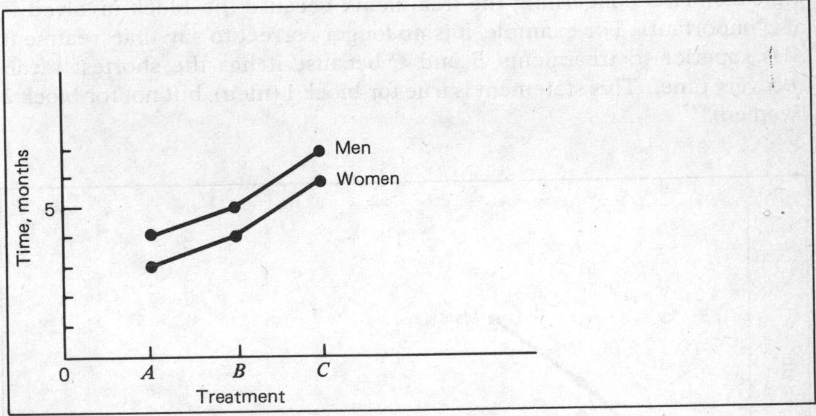


**FIGURE 10.4** No interaction: line segments are parallel.

Figure 10.4 graphs the treatment means shown in the preceding table. When no interaction exists, the line segments joining any two means will be parallel across blocks. Practically speaking, this means that it is possible to make general statements concerning the treatments without having to specify the block involved. For example, it is correct to say that treatment *A* is superior to treatments *B* and *C* in that it has the shortest mean recovery time.

**EXAMPLE 10.4.4** □ Consider Example 10.4.3 with these population means:

| Block | | Treatment A | Treatment B | Treatment C |
|---|---|---|---|---|
| | Men | $\mu_{11} = 4$ | $\mu_{21} = 7$ | $\mu_{31} = 9$ |
| | Women | $\mu_{12} = 3$ | $\mu_{22} = 6$ | $\mu_{32} = 2$ |

This table is not additive. To see this, note that the mean of treatment $A$ is 5 less than that of treatment $C$ in block 1 (men), but 1 more than that of $C$ in block 2. That is, the treatments behave differently in various blocks. In this case, we say that the blocks and treatments interact.

The graph for this table is shown in Figure 10.5. Since not all the line segments are parallel, there is interaction between blocks and treatments. Practically speaking, this means that we must be very careful when making statements concerning the treatments because the block involved is also important. For example, it is no longer correct to say that treatment $A$ is superior to treatments $B$ and $C$ because it has the shortest mean recovery time. This statement is true for block 1 (men), but not for block 2 (women).

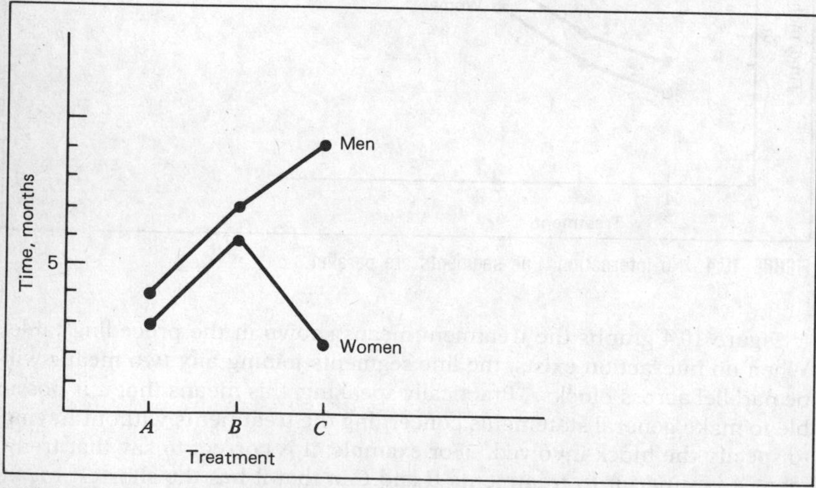


**FIGURE 10.5** Interaction exists: line segments are not parallel.

To derive the sum-of-squares identity for this model, we note that it can be shown that additivity implies that $\mu_{ij} = \mu + (\mu_{i\cdot} - \mu) + (\mu_{\cdot j} - \mu)$. Thus the theoretical model can be written in the form

$$X_{ij} - \mu \equiv (\mu_{i\cdot} - \mu) + (\mu_{\cdot j} - \mu) + \{X_{ij} - [\mu + (\mu_{i\cdot} - \mu) + (\mu_{\cdot j} - \mu)]\}$$

Replacing each of the theoretical means $\mu$, $\mu_{i\cdot}$, $\mu_{\cdot j}$ by their unbiased estimators $\bar{X}_{\cdot\cdot}$, $\bar{X}_{i\cdot}$, $\bar{X}_{\cdot j}$, respectively, we obtain the following identity:

$$X_{ij} - \bar{X}_{\cdot\cdot} \equiv (\bar{X}_{i\cdot} - \bar{X}_{\cdot\cdot}) + (\bar{X}_{\cdot j} - \bar{X}_{\cdot\cdot}) + \{X_{ij} - [\bar{X}_{\cdot\cdot} + (\bar{X}_{i\cdot} - \bar{X}_{\cdot\cdot}) + (\bar{X}_{\cdot j} - \bar{X}_{\cdot\cdot})]\}$$

If each side of this identity is squared and then summed over all possible values of $i$ and $j$, the following sum-of-squares identity for the randomized complete block design results.

**Sum-of-Squares Identity**

$$\sum_{i=1}^{k}\sum_{j=1}^{b}(X_{ij} - \bar{X}_{\cdot\cdot})^2 = \sum_{i=1}^{k}\sum_{j=1}^{b}(\bar{X}_{i\cdot} - \bar{X}_{\cdot\cdot})^2 + \sum_{i=1}^{k}\sum_{j=1}^{b}(\bar{X}_{\cdot j} - \bar{X}_{\cdot\cdot})^2 + \sum_{i=1}^{k}\sum_{j=1}^{b}(X_{ij} - \bar{X}_{i\cdot} - \bar{X}_{\cdot j} + \bar{X}_{\cdot\cdot})^2$$

The practical interpretation for each component is similar to that of the one-way classification model. In particular,

$$\sum_{i=1}^{k}\sum_{j=1}^{b}(X_{ij} - \bar{X}_{\cdot\cdot})^2 = \text{measure of total variability in data} = SS_{\text{Total}}$$

$$\sum_{i=1}^{k}\sum_{j=1}^{b}(\bar{X}_{i\cdot} - \bar{X}_{\cdot\cdot})^2 = \text{measure of variability in data attributable to use of different treatments} = \text{treatment sum of squares} = SS_{\text{Tr}}$$

$$\sum_{i=1}^{k}\sum_{j=1}^{b}(\bar{X}_{\cdot j} - \bar{X}_{\cdot\cdot})^2 = \text{measure of variability in data attributable to use of different blocks} = \text{block sum of squares} = SS_{\text{Blocks}}$$

$$\sum_{i=1}^{k}\sum_{j=1}^{b}(X_{ij} - \bar{X}_{i\cdot} - \bar{X}_{\cdot j} + \bar{X}_{\cdot\cdot})^2 = \text{measure of variability in data due to random factors} = \text{residual, or error, sum of squares} = SS_E$$

Using this notation, we can write the sum-of-squares identity as

$$SS_{\text{Total}} = SS_{\text{Tr}} + SS_{\text{Blocks}} + SS_E$$

Two null hypotheses can be tested:

$H_0$: $\mu_{1\cdot} = \mu_{2\cdot} = \cdots = \mu_{k\cdot}$ (no difference in treatment means)
$H_0'$: $\mu_{\cdot 1} = \mu_{\cdot 2} = \cdots = \mu_{\cdot b}$ (no difference in block means)

The former is the hypothesis of primary concern, since the purpose of the experiment is to detect differences in treatments in the presence of an extraneous variable. It is expected that the latter hypothesis will be rejected; if the block means were not expected to differ, then there would have been no need to block at all. Three mean squares are needed:

$$MS_{\text{Tr}} = \frac{SS_{\text{Tr}}}{k-1} = \text{treatment mean square}$$

$$MS_{\text{Blocks}} = \frac{SS_{\text{Blocks}}}{b-1} = \text{block mean square}$$

$$MS_E = \frac{SS_E}{(k-1)(b-1)} = \text{error mean square}$$

The expected values for these mean squares are

$$E[MS_{\text{Tr}}] = \sigma^2 + \frac{b}{k-1}\sum_{i=1}^{k}(\mu_{i\cdot} - \mu)^2$$

$$E[MS_{\text{Blocks}}] = \sigma^2 + \frac{k}{b-1}\sum_{j=1}^{b}(\mu_{\cdot j} - \mu)^2$$

$$E[MS_E] = \sigma^2$$

To test $H_0$, the hypothesis of equal treatment means, the ratio $MS_{\text{Tr}}/MS_E = F_{k-1,\,(k-1)(b-1)}$ is used. If $H_0$ is true, this ratio should assume a value close to 1 since in this case $\Sigma_{i=1}^{k}(\mu_{i\cdot} - \mu)^2 = 0$ and $MS_{\text{Tr}}$ and $MS_E$ are each estimating $\sigma^2$. If $H_0$ is not true, then the value of this statistic should be larger than 1. Similarly, to test $H_0'$, the hypothesis of equal block means, the ratio $MS_{\text{Blocks}}/MS_E = F_{b-1,\,(k-1)(b-1)}$ is employed with rejection of $H_0'$ occurring for large values of this statistic. The computational formulas used to evaluate these statistics are similar to those of the one-way classification model and are given in Table 10.5.

**TABLE 10.5** ANALYSIS OF VARIANCE: RANDOMIZED COMPLETE BLOCK DESIGN WITH FIXED EFFECTS

| SOURCE OF VARIATION | DEGREES OF FREEDOM | SUM OF SQUARES | MEAN SQUARE | EXPECTED MEAN SQUARE | $F$ RATIO |
|---|---|---|---|---|---|
| Treatment | $k-1$ | $\sum_{i=1}^{k} \frac{T_{i\cdot}^2}{b} - \frac{T_{\cdot\cdot}^2}{N}$ | $\frac{SS_{\mathrm{Tr}}}{k-1}$ | $\sigma^2 + \frac{b}{k-1}\sum_{i=1}^{k}(\mu_{i\cdot} - \mu)^2$ | $\frac{MS_{\mathrm{Tr}}}{MS_E}$ |
| Block | $b-1$ | $\sum_{j=1}^{b} \frac{T_{\cdot j}^2}{k} - \frac{T_{\cdot\cdot}^2}{N}$ | $\frac{SS_{\mathrm{Blocks}}}{b-1}$ | $\sigma^2 + \frac{k}{b-1}\sum_{j=1}^{b}(\mu_{\cdot j} - \mu)^2$ | $\frac{MS_{\mathrm{Blocks}}}{MS_E}$ |
| Error | $(k-1)(b-1)$ | $SS_{\mathrm{Total}} - SS_{\mathrm{Tr}} - SS_{\mathrm{Blocks}}$ | $\frac{SS_E}{(k-1)(b-1)}$ | $\sigma^2$ | |
| **Total** | $kb-1$ | $\sum_{i=1}^{k}\sum_{j=1}^{b} X_{ij}^2 - \frac{T_{\cdot\cdot}^2}{N}$ | | | |

**EXAMPLE 10.4.5** □ The following summary data from Example 10.4.2 are needed to continue the analysis of the energy requirements of running, walking, and bicycling:

$$\begin{array}{lll} k = 3 & T._1 = 3.2 & T._6 = 3.4 \\ b = 8 & T._2 = 3.5 & T._7 = 3.2 \\ N = 24 & T._3 = 3.8 & T._8 = 3.9 \\ T.. = 27.2 & T._4 = 3.8 & \\ & T._5 = 2.4 & \end{array}$$

$$\sum_{i=1}^{3} \sum_{j=1}^{8} X_{ij}^2 = 36.18$$

$$\begin{array}{ll} T_1. = 13.2 & \text{(running)} \\ T_2. = 9.2 & \text{(walking)} \\ T_3. = 4.8 & \text{(bicycling)} \end{array}$$

The ANOVA is as follows:

ANOVA

| SOURCE | *DF* | *SS* | *MS* | *F* |
|---|---|---|---|---|
| Treatment | 2 | 4.41 | 2.205 | 78.75 ($F_{2,14}$) |
| Block | 7 | .55 | .079 | 2.82 ($F_{7,14}$) |
| Error | 14 | .39 | .028 | |
| **Total** | 23 | 5.35 | | |

Since 78.75 exceeds 6.51, the critical point for an $\alpha = .01$ test of

$H_0: \mu_1. = \mu_2. = \mu_3.$ (no difference in mean energy requirements)

we reject $H_0$ and conclude that there are differences in the energy requirements for the three activities. The $P$ value of the test is less than .01. Since 2.82 exceeds 2.76, the critical value for an $\alpha = .05$ test of

$H_0': \mu._1 = \mu._2 = \cdots = \mu._8$ (no differences among blocks)

this hypothesis can be rejected, as expected. The $P$ value lies between .05 and .025 (critical value of 3.38).

Several other points should be made. The analysis of variance presented here assumes no interaction between blocks and treatments. If the data suggest the presence of interaction in that there appears to be some lack of consistency in the behavior of the treatments across blocks or vice versa, then it is desirable to investigate this assumption more carefully. Unfortunately, there is no quick way to do so. Tukey (*Biometrics,* vol. 5,

1949) has suggested a method for testing for interaction. The practical consequences of failing to realize that interaction exists are twofold: general statements concerning the relationship of one treatment to another may be inaccurate, and the probability of committing a Type II error is increased.

If the analysis of variance rejects the null hypothesis of equal treatment means, then the actual differences can be detected by using Duncan's multiple range test. The test is conducted as described in Section 10.2 with

$$SSR_p = r_p\sqrt{\frac{MS_E}{b}}$$

We have assumed that both blocks and treatments are fixed. By so doing, the null hypotheses of no differences among treatments and no differences among blocks can be expressed in terms of equality of treatment and block means, respectively. Three other models can arise. Two are called *mixed* models, and the other is termed *random*. One of the mixed models is encountered often. In this model, the treatments are fixed; that is, they are purposely chosen by the experimenter, but the blocks are selected at random from a larger group of available blocks. Thus the model is mixed in the sense that a different method is employed to choose treatments than to select blocks. The analysis is carried out exactly the same as in the fixed-effects model. The only difference occurs in the statement of $H_0'$, which assumes the form

$$H_0'\colon \sigma^2_{\text{Blocks}} = 0 \qquad \text{(no variability in block effects)}$$

The mixed model in which the blocks are fixed and the treatments are random, and the random model in which both treatments and blocks are selected randomly are outlined in Exercise 10.4.6.

## EXERCISES 10.4

1. For each table of population means, decide whether there is interaction between blocks and treatments.

**a.**

| | | Treatment | | | |
|---|---|---|---|---|---|
| | | *A* | *B* | *C* | *D* |
| Block | 1 | 1 | 3 | 4 | 0 |
| | 2 | 4 | 6 | 7 | 3 |
| | 3 | 2 | 4 | 5 | 1 |

**b.**

| | | Treatment | | | |
|---|---|---|---|---|---|
| | | *A* | *B* | *C* | *D* |
| Block | 1 | 1 | 3 | 0 | 0 |
| | 2 | 4 | 6 | 5 | 3 |
| | 3 | 2 | 4 | 5 | 1 |

**c.**

| | | Treatment | | | |
|---|---|---|---|---|---|
| | | *A* | *B* | *C* | *D* |
| Block | 1 | 1 | 3 | 4 | 0 |
| | 2 | 4 | 5 | 7 | 3 |
| | 3 | 2 | 4 | 5 | 1 |

**2.** The Sitka spruce is economically the most important forest tree in the United Kingdom. However, it exhibits poor natural regeneration as a result of the infrequency of good seed years. There is a definite need to increase seed production. Four hormone treatments are proposed. Since different trees have various natural reproductive characteristics, the effect of tree differences is controlled by blocking. Ten trees are

**TABLE 10.6**

| | | Treatment | | | | BLOCK TOTAL | BLOCK MEAN |
|---|---|---|---|---|---|---|---|
| | | *A* | *B* | *C* | *D* | | |
| Block (tree) | 1 | 89 | 59 | 20 | 51 | | |
| | 2 | 87 | 56 | 15 | 47 | | |
| | 3 | 84 | 52 | 14 | 45 | | |
| | 4 | 92 | 67 | 26 | 56 | | |
| | 5 | 95 | 70 | 28 | 60 | | |
| | 6 | 90 | 62 | 22 | 53 | | |
| | 7 | 89 | 60 | 19 | 51 | | |
| | 8 | 88 | 56 | 17 | 50 | | |
| | 9 | 82 | 50 | 14 | 45 | | |
| | 10 | 94 | 63 | 24 | 53 | | |
| **Treatment Total** | | | | | | | |
| **Treatment Mean** | | | | | | | |

used in the experiment. Four similar branches are selected within each tree. Each branch receives exactly one of the four treatments, with treatments being randomly assigned to branches. Thus each tree constitutes a complete block. The measured response is the number of seeds produced per branch. Assume that this variable, though discrete, is approximately normally distributed. The data are shown in Table 10.6.

**a.** Complete Table 10.6 by computing sample treatment totals and means, block totals and means, and the grand total and grand mean.

**b.** Test the null hypothesis of equal block means to see whether blocking is justified.

**c.** Test the null hypothesis of equal treatment means.

**3.** A study is conducted of the effect of light on the growth of ferns. Since plants grow at various rates at different ages, this variable is controlled by blocking. Four young plants (plants grown in the dark for 4 days) and four older plants (plants grown in the dark for 12 days) are utilized in the study, thus producing two blocks each of size 4. Four different light treatments are investigated. Each treatment is randomly assigned to one plant in each block. The treatments consist of exposing each plant to a single dose of light, returning it to the dark, and measuring the cross-sectional area of the fern tip 24 hr after the light is administered. These data resulted (cross-sectional area is given in square micrometers):

| Block (age) | Treatment (Wavelength of Light) 420 nm | 460 nm | 600 nm | 720 nm |
|---|---|---|---|---|
| Young | 1017.6 | 929.0 | 939.8 | 1081.5 |
| Old | 854.7 | 689.9 | 841.5 | 797.4 |

**a.** Find the sample treatment, block, and grand totals and means.

**b.** Test the null hypothesis of equal block means to see whether blocking is justified.

**c.** Test the null hypothesis of equal treatment means.

**4.** Use Duncan's multiple range test to complete the analysis of the data of Example 10.4.5.

**5.** Use Duncan's multiple range test to complete the analysis of the data of Exercise 10.4.2.

**6.** In the mixed model in which the blocks are fixed and treatments are random, how would the null hypothesis of no difference among treatments be expressed? In the random model in which both blocks and treatments are random, how would the null hypothesis of no difference among treatments be expressed? Would Duncan's test be applicable in either case if the null hypothesis were rejected? Explain.

**Computing Supplement**

PROC GLM also can be used to analyze data in a randomized complete block design. The method for doing so is illustrated with the data from Example 10.4.5. Slight discrepancies occur between the printout and the figures reported in ANOVA table of Example 10.4.5. These are due to roundoff that occurs when a handheld calculator is used.

| **Statement** | **Function** |
|---|---|
| DATA EXERCISE; | names data set |
| INPUT BLOCK TRTMENT KILOCAL; | indicates each card will contain values of three variables: block number, treatment number, and kilocalories expended |
| CARDS; | signals that data follow |
| 1 1 1.4<br>2 1 1.5<br>3 1 1.8<br>4 1 1.7<br>. . .<br>7 3 .4<br>8 3 .6 | data |
| | signals end of data |
| PROC GLM; | calls on procedure for analysis of variance |
| CLASSES BLOCK TRTMENT; | indicates observations are grouped according to value of variables BLOCK and TRTMENT |
| MODEL KILOCAL=BLOCK TRTMENT; | identifies variable on left, KILOCAL, as dependent, or response, variable |
| MEANS TRTMENT/DUNCAN; | asks for appropriate Duncan's multiple range test to be run to compare means for KILOCAL across values of TRTMENT |
| TITLE RANDOMIZED COMPLETE BLOCKS; | titles output |

The output of this program follows. Note that the value of the $F$ statistic used to test $H_0$: $\mu_{1\cdot} = \mu_{2\cdot} = \mu_{3\cdot}$ (no difference in treatment means) is given by (1), and its $P$ value is given by (2). Since the $P$ value is small (.000 1), we reject $H_0$ and conclude that the mean number of kilocalories expended differs among the three exercises. To see what these differences are, we run Duncan's test. As can be seen by (3), each of the treatment means differs from each of the others. The $F$ ratio used to test

$$H_0': \mu_{\cdot 1} = \mu_{\cdot 2} = \cdots = \mu_{\cdot 8} \qquad \text{(no differences among block means)}$$

is given by (4), and its $P$ value is given by (5). As expected, this hypothesis can be rejected ($P = .044\,6$).

```
                    RANDCMIZED COMPLETE BLCCKS

                 GENERAL LINEAR MCDELS PRCCEDURE

                    CLASS LEVEL INFCRMATION

              CLASS       LEVELS      VALUES

              BLCCK          8          1 2 3 4 5 6 7 8

              TRTMENT        3          1 2 3

             NUMBER CF CBSERVATICNS IN CATA SET = 24



                    RANDOMIZED COMPLETE BLOCKS

                 GENERAL LINEAR MODELS PROCEDURE

DEPENDENT VARIABLE: KILCCAL

SOURCE                DF     SUM OF SQUARES        MEAN SQUARE       F VALUE

MODEL                  9         4.96666667         0.55185185         19.98

ERROR                 14         0.38666667         0.02761905        PR > F

CORRECTED TOTAL       23         5.35333333                           0.0001


R-SQUARE            C.V.            STD DEV        KILCCAL MEAN

0.927771         14.6638         0.16618579          1.13333333


SOURCE                DF        TYPE I SS    F VALUE    PR > F

BLOCK                  7       0.55333333       2.86    0.0446
TRTMENT                2       4.41333333      79.90    0.0001


SOURCE                DF       TYPE IV SS    F VALUE    PR > F

BLOCK                  7       0.55333333       2.86 (4)  0.0446 (5)
TRTMENT                2       4.41333333      79.90 (1)  0.0001 (2)



                    RANDCMIZED COMPLETE BLCCKS

                 GENERAL LINEAR MODELS PRCCEDURE

           DUNCAN'S MULTIPLE RANGE TEST FCR VARIABLE KILOCAL


       MEANS WITH THE SAME LETTER ARE NCT SIGNIFICANTLY DIFFERENT.

             ALPHA LEVEL=.05        CF=14        MS=0.027619

             GRCUPING                 MEAN       N     TRTMENT

                    A             1.650000       8     1

        (3)         B             1.150000       8     2

                    C             0.600000       8     3
```

## FACTORIAL EXPERIMENTS

**10.5** □ In many experiments, two or more variables are being actively investigated. Neither variable is considered extraneous; each is of equal concern. When this occurs, the experiment is called a *factorial experiment,* to emphasize the fact that interest is centered on the effect of two or more factors on a measured response. We present here the *two-way classification, completely random design with fixed effects.* Thus we deal with a model in which two factors, $A$ and $B$, are studied with the levels of each factor being purposely, rather than randomly, selected by the experimenter. No matching of like experimental units is done.

---

**EXAMPLE 10.5.1** □ The *Mirogrex terrae-sanctae* is a commercial sardine-like fish found in the Sea of Galilee. A study is conducted to determine the effect of light and temperature on the gonadosomatic index (GSI), which is a measure of the growth of the ovary. Two photoperiods—14 hours of light, 10 hours of dark and 9 hours of light, 15 hours of dark—and two temperature levels—16 and 27°C—are used. In this way, the experimenter can simulate both summer and winter conditions in the region. This is a factorial experiment with two factors, light and temperature, each being investigated at two levels.

---

The data collected in a two-way classification design are conveniently recorded in the following format:

DATA LAYOUT OF TWO-WAY CLASSIFICATION

| | | Factor $A$ Level | | | | |
|---|---|---|---|---|---|---|
| | | 1 | 2 | 3 | $\cdots$ | $a$ |
| Factor $B$ | 1 | $X_{111}$ | $X_{211}$ | $X_{311}$ | $\cdots$ | $X_{a11}$ |
| | | $X_{112}$ | $X_{212}$ | $X_{312}$ | $\cdots$ | $X_{a12}$ |
| | | $\cdots$ | $\cdots$ | $\cdots$ | $\cdots$ | $\cdots$ |
| | | $X_{11n}$ | $X_{21n}$ | $X_{31n}$ | $\cdots$ | $X_{a1n}$ |
| | 2 | $X_{121}$ | $X_{221}$ | $X_{321}$ | $\cdots$ | $X_{a21}$ |
| | | $X_{122}$ | $X_{222}$ | $X_{322}$ | $\cdots$ | $X_{a22}$ |
| | | $\cdots$ | $\cdots$ | $\cdots$ | $\cdots$ | $\cdots$ |
| | | $X_{12n}$ | $X_{22n}$ | $X_{32n}$ | $\cdots$ | $X_{a2n}$ |
| | $\vdots$ | $\cdots$ | $\cdots$ | $\cdots$ | $\cdots$ | $\cdots$ |
| | | $X_{1b1}$ | $X_{2b1}$ | $X_{3b1}$ | $\cdots$ | $X_{ab1}$ |
| | $b$ | $X_{1b2}$ | $X_{2b2}$ | $X_{3b2}$ | $\cdots$ | $X_{ab2}$ |
| | | $\cdots$ | $\cdots$ | $\cdots$ | $\cdots$ | $\cdots$ |
| | | $X_{1bn}$ | $X_{2bn}$ | $X_{3bn}$ | $\cdots$ | $X_{abn}$ |

Note that $a$ denotes the number of levels of factor $A$ used in the experiment, $b$ denotes the number of levels of factor $b$, and $a \cdot b$ is the total number of treatment combinations, where a treatment combination is a level of factor $A$ applied in conjunction with a level of $B$. We assume that there are $n$ observations for each treatment combination. Thus the total number of responses is $N = a \cdot b \cdot n$. $X_{ijk}$, $i = 1, 2, \ldots, a$, $j = 1, 2, \ldots, b$, $k = 1, 2, \ldots, n$, is a random variable denoting the response of the $k$th experimental unit to the $i$th level of factor $A$ and the $j$th level of factor $B$. These sample statistics are needed in analyzing the data. Recall that the dot indicates the subscript over which summation is being conducted.

$$T_{ij\cdot} = \sum_{k=1}^{n} X_{ijk} = \text{total of all responses to } i\text{th level of factor } A \text{ and } j\text{th level of factor } B$$

$$= \text{total of all responses to the } (i-j)\text{th treatment combination}$$

$$\bar{X}_{ij\cdot} = \frac{T_{ij\cdot}}{n} = \text{sample mean for } (i-j)\text{th treatment combination}$$

$$T_{i\cdot\cdot} = \sum_{j=1}^{b} T_{ij\cdot} = \text{total of all responses to } i\text{th level, } i = 1, 2, \ldots, a, \text{ of factor } A$$

$$\bar{X}_{i\cdot\cdot} = \frac{T_{i\cdot\cdot}}{bn} = \text{sample mean for } i\text{th level of factor } A$$

$$T_{\cdot j\cdot} = \sum_{i=1}^{a} T_{ij\cdot} = \text{total of all responses to } j\text{th level, } j = 1, 2, \ldots, b, \text{ of factor } B$$

$$\bar{X}_{\cdot j\cdot} = \frac{T_{\cdot j\cdot}}{an} = \text{sample mean for } j\text{th level of factor } B$$

$$T_{\cdots} = \sum_{i=1}^{a} T_{i\cdot\cdot} = \sum_{j=1}^{b} T_{\cdot j\cdot} = \sum_{i=1}^{a}\sum_{j=1}^{b} T_{ij\cdot} = \text{total of all responses}$$

$$\bar{X}_{\cdots} = \frac{T_{\cdots}}{abn} = \text{sample mean for all responses}$$

$$\sum_{i=1}^{a}\sum_{j=1}^{b}\sum_{k=1}^{n} X_{ijk}^2 = \text{sum of square of each response}$$

These statistics are evaluated in Example 10.5.2.

---

**EXAMPLE 10.5.2** □ The experiment of Example 10.5.1 was conducted by collecting 20 females in June. Then this group was randomly divided into four subgroups, each of size 5. Each subgroup received one of the four possible treatment combinations. At the end of 3 months, the GSI for each fish was determined. These data resulted:

| Factor B (temperature) | | Factor A (photoperiod) 9 HOURS | Factor A (photoperiod) 14 HOURS | TOTAL (FACTOR $B$) |
|---|---|---|---|---|
| 27°C | | (unnatural)<br>.90<br>1.06<br>.98<br>1.29<br>1.12<br>$T_{11\cdot} = 5.35$<br>$\bar{X}_{11\cdot} = 1.07$ | (simulated summer)<br>.83<br>.67<br>.57<br>.47<br>.66<br>$T_{21\cdot} = 3.2$<br>$\bar{X}_{21\cdot} = .64$ | $T_{\cdot 1\cdot} = T_{11\cdot} + T_{21\cdot}$<br>$= 8.55$<br>$\bar{X}_{\cdot 1\cdot} = .855$ |
| 16°C | | (simulated winter)<br>1.30<br>2.88<br>2.42<br>2.66<br>2.94<br>$T_{12\cdot} = 12.20$<br>$\bar{X}_{12\cdot} = 2.44$ | (unnatural)<br>1.01<br>1.52<br>1.02<br>1.32<br>1.63<br>$T_{22\cdot} = 6.5$<br>$\bar{X}_{22\cdot} = 1.3$ | $T_{\cdot 2\cdot} = T_{12\cdot} + T_{22\cdot}$<br>$= 18.7$<br>$\bar{X}_{\cdot 2\cdot} = 1.87$ |
| Total (Factor $A$) | | $T_{1\cdot\cdot} = T_{11\cdot} + T_{12\cdot}$<br>$= 17.55$<br>$\bar{X}_{1\cdot\cdot} = 1.755$ | $T_{2\cdot\cdot} = T_{21\cdot} + T_{22\cdot}$<br>$= 9.7$<br>$\bar{X}_{2\cdot\cdot} = .97$ | $T_{\cdots} = 27.25$<br>(grand total)<br>$\bar{X}_{\cdots} = 1.36$ |

For these data, $a = 2$, $b = 2$, $n = 5$, and $N = a \cdot b \cdot n = 20$. Also

$$\sum_{i=1}^{2} \sum_{j=1}^{2} \sum_{k=1}^{5} X_{ijk}^2 = 48.26$$

The following notation is needed to write the model for the design:

$\mu$ = overall mean effect

$\mu_{i\cdot\cdot}$ = mean for $i$th level of factor $A$, $i = 1, 2, \ldots, a$

$\mu_{\cdot j\cdot}$ = mean for $j$th level of factor $B$, $j = 1, 2, \ldots, b$

$\mu_{ij\cdot}$ = mean for $(i - j)$th treatment combination

$\alpha_i = \mu_{i\cdot\cdot} - \mu$ = effect due to fact that experimental unit was in $i$th level of factor $A$

$\beta_j = \mu_{\cdot j\cdot} - \mu$ = effect due to fact that experimental unit was in $j$th level of factor $B$

$$(\alpha\beta)_{ij} = \mu_{ij\cdot} - \mu_{i\cdot\cdot} - \mu_{\cdot j\cdot} + \mu = \text{effect of interaction between } i\text{th level of factor } A \text{ and } j\text{th level of factor } B$$

$$E_{ijk} = X_{ijk} - \mu_{ij\cdot} = \text{residual, or random, error}$$

Using this notation, we can express the model as follows:

**Model**

$$X_{ijk} \equiv \mu + \alpha_i + \beta_j + (\alpha\beta)_{ij} + E_{ijk} \qquad \begin{aligned} i &= 1, 2, \ldots, a \\ j &= 1, 2, \ldots, b \\ k &= 1, 2, \ldots, n \end{aligned}$$

This model expresses symbolically the idea that each observation can be partitioned into five components: an overall mean effect ($\mu$), an effect due to factor $A$ ($\alpha_i$), an effect due to factor $B$ ($\beta_j$), an effect due to interaction $(\alpha\beta)_{ij}$, and a random deviation due to unexplained sources ($E_{ijk}$). We make the following assumptions:

**Model Assumptions**

1. The observations for each treatment combination constitute independent random samples, each of size $n$, from $a \cdot b$ populations with means $\mu_{ij\cdot}$, $i = 1, 2, \ldots, a$, $j = 1, 2, \ldots, b$.
2. Each of the $a \cdot b$ populations is normal.
3. Each of the $a \cdot b$ populations has the same variance, $\sigma^2$.

The sum-of-squares identity obtained by replacing each of the theoretical means $\mu$, $\mu_{i\cdot\cdot}$, $\mu_{\cdot j\cdot}$, $\mu_{ij\cdot}$ by their unbiased estimators $\bar{X}_{\cdot\cdot\cdot}$, $\bar{X}_{i\cdot\cdot}$, $\bar{X}_{\cdot j\cdot}$, $\bar{X}_{ij\cdot}$, respectively, squaring, and summing over $i$, $j$, and $k$ is as follows:

**Sum-of-Squares Identity**

$$SS_{\text{Total}} = SS_A + SS_B + SS_{AB} + SS_E$$

In this identity,

$$SS_{\text{Total}} = \sum_{i=1}^{a}\sum_{j=1}^{b}\sum_{k=1}^{n} (X_{ijk} - \bar{X}_{\cdot\cdot\cdot})^2 = \text{measure of total variability in data}$$

$$SS_A = \sum_{i=1}^{a}\sum_{j=1}^{b}\sum_{k=1}^{n} (\bar{X}_{i\cdot\cdot} - \bar{X}_{\cdot\cdot\cdot})^2 = \text{measure of variability in data attributable to use of different levels of factor } A$$

$$SS_B = \sum_{i=1}^{a}\sum_{j=1}^{b}\sum_{k=1}^{n} (\bar{X}_{\cdot j\cdot} - \bar{X}_{\cdots})^2 = \text{measure of variability in data attributable to use of different levels of factor } B$$

$$SS_{AB} = \sum_{i=1}^{a}\sum_{j=1}^{b}\sum_{k=1}^{n} (\bar{X}_{ij\cdot} - \bar{X}_{i\cdot\cdot} - \bar{X}_{\cdot j\cdot} + \bar{X}_{\cdots})^2 = \text{measure of variability in data due to interaction between levels of factors } A \text{ and } B$$

$$SS_E = \sum_{i=1}^{a}\sum_{j=1}^{b}\sum_{k=1}^{n} (X_{ijk} - \bar{X}_{ij\cdot})^2 = \text{measure of variability in data due to random, or unexplained, sources}$$

The first null hypothesis to be tested is the null hypothesis of no interaction. Mathematically, this hypothesis is

$$H_0: (\alpha\beta)_{ij} = 0 \qquad i = 1, 2, \ldots, a;\ j = 1, 2, \ldots, b$$

If this hypothesis is not rejected, then the analysis is continued by testing the null hypothesis of no difference among levels of factor $A$,

$$H_0': \mu_{1\cdot\cdot} = \mu_{2\cdot\cdot} = \cdots = \mu_{a\cdot\cdot}$$

and the null hypothesis of no difference among levels of factor $B$,

$$H_0'': \mu_{\cdot 1\cdot} = \mu_{\cdot 2\cdot} = \cdots = \mu_{\cdot b\cdot}$$

However, if the null hypothesis of no interaction is rejected, then we do not test $H_0'$ and $H_0''$. In this case, since the levels of factor $A$ do not behave consistently across the levels of factor $B$, and vice versa, we look for the best treatment combination. That is, we run a one-way classification, analysis of variance to test the null hypothesis of equal treatment combination means. This hypothesis is expressed mathematically as

$$H_0''': \mu_{11\cdot} = \mu_{12\cdot} = \cdots = \mu_{ab\cdot}$$

The computational formulas used to compute $SS_A$, $SS_B$, and $SS_{\text{Total}}$ are similar to those of previous models:

$$SS_A = \sum_{i=1}^{a} \frac{T_{i\cdot\cdot}^2}{bn} - \frac{T_{\cdots}^2}{abn}$$

$$SS_B = \sum_{j=1}^{b} \frac{T_{\cdot j\cdot}^2}{an} - \frac{T_{\cdots}^2}{abn}$$

$$SS_{\text{Total}} = \sum_{i=1}^{a}\sum_{j=1}^{b}\sum_{k=1}^{n} X_{ijk}^2 - \frac{T_{\cdots}^2}{abn}$$

The interaction sum of squares is found by first computing what is called the treatment sum of squares. This is the usual treatment sum of squares that would be obtained if the $a \cdot b$ treatment combinations were analyzed as a one-way classification design. That is,

$$SS_{Tr} = \sum_{i=1}^{a} \sum_{j=1}^{b} \frac{T_{ij\cdot}^2}{n} - \frac{T_{\dots}^2}{abn}$$

It can be shown that $SS_{Tr} = SS_A + SS_B + SS_{AB}$. This allows us to compute the interactions sum of squares by subtraction:

$$SS_{AB} = SS_{Tr} - SS_A - SS_B$$

The error sum of squares can also be obtained by subtraction:

$$SS_E = SS_{Total} - SS_{Tr}$$

The analysis-of-variance table for this design is Table 10.7.

The first $F$ ratio to consider in any experiment is

$$F_{(a-1)(b-1),\, ab(n-1)} = \frac{MS_{AB}}{MS_E}$$

This ratio is used to test the null hypothesis of no interaction. If this hypothesis is not rejected, then the $F$ statistics

$$F_{a-1,\, ab(n-1)} = \frac{MS_A}{MS_E}$$

and

$$F_{b-1,\, ab(n-1)} = \frac{MS_B}{MS_E}$$

are used to test the null hypotheses of no difference among the means of levels of factors $A$ and $B$, respectively. If the null hypothesis of no interaction is rejected, then the $F$ statistic

$$F_{ab-1,\, ab(n-1)} = \frac{MS_{Tr}}{MS_E}$$

is used to test the null hypothesis of no difference among treatment combination means. In each case, rejection occurs for values of the $F$ ratio that are too large to have occurred by chance.

We illustrate these ideas by completing the analysis of the data of Example 10.5.2.

**TABLE 10.7** ANALYSIS OF VARIANCE: TWO-WAY CLASSIFICATION, COMPLETELY RANDOM DESIGN WITH FIXED EFFECTS

| SOURCE OF VARIATION | DEGREES OF FREEDOM | SUM OF SQUARES | MEAN SQUARE | EXPECTED MEAN SQUARE | $F$ RATIO |
|---|---|---|---|---|---|
| Treatment | $ab-1$ | $\sum_{i=1}^{a}\sum_{j=1}^{b}\frac{T_{ij\cdot}^2}{n}-\frac{T_{\dots}^2}{abn}$ | $\frac{SS_{\text{Tr}}}{ab-1}$ | $\sigma^2+n\sum_{i=1}^{a}\sum_{j=1}^{b}\frac{(\mu_{ij\cdot}-\mu_{\dots})^2}{ab-1}$ | $\frac{MS_{\text{Tr}}}{MS_E}$ |
| $A$ | $a-1$ | $\sum_{i=1}^{a}\frac{T_{i\cdot\cdot}^2}{bn}-\frac{T_{\dots}^2}{abn}$ | $\frac{SS_A}{a-1}$ | $\sigma^2+nb\sum_{i=1}^{a}\frac{(\mu_{i\cdot\cdot}-\mu_{\dots})^2}{a-1}$ | $\frac{MS_A}{MS_E}$ |
| $B$ | $b-1$ | $\sum_{j=1}^{b}\frac{T_{\cdot j\cdot}^2}{an}-\frac{T_{\dots}^2}{abn}$ | $\frac{SS_B}{b-1}$ | $\sigma^2+na\sum_{j=1}^{b}\frac{(\mu_{\cdot j\cdot}-\mu_{\dots})^2}{b-1}$ | $\frac{MS_B}{MS_E}$ |
| $AB$ | $(a-1)(b-1)$ | $SS_{\text{Tr}}-SS_A-SS_B$ | $\frac{SS_{AB}}{(a-1)(b-1)}$ | $\sigma^2+n\sum_{i=1}^{a}\sum_{j=1}^{b}\frac{(\alpha\beta)_{ij}^2}{(a-1)(b-1)}$ | $\frac{MS_{AB}}{MS_E}$ |
| Error | $ab(n-1)$ | $SS_{\text{Total}}-SS_{\text{Tr}}$ | $\frac{SS_E}{ab(n-1)}$ | $\sigma^2$ | |
| **Total** | $abn-1$ | $\sum_{i=1}^{a}\sum_{j=1}^{b}\sum_{k=1}^{n}X_{ijk}^2-\frac{T_{\dots}^2}{abn}$ | | | |

**EXAMPLE 10.5.3** □ The following totals were obtained in Example 10.5.2:

$$T_{11\cdot} = 5.35 \qquad T_{22\cdot} = 6.5 \qquad T_{\cdot 1\cdot} = 8.55$$
$$T_{21\cdot} = 3.2 \qquad T_{1\cdot\cdot} = 17.55 \qquad T_{\cdot 2\cdot} = 18.7$$
$$T_{12\cdot} = 12.20 \qquad T_{2\cdot\cdot} = 9.7 \qquad T_{\cdots} = 27.25$$

$$\sum_{i=1}^{2}\sum_{j=1}^{2}\sum_{k=1}^{5} X_{ijk}^2 = 48.26$$

These totals are used to obtain the needed sums of squares:

$$SS_{\text{Tr}} = \frac{(5.35)^2}{5} + \frac{(3.2)^2}{5} + \frac{(12.20)^2}{5} + \frac{(6.5)^2}{5} - \frac{(27.25)^2}{20} = 8.86$$

$$SS_A = \frac{(17.55)^2}{10} + \frac{(9.7)^2}{10} - \frac{(27.25)^2}{20} = 3.08$$

$$SS_B = \frac{(8.55)^2}{10} + \frac{(18.7)^2}{10} - \frac{(27.25)^2}{20} = 5.15$$

$$SS_{AB} = SS_{\text{Tr}} - SS_A - SS_B = 8.86 - 3.08 - 5.15 = .63$$

$$SS_{\text{Total}} = 48.26 - \frac{(27.25)^2}{20} = 11.13$$

$$SS_E = SS_{\text{Total}} - SS_{\text{Tr}} = 11.13 - 8.86 = 2.27$$

The ANOVA is given here:

ANOVA

| SOURCE | *DF* | *SS* | *MS* | *F* |
|---|---|---|---|---|
| Treatment | 3 | 8.86 | 2.95 | 21.07 + |
| *A* | 1 | 3.08 | 3.08 | 22.0 |
| *B* | 1 | 5.15 | 5.15 | 36.79 |
| *AB* | 1 | .63 | .63 | 4.5 * |
| Error | 16 | 2.27 | .14 | |
| **Total** | 19 | 11.13 | | |

We look first at the $F$ ratio used to test for interaction (* in the table). The $P$ value for this statistic is approximately .05 (critical point for $F_{1,16}$ is 4.49). Since this probability is small, we reject the null hypothesis of no interaction and conclude that there is interaction between the light cycle used and the temperature. In this case, we do not look at the levels of factor $A$ and $B$, but instead concentrate on trying to compare the four treatment combinations. That is, we test

$$H_0''': \mu_{11\cdot} = \mu_{12\cdot} = \mu_{21\cdot} = \mu_{22\cdot}$$

This hypothesis is tested by considering the $F$ ratio for treatments (+ in the previous table). The $P$ value in this case is less than .01. Therefore, we reject $H_0'''$ and conclude that there are differences among the treatment combinations. These differences can be pinpointed by using Duncan's multiple range test with

$$SSR_p = r_p\sqrt{\frac{MS_E}{n}}$$

For these data,

$$\sqrt{\frac{MS_E}{n}} = \sqrt{\frac{.14}{5}} = .167\,3$$

The shortest significant ranges for various comparisons are found with the aid of Table VIII in Appendix B ($\alpha = .05$, $DF = 16$):

| $p$ | 2 | 3 | 4 |
|---|---|---|---|
| $r_p$ | 2.998 | 3.144 | 3.235 |
| $SSR_p$ | .501 6 | .526 0 | .541 2 |

The treatment sample means, linearly ordered, are

| Summer | Unnatural | Unnatural | Winter |
|---|---|---|---|
| $\bar{x}_{21\cdot}$ | $\bar{x}_{11\cdot}$ | $\bar{x}_{22\cdot}$ | $\bar{x}_{12\cdot}$ |
| .64 | 1.07 | 1.3 | 2.44 |

In summary, the treatment combination simulating winter conditions produced the highest mean GSI.

One further comment needs to be made. If the null hypothesis of no interaction is not rejected, then interest centers on comparing the levels of factors $A$ and $B$. If differences are detected, then Duncan's multiple range test is again applicable. To pinpoint differences among the levels of factor $A$,

$$SSR_p = r_p\sqrt{\frac{MS_E}{bn}}$$

To determine what differences exist among levels of factor $B$,

$$SSR_p = r_p\sqrt{\frac{MS_E}{an}}$$

## EXERCISES 10.5

1. A study is conducted to determine the effect of water level and type of plant on the overall stem length of pea plants. Three water levels and two plant types are used. Eighteen leafless plants are available for study. These plants are randomly divided into three subgroups, and then water levels are randomly assigned to the groups. A similar procedure is followed with 18 conventional plants. These data resulted (stem length is given in centimeters):

| | | Factor $A$ (Water Level) | | | |
|---|---|---|---|---|---|
| | | LOW | MEDIUM | HIGH | TOTAL (FACTOR $B$) |
| Factor $B$ (plant type) | Leafless | 69.0<br>71.3<br>73.2<br>75.1<br>74.4<br>75.0 (438) | 96.1<br>102.3<br>107.5<br>103.6<br>100.7<br>101.8 (612) | 121.0<br>122.9<br>123.1<br>125.7<br>125.2<br>120.1 (738) | 1788 |
| | Conventional | 71.1<br>69.2<br>70.4<br>73.2<br>71.2<br>70.9 (426) | 81.0<br>85.8<br>86.0<br>87.5<br>88.1<br>87.6 (516) | 101.1<br>103.2<br>106.1<br>109.7<br>109.0<br>106.9 (636) | 1578 |
| | **Total (Factor $A$)** | 864 | 1128 | 1374 | 3366 |

a. Verify the totals given.

b. For these data,

$$\sum_{i=1}^{3}\sum_{j=1}^{2}\sum_{k=1}^{6} X_{ijk}^2 = 237{,}431.42$$

Use this to find $SS_{\text{Total}}$.

c. Find $SS_{\text{Tr}}$. Use this and $SS_{\text{Total}}$ to find $SS_E$.

d. Find $SS_A$ and $SS_B$. Use these and $SS_{\text{Tr}}$ to find $SS_{AB}$.

e. Find the ANOVA table, and use it to test the appropriate hypotheses.

f. If appropriate, continue the analysis, using Duncan's multiple range test.

2. A study is run of the effect of photoperiod and genotype on the latent period of infection of barley mildew isolate AB3. Fifty leaves of each of four genotypes are obtained and

randomly split into five subgroups, each of size 10. Each group is infected and then is exposed to a different photoperiod. The response noted is the number of days until the appearance of visible symptoms. The following treatment and level ***totals*** are found:

Factor $A$ (photoperiod: hours darkness per 24-hr cycle)

| Factor B (genotype) | | 0 | 2 | 4 | 8 | 16 | TOTAL (FACTOR $B$) |
|---|---|---|---|---|---|---|---|
| | Armelle | 630 | 610 | 560 | 570 | 590 | 2,960 |
| | Golden Promise | 640 | 630 | 600 | 620 | 620 | 3,110 |
| | Emir | 640 | 630 | 650 | 620 | 580 | 3,120 |
| | Vacla | 660 | 660 | 620 | 610 | 630 | 3,180 |
| | **Total (Factor $A$)** | 2,570 | 2,530 | 2,430 | 2,420 | 2,420 | 12,370 |

**a.** For these data,

$$\sum_{i=1}^{5}\sum_{j=1}^{4}\sum_{k=1}^{10} X_{ijk}^2 = 773{,}377.2$$

Use this to find $SS_{\text{Total}}$.

**b.** Find $SS_{\text{Tr}}$. Use this and $SS_{\text{Total}}$ to find $SS_E$.

**c.** Find $SS_A$ and $SS_B$. Use these and $SS_{\text{Tr}}$ to find $SS_{AB}$.

**d.** Find the ANOVA table, and test the appropriate hypotheses.

**e.** Where appropriate, continue the analysis using Duncan's multiple range test.

**3.** A study is run of the capsular solubility in biological fluids of two of the most commonly encapsulated enzyme preparations. The purpose is to determine the effect of capsule type and biological fluid on the time until dissolution of the capsule. Two biological fluids, gastric and duodenal juices, and two capsule types, $C$ and $V$, are used. Thus two factors are involved, each being studied at two levels. To conduct the study, 10 empty capsules of each type are obtained and randomly divided into two subgroups, each of size 5. One group is dissolved in gastric juices; the other, in duodenal juices. The response noted is the time at which the first air bubbles are released through perforations in the capsules. These data resulted (time is in minutes):

| | | Factor $A$ (Fluid Type) | | |
|---|---|---|---|---|
| | | GASTRIC | DUODENAL | TOTAL (FACTOR $B$) |
| Factor $B$ (capsule type) | $C$ | 39.5<br>45.7<br>49.8<br>50.2<br>63.8 (249) | 31.2<br>33.5<br>36.7<br>42.0<br>38.1 (181.5) | 430.5 |
| | $V$ | 47.4<br>43.5<br>39.8<br>36.1<br>41.2 (208) | 44.0<br>41.2<br>47.3<br>45.3<br>42.7 (220.5) | 428.5 |
| | **Total (Factor *A*)** | 457 | 402 | 859 |

**a.** Verify the totals given.

**b.** For these data.

$$\sum_{i=1}^{2}\sum_{j=1}^{2}\sum_{k=1}^{5} X_{ijk}^2 = 37{,}847.26$$

Use this value to find $SS_{\text{Total}}$.

**c.** Find $SS_{\text{Tr}}$. Use this and $SS_{\text{Total}}$ to find $SS_E$.

**d.** Find $SS_A$ and $SS_B$. Use these and $SS_{\text{Tr}}$ to find $SS_{AB}$.

**e.** Sketch a graph of the sample means for the levels of factor $A$ for each level of factor $B$. Does this lead you to suspect the presence of interaction? Explain.

**f.** Complete the analysis of the data by finding the ANOVA table and testing the appropriate hypotheses.

---

**Computing Supplement**

We illustrate the use of SAS in running a two-way classification analysis with the data of Examples 10.5.2 and 10.5.3. First we run a two-way classification with Duncan's tests requested. If there is *no* interaction, then the output of this program is applicable. However, if interaction is present based on this analysis, then a one-way classification based on cells is necessary. This program is included also.

| Statement | Function |
|---|---|
| DATA MIROGREX; | names data set |
| INPUT PHOTOPRD TEMP CELL Y1-Y5; | each card will contain a value for photoperiod, temperature, treatment combination or cell number, and all five values of dependent variable for that cell |
| ARRAY OUT Y1-Y5;<br>DO OVER OUT;<br>Y=OUT;<br>OUTPUT;<br>END; | these steps allow data to be read without having to punch values of PHOTOPRD, TEMP, and CELL for *each* value of dependent variable and thus saves time |
| CARDS; | signals that data follow |
| 9 27 1 .9 1.06 .98 1.29 1.12<br>9 16 2 1.3 2.88 2.42 2.66 2.94<br>14 27 3 .83 .67 .57 .47 .66<br>14 16 4 1.01 1.52 1.02 1.32 1.63 | data |
| ; | signals end of data |
| PROC GLM; | calls for general linear models procedure |
| CLASSES PHOTOPRD TEMP; | indicates that data considered grouped according to values of PHOTOPRD and TEMP |
| MODEL Y=PHOTOPRD TEMP PHOTOPRD*TEMP; | identifies model as two-way classification with main effects PHOTOPRD and TEMP; PHOTOPRD*TEMP indicates that interaction term for these two variables is to be included; $Y$ is identified as dependent variable |
| TITLE TWO WAY CLASSIFICATION; | titles output |
| MEANS PHOTOPRD/DUNCAN; | asks for Duncan's test on levels of PHOTOPRD; |
| MEANS TEMP/DUNCAN; | asks for Duncan's test on levels of TEMP |
| PROC GLM; | calls for general linear models procedure |
| CLASSES CELL; | indicates data considered grouped according to value of variable CELL |

| | |
|---|---|
| MODEL Y=CELL; | identifies model as one-way classification with dependent variable $Y$ and independent variable CELL |
| MEANS CELL/DUNCAN; | asks for Duncan's test for equality of cell means |
| TITLE1 ONE WAY CLASSIFICATION; | titles output |
| TITLE2 IF INTERACTION; | |
| TITLE3 is Detected; | |

The output of this program follows. Note that in the two-way ANOVA, the source referred to as "treatment" is called MODEL (1) by SAS. The breakdown of the model, or treatment, sum of squares into factors $A$ (photoperiod), $B$ (temperature), and $AB$ (interaction) is given by (2) on the printout. To interpret the data, we look first at the $F$ ratio used to test for interaction (3) and its $P$ value (4). Since this $P$ value is small (.051 3), we decide to reject the null hypothesis of no interaction. We do ***not*** bother to look at (5) and (6), the $F$ ratios used to test the null hypotheses of no difference between mean photoperiod levels and no difference between mean temperature levels, respectively. We also do ***not*** bother to interpret the Duncan's tests on these variables given by (7) and (8). Instead, we move on to the one-way classification analysis by cells. The $F$ ratio for testing the null hypothesis of no difference among all means and its $P$ value are given by (9) and (10), respectively. Since the $P$ value is very small (.000 1), we conclude that there are differences among the cell means. To pinpoint these differences, we consider the results of the Duncan's test given by (11). They indicate that the mean for cell 2 (simulated winter) is different from all others at the $\alpha = .05$ level; cells 4 and 1 are grouped, and cells 3 and 1 are grouped. Note that these results agree with those of Example 10.5.3.

```
                TWO WAY CLASSIFICATION

             GENERAL LINEAR MODELS PROCEDURE

                CLASS LEVEL INFORMATION

                CLASS      LEVELS    VALUES

                PHOTOPRD     2       9 14

                TEMP         2       16 27

        NUMBER OF OBSERVATIONS IN DATA SET = 20
```

```
                              TWO WAY CLASSIFICATION

                         GENERAL LINEAR MODELS PROCEDURE

DEPENDENT VARIABLE: Y

SOURCE                  DF        SUM OF SQUARES           MEAN SQUARE          F VALUE

MODEL (1)                3            8.86237500            2.95412500            20.81

ERROR                   16            2.27140000            0.14196250           PR > F

CORRECTED TOTAL         19           11.13377500                                 0.0001

R-SQUARE              C.V.               STD DEV                Y MEAN

0.795990           27.6535            0.37677911            1.36250000

SOURCE                  DF           TYPE I SS    F VALUE     PR > F

PHOTOPRD                 1          3.08112500      21.70     0.0003
TEMP                     1          5.15112500      36.29     0.0001
PHOTOPRD*TEMP            1          0.63012500       4.44     0.0513

SOURCE                  DF          TYPE IV SS    F VALUE     PR > F
                                                      (5)
PHOTOPRD (2)             1          3.08112500      21.70     0.0003
TEMP                     1          5.15112500      36.29 (6) 0.0001
PHOTOPRD*TEMP            1          0.63012500       4.44     0.0513 (4)
                                                              (3)


                              TWO WAY CLASSIFICATION

                         GENERAL LINEAR MODELS PROCEDURE

                    DUNCAN'S MULTIPLE RANGE TEST FOR VARIABLE Y

            MEANS WITH THE SAME LETTER ARE NOT SIGNIFICANTLY DIFFERENT.

                    ALPHA LEVEL=.05        DF=16        MS=0.141963

                    GROUPING                     MEAN       N     PHOTOPRD

              (7)          A                 1.755000      10     9

                           B                 0.970000      10     14


                              TWO WAY CLASSIFICATION

                         GENERAL LINEAR MODELS PROCEDURE

                    DUNCAN'S MULTIPLE RANGE TEST FOR VARIABLE Y

            MEANS WITH THE SAME LETTER ARE NOT SIGNIFICANTLY DIFFERENT.

                    ALPHA LEVEL=.05        DF=16        MS=0.141963

                      GROUPING                     MEAN       N     TEMP

                 (8)         A                 1.870000      10     16

                             B                 0.855000      10     27
```

```
                    ONE WAY CLASSIFICATION
                       IF INTERACTION
                        IS DETECTED

               GENERAL LINEAR MODELS PROCEDURE

                   CLASS LEVEL INFORMATION

                 CLASS      LEVELS    VALUES

                 CELL          4      1 2 3 4

          NUMBER OF OBSERVATIONS IN DATA SET = 20


                    ONE WAY CLASSIFICATION
                       IF INTERACTION
                        IS DETECTED

               GENERAL LINEAR MODELS PROCEDURE

DEPENDENT VARIABLE: Y
SOURCE                DF     SUM OF SQUARES       MEAN SQUARE      F VALUE

MODEL                  3         8.86237500        2.95412500        20.81  (9)

ERROR                 16         2.27140000        0.14196250      PR > F

CORRECTED TOTAL       19        11.13377500                        0.0001  (10)

R-SQUARE             C.V.           STD DEV            Y MEAN

0.795990          27.6535        0.37677911        1.36250000

SOURCE                DF        TYPE I SS    F VALUE    PR > F

CELL                   3       8.86237500      20.81    0.0001

SOURCE                DF       TYPE IV SS    F VALUE    PR > F

CELL                   3       8.86237500      20.81    0.0001


                    ONE WAY CLASSIFICATION
                       IF INTERACTION
                        IS DETECTED

               GENERAL LINEAR MODELS PROCEDURE

           DUNCAN'S MULTIPLE RANGE TEST FOR VARIABLE Y

      MEANS WITH THE SAME LETTER ARE NOT SIGNIFICANTLY DIFFERENT.

           ALPHA LEVEL=.05        DF=16        MS=0.141963

             GROUPING                   MEAN       N    CELL

                    A               2.440000       5     2

                    B               1.300000       5     4
                    B
      (11)   C      B               1.070000       5     1
             C
             C                      0.640000       5     3
```

# REGRESSION AND CORRELATION

# 11.

In this chapter we discuss two types of problems. The first, called regression, entails developing an equation by which the value of a variable $Y$ can be predicted from knowledge of the values assumed by one or more variables $X_1, X_2, \ldots, X_n$. In this context, the variable $Y$ is assumed to be random. Since its value is influenced by the values of variables $X_1, X_2, \ldots, X_n$, $Y$ is called a *dependent* variable. Variables $X_1, X_2, \ldots, X_n$ are called *independent* variables; they can be random or under the direct control of the experimenter. This point is illustrated in Examples 11.1.1 and 11.1.2. The second problem, called correlation, involves measuring the strength of the linear relationship between two random variables. Although these problems are conceptually different, they are closely related.

## INTRODUCTION TO SIMPLE LINEAR REGRESSION

**11.1** □ We begin by considering two typical regression problems.

---

**EXAMPLE 11.1.1** □ A physician wants to predict the concentration of a particular drug in the bloodstream 5 minutes after its administration ($Y$) based on knowledge of the size of the initial dose ($X$). In this case, the random variable $Y$ is the dependent variable; $X$ is the independent variable. In a controlled laboratory experiment, the values assumed by $X$ are selected by the experimenter. For example, we might choose to experiment with doses of .05, .10, .20, and .30 ml. In this case, $X$ is not a random variable. Its value at any given time is being determined not by chance, but by design.

---

Example 11.1.2 differs from Example 11.1.1 in that both the dependent and independent variables are random variables.

**EXAMPLE 11.1.2** □ An ecologist wishes to predict the change in water temperature that occurs at a point 1 mile below an industrial plant after the introduction of hot wastewater into the stream ($Y$). The prediction is to be based on the amount of water released ($X$). In this case, the dependent random variable is $Y$, and the independent variable is $X$. Since the amount of hot water released varies depending on the level of activity in the plant, $X$ is a random variable–it is not being directly controlled by the experimenter.

Regardless of the status of the independent variable $X$, the problem of regression is the same–to find a reasonable prediction equation. The mathematical procedures used in the two cases are identical. Example 11.1.3 introduces some notational conventions used in regression analysis. It also provides the motivation for the definition of the term *curve of regression of Y on X*.

**EXAMPLE 11.1.3** □ Suppose that we intend to administer a drug dose of size $x$ to a given patient. What is the best choice for the predicted concentration of the drug in the patient's bloodstream 5 minutes later? That is, what is the predicted value of $Y$, given that $X = x$?

To answer this question, we first note that not all people have the same reaction to a given drug dose. Hence $Y$ will vary from individual to individual even though the amount of drug received is the same in each case. That is, when $X = x$, $Y$ is a *random variable*. We denote this random variable by $Y|x$ (this is read, "$Y$ given that $X = x$"). This random variable has a theoretical average, or mean, value which we denote $\mu_{Y|x}$. Common sense indicates that the best predicted response for a given dose is the mean response for that dosage level. Thus, ideally *we use* $\mu_{Y|x}$ *as the predicted value of Y for a given value of X*. For example, suppose that from past experience we know that the mean response to a dose of .1 ml is a concentration of 200 mg drug/dl blood. The predicted response of the next patient receiving a dose of .1 ml is 200 mg/dl.

Now we can define the term *curve of regression of Y on X*.

**Definition 11.1.1** *Regression of Y on X*. Let $X$ be a variable, and let $Y$ be a random variable. The curve of *regression of Y on X* is the graph of the function $\mu_{Y|x}$.

Typical regression curves are shown in Figure 11.1. Note that these curves are theoretical. They are the graphs of the theoretical mean for the dependent variable $Y$ for given values of the independent variable $X$.

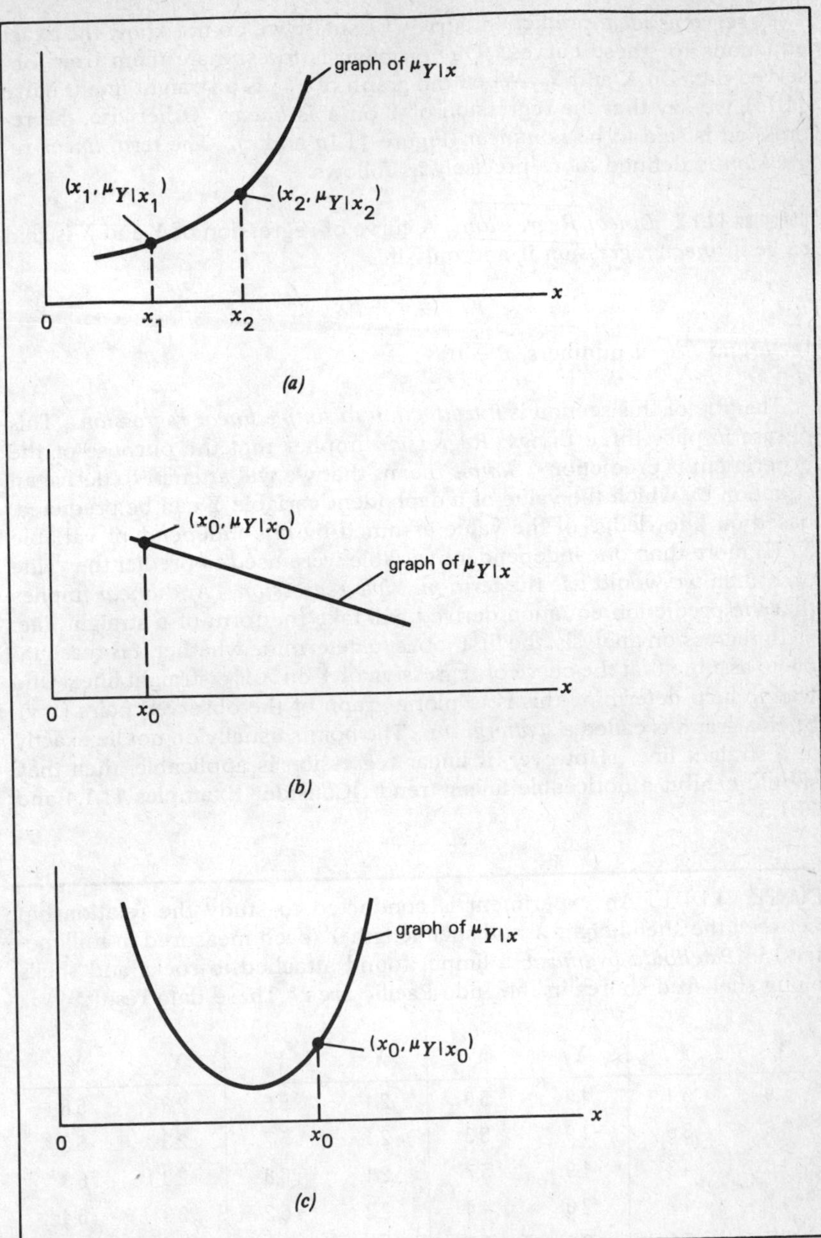


**FIGURE 11.1** (*a*) Nonlinear curve of regression; (*b*) linear curve of regression; (*c*) nonlinear curve of regression.

They serve as *ideal* prediction curves. Usually we do not know the exact equations for these curves. Our problem is to estimate them from observed data on $X$ and $Y$. When the graph of $\mu_{Y|x}$ is a straight line (Figure 11.1*b*), we say that the regression of $Y$ on $X$ is *linear*. Otherwise, the regression is said to be *nonlinear* (Figure 11.1*a* and *c*). The term *linear regression* is defined more precisely as follows:

**Definition 11.1.2** *Linear Regression.* A curve of regression of $Y$ and $X$ is said to be a *linear regression* if and only if

$$\mu_{Y|x} = \alpha + \beta x$$

for $\alpha$ and $\beta$ real numbers, $\beta \neq 0$.

The title of this section is *introduction to simple linear regression.* This phrase implies three things: *Regression* implies that the purpose of the experiment is prediction. *Simple* means that we will attempt to derive an equation by which the value of a dependent variable $Y$ can be predicted, based on knowledge of the value assumed by *one* independent variable $X$. If more than one independent variable were used to predict the value of $Y$, then we would use the term *multiple regression.* And *linear* implies that the prediction equation derived will take the form of a straight line.

In regression analysis, the first job is to determine whether it is reasonable to assume that the curve of regression of $Y$ on $X$ is a straight line. One way to help determine this is to plot a graph of the observed pairs $(x, y)$. Such a graph is called a *scattergram.* The points usually do not lie exactly in a straight line. However, if linear regression is applicable, then they should exhibit a noticeable linear trend. Consider Examples 11.1.4 and 11.1.5.

---

**EXAMPLE 11.1.4** □ An experiment is conducted to study the relationship between the shell height $X$ and shell length $Y$ (each measured in millimeters) in *Patelloida pygmaea,* a limpet found attached to rocks and shells along sheltered shores in the Indo-Pacific area. These data result:

| $X$ | $Y$ | $X$ | $Y$ | $X$ | $Y$ | $X$ | $Y$ |
|---|---|---|---|---|---|---|---|
| .9 | 3.1 | 1.9 | 5.0 | 2.1 | 5.6 | 2.3 | 5.8 |
| 1.5 | 3.6 | 1.9 | 5.3 | 2.1 | 5.7 | 2.3 | 6.2 |
| 1.6 | 4.3 | 1.9 | 5.7 | 2.1 | 5.8 | 2.3 | 6.3 |
| 1.7 | 4.7 | 2.0 | 4.4 | 2.2 | 5.2 | 2.3 | 6.4 |
| 1.7 | 5.5 | 2.0 | 5.2 | 2.2 | 5.3 | 2.4 | 6.4 |
| 1.8 | 5.7 | 2.0 | 5.3 | 2.2 | 5.6 | 2.4 | 6.3 |
| 1.8 | 5.2 | 2.1 | 5.4 | 2.2 | 5.8 | 2.7 | 6.3 |

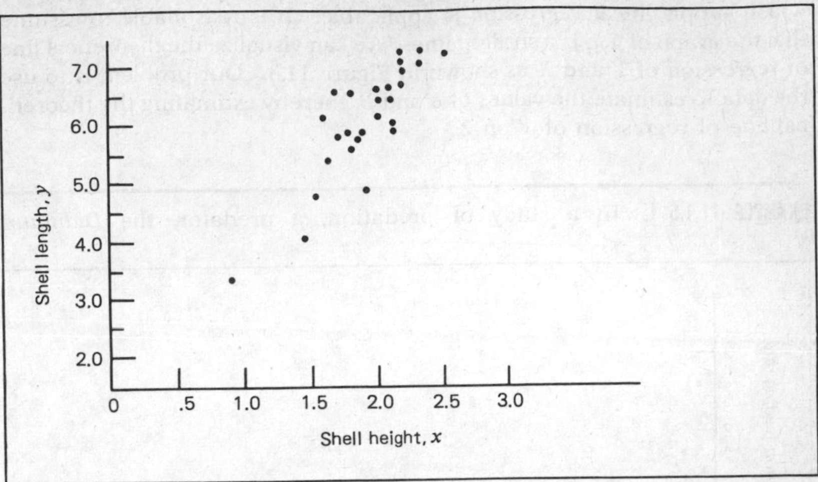


**FIGURE 11.2** Scattergram of shell height versus shell length exhibits a linear trend.

The scattergram shown in Figure 11.2 is obtained by plotting the values of the independent variable $X$ along the horizontal axis and those of the dependent variable $Y$ along the vertical axis. Even though these points do not lie on a single straight line, there is a definite linear trend to the data. The trend is what we are looking for. It identifies the problem as one in

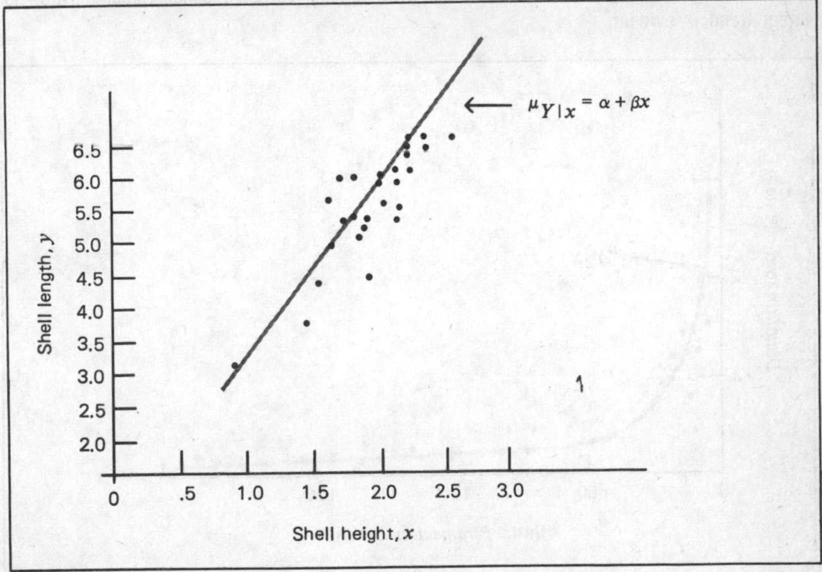


**FIGURE 11.3** Theoretical linear curve of regression and ideal curve for predicting shell length based on shell height.

which simple linear regression is applicable. It is reasonable to assume that the graph of $\mu_{Y|x}$ is a straight line. We can visualize the theoretical line of regression of $Y$ and $X$ as shown in Figure 11.3. Our problem is to use the data to estimate the values of $\alpha$ and $\beta$, thereby estimating the theoretical line of regression of $Y$ on $X$.

---

**EXAMPLE 11.1.5** □ In a study of predation, a predator, the *Didinium*

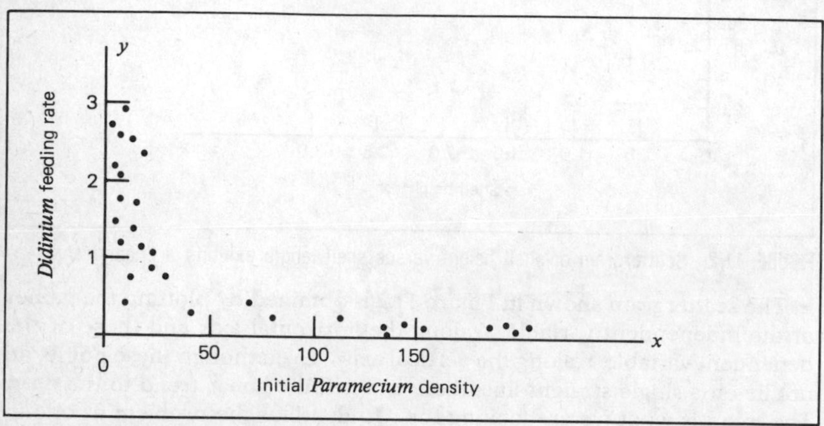


**FIGURE 11.4** Scattergram of initial *Paramecium* density versus *Didinium* feeding rate—no linear trend is evident.

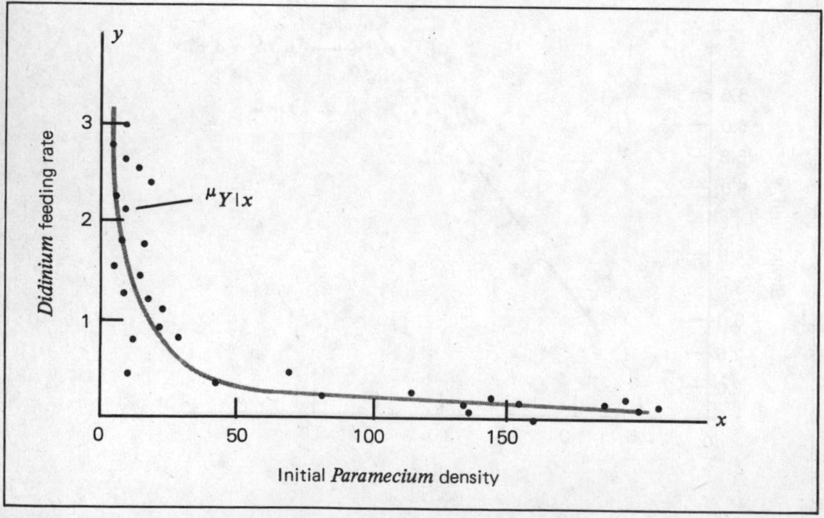


**FIGURE 11.5** Theoretical nonlinear curve of regression and ideal curve for predicting *Didinium* feeding rate based on initial *Paramecium* density.

*nasutum*, is introduced to a medium containing its natural prey, the *Paramecium caudatum*. The purpose is to predict the feeding rate of the *Didinium* ($Y$), based on knowledge of the initial density of the *Paramecium* in the medium ($X$). The scattergram of the data obtained is shown in Figure 11.4. Clearly, the points do *not* exhibit a linear trend. In this case, it is inappropriate to assume that the graph of $\mu_{Y|x}$ is linear. A more reasonable choice is a hyperbolic curve shown in Figure 11.5. We would *not* use the techniques of simple linear regression to estimate $\mu_{Y|x}$.

Our problem in Example 11.1.4 is to estimate mathematically the equation for $\mu_{Y|x}$ based on the observed data. Note that several straight lines that pass through some of the data points can be drawn through the scattergram; others can be drawn that are "close" to most of the data points. Which of these lines should we choose as our estimate for $\mu_{Y|x}$? Which of the lines best "fits" the data? These questions are answered in Section 11.2.

## EXERCISES 11.1

1. Consider the following observations on a dependent variable $Y$ and independent variable $X$:

| $X$ | $Y$ | $X$ | $Y$ |
|---|---|---|---|
| 1.0 | 3.0 | 3.0 | 7.0 |
| 1.1 | 3.2 | 3.0 | 7.1 |
| 1.5 | 4.1 | 3.1 | 7.4 |
| 1.7 | 4.2 | 3.2 | 6.0 |
| 2.0 | 5.0 | 3.5 | 8.1 |
| 2.5 | 6.2 | 3.6 | 8.0 |
| 3.0 | 7.3 | 4.0 | 9.0 |

Plot the scattergram for these data. Does linear regression appear to be applicable?

2. Consider the following observations on the dependent variable $Y$, the attention span of a child in minutes, and $X$, the child's IQ.

| $X$ | $Y$ | $X$ | $Y$ | $X$ | $Y$ | $X$ | $Y$ |
|---|---|---|---|---|---|---|---|
| 75 | 2.0 | 95 | 5.2 | 110 | 7.2 | 130 | 3.8 |
| 80 | 3.0 | 100 | 5.5 | 115 | 6.8 | 135 | 2.9 |
| 85 | 4.5 | 105 | 6.0 | 115 | 6.4 | 140 | 2.0 |
| 85 | 4.7 | 110 | 6.5 | 120 | 5.5 | | |
| 90 | 5.0 | 110 | 6.7 | 125 | 4.2 | | |

Plot the scattergram for these data. Does linear regression appear to be applicable?

3. An experiment is run to study the relationship between the incubation stage (number of days since the eggs were laid) and the mean incubation spell (mean number of minutes of uninterrupted nesting) in the gull-billed tern. The purpose is to derive an equation by which the mean incubation spell $Y$ can be predicted, based on knowledge of the stage of incubation $X$. By using time-lapse photography, these data are obtained:

| $X$ | $Y$ | $X$ | $Y$ | $X$ | $Y$ |
|---|---|---|---|---|---|
| .25 | 30 | 4 | 18 | 12 | 38 |
| .50 | 18 | 5 | 26 | 18 | 55 |
| .50 | 25 | 6 | 21 | 19 | 35 |
| 1.0 | 21 | 7 | 52 | 20 | 30 |
| 1.0 | 22 | 8 | 62 | 20 | 50 |
| 1.0 | 40 | 9 | 45 | 20 | 155 |
| 1.5 | 19 | 10 | 39 | 21 | 35 |
| 2 | 10 | 10 | 120 | 21 | 38 |
| 2.5 | 55 | 11 | 18 | | |
| 3 | 23 | 11 | 50 | | |

Plot the scattergram for these data. Does linear regression appear to be applicable?

**Computing Supplement**

A simple SAS procedure called PLOT is available for plotting the scattergram for a data set. Its use is illustrated in the following program, which plots a scattergram for the data of Exercise 11.1.2.

| **Statement** | **Function** |
|---|---|
| DATA CHILDREN; | names data set |
| INPUT IQ SPAN; | names variables; they will appear on cards in order IQ, then SPAN |
| CARDS; | signifies beginning of data |
| 75 2 | data |
| 80 3 | |
| 85 4.5 | |
| . . . | |
| 140 2 | |
| ; | signals end of data |
| TITLE IS THE REGRESSION LINEAR?; | titles output |
| PROC PLOT; | calls on PLOT procedure |

| | |
|---|---|
| PLOT SPAN*IQ; | asks dependent variable SPAN to be plotted on vertical axis and independent variable IQ on horizontal axis |

The output of this program is as follows:

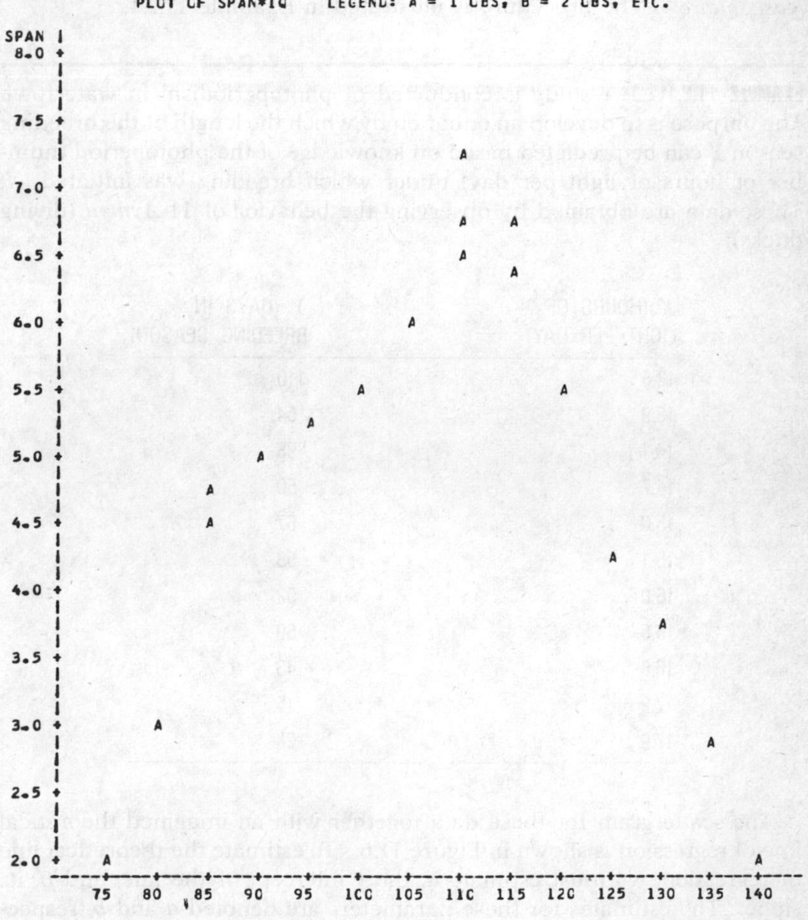

## METHOD OF LEAST SQUARES

**11.2** □ Recall that in simple linear regression we assume that the graph of the mean of the dependent variable $Y$ for given values of the independent variable $X$ is a straight line. That is, we assume

$$\mu_{Y|x} = \alpha + \beta x$$

where $\alpha$ and $\beta$ are unknown parameters whose values are to be estimated. The method employed to estimate $\alpha$ and $\beta$ is called the *method of least squares*. The procedure is illustrated in Example 11.2.1.

---

**EXAMPLE 11.2.1** □ A study is conducted of photoperiodism in waterfowl. The purpose is to develop an equation by which the length of the breeding season $Y$ can be predicted based on knowledge of the photoperiod (number of hours of light per day) under which breeding was initiated, $X$. These data are obtained by observing the behavior of 11 *Aythya* (diving ducks):

| $X$ (HOURS OF LIGHT PER DAY) | $Y$ (DAYS IN BREEDING SEASON) |
|---|---|
| 12.8 | 110 |
| 13.9 | 54 |
| 14.1 | 98 |
| 14.7 | 50 |
| 15.0 | 67 |
| 15.1 | 58 |
| 16.0 | 52 |
| 16.5 | 50 |
| 16.6 | 43 |
| 17.2 | 15 |
| 17.9 | 28 |

The scattergram for these data together with an imagined theoretical line of regression is shown in Figure 11.6. To estimate the theoretical line of regression, we must estimate $\alpha$, the $y$ intercept of the line, and $\beta$, its slope. The estimates for these parameters are denoted $a$ and $b$, respectively. Thus the estimated line of regression is given by

$$\widehat{\mu}_{Y|x} = a + bx$$

Since we use the estimated mean of $Y$ for a given value of $X$ as the predicted value of $Y$ for that value of $X$, we also write

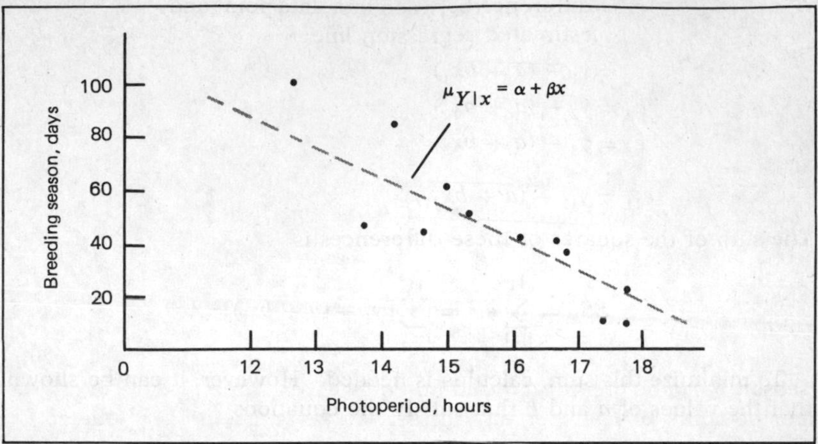


**FIGURE 11.6** Theoretical line of regression and ideal curve for predicting the length of the breeding season based on the photoperiod, which is unknown to the experimenter.

$$\hat{y}(\text{predicted value of } Y|x) = \hat{\mu}_{Y|x} = a + bx$$

The reasoning behind the method of least squares is quite simple. From the many straight lines that can be drawn through the scattergram, we wish to pick the one that "best fits" the data. The fit is "best" in the sense that the values of $a$ and $b$ chosen will be those that minimize the sum of the squares of the distances between the data points and the fitted regression line. In this way, we are picking the straight line that comes as close as it can to all data points simultaneously. This idea is illustrated in Figure 11.7. Note that

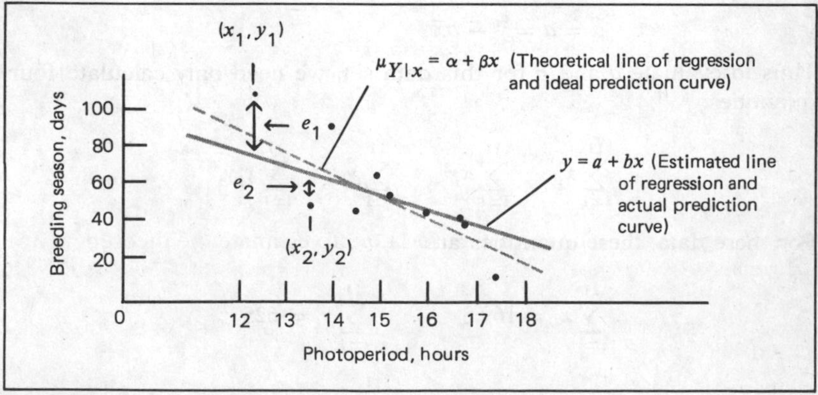


**FIGURE 11.7** The actual prediction curve minimizes the sum of the squares of the distances $e_i$.

$$
\begin{aligned}
e_1 &= \text{difference between first data point and} \\
&\quad\ \text{estimated regression line} \\
&= y_1 - (a + bx_1) \\
e_2 &= y_2 - (a + bx_2) \\
e_3 &= y_3 - (a + bx_3) \\
&\ \vdots \\
e_{11} &= y_{11} - (a + bx_{11})
\end{aligned}
$$

The sum of the squares of these differences is

$$SS_E = \sum_{i=1}^{11} e_i^2 = \sum_{i=1}^{11} [y_i - (a + bx_i)]^2$$

To minimize this sum, calculus is needed. However, it can be shown that the values of $a$ and $b$ that satisfy the equations

$$\sum_{i=1}^{11} y_i = 11a + b \sum_{i=1}^{11} x_i$$

$$\sum_{i=1}^{11} x_i y_i = a \sum_{i=1}^{11} x_i + b \sum_{i=1}^{11} x_i^2$$

minimize $SS_E$. These equations are called the *normal equations*. They can be solved for $a$ and $b$ to obtain

$$\widehat{\beta} = b = \frac{11 \sum_{i=1}^{11} x_i y_i - \sum_{i=1}^{11} x_i \sum_{i=1}^{11} y_i}{11 \sum_{i=1}^{11} x_i^2 - \left[\sum_{i=1}^{11} x_i\right]^2}$$

$$\widehat{\alpha} = a = \overline{y} - b\overline{x}$$

Thus to evaluate $a$ and $b$ for this data set, we need only calculate four quantities:

$$\sum_{i=1}^{11} x_i \qquad \sum_{i=1}^{11} x_i^2 \qquad \sum_{i=1}^{11} y_i \qquad \sum_{i=1}^{11} x_i y_i$$

For these data, these quantities are

$$\sum_{i=1}^{11} x_i = 169.8 \qquad \sum_{i=1}^{11} y_i = 625$$

$$\sum_{i=1}^{11} x_i^2 = 2645.02 \qquad \sum_{i=1}^{11} x_i y_i = 9286.2$$

Thus

$$\hat{\beta} = b = \frac{11(9286.2) - 169.8(625)}{11(2645.02) - (169.8)^2} = -15.11$$

$$\hat{\alpha} = a = \frac{625}{11} - (-15.11)\frac{169.8}{11} = 290.06$$

The estimated line of regression and actual prediction equation based on these data is

$$\hat{y} = \hat{\mu}_{Y|x} = 290.06 - 15.11x$$

To predict the length of the breeding season when the photoperiod under which breeding is initiated is 14.5 hours, we substitute $x = 14.5$ into the above equation. Thus our predicted value is

$$\hat{y} = 290.06 - 15.11(14.5) = 70.97 \text{ days}$$

---

The normal equations and the estimates for $\alpha$ and $\beta$ given in Example 11.2.1 are generalized by replacing the number 11, the sample size for the given data set, by $n$, the sample size for a general data set. Thus the normal equations for the simple linear regression model are

Normal Equations

$$\sum_{i=1}^{n} y_i = na + b \sum_{i=1}^{n} x_i$$

$$\sum_{i=1}^{n} x_i y_i = a \sum_{i=1}^{n} x_i + b \sum_{i=1}^{n} x_i^2$$

The general formulas for $\hat{\alpha}$ and $\hat{\beta}$ are

Estimates for $\alpha$ and $\beta$

$$\hat{\alpha} = a = \bar{y} - b\bar{x}$$

$$\hat{\beta} = b = \frac{n \sum_{i=1}^{n} x_i y_i - \sum_{i=1}^{n} x_i \sum_{i=1}^{n} y_i}{n \sum_{i=1}^{n} x_i^2 - \left[\sum_{i=1}^{n} x_i\right]^2}$$

A word of caution must be added. A given data set gives evidence of linearity only over those values of $X$ covered by the data set. For values of $X$ beyond those covered, there is no evidence of linearity. Thus it is dangerous to use an estimated regression line to predict values of $Y$ corresponding to values of $X$ lying beyond the range of the $X$ values covered by the data set. We illustrate this point in Example 11.2.2.

**EXAMPLE 11.2.2** □ The following data are obtained on the fastest mile-run times $Y$ (in seconds) of world-class runners from 1954 to 1972:

| $X$ (YEAR) | $Y$ (TIME OF RUN) |
|---|---|
| 54 | 239.4 (Bannister breaks 4-min mile) |
| 54 | 238.0 |
| 56 | 238.1 |
| 56 | 238.5 |
| 58 | 234.5 |
| 58 | 236.2 |
| 60 | 235.3 |
| 60 | 234.8 |
| 62 | 235.1 |
| 62 | 234.4 |
| 64 | 234.1 |
| 64 | 234.9 |
| 66 | 231.3 (Ryan) |
| 66 | 232.7 |
| 68 | 231.4 |
| 68 | 231.8 |
| 70 | 232.0 |
| 70 | 231.9 |
| 72 | 231.4 |
| 72 | 231.5 |

The scattergram for these data is shown in Figure 11.8. There does appear to be a linear trend. To fit a regression line to the data, these quantities are needed:

$$\sum_{i=1}^{20} x_i = 1260 \qquad \sum_{i=1}^{20} y_i = 4687.3$$

$$\sum_{i=1}^{20} x_i^2 = 80{,}040 \qquad \sum_{i=1}^{20} x_i y_i = 295{,}024.2$$

$$\bar{x} = 63 \qquad \bar{y} = 234.37$$

$$\widehat{\beta} = b = \frac{n\Sigma x_i y_i - \Sigma x \Sigma y}{n\Sigma x^2 - (\Sigma x)^2} = \frac{20(295{,}024.2) - (1260)(4687.3)}{20(80{,}040) - 1260^2}$$

$$= -.42$$

$$\widehat{\alpha} = a = \bar{y} - b\bar{x} = 234.37 - (-.42)(63) = 260.83$$

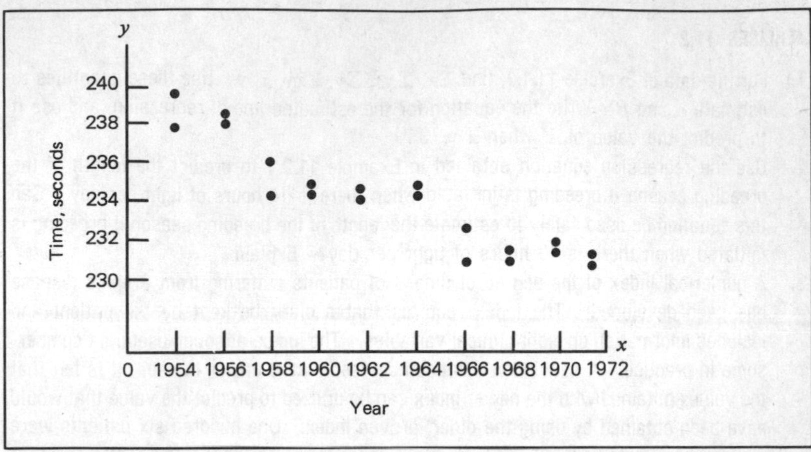


**FIGURE 11.8** Scattergram of year versus time for the mile run for world-class runners.

The estimated regression line is

$$\widehat{y} = \widehat{\mu}_{Y|x} = 260.83 - .42x$$

The line can be used safely to predict the time for a world-class mile runner from 1954 to 1972, the years covered by the data set. The danger lies in using this equation to predict mile-run times much beyond 1972, because there is no evidence from the data set that a linear trend continues indefinitely. In particular, suppose that we erroneously assume that the linear trend continues, and so we try to predict the run time for a runner in the year 2521. For the year 2521, $x = 621$. Thus the predicted value of $y$ is

$$\widehat{y} = 260.83 - .42(621) = .01 \text{ second}$$

This value is inconceivable as a possible time for running 1 mile! The problem arises because at some point beyond 1972, the linear trend ceases and the times level off at some reasonable value.

---

We have provided a logical way to estimate $\alpha$ and $\beta$ and thus fit a straight line to any data set. We also have seen that a scattergram gives some indication of whether linear regression is applicable. However, one important question still must be answered: Does *linear* regression really make sense, or would some other type of curve actually fit the data more closely and thus provide a better prediction equation? This question cannot be ignored. We address it in Section 11.4.

## EXERCISES 11.2

1. For the data of Exercise 11.1.1, find $\Sigma x$, $\Sigma x^2$, $\Sigma y$, $\Sigma xy$, $\bar{x}$, $\bar{y}$. Use these quantities to estimate $\alpha$ and $\beta$. Write the equation for the estimated line of regression, and use it to predict the value of $Y$ when $x = 3.7$.
2. Use the regression equation obtained in Example 11.2.1 to predict the length of the breeding season if breeding is initiated when there is 14 hours of light per day. Can this equation be used safely to estimate the length of the breeding season if breeding is initiated when there is 10 hours of light per day? Explain.
3. A numerical index of the degree of illness of patients suffering from Crohn's disease has been developed. The index requires that a diary be kept by the patient and includes information on eight clinical variables. The index, although useful, is cumbersome in practice. A new index has been devised that is easier to use. It is felt that the values obtained with the newer index can be utilized to predict the value that would have been obtained by using the older, proven index. One hundred six patients were evaluated by using both indices. $X$ values range from .5 to 14.0. The scattergram for the data exhibits a linear trend. For these data,

$$\Sigma x = 366.1 \qquad \Sigma y = 12{,}623$$
$$\Sigma x^2 = 2435.63 \qquad \bar{y} = 119.08$$
$$\bar{x} = 3.45 \qquad \Sigma xy = 75{,}989.6$$

   Use this information to estimate $\alpha$, $\beta$, and $\mu_{Y|x}$. What is the predicted rating on the old index for a patient whose rating on the new index is 5.5? Can we safely predict the rating on the old index for a patient who is rated at $x = 16$ on the new index? Explain.
4. A study is run to develop an equation by which the concentration of estrone in saliva can be used to predict the concentration of this steroid in free plasma. The data are obtained on 14 healthy males:

| $X$ (CONCENTRATION OF ESTRONE IN SALIVA, pg/ml) | $Y$ (CONCENTRATION OF ESTRONE IN FREE PLASMA, pg/ml) |
|---|---|
| 7.4 | 30.0 |
| 7.5 | 25.0 |
| 8.5 | 31.5 |
| 9.0 | 27.5 |
| 9.0 | 39.5 |
| 11.0 | 38.0 |
| 13.0 | 43.0 |
| 14.0 | 49.0 |
| 14.5 | 55.0 |
| 16.0 | 48.5 |
| 17.0 | 51.0 |
| 18.0 | 64.5 |
| 20.0 | 63.0 |
| 23.0 | 68.0 |

a. Sketch a scattergram for these data.
b. Find $\Sigma x$, $\Sigma x^2$, $\Sigma y$, $\Sigma xy$.
c. Estimate $\alpha$, $\beta$, $\mu_{Y|x}$.
d. Use the estimated line of regression to predict the estrone level in the free plasma in a male whose saliva estrone level is 17.5 pg/ml.

**5.** Use the data of Example 11.1.4.
a. Find $\Sigma x$, $\Sigma X^2$, $\Sigma y$, $\Sigma xy$.
b. Estimate $\alpha$, $\beta$, $\mu_{Y|x}$.
c. Use the estimated line of regression to predict the shell length of a limpet whose shell height is 2.25 millimeters.

---

**Computing Supplement**

The SAS program PROC GLM is available for handling regression problems. It estimates $\alpha$ and $\beta$ and predicts the value of $Y$ for any specified value of $X$. The procedure is illustrated by allowing SAS to analyze the data of Example 11.2.1.

| Statement | Function |
|---|---|
| DATA WATERFWL; | names data set |
| INPUT PHOTOPRD LENGTH; | names variables; they will appear on cards in order PHOTOPRD, then LENGTH |
| CARDS; | signals beginning of data |
| 12.8 110 | data |
| 13.9 54 | |
| . . . . | |
| 17.9 28 | |
| 14.5 • | single dot indicates $Y$ value is missing for $X$ value of 14.5; allows SAS to predict $Y$ value |
| ; | signals end of data |
| TITLE IS THE REGRESSION LINEAR?; | titles first page of output |
| PROC PLOT; | asks for scattergram |
| PLOT LENGTH*PHOTOPRD; | |
| PROC GLM; | calls for analysis of regression problems |
| MODEL LENGTH=PHOTOPRD; | identifies variable first named, LENGTH, as dependent; variable(s) appearing after equals sign are identified as independent |
| OUTPUT OUT=NEW P=PREDICT; | forms new data set, NEW, that contains predicted values of PHOTOPRD |
| PROC PRINT; | asks SAS to print values of dependent variable predicted by fitted regression line |

The output of this program follows. Note that $a = \widehat{\alpha}$ is given by (1) and $b = \widehat{\beta}$ is given by (2). Thus the estimated regression line based on these data is

$$\widehat{y} = \widehat{\mu}_{Y|x} = 290.07 - 15.11x$$

This equation differs very slightly from that obtained in Example 11.2.1 as a result of roundoff differences when a handheld calculator is used. The predicted value of $Y$ when $x = 14.5$ is given by (3).

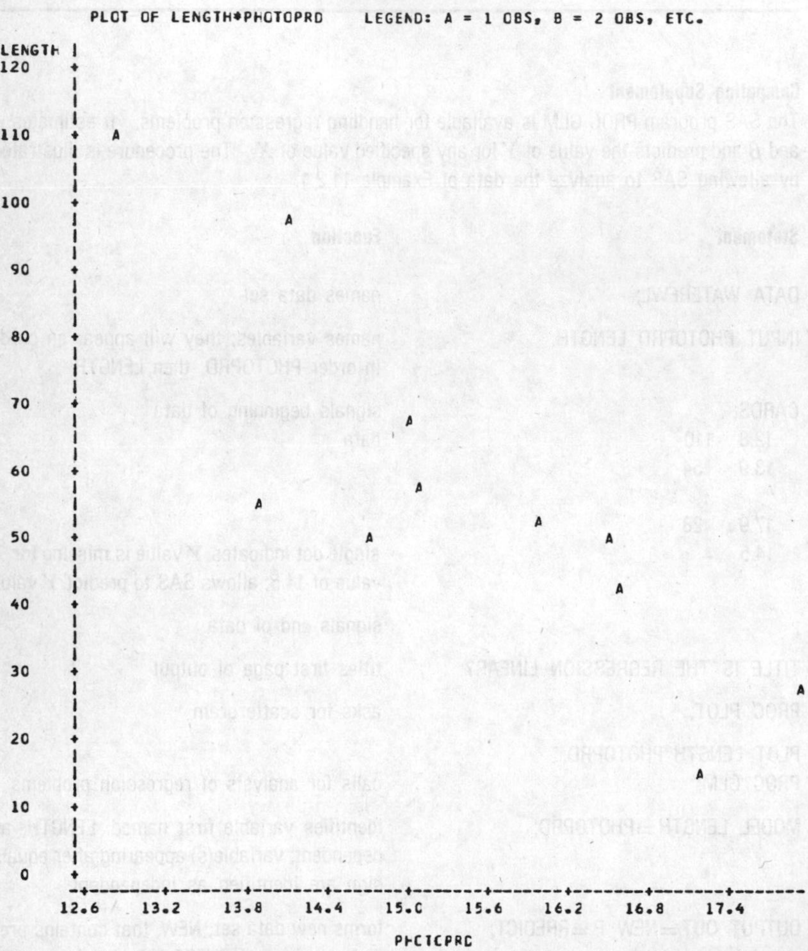

```
                         IS THE REGRESSION LINEAR?
                     GENERAL LINEAR MODELS PROCEDURE
DEPENDENT VARIABLE: LENGTH
SOURCE                DF     SUM OF SQUARES        MEAN SQUARE       F VALUE
MODEL                  1     5462.88341888      5462.88341888         23.86
ERROR                  9     2060.75294475       228.97254942        PR > F
CORRECTED TOTAL       10     7523.63636364                           0.0009

R-SQUARE            C.V.            STD DEV           LENGTH MEAN
0.726096         26.6320       15.13183853        56.81818182

SOURCE                DF      TYPE I SS      F VALUE     PR > F
PHOTOPRD               1    5462.88341888     23.86      0.0009

SOURCE                DF      TYPE IV SS     F VALUE     PR > F
PHOTOPRD               1    5462.88341888     23.86      0.0009

                                  T FOR H0:       PR > |T|     STD ERROR OF
PARAMETER          ESTIMATE     PARAMETER=0                     ESTIMATE
INTERCEPT       290.07044608 (1)       6.05      0.0002       47.97110790
PHOTOPRD        -15.11057071 (2)      -4.88      0.0009        3.09358185

                         IS THE REGRESSION LINEAR?
                 OBS     PHOTOPRD    LENGTH     PREDICT
                  1        12.8       110       96.6551
                  2        13.9        54       80.0335
                  3        14.1        98       77.0114
                  4        14.7        50       67.9451
                  5        15.0        67       63.4119
                  6        15.1        58       61.9008
                  7        16.0        52       48.3013
                  8        16.5        50       40.7460
                  9        16.6        43       39.2350
                 10        17.2        15       30.1686
                 11        17.9        28       19.5912
                 12        14.5                 70.9672 (3)
```

## INTRODUCTION TO CORRELATION

**11.3** □ Recall that statistical regression analysis deals with the relationship between an independent variable $X$ and the *mean* $\mu_{Y|x}$ of a dependent variable $Y$. We have been particularly concerned with situations in which this relationship is linear. In regression analysis, the variable $X$ can be random or designed. In correlation analysis, the variable $X$ is always assumed to be *random*. We seek a parameter that will help us determine whether $Y$ itself is linearly related to $X$. That is, we seek a parameter that will allow us to answer the question, Do real numbers $\alpha$ and $\beta$, $\beta \neq 0$, exist such that $Y = \alpha + \beta X$? If this is true, then the regression of $Y$ on $X$ will be linear also.

The most often used measure of linear association between two random variables is $\rho$, the Pearson product-moment coefficient of correlation. This parameter is defined in terms of the covariance between $X$ and $Y$, where the covariance is a measure of the manner in which $X$ and $Y$ vary together. We define it as follows:

**Definition 11.3.1** *Covariance.* Let $X$ and $Y$ be random variables with means $\mu_X$ and $\mu_Y$, respectively. The *covariance* between $X$ and $Y$, denoted Cov $(X, Y)$, is given by

$$\text{Cov}\,(X, Y) = E[(X - \mu_X)(Y - \mu_Y)] = E[XY] - E[X]E[Y]$$

Note that if small values of $X$ tend to be associated with small values of $Y$ and large values of $X$ with large values of $Y$, then $X - \mu_X$ and $Y - \mu_Y$ will tend to have the same algebraic sign. This implies that $(X - \mu_X)(Y - \mu_Y)$ will tend to be positive, yielding a positive covariance. If the reverse is true and small values of $X$ tend to be associated with large values of $Y$ and vice versa, then $X - \mu_X$ and $Y - \mu_Y$ will tend to have opposite algebraic signs. This results in a tendency for $(X - \mu_X)(Y - \mu_Y)$ to be negative, yielding a negative covariance. This observation helps in interpreting the Pearson correlation coefficient, which is defined now.

**Definition 11.3.2** *Pearson Correlation Coefficient.* Let $X$ and $Y$ be random variables with means $\mu_X$ and $\mu_Y$ and variances $\sigma_X{}^2$ and $\sigma_Y{}^2$, respectively. The *correlation* $\rho$ between $X$ and $Y$ is

$$\rho = \frac{\text{Cov}\,(X, Y)}{\sqrt{(\text{Var}\,X)(\text{Var}\,Y)}}$$

That $\rho$ measures the linear association between $X$ and $Y$ is pointed out in Theorem 11.3.1.

**THEOREM 11.3.1** □ Let $X$ and $Y$ be random variables. Then for $\beta \neq 0$, $Y = \alpha + \beta X$ if and only if $\rho = 1$ or $\rho = -1$.

The point of this theorem is twofold. First, if there is a linear relationship between $X$ and $Y$, then this fact is reflected in a correlation coefficient of $+1$ or $-1$. Second, if $\rho = 1$ or $-1$, then a linear relationship exists between $X$ and $Y$. If $\rho = 1$, then we say that $X$ and $Y$ have *perfect positive correlation;* if $\rho = -1$, then $X$ and $Y$ are said to have *perfect negative correlation.* Perfect positive correlation implies that $Y = \alpha + \beta X$, where $\beta > 0$. This in turn implies that small values of $X$ are associated with small values of $Y$, and large values of $X$ with large values of $Y$. Perfect negative correlation implies that $Y = \alpha + \beta X$, where $\beta < 0$. Practically speaking, this means that small values of $X$ are associated with large values of $Y$, and vice versa. It is equally important to realize what Theorem 11.3.1 is not saying. If $\rho = 0$, we say that $X$ and $Y$ are uncorrelated, but we are *not* saying that $X$ and $Y$ are unrelated. We are saying that if a relationship exists, then it is *not linear*. These ideas are shown graphically in Figure 11.9.

Keep in mind that Cov $(X, Y)$ and $\rho$ are *theoretical* parameters. Neither can be calculated without knowledge of the probability distribution of the pair of variables $(X, Y)$. The statistical problem is to estimate their values from a data set. Since Cov $(X, Y)$ can be expressed as the difference in the theoretical means $E[XY]$ and $E[X]E[Y]$, it can be estimated easily by replacing each theoretical mean by its corresponding sample mean. Thus we estimate

$$E[XY] \quad \text{by} \quad \frac{\sum_{i=1}^{n} x_i y_i}{n}$$

$$E[X] \quad \text{by} \quad \frac{\sum_{i=1}^{n} x_i}{n}$$

$$E[Y] \quad \text{by} \quad \frac{\sum_{i=1}^{n} y_i}{n}$$

By substituting, the estimated covariance becomes

$$\widehat{\text{Cov}(X, Y)} = \sum_{i=1}^{n} \frac{x_i y_i}{n} - \sum_{i=1}^{n} \frac{x_i}{n} \sum_{i=1}^{n} \frac{y_i}{n}$$

$$= \frac{n \sum_{i=1}^{n} x_i y_i - \sum_{i=1}^{n} x_i \sum_{i=1}^{n} y_i}{n^2}$$

Similarly, since Var $X = E[X^2] - (E[X])^2$,

$$\widehat{\text{Var } X} = \frac{\sum_{i=1}^{n} x_i^2}{n} - \left[\sum_{i=1}^{n} \frac{x_i}{n}\right]^2$$

$$= \frac{n \sum_{i=1}^{n} x_i^2 - \left[\sum_{i=1}^{n} x_i\right]^2}{n^2}$$

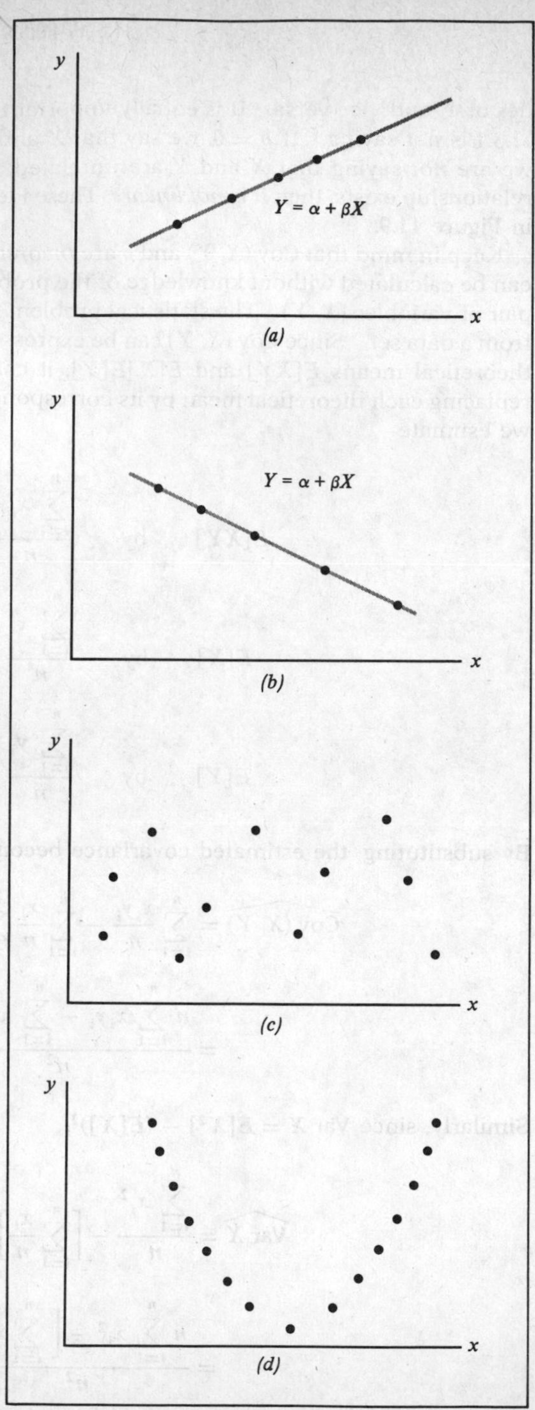


**FIGURE 11.9** (*a*) Perfect positive correlation: $\rho = 1$, $\beta > 0$, all points lie on a straight line with positive slope; (*b*) perfect negative correlation: $\rho = 1$, $\beta < 0$, all points lie on a straight line with negative slope; (*c*) uncorrelated: $\rho = 0$, points are randomly scattered; (*d*) uncorrelated; $\rho = 0$, points indicate a relationship between $X$ and $Y$, but the relationship is not linear.

Combining these results, we get a logical estimate for the correlation coefficient $\rho$:

$$\widehat{\rho} = \frac{\dfrac{n \sum_{i=1}^{n} x_i y_i - \sum_{i=1}^{n} x_i \sum_{i=1}^{n} y_i}{n^2}}{\sqrt{\left[\dfrac{n \sum_{i=1}^{n} x_i^2 - \left[\sum_{i=1}^{n} x_i\right]^2}{n^2}\right]\left[\dfrac{n \sum_{i=1}^{n} y_i^2 - \left[\sum_{i=1}^{n} y_i\right]^2}{n^2}\right]}}$$

By simplifying the estimate for $\rho$ can be as given in Definition 11.3.3.

**Definition 11.3.3** *Estimate for $\rho$.* The *estimate for $\rho$*, the Pearson coefficient of correlation, denoted $r$, is

$$\widehat{\rho} = r = \frac{n\Sigma xy - \Sigma x \Sigma y}{\sqrt{[n\Sigma x^2 - (\Sigma x)^2][n\Sigma y^2 - (\Sigma y)^2]}}$$

These ideas are illustrated in Example 11.3.1.

---

**EXAMPLE 11.3.1** □ Researchers are investigating the correlation between obesity and an individual's response to pain. Obesity is measured as the percentage over ideal weight ($X$). Response to pain is measured by using the threshold of the nociceptive flexion reflex ($Y$), which is a measure of the pricking pain sensation in an individual. Note that both $X$ and $Y$ are random variables. We want to estimate $\rho$, the correlation coefficient for these variables. These data are obtained:

| $X$ (PERCENTAGE OVERWEIGHT) | $Y$ (THRESHOLD OF NOCICEPTIVE FLEXION REFLEX) |
|---|---|
| 89 | 2 |
| 90 | 3 |
| 75 | 4 |
| 30 | 4.5 |
| 51 | 5.5 |
| 75 | 7 |
| 62 | 9 |
| 45 | 13 |
| 90 | 15 |
| 20 | 14 |

The scattergram for these data is shown in Figure 11.10. There appears to be some tendency for small values of $X$ to be associated with large values of $Y$, and vice versa. However, the tendency is not strong as evidenced by points (30, 4.5), for which a small value of $X$ is paired with a small value of $Y$, and (90, 15), for which the reverse is true. Based on these comments, we would expect $r$, the estimate for $\rho$, to be negative; but we would not expect it to be very close to $-1$. That is, we would expect $X$ and $Y$ to be *slightly* negatively correlated. To verify these observations, let us estimate $\rho$, using Definition 11.3.3. These sample statistics are needed:

$$\Sigma x = 627 \qquad \Sigma y = 77 \qquad \Sigma xy = 4461.5$$
$$\Sigma x^2 = 45{,}141 \qquad \Sigma y^2 = 799.5$$

$$\begin{aligned}\hat{\rho} = r &= \frac{n\Sigma xy - \Sigma x \Sigma y}{\sqrt{[n\Sigma x^2 - (\Sigma x)^2][n\Sigma y^2 - (\Sigma y)^2]}} \\ &= \frac{10(4461.5) - 627(77)}{\sqrt{[10(45{,}141) - 627^2][10(799.5) - 77^2]}} \\ &= -.33\end{aligned}$$

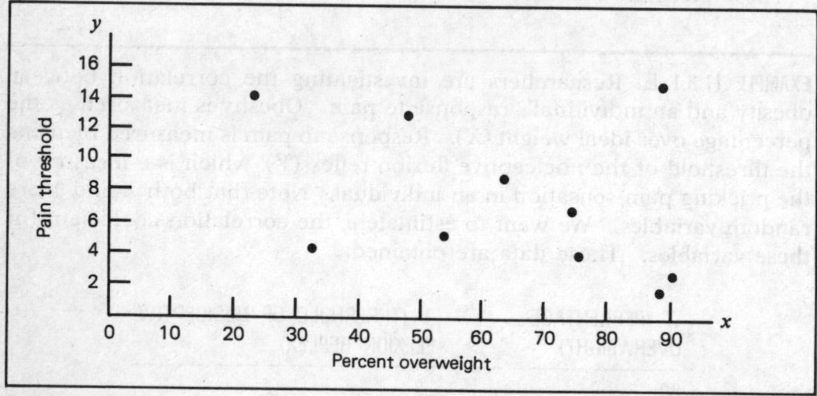


**FIGURE 11.10** Scattergram of percentage overweight versus threshold of nociceptive flexion reflex, indicating a slight negative correlation.

A word of caution is in order. We have provided a logical point estimator for $\rho$ and a very rough notion as to how to interpret the estimated value. There is still a problem to be solved. Since we are estimating $\rho$

from a data set, it is unlikely that $\widehat{\rho}$ will ever assume the easily interpreted values of 1, $-1$, or 0. We are almost always faced with the problem of interpreting a value such as that obtained in Example 11.3.1 ($-.33$), which is not clearly close to any of the extreme values 1, $-1$, or 0. We need to determine whether the value obtained is "close enough" to any of the extreme values to have any practical consequences. We discuss this problem in detail in Section 11.4. For now, beware of putting too much importance on estimated correlations such as $-.33$!

## EXERCISES 11.3

1. Consider the following observations on the random variables $X$ and $Y$:

| $x$ | $y$ |
|---|---|
| 2.0 | 5.0 |
| 2.5 | 5.5 |
| 3.0 | 6.2 |
| 3.5 | 6.4 |
| 4.0 | 7.0 |

   a. Plot a scattergram for these data.
   b. On the basis of the scattergram, do you expect $r$, the estimated correlation coefficient, to be close to 1, $-1$, or 0?
   c. Find $\Sigma x$, $\Sigma x^2$, $\Sigma y$, $\Sigma y^2$, $\Sigma xy$.
   d. Find $r$.

2. Consider the following observations on the random variables $X$ and $Y$:

| $x$ | $y$ |
|---|---|
| 2.0 | 7.2 |
| 2.5 | 7.0 |
| 3.0 | 6.5 |
| 3.5 | 6.0 |
| 4.0 | 5.3 |

   a. Plot a scattergram for these data.
   b. On the basis of the scattergram, do you expect $r$ to be close to 1, $-1$, or 0?
   c. Find $\Sigma x$, $\Sigma x^2$, $\Sigma y$, $\Sigma y^2$, $\Sigma xy$.
   d. Determine $r$.

3. Consider the following observations on the random variables $X$ and $Y$:

| $x$ | $y$ |
|---|---|
| 2.0 | 4.0 |
| 2.1 | 4.4 |
| 2.5 | 6.3 |
| 3.0 | 9.0 |
| 3.5 | 6.2 |
| 3.9 | 4.3 |
| 4.0 | 4.0 |

**a.** Plot a scattergram for these data.
**b.** On the basis of the scattergram, do you expect $r$ to be close to 1, $-1$, or 0?
**c.** Find $\Sigma x$, $\Sigma x^2$, $\Sigma y$, $\Sigma y^2$, $\Sigma xy$.
**d.** Calculate $r$.

4. A study is conducted to estimate the correlation between the random variables $X$, an individual's score on an obesity index, and $Y$, the individual's resting metabolic rate. On the obesity index, a high score indicates a high degree of obesity; the metabolic rate is measured in milliliters of oxygen consumed per minute. Each variable is measured on 43 subjects. These sample statistics result:

$$\Sigma x = 1482.5 \qquad \Sigma y = 10{,}719 \qquad \Sigma xy = 379{,}207.5$$
$$\Sigma x^2 = 53{,}515.25 \qquad \Sigma y^2 = 2{,}736{,}063$$

Find $r$.

5. In studying the effect of sewage effluent on a lake, measurements are taken of the nitrate concentration of the water. An older manual method has been used to monitor this variable. A new automated method has been devised. If a high positive correlation can be shown between the measurements taken by using the two methods, then the automated method will be put into routine use. These data are obtained (units are micrograms of nitrate per liter of water):

| $x$ (MANUAL) | $y$ (AUTOMATED) |
|---|---|
| 25 | 30 |
| 40 | 80 |
| 120 | 150 |
| 75 | 80 |
| 150 | 200 |
| 300 | 350 |
| 270 | 240 |
| 400 | 320 |
| 450 | 470 |
| 575 | 583 |

**a.** Find $\Sigma x$, $\Sigma x^2$, $\Sigma y$, $\Sigma y^2$, $\Sigma xy$.
**b.** Estimate $\rho$.

---

**Computing Supplement**

The SAS procedure PROC CORR estimates the value of the Pearson coefficient of correlation. The data of Example 11.3.1 are used.

| Statement | Function |
|---|---|
| DATA OBESITY; | names data set |
| INPUT PERCENT PAIN; | each card will contain value of percentage overweight of patient, followed by measure of response to pain |
| CARDS; | signals beginning of data |
| 89 2 | data |
| 90 3 | |
| 75 4 | |
| . . . . | |
| 20 14 | |
| ; | signals end of data |
| PROC CORR; | calls for correlation procedure |
| TITLE ARE PAIN AND OBESITY CORRELATED?; | titles output |

The output of this program follows. Note that the value of $r$, the estimated correlation ($-.333\,91$) between $X$, percentage overweight, and $Y$, threshold of the nociceptive flexion reflex, is given by (1). The value (.345 7) given by (2) is the $P$ value for testing

$$H_0\colon \rho = 0 \qquad (X \text{ and } Y \text{ are uncorrelated})$$
$$H_1\colon \rho \neq 0$$

Since this value is large, we do not reject $H_0$. We are unable to detect a linear relationship between $X$ and $Y$ based on these data.

```
                        ARE PAIN AND OBESITY CORRELATED
VARIABLE        N          MEAN        STD DEV           SUM        MINIMUM      MAXIMUM

PERCENT        10 62.70000000 25.44733123 627.0000000 20.00000000 90.00000000
PAIN           10  7.70000000  4.79119563  77.0000000  2.00000000 15.00000000

       CORRELATION COEFFICIENTS / PROB > |R| UNDER HO:RHO=0 / N = 10
                             PERCENT      PAIN

              PERCENT       1.00000   -0.33391  (1)
                            0.0000     0.3457   (2)

              PAIN         -0.33391    1.00000
                            0.3457     0.0000
```

## *EVALUATING THE STRENGTH OF THE LINEAR RELATIONSHIP

**11.4** □ As we pointed out in Section 11.2, the method of least squares can be used to fit a straight line to *any* data set. However, the utility of this line as a predictor of future values of the dependent variable $Y$ depends entirely on *whether the assumption of linearity is appropriate.* For this reason we need an analytic method for determining how well a straight line fits the data points. We present two methods here. The first employs a statistic called the coefficient of determination; the second uses an analysis-of-variance technique to discover whether the variability in $Y$ is well explained by a linear relationship with $X$.

Similarly, we can always calculate $r$, the estimated correlation coefficient between $X$ and $Y$. It is not always easy to attach a practical meaning to the value obtained. The coefficient of determination is useful in that it allows us to interpret more precisely those values of $r$ that clearly are not close to the easily interpreted values of $-1$, 1, or 0. Since this coefficient is associated with both regression and correlation analysis, it provides a link between the two procedures. To define this statistic, we must determine the relationship between $r$, the estimated correlation coefficient, and $b$, the estimated slope of the least-squares regression line. We use the following notation:

$$S_{xy} = \Sigma(x - \bar{x})(y - \bar{y})$$

$$= \frac{n\Sigma xy - \Sigma x \Sigma y}{n} = \text{measure of covariance between } X \text{ and } Y$$

$$S_{xx} = \Sigma(x - \bar{x})^2$$

$$= \frac{n\Sigma x^2 - (\Sigma x)^2}{n} = \text{measure of variability in } X$$

$$S_{yy} = \Sigma(y - \bar{y})^2$$
$$= \frac{n\Sigma y^2 - (\Sigma y)^2}{n} = \text{measure of variability in } Y$$

Using this notation, we can express $b$ and $r$ as

$$b = \frac{n\Sigma xy - \Sigma x \Sigma y}{n\Sigma x^2 - (\Sigma x)^2} = \frac{S_{xy}}{S_{xx}}$$
$$r = \frac{n\Sigma xy - \Sigma x \Sigma y}{\sqrt{[n\Sigma x^2 - (\Sigma x)^2][n\Sigma y^2 - (\Sigma y)^2]}} = \frac{S_{xy}}{\sqrt{S_{xx}S_{yy}}}$$

Note that

$$b\frac{\sqrt{S_{xx}}}{\sqrt{S_{yy}}} = \frac{S_{xy}}{S_{xx}}\frac{\sqrt{S_{xx}}}{\sqrt{S_{yy}}} = \frac{S_{xy}}{\sqrt{S_{xx}S_{yy}}} = r$$

Thus the equation relating $b$ and $r$ is

$$r = b\frac{\sqrt{S_{xx}}}{\sqrt{S_{yy}}}$$

The practical implication of this relationship is that $b$ and $r$ always have the *same* algebraic sign. Thus a positive correlation implies a regression line with positive slope (a line that rises from left to right); a negative correlation implies a regression line with negative slope (a line that falls from left to right).

Let us now reconsider the sum of squares $SS_E$ that is being minimized in the least-squares procedure:

$$SS_E = \sum_{i=1}^{n} e_i^2 = \sum_{i=1}^{n} [y_i - (a + bx_i)]^2$$

This sum measures the variability of the data points $y_i$ about the fitted regression line $a + bx_i$. If the line closely fits the data points, then $SS_E$ will be small; otherwise, it will be large. By using the rules of summation (Appendix A),

$$SS_E = S_{yy} - bS_{xy}$$

Dividing each side of the equation by $S_{yy}$, we obtain

$$\frac{SS_E}{S_{yy}} = 1 - b\frac{S_{xy}}{S_{yy}}$$

Substituting $S_{xy}/S_{xx}$ into this equation for $b$, we have

$$\frac{SS_E}{S_{yy}} = 1 - \frac{S_{xy}^2}{S_{xx}S_{yy}}$$

Since $r = S_{xy}/\sqrt{S_{xx}S_{yy}}$, we conclude that

$$\frac{SS_E}{S_{yy}} = 1 - r^2$$

or that

$$r^2 = 1 - \frac{SS_E}{S_{yy}} = \frac{S_{yy} - SS_E}{S_{yy}}$$

Since $S_{yy}$ measures the total variation in $Y$ and $SS_E$ measures the random variation of $Y$ about the regression line, $S_{yy} - SS_E$ is a measure of the variation in $Y$ that is not random. That is, $S_{yy} - SS_E$ is a measure of the variability in $Y$ that can be attributed to a linear association with $X$.

The statistic $r^2$ is called the *coefficient of determination*. Thus, in a practical sense,

$$r^2 = \frac{\text{variation in } Y \text{ due to linearity}}{\text{total variation in } Y}$$

If we multiply $r^2$ by 100, we obtain the percentage of the variation in $Y$ that can be attributed to a linear relationship between $X$ and $Y$. Thus if $r^2$ is large, we may conclude that there is a strong linear association between $X$ and $Y$ and that predictions obtained by using the fitted regression equation should be quite good. These ideas are illustrated in Examples 11.4.1 and 11.4.2.

---

**EXAMPLE 11.4.1** □ Let us reexamine the relationship between $X$, the percentage over ideal weight, and $Y$, an individual's threshold of pain. In Example 11.3.1 we found that $r = -.33$ and interpreted this to indicate a *slight* negative correlation between the two variables. To get a better idea of the strength of the linear relationship, we compute $r^2$, the coefficient of determination. The value of this statistic is $r^2 = (-.33)^2 = .108\,9$. Multiplying by 100, we conclude that only 10.89% of the variation in $Y$ is attributed to a linear association with $X$. Since this percentage is small, clearly a correlation of $-.33$ is not really very strong. It does not indicate a strong tendency for obese individuals to exhibit a low threshold of pain, and vice versa. Also, even though a regression line can be fit to the data, it should not be expected to accurately predict the value of $Y$ based on knowledge of the value of $X$.

---

An analysis-of-variance technique is available for testing whether a straight line explains a significant amount of the observed variability in $Y$. As in any analysis-of-variance procedure, the idea is to partition the total variability in $Y$, $S_{yy}$, into components that can be attributed to recognizable sources. This can be done easily since we already established that $SS_E$, the random variability about the fitted regression line, can be written in the form

$$SS_E = S_{yy} - bS_{xy}$$

Solving this equation for $S_{yy}$, we see that

$$S_{yy} = bS_{xy} + SS_E$$

The second component on the right, $SS_E$, is called the *error*, or *residual, sum of squares;* it is a measure of the variability in $Y$ that is random or unexplained. The first component on the right, $bS_{xy}$, the *regression sum of squares,* measures the variability in $Y$ attributable to the linear association between $X$ and $Y$. The regression sum of squares is denoted $SS_R$. Thus we have partitioned $S_{yy}$ into two components:

$$\underset{\text{(total variability in } Y)}{S_{yy}} = \underset{\text{(variability in } Y \text{ due to regression on } X)}{SS_R} + \underset{\text{(unexplained, or random, variation)}}{SS_E}$$

Logically, if the assumption of linear regression is valid, then $SS_R$ should account for most of the variability in $Y$, with only a small portion being random or unexplained. Thus we should be able to use the relative sizes of $SS_R$ and $SS_E$ is some way to decide whether the assumption of linear regression is reasonable.

This can be done by making some further assumptions concerning the dependent variable $Y$. Assume that we are dealing with $k$ specific values of the independent variable $x_1, x_2, x_3, \ldots, x_k$. This implies that we are dealing with $k$ random variables $Y|x_1, Y|x_2, Y|x_3, \ldots, Y|x_k$. We assume that these variables are independent normal random variables, each with the same variance, $\sigma^2$. If linear regression is valid, then the means of these variables lie on the straight line $\mu_{Y|x} = \alpha + \beta x$. This idea is illustrated in Figure 11.11.

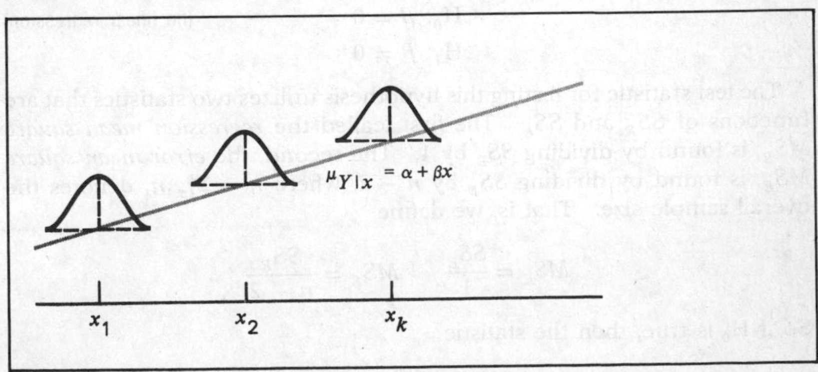


**FIGURE 11.11** Each variable $Y|x_i$ is normally distributed with the same variance.

Now assume that a random sample of size $n_i$, $i = 1, 2, \ldots, k$, is selected from each distribution. Let $Y_{ij}$ denote the $j$th element of the random sample from the distribution of $Y|x_i$. The variable $Y_{ij}$ is a random variable with mean $\alpha + \beta x_i$ and variance $\sigma^2$. Its observed value is not expected to lie exactly at the mean value, but is expected to deviate from this value by some random amount, $E_{ij}$. Thus we may write the following expression, which serves as the model for simple linear regression:

**Model**

$$Y_{ij} = \alpha + \beta x_i + E_{ij} \qquad \begin{array}{l} i = 1, 2, \ldots, k \\ j = 1, 2, \ldots, n_i \end{array}$$

$$\begin{bmatrix} \text{observed value} \\ \text{of } Y \text{ for} \\ \text{particular value} \\ \text{of } X \end{bmatrix} = \begin{bmatrix} \text{mean value of } Y \\ \text{for that value} \\ \text{of } X \\ \end{bmatrix} + \begin{bmatrix} \text{random} \\ \text{deviation} \\ \text{from mean} \\ \end{bmatrix}$$

The assumptions made concerning $Y$ imply these model assumptions:

**Model Assumptions** The random deviations $E_{ij}$ are independent normal random variables, each with mean 0 and variance $\sigma^2$.

With these assumptions it is possible to formulate the desired null and alternative hypotheses mathematically and test the null hypothesis by using $SS_R$ and $SS_E$. We wish to test

$H_0$: variation in $Y$ not explained by linear model

$H_1$: significant portion of variation in $Y$ explained by linear model

Note that if $\beta = 0$, the model becomes $Y_{ij} = \alpha + E_{ij}$. That is, if $\beta = 0$, then *all* the variability in $Y$ is assumed to be random; if $\beta \neq 0$, then at least a portion of the variability is assumed to be due to the linear regression of $Y$ on $X$. Thus the null hypothesis of no linear regression can be expressed in the form $H_0$: $\beta = 0$. So we are interested in testing

$$H_0: \beta = 0 \qquad \text{(no linear regression)}$$
$$H_1: \beta \neq 0$$

The test statistic for testing this hypothesis utilizes two statistics that are functions of $SS_R$ and $SS_E$. The first, called the *regression mean square* $MS_R$, is found by dividing $SS_R$ by 1. The second, the *error mean square* $MS_E$, is found by dividing $SS_E$ by $n - 2$, where $n = \sum_{i=1}^{k} n_i$ denotes the overall sample size. That is, we define

$$MS_R = \frac{SS_E}{1} \qquad MS_E = \frac{SS_R}{n-2}$$

So if $H_0$ is true, then the statistic

$$\frac{MS_R}{MS_E}$$

follows an $F$ distribution with 1 and $n-2$ degrees of freedom. Furthermore, if $H_0$ is true, then the observed value of this statistic should lie close to 1; otherwise, its value should be inflated. Thus the null hypothesis of no linear regression is rejected if the observed value of the $F$ ratio is too *large* to have reasonably occurred by chance.

Everything that has been said can be summarized conveniently in an analysis-of-variance table. The table includes the formulas needed to compute $S_{yy}$, the total sum of squares, and $SS_R$, the regression sum of squares. The error sum of squares $SS_E$ is obtained by subtracting $SS_R$ from $S_{yy}$. Recall that

$$S_{xy} = \frac{n\Sigma xy - \Sigma x \Sigma y}{n} \qquad S_{xx} = \frac{n\Sigma x^2 - (\Sigma x)^2}{n}$$

$$S_{yy} = \frac{n\Sigma y^2 - (\Sigma y)^2}{n} \qquad b = \frac{S_{xy}}{S_{xx}}$$

ANALYSIS OF VARIANCE: SIMPLE LINEAR REGRESSION

| SOURCE OF VARIATION | DEGREES OF FREEDOM $DF$ | SUM OF SQUARES $SS$ | MEAN SQUARE $MS$ | $F$ RATIO |
|---|---|---|---|---|
| Regression (model) | 1 | $bS_{xy}$ | $\frac{SS_R}{1}$ | $F_{1,n-2} = \frac{MS_R}{MS_E}$ |
| Error | $n-2$ | $S_{yy} - bS_{xy}$ | $\frac{SS_E}{n-2}$ | |
| **Total** | $n-1$ | $S_{yy}$ | | |

Now we show how to use the analysis-of-variance procedure to test the hypothesis of no linear regression for the data of Example 11.1.4.

**EXAMPLE 11.4.2** □ In Example 11.1.4, the variables of interest are $X$ and $Y$, the shell height and length, respectively, in the limpet *Patelloida pygmaea*. The scattergram indicates that the assumption of linear regression is valid. We now test that assumption statistically, instead of relying solely on the visual pattern of the data. These quantities are needed:

$$\Sigma x = 56.6 \qquad \Sigma y = 151.1 \qquad \Sigma xy = 311.96$$
$$\Sigma x^2 = 117.68 \qquad \Sigma y^2 = 832.85 \qquad S_{xy} = 6.52$$
$$S_{xx} = 3.27 \qquad S_{yy} = 17.45 \qquad n = 28$$

From these quantities we may conclude that

$$\hat{\alpha} = a = 1.36 \qquad r = .863\,8$$
$$\hat{\beta} = b = 1.99 \qquad r^2 = .746\,1$$

Since $r^2 = .746\,1$, we may conclude that 74.61% of the variation in $Y$ can be attributed to a linear association with $X$. Is this percentage high enough to conclude that a significant amount of the variability in $Y$ is explained by the linear model?

To answer this question, we test

$$\begin{aligned} H_0&: \beta = 0 \quad \text{(no linear regression)} \\ H_1&: \beta \neq 0 \end{aligned}$$

using the analysis-of-variance technique. Here is the ANOVA table:

ANOVA

| SOURCE | $DF$ | $SS$ | $MS$ | $F$ |
|---|---|---|---|---|
| Regression | 1 | $bS_{xy} = 12.97$ | 12.97 | $\frac{12.97}{.17} = 76.29$ |
| Error | 26 | $17.45 - 12.97 = 4.48$ | $\frac{4.48}{26} = .17$ | |
| **Total** | 27 | $S_{yy} = 17.45$ | | |

We now compare the observed value of the $F$ statistic, 76.29, with the tabled probabilities of the $F_{1,\,26}$ distribution. Since the critical point for an $\alpha = .01$ test is 7.72, and since 76.29 is much larger than this, we can reject $H_0$ and conclude that, as expected, the assumption of linear regression is valid. Practically speaking, this means that predictions based on the estimated regression line

$$\hat{y} = 1.36 + 1.99x$$

should be acceptable.

Note that when the null hypothesis of no linear regression is rejected, we have concluded that a significant portion of the variability in $Y$ has been explained by the linear model. This does not mean that the linear model is necessarily the best model to use; it does mean that it is at least reasonable.

## EXERCISES 11.4

1. A study of body characteristics and performance is conducted among master- and first-class Olympic weight lifters. Two variables studied are $X$, the subject's body weight, and $Y$, his best reported clean and jerk lift. These data (in pounds) are obtained:

| $X$ | $Y$ | $X$ | $Y$ |
|---|---|---|---|
| 134 | 185 | 190 | 336 |
| 138 | 238 | 190 | 339 |
| 154 | 260 | 205 | 341 |
| 178 | 290 | 205 | 358 |
| 176 | 312 | 206 | 359 |

**a.** Plot a scattergram for these data. Based on the scattergram, do you expect $r$ to lie close to 1, −1, or 0?

**b.** Find $\Sigma x$, $\Sigma x^2$, $\Sigma y$, $\Sigma y^2$, $\Sigma xy$, and $r$.

**c.** Find and interpret the coefficient of determination.

**d.** Test the appropriateness of the linear regression model. If it is appropriate, find the estimated line of regression of $Y$ on $X$ and use this to estimate the best clean and jerk lift for a weight lifter who weighs 200 pounds.

**2.** A study of the body's ability to absorb iron and lead is conducted by using radioactive tracer techniques. Ten subjects participate in the study. Each is given an identical oral dose of iron (ferrous sulfate) and lead (lead-203 chloride). After 12 days, the amount of each compound retained in the system is measured, and from this the percentage absorbed by the body is determined. These data result:

| $X$ (PERCENTAGE IRON ABSORBED) | $Y$ (PERCENTAGE LEAD ABSORBED) |
|---|---|
| 17 | 8 |
| 22 | 17 |
| 35 | 18 |
| 43 | 25 |
| 80 | 58 |
| 85 | 59 |
| 91 | 41 |
| 92 | 30 |
| 96 | 43 |
| 100 | 58 |

**a.** Plot a scattergram for these data. Based on the scattergram, do you expect $r$ to lie close to 1, −1, or 0?

**b.** Find $\Sigma x$, $\Sigma x^2$, $\Sigma y$, $\Sigma y^2$, $\Sigma xy$, and $r$.

**c.** Find and interpret the coefficient of determination.

**d.** Test the appropriateness of the linear regression model. If it is appropriate, estimate the true regression line and use it to predict the percentage of iron absorbed by an individual whose system absorbs 15% of the lead ingested.

3. Test the appropriateness of the linear regression model, using the data of Example 11.3.1. Did you anticipate this result?
4. a. Find and interpret the coefficient of determination for the data of Exercise 11.2.4.
   b. Test the appropriateness of the linear regression model, using the data of Exercise 11.2.4. Do you think that the prediction given in Exercise 11.2.4*d* is likely to be accurate? Explain.
5. a. Use the data of Exercise 11.3.5 to find the coefficient of determination for variables $X$, the nitrate reading taken by an older manual technique, and $Y$, the reading taken by a new automated method. On the basis of this value, do you think that the new method will accurately reflect the readings that would have been obtained with the older technique?
   b. Test the appropriateness of the linear regression model, using the data of Exercise 11.3.5. If the model is appropriate, find the estimated line of regression of $Y$ on $X$ and use it to predict the reading that would be obtained by using the automated technique for a water sample whose manual reading is 100.

---

**Computing Supplement**

The SAS program PROC GLM is used to test for the appropriateness of the linear model by analysis of variance. It also computes the coefficient of determination $r^2$. We use the data of Examples 11.4.2 and 11.1.4.

| **Statement** | **Function** |
|---|---|
| DATA LIMPET; | names data set |
| INPUT HEIGHT LENGTH; | each card will contain two values; height, then length |
| CARDS; | signals beginning of data |
| .9 3.1<br>1.5 3.6<br>1.6 4.3<br>. . . .<br>2.7 6.3 | data |
| ; | signals end of data |
| PROC PLOT;<br>PLOT LENGTH*HEIGHT; | asks for scattergram with variable length plotted on vertical axis |
| TITLE LIMPET STUDY; | titles output |
| PROC GLM; | calls for general linear models procedure |
| MODEL LENGTH=HEIGHT; | identifies left variable, LENGTH, as dependent, or response, variable |

The output of this program is shown on pages 369 and 370. Note that the source that we referred to as "regression" is called MODEL by SAS (1). The value of the coefficient of determination $r^2$ is given by (2). The value of the $F$ statistic used to test

$$\begin{aligned} H_0&: \beta = 0 \qquad \text{(no linear regression)} \\ H_1&: \beta \neq 0 \end{aligned}$$

and its $P$ value are given by (3) and (4), respectively. Note that the $F$ value agrees quite well with that obtained by using a handheld calculator. The estimates for $\alpha$ and $\beta$ are given by (5) and (6), respectively.

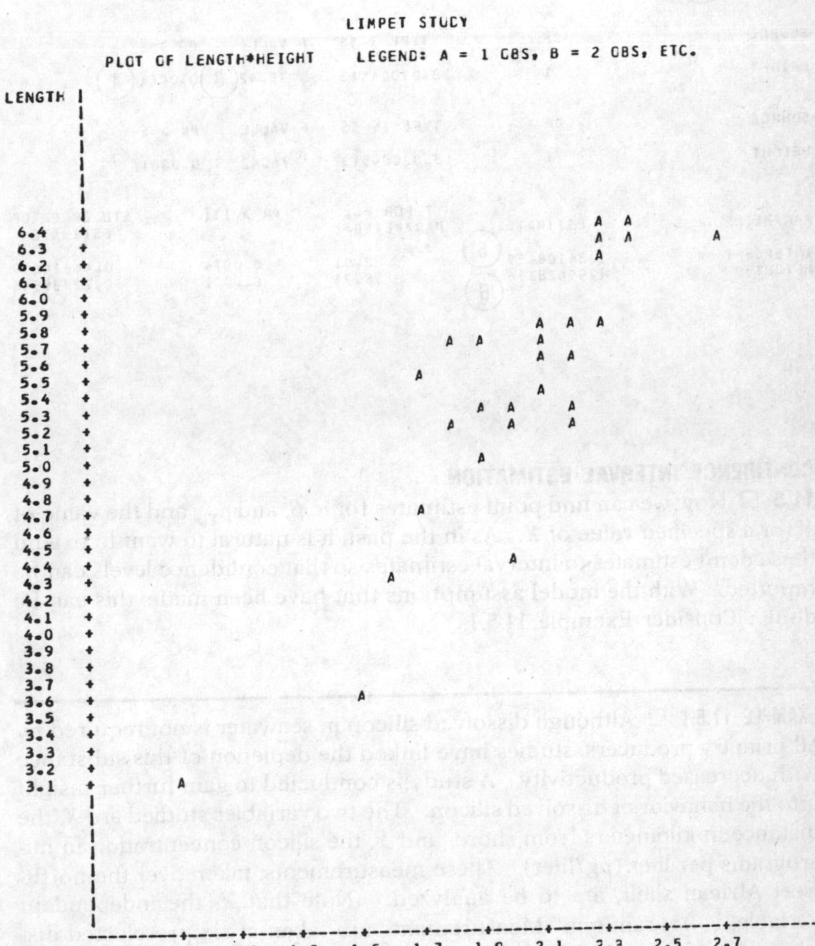

```
                                LIMPET STUDY

                        GENERAL LINEAR MODELS PROCEDURE

DEPENDENT VARIABLE: LENGTH

SOURCE              DF      SUM OF SQUARES        MEAN SQUARE        F VALUE

MODEL (1)            1         13.02004513        13.02004513          76.42

ERROR               26          4.42959773         0.17036914        PR > F

CORRECTED TOTAL     27         17.44964286                            0.0001

R-SQUARE            C.V.           STD DEV             LENGTH MEAN

0.746150 (2)      7.6487        0.41275797              5.39642857

SOURCE              DF           TYPE I SS    F VALUE     PR > F

HEIGHT               1         13.02004513    76.42 (3)   0.0001 (4)

SOURCE              DF          TYPE IV SS    F VALUE     PR > F

HEIGHT               1         13.02004513    76.42       0.0001

                                 T FOR H0:      PR > |T|        STD ERROR OF
PARAMETER         ESTIMATE      PARAMETER=0                        ESTIMATE

INTERCEPT       1.36108439 (5)      2.91         0.0074          0.46814859
HEIGHT          1.99628334 (6)      8.74         0.0001          0.22835546
```

## *CONFIDENCE INTERVAL ESTIMATION

**11.5** □ Now we can find point estimates for $\alpha$, $\beta$, and $\mu_{Y|x}$ and the value of $Y$ for a specified value of $X$. As in the past, it is natural to want to extend these point estimates to interval estimates so that confidence levels can be reported. With the model assumptions that have been made, this can be done. Consider Example 11.5.1.

---

**EXAMPLE 11.5.1** □ Although dissolved silicon in seawater is not required by all primary producers, studies have linked the depletion of this substance with decreased productivity. A study is conducted to gain further insight into the behavior of dissolved silicon. The two variables studied are $X$, the distance in kilometers from shore, and $Y$, the silicon concentration in micrograms per liter ($\mu$g/liter). These measurements, taken over the northwest African shelf, are to be analyzed. (Note that $X$, the independent variable, is *not* random. Measurements are taken at six preselected distances from shore with four measurements taken at each distance.)

| $x$ | $y$ | $x$ | $y$ | $x$ | $y$ |
|---|---|---|---|---|---|
| 5 | 6.1 | 25 | 3.7 | 42 | 3.4 |
| 5 | 6.2 | 25 | 3.7 | 42 | 3.6 |
| 5 | 6.1 | 25 | 3.8 | 42 | 3.5 |
| 5 | 6.0 | 25 | 3.9 | 42 | 3.2 |
| 15 | 5.2 | 32 | 3.9 | 55 | 3.7 |
| 15 | 5.0 | 32 | 3.8 | 55 | 3.9 |
| 15 | 4.9 | 32 | 3.9 | 55 | 3.6 |
| 15 | 5.1 | 32 | 3.7 | 55 | 3.8 |

The scattergram for these data is shown in Figure 11.12. There does appear to be a downward linear trend. Therefore, we anticipate a negative slope for thc estimated line of regression. We first test the appropriateness of the linear regression model. For these data,

$$\Sigma x = 696 \qquad \Sigma y = 103.7 \qquad \Sigma xy = 2692.5$$

$$\Sigma x^2 = 26{,}752 \qquad \Sigma y^2 = 469.81 \qquad S_{xy} = -314.8$$

$$\bar{x} = 29 \qquad \bar{y} = 4.32 \qquad b = \frac{S_{xy}}{S_{xx}} = -.048$$

$$S_{xx} = 6568 \qquad S_{yy} = 21.74 \qquad a = \bar{y} - b\bar{x} = 5.71$$

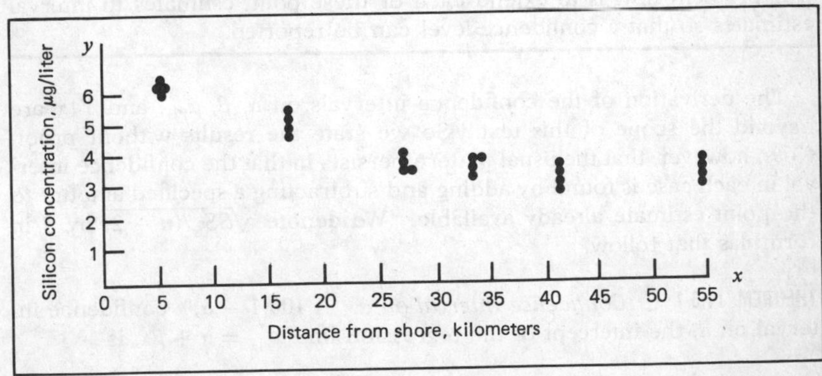


**FIGURE 11.12** Scattergram of distance from the shore versus silicon concentration in waters over the northwest African shelf.

The analysis-of-variance table is as follows:

ANOVA

| SOURCE | *DF* | *SS* | *MS* | *F* |
|---|---|---|---|---|
| Regression | 1 | 15.11 | 15.11 | 50.37 |
| Error | 22 | 6.63 | .30 | |
| **Total** | 23 | 21.74 | | |

The critical point for an $\alpha = .01$ test of

$$H_0: \beta = 0 \qquad \text{(regression is not linear)}$$
$$H_1: \beta \neq 0$$

is 7.95, based on the $F_{1,\,22}$ statistic. Since 50.37, the observed value of the $F$ ratio, exceeds this critical value, we may reject $H_0$ and conclude that the assumption of linearity is warranted. We now have *point* estimates for $\alpha$ and $\beta$, namely, $\widehat{\alpha} = a = 5.71$ and $\widehat{\beta} = b = -.048$.

Assume that we are particularly interested in the silicon concentration at a distance of 10 kilometers from shore. Two questions can be asked: What is the *mean* concentration at this distance? and If a *single* water sample is drawn at this distance, what will be the silicon concentration for this sample? These questions already can be answered by using point estimation. In particular, we are being asked to estimate $\mu_{Y|x=10}$ and $Y|_{x=10}$. Each of these estimates is the same, namely,

$$\begin{aligned}\widehat{\mu}_{Y|x} &= \widehat{y} = a + bx \\ &= 5.71 - .048x = 5.23\ \mu\text{g/liter}\end{aligned}$$

Our problem now is to extend each of these point estimates to interval estimates so that a confidence level can be reported.

---

The derivation of the confidence intervals on $\alpha$, $\beta$, $\mu_{Y|x}$, and $Y|x$ are beyond the scope of this text. So we state the results without proof. Note, however, that the usual pattern persists in that the confidence interval in each case is found by adding and subtracting a specified amount to the point estimate already available. We denote $\sqrt{SS_E/(n-2)}$ by $S$ in formulas that follow.

**THEOREM 11.5.1** □ *Confidence Interval on α.* A $100(1-\alpha)\%$ confidence interval on $\alpha$, the intercept of the regression line $\mu_{Y|x} = \alpha + \beta x$, is

$$a \pm t_{\alpha/2} \frac{S\sqrt{\Sigma x^2}}{\sqrt{nS_{xx}}}$$

where the point $t_{\alpha/2}$ is a point from the $T$ distribution with $n - 2$ degrees of freedom.

---

**EXAMPLE 11.5.2** □ To construct a 95% confidence interval on $\alpha$ based on the data of Example 11.5.1, we need only substitute the appropriate values into the formula

$$a \pm t_{\alpha/2} \frac{S\sqrt{\Sigma x^2}}{\sqrt{nS_{xx}}}$$

For the data given,

$$\Sigma x^2 = 26{,}752 \qquad n = 24 \qquad a = 5.71$$

$$S_{xx} = 6568 \qquad S = \sqrt{\frac{SS_E}{n-2}} = \sqrt{.30} = .547\,7$$

The point $t_{\alpha/2} = t_{.025} = 2.074$ is found from the table of the $T$ distribution with $n - 2 = 22$ degrees of freedom. The confidence interval is therefore

$$5.71 \pm 2.074 \frac{\sqrt{.3}\sqrt{26{,}752}}{\sqrt{24(6568)}} = 5.71 \pm .47$$

That is, we can be 95% confident that the intercept of the regression line lies between 5.24 and 6.18.

---

**THEOREM 11.5.2** □ *Confidence Interval on $\beta$.* A $100(1 - \alpha)\%$ confidence interval on $\beta$, the slope of the regression line $\mu_{Y|x} = \alpha + \beta x$, is

$$b + t_{\alpha/2} \frac{S}{\sqrt{S_{xx}}}$$

where the point $t_{\alpha/2}$ is a point from the $T$ distribution with $n - 2$ degrees of freedom.

---

**EXAMPLE 11.5.3** □ A 95% confidence interval on $\beta$ based on the data of Example 11.5.1 is found by substituting the values $t_{\alpha/2} = 2.074$, $S = \sqrt{.3}$, $S_{xx} = 6568$, and $b = -.048$ into

$$b \pm t_{\alpha/2} \frac{S}{\sqrt{S_{xx}}}$$

The resulting confidence interval is

$$-.048 \pm 2.074 \frac{\sqrt{.3}}{\sqrt{6568}} = -.048 \pm .014$$

We can be 95% confident that the slope of the regression line lies between −.062 and −.034. Note that the analysis-of-variance procedure already has indicated that $\beta \neq 0$. Thus it should not be surprising that the confidence interval on $\beta$ does *not* contain the number 0.

---

**THEOREM 11.5.3** □ *Confidence Interval on* $\mu_{Y|x}$. A $100(1-\alpha)\%$ confidence interval on $\mu_{Y|x}$, the mean value of $Y$ for a specific value $x$ of $X$, is given by

$$\widehat{\mu}_{Y|x} \pm t_{\alpha/2} S \sqrt{\frac{1}{n} + \frac{(x-\bar{x})^2}{S_{xx}}}$$

where the point $t_{\alpha/2}$ is a point from the $T$ distribution with $n-2$ degrees of freedom.

---

**EXAMPLE 11.5.4** □ A 95% confidence interval on the mean silicon concentration drawn 10 kilometers from shore is found by substituting the values $t_{\alpha/2} = 2.074$, $S = \sqrt{.3}$, $n = 24$, $x = 10$, $\bar{x} = 29$, $S_{xx} = 6568$, and $\widehat{\mu}_{Y|x} = 5.23$ into

$$\widehat{\mu}_{Y|x} \pm t_{\alpha/2} S \sqrt{\frac{1}{n} + \frac{(x-\bar{x})^2}{S_{xx}}}$$

The resulting confidence interval is

$$5.23 \pm 2.074\sqrt{.3}\sqrt{\frac{1}{24} + \frac{(10-29)^2}{6568}} = 5.23 \pm .35$$

We can be 95% confident that the *mean* silicon concentration at this distance is between 4.88 and 5.58 $\mu$g/liter.

---

**THEOREM 11.5.4** □ *Confidence Interval on* $Y|x$. A $100(1-\alpha)\%$ confidence interval on $Y|x$, the value of $Y$ for a specific value $x$ of $X$, is given by

$$\widehat{y} \pm t_{\alpha/2} S \sqrt{1 + \frac{1}{n} + \frac{(x-\bar{x})^2}{S_{xx}}}$$

where the point $t_{\alpha/2}$ is a point from the $T$ distribution with $n-2$ degrees of freedom.

---

**EXAMPLE 11.5.5** □ A 95% confidence interval on the silicon concentration for a single water sample drawn 10 kilometers from shore is found by substituting the values $t_{\alpha/2} = 2.074$, $S = \sqrt{.3}$, $n = 24$, $x = 10$, $\bar{x} = 29$, $S_{xx} = 6568$, and $\widehat{y} = 5.23$ into

$$\widehat{y} \pm t_{\alpha/2} S \sqrt{1 + \frac{1}{n} + \frac{(x-\bar{x})^2}{S_{xx}}}$$

The resulting interval is

$$5.23 \pm 2.074\sqrt{.3}\sqrt{1 + \frac{1}{24} + \frac{(10 - 29)^2}{6568}} = 5.23 \pm 1.19$$

We can be 95% confident that the silicon concentration for the next sample taken 10 kilometers from shore will be between 4.04 and 6.42 $\mu$g/liter.

## EXERCISES 11.5

1. These data are obtained on $X$, the latitude of the natural breeding range, and $Y$, the length of the breeding season in days, of 11 species of diving ducks:

| $x$ | $y$ |
|---|---|
| 29 | 112 |
| 42 | 98 |
| 45 | 58 |
| 45 | 68 |
| 50 | 28 |
| 50 | 46 |
| 53 | 42 |
| 54 | 50 |
| 55 | 18 |
| 60 | 51 |
| 65 | 49 |

   **a.** Plot a scattergram for these data. Based on the scattergram, do you feel that linear regression is applicable?
   **b.** Use the analysis-of-variance procedure to test the appropriateness of the linear model.
   **c.** Find point estimates for $\alpha$ and $\beta$.
   **d.** Find 95% confidence intervals on $\alpha$ and $\beta$.
   **e.** Find a point estimate for the mean length of the breeding season for birds whose natural breeding range is at a latitude of 35 degrees. Find a 95% confidence interval on this parameter.
   **f.** Find a point estimate for the length of the breeding season for a single bird whose natural breeding range is at a latitude of 35 degrees. Find a 95% confidence interval on this predicted value.

2. Teaching diabetics to measure their own blood glucose has been of great benefit. A new technique that is less expensive than the current procedure is under investigation. The technique uses a glucose oxidase stick. The stick develops two colors

simultaneously, and these colors are matched by eye to a chart that gives the glucose level. If this procedure can be shown to be accurate, it can be put into widespread use. These data are obtained on $X$, the blood glucose level as measured by a diabetic patient using the new glucose oxidase stick, and $Y$, the patient's blood glucose level as measured in a laboratory test.

(DATA ARE GIVEN IN MILLIMOLES PER LITER.)

| $x$ | $y$ | $x$ | $y$ | $x$ | $y$ | $x$ | $y$ |
|---|---|---|---|---|---|---|---|
| 1.3 | 2.4 | 3.2 | 4.4 | 7.0 | 7.7 | 15.0 | 14.9 |
| 2.0 | 3.0 | 3.6 | 4.3 | 8.0 | 8.0 | 15.0 | 13.8 |
| 2.4 | 2.3 | 3.7 | 4.3 | 8.0 | 10.0 | 17.5 | 17.6 |
| 2.6 | 3.0 | 3.7 | 5.0 | 10.0 | 10.0 | 18.7 | 17.5 |
| 2.5 | 2.2 | 3.8 | 4.4 | 10.2 | 9.5 | 6.0 | 6.0 |
| 2.6 | 2.4 | 4.4 | 4.5 | 10.2 | 11.2 | 8.7 | 8.8 |
| 2.7 | 2.5 | 4.3 | 5.0 | 12.5 | 11.0 | 5.6 | 5.7 |
| 3.0 | 3.8 | 5.0 | 4.5 | 11.3 | 13.0 | 9.1 | 9.0 |
| 3.7 | 2.5 | 5.0 | 6.2 | 13.0 | 13.1 | 16.2 | 12.5 |
| 3.7 | 3.5 | 6.3 | 6.2 | 14.5 | 13.8 | 9.0 | 14.0 |

For these data,

$$\Sigma x = 295 \qquad \Sigma y = 303.5 \qquad \Sigma xy = 3073.55$$
$$\Sigma x^2 = 3090.96 \qquad \Sigma y^2 = 3120.59$$
$$\bar{x} = 7.375 \qquad \bar{y} = 7.587$$

**a.** Plot a scattergram for the data. Based on the scattergram, do you feel that there is a strong positive correlation between the blood glucose level reported by the patient and the glucose level measured in the laboratory?
**b.** Find $r$ and the coefficient of determination.
**c.** Use the analysis-of-variance procedure to test the appropriateness of the linear model.
**d.** Find point estimates for $\alpha$ and $\beta$.
**e.** Find 90% confidence intervals on $\alpha$ and $\beta$.
**f.** Find a point estimate for the laboratory-reported glucose level of a patient who reports the level to be 4.0 mmol/liter. Find a 90% confidence interval on this value.

---

**Computing Supplement**

We utilize the data of Example 11.5.1 to show how to use PROC GLM to obtain confidence intervals on $\mu_{Y|x_0}$ and $Y|x_0$.

| **Statement** | **Function** |
|---|---|
| DATA SILICON; | names data set |
| INPUT DIST Y1–Y4; | each card will contain value for distance from shore (DIST) and all four values of variable $Y$ (silicon concentration) |
| ARRAY OUT Y1–Y4;<br>DO OVER OUT;<br>Y=OUT;<br>OUTPUT;<br>END; | these steps allow data to be read without having to punch value of DIST for each value of dependent variable |
| CARDS; | signals that data follow |
| 5 6.1 6.2 6.1 6.0<br>15 5.5 5.0 4.9 5.1<br>. . . . . | data |
| 55 3.7 3.9 3.6 3.8 | last actual data reported |
| 10 • • • • | allows us to predict value of $Y$ when DIST is 10; dot indicates that we have ***no*** reported values of $Y$ at this distance |
| ; | signals end of data |
| PROC PLOT;<br>PLOT Y*DIST; | asks for scattergram with $Y$ on vertical axis |
| TITLE1 CONFIDENCE INTERVALS;<br>TITLE2 FOR REGRESSION PARAMETERS; | titles the output |
| PROC GLM; | calls for general linear models procedure |
| MODEL Y=DIST/P CLM; | identifies $Y$ as dependent variable; asks for predicted values to be printed for each value of independent variable DIST; asks for confidence interval on $\mu_{Y\|x}$ for each value of DIST |

The output of this program is shown on pages 378 to 380. Note that the scattergram indicates a linear trend. The value of the $F$ statistic used to test the null hypothesis of no linear relationship is given by (1). Its $P$ value is given by (2). Since this $P$ value is small, we reject $H_0$ and conclude that linear regression is applicable. The estimated values of $\alpha$ and $\beta$ are given by (3) and (4), respectively. By using these values, when the distance from shore is 10 kilometers, the predicted value of $Y$ is given by (5). The lower and upper bounds for a 95% confidence interval on the mean silicon concentration at a distance of 10 kilometers are shown by (6) and (7), respectively. If we want a confidence interval on the value of the silicon concentration at 10 kilometers rather than the *mean* value when DIST=10, we make one change in the above program. We change the model statement to read

```
MODEL Y=DIST/P CLI;
```

Although the printout does not give the bounds for confidence intervals on $\alpha$ and $\beta$, it does give most of the quantities needed to construct these intervals. In particular, $a$ and $b$ are given by (3) and (4), respectively; $S$ is given by (8); the term $S\sqrt{\Sigma x^2}/\sqrt{nS_{xx}}$ needed to find a confidence interval on $\alpha$ is shown by (9); and the term $S/\sqrt{S_{xx}}$ needed for a confidence interval on $\beta$ is found at (10). Thus to construct a confidence interval on either parameter, all you must do is find the appropriate value for $t_{\alpha/2}$ and apply the formulas of Theorems 11.5.1 and 11.5.2. Also note that, unless specified otherwise, the confidence intervals constructed by GLM are 95%. If you want 99% (or 90%) intervals, the model statement should read

MODEL Y=DIST/P CLM ALPHA=.01 (or .10);

CONFIDENCE INTERVALS
FOR REGRESSION PARAMETERS

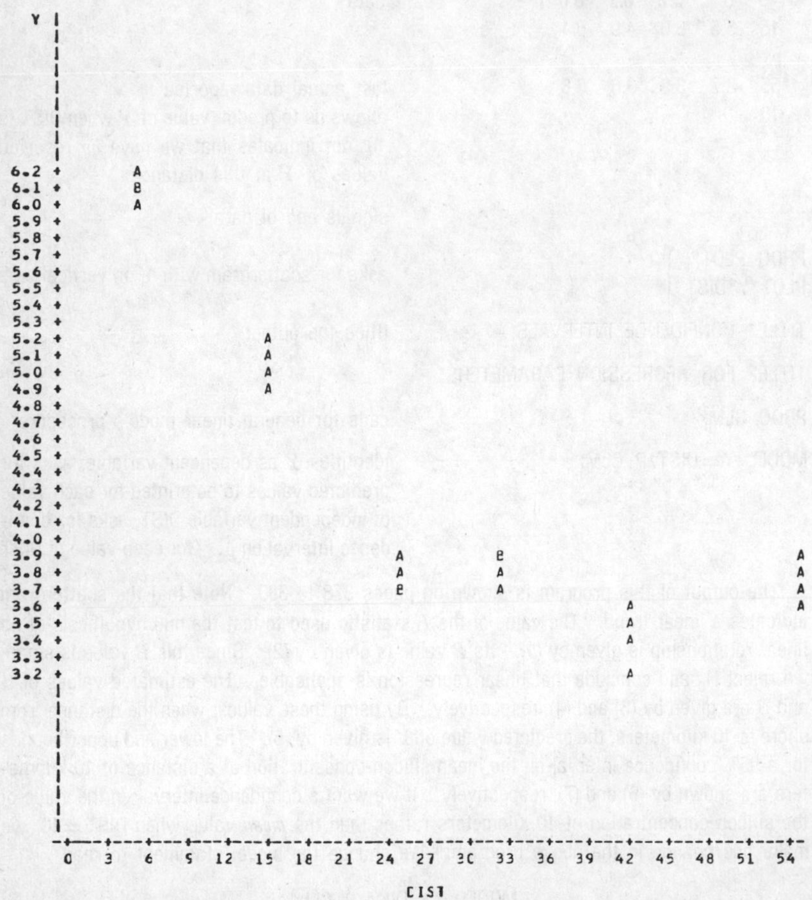


NOTE:     4 OBS HAD MISSING VALUES

```
                         CONFIDENCE INTERVALS
                       FOR REGRESSION PARAMETERS

                    GENERAL LINEAR MODELS PROCEDURE

DEPENDENT VARIABLE: Y

SOURCE              DF      SUM OF SQUARES       MEAN SQUARE         F VALUE

MODEL                1         15.08816078       15.08816078           49.91  (1)

ERROR               22          6.65142255        0.30233739          PR > F  (2)

CORRECTED TOTAL     23         21.73958333                            0.0001

R-SQUARE          C.V.             STD DEV            Y MEAN

0.694041       12.7256          0.54985215 (8)    4.32083333

SOURCE              DF           TYPE I SS    F VALUE     PR > F

DIST                 1         15.08816078      49.91     0.0001

SOURCE              DF          TYPE IV SS    F VALUE     PR > F

DIST                 1         15.08816078      49.91     0.0001

                                         T FOR H0:    PR > |T|       STD ERROR OF
PARAMETER               ESTIMATE       PARAMETER=0                     ESTIMATE
                                  (3)                                          (9)
INTERCEPT             5.71078461             25.21      0.0001         0.22651755
DIST                 -0.04792935             -7.06      0.0001         0.00678468
                                  (4)                                          (10)

OBSERVATION             OBSERVED            PREDICTED          LOWER 95% CLM
                                             RESIDUAL          UPPER 95% CLM

      1               3.70000000           4.51255075             4.27307743
                                          -0.81255075             4.75202407
      2               3.70000000           4.51255075             4.27307743
                                          -0.81255075             4.75202407
      3               3.80000000           4.51255075             4.27307743
                                          -0.71255075             4.75202407
      4               3.90000000           4.51255075             4.27307743
                                          -0.61255075             4.75202407
      5               3.90000000           4.17704527             3.94048317
                                          -0.27704527             4.41360737
      6               3.80000000           4.17704527             3.94048317
                                          -0.37704527             4.41360737
      7               3.90000000           4.17704527             3.94048317
                                          -0.27704527             4.41360737
      8               3.70000000           4.17704527             3.94048317
                                          -0.47704527             4.41360737
      9               3.40000000           3.69775173             3.40171453
                                          -0.29775173             3.99378892

     10               3.60000000           3.69775173             3.40171453
                                          -0.09775173             3.99378892
     11               3.50000000           3.69775173             3.40171453
                                          -0.19775173             3.99378892
     12               3.20000000           3.69775173             3.40171453
                                          -0.49775173             3.99378892
     13               6.10000000           5.47113784             5.06099781
                                           0.62886216             5.88127787
     14               6.20000000           5.47113784             5.06099781
                                           0.72886216             5.88127787
     15               6.10000000           5.47113784             5.06099781
                                           0.62886216             5.88127787
     16               6.00000000           5.47113784             5.06099781
                                           0.52886216             5.88127787
     17               5.20000000           4.99184430             4.68691248
                                           0.20815570             5.29677611
     18               5.00000000           4.99184430             4.68691248
                                           0.00815570             5.29677611
```

CONFIDENCE INTERVALS
FOR REGRESSION PARAMETERS

GENERAL LINEAR MODELS PROCEDURE

DEPENDENT VARIABLE: Y

| OBSERVATION | OBSERVED | PREDICTED<br>RESIDUAL | LOWER 95% CLM<br>UPPER 95% CLM |
|---|---|---|---|
| 19 | 4.90000000 | 4.99184430<br>-0.09184430 | 4.68691248<br>5.29677611 |
| 20 | 5.10000000 | 4.99184430<br>0.10815570 | 4.68691248<br>5.29677611 |
| 21 | 3.70000000 | 3.07467012<br>0.62532988 | 2.64106593<br>3.50827430 |
| 22 | 3.90000000 | 3.07467012<br>0.82532988 | 2.64106593<br>3.50827430 |
| 23 | 3.60000000 | 3.07467012<br>0.52532988 | 2.64106593<br>3.50827430 |
| 24 | 3.80000000 | 3.07467012<br>0.72532988 | 2.64106593<br>3.50827430 |
| 25 * | . | 5.23149107<br>. | 4.87702007<br>5.58596207 (6) |
| 26 * | . | 5.23149107 (5)<br>. | 4.87702007<br>5.58596207 |
| 27 * | . | 5.23149107<br>. | 4.87702007 (7)<br>5.58596207 |
| 28 * | . | 5.23149107<br>. | 4.87702007<br>5.58596207 |

* OBSERVATION WAS NOT USED IN THIS ANALYSIS

| | |
|---|---|
| SUM OF RESIDUALS | 0.00000000 |
| SUM OF SQUARED RESIDUALS | 6.65142255 |
| SUM OF SQUARED RESIDUALS - ERROR SS | -0.00000000 |
| PRESS STATISTIC | 8.17395402 |
| FIRST ORDER AUTOCORRELATION | 0.73835425 |
| DURBIN-WATSON D | 0.34493233 |

# CATEGORICAL DATA

# 12.

In this chapter we are concerned with the analysis of data characterized by the fact that each observation in the data set can be classed as falling into exactly one of several mutually exclusive "cells," or categories. Interest centers on the number of observations falling into each category. The statistical problem is to determine whether the observed category frequencies tend to support or refute a stated hypothesis. We are concerned with two problems in particular:

1. Testing to see whether a set of observations was drawn from a specified probability distribution

2. Testing to see whether there is an association between variables used for classification purposes

The statistical procedures used in each problem utilize the *multinomial* distribution. This distribution is described briefly now.

## MULTINOMIAL DISTRIBUTION

**12.1** □ To develop the definition of a multinomial random variable we need to consider first the idea of a multinomial trial.

**Definition 12.1.1** *Multinomial Trial.* A *multinomial trial* with parameters $p_1$, $p_2, \ldots, p_k$ is a trial that can result in exactly one of $k$ possible outcomes. The probability that outcome $i$ will occur on a given trial is $p_i$ for $i = 1, 2, 3, \ldots, k$.

Note that since parameters $p_1, p_2, \ldots, p_k$ are probabilities, they each lie between 0 and 1, inclusive. Furthermore, they must sum to 1.

---

**EXAMPLE 12.1.1** □ The blood-type distribution in the general U.S. population is type A, 41%; type B, 9%; type AB, 4%; and type O, 46%. One individual is selected at random and the blood type noted. Since exactly one of four possible outcomes can result, this experiment can be viewed as constituting a single multinomial trial with parameters $p_1 = .41$, $p_2 = .09$,

$p_3 = .04$, and $p_4 = .46$. Note that these probabilities sum to 1.00, as required.

---

**Definition 12.1.2** *Multinomial Random Variable.* Let an experiment consist of $n$ independent and identical multinomial trials with parameters $p_1, p_2, \ldots, p_k$. Let $X_i$ denote the number of trials that result in outcome $i$ for $i = 1, 2, \ldots, k$. The $k$-tuple $(X_1, X_2, \ldots, X_k)$ is called a *multinomial random variable* with parameters $n, p_1, p_2, \ldots, p_k$.

---

**EXAMPLE 12.1.2** □ Assume that a random sample of 10 individuals is selected and the blood type of each noted. This experiment can be viewed as consisting of $n = 10$ independent multinomial trials, each with parameters $p_1 = .41$, $p_2 = .09$, $p_3 = .04$, and $p_4 = .46$. (See Example 12.1.1.) Let $X_1$ denote the number of individuals in the sample with type A blood; $X_2$, the number with type B; $X_3$, the number with type AB; and $X_4$, the number with type O. The 4-tuple $(X_1, X_2, X_3, X_4)$ is a multinomial random variable with parameters 10, .41, .09, .04, and .46.

---

Consider a single multinomial trial and any fixed outcome $i$. This trial either does or does not result in outcome $i$. If outcome $i$ does occur, we consider the trial a *success;* otherwise, it is a *failure.* Thus the probability of success is $p_i$, and the probability of failure is $1 - p_i$. Consider now a series of $n$ independent and identical multinomial trials. Let $X_i$ denote the number of trials that result in outcome $i$. In fact, $X_i$ denotes the number of successes in $n$ independent trials, each with probability $p_i$ of success. Therefore, $X_i$ is a binomial random variable with parameters $n$ and $p_i$. From the discussion of Chapter 5, we know, then, that for each $i$, $E[X_i] = np_i$. This result plays an important role in analyzing categorical data in the following sections, and it is illustrated in Example 12.1.3.

---

**EXAMPLE 12.1.3** □ In a random sample of 10 individuals, the expected number falling into each of the blood groups, based on the percentages of Example 12.1.1, are

$$E[X_1] = np_1 = 10(.41) = 4.1$$
$$E[X_2] = np_2 = 10(.09) = .9$$
$$E[X_3] = np_3 = 10(.04) = .4$$
$$E[X_4] = np_4 = 10(.46) = 4.6$$

That is, for samples of size 10, we would expect *on the average* to see 4.1 with type A blood, .9 with type B, .4 with type AB, and 4.6 with type O.

---

## EXERCISES 12.1

1. Based on recent information, it is thought that 40% of all people in the United States between the ages of 10 and 18 do not drink at all, 45% drink occasionally, and the rest drink frequently. A random sample of 75 is selected. If these figures are accurate, how many would you expect to see in each category?
2. A study is run to determine whether the general public favors the construction of a dam for the generation of electricity and flood control. It is thought that 40% favor dam construction, 30% are neutral, 20% oppose the dam, and the rest have given the issue no thought. A random sample of 150 individuals in the affected area is selected and interviewed. If the above figures accurately reflect public opinion, how many individuals are expected in each category? If in the sample 42 are in favor, 61 are neutral, 33 are opposed, and the rest have given the issue no thought, do you think, on an intuitive basis, that the proposed percentages have been refuted? Explain briefly.
3. A medical journal reported that patients are, on the whole, happy with the care they receive and that, in fact, 92% have never considered suing for malpractice, 7% have considered such action, and 1% have no opinion. To verify these figures, a random sample of 250 patients seen at a large clinic is selected and interviewed. If the experience of the patients at this clinic is similar to the reported figures, how many are expected to fall into each of the three categories? If, in fact, 240 claimed that they had never considered suing, 9 had considered such action, and 1 had no opinion, do you think that there may be reason to doubt the stated percentages? Explain.

## CHI-SQUARE GOODNESS OF FIT TEST

**12.2** □ The purpose of the chi-square goodness of fit test is to test the null hypothesis that a given set of observations is drawn from, or "fits," a specified probability distribution against the alternative, that it is not. We consider two distinct situations:

1. The hypothesized distribution is completely specified before the sampling is actually done.
2. The hypothesized distribution is completely specified only after the sampling is done.

Case 1 is useful, but case 2 is particularly interesting because it provides a method for testing whether a given data set is drawn from a normal distribution. Recall that normality is an underlying assumption in virtually every procedure discussed in Chapters 7 through 10. Thus we obtain a procedure for determining the appropriateness of the tests discussed in those chapters to a given data set.

The procedure for handling case 1 is based on Theorem 12.2.1, which is offered without proof.

**THEOREM 12.2.1** □ Let $(X_1, X_2, \ldots, X_k)$ be a multinomial random variable with parameters $n, p_1, p_2, \ldots, p_k$. For large $n$, the random variable

$$\sum_{i=1}^{k} \frac{(X_i - np_i)^2}{np_i}$$

follows an approximate chi-square distribution with $k - 1$ degrees of freedom.

We make two notational changes in order to make this random variable easier to remember. Since in the multinomial context $X_i$ is the actual, or "observed," number of trials resulting in outcome $i$ or falling into category $i$, we denote $X_i$ by $O_i$. Recall that $np_i$ is the theoretical expected number of trials resulting in outcome $i$, and so we let $np_i = E[X_i] = E_i$. Thus Theorem 12.2.1 states that

$$\sum_{i=1}^{k} \frac{(O_i - E_i)^2}{E_i} = \sum_{i=1}^{k} \frac{\left[\begin{matrix}\text{(observed} \\ \text{frequency)}\end{matrix} - \begin{matrix}\text{(expected} \\ \text{frequency)}\end{matrix}\right]^2}{\begin{matrix}\text{expected} \\ \text{frequency}\end{matrix}}$$

is, for large $n$, approximately chi-square with $k - 1$ degrees of freedom, where $k$ is the number of mutually exclusive categories involved. This naturally brings up the question, How large is large? It is generally felt that $n$ should be large enough that *no expected frequency is less than 1 and no more than 20% of the expected frequencies are less than 5.* If this condition is not met, either categories should be combined or redefined or the sample size should be increased so that the expected frequencies will be of adequate size.

This random variable serves quite logically as a test statistic for testing a null hypothesis that a given set of observations is drawn from a specified probability distribution. If $H_0$ is true, the value of $p_i$ will be known for each $i$, and hence $E_i$ can be computed easily. In effect, the above statistic compares the observed number of observations per category with the number expected under $H_0$. If these figures agree fairly well (there is a good fit), then the term $(O_i - E_i)^2$ will be small for each $i$ and $H_0$ should not be rejected. If the observed and expected frequencies differ greatly, then $(O_i - E_i)^2$ will be large for some $i$, indicating a poor fit. This calls for rejection of $H_0$. The test is to reject $H_0$ at the appropriate $\alpha$ level if and only if the observed value of the statistic

$$\sum_{i=1}^{k} \frac{(O_i - E_i)^2}{E_i}$$

is too large to have occurred by chance, based on the $X^2_{k-1}$ distribution.

**EXAMPLE 12.2.1** □ It is suspected that the blood-type distribution may not be the same among persons suffering from stomach cancer as in the general population. (See Example 12.1.1.) A sample of 200 patients reveals 80 with type A blood, 20 with type B, 9 with type AB, and the rest with type O. Do these data tend to support the suspected theory?

Since the contention to be supported is always taken as the alternative hypothesis, we wish to test

$H_0$: blood-type distribution among patients with stomach cancer is same as in general population

$H_1$: blood-type distribution among stomach cancer patients is different from that of general population

Statistically, we are testing

$$H_0: p_1 = .41,\ p_2 = .09,\ p_3 = .04,\ p_4 = .46$$
$$H_1: p_i \text{ is not as stated for some } i = 1, 2, 3, 4$$

If $H_0$ is true, then

$$E[X_1] = E_1 = np_1 = 200(.41) = 82$$
$$E[X_2] = E_2 = np_2 = 200(.09) = 18$$
$$E[X_3] = E_3 = np_3 = 200(.04) = 8$$
$$E[X_4] = E_4 = np_4 = 200(.46) = 92$$

The situation is summarized here:

| CATEGORY | 1 (TYPE A) | 2 (TYPE B) | 3 (TYPE AB) | 4 (TYPE O) |
|---|---|---|---|---|
| Observed frequency | 80 | 20 | 9 | 91 |
| Expected frequency under $H_0$ | 82 | 18 | 8 | 92 |

Since $E_i > 5$ for each $i = 1, 2, 3, 4$, the test statistic

$$\sum_{i=1}^{4} \frac{(O_i - E_i)^2}{E_i}$$

follows an approximate $X^2_{k-1} = X_3{}^2$ distribution. The observed value of this statistic is

$$\frac{(80-82)^2}{82} + \frac{(20-18)^2}{18} + \frac{(9-8)^2}{8} + \frac{(91-92)^2}{92} = .406\,9$$

This result is not significant even at the $\alpha = .1$ level (critical point, 2.71); hence we are unable to reject $H_0$. Based on the data given, there is no evidence of a difference in blood-type distribution among those with stomach cancer.

Now let us turn our attention to the question of testing for normality. We assume that we have available a random sample $Y_1, Y_2, \ldots, Y_n$ from a distribution $Y$ with *unknown* mean $\mu_Y$ and *unknown* variance $\sigma_Y^2$. We want to see whether there is evidence that the distribution is not normal. The test is similar to that already considered with just three changes:

1. The $k$ categories themselves are not natural ones; they must be defined by the investigator.

2. The number of degrees of freedom associated with the test statistic

$$\sum_{i=1}^{k} \frac{(O_i - E_i)^2}{E_i}$$

is not $k - 1$, but $k - 3$. This change is necessitated by the fact that 1 degree of freedom is lost for each parameter estimated from the data used in computing expected frequencies. In this case, we estimate from the data both the unknown mean $\mu_Y$ and the unknown variance $\sigma_Y^2$.

3. The test is acceptable as long as *no expected category frequency is less than 1.*

Otherwise, the idea behind the test is the same, namely, to compare the observed frequencies with those expected under the assumption that $H_0$ is true, rejecting $H_0$ only if the observed value of the test statistic is too large to have occurred by chance. The steps followed in this test are outlined below for future reference. They are carefully illustrated in Example 12.2.2.

**Chi-Square Test for Normality**

1. Break the real line into $k$ mutually exclusive categories.

2. Estimate $\mu_Y$ and $\sigma_Y^2$ from the data using the procedure of Definition 1.4.1. In particular,

$$\widehat{\mu}_Y = \sum_{i=1}^{k} \frac{O_i M_i}{n}$$

where $O_i$ is the observed number of observations in the $i$th category, $M_i$ is the midpoint of the $i$th category, and $n$ is the sample size. And

$$\widehat{\sigma}_Y^2 = \frac{n \sum_{i=1}^{k} O_i M_i^2 - \left(\sum_{i=1}^{k} O_i M_i\right)^2}{n(n-1)}$$

3. Estimate the probability of an observation falling into the $i$th category by $\widehat{p}_i$; the method for doing so is presented later.

**4.** Estimate the expected number of observations falling into the $i$th category by

$$\widehat{E}_i = n\widehat{p}_i$$

**5.** Test

H$_0$: data drawn from normal distribution
H$_1$: data drawn from distribution that is not normal

using

$$\sum_{i=1}^{k} \frac{(O_i - \widehat{E}_i)^2}{\widehat{E}_i}$$

which follows an approximate chi-square distribution with $k - 3$ degrees of freedom as the test statistic.

Example 12.2.2 illustrates this procedure.

---

**EXAMPLE 12.2.2** □ A new drug is being tested for possible use in relieving nausea associated with motion sickness. The variable studied is $Y$, the time in minutes needed to obtain relief. Test $Y$ for normality, based on the following 40 observations:

| | | | | |
|---|---|---|---|---|
| 2.2 | 1.5 | 3.4 | 4.4 | 3.9 |
| 3.4 | 4.3 | 3.7 | 2.6 | 4.2 |
| 2.5 | 3.1 | 3.2 | 1.9 | 3.7 |
| 3.3 | 3.8 | 3.9 | 3.5 | 3.1 |
| 4.8 | 4.7 | 3.4 | 3.2 | 3.3 |
| 3.0 | 3.1 | 4.5 | 3.8 | 4.1 |
| 3.7 | 3.5 | 3.3 | 2.9 | 3.0 |
| 4.1 | 3.1 | 3.6 | 3.2 | 2.6 |

**1.** First we must divide the real line into mutually exclusive categories in such a way that the expected frequency in each category is at least 1. Generally 5 to 20 categories are desirable, with each finite category being the same length. Since this data set is not large, let us use six categories. Note that the largest observation is 4.8 and the smallest 1.5. The observations cover an interval of length $4.8 - 1.5 = 3.3$ units. To cover this interval, each finite category must have length at least $3.3/6 = .55$. This length should be rounded *up* to the same number of decimal places as the data, to get the actual length of each finite category. In this case, the actual length is .6. The lower boundary for the first category should start $\frac{1}{2}$ unit below the smallest observation. Since the data are reported to the nearest $\frac{1}{10}$, we take $\frac{1}{10}$ as a unit. Since $\frac{1}{2} \cdot \frac{1}{10} = \frac{1}{20} = .05$, we begin the first category at $1.5 - .05 = 1.45$. (If the data were reported to the nearest $1/100$, we would start $1/2 \cdot 1/100 = .005$ units below the smallest observation.) The remaining category boundaries are found by adding .6 successively to the preceding boundary value until all data points are covered. In this manner, we obtain six finite categories and observed frequencies:

| CATEGORY | BOUNDARIES | OBSERVED FREQUENCY $O_i$ | MIDPOINT $M_i$ |
|---|---|---|---|
| 1 | 1.45 to 2.05 | 2 | 1.75 |
| 2 | 2.05 to 2.65 | 4 | 2.35 |
| 3 | 2.65 to 3.25 | 10 | 2.95 |
| 4 | 3.25 to 3.85 | 14 | 3.55 |
| 5 | 3.85 to 4.45 | 7 | 4.15 |
| 6 | 4.45 to 5.05 | 3 | 4.75 |

Note that this method of defining categories guarantees that the boundary values have one more decimal point than the data; hence no data point can fall on a boundary. This creates $k$ mutually exclusive categories, as required.

**2.** Next we estimate $\mu_Y$ and $\sigma_Y^2$, using the estimators given. In particular,

$$\widehat{\mu}_Y = \sum_{i=1}^{6} \frac{O_i M_i}{n} = \frac{2(1.75) + 4(2.35) + \cdots + 3(4.75)}{40} = \frac{135.4}{40} = 3.385$$

$$\widehat{\sigma}_Y^2 = \frac{n \sum_{i=1}^{6} O_i M_i^2 - \left( \sum_{i=1}^{6} O_i M_i \right)^2}{n(n-1)}$$

$$= \frac{40[2(1.75)^2 + 4(2.35)^2 + \cdots + 3(4.75)^2] - (135.4)^2}{40(39)}$$

$$= .553\,6$$

This implies that

$$\widehat{\sigma}_Y = \sqrt{.553\,6} \doteq .744$$

**3.** The first and last categories are, in practice, considered open-ended. Hence to estimate $p_1$, the probability of an observation falling into category 1, we need to find

$$P[Y \leq 2.05 \mid Y \text{ is normal}]$$

This probability is found by using $\widehat{\mu}_Y$ and $\widehat{\sigma}_Y$ to standardize $Y$. From Table III of Appendix B:

$$\begin{aligned}\widehat{p}_1 &= P[Y \le 2.05 \mid Y \text{ is normal}] \\ &= P\left[\frac{Y - 3.385}{.744} < \frac{2.05 - 3.385}{.744} \middle| Y \text{ is normal}\right] \\ &= P[Z \le -1.79] \\ &= .036\,7\end{aligned}$$

Similarly, the probability of an observation falling into category 2 is

$$\begin{aligned}\widehat{p}_2 = P[2.05 \le Y \le 2.65] &= P[-1.79 \le Z \le -.99] \\ &= .161\,1 - .036\,7 \\ &= .124\,4\end{aligned}$$

It can be shown that

$$\widehat{p}_3 = .267\,5 \qquad \widehat{p}_4 = .307\,1 \qquad \widehat{p}_5 = .187\,9 \qquad \widehat{p}_6 = .076\,4$$

**4.** Since $\widehat{E}_i = n\widehat{p}_i = 40\widehat{p}_i$, now we can compute the estimated expected frequencies in each category under the assumption that the data are normally distributed:

$$\begin{aligned}\widehat{E}_1 &= 40\widehat{p}_1 = 40(.036\,7) = 1.468 \\ \widehat{E}_2 &= 40\widehat{p}_2 = 40(.124\,4) = 4.976 \\ \widehat{E}_3 &= 40\widehat{p}_3 = 40(.267\,5) = 10.7 \\ \widehat{E}_4 &= 40\widehat{p}_4 = 40(.307\,1) = 12.284 \\ \widehat{E}_5 &= 40\widehat{p}_5 = 40(.187\,9) = 7.516 \\ \widehat{E}_6 &= 40\widehat{p}_6 = 40(.076\,4) = 3.056\end{aligned}$$

Note that all categories have expected frequencies greater than 1. If this were not the case, adjacent categories would have to be combined to satisfy this requirement.

**5.** The situation is summarized thus:

| CATEGORY | BOUNDARIES | $O_i$ | $E_i$ |
|---|---|---|---|
| 1 | $-\infty$ to 2.05 | 2 | 1.468 |
| 2 | 2.05 to 2.65 | 4 | 4.976 |
| 3 | 2.65 to 3.25 | 10 | 10.700 |
| 4 | 3.25 to 3.85 | 14 | 12.284 |
| 5 | 3.85 to 4.45 | 7 | 7.516 |
| 6 | 4.45 to $\infty$ | 3 | 3.056 |

The observed value of the test statistic

$$X^2_{k-3} = X^2_{6-3} = X_3{}^2 = \sum_{i=1}^{6} \frac{(O_i - \widehat{E}_i)^2}{\widehat{E}_i}$$

is .706 2. This result is not significant even at the $\alpha = .1$ level (critical point, 6.25). We are unable to reject the null hypothesis that the data are drawn from a normal distribution.

---

Keep in mind the fact that both tests introduced here are large-sample tests. The chi-square distribution provides a good approximation to the distribution of the test statistic whenever the stated guidelines on the expected cell frequencies are satisfied. If these guidelines are not met, then the chi-square goodness of fit test should not be employed. Instead, a small-sample procedure such as the Kolmogorov-Smirnov test [3] is recommended.

---

**EXAMPLE 12.2.3** □ It is instructive to sketch a bar graph of the data set of Example 12.2.2. We use six bars, one for each of the six categories de-

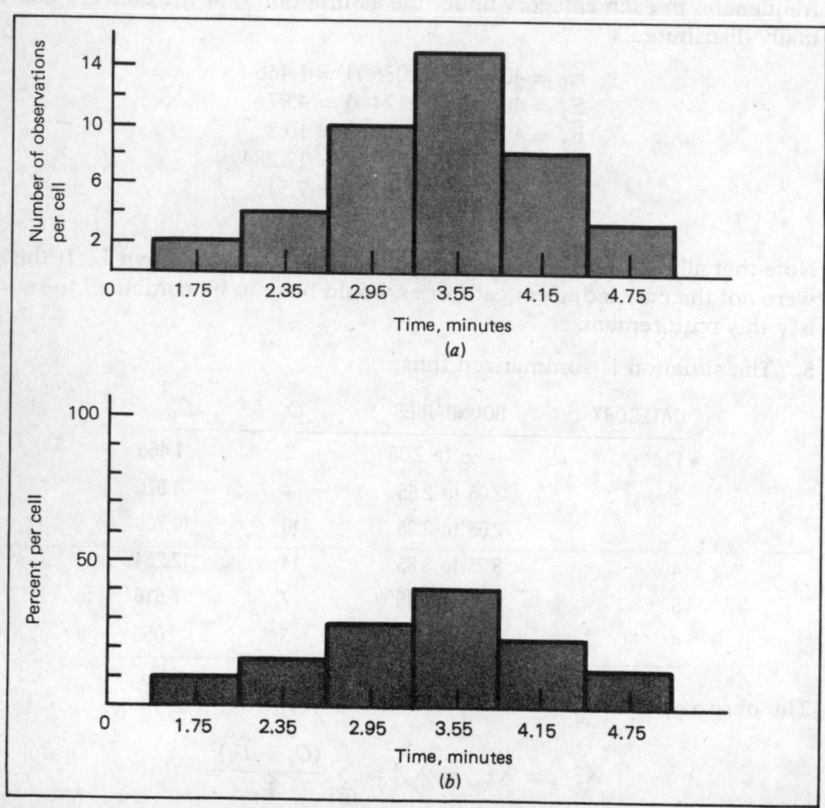


**FIGURE 12.1** (*a*) Frequency histogram. (*b*) Relative frequency histogram.

fined. The bars are .6 unit wide and are centered at the midpoints of their respective categories. The height of each bar can represent either the number or the percentage of observations in the category. In the former case, the graph produced is called a *frequency histogram;* in the latter, it is referred to as a *relative frequency histogram.* Each is shown in Figure 12.1.

It is not hard to see that the histograms in Figure 12.1 assume a rough bell shape. Thus it is not surprising that the chi-square test failed to reject the null hypothesis of normality. When you run any statistical test that has normality as an underlying assumption, you should construct a histogram of the data. In this way, a quick visual check can be made of the validity of this assumption.

## EXERCISES 12.2

1. In 1970 it was estimated that 41% of all males in the 17 to 24 years old group smoked at the time, 9% were former smokers but no longer smoked, and 50% never smoked. A newer survey was done in 1974. Of 200 men in this age group who were interviewed, 72 smoked at the time, 20 were former smokers, and 108 never smoked.
   - **a.** Set up the appropriate null and alternative hypotheses for gaining statistical evidence to support the contention that there has been a shift in the smoking pattern in the age group over the 4-year period.
   - **b.** Find the expected number falling into each category under the assumption that $H_0$ is true.
   - **c.** Does the chi-square goodness of fit test apply?
   - **d.** Find the critical point for an $\alpha = .1$ test.
   - **e.** Test the hypothesis of part **a**, and comment on the result in a practical sense.
2. A random sample of 75 people between the ages of 10 and 18 yielded 35 who do not drink at all, 34 who drink occasionally, and 6 who drink frequently. Do these data tend to support or refute the hypothesized percentages of Exercise 12.1.1? Explain your answer on the basis of the $P$ value of the test.
3. Use the data of Exercise 12.1.2 to test the accuracy of the hypothesized percentages. What is the $P$ value of the test?
4. Do you think that the chi-square goodness of fit test could be used safely on the data of Exercise 12.1.3 as they stand? If not, explain why not and suggest a way to overcome the problem. If so, use the data to test the accuracy of the hypothesized percentages.
5. Consider the cross between two pea plants, each of genotype $RrYy$. The dominant gene $R$ causes the seed to be round, while the recessive gene $r$ leads to a wrinkled seed. The dominant gene $Y$ yields a yellow seed; its recessive allele $y$ results in a green seed.
   - **a.** Let stage 1 in the experiment represent the inheritance of a shape allele from the first parent; stage 2, the inheritance of a shape allele from the second parent; stage

3, the inheritance of a color allele from the first parent; and stage 4, the inheritance of a color allele from the second parent. Construct the 16-path tree corresponding to this four-stage process.

**b.** For each path in the tree, determine the type of pea produced.

**c.** Assuming that each path in the tree is equally likely, show that the theoretical distribution of seeds is as follows:

| TYPE | PERCENTAGE |
|---|---|
| Round, yellow | $9/16$ |
| Round, green | $3/16$ |
| Wrinkled, yellow | $3/16$ |
| Wrinkled, green | $1/16$ |

**d.** When the experiment is run, 85 seeds are obtained. The following distribution is observed:

| TYPE | NUMBER |
|---|---|
| Round, yellow | 48 |
| Round, green | 16 |
| Wrinkled, yellow | 14 |
| Wrinkled, green | 7 |

Use these data to test the accuracy of the hypothesized distribution at the $\alpha =$ .05 level.

**6.** The following are observations on random variable $Y$, the percentage of income spent by surgeons in 1972 for malpractice insurance. Test at the $\alpha = .05$ level the null hypothesis that $Y$ is normally distributed. (Begin with six categories.)

| | | | | | | |
|---|---|---|---|---|---|---|
| 3.4 | 4.3 | 3.3 | 7.1 | 5.8 | 6.7 | 8.2 |
| 6.1 | 4.7 | 2.9 | 5.1 | 9.4 | 4.6 | 5.3 |
| 4.8 | 6.9 | 5.8 | 5.7 | 8.6 | 5.9 | 4.9 |
| 7.7 | 2.8 | 3.2 | 4.8 | 3.3 | 7.3 | 7.0 |
| 5.9 | 3.7 | 6.0 | 4.3 | 5.0 | 6.4 | 5.3 |
| 2.8 | 7.1 | 4.4 | 4.5 | 5.1 | 4.0 | 6.9 |

**7.** The following are observations on random variables $X$, the creatinine level (in milligrams per deciliter of blood) in 40 nonalcoholic subjects, and $Y$, the creatinine level in 40 medical ward alcoholics. The purpose is to compare the mean creatinine levels for these two groups by using a two-sample $T$ test.

| NONALCOHOLIC SUBJECTS $x$ | | | | |
|---|---|---|---|---|
| 1.16 | 1.04 | 1.34 | 1.61 | 1.04 |
| 1.30 | 1.35 | 1.18 | 1.54 | 1.41 |
| .87 | .62 | 1.27 | .69 | .78 |
| 1.74 | 1.01 | 1.56 | .12 | 1.18 |
| .95 | 1.23 | .94 | .74 | 1.11 |
| 1.56 | 1.09 | 1.26 | 1.22 | 1.32 |
| .28 | .86 | 1.32 | 1.20 | 1.16 |
| .70 | 1.07 | .94 | .84 | 1.40 |

| MEDICAL WARD ALCOHOLICS $y$ | | | | |
|---|---|---|---|---|
| 1.01 | .87 | .63 | 1.12 | 1.21 |
| .85 | 1.19 | .21 | 1.15 | .77 |
| .78 | .81 | .72 | 1.04 | .64 |
| 1.31 | 1.11 | .81 | 1.00 | .89 |
| 1.47 | .69 | 1.17 | 1.40 | .87 |
| 1.07 | .79 | 1.07 | 1.26 | 1.47 |
| 1.35 | .74 | 1.48 | 1.15 | 1.42 |
| 1.42 | .90 | .31 | 1.04 | 1.61 |

Test both $X$ and $Y$ for normality by using the chi-square goodness of fit test as illustrated. Begin with six categories. (Note that 1 unit is $\frac{1}{100}$ and $\frac{1}{2}$ unit is $\frac{1}{200} = .005$.) Is the normality assumption rejected in either case? If so, what is the $P$ value of the test? Is there reason to suspect that the $T$ test for equality of means is not appropriate? Construct a frequency histogram for each data set. Does the histogram look as you expected, based on the results of your test for normality?

## 2 × 2 CONTINGENCY TABLES

**12.3** □ In this section, we discuss a problem involving categorical data that is somewhat different from that considered earlier. However, the idea behind the test procedure used is identical to that studied earlier. Namely, the test statistic used compares observed category frequencies with those expected under the assumption that a stated null hypothesis is true, with rejection coming if these differ too much to have occurred by chance alone.

The name *2 × 2 contingency table* refers to that fact that each observation is classed according to two characteristics, with each characteristic having two levels of classification. Thus each observation falls into exactly one of four mutually exclusive "cells," or categories. The data analysis is based on an examination of the number of observations falling into each category. We illustrate this idea in Example 12.3.1.

**EXAMPLE 12.3.1** □ In a study of a new hepatitis vaccine, 1083 male volunteers are used. Five-hundred and forty-nine are randomly chosen and vaccinated with the new drug. The remaining 534 are not vaccinated. After a time it is found that 70 of the 534 unvaccinated volunteers contracted hepatitis, whereas only 11 of the 549 vaccinated had done so. We are dealing with two characteristics, the vaccination status and the health status of each subject. Each volunteer either was vaccinated ($V$) or was not vaccinated ($V'$). Similarly, each either did contract hepatitis ($H$) or did not ($H'$). Thus these two characteristics define four categories:

$V \cap H$: vaccinated and contracted hepatitis
$V' \cap H$: not vaccinated and contracted hepatitis
$V \cap H'$: vaccinated and did not contract hepatitis
$V' \cap H'$: not vaccinated and did not contract hepatitis

Each volunteer falls into exactly one category.

Since we are concerned with the number of observations falling into each cell, we need a notational convention for these cell frequencies. We also need a notational convention to indicate the number of observations falling into each level of each of the two classification variables. We use the following:

$n_{11}$ = number of observations falling into cell in row 1 and column 1
$n_{12}$ = number of observations falling into cell in row 1 and column 2
$n_{21}$ = number of observations falling into cell in row 2 and column 1
$n_{22}$ = number of observations falling into cell in row 2 and column 2
$n_{1\cdot} = n_{11} + n_{12}$ = number of observations in row 1
$n_{2\cdot} = n_{21} + n_{22}$ = number of observations in row 2
$n_{\cdot 1} = n_{11} + n_{21}$ = number of observations in column 1
$n_{\cdot 2} = n_{12} + n_{22}$ = number of observations in column 2
$n$ = total number of observations

This notational convention is illustrated in Example 12.3.2.

**EXAMPLE 12.3.2** □ Table 12.1 summarizes the data of Example 12.3.1 with the appropriate notation indicated. Note that $n_{\cdot 1}$ and $n_{\cdot 2}$ are column totals that appear along the margins of the 2 × 2 table. They are called *marginal*

**TABLE 12.1**

| | $V$ | $V'$ | |
|---|---|---|---|
| $H$ | $11 = n_{11}$ | $70 = n_{12}$ | $81 = n_{1\cdot}$ |
| $H'$ | $538 = n_{21}$ | $464 = n_{22}$ | $1002 = n_{2\cdot}$ |
| | $549 = n_{\cdot 1}$ | $534 = n_{\cdot 2}$ | $1083 = n$ |

column totals. Similarly, $n_{1\cdot}$ and $n_{2\cdot}$ are *marginal* row totals. A table such as Table 12.1 is called a 2 × 2 contingency table.

The general null hypothesis to be tested by a 2 × 2 contingency table is that there is "no association" between the two classification variables. The alternative is that there is an association. The exact form of the null hypothesis depends on the design of the experiment. We study two different experimental settings that lead to 2 × 2 contingency tables:

1. One set of marginal totals is fixed; the other is free to vary.
2. All marginal totals are variable.

Examples 12.3.3 and 12.3.4 illustrate the two designs.

**EXAMPLE 12.3.3** □ A large number of people living in a particular section of a community have been exposed over the last 10 years to radioactivity from an atomic waste storage dump. A study is run to find out whether there is any apparent association between this exposure and the development of a specific blood disorder. To conduct the experiment, random samples are chosen of 300 persons from the community who have been

**TABLE 12.2**

| | $D$ (HAS DISEASE) | $D'$ (DOES NOT HAVE DISEASE) | |
|---|---|---|---|
| $E$ (exposed to hazard) | | | $n_{1\cdot} = 300$ (fixed prior to experiment) |
| $E'$ (not exposed to hazard) | | | $n_{2\cdot} = 320$ (fixed prior to experiment) |
| | $n_{\cdot 1} = ?$ (random) | $n_{\cdot 2} = ?$ (random) | $n = 620$ |

exposed to the hazard and 320 persons not so exposed. Each subject is screened to determine whether he or she has the blood disorder. This experiment generates a 2 × 2 table of the form shown in Table 12.2. Note that the marginal row totals are fixed at 300 and 320, since these sample sizes are predetermined by the investigator. The marginal column totals are free to vary; that is, they are random variables whose numerical values are known only at the conclusion of the experiment.

**EXAMPLE 12.3.4** □ A study is run to determine whether there is any apparent association between a child's weight and early success in school, as judged by a school psychologist. A random sample is selected consisting of 500 students in grades 1 to 3. Each child is classed according to two criteria, weight and success in school. The 2 × 2 contingency table generated is shown in Table 12.3. In this design, the only fixed quantity is $n$, the total sample size. Both the row and column marginal totals are free to vary; neither set is fixed by the investigator prior to the experiment.

**TABLE 12.3**

| | $W$ (OVERWEIGHT) | $W'$ (NOT OVERWEIGHT) | |
|---|---|---|---|
| $S$ (successful) | | | $n_{1\cdot} = ?$ (random) |
| $S'$ (unsuccessful) | | | $n_{2\cdot} = ?$ (random) |
| | $n_{\cdot 1} = ?$ (random) | $n_{\cdot 2} = ?$ (random) | $n = 500$ (fixed) |

There are two ways to think of the null hypothesis of no association between classification variables. Each can be expressed in terms of appropriately chosen probabilities. The form selected depends on the design of the experiment.

1. *One set of marginal totals fixed.* Let us denote the two classification variables $A$ and $B$, and let us assume that the marginal totals for characteristic $B$ are fixed by the investigator prior to the experiment. The proportion of those with characteristic $B$ that have characteristic $A$ is denoted $p_1$. Thus the proportion of those with characteristic $B$ that do not have characteristic $A$ is $1 - p_1$. Similarly, the proportions of those that do not have characteristic $B$ but do have characteristics $A$ and $A'$ are $p_2$ and $1 - p_2$, respectively. These proportions are shown in Table 12.4. In this context, the null hypothesis of no association is stated as

$H_0$: proportion of objects with trait $A$ among those with trait $B$ = proportion of objects with trait $A$ among those without trait $B$

**TABLE 12.4**

| | $A$ | $A'$ | |
|---|---|---|---|
| $B$ | $p_1$ | $1 - p_1$ | $n_{1\cdot}$ (fixed) |
| $B'$ | $p_2$ | $1 - p_2$ | $n_{2\cdot}$ (fixed) |
| | $n_{\cdot 1}$ (random) | $n_{\cdot 2}$ (random) | $n$ |

or

$$H_0: p_1 = p_2$$

This implies that characteristic $A$ is no more prevalent among those with characteristic $B$ than among those without characteristic $B$; hence there is no apparent association between $A$ and $B$. For instance, in Example 12.3.3 the null hypothesis is that the proportion of persons with the blood disorder is the same among those exposed to the radioactive source as among those not exposed. That is, there is no apparent association between exposure to this form of radiation and development of the disorder. When the null hypothesis is expressed in this way, the test is referred to as a *test of homogeneity*.

**2.** *Marginal totals random.* When both sets of marginal totals are random, the null hypothesis of no association is stated in the form

$$H_0: A \text{ and } B \text{ are independent}$$

This means that knowledge of the classification level of an object relative to characteristic $A$ has no bearing on its level relative to characteristic $B$. For instance, in Example 12.3.4, the null hypothesis is that being overweight is independent of early success in school; knowing that a child is overweight does not help predict success in school. To express this idea mathematically, we use the table of probabilities given in Table 12.5. Note that $p_{11}$ denotes the proportion of objects with both $A$ and $B$, $p_{\cdot 1}$ denotes the proportion with characteristic $A$, and $p_{1\cdot}$ denotes the proportion with characteristic $B$. Recall that $A$ and $B$ are independent if and only if

$$P[A \cap B] = P[A] \cdot P[B]$$

**TABLE 12.5**

| | $A$ | $A'$ | |
|---|---|---|---|
| $B$ | $p_{11}$ | $p_{12}$ | $p_{1\cdot}$ |
| $B'$ | $p_{21}$ | $p_{22}$ | $p_{2\cdot}$ |
| | $p_{\cdot 1}$ | $p_{\cdot 2}$ | 1 |

Thus the null hypothesis that $A$ and $B$ are independent can be expressed as

$$H_0: p_{11} = p_{\cdot 1} p_{1\cdot}$$

This implies that $p_{ij} = p_{i\cdot} p_{\cdot j}$ for $i = 1, 2$ and $j = 1, 2$. That is, $A$ and $B$ are independent if and only if the cell probability for any cell can be found by multiplying the corresponding row and column probabilities.

Although there is a difference in the way that the null hypothesis is expressed in the two cases, both imply a lack of association between the classification variables. Mathematically, they are tested in the same manner. In particular, the analysis is based on the chi-square approximation to the multinomial distribution discussed in Section 12.2.

Consider a $2 \times 2$ table in which all marginal totals are random. Since each observation falls into exactly one of four mutually exclusive categories, a random sample of size $n$ can be viewed as constituting a series of $n$ independent multinomial trials, each with parameters $p_{11}$, $p_{12}$, $p_{21}$, and $p_{22}$. Hence the set $(n_{11}, n_{12}, n_{21}, n_{22})$ of observed cell frequencies is a multinomial random variable with parameters $n$, $p_{11}$, $p_{12}$, $p_{21}$, and $p_{22}$. Thus the expected cell frequencies are given by

$$E_{ij} = np_{ij}$$

where $p_{ij}$ is the probability of an observation falling into the $(ij)$th cell and $n$ is the sample size. These probabilities are not known and must be estimated from the data under the assumption that the null hypothesis is true.

How can this be done? Quite simply! Note, for instance, that if $H_0$ is true and characteristics $A$ and $B$ are independent, then

$$p_{11} = p_{1\cdot} p_{\cdot 1}$$

Since $p_{1\cdot}$ is the probability of an observation falling into row 1, it is logical to estimate $p_{1\cdot}$ by

$$\widehat{p}_{1\cdot} = \frac{\text{number of elements in row 1}}{\text{sample size}} = \frac{n_{1\cdot}}{n}$$

Similarly, since $p_{\cdot 1}$ is the probability of an observation falling into column 1, we estimate $p_{\cdot 1}$ by

$$\widehat{p}_{\cdot 1} = \frac{\text{number of elements in column 1}}{\text{sample size}} = \frac{n_{\cdot 1}}{n}$$

Thus

$$\widehat{p}_{11} = \widehat{p}_{1\cdot} \widehat{p}_{\cdot 1} = \frac{n_{1\cdot}}{n} \frac{n_{\cdot 1}}{n}$$

This, in turn, implies that

$$\widehat{E}_{11} = \widehat{p}_{11} n = \frac{n_{1\cdot}}{n} \frac{n_{\cdot 1}}{n} n$$

$$= \frac{n_{1}.n._{1}}{n} = \frac{\begin{pmatrix}\text{marginal}\\ \text{row total}\end{pmatrix}\begin{pmatrix}\text{marginal}\\ \text{column total}\end{pmatrix}}{\text{sample size}}$$

A similar argument holds for other cell probabilities.

Thus we conclude that for each $i$ and $j$,

$$\widehat{E}_{ij} = \frac{n_{i}.n._{j}}{n} = \frac{\begin{pmatrix}\text{marginal}\\ \text{row total}\end{pmatrix}\begin{pmatrix}\text{marginal}\\ \text{column total}\end{pmatrix}}{\text{sample size}}$$

Recall from Section 12.2 that for large samples,

$$\sum_{i=1}^{2}\sum_{j=1}^{2}\frac{(O_{ij} - \widehat{E}_{ij})^2}{\widehat{E}_{ij}} = \sum_{i=1}^{2}\sum_{j=1}^{2}\frac{(n_{ij} - \widehat{E}_{ij})^2}{\widehat{E}_{ij}}$$

follows an approximate chi-square distribution. The number of degrees of freedom is $k - 1 - m$, where $m$ is the number of parameters estimated from the data used in computing the expected cell frequencies. Note that we actually need estimate only $p_{1}.$ and $p._{1}$ from the data, since $p._{2} = 1 - p._{1}$ and $p_{2}. = 1 - p_{1}.$. Hence the number of degrees of freedom associated with the test statistic is

$$k - 1 - m = 4 - 1 - 2 = 1$$

In this case, to satisfy the rule that no expected frequency be less than 1 and no more than 20% be less than 5, we must, in fact, have *no expected frequency less than 5*. If this rule cannot be satisfied, then the data should be analyzed by a procedure called *Fisher's exact test*.

---

**EXAMPLE 12.3.5** □ When the experiment of Example 12.3.4 is run, the data in Table 12.6 are found. Let us test the null hypothesis

$H_0$: Being overweight is independent of success in school

at the $\alpha = .1$ level. The critical point based on the $X_1{}^2$ distribution is 2.71. We reject the null hypothesis if and only if the observed value of the test statistic

**TABLE 12.6**

| | $W$ (OVERWEIGHT) | $W'$ (NOT OVERWEIGHT) | |
|---|---|---|---|
| $S$ (successful) | $n_{11} = 162$ | $n_{12} = 263$ | $n_{1}. = 425$ |
| $S'$ (not successful) | $n_{21} = 38$ | $n_{22} = 37$ | $n_{2}. = 75$ |
| | $n._{1} = 200$ | $n._{2} = 300$ | $n = 500$ |

$$\sum_{i=1}^{2}\sum_{j=1}^{2}\frac{(n_{ij}-\widehat{E}_{ij})^2}{\widehat{E}_{ij}}$$

falls on or above this point. The expected cell frequencies under $H_0$ are given by

$$\widehat{E}_{11}=\frac{n_1.n._1}{n}=\frac{425(200)}{500}=170$$

$$\widehat{E}_{12}=\frac{n_1.n._2}{n}=\frac{425(300)}{500}=255$$

$$\widehat{E}_{21}=\frac{n_2.n._1}{n}=\frac{75(200)}{500}=30$$

$$\widehat{E}_{22}=\frac{n_2.n._2}{n}=\frac{75(300)}{500}=45$$

We summarize the situation in Table 12.7. Note that there are some differences between what is expected if $H_0$ is true (listed in parentheses) and what is actually observed. The question is, Are these differences too large to have occurred strictly by chance? Note that all cell frequencies are well above 5, as required. The observed value of the test statistic is given by

$$\sum_{i=1}^{2}\sum_{j=1}^{2}\frac{(n_{ij}-\widehat{E}_{ij})^2}{\widehat{E}_{ij}}=\frac{(162-170)^2}{170}+\frac{(263-255)^2}{255}+\frac{(38-30)^2}{30}+\frac{(37-45)^2}{45}$$
$$=4.18$$

Since this value is above the critical point of 2.71, we reject $H_0$ and conclude that a child's success in school is not independent of weight.

**TABLE 12.7**

| | $W$ | $W'$ | |
|---|---|---|---|
| $S$ | 162 (170) | 263 (255) | 425 |
| $S'$ | 38 (30) | 37 (45) | 75 |
| | 200 | 300 | 500 |

**EXAMPLE 12.3.6** □ Table 12.8 summarizes the data of Example 12.3.3. Since the marginal row totals are fixed, the null hypothesis of interest is

**TABLE 12.8**

| | $D$ (HAS DISEASE) | $D'$ (DOES NOT HAVE DISEASE) | |
|---|---|---|---|
| $E$ (exposed) | 52 (48.39) | 248 (251.61) | 300 |
| $E'$ (not exposed) | 48 (51.61) | 272 (268.39) | 320 |
| | 100 | 520 | 620 |

$H_0$: proportion of persons with disease among those exposed to radioactivity = proportion of persons with disease among those not exposed

The observed value of the $X_1{}^2$ statistic is .62. This value is not significant even at the $\alpha = .25$ level (critical point, 1.32), so $H_0$ cannot be rejected. There is no evidence of an association between the blood disease and exposure to this source of radioactivity.

There is an easy computational shortcut for evaluating the test statistic in the 2 × 2 table. Namely, it can be shown algebraically that

$$\sum_{i=1}^{2}\sum_{j=1}^{2}\frac{(n_{ij}-\widehat{E}_{ij})^2}{\widehat{E}_{ij}} = \frac{n(n_{11}n_{22}-n_{12}n_{21})^2}{n_{1}.n_{2}.n._{1}n._{2}}$$

**EXAMPLE 12.3.7** □ Consider the data of Example 12.3.6 shown in Table 12.9. Using the computational shortcut, we have

$$\sum_{i=1}^{2}\sum_{j=1}^{2}\frac{(n_{ij}-\widehat{E}_{ij})^2}{\widehat{E}_{ij}} = \frac{n(n_{11}n_{22}-n_{12}n_{21})^2}{n_{1}.n_{2}.n._{1}n._{2}}$$

$$= \frac{620(52\cdot 272 - 48\cdot 248)^2}{300(320)(100)(520)} = .62$$

**TABLE 12.9**

| | $D$ | $D'$ | |
|---|---|---|---|
| $E$ | $n_{11} = 52$ | $n_{12} = 248$ | $n_{1}. = 300$ |
| $E'$ | $n_{21} = 48$ | $n_{22} = 272$ | $n_{2}. = 320$ |
| | $n._{1} = 100$ | $n._{2} = 520$ | $n = 620$ |

One other point should be made about the analysis of data in the large-sample case. The chi-square distribution is being utilized to approximate the multinomial. That is, a continuous distribution (chi square) is being used to approximate one that is discrete (multinomial). This was seen once before, when we employed the normal curve (continuous) to approximate binomial probabilities (discrete). In that case, we found that the approximation could be improved by using a "correction factor" for continuity. You might ask whether the same should be done here. Dr. Frank Yates in 1934 proposed the following "corrected" chi-square statistic:

$$X^2_{\text{corr}} = \frac{n(|n_{11}n_{22} - n_{12}n_{21}| - \frac{1}{2}n)^2}{n_{1\cdot}n_{2\cdot}n_{\cdot 1}n_{\cdot 2}}$$

Recent studies [5] indicate that in the two cases considered, this should *not* be done. However, occasionally the correction factor is utilized in the literature. Be aware of the fact that when this is done, the test is conservative in the sense that the actual $P$ value of the test usually is lower than that reported.

"Hello, FDA? I'd like to report research that directly links cheese with death in rats"

(Copyright 1977 *Chicago Tribune;* reprinted by permission.)

## EXERCISES 12.3

1. A study is run of a new flu vaccine. A random sample of 900 individuals is chosen, and each is classified according to whether the flu had been contracted during the last year and whether each person had been innoculated. The following information is obtained:

| | CONTRACTED FLU | DID NOT CONTRACT FLU | |
|---|---|---|---|
| Innoculated | 150 | 200 | |
| Not innoculated | 300 | 250 | |
| | | | |

**a.** Are any of the marginal totals fixed?
**b.** Set up appropriate null hypothesis to test for association between variables.
**c.** Find the expected frequency for each cell.
**d.** Can $H_0$ be rejected? What is the $P$ value of the test?
**e.** Verify the value of the test statistic, using the computational shortcut.

**2.** In a study to determine the association, if any, between maternal rubella and congenital cataracts, a sample is selected of 20 children with the defect and 25 children of similar background and age who do not have the defect. The mother of each child is interviewed to determine whether she had rubella while carrying the child. The following data are obtained:

| | HAVE CONGENITAL CATARACT | CONTROL | |
|---|---|---|---|
| Mother had rubella | 14 | 10 | |
| Mother did not have rubella | 6 | 15 | |
| | | | |

**a.** Are any of the marginal totals fixed?
**b.** Set up appropriate null hypothesis to test for association between variables.
**c.** Find the expected frequency for each cell.
**d.** Test the null hypothesis at the $\alpha = .01$ level.

**3.** It has long been thought that peptic ulcers are caused by both genetic and environmental factors. A recent study considered the association between the pepsinogen I level in the blood and the presence of peptic ulcers; 14 patients who had duodenal ulcers were compared with 49 individuals who did not. The pepsinogen I level in the blood of each was determined and classified as high or low. The following was obtained:

| Ulcer | Pepsinogen Level: HIGH | LOW | |
|---|---|---|---|
| Present | 12 | | 14 |
| Absent | | 31 | 49 |
| | | | |

**a.** Complete the table.
**b.** Set up appropriate null hypothesis to test for association between variables.
**c.** Find the expected number of observations for each cell.
**d.** Test the null hypothesis at the $\alpha = .01$ level.

**4.** A small pilot study is run to determine the association between the occurrence of leukemia and a history of allergy. A sample of 19 leukemia patients and 17 controls is selected, and their history of allergy is determined. The following data result:

| | HISTORY OF ALLERGY | NO HISTORY OF ALLERGY | |
|---|---|---|---|
| Control | 5 | 12 | |
| Patient | 17 | 2 | |
| | | | |

**a.** Are any of the marginal totals fixed?
**b.** Set up the appropriate null hypothesis to test for association between classification variables.
**c.** Find the expected frequency for each cell.
**d.** Is there evidence of an association between history of allergy and leukemia? Explain your answer based on the $P$ value of the test.

**5.** Use the data of Example 12.3.1 to determine whether contracting hepatitis is independent of receiving the hepatitis vaccine.

---

**Computing Supplement**

The SAS procedure PROC FREQ analyzes categorical data. We use the data of Exercise 12.3.2.

| Statement | Function |
|---|---|
| DATA DEFECT; | names data set |
| INPUT RUBELLA \$ CATARACT \$; | two variables are read from each card; \$ indicates variable is nonnumeric |
| CARDS; | signals beginning of data |
| yes yes<br>yes yes<br>. . .<br>yes yes | 14 cards |
| yes no<br>. . .<br>yes no | 10 cards |
| no no<br>. . .<br>no no | 15 cards |
| no yes<br>. . .<br>no yes | 6 cards |

| | |
|---|---|
| | signals end of data |
| PROC FREQ; | calls for procedure to analyze categorical data |
| TABLES RUBELLA*CATARACT/EXPECTED CHISQ NOPERCENT NOROW NOCOL; | asks for frequency table for variables RUBELLA versus CATARACT; asks for expected number of observations per cell to be printed; suppresses printing of cell, column, and row percentages; asks for chi-square goodness of fit test |
| TITLE TESTING FOR ASSOCIATION; | titles output |

The output of this program is shown below. Note that the top number in each cell is the observed number in the cell; immediately under this is the expected number per cell, under the assumption that there is no association between the two variables. The observed value of the chi-square statistic used to test for association is given by (1); its $P$ value is given by (2). Note that since $P$ is small (.045.0), $H_0$ is rejected. There does appear to be an association between maternal rubella and congenital cataracts.

```
                         TESTING FOR ASSOCIATION

                       TABLE OF RUBELLA BY CATARACT

              RUBELLA         CATARACT

              FREQUENCY|
              EXPECTED |NO      |YES     |  TOTAL
              ---------+--------+--------+
              NO       |     15 |      6 |     21
                       |   11.7 |    9.3 |
              ---------+--------+--------+
              YES      |     10 |     14 |     24
                       |   13.3 |   10.7 |
              ---------+--------+--------+
              TOTAL          25       20       45

                       STATISTICS FOR 2-WAY TABLES

      CHI-SQUARE                      (1) 4.018   DF=   1   PROB=0.0450 (2)
      PHI                                 0.299
      CONTINGENCY COEFFICIENT             0.286
      CRAMER'S V                          0.299
      LIKELIHOOD RATIO CHISQUARE          4.098   DF=   1   PROB=0.0429
      CONTINUITY ADJ. CHI-SQUARE          2.903   DF=   1   PROB=0.0884
      FISHER'S EXACT TEST (2-TAIL)                          PROB=0.0199
                          (1-TAIL)                          PROB=0.9901
```

## $r \times c$ CONTINGENCY TABLES

**12.4** □ In this section we extend the methods of Section 12.3 to situations in which the number of rows or columns in the contingency table is greater than 2. The purpose of the experiment is as before, namely, to test for association between classification variables by comparing observed cell frequencies with those expected if there is no association. Two classi-

**TABLE 12.10** TABLE OF FREQUENCIES

| Variable B | | Variable A 1 | 2 | 3 | ... | $c$ | |
|---|---|---|---|---|---|---|---|
| | 1 | $n_{11}$ | $n_{12}$ | $n_{13}$ | ... | $n_{1c}$ | $n_{1\cdot}$ |
| | 2 | $n_{21}$ | $n_{22}$ | $n_{23}$ | ... | $n_{2c}$ | $n_{2\cdot}$ |
| | ⋮ | ... | ... | ... | ... | ... | ... |
| | $r$ | $n_{r1}$ | $n_{r2}$ | $n_{r3}$ | ... | $n_{rc}$ | $n_{r\cdot}$ |
| | | $n_{\cdot 1}$ | $n_{\cdot 2}$ | $n_{\cdot 3}$ | ... | $n_{\cdot c}$ | $n$ |

fication variables, $A$ and $B$, are used. We assume that there are $c$ levels relative to variable $A$ and $r$ levels relative to $B$. Thus the contingency table generated has $r$ rows, $c$ columns, and $rc$ cells, or categories. The notation used is shown in Table 12.10. Note that

$$n_{ij} = \text{observed frequency in } (ij)\text{th cell}$$
$$n_{i\cdot} = \text{marginal row total for } i\text{th row, } i = 1, 2, \ldots, r$$
$$n_{\cdot j} = \text{marginal column total } j\text{th column, } j = 1, 2, \ldots, c$$

We illustrate the use of this notation in Example 12.4.1.

**EXAMPLE 12.4.1** □ A study is run to determine whether there is an association between blood type and duodenal ulcers. A sample of 1301 patients and 6313 controls is selected, and the blood type of each is determined. Among the patients, 698 have type O blood, 472 have type A, 102 have type B, and the rest have type AB. Among controls the figures are 2892, 2625, 570, and 226, respectively. These data are conveniently displayed as a $2 \times 4$ (two rows and four columns) contingency table, as shown in Table 12.11.

**TABLE 12.11**

| | Blood Type: O | A | B | AB | |
|---|---|---|---|---|---|
| Patients | $n_{11} = 698$ | $n_{12} = 472$ | $n_{13} = 102$ | $n_{14} = 29$ | $n_{1\cdot} = 1301$ (fixed) |
| Controls | $n_{21} = 2892$ | $n_{22} = 2625$ | $n_{23} = 570$ | $n_{24} = 226$ | $n_{2\cdot} = 6313$ (fixed) |
| | $n_{\cdot 1} = 3590$ | $n_{\cdot 2} = 3097$ | $n_{\cdot 3} = 672$ | $n_{\cdot 4} = 255$ | $n = 7614$ |

Once again, there are two commonly encountered ways of expressing the null hypothesis of no association. The form chosen depends on

TABLE 12.12

| | | Variable $A$ | | | | | |
|---|---|---|---|---|---|---|---|
| | | 1 | 2 | 3 | ⋯ | $c$ | |
| Variable $B$ | 1 | $p_{11}$ | $p_{12}$ | $p_{13}$ | ⋯ | $p_{1c}$ | 1 |
| | 2 | $p_{21}$ | $p_{22}$ | $p_{23}$ | ⋯ | $p_{2c}$ | 1 |
| | 3 | $p_{31}$ | $p_{32}$ | $p_{33}$ | ⋯ | $p_{3c}$ | 1 |
| | ⋮ | ⋯ | ⋯ | ⋯ | ⋯ | ⋯ | ⋮ |
| | $r$ | $p_{r1}$ | $p_{r2}$ | $p_{r3}$ | ⋯ | $p_{rc}$ | 1 |

whether all marginal totals are random or some are fixed. The analysis is the same in either case.

**1.** *One set of marginal totals fixed.* Assume that the row totals are fixed. Let $p_{ij}$ denote the proportion of objects in the $i$th level relative to variable $B$ that are in the $j$th level relative to $A$. These proportions are shown in Table 12.12. Note that the proportions within each row sum to 1. The null hypothesis of no association essentially states that within each column, no row classification is more prevalent than any other. The alternative is that for some columns, this is not the case. Statistically, this null hypothesis takes the form

$$H_0: p_{1j} = p_{2j} = p_{3j} = \cdots = p_{rj} \qquad j = 1, 2, 3, \ldots, c$$

For instance, in Example 12.4.1 we are testing the null hypothesis of no association between blood type and duodenal ulcers; that is, for *each* blood type, the proportion of patients with the type is the same as that of the controls. The alternative is that there is an association between blood type and the disease—that there is a difference in percentages between patients and controls for at least one blood type. When the null hypothesis takes this form, we refer to the test as a *test of homogeneity.*

**2.** *Marginal totals random.* If all marginal totals are random, then the null hypothesis of no association between classification variables is expressed as

$$H_0: A \text{ and } B \text{ are independent}$$

Statistically, this is expressed in the form

$$H_0: p_{ij} = p_{i\cdot}p_{\cdot j} \qquad \begin{matrix} i = 1, 2, \ldots, r \\ j = 1, 2, \ldots, c \end{matrix}$$

The test statistic for testing the null hypothesis of no association, regardless of the design, is

$$X^2_{(r-1)(c-1)} = \sum_{i=1}^{r}\sum_{j=1}^{c} \frac{(n_{ij} - \widehat{E}_{ij})^2}{\widehat{E}_{ij}}$$

where $\widehat{E}_{ij}$ is the estimated expected frequency in the $(ij)$th cell. As before,

$$\widehat{E}_{ij} = \frac{\text{(marginal row total)(marginal column total)}}{\text{sample size}}$$

The test is to reject $H_0$ for values of the test statistic too large to have occurred by chance. The test is applicable for sample sizes large enough that no expected frequency is less than 1 and no more than 20% are less than 5. We illustrate this procedure in Example 12.4.2.

---

**EXAMPLE 12.4.2** □ When the data of Example 12.4.1 are analyzed, the observed and expected frequencies shown in Table 12.13 result. The observed value of the test statistic is

$$\frac{(698 - 613.42)^2}{613.42} + \frac{(2892 - 2976.58)^2}{2976.58} + \cdots + \frac{(226 - 211.43)^2}{211.43} = 29.12$$

The number of degrees of freedom involved is

$$(r - 1)(c - 1) = (2 - 1)(4 - 1) = 3$$

Hypothesis $H_0$ can be rejected at the $\alpha = .005$ level (critical point, 12.8). There is evidence of an association between the disease and blood type. To get an intuitive idea of what differences exist between patients and controls, note that the estimated probability of a patient falling into blood group O is given by

$$\frac{\text{Number of patients in group O}}{\text{Number of patients}} = \frac{698}{1301} = .54$$

**TABLE 12.13**

| | Blood Type O | A | B | AB | |
|---|---|---|---|---|---|
| Patients | 698 (613.42) | 472 (529.18) | 102 (114.82) | 29 (43.57) | 1301 |
| Controls | 2892 (2976.58) | 2625 (2567.82) | 570 (557.18) | 226 (211.43) | 6313 |
| | 3590 | 3097 | 672 | 255 | 7614 |

Similarly, the estimated probability of a control falling into group O is

$$\frac{\text{Number of controls in group O}}{\text{number of controls}} = \frac{2892}{6313} = .46$$

It appears that the proportion of persons with type O blood is not the same among patients as among controls. That is,

$$p_{11} \neq p_{21}$$

## EXERCISES 12.4

1. Consider the data of Example 12.4.2. Estimate the proportion of patients falling into blood group A and the proportion of controls falling into this group. Do the same for blood groups B and AB. Comment on the results.
2. To try to convince the public to use safety equipment in automobiles, a random sample of 1000 accidents is chosen from the records. Each accident is classed according to type of safety restraint used by the occupants and severity of injuries received. These data result:

| | | Type of Restraint | | |
|---|---|---|---|---|
| | | SEAT BELT ONLY | SEAT BELT AND HARNESS | NONE |
| **Extent of Injury** | None | 75 | 60 | 65 |
| | Minor | 160 | 115 | 175 |
| | Major | 100 | 65 | 135 |
| | Death | 15 | 10 | 25 |
| | | | | 1000 |

   a. State and test the appropriate null hypothesis of no association. What is the $P$ value?
   b. Estimate the probability of death occurring when no restraint is used, the seat belt and harness are used, and only the seat belt is used. Comment on the practical implications of your findings.
   c. Estimate the probability of no injury, minor injuries, major injuries, and death when no restraint is utilized. Estimate the same probabilities when a seat belt and harness are used, and comment on the practical implications.
3. A study is run to investigate the association between flower color and fragrance in wild azaleas. Two hundred randomly selected, blooming plants yield the following data:

| | | Flower Color | | |
|---|---|---|---|---|
| | | WHITE | PINK | ORANGE |
| **Fragrance** | Yes | 12 | 60 | 58 |
| | No | 50 | 10 | 10 |

**a.** State the appropriate null hypothesis.

**b.** Can $H_0$ be rejected? What is the $P$ value of the test? What practical conclusion can be drawn trom these data?

**4.** In a study of goiter, random samples of specified size are selected from 10 states. The persons chosen are examined for goiter, and the number of cases found is recorded. The following data are obtained:

| | Goiter Test | |
|---|---|---|
| | POSITIVE | NEGATIVE |
| California | 36 | 500 |
| Kentucky | 17 | 350 |
| Louisiana | 12 | 300 |
| Massachusetts | 1 | 300 |
| Michigan | 4 | 350 |
| New York | 14 | 500 |
| South Carolina | 7 | 200 |
| Texas | 27 | 500 |
| Washington | 2 | 200 |
| West Virginia | 4 | 200 |
| | | 3400 |

**a.** State the null hypothesis of interest.

**b.** Test $H_0$ at the $\alpha = .05$ level.

**c.** Estimate the probability of a randomly selected individual from California having goiter. Estimate the probability of a randomly selected individual from Massachusetts having goiter.

**5.** A study is conducted to consider the association between the sulfur dioxide level in the air and the mean number of chloroplasts per leaf cell of trees in the area. A sample is chosen of 10 areas known to have a high sulfur dioxide concentration, 10 known to have a normal level of sulfur dioxide, and 10 known to have a low sulfur dioxide concentration. Twenty trees are randomly selected within each area, and the mean number of chloroplasts per leaf cell is determined for each tree. On this basis, each tree is classified as having a low, normal, or high chloropiast count. The following data result:

| | | Chloroplast Level | | | |
|---|---|---|---|---|---|
| | | HIGH | NORMAL | LOW | |
| **$SO_2$ Level** | High | 3 | 4 | 13 | 20 |
| | Normal | 5 | 10 | 5 | 20 |
| | Low | 7 | 11 | 2 | 20 |
| | | | | | |

**a.** State the appropriate null hypothesis.

**b.** Test the null hypothesis at the $\alpha = .05$ level.

**c.** Estimate the probability that a randomly selected tree will have a low chloroplast level, given that it is from an area with a high sulfur dioxide concentration. Estimate the probability that a randomly selected tree from an area of normal sulfur dioxide concentration will have a low chloroplast level. Estimate this probability for a randomly selected tree growing in an area of low sulfur dioxide concentration. Comment on the practical implications of these estimates.

# DISTRIBUTION-FREE METHODS

# 13.

Recall that most of the statistical procedures introduced thus far have an underlying assumption of normality. That is, we generally assume that the samples are drawn from distributions that are normal, or at least approximately so. For this reason, the procedures presented that are based on the $Z$, $T$, $X^2$, and $F$ distributions are referred to as constituting the body of *normal theory statistics*. We have seen how to test the validity of this assumption visually by using a histogram and statistically by using the chi-square goodness of fit test.

The natural question to ask is, What do you do if it appears that the normality assumption is not valid? Studies have shown that the use of the normal theory statistics in this case leads to tests that are approximate. In many cases, the approximations are excellent; in others, they are so bad as to be unacceptable. In any case, using normal theory statistics in situations in which the normal theory assumptions are violated leads to results that are suspect. There are two possible courses of action. First, we can try to transform the data so that the normal theory assumptions are met. Some methods for doing so are presented in [2], [12], [13]. Second, we can develop a body of statistical methods that presupposes little about the distribution of the sampled population. Such methods are called *distribution-free*. In this chapter we discuss some of the more frequently encountered distribution-free techniques. In particular, we include techniques paralleling those presented earlier. In this way, you have a viable alternative to many normal theory procedures.

Distribution-free statistical procedures have several appealing characteristics. In particular, the derivation of the test statistic in most cases depends only on counting methods, such as those presented in Chapters 2 and 3. Thus the logic behind each test generally is easy to follow. Distribution-free tests often require little computation and can be performed quickly. When sample sizes are small ($n \leq 10$), violations of the normal theory assumptions are hard to detect, but they can have disastrous effects. However, for these small samples, distribution-free tests compare very well with normal theory tests even when all the normal theory assumptions are met. If they are not met, the distribution-free procedure is usually superior. Thus unless all classical assumptions have been met, for small samples the wiser choice is a distribution-free test. One further advantage of distribution-free techniques should be pointed out. Many distribution-free methods involve analyzing the ranks of the observations, rather than the observations themselves. Thus these techniques are particularly useful with data that consist of ranks rather than measurements or counts.

## TESTS OF LOCATION: ONE SAMPLE

**13.1** □ In normal theory procedures, the usual measure of the center of location of the distribution of a random variable is its mean. In most distribution-free tests, the center of location is measured by the median of the random variable. The *median* of a random variable $X$ is defined to be the number $M$ such that

$$P[X < M] \leq \tfrac{1}{2} \qquad \text{and} \qquad P[X \leq M] \geq \tfrac{1}{2}$$

Note that if $X$ is continuous, then

$$P[X < M] = P[X \leq M] = \tfrac{1}{2}$$

That is, for a continuous random variable, the median is the point $M$ such that 50% of the time $X$ lies below $M$ and 50% of the time above $M$.

We discuss two tests for the median of a continuous random variable. The first, called the *sign test,* is based on the binomial distribution. It assumes only that the random variable under study is continuous.

### Sign Test for Median

Assume that $X$ is a continuous random variable with median $M$. Let $X_1$, $X_2, \ldots, X_n$ denote a random sample of size $n$ from the distribution of $X$. If we let $M_0$ denote the hypothesized value of the median, tests of hypotheses can take any of the usual three forms:

| Right-tailed test | Left-tailed test | Two-tailed test |
|---|---|---|
| $H_0: M \leq M_0$ | $H_0: M \geq M_0$ | $H_0: M = M_0$ |
| $H_1: M > M_0$ | $H_1: M < M_0$ | $H_1: M \neq M_0$ |

Note that if $H_0$ is true ($M = M_0$), then each of the continuous random variables $X_1, X_2, \ldots, X_n$ has probability $\tfrac{1}{2}$ of lying below $M_0$, probability $\tfrac{1}{2}$ of lying above $M_0$, and probability 0 of assuming the value $M_0$. This implies that each of the differences $X_1 - M_0, X_2 - M_0, \ldots, X_n - M_0$ has probability $\tfrac{1}{2}$ of being negative, probability $\tfrac{1}{2}$ of being positive, and probability 0 of assuming the value 0. Let $N$ and $N'$ denote the number of

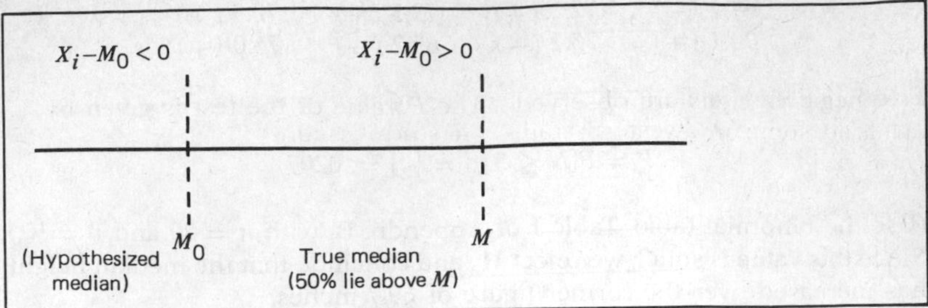


**FIGURE 13.1** Relationship between $M$ and $M_0$ (right-tailed test: $H_1$: $M > M_0$).

negative and positive signs obtained, respectively. If $H_0$ is true, each of these random variables has a binomial distribution with parameters $n$ and $1/2$ and expected value $n \cdot 1/2$. That is, if $H_0$ is true, we expect half the signs to positive and half to be negative.

Now consider the diagram of the relationship between $M$ and $M_0$ for a right-tailed test, shown in Figure 13.1. Clearly, if $H_1$ is true, then we should observe more positive signs and fewer negative signs than expected. In this case, we use $N$, the number of negative signs observed, as our test statistic. We reject $H_0$ ($M \leq M_0$) in favor of $H_1$ ($M > M_0$) if the observed value of $N$ is too small to have occurred by chance under the assumption that $H_0$ is true. For a left-tailed test, the situation is reversed. In this case, the test statistic is $N'$, the number of positive signs observed. Once again, $H_0$ is rejected in favor of $H_1$ if the observed value of the test statistic is too small to have occurred by chance. The test statistic for a two-tailed test is the smaller of $N$ and $N'$, with rejection of $H_0$ occurring for small values of this statistic.

We use the sign test for the median in Example 13.1.1.

---

**EXAMPLE 13.1.1** □ A study of growth based on data gathered from 1971 to 1974 indicates that the median height of men in the 18 to 24 years old group was 69.7 inches. It is felt that as a result of improvements in health care and nutrition, the median height among young men in this age group is currently larger than 69.7. So we wish to test

$$H_0: M \leq 69.7 \qquad H_1: M > 69.7$$

Since the test is right-tailed, the test statistic is $N$, the number of negative differences obtained when the hypothesized median (69.7) is subtracted from each observation. These data result:

|  |  |  |  |
|---|---|---|---|
| 70.2 (+) | 65.8 (−) | 78.0 (+) | 74.4 (+) |
| 71.4 (+) | 67.3 (−) | 72.6 (+) | 67.5 (−) |
| 69.8 (+) | 71.4 (+) | 69.9 (+) | 70.5 (+) |

| | | | |
|---|---|---|---|
| 67.2 (−) | 72.1 (+) | 73.5 (+) | 70.9 (+) |
| 70.1 (+) | 73.2 (+) | 65.2 (−) | 76.0 (+) |

Five negative signs are observed. The $P$ value of the test is given by

$$P = P[N \leq 5 \mid p = \tfrac{1}{2}] = .0207$$

(Use the binomial table, Table I of Appendix B, with $n = 20$ and $p = \tfrac{1}{2}$.) Since this value is small, we reject $H_0$ and conclude that the median height has increased over the former figure of 69.7 inches.

---

Several points should be made about the sign test for median. The rationale behind the test is quite logical. It requires very little computation and therefore is quick and easy to apply. It presupposes very little about the distribution of the population from which the sampling is done, requiring only that it be continuous. If, in fact, the distribution is also normal, then the mean and the median are the same. In this case, the sign test is testing the same hypothesis as that tested previously by using the one-sample $T$ test (Chapter 7).

Now we discuss the Wilcoxon signed-rank test for the median. This test, developed by F. Wilcoxon in 1945, tests the null hypothesis that a continuous distribution is symmetric about a hypothesized median $M_0$.

**Wilcoxon Signed-Rank Test**

Let $X_1, X_2, X_3, \ldots, X_n$ be a random sample of size $n$ from a continuous distribution. Consider the set of differences $X_1 - M_0, X_2 - M_0, \ldots, X_n - M_0$, where $M_0$ is the hypothesized median of the distribution from which the sample is drawn. If the null hypothesis is true, then these differences are drawn from a distribution that is symmetric about zero. To conduct the test, we first consider the set of $n$ absolute differences $|X_i - M_0|$ and order them from smallest to largest. We then rank them from 1 to $n$, with the smallest absolute difference receiving the rank of 1. Each rank $R_i$ is assigned the algebraic sign of the difference score that generated the rank. If the null hypothesis is true and the differences are symmetric about zero, then each rank is just as likely to be assigned a positive sign as a negative sign.

Consider the statistics

$$W_+ = \sum_{\substack{\text{all} \\ \text{positive} \\ \text{ranks}}} R_i \quad \text{and} \quad |W_-| = \left| \sum_{\substack{\text{all} \\ \text{negative} \\ \text{ranks}}} R_i \right|$$

If $H_0$ is true, each of these should be about the same size. If the true population median is actually larger than the hypothesized median, then we will obtain too many positive differences, too many positive ranks, $W_+$ will be larger than expected, and $|W_-|$ will be smaller than expected. If the true median is smaller than the hypothesized value, then the situation is reversed. Thus we can use as our test statistic $W$, the smaller of $W_+$ and $|W_-|$. The distribution of this statistic has been tabled for various values of $\alpha$ and $n$. One such table is Table IX of Appendix B. The null hypothesis is always rejected for values of $W$ that are too small to have occurred by chance. Thus we reject $H_0$ if the observed value of $W$ falls on or below the critical point listed in Table IX.

We show how to use the Wilcoxon signed-rank test in Example 13.1.2.

---

**EXAMPLE 13.1.2** □ The current median survival time of patients with acute myelogenous leukemia who achieve complete remission from conventional treatment is 21 months. A new procedure is being studied. It is hoped that the median survival time will be improved. These survival times are noted for 10 patients who received the new treatment:

| | | | | |
|---|---|---|---|---|
| 24.1 | 25.8 | 20.5 | 20.9 | 27.3 |
| 21.5 | 20.1 | 28.9 | 19.2 | 26.3 |

To test for symmetry about 21, first we form the set of 10 differences by subtracting 21 from each observed survival time:

| $X_i$ | 24.1 | 21.5 | 25.8 | 20.1 | 20.5 | 28.9 | 20.9 | 19.2 | 27.3 | 26.3 |
|---|---|---|---|---|---|---|---|---|---|---|
| $X_i - 21$ | 3.1 | .5 | 4.8 | −.9 | −.5 | 7.9 | −.1 | −1.8 | 6.3 | 5.3 |

Now we order the absolute values of these differences from smallest to largest, rank them from 1 to 10, and assign to each rank the algebraic sign of the difference that generated the rank. Note that because of the continuity assumption, no ties should occur. However, in practice, ties do occur. For example, the absolute difference of .5 is obtained twice. When this happens, all tied scores are assigned the average group rank. This idea is illustrated here:

| $\lvert X_i - 21\rvert$ | .1 | .5 | .5 | .9 | 1.8 | 3.1 | 4.8 | 5.3 | 6.3 | 7.9 |
|---|---|---|---|---|---|---|---|---|---|---|
| Rank $R_i$ | 1 | 2.5 | 2.5 | 4 | 5 | 6 | 7 | 8 | 9 | 10 |
| Signed rank | −1 | −2.5 | 2.5 | −4 | −5 | 6 | 7 | 8 | 9 | 10 |

The observed values of $W_+$ and $|W_-|$ are

$$W_+ = \sum_{\substack{\text{all} \\ \text{positive} \\ \text{ranks}}} R_i = 2.5 + 6 + 7 + 8 + 9 + 10 = 42.5$$

and

$$|W_-| = \left| \sum_{\substack{\text{all}\\ \text{negative}\\ \text{ranks}}} R_i \right| = |-1 + (-2.5) + (-4) + (-5)| = 12.5$$

Our test statistic is $W$, the smaller of the two. From Table IX in Appendix B, we see that for a sample of size 10, $P[W \leq 12.5]$ is larger than .05. (The critical point for an $\alpha = .05$ test is 11.) Thus we do not have sufficient evidence based on this sample that the new procedure has increased the median survival time.

---

Several things are notable concerning the Wilcoxon signed-rank test. It, like the sign test, assumes that the distribution from which the sampling is done is continuous. If the distribution is also symmetric, then the test is a test for both the median and the mean of the distribution, since in this case these two parameters are identical. Occasionally from past experience we know that a population is symmetric, but more often we do not. When the latter is the case, the sign test is preferred as a test for location. If there is evidence that the distribution is normal, then the Wilcoxon signed-rank test is testing the same hypothesis as that tested by the one-sample $T$ test in normal theory statistics.

---

## EXERCISES 13.1

1. Recent studies of private practices that handle no Medicaid patients indicate that the median length of a patient visit is 22 minutes. It is thought that the median visit length in practices with a large Medicaid load is smaller than this figure. These data are obtained on 20 randomly selected patient visits for one such practice:

| LENGTH OF PATIENT VISIT, MINUTES | | | |
|---|---|---|---|
| 21.6 | 13.4 | 20.4 | 16.4 |
| 23.5 | 26.8 | 24.8 | 19.3 |
| 23.4 | 9.4 | 16.8 | 21.9 |
| 24.9 | 15.6 | 20.1 | 16.2 |
| 18.7 | 18.1 | 19.1 | 18.9 |

Based on the sign test, is there sufficient evidence to conclude that for this practice the median length of a patient visit is less than 22 minutes? Explain your answer on the basis of the expected number of positive signs under $H_0$ and the $P$ value of the test.

2. A study is conducted of nutrition among patients with respiratory failure who require ventilatory support. One variable considered is the creatinine height index, which is a measure of the patient's protein level. An index value less than 6 is considered indicative of a serious protein deficiency. If the median index value among this type of patient is shown to lie below 6, then a new dietary program will be put into effect to correct the problem. These values are obtained from a random sample of 15 patients:

| | | | |
|---|---|---|---|
| 5.7 | 4.2 | 4.7 | 4.6 |
| 5.3 | 5.4 | 6.8 | 4.9 |
| 4.9 | 5.8 | 4.1 | 5.5 |
| 6.4 | 5.1 | 4.7 | |

Based on the sign test, is there evidence that the median index reading is below 6? Explain your answer based on the expected number of positive signs under $H_0$ and the $P$ value of the test.

3. Well-developed pasture soils should contain indigenous mycorrhizal fungi, which greatly stimulate the growth of clover and rye grass. The median number of spores per gram of soil in good pastureland is 9. In eroded areas, the mycorrhizal infectivity is thought to be highly reduced. Do these data, obtained from 20 eroded areas, tend to support this contention? Explain on the basis of the $P$ value of the sign test.

| | | | | |
|---|---|---|---|---|
| .01 | .12 | .28 | .54 | 2.7 |
| .02 | .15 | .30 | .92 | 2.7 |
| .06 | .16 | .32 | 1.52 | 8.24 |
| .08 | .24 | .48 | 1.64 | 9.3 |

4. A study is made of alarm calling in ground squirrels. One variable considered is the maximal audible range of a warning call. The median maximal audible range is thought to be more than 87 meters. Do these data support this contention? Explain your answer based on the expected number of negative signs under $H_0$ and the $P$ value of the test. (The $P$ value can be found by using the normal approximation to the binomial distribution, explained in Chapter 5.)

MAXIMAL AUDIBLE RANGE, METERS

| | | | | | | | |
|---|---|---|---|---|---|---|---|
| 88.7 | 76.9 | 90.8 | 79.4 | 94.4 | 96.7 | 85.9 | 84.1 |
| 92.6 | 95.9 | 91.9 | 94.3 | 95.1 | 84.5 | 85.6 | 78.0 |
| 93.3 | 85.8 | 85.2 | 89.7 | 82.0 | 88.2 | 81.2 | 90.5 |
| 82.1 | 85.9 | 88.6 | 95.6 | 89.4 | 87.3 | 83.5 | 90.6 |
| 87.8 | 87.1 | 98.5 | 87.1 | 82.1 | 86.7 | 82.4 | 88.1 |

*5. Note that $W_+ + |W_-| = 1 + 2 + 3 + \cdots + n$. From high school algebra this sum is given by $n(n+1)/2$. This fact can be used as a check on the accuracy of your ranking and computation of the values of $W_+$ and $|W_-|$ when the Wilcoxon test is utilized. Verify this result for the data of Example 13.1.2, in which $n = 10$.

***6.** If the null hypothesis is that the distribution from which we are sampling is symmetric about the hypothesized median $M_0$, then the expected value of $W_+$ is given by

$$E[W_+] = \frac{n(n+1)}{4}$$

Find the expected value of $W_+$ for Example 13.1.2 ($n = 10$).

**7.** Whirligig beetles aggregate in the daytime into dense, single-species and multispecies groups, called ***rafts,*** of hundreds of individuals. The median distance between rafts is thought to be less than .8 km. Use the Wilcoxon signed-rank test to test this hypothesized value, based on these data. Assume symmetry.

| | | | | |
|---|---|---|---|---|
| .71 | .65 | .51 | .32 | .21 |
| .13 | .21 | 1.10 | .71 | 1.63 |
| .16 | 1.00 | 1.11 | .40 | |

**8.** Preliminary studies on black widows indicate that the median time spent on the ground when the spider touches down to attach a fiber during web building is less than 16 seconds. To verify this finding, spiders engaged in active web building are observed. These data result (assume symmetry):

| TIME ON GROUND, SECONDS | | | | |
|---|---|---|---|---|
| 18.9 | 9.3 | 10.8 | 20.0 | 11.9 |
| 11.7 | 19.8 | 11.1 | 15.5 | 9.8 |
| 15.9 | 13.1 | 23.7 | 10.4 | 11.9 |
| 25.2 | 13.5 | 8.9 | 12.5 | 19.9 |
| 21.3 | 8.5 | 17.5 | 18.9 | 13.4 |

If the true median is 16 seconds, what is the expected value of $W_+$? (See Exercise 13.1.6.) What is the observed value of $W_+$? Do the data tend to support the contention that the median time spent on the ground is less than 16 seconds? Explain your answer based on the $P$ value of the Wilcoxon test.

**9.** The median age of onset of diabetes is thought to be 45 years. Assume that the distribution of the variable age of onset is symmetric. We wish to test

$$H_0\!: M = 45 \qquad H_1\!: M \neq 45$$

at the $\alpha = .05$ level, using the Wilcoxon signed-rank test based on a sample of size 30.

**a.** What is the critical point for the test?

**b.** What is the test statistic for the test?

**c.** These data result from a study of 30 randomly selected diabetics:

| | | | | |
|---|---|---|---|---|
| 35.5 | 30.5 | 40.1 | 59.8 | 47.3 |
| 44.5 | 48.9 | 36.8 | 52.4 | 36.6 |
| 39.8 | 42.1 | 39.3 | 26.2 | 55.6 |
| 33.3 | 40.3 | 65.4 | 60.9 | 45.1 |
| 51.4 | 46.8 | 42.6 | 45.6 | 52.2 |
| 51.3 | 38.0 | 42.8 | 27.1 | 43.5 |

Can $H_0$ be rejected? To what type of error are we now subject?

**10.** In 1970 it was reported that the median cost of an initial office visit to a physician was \$14.23. Although the cost for such a visit is certainly higher in current dollars, with inflation taken into account there may not have been a real rise in price relative to the economy as a whole. These data represent the current cost of an initial office visit, adjusted to 1970 dollars. Assuming symmetry, do the data indicate that the median cost is now higher than the 1970 median? Explain your answer on the basis of the $P$ value of the Wilcoxon test.

| CURRENT COST, 1970 DOLLARS | | | | |
|---|---|---|---|---|
| 16.14 | 15.71 | 16.23 | 17.44 | 16.88 |
| 15.79 | 15.10 | 15.82 | 15.89 | 16.99 |
| 14.08 | 16.30 | 14.88 | 14.02 | 14.22 |
| 17.22 | 14.39 | 16.04 | 14.56 | 15.32 |
| 16.18 | 15.26 | 16.73 | 16.03 | 13.94 |

***11.** *Normal Approximation to* $W_+$. For large values of $n$, $W_+$ and $|W_-|$ are each approximately normally distributed with mean $n(n+1)/4$ and variance

$$\frac{n(n+1)(2n+1)}{24}$$

This fact can be used to approximate $P$ values for values of $n$ not listed in Table IX of Appendix B. We need only standardize $W_+$ or $|W_-|$ and approximate $P$, using the standard normal table. Since we are approximating a discrete distribution, the $\frac{1}{2}$-unit correction factor for continuity should be used.

**a.** For a sample of size 70, find $P[W_+ \leq 1000]$.

**b.** For a sample of size 80, find $P[|W_-| \leq 1500]$.

## TESTS OF LOCATION: PAIRED DATA

**13.2** □ We consider now two tests for location that use paired observations. The first, the sign test for median difference, is an extension of the sign test just presented.

### Sign Test for Median Difference

Let $X$ and $Y$ be continuous random variables. Let $(X_1, Y_1), (X_2, Y_2), \ldots, (X_n, Y_n)$ be a random sample of size $n$ from the distribution of $(X, Y)$. Consider the set of $n$ continuous differences $X_1 - Y_1, X_2 - Y_2, \ldots,$

$X_n - Y_n$. The null hypothesis is that the median difference is zero. That is, we are testing

$$H_0: M_{X-Y} = 0$$

If $H_0$ is true, each of the differences $X_i - Y_i$ has probability $1/2$ of being positive, probability $1/2$ of being negative, and probability 0 of assuming the value 0. Let $N$ and $N'$ denote the number of negative and positive signs obtained, respectively. If $H_0$ is true, then each of these random variables is binomially distributed with parameters $n$ and $1/2$. Thus if $H_0$ is true, we expect half the observed differences to be positive and half to be negative. If the median difference is actually positive, then we should obtain too many positive signs and too few negative signs. If the actual median difference is negative, then the situation is reversed. Thus we may use as our test statistic the smaller of $N$ and $N'$. We reject $H_0$ in favor of the appropriate alternative if the observed value of the test statistic is too small to have occurred by chance under the assumption that $H_0$ is true.

The use of this test is illustrated in Example 13.2.1.

---

**EXAMPLE 13.2.1** □ In a study of the use of Captopril with diuretic-treated hypertensive patients, a 6.25-mg dose is used. Each patient's systolic blood pressure is noted before she or he receives the drug ($X$) and again 70 min after the drug is administered ($Y$). To determine whether the drug is effective in reducing blood pressure in these patients, we test

$$H_0: M_{X-Y} \le 0 \qquad H_1: M_{X-Y} > 0$$

If $H_1$ is true, we expect very few negative differences. The test statistic is therefore $N$, the number of negative signs obtained. These data result:

| $X$ (BEFORE) | $Y$ (AFTER) | SIGN OF $X - Y$ |
|---|---|---|
| 175 | 140 | + |
| 179 | 143 | + |
| 165 | 135 | + |
| 170 | 133 | + |
| 160 | 162 | − |
| 180 | 150 | + |
| 177 | 182 | − |
| 178 | 139 | + |
| 173 | 140 | + |
| 176 | 141 | + |

The observed value of $N$ is 2. The $P$ value for the test is given by

$$P = P[N \leq 2 \mid p = \tfrac{1}{2}] = .0547$$

(Use Table I of Appendix B with $n = 10$ and $p = \tfrac{1}{2}$.) Since this probability is fairly small, we reject $H_0$ and conclude that Captopril is effective in reducing systolic blood pressure in diuretic-treated hypertensive patients.

---

Note that the sign test for median difference assumes only that both $X$ and $Y$ are continuous. If each is also normal, then $X - Y$ is normal. In this case, the median difference is equal to the mean difference, which, in turn, is equal to the difference in the population means. That is,

$$M_{X-Y} = \mu_{X-Y} = \mu_X - \mu_Y$$

Thus if $X$ and $Y$ are normal, then testing the null hypothesis $H_0$: $M_{X-Y} = 0$ is equivalent to testing the null hypothesis of equal population means. This is the same hypothesis as that tested by the paired $T$ test in normal theory statistics.

The next test that we consider for use with paired data is the Wilcoxon signed-rank test for matched observations. This test is conducted in exactly the same manner as the signed-rank test for the median illustrated in Section 13.1.

### Wilcoxon Signed-Rank Test: Paired Data

Let $X$ and $Y$ be continuous random variables. Let $(X_1, Y_1), (X_2, Y_2), \ldots, (X_n, Y_n)$ be a random sample of size $n$ from the distribution of $(X, Y)$. Consider the set of continuous differences $X_1 - Y_1$, $X_2 - Y_2$, $\ldots, X_n - Y_n$. The null hypothesis is that these differences are drawn from a population that is symmetric about zero. The test is performed by ordering the absolute values of these differences from smallest to largest and ranking them from 1 to $n$ (assigning tied scores the average group rank). Then each rank is assigned the sign of the difference that generated the rank, and the value is computed of

$$W_+ = \sum_{\substack{\text{all}\\ \text{positive}\\ \text{ranks}}} R_i \qquad \text{and} \qquad |W_-| = \left| \sum_{\substack{\text{all}\\ \text{negative}\\ \text{ranks}}} R_i \right|$$

The test statistic is $W$, the smaller of $W_+$ and $|W_-|$. Hypothesis $H_0$ is rejected in favor of the appropriate alternative for values of $W$ that are too small to have occurred by chance, based on Table IX of Appendix B.

Example 13.2.2 illustrates the use of Wilcoxon's procedure with paired data.

**EXAMPLE 13.2.2** □ The accidental incorporation of polybrominated biphenyl (PBB) compounds into high-protein dairy pellets led to the contamination of dairy herds in some midwestern states. A study is conducted to determine whether cooking reduces the PBB level in meat from contaminated animals. The experiment is conducted by measuring the PBB level in raw roast sirloin tip ($X$), cooking the roast, and then measuring the PBB level in the cooked meat ($Y$). If cooking reduces the PBB level, then we expect very few negative differences when subtraction is done in the order $X - Y$. Our test statistic is therefore $|W_-|$. We conclude that cooking effectively reduces the PBB level if the observed value of this statistic is too *small* to have occurred by chance. These data (in ppm) result (assume symmetry):

| $X$ (RAW) | $Y$ (COOKED) | $X - Y$ (DIFFERENCE) |
|---|---|---|
| .19 | .15 | .04 |
| .20 | .10 | .10 |
| .01 | .02 | −.01 |
| .16 | .18 | −.02 |
| .15 | .10 | .05 |
| .27 | .04 | .23 |
| .08 | .01 | .07 |
| .23 | .15 | .08 |
| .07 | .04 | .03 |
| .10 | .10 | 0 |

We now order the absolute values of the differences smallest to largest and rank them from 1 to 10. In assigning signs to the ranks, there is one problem. What algebraic sign is associated with the difference 0, which is neither positive nor negative? Theoretically, because of the continuity of both $X$ and $Y$, a zero difference should not occur. However, in practice, as a result of difficulties in measurement, a zero difference does arise occasionally. There are various suggestions as to how to handle the problem. We take a conservative approach. Since the null hypothesis is that the population of differences is symmetric about 0, a zero difference tends to support $H_0$. Thus logically we should assign to the 0 difference the sign least conducive to the rejection of $H_0$. In this case, we assign a negative sign, since this will increase the size of $|W_-|$ and make it harder to reject $H_0$. The results of the signed ranking are as follows:

| $\lvert X_i - Y_i \rvert$ | 0 | .01 | .02 | .03 | .04 | .05 | .07 | .08 | .10 | .23 |
|---|---|---|---|---|---|---|---|---|---|---|
| Rank $R_i$ | 1 | 2 | 3 | 4 | 5 | 6 | 7 | 8 | 9 | 10 |
| Signed rank | −1 | −2 | −3 | 4 | 5 | 6 | 7 | 8 | 9 | 10 |

The observed value of $|W_-|$ is

$$|W_-| = \left|\sum_{\substack{\text{all}\\\text{negative}\\\text{ranks}}} R_i\right| = |-1 + (-2) + (-3)| = 6$$

From Table IX of Appendix B, the $P$ value of the test ($P[|W_-| \leq 6]$) lies between .01 (critical point, 5) and .025 (critical point, 8). Since this value is small, we reject $H_0$ and conclude that cooking does tend to reduce the PBB level in contaminated meat.

---

Again, it is important to note the relationship between this test and others previously presented. If the population of differences is known to be symmetric, then you are testing the null hypothesis that the median difference is zero. This is the same hypothesis as that tested by the sign test. If you do not know that the population is symmetric and wish to test a hypothesis about the median, then the sign test is preferable to the Wilcoxon test. If there is evidence that the population of differences is normally distributed, then you are testing $H_0$: $\mu_X = \mu_Y$, the same hypothesis as that tested by the paired $T$ test in normal theory statistics.

---

## EXERCISES 13.2

**1.** A 20-week physical conditioning program for women is conducted. One variable studied is the maximal oxygen uptake of the subject. This is measured while she is using a treadmill both before ($X$) and after ($Y$) the training period. It is hoped that the training will increase the value of this variable for most subjects.

**a.** The research hypothesis is $H_1$: $M_{X-Y} < 0$. What is the test statistic for detecting this situation?

**b.** These data result:

Maximal Oxygen Uptake, liters/minute

| SUBJECT | BEFORE ($X$) | AFTER ($Y$) |
|---|---|---|
| 1 | 1.98 | 2.26 |
| 2 | 1.57 | 1.83 |
| 3 | 1.89 | 2.31 |
| 4 | 1.42 | 1.79 |
| 5 | 1.73 | 1.65 |
| 6 | 1.95 | 2.26 |
| 7 | 1.69 | 2.10 |
| 8 | 1.92 | 2.15 |
| 9 | 1.96 | 1.54 |
| 10 | 1.94 | 1.87 |

Use the sign test to test

$$H_0: M_{X-Y} \geq 0 \qquad H_1: M_{X-Y} < 0$$

Can we conclude that the training tends to increase the maximal oxygen uptake? Explain on the basis of $P$ value of the test.

2. A study of hand reaction time among Indian hockey players is conducted. The purpose is to compare visual with auditory reaction time. Visual reaction time is measured by noting the time needed to respond to a light signal; auditory reaction time is the time needed to respond to the click of an electric switch. These times are noted for 15 subjects:

| | Reaction Time, milliseconds | |
|---|---|---|
| SUBJECT | VISUAL | AUDITORY |
| 1 | 165.75 | 162.32 |
| 2 | 207.57 | 211.84 |
| 3 | 240.21 | 202.65 |
| 4 | 180.50 | 166.14 |
| 5 | 205.89 | 239.14 |
| 6 | 192.96 | 201.51 |
| 7 | 233.16 | 184.88 |
| 8 | 215.86 | 170.48 |
| 9 | 195.76 | 207.34 |
| 10 | 182.82 | 198.44 |
| 11 | 164.37 | 177.82 |
| 12 | 232.54 | 142.28 |
| 13 | 197.55 | 187.09 |
| 14 | 196.58 | 164.42 |
| 15 | 216.09 | 161.39 |

Is there evidence, based on the sign test, that the visual reaction time tends to be slower than the auditory reaction time? Explain on the basis of the $P$ value of the test.

3. A study is run to determine the effects of removing a renal blockage in patients whose renal function is impaired because of advanced metastatic malignancy of nonurologic cause. The arterial blood pressure of each patient is measured before ($X$) and after ($Y$) surgery. These data are found:

Arterial Blood Pressure, mmHg

| PATIENT | BEFORE ($X$) | AFTER ($Y$) |
|---|---|---|
| 1 | 150 | 90 |
| 2 | 132 | 102 |
| 3 | 130 | 80 |
| 4 | 116 | 82 |
| 5 | 107 | 90 |
| 6 | 100 | 94 |
| 7 | 101 | 84 |
| 8 | 96 | 93 |
| 9 | 90 | 89 |
| 10 | 78 | 85 |

Based on the sign test, can you conclude that the surgery tends to lower arterial blood pressure? Explain on the basis of the $P$ value of the test.

**4.** A study of the effects of physical training on postcoronary patients included measurements on maximum oxygen uptake, which was determined for each patient before training began ($X$). After 6 months of bicycle exercise 3 times per week, each person's oxygen uptake was determined again ($Y$). These data result (assume symmetry):

Maximum Oxygen Uptake, ml/(kg)(min)

| PATIENT | BEFORE ($X$) | AFTER ($Y$) |
|---|---|---|
| 1 | 46.98 | 40.96 |
| 2 | 23.98 | 26.21 |
| 3 | 48.25 | 57.25 |
| 4 | 41.24 | 38.83 |
| 5 | 42.90 | 52.17 |
| 6 | 42.45 | 54.02 |
| 7 | 23.00 | 24.58 |
| 8 | 30.39 | 51.51 |
| 9 | 33.80 | 31.62 |
| 10 | 47.41 | 54.83 |

Based on the Wilcoxon signed-rank test, can you conclude at the $\alpha = .05$ level that exercise tends to increase the maximum oxygen uptake in these patients?

5. A study of the courtship behavior of domesticated zebra finches is run to determine the effect of beak color in the female on the number of song patterns sung by the male during courtship. It is thought that the red beak, a sign of maturity, will elicit more patterns than the black beak, which is found in juvenile birds. Each of 10 mature males is presented separately with a live red-beaked and live black-beaked female bird. The male's behavior is observed in each case. The measured variable is the mean number of song patterns over three 10-minute observation periods with each female:

| | Mean Number of Song Patterns | |
|---|---|---|
| BIRD NUMBER | RED BEAK ($X$) | BLACK BEAK ($Y$) |
| 1 | 11.24 | 2.19 |
| 2 | 12.21 | 1.69 |
| 3 | 11.7 | 9.84 |
| 4 | 14.09 | 13.98 |
| 5 | 15.7 | 12.66 |
| 6 | 16.9 | 7.9 |
| 7 | 17.08 | 14.78 |
| 8 | 11.17 | 15.66 |
| 9 | 15.18 | 11.06 |
| 10 | 14.72 | 20.08 |

**a.** Assume symmetry and use the Wilcoxon signed-rank test to test

$$H_0: M_{X-Y} \leq 0 \qquad H_1: M_{X-Y} > 0$$

at the $\alpha = .05$ level.

**b.** If we do not assume symmetry, then the hypothesis

$$H_0: M_{X-Y} \leq 0 \qquad H_1: M_{X-Y} > 0$$

is best tested by the sign test. If the sign test is used, can $H_0$ be rejected at the $\alpha = .05$ level?

6. In a study of mild hypertension among patients aged 21 to 29 years, two groups are used. An experimental group receives chlorthalidone plus reserpine; a second group receives a placebo. The total cholesterol level for each patient is determined at the outset of the study and again at the end of 1 year of treatment. The following data result:

TOTAL CHOLESTEROL LEVEL (MG/DL)

| Chlorthalidone and Reserpine | | Placebo | |
|---|---|---|---|
| BEFORE TREATMENT ($X$) | AFTER TREATMENT ($Y$) | BEFORE TREATMENT ($X$) | AFTER TREATMENT ($Y$) |
| 192.3 | 172.1 | 180.5 | 182.3 |
| 178.6 | 164.1 | 170.1 | 170.9 |
| 185.7 | 171.4 | 174.1 | 170.2 |
| 175.3 | 152.9 | 180.4 | 178.3 |
| 183.9 | 163.9 | 175.4 | 175.8 |
| 182.6 | 170.7 | 188.4 | 186.1 |
| 180.9 | 165.3 | 182.8 | 185.1 |
| 184.2 | 164.2 | 181.0 | 177.6 |

Assuming symmetry, use Wilcoxon's signed-rank test to test

$$H_0\colon M_{X-Y} \leq 0 \qquad H_1\colon M_{X-Y} > 0$$

at the $\alpha = .05$ level for each group.

## TESTS OF LOCATION: UNMATCHED DATA

**13.3** □ In this section we discuss a distribution-free test that can be used to compare the locations of two continuous populations based on independent sample sizes $m$ and $n$ drawn from those populations. The test is called the *Wilcoxon rank-sum test.*

### Wilcoxon Rank-Sum Test

Let $X$ and $Y$ be continuous random variables. Let $X_1, X_2, \ldots, X_m$ and $Y_1, Y_2, \ldots, Y_n$ be independent random samples of size $m$ and $n$ from the distribution of $X$ and $Y$, respectively. Assume that $m \leq n$. That is, assume that the $X$'s represent the smaller sample. The null hypothesis is that the $X$ and $Y$ populations are identical. We wish to test this hypothesis with a test that is especially likely to reject $H_0$ if the populations differ in location. The $m + n$ observations are pooled to form a single sample. These observations are linearly ordered and ranked from 1 to $m + n$, retaining their group identity. Tied scores receive the average group rank, as in previous Wilcoxon tests.

The test statistic is $W_m$, the sum of the ranks associated with the observations that originally constituted the *smaller* sample ($X$ values). The logic behind this choice of test statistic is as follows. If the $X$ population is located below the $Y$ population, then the smaller ranks will tend to be associated with the $X$ values. This will produce a small value for $W_m$. If the reverse is true (the $X$ population is located above the $Y$ population), then the larger ranks will be found among the $X$ values, producing a large value of $W_m$. Thus we should reject $H_0$ if the observed value of $W_m$ is too small or too large to have occurred by chance. Table X of Appendix B gives the probabilities for selected values of $m$ and $n$. We show how to use this table in Example 13.3.1.

---

**EXAMPLE 13.3.1** □ In a study of smoking and its effects on sleep patterns, one variable is the time that it takes to fall asleep. A random sample of size 12 is drawn from the population of smokers; an independent sample of size 15 is drawn from the population of nonsmokers. These data result:

Time to Sleep, minutes

| SMOKERS (*S*) | | NONSMOKERS (*N*) | |
|---|---|---|---|
| 69.3 | 52.7 | 28.6 | 30.6 |
| 56.0 | 34.4 | 25.1 | 31.8 |
| 22.1 | 60.2 | 26.4 | 41.6 |
| 47.6 | 43.8 | 34.9 | 21.1 |
| 53.2 | | 29.8 | 36.0 |
| 48.1 | | 28.4 | 37.9 |
| 23.2 | | 38.5 | 13.9 |
| 13.8 | | 30.2 | |

Do these data indicate that smokers tend to take longer to fall asleep than nonsmokers?

To answer this question, we pool the two samples, order the observations from smallest to largest, retaining their group identity, and rank them from 1 to 27:

| OBSERVATION | 13.8 | 13.9 | 21.1 | 22.1 | 23.2 | 25.1 | 26.4 | 28.4 | 28.6 |
|---|---|---|---|---|---|---|---|---|---|
| Group | S | N | N | S | S | N | N | N | N |
| Rank | 1 | 2 | 3 | 4 | 5 | 6 | 7 | 8 | 9 |

| OBSERVATION | 29.8 | 30.2 | 30.6 | 31.8 | 34.4 | 34.9 | 36.0 | 37.9 | 38.5 |
|---|---|---|---|---|---|---|---|---|---|
| Group | N | N | N | N | S | N | N | N | N |
| Rank | 10 | 11 | 12 | 13 | 14 | 15 | 16 | 17 | 18 |

| OBSERVATION | 41.6 | 43.8 | 47.6 | 48.1 | 52.7 | 53.2 | 56.0 | 60.2 | 69.3 |
|---|---|---|---|---|---|---|---|---|---|
| Group | N | S | S | S | S | S | S | S | S |
| Rank | 19 | 20 | 21 | 22 | 23 | 24 | 25 | 26 | 27 |

Since the sample from the population of smokers ($m = 12$) is smaller than that of nonsmokers ($n = 15$), the test statistic $W_m$ is the sum of the ranks associated with the smokers. Since we suspect that smokers take longer to fall asleep than nonsmokers, we reject the null hypothesis of no difference between the two groups if the observed value of $W_m$ is too large to have occurred by chance. For these data

$$W_m = 1 + 4 + 5 + 14 + 20 + 21 + 22 + 23 + 24 + 25 + 26 + 27$$
$$= 212$$

We now turn to Table X in Appendix B, entering with $m = 12$ and $n = m + 3 = 15$. The critical point for an $\alpha = .05$, right-tailed test is 202. Since $212 > 202$, we reject $H_0$ and conclude that smokers do tend to take longer to fall asleep than nonsmokers.

If both the $X$ and $Y$ populations are assumed normal, then the Wilcoxon rank-sum test tests the same hypothesis as the pooled $T$ test in normal theory statistics.

Several other distribution-free tests are equivalent to the Wilcoxon rank-sum test. The best known alternative is the Mann-Whitney test. This test also depends on linearly ordering the $X$ and $Y$ observations. The test statistic in this case is $U$, the number of times that an $X$ value precedes a $Y$ value. If the $X$ population is located below the $Y$ population, then $U$ will be large; if the reverse is true, $U$ will be small. The probability distribution for $U$ also has been tabulated for selected sample sizes. Since the test is equivalent to the Wilcoxon test, there is no need to present both here.

## EXERCISES 13.3

1. Nerve growth factor (NGF) is a protein that has been shown to play a role in the development and maintenance of peripheral sympathetic neurons. One approach to the study of NGF is to deprive the animal of NGF and study the effect of this deprivation on various cell types. In this study, the effect on the total protein content in the dorsal root ganglia of rats is considered. Two groups of rats are compared: those born to NGF-deficient females (in utero) and those born to normal females but nursed by NGF-deficient females (in milk). These data result:

Total Protein Content, milligrams of protein per dorsal root ganglion

| IN UTERO ($U$) | | IN MILK ($M$) | |
|---|---|---|---|
| .12 | .09 | .19 | .20 |
| .19 | .13 | .21 | .22 |
| .17 | .21 | .21 | |
| .20 | | .23 | |

Do these data indicate at the $\alpha = .05$ level that the total protein content tends to be smaller among rats deprived of NGF in utero than among those deprived of the growth factor in milk?

2. Polychlorinated biphenyls (PCBs) are worldwide environmental contaminants of industrial origin that are related to DDT. They are being phased out in the United States, but they will remain in the environment for many years. An experiment is run to study the effects of PCB on the reproductive ability of screech owls. The purpose is to compare the shell thickness of eggs produced by birds exposed to PCB with that of birds not exposed to the contaminant. It is thought that shells of the former group will be thinner than those of the latter. Do these data support this research hypothesis? Explain.

Shell Thickness, mm

| EXPOSED TO PCB ($E$) | | FREE OF PCB ($F$) | |
|---|---|---|---|
| .21 | .226 | .22 | .27 |
| .223 | .215 | .265 | .18 |
| .25 | .24 | .217 | .187 |
| .19 | .136 | .20 | .256 |
| .20 | | .23 | |

3. In a study of characteristics of patients experiencing myocardial infarction, the cardiac volume of those whose duration of pain is less than 8 hr is compared with that of patients whose pain lasted 8 hr or more. These data result:

Cardiac Volume, ml

| LESS THAN 8 HR ($<$) | | 8 HR OR MORE ($\geq$) | |
|---|---|---|---|
| 793.4 | 760.5 | 979.1 | 940.7 |
| 906.5 | 856.6 | 797.0 | 1009.9 |
| 604.1 | 899.1 | 961.8 | 1330.3 |
| 646.8 | 806.8 | 1100.6 | 909.3 |
| 688.1 | 968.1 | 843.6 | 812.4 |
| | | 739.4 | 850.0 |
| | | 1335.8 | 818.9 |

Do these data support the research hypothesis that the cardiac volume of those who experience pain for less than 8 hr tends to be smaller than that of those who experience pain for 8 hr or more with myocardial infarction?

**4.** Sickle cell anemia is a disease associated with impaired urinary potassium excretion. A study is run to compare the responses of subjects with normal hemoglobin and sickle cell disease to an oral potassium chloride (KCl) load (.75 meq/kg body weight). Before patients receive the KCl load, no differences in urine pH are detected. These data are obtained at the end of the study. Do they indicate that there is a difference in the way that these groups respond to an oral KCl load relative to the variable urine pH?

| Urine pH | | | |
|---|---|---|---|
| NORMAL ($N$) | | SICKLE CELL ($S$) | |
| 6.6 | 5.9 | 5.7 | 5.2 |
| 6.1 | 5.4 | 5.6 | 5.6 |
| 6.2 | 5.7 | 5.3 | 5.9 |
| 5.8 | 4.7 | 5.4 | 6.0 |
| | | 4.8 | |

***5.** *Normal Approximation to $W_m$.* For large samples, $W_m$ is approximately normally distributed with mean $\mu = m(m + n + 1)/2$ and variance $\sigma^2 = mn(m + n + 1)/12$. These facts can be used to test hypotheses that call for the use of the Wilcoxon procedure for sample sizes not listed in Table X of Appendix B. We need only standardize $W_m$ and use the standard normal table (Table III of Appendix B) to approximate the $P$ value of the test.

**a.** Let $m = 30$ and $n = 60$. Find $P[W_m \leq 1350]$.
**b.** Let $m = 40$ and $n = 50$. Find $P[W_m \geq 2000]$.

## KRUSKAL-WALLIS *k*-SAMPLE TEST FOR LOCATION: UNMATCHED DATA

**13.4** □ The idea of using rank sums for comparing two populations based on independent random samples drawn from the populations can be extended to more than two populations. The resulting test was developed by W. H. Kruskal and W. A. Wallis in 1952.

### Kruskal-Wallis *k*-Sample Test

Assume that independent random samples of sizes $n_1, n_2, n_3, \ldots, n_k$ are drawn from $k$ continuous populations, respectively. We wish to test the null hypothesis that these populations are identical with a test that is especially sensitive to differences in location. To do so, the $n_1 + n_2 + n_3 + \cdots + n_k = N$ observations are pooled and ordered from smallest to largest. Then they are ranked from 1 to $N$, with tied scores receiving the average group rank, as in the Wilcoxon procedures.

Let $R_i$, $i = 1, 2, \ldots, k$, denote the sum of the ranks associated with the observations drawn from the $i$th population. If the null hypothesis of no difference among populations is true, then the higher ranks should scatter randomly across the $k$ samples; if one or more populations is located above the others, then the higher ranks should cluster in the samples drawn from those populations. Thus, if $H_0$ is true, the average rank associated with each group should be moderate in size; otherwise, one or more of these mean ranks should be inflated. The Kruskal-Wallis statistic is given by

$$H = \frac{12}{N(N+1)} \sum_{i=1}^{k} n_i \left( \bar{R}_i - \frac{N+1}{2} \right)^2$$

where $\bar{R}_i = R_i / n_i$, the average rank of the observations drawn from the $i$th population. Using the methods of Chapters 2 and 4, we can show that if the null hypothesis is true, then $E[\bar{R}_i] = (N+1)/2$. Thus, the Kruskal-Wallis statistic essentially compares the observed average ranks for the $k$ samples with that expected under $H_0$. If there is a wide discrepancy, then $H$ will be inflated. This implies that $H_0$ should be rejected for large values of $H$. It has been found that if $H_0$ is true, $H$ follows an approximate chi-square distribution with $k - 1$ degrees of freedom. Therefore, $P$ values for the test are found in Table VI of Appendix B. As in other cases, there is a form for $H$ is arithmetically equivalent, but computationally easier to handle: This form is

$$H = \frac{12}{N(N+1)} \sum_{i=1}^{k} \frac{R_i^2}{n_i} - 3(N+1)$$

This is the form that we use in practice.

---

**EXAMPLE 13.4.1** □ To determine the effect of hemodialysis on the size of the liver, three populations are studied: normal controls, nondialyzed uremic patients, and patients on dialysis. Random samples are obtained from each population, and liver scans are used to determine the area of the liver (in square centimeters) for each subject. These data result (the rank of each observation is given in parentheses):